with MyEconLab

D0066557

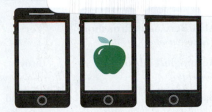

- **Learning Catalytics**—Generates classroom discussion, guides lectures, and promotes peer-to-peer learning with real-time analytics. Students can use any device to interact in the classroom, engage with content, and even draw and share graphs.

- **Real-Time Data Analysis Exercises**—Using current macro data to help students understand the impact of changes in economic variables, Real-Time Data Analysis Exercises communicate directly with the Federal Reserve Bank of St. Louis's FRED® site and update as new data are available.

- **Current News Exercises**—Every week, current microeconomic and macroeconomic news stories, with accompanying exercises, are posted to MyEconLab. Assignable and auto-graded, these multi-part exercises ask students to recognize and apply economic concepts to real-world events.

- **Reporting Dashboard**—View, analyze, and report learning outcomes clearly and easily. Available via the Gradebook and fully mobile-ready, the Reporting Dashboard presents student performance data at the class, section, and program levels in an accessible, visual manner.

- **LMS Integration**—Link from any LMS platform to access assignments, rosters, and resources, and synchronize MyLab grades with your LMS gradebook. For students, new direct, single sign-on provides access to all the personalized learning MyLab resources that make studying more efficient and effective.

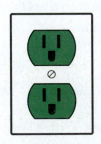

- **Mobile Ready**—Students and instructors can access multimedia resources and complete assessments right at their fingertips, on any mobile device.

PEARSON

The Pearson Series in Economics

Abel/Bernanke/Croushore
Macroeconomics*

Acemoglu/Laibson/List
Economics*

Bade/Parkin
Foundations of Economics*

Berck/Helfand
The Economics of the Environment

Bierman/Fernandez
Game Theory with Economic Applications

Blanchard
Macroeconomics*

Blau/Ferber/Winkler
The Economics of Women, Men, and Work

Boardman/Greenberg/Vining/Weimer
Cost-Benefit Analysis

Boyer
Principles of Transportation Economics

Branson
Macroeconomic Theory and Policy

Bruce
Public Finance and the American Economy

Carlton/Perloff
Modern Industrial Organization

Case/Fair/Oster
Principles of Economics*

Chapman
Environmental Economics: Theory, Application, and Policy

Cooter/Ulen
Law & Economics

Daniels/VanHoose
International Monetary & Financial Economics

Downs
An Economic Theory of Democracy

Ehrenberg/Smith
Modern Labor Economics

Farnham
Economics for Managers

Folland/Goodman/Stano
The Economics of Health and Health Care

Fort
Sports Economics

Froyen
Macroeconomics

Fusfeld
The Age of the Economist

Gerber
International Economics*

González-Rivera
Forecasting for Economics and Business

Gordon
Macroeconomics*

Grant
Economic Analysis of Social Issues*

Greene
Econometric Analysis

Gregory
Essentials of Economics

Gregory/Stuart
Russian and Soviet Economic Performance and Structure

Hartwick/Olewiler
The Economics of Natural Resource Use

Heilbroner/Milberg
The Making of the Economic Society

Heyne/Boettke/Prychitko
The Economic Way of Thinking

Holt
Markets, Games, and Strategic Behavior

Hubbard/O'Brien
Economics*

Money, Banking, and the Financial System*

Hubbard/O'Brien/Rafferty
Macroeconomics*

Hughes/Cain
American Economic History

Husted/Melvin
International Economics

Jehle/Reny
Advanced Microeconomic Theory

Johnson-Lans
A Health Economics Primer

Keat/Young/Erfle
Managerial Economics

Klein
Mathematical Methods for Economics

Krugman/Obstfeld/Melitz
International Economics: Theory & Policy*

Laidler
The Demand for Money

Leeds/von Allmen
The Economics of Sports

Leeds/von Allmen/Schiming
Economics*

Lynn
Economic Development: Theory and Practice for a Divided World

Miller
Economics Today*

Understanding Modern Economics

Miller/Benjamin
The Economics of Macro Issues

Miller/Benjamin/North
The Economics of Public Issues

Mills/Hamilton
Urban Economics

Mishkin
The Economics of Money, Banking, and Financial Markets*

The Economics of Money, Banking, and Financial Markets, Business School Edition*

Macroeconomics: Policy and Practice*

Murray
Econometrics: A Modern Introduction

O'Sullivan/Sheffrin/Perez
Economics: Principles, Applications and Tools*

Parkin
Economics*

Perloff
Microeconomics*

Microeconomics: Theory and Applications with Calculus*

Perloff/Brander
Managerial Economics and Strategy*

Phelps
Health Economics

Pindyck/Rubinfeld
Microeconomics*

Riddell/Shackelford/Stamos/Schneider
Economics: A Tool for Critically Understanding Society

Roberts
The Choice: A Fable of Free Trade and Protection

Rohlf
Introduction to Economic Reasoning

Roland
Development Economics

Scherer
Industry Structure, Strategy, and Public Policy

Schiller
The Economics of Poverty and Discrimination

Sherman
Market Regulation

Stock/Watson
Introduction to Econometrics

Studenmund
Using Econometrics: A Practical Guide

Tietenberg/Lewis
Environmental and Natural Resource Economics

Environmental Economics and Policy

Todaro/Smith
Economic Development

Waldman/Jensen
Industrial Organization: Theory and Practice

Walters/Walters/Appel/Callahan/Centanni/Maex/O'Neill
Econversations: Today's Students Discuss Today's Issues

Weil
Economic Growth

Williamson
Macroeconomics

Economic Analysis

OF SOCIAL ISSUES

Vice President, Business Publishing: Donna Battista
Executive Editor: David Alexander
Executive Development Editor: Lena Buonanno
Editorial Assistant: Courtney Turcotte
Vice President, Product Marketing: Maggie Moylan
Director of Marketing, Digital Services and Products: Jeanette Koskinas
Senior Product Marketing Manager: Alison Haskins
Executive Field Marketing Manager: Lori DeShazo
Senior Strategic Marketing Manager: Erin Gardner
Team Lead, Program Management: Ashley Santora
Program Manager: Lindsey Sloan
Team Lead, Project Management: Jeff Holcomb
Project Manager: Liz Napolitano
Operations Specialist: Carol Melville
Creative Director: Blair Brown
Art Director: Jon Boylan
Vice President, Director of Digital Strategy and Assessment: Paul Gentile
Manager of Learning Applications: Paul DeLuca
Digital Editor: Denise Clinton

Director, Digital Studio: Sacha Laustsen
Digital Studio Manager: Diane Lombardo
Digital Studio Project Manager: Melissa Honig
Product Manager: Elizabeth Cameron
Digital Content Team Lead: Noel Lotz
Digital Content Project Lead: Courtney Kamauf
Full-Service Project Management and Composition: Cenveo® Publisher Services
Interior Design: Cenveo® Publisher Services
Cover Designer: Jon Boylan
Cover Art: TOP ROW, left to right: George Spade/Shutterstock; ImageSource/Getty Images; Ricon16/Fotolia; nimon_t/Fotolia; CENTER: David Malan/Getty Images; BOTTOM ROW, left to right: Monkey Business/Fotolia; Serguei Vlassov/123RF; Age fotostock Spain, S.L./Alamy; karichs/Fotolia
Printer/Binder/Cover Printer: Courier Corp./Kendallville
Typeface: 10/12 Janson Text LT Std

Library of Congress Cataloging-in-Publication Data
Grant, Alan P.
  Economic analysis of social issues / Alan Grant.
     pages cm
  Includes index.
  ISBN 978-0-13-302303-9 – ISBN 0-13-302303-6
1. Welfare economics. 2. Social choice. 3. Economic development—Social aspects. 4. Economics—Sociological aspects. I. Title.
  HB99.3.G73 2016
  361—dc23
                              2014043326

10 9 8 7 6 5 4 3 2

ISBN 10: 0-13-302303-6
ISBN 13: 978-0-13-302303-9

Economic Analysis

OF SOCIAL ISSUES

Alan Grant

Baker University, Kansas

PEARSON

Boston   Columbus   Indianapolis   New York   San Francisco   Hoboken
Amsterdam   Cape Town   Dubai   London   Madrid   Milan   Munich   Paris   Montréal   Toronto
Delhi   Mexico City   São Paulo   Sydney   Hong Kong   Seoul   Singapore   Taipei   Tokyo

For Emily and Cooper

Brief Contents

Part 1 The Basic Building Blocks

1 Fundamental Concepts in Economics 1

Appendix: Supply and Demand 19

2 Cost–Benefit Analysis and the Value of a Life 36

3 Basic Game Theory: Games Between Two Players 56

4 Game Theory: Games Between Three or More Players 79

Part 2 Markets and Government: A Recipe for Producing Wealth

5 Free Exchange: Individual and International Trade 98

6 The Market System: Functions, Structure, and Institutions 119

Part 3 The Environment: Property Rights, Transactions Costs, and the Role of Government

7 The Nature of Pollution Problems 141

8 Government Policies to Regulate Pollution 159

9 Resource Depletion and Sustainability 179

Part 4 Public Goods and the Public Sector

10 Public Goods and the Role of Government 197

11 Public Goods: Tackling Large Projects and Eminent Domain 215

12 The Volunteer's Dilemma: A Collective Inaction Problem 230

13 Voting: You Can't Always Get What You Want 252

Part 5 Health Care and Discrimination: Problems of Incomplete Information

14 The Economics of Health Insurance and Health Care 275

15 Segregation and Discrimination 300

Part 6 Macroeconomics

16 Gross Domestic Product and the Wealth of Nations: An Introduction to the Macroeconomy 325

17 Unemployment 355

18 An Introduction to Money, Banks, and the Financial System 379

19 The Federal Reserve: Monetary Policy, Economic Activity, and Inflation 400

20 The Federal Government: Taxes, Spending, and Fiscal Policy 427

21 Income Inequality and the Redistribution of Income 455

Contents

Preface xxvii

Part 1

The Basic Building Blocks

1 Fundamental Concepts in Economics 1

What Is Economics? 2

Key Features of an Economy 2

The Two Key Questions Every Economy Must Answer: What Gets Produced? And for Whom? 3

Key Principles of Economics: Scarcity, Trade-offs, and Opportunity Costs 4

Scarcity 4

Trade-offs and Opportunity Costs 4

■ Application 1.1 Even Superheroes Face Trade-offs 6

Government, Public Policy, and Trade-offs 7

■ Application 1.2 Rolling Out the Barrels, North Korean Style 8

Key Principle of Economics: People Respond to Incentives 9

■ Application 1.3 Dying to Save Taxes 10

A Brief Introduction to Collective Action Problems 11

How Economists Analyze Economic Issues 12

Positive and Normative Economics 12

The Benevolent Social Planner and the Best Use of Scarce Resources 13

Conclusion 13

CHAPTER SUMMARY AND PROBLEMS 14

1.1 WHAT IS ECONOMICS? 14

1.2 KEY PRINCIPLES OF ECONOMICS: SCARCITY, TRADE-OFFS, AND OPPORTUNITY COSTS 15

1.3 KEY PRINCIPLE OF ECONOMICS: PEOPLE RESPOND TO INCENTIVES 16

1.4 A BRIEF INTRODUCTION TO COLLECTIVE ACTION PROBLEMS 16

1.5 HOW ECONOMISTS ANALYZE ECONOMIC ISSUES 17

EXPERIMENT: THE ULTIMATUM GAME: ARE YOU GENEROUS OR GREEDY? 18

1 APPENDIX: Supply and Demand 19

Demand 20

Supply 21

Equilibrium 21

Changes in Supply and Demand 23

Factors That Shift Supply and Demand 26

Factors That Shift the Demand Curve 26

Factors That Shift the Supply Curve 27

Putting the Pieces Together 28

The Price Elasticity of Supply and Demand 29

APPENDIX SUMMARY AND PROBLEMS 32

1A.1 DEMAND 32

1A.2 SUPPLY 32

1A.3 EQUILIBRIUM 33

1A.4 CHANGES IN SUPPLY AND DEMAND 33

1A.5 FACTORS THAT SHIFT SUPPLY AND DEMAND 34

1A.6 THE PRICE ELASTICITY OF SUPPLY AND DEMAND 35

2 **Cost–Benefit Analysis and the Value of a Life 36**

Cost–Benefit Analysis 37

Cost–Benefit Analysis: The Basics 37

Using Cost–Benefit Analysis to Select Among Competing Alternatives 37

Evaluating Alternatives at the Margin 38

■ Application 2.1 Cost–Benefit Analysis and the Tobacco Settlement 39

Applying Cost–Benefit Analysis to Life 40

Corporations Do It: The Ford Pinto 40

You Do It: Exposing Yourself and Others to Risk 41

Using Cost–Benefit Analysis to Determine an Appropriate Level of Safety 41

■ Application 2.2 What Is the Value of a Child Safety Seat? 42

Problems and Pitfalls of Cost–Benefit Analysis When Life Is Involved 44

Mistakes in Estimating Risk 44

■ Application 2.3 Better Safe Than Sorry? 46

Mistakes in Estimating the True Value of a Life 47

Approaches to Valuing a Life 47

The Lost-Income Approach 47

The Compensating Differential Approach 48

Conclusion 50

CHAPTER SUMMARY AND PROBLEMS 50

2.1 COST–BENEFIT ANALYSIS 51

2.2 APPLYING COST–BENEFIT ANALYSIS TO LIFE 51

2.3 USING COST–BENEFIT ANALYSIS TO DETERMINE AN APPROPRIATE LEVEL OF SAFETY 52

2.4 PROBLEMS AND PITFALLS OF COST–BENEFIT ANALYSIS WHEN LIFE IS INVOLVED 53

2.5 APPROACHES TO VALUING A LIFE 54

EXPERIMENT: THE DICTATOR GAME 55

3 **Basic Game Theory: Games Between Two Players 56**

What Is Game Theory? 57

The Basic Structure of Games 58

Setting Up a Game 58

Nash Equilibrium 60

Strategies for Finding Equilibria 60

■ The People Behind the Theory John Nash 61

The Basic Types of Games 63

Prisoner's Dilemma Games 63

Pure Coordination Games 64

■ Application 3.1 Game Theory and the Tobacco Advertising Ban 65

Assurance Games 69

Battle of the Sexes Games 70

■ Application 3.2 Meeting Your Problems Head On 71

Games of Chicken 72

Conclusion 74

CHAPTER SUMMARY AND PROBLEMS 74

3.1 WHAT IS GAME THEORY? 74

3.2 THE BASIC STRUCTURE OF GAMES 74

3.3 THE BASIC TYPES OF GAMES 76

EXPERIMENT: THE PUSH–PULL GAME 78

4   Game Theory: Games Between Three or More Players 79

Introduction to Three-Player Games 80

Finding Nash Equilibria in Three-Player Games 82

Dominance in Three-Player Games 82

Best-Response Analysis in Three-Player Games 83

■ Application 4.1 Blondes Have Less Fun: Game Theory in *A Beautiful Mind* 85

Depicting Games with More Than Three Players 87

Finding Equilibria in Games with More Than Three Players 88

■ Application 4.2 Breaking Facebook's Stranglehold 92

Conclusion 93

CHAPTER SUMMARY AND PROBLEMS 93

4.1 INTRODUCTION TO THREE-PLAYER GAMES 93

4.2 FINDING NASH EQUILIBRIA IN THREE-PLAYER GAMES 94

4.3 DEPICTING GAMES WITH MORE THAN THREE PLAYERS 94

4.4 FINDING EQUILIBRIA IN GAMES WITH MORE THAN THREE PLAYERS 95

EXPERIMENT: THE RED–GREEN GAME 97

Part 2

Markets and Government: A Recipe for Producing Wealth

5   Free Exchange: Individual and International Trade 98

Comparative Advantage, Exchange, and Wealth Creation 99

Comparative Advantage and Specialization: Catalysts for Exchange 99

Exchange and Cooperative Surplus 101

Cooperative Surplus as a Measure of Wealth Creation 102

■ Application 5.1 The Globalization of Wine—Our Cups Runneth Over 103

■ The People Behind the Theory Adam Smith 104

Restrictions on Free Exchange 105

Taxes 105

Deadweight Losses 106

Subsidies 107

■ Application 5.2 Something Stinks in Louisiana's Floral-Arranging Industry 108

International Trade and Not-So-Free Exchange 109

Tariffs 110

Quotas 112

■ Application 5.3 Chickens, Turkey, and the Transit Connect 113

Conclusion 114

CHAPTER SUMMARY AND PROBLEMS 114

5.1 COMPARATIVE ADVANTAGE, EXCHANGE, AND WEALTH CREATION 115

5.2 RESTRICTIONS ON FREE EXCHANGE 115

5.3 INTERNATIONAL TRADE AND NOT-SO-FREE EXCHANGE 116

EXPERIMENT: THE GAINS-FROM-TRADE GAME 118

6   The Market System: Functions, Structure, and Institutions 119

The Market System: Its Functions and Structure 120

Markets Are More Than Places to Trade 120

Market Structures 120

The Four Functions of Prices in the Market System 122

Measuring Desire 122

Reflecting Scarcity 122

A Means of Communication 122

Coordinating Production Decisions 123

The Foundations of Well-Functioning Markets: A Role for Government 124

Competition 124

Honesty 126

■ Application 6.1 Enforcing Honesty in India: Justice Delayed and Justice Denied 127

Information 128

Property Rights 130

■ Application 6.2 Private Property and the Pilgrims' Progress 132

Connecting Effort and Reward: An Illustration 132

■ Application 6.3 Property Rights and the Chinese Agricultural Revolution 134

Conclusion 135

CHAPTER SUMMARY AND PROBLEMS 135

6.1 THE MARKET SYSTEM: ITS FUNCTIONS AND STRUCTURE 136

6.2 THE FOUR FUNCTIONS OF PRICES IN THE MARKET SYSTEM 136

6.3 THE FOUNDATIONS OF WELL-FUNCTIONING MARKETS: A ROLE FOR GOVERNMENT 137

6.4 CONNECTING EFFORT AND REWARD: AN ILLUSTRATION 138

EXPERIMENT: CAPITALISM AND COMMUNISM GAMES 140

Part 3

The Environment: Property Rights, Transactions Costs, and the Role of Government

7   The Nature of Pollution Problems 141

Externalities 142

Negative Externalities 142

■ Application 7.1 Property Values and Megan's Law 143

Positive Externalities 143

Pollution Problems (Negative Externalities) and Disagreements over the Competing Uses of Scarce Resources 144

How Much Pollution Is the Right Amount of Pollution? 145

The Benevolent Social Planner and the Socially Optimal Amount of Pollution 145

The Law, Bargaining, and the Socially Optimal Amount of Pollution 145

■ Application 7.2 The Salk Vaccine Versus the Sabin Vaccine 147

The Coase Theorem 148

■ Application 7.3 The Nature Conservancy 149

The Coase Theorem, Applied 150

The Coase Theorem: A Second Example 150

Why the Coase Theorem May Not Work: Transactions Costs 151

Conclusion 152

■ The People Behind the Theory Ronald Coase 153

CHAPTER SUMMARY AND PROBLEMS 154

7.1 EXTERNALITIES 154

7.2 POLLUTION PROBLEMS (NEGATIVE EXTERNALITIES) AND DISAGREEMENTS

OVER THE COMPETING USES OF SCARCE
RESOURCES 155

7.3 HOW MUCH POLLUTION IS THE RIGHT
AMOUNT OF POLLUTION? 155

7.4 THE COASE THEOREM 156

7.5 WHY THE COASE THEOREM MAY
NOT WORK: TRANSACTIONS COSTS 157

EXPERIMENT: THE HERD IMMUNITY
GAME 158

8 Government Policies to Regulate
Pollution 159

Four Major Types of Transactions Costs 160

Search Costs 160

Collectivization Costs 161

Negotiation Costs 162

Monitoring and Enforcement Costs 162

Regulating Pollution in an Ideal World 163

Principle 1: Regulation is Necessary Only
When Transactions Costs Preclude Bargaining
Between Polluter and Victim 163

Principle 2: The Regulation Should Achieve the
Outcome the Affected Parties Would Have
Reached Had Transactions Costs Not Been So
High 164

Principle 3: The Regulation Should Be Designed
to Make the Polluter Internalize the Cost of the
Externality 164

Principle 4: Eliminating Pollution Entirely Should
Not Be the Goal of Regulation 165

Application 8.1 Alternative Approaches to
Reducing Auto Emissions 166

Tools Governments Use to Regulate
Pollution 167

Taxes 167

Application 8.2 Dealing with Climate Change 168

Subsidies 169

Cap-and-Trade Systems 171

Conclusion 173

CHAPTER SUMMARY AND PROBLEMS 174

8.1 FOUR MAJOR TYPES OF TRANSACTIONS
COSTS 174

8.2 REGULATING POLLUTION IN AN IDEAL
WORLD 175

8.3 TOOLS GOVERNMENTS USE TO REGULATE
POLLUTION 176

EXPERIMENT: THE JUDGE-ME-NOT
GAME 178

9 Resource Depletion and
Sustainability 179

Will the World Run Out of Oil? 180

Depicting the World's Supply of Oil 180

Depletion and the Role of Prices 181

What Resources Are in Danger of
Depletion? 184

Application 9.1 How to Turn a Rhino into a
Chicken 185

The Tragedy of the Commons 186

The Tragedy of the Commons: An
Illustration 186

Application 9.2 Good to the Last Drop 187

Depletion and Pollution: Mirror Images of the
Same Problem 188

How Can Society Fix Depletion Problems? 188

Restricting the Access to Endangered Resources
and Their Use 188

Creating Absolute Property Rights 189

Application 9.3 Not Just a Fish Tale: Cap-and-
Trade Brings Fisheries Back from the Brink 190

Conclusion 191

■ The People Behind the Theory Elinor Ostrom 192

CHAPTER SUMMARY AND PROBLEMS 193

9.1 WILL THE WORLD RUN OUT OF OIL? 193

9.2 WHAT RESOURCES ARE IN DANGER OF DEPLETION? 194

9.3 THE TRAGEDY OF THE COMMONS 194

9.4 HOW CAN SOCIETY FIX DEPLETION PROBLEMS? 195

EXPERIMENT: THE "GONE FISHING" GAME 196

Part 4

Public Goods and the Public Sector

10 Public Goods and the Role of Government 197

Public Versus Private Goods 198

Rival and Nonrival Goods 199

Excludable and Nonexcludable Goods 199

Four Different Classes of Goods 199

How Nonexcludability Leads to Free Riding and the Public Goods Problem 200

■ Application 10.1 The Not-So-Friendly Confines of Wrigley Field 201

The Free Ridership "Game" 202

The Public Goods Problem 204

Property Rights and the Public Goods Problem 204

How Governments Can Overcome the Public Goods Problem 205

Government's Tax Powers and Free Ridership 205

■ Application 10.2 Paying for Big Sugar's Sweet Deal 206

Some General Guidelines for the Government Provision of Public Goods 207

■ Application 10.3 Government-Provided Salt in Turkmenistan 209

Conclusion 209

CHAPTER SUMMARY AND PROBLEMS 210

10.1 PUBLIC VERSUS PRIVATE GOODS 210

10.2 HOW NONEXCLUDABILITY LEADS TO FREE RIDING AND THE PUBLIC GOODS PROBLEM 211

10.3 PROPERTY RIGHTS AND THE PUBLIC GOODS PROBLEM 212

10.4 HOW GOVERNMENTS CAN OVERCOME THE PUBLIC GOODS PROBLEM 212

EXPERIMENT: THE GARDEN GAME 214

11 Public Goods: Tackling Large Projects and Eminent Domain 215

The Role of Individuals in Large Projects 216

The Holdout Problem 217

Transactions Costs 219

The Role of Government in Large Projects 219

Takings Power and the Fifth Amendment 219

Conditions for the Use of Eminent Domain 219

■ Application 11.1 Steel Company Can't Get Homeowner to Sell 220

■ Application 11.2 The Robber Barons of Merriam, Kansas 223

Conclusion 225

CHAPTER SUMMARY AND PROBLEMS 226

11.1 THE ROLE OF INDIVIDUALS IN LARGE PROJECTS 226

11.2 THE ROLE OF GOVERNMENT IN LARGE PROJECTS 226

EXPERIMENT: THE "ASK AND YOU MIGHT RECEIVE" GAME 229

12 The Volunteer's Dilemma: A Collective Inaction Problem 230

What Is the Volunteer's Dilemma? 231

■ Application 12.1 Curt Flood Knocks the Volunteer's Dilemma Out of the Park 232

If Apathy Doesn't Explain the Volunteer's Dilemma, What Does? 233

Pluralistic Ignorance 233

Diffusion of Responsibility 233

■ Application 12.2 Bill Nye, the Science Guy, Weighs in on the Volunteer's Dilemma 234

Game Theory and the Volunteer's Dilemma 237

Mixed-Strategy Games: An Overview 237

Finding the Mixed-Strategy Equilibrium in a Zero-Sum Game 241

Mixed-Strategy Play and the Volunteer's Dilemma 242

Overcoming the Volunteer's Dilemma 244

Compulsory Volunteerism 245

Coalition Building and Bargaining 245

Conclusion 245

■ Application 12.3 Should There Be a Duty to Rescue? 246

CHAPTER SUMMARY AND PROBLEMS 247

12.1 WHAT IS THE VOLUNTEER'S DILEMMA? 247

12.2 IF APATHY DOESN'T EXPLAIN THE VOLUNTEER'S DILEMMA, WHAT DOES? 247

12.3 GAME THEORY AND THE VOLUNTEER'S DILEMMA 248

12.4 MIXED-STRATEGY PLAY AND THE VOLUNTEER'S DILEMMA 249

12.5 OVERCOMING THE VOLUNTEER'S DILEMMA 250

EXPERIMENT: THE "SAVE FERRIS!" GAME 251

13 Voting: You Can't Always Get What You Want 252

An Introduction to Voting Methods 253

The Plurality-Rule Method 254

The Condorcet Method 255

The Borda-Count Method 256

The Instant Runoff Method 258

■ Application 13.1 U.S. Presidential Elections and the Will of the People 260

Voting Methods and Arrow's Impossibility Theorem 261

Conventional Political Elections and the Median Voter Theorem 261

Candidate Positioning and the Median Voter Theorem 262

Why the Median Voter Theorem Might Fail 264

■ Application 13.2 Dangerous Voters: Rational, Irrational, or Both? 265

Strategic Voting and the Order of Events in Runoff Elections 268

The Agenda Paradox 269

Strategic and Naive Voting 269

■ **Application 13.3** Choosing Planes: Agenda Influence in the Real World 270

Conclusion 271

CHAPTER SUMMARY AND PROBLEMS 271

13.1 AN INTRODUCTION TO VOTING METHODS 271

13.2 CONVENTIONAL POLITICAL ELECTIONS AND THE MEDIAN VOTER THEOREM 272

13.3 STRATEGIC VOTING AND THE ORDER OF EVENTS IN RUNOFF ELECTIONS 273

EXPERIMENT: LOOKING FOR A "GOLDILOCKS" LOCATION 274

Part 5

Health Care and Discrimination: Problems of Incomplete Information

14   The Economics of Health Insurance and Health Care 275

The Current State of the U.S. Health Care System 276

Health Care Spending in the United States 276

Health Care Outcomes in the United States 277

An International Comparison of Health Care Costs and Outcomes 278

■ **Application 14.1** Explaining the Gap in Measured Health Care Outcomes Between the United States and Canada 280

Health Care Delivery and Finance Systems: An International Comparison 281

The United Kingdom's Nationalized Health Care System 281

Canada's Single-Payer System 281

Japan's Universal Care System 282

The U.S. Private Health Care System 282

■ **Application 14.2** Why Do Americans Get Health Insurance from Their Employers? 283

How Health Care Finance May Affect the Affordability of Health Care 284

Insurance: The Fundamentals 284

Asymmetric Information and the Adverse Selection Problem 285

■ **Application 14.3** How Big a Problem Is Adverse Selection? 288

The Moral Hazard Problem 288

■ **Application 14.4** Using Information to Overcome Moral Hazard 292

How Pricing Variability May Contribute to High Health Care Costs 292

Conclusion 294

CHAPTER SUMMARY AND PROBLEMS 295

14.1 THE CURRENT STATE OF THE U.S. HEALTH CARE SYSTEM 295

14.2 HEALTH CARE DELIVERY AND FINANCE SYSTEMS: AN INTERNATIONAL COMPARISON 296

14.3 HOW HEALTH CARE FINANCE MAY AFFECT THE AFFORDABILITY OF HEALTH CARE 296

EXPERIMENT: THE RESTAURANT GAME 299

15   Segregation and Discrimination 300

The Segregation of Neighborhoods and Schelling's Checkerboard 301

Unraveling and Equilibrium 303

Is Neighborhood Segregation Inevitable? 304

Does Your Neighborhood Determine Your Future Well-Being? 304

■ The People Behind the Theory Thomas Schelling 305

The Link Between Neighborhoods and Outcomes: Correlation or Causation? 305

Moving to Opportunity: A Housing Experiment to Determine Causation 306

Labor Market Discrimination 308

An Initial Observation: Outcomes Differ Across Demographic Groups 308

■ Application 15.1 Can You Avoid Being Short-Changed in the Labor Market? 309

Types of Discrimination in the Labor Market 310

How Discrimination Harms Individuals and Society 312

How Economists Detect and Measure Discrimination 312

The Audit Method 312

Regression Analysis 313

■ Application 15.2 What's in a Name? Comparing Regression Analysis and Audit Studies in Detecting Discrimination 315

Anti-Discrimination Legislation 316

Affirmative Action Programs 317

Some Benefits and Costs of Affirmative Action Programs 318

Conclusion 319

CHAPTER SUMMARY AND PROBLEMS 320

15.1 THE SEGREGATION OF NEIGHBORHOODS AND SCHELLING'S CHECKERBOARD 320

15.2 DOES YOUR NEIGHBORHOOD DETERMINE YOUR FUTURE WELL-BEING? 320

15.3 LABOR MARKET DISCRIMINATION 321

15.4 HOW ECONOMISTS DETECT AND MEASURE DISCRIMINATION 322

15.5 ANTI-DISCRIMINATION LEGISLATION 323

EXPERIMENT: SCHELLING'S CHECKERBOARD 324

Part 6

Macroeconomics

16 Gross Domestic Product and the Wealth of Nations: An Introduction to the Macroeconomy 325

Macroeconomics and How It Differs from Microeconomics 326

Material Well-Being and Gross Domestic Product 326

Gross Domestic Product: A Measuring Stick for Production 327

The Components of GDP and the Expenditures Approach 329

The Income Approach 332

Nominal GDP and Real GDP 333

How Rising Prices Affect Nominal GDP 333

Adjusting GDP for Increasing Prices: Real GDP 334

Adjusting for a Country's Size and Real GDP per Capita 334

Shortcomings of GDP 335

GDP Doesn't Include the Underground Economy 335

GDP Doesn't Include Household Production 336

GDP Doesn't Account for the Value of Leisure 336

GDP Doesn't Account for Economic "Bads" 337

GDP Reveals Nothing About the Distribution of Income 337

GDP Redeemed 337

■ Application 16.1 Don't Care Too Much for Money 339

Economic Growth 340

How Small Differences in Growth Rates Can Cause Large Differences in Well-Being 341

Essential Ingredients for Economic Growth 342

Business Cycles and Recessions 343

Business Cycles and Recessions
Defined 344

■ **Application 16.2** Who Says We're in a
Recession? 345

Supply Shocks as a Cause of Recessions 345

Demand Shocks as a Cause of Recessions 346

■ **Application 16.3** The Origins of the Great
Recession 347

Conclusion 348

CHAPTER SUMMARY AND PROBLEMS 349

16.1 MACROECONOMICS AND
HOW IT DIFFERS FROM
MICROECONOMICS 349

16.2 MATERIAL WELL-BEING AND
GROSS DOMESTIC PRODUCT 349

16.3 NOMINAL GDP AND REAL GDP 350

16.4 SHORTCOMINGS OF GDP 351

16.5 ECONOMIC GROWTH 352

16.6 BUSINESS CYCLES AND
RECESSIONS 353

MYECONLAB REAL-TIME DATA
ACTIVITY: GROSS DOMESTIC
PRODUCT AND BUSINESS CYCLES 354

17 Unemployment 355

What Is Unemployment? 356

Determining a Person's Labor Status 356

Calculating the Unemployment Rate 357

■ **Application 17.1** What Caused
the Dramatic Increase in Women's
Labor Force Participation Rates in
the 1970s? 358

**Shortcomings of the Measured
Unemployment Rate 359**

The Unemployment Rate Doesn't Include People
Who Work Part Time 359

The Unemployment Rate Doesn't Include People
Who Are Underemployed 360

The Unemployment Rate Doesn't Include People
Who Are Discouraged Workers 360

The Unemployment Rate Doesn't Include People
Who Work in the Underground Economy 361

Why Not Fix the Shortcomings of the
Unemployment Rate? 361

Types of Unemployment 362

Frictional Unemployment 362

Structural Unemployment 363

■ **Application 17.2** Mixed Blessing: Unemployment
Insurance Makes the Labor Market Work Better.
And Worse. 367

The Natural Rate of Unemployment 368

Cyclical Unemployment 368

Policy Implications of Unemployment 370

Why the Appropriate Policy Prescription
Depends on the Type of Unemployment 370

Data Issues and the Appropriate Policy
Prescription 371

■ **Application 17.3** Unemployment During the
Great Recession 372

Conclusion 373

CHAPTER SUMMARY AND PROBLEMS 373

17.1 WHAT IS UNEMPLOYMENT? 373

17.2 SHORTCOMINGS OF THE MEASURED
UNEMPLOYMENT RATE 374

17.3 TYPES OF UNEMPLOYMENT 374

17.4 POLICY IMPLICATIONS OF
UNEMPLOYMENT 375

MYECONLAB REAL-TIME DATA ACTIVITY: UNEMPLOYMENT RATES 377

NOTES 378

18 An Introduction to Money, Banks, and the Financial System 379

Money and Its Functions 380

The Medium of Exchange Function 380

The Store of Value Function 380

The Standard of Value Function 381

The Evolution of Money and the Origins of the Modern Banking System 381

Commodity Money 381

Representative Commodity Money 382

Partially Backed Representative Commodity Money 382

Fiat Money 383

■ Application 18.1 Funny Money Meets Serious Need 384

Commercial Banks, Central Banks, and Money Creation 384

Commercial Banks 385

Central Banks 385

The Banking System and the Money Supply 385

The Central Bank's Role in Money Creation 386

The Commercial Banking System's Role in Money Creation 386

Measuring the Money Supply 387

Financial Instruments and Their Functions 388

Raising Capital 389

Storing Wealth Across Time 390

Reducing Risk 391

Enabling Speculation 392

■ Application 18.2 Financial Instruments and the Origins of the Great Recession 393

Conclusion 394

CHAPTER SUMMARY AND PROBLEMS 395

18.1 MONEY AND ITS FUNCTIONS 395

18.2 THE EVOLUTION OF MONEY AND THE ORIGINS OF THE MODERN BANKING SYSTEM 396

18.3 COMMERCIAL BANKS, CENTRAL BANKS, AND MONEY CREATION 396

18.4 THE BANKING SYSTEM AND THE MONEY SUPPLY 397

18.5 FINANCIAL INSTRUMENTS AND THEIR FUNCTIONS 397

MYECONLAB REAL-TIME DATA ACTIVITY: MONEY AND THE FINANCIAL SYSTEM 399

19 The Federal Reserve: Monetary Policy, Economic Activity, and Inflation 400

The Origins of the Federal Reserve and Its Tools of Policy 401

Runs, Clearinghouses, Panics, and the Fed 402

■ Application 19.1 The Fed's Role as a Lender of Last Resort During the Great Recession 403

The Federal Reserve, Its Tools of Policy, and the Money Supply 404

The Money Supply, Interest Rates, and Monetary Policy 406

The Money Supply and Interest Rates 406

Interest Rates and Real Economic Activity 407

The Natural Limits of Monetary Policy 407

■ **Application 19.2** The Fed's Job Is Easing, but It Isn't Easy 408

When Monetary Policy Is Most Effective 409

The Art and Implementation of Monetary Policy 409

The Lags of Policy 409

Why the Lags of Policy Make Monetary Policy Difficult 411

■ **The People Behind the Theory** Milton Friedman 413

Money and Inflation 415

How Is Inflation Calculated? 415

The Link Between Money Growth and Inflation 416

■ **Application 19.3** Should the United States Return to the Gold Standard? 416

The Costs of Inflation 417

The End of Inflation 419

If Inflation Is Bad, Is Deflation Good? 420

Conclusion 421

CHAPTER SUMMARY AND PROBLEMS 421

19.1 THE ORIGINS OF THE FEDERAL RESERVE AND ITS TOOLS OF POLICY 421

19.2 THE MONEY SUPPLY, INTEREST RATES, AND MONETARY POLICY 422

19.3 THE ART AND IMPLEMENTATION OF MONETARY POLICY 423

19.4 MONEY AND INFLATION 424

MYECONLAB REAL-TIME DATA ACTIVITY: MONETARY POLICY AND INFLATION 425

NOTES 426

20 The Federal Government: Taxes, Spending, and Fiscal Policy 427

Government Revenue 428

Payroll Taxes 429

Income Taxes 430

■ **Application 20.1** Why Do Americans Work So Much? 433

■ **Application 20.2** Big Profits, No Taxes: Incentives and the Corporate Tax Code 434

Government Expenditures, Deficits, and Debt 435

Discretionary Expenditures 435

Mandatory Spending and Entitlements 436

Surpluses, Deficits, and Debt 437

The Future of the Federal Budget 440

Demographic Challenges 440

Meeting Future Demographic Challenges 441

The Federal Government and Fiscal Stabilization Policy 442

Fiscal Policy: The Basics 442

The Multiplier Effect 443

■ **The People Behind the Theory** John Maynard Keynes 443

Potential Pitfalls of Fiscal Policy 444

■ **Application 20.3** Fiscal Policy During the Great Recession 446

Conclusion 448

CHAPTER SUMMARY AND PROBLEMS 449

20.1 GOVERNMENT REVENUE 449

20.2 GOVERNMENT EXPENDITURES, DEFICITS, AND DEBT 450

20.3 THE FUTURE OF THE FEDERAL BUDGET 451

20.4 THE FEDERAL GOVERNMENT AND FISCAL STABILIZATION POLICY 452

MYECONLAB REAL-TIME DATA ACTIVITY: BUDGET DEFICITS AND THE FEDERAL DEBT 453

NOTES 454

21 Income Inequality and the Redistribution of Income 455

How Is Inequality Measured? 456

Means and Medians: A First Step Toward Measuring Inequality 456

Quintiles: A More Detailed Look at the Income Distribution 458

Lorenz Curves and Gini Coefficients 458

How Unequal Is the Distribution of Income in the United States? 461

U.S. Income Inequality, Past and Present 461

U.S. Income Inequality Compared to Other Countries 463

Are the Rich Getting Richer and the Poor Getting Poorer in the United States? 464

Is Economic Mobility Decreasing in the United States? 465

What Are the Causes and Effects of Income Inequality? 466

Inequality and Productivity 466

Inequality, Globalization, and Technology 467

Inequality, Technology, and Tournament-Style Markets 467

Inequality and Rent Seeking 468

The Economic Effects of Inequality 468

■ Application 21.1 Keeping Up with Your Co-workers Is Important 469

What Is the Role of Government in Promoting Equality? 470

Philosophical Justifications for Redistribution 470

■ Application 21.2 What Does the Ideal Wealth Distribution Look Like? 472

Progressive Taxation 473

Conclusion 474

CHAPTER SUMMARY AND PROBLEMS 475

21.1 HOW IS INEQUALITY MEASURED? 475

21.2 HOW UNEQUAL IS THE DISTRIBUTION OF INCOME IN THE UNITED STATES? 475

21.3 WHAT ARE THE CAUSES AND EFFECTS OF INCOME INEQUALITY? 476

21.4 WHAT IS THE ROLE OF GOVERNMENT IN PROMOTING EQUALITY? 477

EXPERIMENT: UNVEILING IGNORANCE 478

NOTES 479

Glossary 481

Credits 489

Index 491

Flexibility Chart

The following table will help you organize your syllabus based on your teaching objectives. As you review the table, please keep these points in mind:

1. Despite the fact that Chapter 4 is optional, you can conduct the Red/Green Experiment without going through the concepts of that chapter. The experiment is very useful in helping students' understanding of the outcomes of experiments with more than two players.

Core Topics in Micro	Optional Topics in Micro
Chapter 1: Fundamental Concepts in Economics *Experiment:* The Ultimatum Game: Are You Generous or Greedy?	
	Chapter 1 Appendix: Supply and Demand
Chapter 2: Cost–Benefit Analysis and the Value of a Life *Experiment:* The Dictator Game	
Chapter 3: Basic Game Theory: Games Between Two Players *Experiment:* The Push–Pull Game	
	Chapter 4: Game Theory: Games Between Three or More Players *Experiment:* The Red–Green Game
Chapter 5: Free Exchange: Individual and International Trade *Experiment:* The Gains-from-Trade Game	
Chapter 6: The Market System: Functions, Structure, and Institutions *Experiment:* Capitalism and Communism Games	
Chapter 7: The Nature of Pollution Problems *Experiment:* The Herd Immunity Game	
Chapter 8: Government Policies to Regulate Pollution *Experiment:* The Judge-Me-Not Game	
	Chapter 9: Resource Depletion and Sustainability *Experiment:* The "Gone Fishing" Game
Chapter 10: Public Goods and the Role of Government *Experiment:* The Garden Game	
	Chapter 11: Public Goods: Tackling Large Projects and Eminent Domain *Experiment:* The "Ask and You Might Receive" Game
	Chapter 12: The Volunteer's Dilemma: A Collective Inaction Problem *Experiment:* The "Save Ferris!" Game
	Chapter 13: Voting: You Can't Always Get What You Want *Experiment:* Looking for a "Goldilocks" Location
	Chapter 14: The Economics of Health Insurance and Health Care *Experiment:* The Restaurant Game
	Chapter 15: Segregation and Discrimination *Experiment:* Schelling's Checkerboard

2. The macro chapters de-emphasize game theory. You will see game theory in segments of Chapters 5, 6, 10, 13, and 14, but it's not vital to the understanding of most of the material in those chapters. Nevertheless, the collective action material and the material on the divergence between individual and social incentives that Chapter 1 presents can be illustrated with the experiments in Chapters 3, 4, 6, 10, 11, 13, and 14, even if students don't have the formal background in game theory.

Core Topics in Macro	Optional Topics in Macro
Chapter 1: Fundamental Concepts in Economics *Experiment:* The Ultimatum Game: Are You Generous or Greedy?	
	Chapter 1 Appendix: Supply and Demand
Chapter 2: Cost–Benefit Analysis and the Value of a Life *Experiment:* The Dictator Game	
	Chapter 3: Basic Game Theory: Games Between Two Players *Experiment:* The Push–Pull Game
	Chapter 4: Game Theory: Games Between Three or More Players *Experiment:* The Red–Green Game
Chapter 5: Free Exchange: Individual and International Trade *Experiment:* The Gains-from-Trade Game	
Chapter 6: The Market System: Functions, Structure, and Institutions *Experiment:* Capitalism and Communism Games	
Chapter 10: Public Goods and the Role of Government *Experiment:* The Garden Game	
	Chapter 11: Public Goods: Tackling Large Projects and Eminent Domain *Experiment:* The "Ask and You Might Receive" Game
	Chapter 13: Voting: You Can't Always Get What You Want *Experiment:* Looking for a "Goldilocks" Location
	Chapter 14: The Economics of Health Insurance and Health Care *Experiment:* The Restaurant Game
Chapter 16: Gross Domestic Product and the Wealth of Nations: An Introduction to the Macroeconomy MyEconLab Real-Time Data Activity: Gross Domestic Product and Business Cycles	
Chapter 17: Unemployment MyEconLab Real-Time Data Activity: Unemployment Rates	
Chapter 18: An Introduction to Money, Banks, and the Financial System MyEconLab Real-Time Data Activity: Money and the Financial System	
Chapter 19: The Federal Reserve: Monetary Policy, Economic Activity, and Inflation MyEconLab Real-Time Data Activity: Monetary Policy and Inflation	
Chapter 20: The Federal Government: Taxes, Spending, and Fiscal Policy MyEconLab Real-Time Data Activity: Budget Deficits and the Federal Debt	
	Chapter 21: Income Inequality and the Redistribution of Income *Experiment:* Unveiling Ignorance

Preface

The Audience and Focus of This Book

This book is written for a one-semester course in economic issues and is tailored to non-majors who are passionate about contemporary social problems. Most of the students who take this course are freshmen or sophomores with little mathematical training and little background in economics.

It is important for instructors of the issues course to remember that students who take the issues course aren't priming themselves to become theorists: They are concerned citizens who want to understand more about the problems society faces. Largely, these students are interested in becoming economically literate without subjecting themselves to the theory, graphs, and rigorous math they might find in a principles of economics course.

Many existing issues books fall back on teaching students to manipulate graphs—largely the same approach used in principles courses. Mastering the technical skills required by that approach is time-consuming, difficult for many students, and alienating for others. Other issues books offer short treatments of scattered topics, using ad hoc methods to analyze those topics. Students often leave those courses without a unified method of analysis that they can apply to problems that weren't covered in the course.

In contrast, this book uses fun, simple tools from game theory to analyze some of society's most vexing problems and depends less on mathematical and graphical models than do other issues texts. Students enjoy learning game theory, and it is an analytical framework that is applicable to a broad class of social problems such as pollution, health care, and the depletion of natural resources. Using the tools of game theory helps students discover that, ultimately, those problems have similar origins.

This textbook is substantially different from other issues of economics textbooks and will appeal to the teacher who wants to:

- Use a modern analytical approach based on the **tools of game theory**. Students will leave the course with a solid grasp of strategic behavior and how such behavior, exercised in the pursuit of individual incentives, can lead to poor collective outcomes.
- Conduct **economics experiments, games, and real-time data analysis exercises** so that students *learn by doing*. Innovative teachers will find activities in this book that cannot be found in any competing text. For example, in the "Judge Me Not" experiment, each student assumes the role of a producer who can choose polluting technology or clean technology. Individual incentives encourage each producer to choose polluting technology, so the collective outcome is a welfare-destroying volume of pollution that drives

up everyone's health care costs. Additional single and multiplayer experiments, interactives, and data exercises are available in **MyEconLab®**—Pearson Education's powerful assessment and tutorial system. *What students do, they remember.*

- Help students learn to *analyze* social problems rather than *memorize* facts that will soon become dated or irrelevant.
- Motivate students to read. The textbook blends a user-friendly, conversational writing style with analytical rigor.

About the Cover

Rock-paper-scissors is a game that even kids can master. In the game, two players use hand gestures to signal whether they'd like to play rock, paper, or scissors: rock beats scissors, scissors beats paper, and paper beats rock. It's a simple game, but understanding the strategies involved in rock-paper-scissors and other kids' games can lend tremendous insights into many of society's most serious problems—problems that result when people strategically trade society's best interests for individual gain. This book extensively applies the tools of game theory to develop those insights.

Organization

This textbook uses a core of basic game theory to analyze many social issues, such as how to preserve endangered species and why U.S. health care is so expensive. The book covers both microeconomics and macroeconomics:

Chapters 1–4 present fundamental economic concepts, such as scarcity, trade-offs, and opportunity costs. The Chapter 1 appendix covers demand and supply.

Chapters 5–15 discuss contemporary microeconomic issues such as pollution, health care, and discrimination. These chapters emphasize the roles that property rights, transactions costs, and information play in creating those social problems.

Chapters 16–21 explain how the macroeconomy works and address critical macroeconomic issues such as monetary policy, fiscal policy, unemployment, and income inequality.

For instructors who emphasize the macroeconomy, the textbook offers a user-friendly introduction. Rather than emphasize graphical analysis, the macro portion of this book presents a straightforward textual description of how the macroeconomy works. That description is easy for students to understand and remember, and it will give them an understanding of business cycles, stabilization policy, and other macro issues that will be useful for years to come. Each macro chapter is accompanied by an active-learning data collection and analysis exercise, and each chapter includes coverage of the Great Recession of 2007–2009.

Economic Experiments and Interactive Data Activities That Promote Knowledge and Self-Discovery

It can be challenging to help students make connections between what they learn in the classroom and what they see in the real world. One of the best ways for students to learn about economics is for them to "get their hands dirty" by *doing* economics. *What students do, they remember.*

This book contains 21 experiments and data activities. Most of the experiments place students in a scenario where they have to make an important real-world decision. The outcome of each experiment depends on both the individual student's decisions and the collective decisions of his or her classmates. These experiments are designed to show students that social problems may arise when many individuals collectively behave in a certain way. Students also learn something about themselves and their decision-making process along the way.

Each microeconomics chapter includes an experiment or game designed to represent an important social problem. For example, the "Save Ferris!" experiment in Chapter 12 illustrates one reason there aren't enough organ donors; the Garden Game experiment in Chapter 10 illustrates the difficulty in getting groups to work together toward a common goal. By combining a discussion of the theory behind these problems with experiential learning, students discover why social problems such as global warming and discrimination occur and why the incentives inherent in those problems make them so difficult for societies to solve.

Chapters 16–20 cover macroeconomic topics students hear about in the news, including gross domestic product (GDP), growth, unemployment, and inflation. Each of these chapters ends with a Real-Time Data Activity exercise that  teaches students how to locate, read, and interpret data about the economy from FRED® (Federal Reserve Economic Data), a comprehensive, up-to-date data set maintained by the Federal Reserve Bank of St. Louis.

The *Instructor's Manual* provides step-by-step instructions on how to set up, conduct, analyze, and grade each experiment for various class sizes.

Here are just a few of the unique experiments and interactive activities that accompany this text. These activities cannot be found in any other book! Please refer to the detailed table of contents for a complete listing of the experiments and Real-Time Data Activities.

Chapter 4: Game Theory: Games Between Three or More Players

Experiment: The Red–Green Game is a multiplayer prisoner's dilemma game in which students choose between two colors for a cash reward.

Chapter 5: Free Exchange: Individual and International Trade

Experiment: The Gains-from-Trade Game asks students to rate a snack they receive, and then trade with other students who have different snacks.

Chapter 6: The Market System: Functions, Structure, and Institutions

Experiment: The Capitalism and Communism Games explore how incentives shape student behavior and attitude toward work.

Chapter 7: The Nature of Pollution Problems

Experiment: The Herd Immunity Game explores positive externalities using the example of whether students would get a vaccine for a flu that is rampaging through their class.

Chapter 11: Public Goods: Tackling Large Projects and Eminent Domain

Experiment: The "Ask and You Might Receive" Game explores the holdout problem by asking students to claim a share of a fixed amount of money. If students claim more than is available, nobody gets anything.

Chapter 12: The Volunteer's Dilemma: A Collective Inaction Problem

Experiment: The "Save Ferris!" Game uses the prisoner's dilemma to explore whether a student would donate a kidney to save a beloved school administrator.

Chapter 16: Gross Domestic Product and the Wealth of Nations: An Introduction to the Macroeconomy

Real-Time Data Activity: Gross Domestic Product and the Business Cycles asks students to examine the behavior of GDP and its components over both the long term and the course of the business cycle.

Chapter 21: Income Inequality and the Redistribution of Income

Experiment: The Unveiling Ignorance Game randomly assigns students to an income quintile, where income is measured as extra credit points. Students can propose alternative social contracts, which the class votes on.

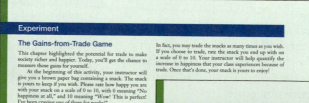

Experiment

The Gains-from-Trade Game

This chapter highlighted the potential for trade to make society richer and happier. Today, you'll get the chance to measure those gains for yourself.

At the beginning of this activity, your instructor will give you a brown paper bag containing a snack. The snack is yours to keep if you wish. Please rate how happy you are with your snack on a scale of 0 to 10, with 0 meaning "No happiness at all," and 10 meaning "Wow! This is perfect! I've been craving one of these for weeks!"

Other students in your class have different snacks. You have the option to trade your snack with any other student.

In fact, you may trade the snacks as many times as you wish. If you choose to trade, rate the snack you end up with on a scale of 0 to 10. Your instructor will help quantify the increase in happiness that your class experiences because of trade. Once that's done, your snack is yours to enjoy!

MyEconLab Real-Time Data Activity

Gross Domestic Product and Business Cycles

This chapter introduced you to gross domestic product (GDP), which is the most fundamental and important indicator of a country's economic performance. You learned that GDP has four components: Consumption, investment, government spending, and net exports. Here are some news headlines about GDP that you may have noticed:

- U.S. GDP expanded in last quarter.
- Ireland's GDP leads the Eurozone.
- Hong Kong's GDP contracted last quarter.

The chapter also discussed the nature and origins of business cycles, which refer to the ups and downs of the economy. Here are some news headlines about business cycles that you may have noticed:

- Fears of recession linger.
- Is the Eurozone recession over?
- Economic recovery expected, but uncertain.

Collecting and analyzing data about GDP and business cycles are an important part of what economists do and are of great interest to government officials and the general public. The activities at the ends of Chapters 16–20 therefore focus on data.

In this real-time data analysis activity, you'll revisit the fundamental ideas of GDP and business cycles using data from Federal Reserve Economic Data (FRED), a comprehensive, up-to-date data set maintained by the Federal Reserve Bank of St. Louis.

1. Visit the FRED website located at www.stlouisfed.org/fred2.
2. Examine the data for each component of GDP and track how each component has changed over time.
3. Explore how each component of GDP behaves during economic recessions, paying particular attention to the behavior of consumption and investment spending.

MyEconLab
Please visit http://www.myeconlab.com for support material to conduct this experiment if assigned by your instructor.

By applying the tools of game theory within the chapters and completing the hands-on experiments at the end of the chapters, students have experiences that help them understand why many social problems—problems as diverse as neighborhood segregation and measles epidemics—result from individual incentives that lead people to behave in ways that, when aggregated, produce undesirable results.

Additional single and multiplayer experiments, interactives, and data exercises are available in MyEconLab—Pearson Education's powerful assessment and tutorial system. See page xxx for a full description of MyEconLab and its resources.

Pedagogy

This book contains a number of features designed to pique student interest and enhance student learning.

Learning Objectives

Each chapter opens with a chapter outline and numbered learning objectives. The content within the chapter is organized by those numbered objectives so that professors can design the class and prepare reading assignments for the class. The end-of-chapter problems and the separate Test Item File are also organized by learning objective to help professors assign homework and assess student learning in exams.

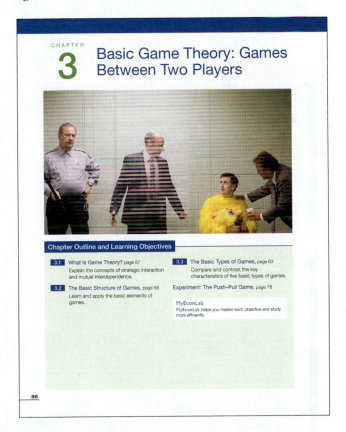

Application Feature

Each chapter contains two or more boxed Application features that present real-world reinforcement of key concepts from the chapter. Each Application box includes a supporting problem

at the end of the chapter, so instructors can use it to generate in-class discussion or assign it as homework. Each of the macroeconomics chapters (Chapters 16–20) features an Application box that explores the Great Recession of 2007–2009.

The People Behind the Theory Feature

Approximately half the chapters include a boxed feature that explores the people behind the theory, including vignettes on John Nash (Chapter 3), Adam Smith

(Chapter 5), Thomas Schelling (Chapter 15), and Milton
Friedman (Chapter 19).

Questions and Problems Grouped by Learning Objectives

Each chapter closes with the following features:

- Summary
- Key Terms list
- Review Questions consisting of fill-in-the-blank questions and multiple-choice questions
- Problems and Applications

The Summary, Review Questions, and Problems and Applications are grouped under *learning objectives*. The goals of this organization are to (1) make it easier for instructors to assign problems based on learning objectives, both in the book and in MyEconLab, and (2) help students efficiently locate and review material that they find difficult.

MyEconLab

MyEconLab is a unique online course management, homework, quizzing, testing, activity, and tutorial resource.

For Instructors

Instructors can choose how much or how little time to spend setting up and using MyEconLab. Here is a snapshot of what instructors are saying about MyEconLab:

MyEconLab's eText is great—particularly in that it helps offset the skyrocketing cost of textbooks. Naturally, students love that.

—Doug Gehrke, Moraine Valley Community College

MyEconLab offers [students] a way to practice every week. They receive immediate feedback and a feeling of personal attention. As a result, my teaching has become more targeted and efficient.

—Kelly Blanchard, Purdue University

Students tell me that offering them MyEconLab is almost like offering them individual tutors.

—Jefferson Edwards, Cypress Fairbanks College

With comprehensive homework, quiz, test, activity, practice, and tutorial options, instructors can manage all their assessment and online activity needs in one place. MyEconLab saves time by automatically grading questions and activities and tracking results in an online gradebook.

Each chapter contains two prebuilt assignments (homework and a quiz). Homework and study plan exercises contain tutorial resources (including instant feedback), links to

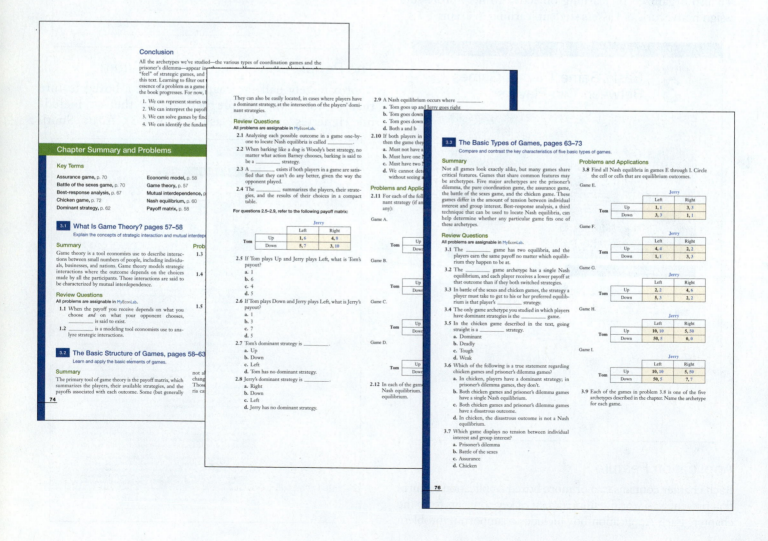

the appropriate learning objective in the eText, and step-by-step guided solutions, where appropriate. The online grade book records each student's performance and time spent on assessments and generates reports by student or by chapter.

Instructors can fully customize MyEconLab, adding reading assignments, homework assignments, media assignments, current news assignments, and quizzes and tests. Assignable resources include preloaded exercise assignments and quizzes for each chapter that are custom-tailored to the text and study plan problems that are similar to the end-of-chapter problems.

Learning Catalytics™ Experiments and Activities: Learning Catalytics is a real-time learning analytics and assessment system that helps faculty connect instantly with student laptops, tablets, smartphones, or other personal devices to engage students and personalize learning. Faculty can easily access Learning Catalytics from MyEconLab. We have created activities and questions specifically to support experiments in this book. With Learning Catalytics you can:

- Engage students in real time, using open-ended tasks to probe student understanding.
- Promote student participation using any modern Web-enabled device students already have—laptop, smartphone, or tablet.
- Address misconceptions before students leave the classroom.
- Understand immediately where students are and adjust your lecture accordingly.
- Improve your students' critical-thinking skills.
- Engage with and record the participation of every student in your classroom.

Learning Catalytics gives you the flexibility to create your own questions to fit your course exactly or choose from a searchable question library Pearson has created.

To learn more about Learning Catalytics, please visit **https://learningcatalytics.com/**.

Digital Interactives help to facilitate experiential learning through a set of interactives focused on core economic concepts. Fueled by data, decision-making, and personal relevance, each interactive progresses through a series of levels that build on foundational concepts, enabling a new immersive learning experience. The flexible and modular setup of each interactive makes Digital Interactives suitable for classroom presentation, auto-graded homework, or both. Digital Interactives can be assigned on their own for a grade, or professors can add additional MyEconLab exercises to the Digital Interactive assignment. To learn more, and for a complete list of Digital Interactives, visit **http://www.myeconlab.com**.

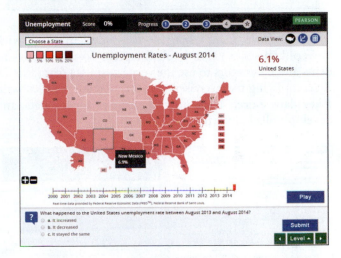

Experiments in MyEconLab provide a fun and engaging way to promote active learning and mastery of important economic concepts. Pearson's Experiments program is flexible and easy for instructors and students to use. Single-player experiments allow your students to play against virtual players from anywhere at any time, as long as they have an Internet connection. Multiplayer experiments allow you to assign and manage a real-time experiment with your class. Pre- and post-questions for each experiment are available for assignment in MyEconLab. For a complete list of available experiments, visit **http://www.myeconlab.com**.

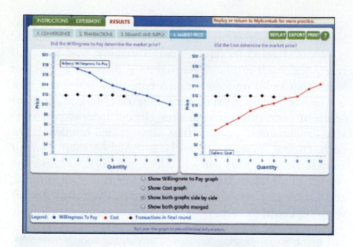

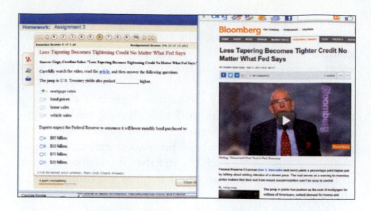

Real-Time Data Analysis Exercises, marked with MyEconLab Real-time data in book Chapters 16–20, allow students and instructors to use the very latest data from FRED. By completing the exercises, students become familiar with a key data source, learn how to locate real-time data, and develop skills in interpreting data.

In the eText available in MyEconLab, select figures labeled MyEconLab Real-Time Data allow students to display a pop-up graph updated with real-time data from FRED®.

Current News Exercises provide a turnkey way to assign gradable news-based exercises in MyEconLab. Each week, Pearson scours the news, finds current microeconomics and macroeconomics articles, creates an exercise around these news articles, and then automatically adds them to MyEconLab. Assigning and grading current news-based exercises that deal with the latest micro and macro events and policy issues has never been more convenient.

Test Item File questions allow you to assign quizzes or homework that look just like your exams.

Econ Exercise Builder allows you to build customized exercises. Exercises include multiple-choice and free-response items, some of which are generated algorithmically so that each time a student works them, a different variation is presented.

Customization and Communication

MyEconLab in MyLab/Mastering provides additional optional customization and communication tools. Instructors who teach distance-learning courses or very large lecture sections find the MyLab/Mastering format useful because they can upload course documents and assignments, customize the order of chapters, and use communication features such as Document Sharing, Chat, ClassLive, and Discussion Board.

For the Student

MyEconLab puts students in control of their learning through a collection of testing, practice, and study tools tied to the online, interactive version of the textbook and other media resources. Here is a snapshot of what students are saying about MyEconLab:

It was very useful because it had EVERYTHING, from practice exams to exercises to reading. Very helpful.
—student, Northern Illinois University

I would recommend taking the quizzes on MyEconLab because it gives you a true account of whether or not you understand the material.
—student, Montana Tech

It made me look through the book to find answers, so I did more reading.
—student, Northern Illinois University

Students can study on their own or can complete assignments created by their instructor. In MyEconLab's structured environment, students practice what they learn, test their understanding, and pursue a personalized study plan generated from their performance on sample tests and from quizzes created by their instructors. In Homework or Study

Plan mode, students have access to a wealth of tutorial features, including:

- Instant feedback on exercises that helps students understand and apply the concepts
- Links to the eText to promote reading of the text just when the student needs to revisit a concept or an explanation
- Links to the important features of the eText
- A graphing tool that is integrated into the various exercises to enable students to build and manipulate graphs to better understand how concepts, numbers, and graphs connect

Additional MyEconLab Tools

MyEconLab includes the following additional features:

- **eText**—In addition to the portions of eText available as pop-ups or links, a fully searchable eText is available for students who wish to read and study in a fully electronic environment.
- **Print upgrade**—For students who wish to complete assignments in MyEconLab but read in print, Pearson offers registered MyEconLab users a loose-leaf version of the print text at a significant discount.
- **Glossary flashcards**—Every key term is available as a flashcard, allowing students to quiz themselves on vocabulary from one or more chapters at a time.
- **MySearchLab**—MySearchLab provides extensive help on the research process and four exclusive databases of credible and reliable source material, including the *New York Times*, the *Financial Times*, and peer-reviewed journals.

Supplements

The *Instructor's Manual*, prepared by the author, includes step-by-step guidance on how to integrate experiments in class and how to discuss the results of the experiments, chapter-by-chapter summaries, teaching outlines incorporating key terms and definitions, teaching tips, topics for class discussion, and solutions to the questions and problems that appear at the end of each chapter. The Instructor's Manual is available for download from the Instructor's Resource Center (**http://www.pearsonhighered.com/Grant**).

The *Test Item File*, prepared by Randy Methenitis of Richland College, includes approximately 1,200 multiple-choice, true/false, short-answer, and graphing questions. The Test Item File is available for download from the Instructor's Resource Center (**http://www.pearsonhighered**

.com/Grant). Test questions are annotated with the following information:

- Difficulty: 1 for straight recall, 2 for some analysis, 3 for complex analysis
- Type: multiple-choice, true/false, short-answer, essay
- Topic: the term or concept the question supports
- Learning outcome
- Page number in the text

The *computerized TestGen* package allows instructors to customize, save, and generate classroom tests. The test program permits instructors to edit, add, or delete questions from the Test Item File; analyze test results; and organize a database of tests and student results. This software allows for extensive flexibility and ease of use. It provides many options for organizing and displaying tests, along with search and sort features. The software and the Test Item File can be downloaded from the Instructor's Resource Center (**http://www.pearsonhighered.com/Grant**).

PowerPoint slides, prepared by Larry McCarthy of Slippery Rock University, can be downloaded from the Instructor's Resource Center (**http://www.pearsonhighered .com/Grant**):

1. A comprehensive set of PowerPoint slides can be used by instructors for class presentations or by students for lecture preview or review. These slides include all the graphs, tables, and equations in the textbook.
2. A student version of the PowerPoint slides is available as .pdf files. This version allows students to print the slides and bring them to class for note taking. Instructors can also download these PowerPoint presentations from the Instructor's Resource Center (**http://www .pearsonhighered.com/Grant**).

Accuracy Review Board

Our accuracy checkers helped us proof the content, figures, and features of the text and the solutions to the end-of-chapter questions and problems. I am grateful for their time and contribution to making this book the best it can be:

CARLOS AGUILAR, *El Paso Community College*

HUGO EYZAGUIRRE, *Northern Michigan University*

BOB GILLETTE, *University of Kentucky*

LARRY MCCARTHY, *Slippery Rock University*

RANDY METHENITIS, *Richland College*

CHRIS PHILLIPS, *Somerset Community College*

Reviewers

I've always believed in surrounding myself with people who are smarter than I am. I benefited greatly from intelligent and thoughtful reviewers who provided feedback and recommendations throughout this book's development. Their contributions were essential to this project, and I am greatly indebted to them.

CARLOS AGUILAR, *El Paso Community College*

OLUBENGA AJILORE, *University of Toledo*

PATRICIA ATKINSON, *Clark College*

CLARE BATTISTA, *California Polytechnic State University–San Luis Obispo*

DANIEL BELL, *Big Sandy Community and Technical College*

DORIS BENNETT, *Jacksonville State University*

ANOOP BHARGAVA, *Finger Lakes Community College*

JOHN BLAIR, *Wright State University*

KELLY BLANCHARD, *Purdue University*

JIM BRUEHLER, *Eastern Illinois University*

STEPHANIE CAMPBELL, *Mineral Area College*

SHAWN CARTER, *Jacksonville State University*

ERIC DODGE, *Hanover College*

HUGO EYZAGUIRRE, *Northern Michigan University*

KAYA FORD, *Northern Virginia Community College*

MELANIE FOX, *Austin College*

GEORGE GOERNER, *Mohawk Valley Community College*

ABBAS GRAMMY, *California State University–Bakersfield*

GARY GRAY, *Umpqua Community College*

GAIL HEYNE HAFER, *St. Louis Community College–Meramec*

WAYNE HICKENBOTTOM, *University of Texas–Austin*

MARK HOLMGREN, *Eastern Washington University*

JIM HUBERT, *Seattle Central Community College*

ERIN HUTTON, *Bob Jones University*

SARAH JEYNK, *Youngstown State University*

SUKANYA KEMP, *University of Akron*

NELSON LAPLANTE, *Everett Community College*

ANTHONY LARAMIE, *Merrimack College*

JIM LEE, *Texas A&M University–Corpus Christi*

JOHN G. MARCIS, *Coastal Carolina University*

WARREN MATTHEWS, *LeTourneau University*

JOHN MCARTHUR, *Wofford College*

LARRY MCCARTHY, *Slippery Rock University*

NEIL MEREDITH, *West Texas A&M University*

MARTIN MILKMAN, *Murray State University*

ANDREW MONACO, *University of Puget Sound*

MICHAEL MORELLI, *Rutgers University at Camden*

RONALD NECOECHEA, *Roberts Wesleyan College*

TOMI OVASKA, *Youngstown State University*

BENNY OVERTON, *Vance Granville Community College*

SUZANNE PALMER, *Albright College*

STEPHEN PAULONE, *Post University*

SHERI PEREZ, *College of Southern Nevada*

WILLIAM PERFIT, *Suffolk County Community College*

NATE PERRY, *Colorado Mesa University*

CHRIS PHILLIPS, *Somerset Community College*

FERNANDO QUIJANO, *Dickinson State University*

JOHN RUDDER, *Blueridge Community & Technical College*

FRED J. RUPPEL, *Eastern Kentucky University*

MARK STEGEMAN, *University of Arizona*

CRAIG WALKER, *Oklahoma Baptist University*

NING WANG, *Arizona State*

CHARLES WASSELL, *Central Washington University*

BASSAM YOUSIF, *Indiana State University*

A Word of Thanks...

When this project began, I thought that writing a book was a solo effort. I couldn't have been more wrong. The team of professionals at Pearson has devoted tremendous time, energy, and thought to this project. I simply could not have done this without them, and I owe them a huge debt of gratitude. Acquisitions editor Noel Seibert took the risk of signing me at the beginning. David Alexander took over the project midway, and he has never failed to show enthusiasm for the project and creativity in how it has developed. Liz Napolitano shepherded the production of the end product in concert with Heidi Allgair at Cenveo® Publisher Services. Jonathan Boylan designed the beautiful cover and interior. Program manager Lindsey Sloan provided guidance on the general look of the book and on the functioning of Learning Catalytics.

I worked most closely with development editors Lena Buonanno and Amy Ray, two brilliant, helpful, and kind people who patiently introduced me to the process of writing a textbook. I can't thank them enough. Noel Lotz and Denise Clinton imagined and developed the MyEconLab resources that provide the interactive activities that are so important to the message of the book. Melissa Honig managed the MyEconLab course content for the book.

I am also indebted to a large group of people outside Pearson who inspired and supported this project. Larry McCarthy of Slippery Rock University reviewed multiple drafts of the manuscript, authored the PowerPoint presentation slides for the finished text, and carefully guided us in developing Learning Catalytic exercises. Randy Methenitis of Richland College wrote the test bank that accompanies this text. Linda Ghent and Andreea Chiritescu at Eastern Illinois University class-tested the developing drafts of this manuscript over several semesters, and they have provided both feedback and enthusiasm over that time. Jim Bruehler, also at Eastern Illinois, has been my biggest inspiration: His intellectual energy and his creativity in using experiments in the classroom encouraged me to try bringing experiments (some of them his!) into my own. My former department chair Ebi Karbassioon gave me the space to figure out what belongs in a course like this one, and Eastern alum Jen Muser wrote an excellent set of end-of-chapter questions.

At Baker University, my former student Justine Greve convinced me that this project was worth pursuing; it never would have gotten off the ground without her. Once under way, I benefitted from a whitespace grant that gave me time to pursue writing. I also appreciate the unwavering support of virtually everyone I work with.

Most importantly, however, I owe thanks and love to Emily and Cooper, who shared the joys and frustrations of writing a book without question or complaint. If this book is written for anyone, it's written for them.

About the Author

Alan Grant is professor of economics at Baker University. Prior to teaching at Baker, he was professor of economics at Eastern Illinois University and served as a visiting professor at Harlaxton College in England. He has taught the economic issues course for more than 15 years. Professor Grant has received a number of teaching awards and has been nationally recognized for teaching excellence. His research has been published in numerous professional journals, including *Public Finance Review*, *National Tax Journal*, *Economics Letters*, *Quarterly Review of Economics and Finance*, *Applied Economics Letters*, and the *Journal of Economic Education*, and he has been highlighted in *The Wall Street Journal*, *Businessweek*, *The Economist*, and the *New York Times*.

Economic Analysis

OF SOCIAL ISSUES

1

Fundamental Concepts in Economics

Chapter Outline and Learning Objectives

1.1 **What Is Economics?** page 2

Define *economics* and explain how a society decides what goods and services to produce and how to distribute them.

1.2 **Key Principles of Economics: Scarcity, Trade-offs, and Opportunity Costs,** page 4

Discuss how scarcity and trade-offs affect individuals and society.

1.3 **Key Principle of Economics: People Respond to Incentives,** page 9

Describe how incentives can affect behavior.

1.4 **A Brief Introduction to Collective Action Problems,** page 11

Define *collective action problems*.

1.5 **How Economists Analyze Economic Issues,** page 12

Explain the difference between positive and normative economics and explain how the benevolent social planner analyzes economic issues.

Experiment: The Ultimatum Game: Are You Generous or Greedy? page 18

MyEconLab
MyEconLab helps you master each objective and study more efficiently.

There is no general shortage of problems—everybody has them. Some people don't have enough time: *"My physics exam is in two hours, and I haven't started studying yet."* Some people don't have enough money: *"I just bought this iPod, but I don't have any money left for downloading music."* Other people wish they were more attractive or better at math. Some problems, of course, are more serious than others: *"I don't have enough to eat."* And other problems, like climate change and access to medical care, have far-reaching consequences that affect large numbers of people.

This book uses the tools of economics to examine some of society's largest and most difficult problems. It explores why those problems arise and why they are often so hard to solve. It also looks at some of the ways that individuals and governments try to deal with those problems and evaluates the effectiveness of those efforts. This chapter lays the foundation for that work by introducing you to some of the most basic, and yet most useful, economic concepts: scarcity, trade-offs, and the power of incentives.

What Is Economics?

1.1 Learning Objective

Define *economics* and explain how a society decides what goods and services to produce and how to distribute them.

Economics The study of how society manages its scarce resources to satisfy its wants.

Resources Items such as land, labor power, raw materials, fuel, factories, machinery, and people's skills that a society uses to create goods and services.

If you're typical of students taking a first course in economics, you might be wondering exactly what economics is. **Economics** is the study of how society manages its scarce resources to satisfy its wants. An economy's **resources** include land, labor power, raw materials, fuel, and factories and machinery (which economists generally call *capital*). But they also include people's time, talent, knowledge, willingness to take risks, and uncountable other traits and abilities that can be used to help meet society's desires.

We can use economics to explain a variety of business-related questions, including why interest rates change and what causes unemployment to increase or decrease. The tools of economics can also be used to answer more arcane (but no less interesting) questions that aren't directly related to business. For example, why do people who buy expensive gym memberships often fail to use them? Why do men traditionally give their fiancées diamond engagement rings? Is online social networking a valuable activity or a big waste of time?

Economics has a reputation for being a difficult and abstract subject, but it can be clear, fascinating, and fun. Throughout this book, you'll tear apart social problems using a small but powerful economics toolkit. You will discover that many of society's big issues—issues like global warming, the shortage of organ donors, and economic recessions—have remarkably similar origins.

Key Features of an Economy

No matter how commonplace or how unusual they are, the topics that economists study all relate in some way to the overall functioning of the economy. But what exactly do we mean by "the economy"? If you spend a lot of time reading newspapers or watching TV, you might have been mistakenly led to believe that the economy consists of little more than a perpetual quest to create jobs and the performance of the stock market.

Economy A type of organization that produces goods and services and then allocates those goods and services to its members.

But "the economy" encompasses much more than just those things. An **economy** is simply some type of organization that produces goods and services and then allocates those goods and services to its members. Economies can be small organizations, such as households, whose job might be to grow a garden to produce vegetables— vegetables that will eventually be transformed into a hearty stew to be ladled out into everyone's bowl come December. In fact, the word *economy* comes from the Greek *oikonomia*, which translates roughly as "household management." Economies can be big organizations, too, like the United States, the European Union, or the Pacific Rim, each of which produces hundreds of thousands of different goods and services. In each of these larger economies, just as in households, you'll find legal and cultural conventions that determine how production and distribution decisions will be made.

The Two Key Questions Every Economy Must Answer: What Gets Produced? And for Whom?

Whether an economy is as big as a continent or as small as a household, it needs to address these two questions:

1. *What* are we going to make with our resources?
2. Once we've made something, how do we decide *who* gets to enjoy it?

In the United States, we generally let the market system decide what is going to be produced and how to distribute goods. The **market system** is a form of economic organization in which individual buyers and sellers are free to exchange goods and services. In a market system, the ultimate decision about what to produce is left to sellers. But sellers do not make that decision in a vacuum; they must satisfy the tastes of buyers if they hope to earn a living. Once goods and services have been produced, they are given only to the buyers who are willing and able to pay for them. This means that the only people who end up getting plaid sweaters are the people who buy them . . . or who receive them as birthday presents.

In the market system, sellers must also decide *how* to produce the things they've decided to make. In other words, sellers determine what resources will be used. Will a furniture maker, for example, build tables and chairs by hand, using only a primitive set of tools? Or will he build those things using a lot of expensive power tools and a relatively small amount of human power? Choosing the right mixture of labor and machinery will help the furniture maker increase his profits and remain competitive in the furniture market.

Markets are only one mechanism society might use to answer the two key questions of what goods to produce and how to distribute them. For example, in North Korea, most decisions about what (and how) to produce are not made by markets but are instead made by a dictator. Economies where production and distribution decisions are made by government are called **command economies**. Do you think it's a bad thing to have a dictator making such important decisions on behalf of society? There are plenty of reasons you might think so, but before rushing to judgment, consider that sometimes command can be a highly effective way to organize production and distribution. This is often true for household-sized economies: If every family decision were open to debate by every family member, you'd spend every waking moment in family meetings, and very little would get done. And sometimes things need to be done quickly. This is why so many children's "Why?" questions are answered by their parents with "Because I said so. Now get moving!"

Just as a command can be used to mobilize households, it can also be used to mobilize nations. That's not always a blessing, but sometimes the ability to say "Because I said so" enables leaders to accomplish extraordinary things that might never be achieved if left to private initiative. It was a series of "Because I said so" orders, for example, that mobilized the labor necessary to build the 13,000 miles of the Great Wall of China, an architectural marvel of such tremendous scale that it is visible from outer space.

Most economies today are neither purely market economies nor purely command economies. Instead, they are hybrids where buyers and sellers make some production decisions and governments make others. Economies like this are called **mixed economies**. Different economies have different mixtures of market and governmental decision making. In the United States, which is fairly market oriented, private firms decide how many shoes, tablet computers, and loaves of bread to produce. The government, on the other hand, generally decides how many miles of highway to build, how many schools to staff, and how many post offices to operate. In more centralized economies, government is responsible for either directly providing or for planning the production of goods and services that the United States leaves to private individuals or firms, like electricity and telephone service, health care services, and food.

Market system A form of economic organization in which individual buyers and sellers are free to exchange goods and services.

Command economy An economy where the government makes production and distribution decisions.

Mixed economies Economies where buyers and sellers make some production decisions and governments make others.

1.2 Learning Objective

Discuss how scarcity and trade-offs affect individuals and society.

Key Principles of Economics: Scarcity, Trade-offs, and Opportunity Costs

Regardless of which system an economy chooses for organizing its production and distribution decisions, those decisions are governed by a common set of principles—principles that are the foundation on which this course is built. Understanding these principles will help you interpret news stories about the economy, make decisions about your life, and, importantly, succeed in this course.

Scarcity

Scarcity A situation where limited resources make it impossible to fulfill all of our wants.

The first of the key economic principles is scarcity. **Scarcity** means that we don't have the resources necessary to fulfill all of our wants. One of the fundamental assumptions we'll rely on in our study of economics is that our wants are virtually unlimited. We are born wanting: *"Hey you—you in the white coat! It sure is cold and bright out here. Can you turn down the lights and turn up the thermostat?"* We die wanting: *"Please just give me a few more weeks to be with my loved ones."* In between, we will spend a lifetime working to fulfill our material and spiritual wants, only to replace them with other desires once they have been satisfied: *"I like my BMW, but would you look at the lines on that Mercedes?"* We're fighting a losing battle. Our desires are virtually unlimited, but the means to satisfy them are not. The most obvious resource we're lacking is cash: Most of us simply don't have enough money to buy everything we would like. But a lack of money is only the top layer of the problem. Peel it away, and we'll find that under the surface, we're lacking other resources, too, and the lack of money is actually a manifestation of those shortfalls. For example, it generally takes some extraordinary ability to become super rich. Most people lack the athletic ability of LeBron James, the technological genius of Bill Gates, the market savvy of Warren Buffett, or the entrepreneurial vision of Mark Zuckerberg. And plain hard work just isn't enough because, after all, there are only 24 hours in a day, and we have only a limited amount of time on this planet.

In fact, time is one of our scarcest resources. If only we could work more hours to satisfy our material wants. If only we had more quality time to spend with our friends and family. If only we could pack a few extra hours into each day, how much happier we might be! But time is both precious and fleeting. A lack of time can make you wish you could be in two places at once, force you to pull an all-nighter before a psychology final, and make you angry about every second you spend stuck in traffic. Even wealthy people like Gates and Buffett still feel the pressure of having too little time.

Trade-offs and Opportunity Costs

Opportunity cost What is sacrificed in order to engage in an activity.

Because of scarcity, we have to make choices about which desires to satisfy and which to leave unfilled. Nobody gets to break the law of scarcity, no matter where they live or what system their economy is based on. We all face *trade-offs* in that we address some needs at the expense of others. Economists have a special term for trade-offs: opportunity costs. The **opportunity cost** of an activity is what you sacrifice to engage in that activity. At its most basic, opportunity cost is a straightforward concept. Suppose you're down to your last $10, and there are two things you really want to do. One is to see *The Hobbit* at the movie theater, and the other is to eat a delicious pulled-pork sandwich at the local barbeque joint. But each of these activities costs about $10, so you can afford one or the other, but you can't afford both. If you choose the movie, you lose the opportunity to eat a great sandwich. If you choose the sandwich, you give up the opportunity to see the movie. The option you do *not* choose is what you'll give up. It is the opportunity cost of your choice.

It is, of course, true that when you decide to go to the movie, you lose other alternatives as well. With the $10 you spend on your movie ticket, you could have gotten a barbeque sandwich. You could also have downloaded a Lady Gaga album, gotten a manicure, or enjoyed a monster-sized half-caf soy latte. It is, however, inaccurate to say that because you went to the movie you gave up a sandwich, a CD, a manicure, *and* a latte, because the $10 would have allowed you to buy any one of those things but not all of those things. So when we talk about measuring the cost of what we gave up, we consider the *best* of the sacrificed options as the opportunity cost. This is why many economists describe the opportunity cost of doing something as the value of your next-best alternative.

The concept of opportunity cost applies to individuals, but it also applies to various levels of society. For example, because resources are scarce, countries have to decide what they will produce and what they won't. Not every country can do everything well: If Finland decides it wants to grow bananas, it's going to have to pump a lot of resources into building, staffing, and heating greenhouses—resources that could have been used to produce other things like softwood lumber and cellular phones. In other words, bananas are expensive in Finland in that they are grown at high opportunity cost. In contrast, bananas are pretty easy to grow in Guatemala, and their opportunity cost is relatively low: Because of its warm climate and a relative lack of skilled labor, the resources used to produce bananas in Guatemala wouldn't be very productive if they were devoted to growing pine trees or making cell phones instead. Such differences in opportunity costs create natural opportunities for countries to gain by trading with one another: Finland can send Guatemala some of its cell phones in exchange for some of Guatemala's bananas. That keeps each country from trying to do something that it's not particularly good at. (That process of exchange is explored in greater depth in Chapter 5.)

Opportunity Cost Is Not About Money When you talk with your friends about how much something costs, you probably mention money. So our movie-versus-sandwich example may puzzle you. Couldn't we simply say that the cost of the movie was $10, and avoid discussing the sandwich?

Economists avoid measuring opportunity cost strictly in terms of money for two reasons. First, as strange as it sounds, money itself does not make us particularly happy. Our money is a contrivance we invented to help facilitate exchange. It has virtually no intrinsic value. It is simply colorful paper, backed by only the expectation that if we accept it in exchange for the things we sell, we will later be able to find someone else to accept it in exchange for the things we wish to buy. That's particularly true when the thing we're selling is our labor: We're generally confident that we'll be able to use the money we earn to buy clothes and food. If we weren't, we'd demand to be paid in blue jeans and sushi.

It's the clothes, and the food, and the other things we enjoy that really matter to us. If you run a $50 bill through the washing machine and it comes out in little linty pieces, you're probably not upset because you ruined the bill. You're upset because you can't use that bill to go out Saturday night with friends, buy books, or pay rent. Fundamentally, the loss of those opportunities is what is important; the loss of fancy colorful paper is not.

The second reason economists sometimes avoid using money as a measure of opportunity cost is because not all opportunities are easily measured in dollars. Suppose it's the night before your chemistry final. You're just settling in for some intensive study when friends down the hall stop by to see if you'd like to join them to see *Plan 9 from Outer Space*. "We've got an extra ticket," they tell you. "One night only—and it won't cost you a dime!"

And they're right—it won't cost you a dime. But it will cost you time. Once again, you're facing a tough choice. If you decide to study, you'll miss a cult classic and some time with your friends. If you go to the movie, you'll sacrifice valuable study time—time that could easily make a difference in your course grade. The opportunity cost—the trade-off—is very real and very important to you, but it is not easily measured in dollars. So, when you consider your trade-offs, all costs matter, not just those measured in dollars.

Explicit costs Costs that are measured in dollars and that typically involve some exchange of money.

Implicit costs Costs that do not involve an exchange of money.

Explicit Costs Versus Implicit Costs Economists use special terminology to describe different types of costs. **Explicit costs** are costs that are measured in dollars and that typically involve some exchange of money. **Implicit costs** are costs that do not involve an exchange of money. Implicit costs can sometimes be difficult to measure, but they are still real costs, and they are still important. When we evaluate trade-offs, accounting for explicit costs is fairly straightforward, but we want to take extra care to account for implicit costs.

Consider, for example, a new program at your university that will provide all students free Subway sandwiches at lunchtime each semester. This may seem like a great deal to you. But is the free lunch program really free to you? After all, Subway isn't going to *give* those sandwiches away. One way that your university might fund the sandwich program is by raising your tuition. In that case, the costs are explicit,

---

Application 1.1

Even Superheroes Face Trade-offs

Everyone faces trade-offs. You face them. Presidents face them. Even dictators face them. But you, presidents, and dictators are mere mortals. Could it be that superheroes, with their superpowers, don't fall prey to the laws of scarcity?

Alas, even superheroes face trade-offs. To illustrate, consider Superman. He can't be in two places at once. So when Lois Lane is being mugged on the south side of Metropolis, and arch-villain Lex Luthor is kidnapping *Daily Planet* editor Perry White on the north side, Superman has to make a choice: Will he save Lois, or will he save Perry?

If Superman is really interested in saving lives, perhaps he should let Lois be mugged *and* let Perry be kidnapped! From society's standpoint, the question is how to apply Superman's superhuman strength and endurance to bring the greatest benefit to humanity. Should he use his strength to disarm evil villains intent on taking a life or two? Or should he use his power to benefit greater numbers of people?

What if society put Superman to work plowing fields in impoverished countries, or hauling water to irrigate crops in remote arid regions where people are starving for a lack of food? That would surely be a better use of Superman's strength than having him waiting around for an isolated crime or two to occur in relatively wealthy Metropolis.

But even that may not be the best use of Superman's resources. If he would apply his superhuman strength to turning a gigantic turbine, he could power the globe, bringing abundant electricity to billions of people and raising living standards worldwide.

Because instead Superman chooses to fight crime one villain at a time, society loses. And because of the daunting trade-offs they face, Superman and his fellow crime fighters also lose. The demands of the job are so incredible, regardless of what tasks these superheroes undertake, that their chances of having normal relationships are slim. Superman loved Lois Lane, Batman loved Vicky Vail, Spider-Man loved Mary Jane Watson, and Wonder Woman has had many love interests over the years. Yet each of those relationships was a rocky, drawn-out affair. Most were doomed to failure. In the end, only Superman ended up with his true love.

Everyone faces trade-offs, including superheroes. Super powers may enable superheroes to defy the law of gravity, but even super powers aren't strong enough to break the law of scarcity.

See related problem 2.10 on page 15 at the end of this chapter.

Based on Zach Weiner's *Saturday Morning Breakfast Cereal*, July 11, 2011, and the Ecocomics blog entry, "Do Superheroes Act in Socially Optimal Ways?" Eco-comics.blogspot.com, November 8, 2010.

and those costs represent the other things you might have spent those tuition dollars on—possibly things you might like more than a few hundred sandwiches.

But your university might choose to hold the line on tuition and not pass the cost of the sandwich program along to you explicitly. That doesn't mean that the sandwich program doesn't cost you something! For starters, you're likely to spend lots of time standing in line waiting for your "free" sandwiches. That's an implicit cost, and it may be very important to you.

You might bear the cost in more subtle ways. Perhaps the expense of the sandwich program forces the university to make cuts elsewhere. Perhaps it will hire fewer professors and, as a result, a course that you'll need in order to graduate won't be offered on schedule. Or perhaps your university will cut a midmorning section of a course you're planning to take, leaving only a 7:30 a.m. section and costing you hours of valuable sleep.

These implicit costs are very real. They matter to you. But even though they're a direct consequence of the sandwich program, that fact is not readily apparent to a casual observer. This is because the sandwich program is one of many university programs, and it can be hard to link cause and effect when all those programs get jumbled together. But more important is the fact that it's hard to account for those implicit costs because they are opportunities that never materialized. Figuring out the size of those lost opportunities is just plain tough.

In the end, though, one conclusion is certain: Your university's sandwich program is not free. Somebody pays, visibly or invisibly, directly or indirectly, for every sandwich that gets eaten. And that someone is likely to be you. This example demonstrates why the most famous saying in all of economics, popularized by the late Nobel Prize–winning economist Milton Friedman, is, "There is no such thing as a free lunch." That wisdom, which is often referred to as the "law of no free lunch," applies to you, your university, and everyone else.

Government, Public Policy, and Trade-offs

The "law of no free lunch" also applies to governments. Some problems, such as pollution and poverty, can be difficult for individuals to solve on their own. Governments can help solve such problems but, like individuals, governments face opportunity costs. A government can't provide us with everything we desire; its resources are limited, and our desires are not. For a given amount of revenue, your government must decide which goods or services to provide for people and which ones people will have to provide for themselves. A harsh winter that requires government to spend a lot of money plowing highways could mean cutting back on summer programs for children. Buying more tanks and Humvees for the military could mean less government funding for national parks.

Governments aren't always the *best* at solving our problems. In fact, sometimes governments can actually make things worse. A government that expends resources trying to solve problems that people can solve for themselves may be wasting those resources. A government that actually makes things worse through its actions definitely is. Throughout this book, we'll explore questions of public policy. **Public policy** is the collection of laws, regulatory measures, and actions concerning a particular topic, such as the environment or health care, that originates with some body of government.

Public policy The collection of laws, regulatory measures, and actions concerning a particular topic that originates with some body of government.

In other words, public policy concerns the collection of choices the government makes. We'll spend considerable time evaluating those choices: Is the government using its scarce resources where they can do the most good? Is it applying its powers to improve society? Or is it squandering its resources by applying them to problems that can be better solved in other ways? Further, governments, policymakers, and politicians have their own sets of motivations that may not align well with society's interests. One simple example is a congressperson who devotes his efforts to pursuing reelection instead of working to pass legislation that everybody agrees is important.

Application 1.2

Rolling Out the Barrels, North Korean Style

North Korea isn't a shopper's paradise. But oddly, it's an okay place to go for a beer; it's been the home of high-quality Taedonggang beer since the year 2000. To fully appreciate the story behind Taedonggang, we need to know how North Korea answers the two questions facing every economy:

1. *What* are we going to make with our resources?
2. Once we've made something, how do we decide *who* gets to enjoy it?

North Korea has a command economy, so when people in 2000 asked, "What will we produce?" the answer was, "Whatever dictator Kim Jong-il desires." When they asked, "How will we distribute it?" the answer was, "However Kim Jong-il desires."

So when Kim Jong-il decided North Korea needed a brewery, it got one. In 2000, his officials negotiated with a centuries-old British brewery to purchase a recently closed plant. The plant was dismantled and reassembled in North Korea as the Taedonggang Beer Factory. Production began soon after.

The typical North Korean, however, is very poor and generally drinks cheap but potent rice liquor rather than more expensive beer. In other words, Kim Jong-il imported an expensive, large-scale brewery to satisfy the few people in North Korea wealthy enough to drink beer. This is nothing new to North Koreans. For example, the country has a massive highway system but essentially no cars.

But even dictators are constrained by scarcity. They have to make choices, and the consequences of those choices can be tough. Take the choice to begin brewing Taedonggang beer. That decision came on the heels of a series of disastrous floods that resulted in a five-year famine in the country. Of the 22 million people living in North Korea in 1994, an estimated 3 million had died by 1998. The famine is officially ended, but quality of life isn't much better today: In 2011, the government's Public Distribution System reduced peoples' daily food rations so drastically that the associated caloric intake fell from 1,400 calories to just 700—about a third of the typical Westerner's. In North Korea, the government makes distribution decisions down to the calorie level.

The choice to brew Taedonggang, then, comes with this trade-off: Beer is made from food. The barley that goes into Taedonggang could be used to feed a chronically malnourished people. There is a cost to Taedonggang beer, and unfortunately, ordinary North Koreans bear the brunt of it. But the leaders bear some, too, because in making a decision to brew beer instead of provide food, they're weakening the very people they depend on to build their highways, patrol their borders, design their missiles, and staff their cult of personality.

In North Korea, the dictator makes the laws. But nobody, not even the dictator, gets to rewrite the law of no free lunch.

See related problem 2.11 on page 15 at the end of this chapter.

Based on "Thirsty Communists Roll Out the Barrels in North Korea," *USA Today*, March 11, 2008, and "A Tasty Brew That Won't Be On Tap in the West; In North Korea, a Favorite Party Project Receives Priority but Little Marketing," *International Herald Tribune*, March 11, 2008.

The *public choice* branch of economics applies the same set of tools economists use to study market transactions to examine the self-interested behavior of politicians, lobbyists, agencies, bureaucrats, and voters.

Answering public policy questions is hard because many government trade-offs are implicit, which makes them subtle and difficult to measure. Consider, for example, the automobile safety regulation "Click It or Ticket," which requires people to wear safety belts. One benefit of the regulation is that it encourages people to use the safety equipment in their cars. Consequently, they will be more likely to survive a crash.

What's the trade-off of the seat belt regulation? It lowers the cost of driving like a maniac. By encouraging drivers to buckle up, the regulation reduces the costs to drivers of being in accidents. For example, they face a lower risk of injury or death, smaller hospital bills, and less pain. Because of that, we can expect some people to drive faster, venture out more often when roads are snowy, and pay less attention while driving. As a result, mandatory seat belt laws *actually create more accidents*.[1] And people—both pedestrians and occupants of other cars—will die in those accidents. This puts government in the odd position of choosing exactly who it is going to save: *"We know the new law will save the lives of drivers who get in accidents, but we also know that the new law will end up causing some entirely innocent people to die in accidents that would otherwise not have occurred. If we pass the law, we save* X *number of lives. If we don't pass the law, we'll save* Y *number of lives."* Now that's a deadly trade-off!

In the case of mandatory seat belt laws, the trade-off is subtle but measurable. The government has numbers to work with: It can compare X and Y and figure out, based on their magnitudes, whether the law produces a net gain. In fact, governments regularly employ economists and statisticians to do just that—estimate how many lives might be both saved and lost as a result of such a policy and make a recommendation based on those estimates.

Sometimes measuring trade-offs can be more difficult. Consider, for example, the U.S. Constitution's protection of free speech. As a society, we value free speech because it gives us the right to express ourselves without fear of sanction by the government. But free speech doesn't come without cost; there's always a trade-off. Free speech gives you the right to speak your mind, but it also gives someone who is loudmouthed, anti-Semitic, misogynistic, and economist-hating the right to speak his. That trade-off isn't particularly subtle, but the costs and benefits are incredibly difficult to quantify.

Key Principle of Economics: People Respond to Incentives

Another major principle of economics is that people respond to incentives. **Incentives** are inducements to act in certain ways. Depending on their structure, incentives can either encourage or discourage particular behaviors. Suppose you're walking down the sidewalk, and you see a penny. Do you stop and pick it up? If not, would you stop for a nickel? A dime? A dollar? Incentives often, as in this case, appear in the form of benefits. Benefits, in turn, encourage rewarded behaviors. Incentives imply that if you want people walking down the sidewalk to stop and bend over, you can get them to do it by leaving a coin on the sidewalk. If you want a greater proportion of the people to bend over, leave a bill instead.

Incentives can also appear in the form of costs. Suppose, gentlemen, that you're one of the cheapskates willing to pick up a penny from the sidewalk. Now, suppose that you're not on the sidewalk when you spot the gleam of copper, but are at the altar exchanging your wedding vows. Do you pick up the penny now? Because no matter what everyone

1.3 Learning Objective

Describe how incentives can affect behavior.

Incentives Inducements to act in certain ways.

---

[1] You may be skeptical of the assertion that safer cars encourage reckless driving. To overcome those doubts, consider a thought experiment proposed by several very prominent economists: Replace every car's driver's side airbag with a sharpened spear pointed directly at the center of the driver's chest. If you agree, as I do, that drivers of such dangerous cars would be *extremely* careful, then you are essentially agreeing that seat belts encourage less caution. If even that isn't convincing enough, Richard Porter's excellent book *Economics at the Wheel* reviews a large number of studies that test the assertion and find strong support for the hypothesis.

Application 1.3

Dying to Save Taxes

Social scientists have long known that people have some ability to control the timing of their deaths. They often remain alive long enough to observe religious holidays, see offspring born, or reach landmark birthdays. So if people can control the timing of their deaths for social and religious reasons, can they do so if it's to their financial advantage? In other words, does death respond to incentives?

Economists Joshua Gans and Andrew Leigh addressed that question by examining changes in Australian estate tax law. The estate tax gives the government a financial claim on the accumulated wealth you leave your heirs. In 1979, Australia reduced its federal estate tax from 27.5% to 0%. The tax was broadly based: About 1 in 10 people were subject to it. So, for significant numbers of Australians, the ability to delay death until the tax expired could add thousands or even millions of dollars to their survivors' inheritances.

Were people able to delay their deaths to take advantage of lower tax rates? After looking at the number of deaths reported in Australia each day, Gans and Leigh say yes. In the week before the estate tax expired, death totals were unexpectedly low: About 50 fewer people died than the long-run trend would have predicted. In the week after the tax was abolished, 50 *extra* people died. This suggests that those 50 people were able to delay their deaths by a week, solely to take advantage of favorable changes in tax law. Given the overall number of deaths in Australia, Gans and Leigh conclude that about *half* of the people who were eligible for the estate tax managed to delay death to avoid taxation!

How did they do that? Some people asked for extra medication, and some delayed removing life-sustaining medical devices. Some may have even asked their doctors to illegally postdate their death certificates. But at least some of the response can be attributed to sheer stubbornness: People simply willed themselves to live a bit longer, until the time and the tax were right.

The results of the Gans and Leigh study have been confirmed using data from Sweden. In addition, using historical data from the United States, economists Joel Slemrod and Wojciech Kopczuk have shown that the opposite holds true as well: Estate tax increases may induce people to accelerate their deaths. This leaves us with little doubt about the deadly effects of January 1, 2011, when the U.S. estate tax rose dramatically from 0% to 35%.

Benjamin Franklin once commented that only two things in life are certain: death and taxes. Now we know that those two things are intertwined. In the words of Gans and Leigh, "Even the super-rich cannot cheat death forever, but some may be able to stay alive long enough to avoid the estate tax."[2]

See related problem 3.7 on page 16 at the end of this chapter.

Based on Joshua Gans and Andrew Leigh, "Toying with Death and Taxes: Some Lessons from Down Under," *The Economist's Voice*, 2006, and Joel Slemrod and Wojciech Kopczuk, "Dying to Save Taxes: Evidence from Estate Tax Returns on the Death Elasticity," *Review of Economics and Statistics*, 2003.

tells you, this day *belongs* to your bride, and she's just being nice by letting you share it. And if you interrupt *her* day in the middle of the "Do you takes" to pick up a penny (or a dime, or a quarter), you will never be allowed to forget it. The simple lesson is that one way to discourage particular behaviors is to increase the costs associated with them.

It's important for policymakers to understand incentives. Governments can use the power of incentives to encourage behaviors that society wants more of and to discourage behaviors that society wants less of. The U.S. government, for example, uses

---

[2]Joshua Gans and Andrew Leigh, "Toying with Death and Taxes: Some Lessons from Down Under," *The Economist's Voice*, 2006.

both benefits and costs to encourage you to drive a more fuel-efficient automobile: You qualify for a tax credit if you purchase a plug-in hybrid car, but you may pay a surtax if you choose a gas guzzler instead. The government also encourages altruism by allowing you to deduct charitable donations from your taxable income; it encourages communities to build large-scale tornado shelters by helping to pay for their construction; it nudges you to lead a healthier lifestyle by taxing cigarette purchases. Not all incentives need to be measured in dollars: The government enacts laws to discourage crime; the incentives those laws create are often measured in time (20 years to life, for example) rather than money.

All incentives, whether they appear as costs or benefits, work by changing the trade-offs individuals face. That makes some options appear more attractive and others less so. If the trade-offs change enough, people may be convinced to act in ways that they ordinarily wouldn't.

A Brief Introduction to Collective Action Problems

1.4 Learning Objective

Define *collective action problems*.

Now that you understand the concepts of scarcity, trade-offs, and incentives, we can preview the kinds of social problems you'll study throughout this book.

Suppose a huge crowd packs a stadium to see Taylor Swift perform. When the performance begins, everyone is sitting. Then a single fan in the front row stands. When she does, she obstructs the view of two or three fans behind her. Those fans stand, too, obstructing the view of another six or seven fans behind them. Before you know it, the entire audience is standing, and they remain this way for the entire show.

This is a very interesting situation! Every individual can improve his or her view by standing. But when everybody stands, nobody can see any better than they could when they were all sitting. The only thing the audience gets for its trouble is a tired back from standing for hours on a hard concrete floor.

If, hypothetically, the audience could vote to either sit or stand, sitting would be the likely winner. But it is unlikely that an audience will put this to a vote, and it is unlikely that members of the audience will unilaterally forgo what is in their best interests as individuals (namely, standing) and choose to act in the best interest of the group, or *collectively*. For that reason, problems like this are referred to as collective action problems. A **collective action problem** exists when naturally occurring incentives encourage sufficient numbers of people to act in a way that makes everybody worse off. Simply put, individual trade-offs are different than the trade-offs for society as a whole.

Collective action problem A problem that exists when naturally occurring incentives encourage sufficient numbers of people to act in a way that makes everybody worse off.

The world is full of collective action problems. In fact, many if not most of the toughest problems society faces today are some type of collective action problem. We'll devote quite a bit of time and paper convincing you of this in the remainder of this book.

The general trouble with collective action problems is that no individual has any incentive to act in the best interests of the group. In other words, private incentives are not properly aligned with collective, or social, goals. In cases like these, individuals may be powerless to solve the problem through individual action. Under those circumstances, we may need a more powerful entity to alter incentives so that individuals are guided to make choices that are in the best interest of society. In our stadium example, that entity might be a fire marshal who orders everyone to sit. In society as a whole, that entity is often, but not always, the government.[3] When a collective action problem exists, the government often has the ability to guide behaviors in ways that make the world better off.

---

[3] In some cases, individuals working together are able to establish organizations and social norms that are strong enough to overcome collective action problems without the help of a formal government. You'll see some of those cases beginning in Chapter 6.

However, it is important to note that not all problems are collective action problems. Often, individual and collective incentives line up quite nicely. (We'll spend a great deal of time talking about an example of this in Chapter 5.) In these situations, government intervention may actually make the world a worse place rather than a better one. So a big part of your job as students of the economy is to ask first under what circumstances the government's attempts to solve problems can potentially make the world better off, and second, what kinds of policies might be necessary to realize that potential.

How Economists Analyze Economic Issues

Let's take a look at the manner in which economists approach the analysis of economic problems and their potential solutions. Generally, economists take an observational approach to studying the world. In other words, economists strive to describe the world as it is, not how they or others would *like* it to be.

Positive and Normative Economics

Positive economics Objective analysis of "what is" in the economy.

This observational approach to economic analysis—describing the world as it is, not how we would *like* it to be—is referred to as **positive economics**. The single defining feature of this approach is that economists do not try to impose their beliefs and preferences on anyone else. There's a big difference, for example, between saying, "Increasing the minimum wage will cause businesses to hire fewer workers," and saying, "The minimum wage is not rising fast enough." The difference is that the first statement is testable: It can be either verified or proven false by collecting data and crunching numbers. The second statement, on the other hand, cannot be tested in any meaningful way: It is a statement of someone's opinion of how the world *should* be rather than an assertion of fact. Economists refer to such statements as **normative economics**.

Normative economics Statements of "what should be" in the economy.

Everybody has opinions, but that doesn't make them right. If you say the minimum wage isn't rising fast enough, not everyone will agree with you. Business owners facing rising labor costs might think that the minimum wage is rising too fast. That, too, is an opinion. Both of these opinions might be based on observed data, but they could just as easily reflect the opinion holder's pro-labor or pro-business sympathies.

In this book, we will take a positive approach. The positive approach prevents us from arbitrarily supporting the interests of the people we happen to like over the interests of people we don't. In our study of the economy, everybody counts, no matter how much we might dislike them.

The positive approach also helps us avoid making judgments about what is "fair." Economist Harold Winter of Ohio University illustrates the difficulty in making such judgments in this way: Suppose your instructor has $1,000 to split between two students in your class (let's call them Velma and Daphne). How should the instructor divide that money? Many of you might say that $500 each, a 50–50 split, is the only fair division. But what if Velma is very rich and Daphne is very poor? Would your answer change? Would it be more fair to give Velma less (say, $100), and Daphne more ($900)?

But one might argue that because Velma already has a lot of money, $500 wouldn't make her much happier. Conversely, because Daphne is poor, even a tiny amount would bring her great happiness. So maybe it's most fair to divide the money in a way that brings each girl the same amount of *happiness*—perhaps $900 to Velma and only $100 to Daphne.

The point is that there isn't really a right or wrong answer to the question of a fair division of the $1,000. Make a decision about how to divide the money, and one person or the other can come up with a reasoned argument why it should be divided differently. That's true for the $1,000, and it's generally true for anything produced in an economy that must then be allocated among that economy's participants. One reason that economists generally stick to the positive approach is because the question of fair division is so hard to decide objectively.

The Benevolent Social Planner and the Best Use of Scarce Resources

There's a bigger problem that appears when scarce resources must be allocated. Sometimes people don't just holler, "That's not fair!" when they receive a smaller slice than they think they deserve; instead, they take action to increase the size of the slice. As this book unfolds, you'll learn that sometimes when people actively pursue bigger slices for themselves, they can cause losses to others that are much larger than their own gains. Cases like these are directly analogous to taking $5 from Velma, giving $3 of it to Daphne, and tearing the remaining $2 into confetti.

At a societal level, these kinds of things happen all the time, and every time they happen, society gets poorer.[4] In those circumstances, it *might* be nice to have an impartial watchdog that cares about society and can offer guidance to help keep society from wasting its scarce resources.

We've got just such a watchdog. She is a hypothetical figure economists call the benevolent social planner (BSP). You will see her often in this book. She is all-seeing and all-knowing, able to process the likes, dislikes, and activities of every individual in every society simultaneously. She's called "benevolent" for a reason: She cares about her people, she understands the environment of scarcity we operate in, and she wants us to extract the greatest amount of happiness from the limited resources we've been given. Her only objective is to maximize the size of the economic pie, and she always knows just how to do that. Despite that knowledge, she has no actual authority: She cannot direct us to do more of the things that make us richer and less of the things that make us poorer. She serves in an advisory role only.

We could use the BSP's advice. This is because we have a natural inclination to focus on our own needs while ignoring the impact we have on others. Consider a policy that makes Kansans $3 richer but Nebraskans $5 poorer. If the Kansas legislature is considering this policy, it makes perfect sense for it to enact it. But if it's the federal government considering that same policy, it looks a bit more foolish: It makes the *nation* $2 poorer.

The benevolent social planner takes that bird's-eye view of our affairs. She understands why Kansans might want such a law but knows that in the end, such a law will ultimately reduce the material well-being of Nebraska, the United States, and the world as a whole. The benevolent social planner considers everybody equally, no matter where they were born or what they do for a living, and she philosophically rejects any policy that makes someone richer at the greater expense of people elsewhere. In other words, the BSP is a positive economist, one that we will look to often when we evaluate the origins of and solutions to social problems.

Conclusion

You've come a great distance in just a few pages. You've learned about scarcity, opportunity cost, incentives, and the nature of collective action problems. This leaves you in a terrific position to begin studying social issues. As you work your way through the book, pay particular attention to these general ideas:

- People face trade-offs, which means they have choices.
- Choices that look attractive to individuals often look less attractive to society as a whole.
- If carefully crafted, a government policy is often capable of altering private incentives to more accurately align them with social goals.

---

[4]Much of this book is devoted to explaining when and why these wealth-destroying events occur.

You will soon discover that you can apply these powerful ideas to describe both the causes of and solutions to many social problems. As mentioned earlier, we're going to discover that the problems we focus on, once stripped of their context, look very much alike. But stripping away the context is difficult. To help with that difficult job, we're going to use a simple but powerful analytical framework called *game theory*. Game theory is a lens we can use to look past the context directly to the problem's core.

Chapter Summary and Problems

Key Terms

Collective action problem, p. 11

Command economy, p. 3

Economics, p. 2

Economy, p. 2

Explicit costs, p. 6

Implicit costs, p. 6

Incentives, p. 9

Market system, p. 3

Mixed economy, p. 3

Normative economics, p. 12

Opportunity cost, p. 4

Positive economics, p. 12

Public policy, p. 7

Resources, p. 2

Scarcity, p. 4

1.1 What Is Economics? pages 2–3

Define *economics* and explain how a society decides what goods and services to produce and how to distribute them.

Summary

Economics is the study of how society manages scarce resources, like land, labor, capital, and human ability, to best fulfill its wants. Any economy must decide first what it will produce and then how it will distribute what it has produced. In a market economy, sellers and buyers interact to make those decisions. In command economies, the government makes those decisions. Most economies are mixed economies where, in varying degrees, some decisions are made by buyers and sellers, but other decisions are made by the government.

Review Questions

All problems are assignable in MyEconLab.

1.1 The study of how to use society's resources to best meet our material wants is called _____.

1.2 An economy where production and distribution decisions are made by buyers and sellers is called a _____ economy.

1.3 An economy's resources include _____.
  a. Land
  b. Labor
  c. Human talent and ingenuity
  d. All of the above

1.4 Which of the following is *not* a fundamental question that every economy has to answer?
  a. What will we produce with our economy's resources?
  b. Why are some people rich and other people poor?

  c. How will we decide who gets the goods we have produced?
  d. Society must answer all of these questions.

1.5 An economy where government makes some production and distribution decisions and buyers and sellers make others is called a _____ economy.
  a. Command
  b. Market
  c. Mixed
  d. Hybrid

Problems and Applications

1.6 In a market system, buyers and sellers collectively decide what will be produced, and those items are then distributed to people who are willing to pay for them. Discuss some basic pros and cons of using a market system to produce and distribute health care.

1.7 In wartime, nations often institute a draft and require individuals to serve in the military. What kind of production and allocation system does the draft represent? Why do you suppose that kind of system might be necessary?

1.2 Key Principles of Economics: Scarcity, Trade-offs, and Opportunity Costs, pages 4–9

Discuss how scarcity and trade-offs affect individuals and society.

Summary

Several key principles govern all of economics. First, all of society's decisions are made in an environment of scarcity. Because of scarcity, we have to sacrifice some options to take advantage of others. The opportunity cost of an action is the value of the next-best option sacrificed, whether that value is measurable in dollars or not.

Review Questions

All problems are assignable in MyEconLab.

2.1 _____ means that society doesn't have enough resources to produce the things it wants.

2.2 To date Michelle, you break up with Susan. Losing Susan is called the _____ of dating Michelle.

2.3 You pay $5 for a slice of pizza. That $5 is called an _____ cost.

2.4 You purchase a new backpack for $75. The cash you sacrificed is a(n) _____.
a. Explicit cost
b. Implicit cost
c. Deferred cost
d. Accrued cost

2.5 You decide to spend spring break digging wells in developing countries and forgo the chance to spend a week on the beach with your friends in Panama City. Losing the chance to be with your friends is the _____ cost of digging wells.
a. Explicit
b. Implicit
c. Deferred
d. Inherent

2.6 When evaluating options, good economists consider _____.
a. Only explicit costs and benefits
b. Only implicit costs and benefits
c. Both implicit and explicit costs and benefits
d. Neither implicit nor explicit costs and benefits

2.7 Who does not face trade-offs?
a. You
b. Super-rich CEOs of high-powered corporations
c. The U.S. government
d. Everybody faces trade-offs.

2.8 While Superman sits around Metropolis waiting to save Lois Lane from Lex Luthor, he sacrifices the opportunity to generate electricity for millions. That forgone opportunity is a(n) _____ cost of protecting Lois Lane.
a. Implicit
b. Explicit
c. Monetary
d. Sunk

Problems and Applications

2.9 Going to college is an expensive proposition. List the basic explicit costs of attending college. Be sure not to include explicit costs you would face anyway, such as food or housing. Then consider the implicit costs of attending college: What opportunity did you pass up, and how much was that opportunity worth? Finally, add implicit and explicit costs to determine the full opportunity cost of attending college.

2.10 [Related to Application 1.1 on page 6] Superman devotes his life to protecting the citizens of Metropolis from crime. Do you suppose society is better off or worse off because of the generous sacrifice Superman has made?

2.11 [Related to Application 1.2 on page 8] Relative to their populations, the former communist countries of East Germany, Romania, and Cuba won a disproportionate number of Olympic medals. Explain how these economies were able to produce such outstanding Olympic teams. Then discuss the opportunity cost of their Olympic success.

2.12 The National Security Agency (NSA) came under attack in 2014 for monitoring individuals' cell phone calls. Discuss the trade-offs of this NSA surveillance.

2.13 In June 2014, Korean pop sensation PSY's "Gangnam Style" video surpassed 2 billion views on YouTube. View the video at the following site: http://youtu.be/9bZkp7q19f0. Then count the number of views and multiply by the length of the video to determine how much time has been spent watching PSY's video. Express your answer in hours and then convert to years. If the Empire State Building took 7 million labor-hours to complete, what is the opportunity cost of Gangnam Style, expressed in Empire State Buildings?

1.3 Key Principle of Economics: People Respond to Incentives, pages 9–11

Describe how incentives can affect behavior.

Summary

Another governing principle of economics is that people respond to incentives. Incentives are inducements to act in certain ways. People are encouraged to do things when the rewards for doing them increase. People are discouraged from doing things when the cost of doing them rises. Many public policy initiatives try to induce desired behaviors by altering the incentives people face.

Review Questions

All problems are assignable in MyEconLab.

3.1 Inducements to act in particular ways are called _____.

  a. Trade-offs
  b. Coercion
  c. Opportunity costs
  d. Incentives

3.2 Joan would like her daughter Emily to get better grades. One way she could encourage Emily to do better in school would be to _____.
  a. Pay Emily for improving her grades
  b. Fine Emily if her grades aren't good enough
  c. Either (a) or (b) will likely work.
  d. Option (a) will work, but (b) will not.

3.3 When government imposes a new tax on gasoline, that tax _____.

  a. Encourages drivers to drive more
  b. Encourages drivers to drive less
  c. Neither encourages nor discourages drivers from driving

Problems and Applications

3.4 The U.S. tax code allows homeowners to deduct the interest they pay on their home loans from their taxable incomes. What effect is this policy likely to have on the size of the average home? Why?

3.5 U.S. agriculture subsidies make food look artificially inexpensive to consumers. What is the likely effect of agriculture subsidies on the size of the typical American? Why?

3.6 To reduce America's dependence on foreign oil, the government decides it wants to encourage people to drive less. Suggest two proposals that the government might use to accomplish that. Is one of your proposals easier to implement than the other? Explain.

3.7 [Related to Application 1.3 on page 10] In 2013, the International Monetary Fund suggested that nations impose a one-time 10% tax on all accumulated individual wealth as a means to solve governments' financial problems. What kind of behaviors would this tax be likely to create?

1.4 A Brief Introduction to Collective Action Problems, pages 11–12

Define *collective action problems*.

Summary

Many social problems are manifestations of collective action problems. A collective action problem exists when the members of a group have incentives to act in ways that are beneficial to the individual but detrimental to the group as a whole: Private incentives are misaligned with social goals. In many cases, collective action problems can be overcome by government action.

Review Questions

All problems are assignable in MyEconLab.

4.1 John is a member of a group working to achieve a goal. But every member of the group has an incentive to skip the group's long and tedious meetings, and that skipping makes the group less likely to succeed. This kind of economic problem is known as a _____ problem.

4.2 Because collective action problems are difficult to solve, society often _____.
  a. Asks the benevolent social planner to step in and fix things
  b. Asks the government to step in and fix things
  c. Succeeds in solving them by asking its members to forgo their own best interests and work for the greater good
  d. Collective action problems are actually not difficult to solve.

Problems and Applications

4.3 Everybody in a residential high-rise building owns his or her own condominium. One day, the elevator breaks. Discuss the collective action problem that fixing the elevator presents. In the real world, how do high-rise condo owners typically overcome that problem? Is that typical real-world solution fair to people who live on the first floor compared to people who live on the top floor?

4.4 Your philosophy professor always grades exams on a curve, so that the top score in class becomes an A. The morning of a big exam, one of your classmates makes the following suggestion to the class: "Let's all leave our papers blank. That way, even though we'll all get zeros, everyone will get an A." Discuss the collective action problem this situation might present.

How Economists Analyze Economic Issues, pages 12–13

Explain the difference between positive and normative economics and explain how the benevolent social planner analyzes economic issues.

Summary

Most economic analysis seeks to describe the world as it is. This approach is called *positive economics*. In some cases, economic reasoning can be used to justify a particular vision of how a particular person thinks the world ought to look. That approach to economics is called *normative economics*. The positive approach is impartial and avoids imposing personal values—values that may not be shared by others—on economic analysis. The benevolent social planner is a fictitious, all-seeing, all-knowing entity who, using positive analysis, provides a benchmark by which to measure whether society is making the best use of its scarce resources.

Review Questions

All problems are assignable in MyEconLab.

5.1 "We must encourage more women to attend graduate school" is an example of a _____ economic statement.

5.2 The imaginary figure who advises us whether society is making the most of its scarce resources is the _____.

5.3 Choose the statement that represents normative economic analysis.

   a. Children who grow up in households with more books are more successful in school.

   b. Legalizing marijuana leads to increases in the number of pot smokers.

   c. If we raise the income tax on the super-rich, they will work less.

   d. Global warming is America's most serious problem.

5.4 Your instructor takes $1 each from 10 of your classmates and gives all $10 to you. Generally speaking, the benevolent social planner _____.

   a. Disapproves of this transaction

   b. Is pleased by this transaction

   c. Neither approves nor disapproves of this transaction

5.5 The benevolent social planner practices _____.

   a. Positive economics

   b. Normative economics

   c. A mix of positive and normative economics

   d. The benevolent social planner does not adhere to a particular style of economic analysis.

Problems and Applications

5.6 The minimum wage makes life more livable for those with jobs at the bottom end of the economic ladder. But it is widely believed to make jobs harder to get for those with few skills or little experience, leading to greater unemployment. Was the decision to implement a minimum wage based on positive economics or normative economics? Why?

5.7 A local supermarket plans to give away canned hams free to the first 100 customers through its door. Do you think the benevolent social planner would support this mechanism for distributing hams? Why or why not?

The Ultimatum Game: Are You Generous or Greedy?

Making connections between what you learn in the classroom and what you see in the real world can be hard. One of the best ways to learn about economics is to "get your hands dirty" by *doing* economics. This book contains 16 games and experiments, including one in each microeconomics chapter. Most of those games and experiments place you and your classmates in a scenario where you have to make an important real-world decision. The outcome of each game or experiment depends on both your individual decision and that of your classmates. These games and experiments are designed to show you that social problems may arise when many individuals collectively behave in a certain way. You'll also learn something about yourself and your decision-making process along the way.

Chapters 16–20 cover macroeconomic topics you hear about in the news: gross domestic product (GDP), growth, unemployment, and inflation. Each of those chapters ends with a Real-Time-Data Analysis Exercise that shows you how to locate, read, and interpret data about the economy.

Your instructor will provide you with detailed instructions, if necessary, and can also help you conduct a post-game analysis of the link between the game and the real world.

In this chapter, you learned that people respond to incentives. In this game, you'll have a chance to explore how your individual incentives can be shaped by the alternatives available to others.

Your instructor will randomly pair you with a classmate. The pairings will be anonymous; no player will know who his or her partner is.

One person in each pair will be designated as the "allocator." The other will be designated as the "receiver." You will get the chance to play both roles during today's game.

At the beginning of the game, the allocator will receive $1,000. However, there is a condition: The allocator must offer some portion of those dollars to the receiver. The allocator may offer as little as $0 or as much as $1,000.

The receiver then has a chance to either accept or reject the allocator's offer. If the offer is accepted, the receiver will receive the amount offered; the allocator will earn whatever is left over ($1,000 minus the amount offered). If the receiver rejects the allocator's offer, neither player will receive anything.

Your instructor will outline the procedures for submitting offers.

MyEconLab

Please visit http://www.myeconlab.com for support material to conduct this experiment if assigned by your instructor.

Supply and Demand

Appendix Outline and Learning Objectives

1A.1 **Demand,** page 20

Define the *law of demand*.

1A.2 **Supply,** page 21

Explain the difference between the supply curve and the demand curve.

1A.3 **Equilibrium,** page 21

Use the supply and demand model to find an equilibrium price and quantity.

1A.4 **Changes in Supply and Demand,** page 23

Analyze the effects on equilibrium price and quantity of a change in demand or a change in supply.

1A.5 **Factors That Shift Supply and Demand,** page 26

List four factors that can cause demand to increase and four factors that can cause supply to increase.

1A.6 **The Price Elasticity of Supply and Demand,** page 29

Demonstrate how the effects on price and quantity of a change in demand or supply depend on the elasticity of demand and the elasticity of supply.

MyEconLab
MyEconLab helps you master each objective and study more efficiently.

Supply and demand model A graphical model used to depict the interaction of consumers and producers in the market for a good or service and to explain how the price of that good or service is determined.

O ne tool that economists often use to depict the interaction of consumers and producers in the market for a good or service is a graphical model called the **supply and demand model**. You can use supply and demand to explain many real-world phenomena. It is particularly useful in explaining why the price of a particular good or service might change.

The supply and demand model makes these assumptions about what the market for a particular good looks like:

• There are many buyers and sellers participating in the market. Competition among them limits the power of both buyers and sellers: A seller can't charge ridiculously high prices if there are other sellers willing to sell for less. Nor can a stingy buyer offer less than everyone else and expect to obtain the product.

• Every unit of the good being offered for sale is identical, which ensures that sellers compete with one another only on the basis of price.

• All buyers and all sellers have perfect information about the market: They know how much each seller is charging and every buyer is paying, and they know about all of the product's attributes.

1A.1 Learning Objective

Define the *law of demand*.

Demand curve A curve that shows how many units of a good or service consumers are willing to buy at various prices.

Demand

The **demand curve**, or *demand relationship*, depicts the buyers' side of the marketplace. It indicates how many units of a good or service consumers are willing to buy at various prices. The demand relationship is based on the key observation that as the price of a product decreases, buyers are willing to purchase more of it. That happens for two reasons. First, as prices decrease, any given buyer might purchase additional units of a good. If you're craving chocolate, you might buy only one Butterfinger at a price of $2, but you might buy two if they only cost 25 cents each. Second, some new buyers might appear once the price gets low enough: Your roommate might never buy a Butterfinger at a price of $2, but if the price fell to 25 cents, he might start buying them.

Let's describe what a demand relationship might look like by considering the market for peanut butter. The demand relationship shows how many jars of peanut butter buyers would like to purchase (called *quantity demanded*) at various prices. The table in Figure 1A.1 presents some hypothetical price/quantity information.

We can plot the numbers in the table, as shown in the graph in Figure 1A.1. The price goes on the vertical axis (or *y*-axis) and the quantity on the horizontal axis (or *x*-axis), and each point on the graph depicts the price and quantity from a particular row of the table. Note that as the price decreases, we move downward along the

▶ **Figure 1A.1**
Price, Quantity Demanded, and the Demand Curve
The demand curve plots the quantity consumers want to buy at the various prices in the table. As the price of a good or service increases, the quantity demanded decreases.

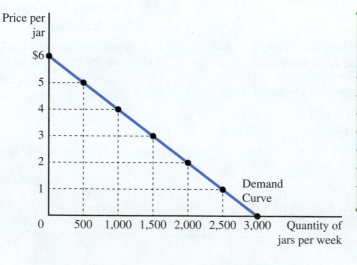

Price (dollars per jar of peanut butter)	Quantity (number of jars of peanut butter the market demands)
$6	0
5	500
4	1,000
3	1,500
2	2,000
1	2,500
0	3,000

demand curve. Economists say that a decrease in price causes an *increase in quantity demanded*. That inverse relationship between quantity demanded and price is known as the **law of demand**.

Supply

The sellers' (or producers') side of the market is represented by the **supply curve**, or *supply relationship*, which indicates how many units of a good or service sellers are willing to offer for sale at various prices. The supply relationship stems from the fact that some units of a good are less costly to produce than others. That can occur because some producers are simply more efficient than other producers: Low-cost producers operate lean and mean, while higher-cost producers spend more money to produce the same product. It can also be the case that a producer can produce a few units at fairly low cost, but as the producer expands output, the cost of production increases. That can happen because of limited space in the factory or because of physical constraints on how fast machinery can be run.

Generally, a producer will offer to make and sell a good only if the price he receives for that good from buyers is greater than what it costs to produce that good. At low prices, only the lowest-cost units can be profitably produced and sold. At higher prices, more costly units can be profitably sold, too. So, the higher the price, the greater the quantity offered for sale. Let's use this idea to depict the supply relationship for peanut butter, as shown in Figure 1A.2.

The table in Figure 1A.2 shows how many jars of peanut butter sellers are willing to offer for sale at various prices. The graph in the figure plots the numbers in the table, with each point corresponding to a particular row. Both the data in the table and the upward slope of the graph reflect the fundamental observation that the higher the price of peanut butter, the more effort producers will devote to producing peanut butter and offering it for sale. Economists generally say that the higher the price, the greater the *quantity supplied*, which is known as the **law of supply**.

Law of demand The inverse relationship between the price of a good or service and the quantity of that good or service that consumers want to buy. When the price of a good rises, there is a decrease in quantity demanded, and when the price of a good falls, there is an increase in quantity demanded.

Supply curve A curve that indicates how many units of a good or service sellers are willing to offer for sale at various prices.

Law of supply The positive relationship between the price of a good or service and the quantity of that good or service that sellers are willing to offer for sale. When the price of a good rises, there is an increase in quantity supplied, and when the price of a good falls, there is a decrease in quantity supplied.

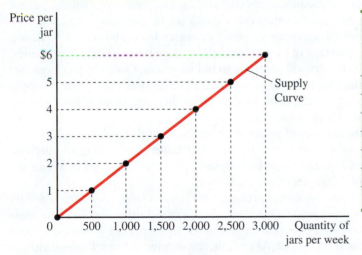

Price (dollars per jar of peanut butter)	Quantity (number of jars of peanut butter the market supplies)
$6	3,000
5	2,500
4	2,000
3	1,500
2	1,000
1	500
0	0

◄ **Figure 1A.2**
Price, Quantity Supplied, and the Supply Curve
The supply curve plots the quantity sellers are willing to offer for sale at the various prices in the table. As the price of a good or service increases, the quantity supplied increases.

Equilibrium

You now have a basic understanding of the motivations of both buyers and sellers. What happens if we put them together in the marketplace? We have some natural intuition about what might happen in the real world: Some buyers and some sellers will work out deals, and peanut butter will change hands. But how many buyers and sellers will work out deals, and at what price?

► **Figure 1A.3**
Equilibrium in the Market for Peanut Butter
The market equilibrium is found at the price where quantity demanded equals quantity supplied. In this market, the equilibrium price is $3, and the equilibrium quantity is 1,500 jars of peanut butter.

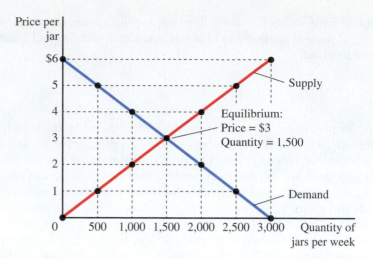

Shortage A condition in which the quantity of a good or service demanded at the existing price is greater than the quantity supplied.

Surplus A condition in which the quantity of a good or service supplied at the existing price is greater than the quantity demanded.

Market equilibrium A condition in a market where there is no upward or downward pressure on price, and where quantity demanded equals quantity supplied.

The supply and demand model can help answer these questions. In Figure 1A.3, we put both the demand curve (representing buyers) and the supply curve (representing sellers) on a single graph.

To begin analyzing the likely outcome in this market, suppose that sellers decide to offer their peanut butter for sale at a price of $1. At this price, sellers are willing to offer only 500 jars for sale, but consumers want to buy 2,500 jars. Because quantity demanded exceeds quantity supplied at the prevailing $1 price, there is a **shortage** of 2,000 jars. You can imagine what happens when the 500th customer comes to the cash register. One of the 2,000 unsatisfied customers behind him, noting that the last jar is about to be sold for a dollar, bids up the price: "Don't sell it to *him* for $1. I'll give you $2!"

The shortage puts upward pressure on the price. As the price rises to $2, some buyers exit the market; they were just there for the super-cheap peanut butter, and now that it's become more expensive, they'll eat ham instead. Quantity demanded falls from 2,500 to 2,000. Also, some producers that couldn't make a profit selling peanut butter when it sold for $1 find that they can make a profit if it sells for $2. So they ramp up production, and the quantity supplied increases from 500 to 1,000. Rising prices have reduced the shortage of peanut butter! But though the shortage is smaller, it has not disappeared, so buyers will continue to bid up prices. Once the price reaches $3, something interesting happens: Buyers demand 1,500 units, and sellers supply 1,500 units, so the shortage disappears! At that point, because there is no shortage, there is no more pressure for prices to rise.

Exactly the opposite happens if prices start at a very high level, like $5. There, sellers offer 2,500 units of peanut butter for sale, but buyers are willing to purchase only 500 of them. Because quantity supplied exceeds quantity demanded at $5, we say that there is a **surplus** of 2,000 jars of peanut butter.

The surplus tends to put downward pressure on the price of peanut butter: Sellers with unsold jars start to compete: "Don't buy *her* peanut butter for $5—buy *mine* for $4!" As the price decreases, buyers start asking for more peanut butter, and some higher-cost producers cut their output. As a result, the surplus shrinks. Prices continue to decrease until, at $3, the surplus disappears.

Note that at $3, buyers want every unit sellers offer, and sellers offer just enough to satisfy all the willing buyers. Because there is no shortage, there is no pressure for prices to increase. Because there is no surplus, there is no pressure for prices to decrease. Economists say that the market is in **market equilibrium**, a condition where there is no upward or downward pressure on price, and where quantity demanded equals quantity supplied. Specifically, $3 is the *equilibrium price* because once the market price hits $3, there's nothing trying to push it to some different level. At that price, the *equilibrium quantity* of 1,500 jars of peanut butter change hands.

Changes in Supply and Demand

One of the primary uses of the supply and demand model is to explain how equilibrium prices and quantities *change* when events in the marketplace alter the position of the supply curve or the position of the demand curve.

Consider, for example, what happens when peanut butter becomes more desired by consumers. (We'll talk about why that might happen in Section 1A.5.) In precise terms, this means that even holding the price constant, consumers now want more peanut butter than they did before. This is called an **increase in demand**, and its effects are shown in Table 1A.1.

1A.4 Learning Objective

Analyze the effects on equilibrium price and quantity of a change in demand or a change in supply.

Increase in demand A condition in which buyers increase the number of units of a good or service they are willing to purchase at each price.

Table 1A.1	An Increase in Demand	
Price per jar	Old quantity demanded by consumers each week	New quantity demanded by consumers each week
$6	0	1,000
5	500	1,500
4	1,000	2,000
3	1,500	2,500
2	2,000	3,000
1	2,500	3,500
0	3,000	4,000

Notice that at each possible price, consumers want more peanut butter than they did before. For example, at a price of $4, they used to want 1,000 units. But now they want 2,000. This change in the demand relationship shifts the *entire position* of the demand curve to the right, as shown in Figure 1A.4.

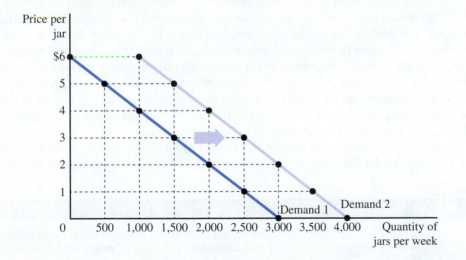

◀ **Figure 1A.4**
An Increase in Demand
An increase in demand shifts the demand curve to the right, from Demand 1 to Demand 2. At each price, consumers want to buy more jars of peanut butter.

How does the increase in demand affect the key things that we observe in the market: price and quantity sold? Let's find out. Begin with the original supply and demand curves. Then shift the demand curve to the right to reflect the increase in demand, as shown in Figure 1A.5. In Figure 1A.5, the original demand curve is labeled "Demand 1," and the new demand curve is labeled "Demand 2."

At the original equilibrium (denoted as P1 and Q1), the price was $3, and 1,500 jars of peanut butter traded hands. But when demand increases, consumers suddenly

▶ **Figure 1A.5**

How an Increase in Demand Affects Price

An increase in demand causes both the equilibrium price and the equilibrium quantity to increase.

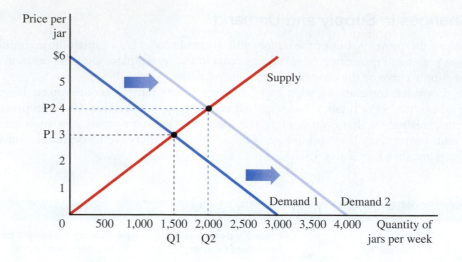

want to buy 2,500 units, while sellers continue to bring the same 1,500 units to market. Suddenly, there is a shortage, and that shortage puts upward pressure on prices.

When do prices stop increasing? When the price hits $4, consumers want to buy 2,000 units—exactly the same quantity producers are willing to supply. We've found a new equilibrium in the peanut butter market: The increase in demand causes the equilibrium price to increase from $3 to $4 and causes the equilibrium quantity to increase from 1,500 to 2,000. Those new equilibrium values are denoted as P2 and Q2, respectively.

A decrease in the desire for peanut butter has exactly the opposite effects: At each quantity, consumers would want to buy fewer units (that's called a *decrease in demand*). At the original price of $3, there would suddenly be a surplus, as producers, unaware of consumers' decreased desire for peanut butter, continue to produce 1,500 units. Prices fall until the surplus disappears. Ultimately, the equilibrium price and the equilibrium quantity sold both decrease. (Illustrating that change with numbers and a graph has been left for exercises 4.3 and 4.4 on page 33 at the end of this appendix.)

What if the change in the marketplace begins with sellers instead of with buyers? Remember that sellers are really only concerned with two things: the price their product will fetch in the marketplace and how much it costs them to produce their product. So changes in producers' cost of production will affect their willingness to supply peanut butter at various prices. For example, suppose that the cost of making peanut butter goes down because of a new, fast machine that removes peanut shells. That makes peanut butter production more profitable for more producers and leads to an increase in the quantity of peanut butter offered for sale at any particular price. Table 1A.2 summarizes the increase in supply at each price.

Note that at each price (except zero—no producer can turn a profit by giving away peanut butter for free!), producers bring 1,000 more jars to the market than they

Table 1A.2 An Increase in Supply		
Price per jar	Old quantity supplied by sellers each week	New quantity supplied by sellers each week
$6	3,000	4,000
5	2,500	3,500
4	2,000	3,000
3	1,500	2,500
2	1,000	2,000
1	500	1,500
0	0	0

used to. This increase in the number of jars offered for sale at every price is called an **increase in supply**, and it shifts the entire position of the supply curve to the right by 1,000 units, as shown in Figure 1A.6.

Increase in supply A condition in which sellers increase the number of units of a good or service they offer for sale at each price.

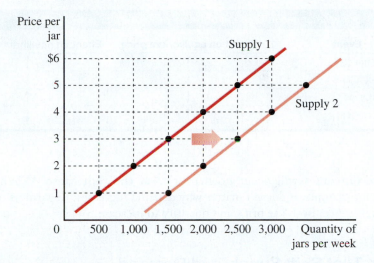

◄ **Figure 1A.6**
An Increase in Supply
An increase in supply shifts the supply curve to the right, from Supply 1 to Supply 2. At each price, sellers offer more jars of peanut butter for sale.

How will this change affect the market price and quantity? Begin with the original supply and demand curves, as shown in Figure 1A.7. The original equilibrium price is $3 (P1), and the original equilibrium quantity is 1,500 (Q1). Then shift the supply curve to the right (to Supply 2) to reflect the increase in supply.

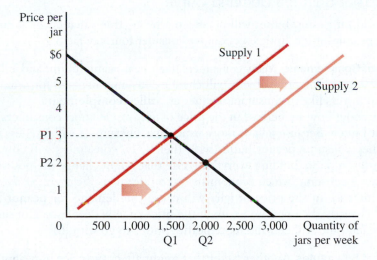

◄ **Figure 1A.7**
An Increase in Supply
An increase in supply causes the equilibrium price to decrease and the equilibrium quantity to increase.

Note what happens as supply increases from Supply 1 to Supply 2. At the original equilibrium price of $3, there is now a surplus: Sellers bring 2,500 units to market, but consumers want only 1,500 of them. That surplus puts downward pressure on prices, which fall until quantity demanded equals quantity supplied. That occurs at a price of $2 (P2), where 2,000 jars of peanut butter (Q2) change hands. So the increase in the supply of peanut butter causes the price of peanut butter to decrease and the quantity sold to increase.

Exactly the opposite happens if supply decreases (as might happen if the cost of producing peanut butter increased): A *decrease in supply* shifts the supply curve to the left, creating a shortage at the initial equilibrium price. That shortage puts upward pressure on prices. At the new equilibrium, prices are higher than they originally were, but the equilibrium quantity is lower. (Showing this graphically is left for exercise 4.5 on page 33 at the end of this appendix.)

Table 1A.3 summarizes the effects that changes in supply and demand have on equilibrium prices and quantities:

Table 1A.3 How Changes in Demand or Supply Affect Price and Quantity		
Event	**Effect on equilibrium price**	**Effect on equilibrium quantity**
Demand increases	↑	↑
Demand decreases	↓	↓
Supply increases	↓	↑
Supply decreases	↑	↓

Those outcomes will occur no matter what the root cause. When demand increases, for example, it doesn't matter why demand increases: Regardless of the reason, you can expect both the price and quantity to increase.

1A.5 Learning Objective

List four factors that can cause demand to increase and four factors that can cause supply to increase.

Factors That Shift Supply and Demand

A thorough understanding of the supply and demand model includes knowing *why* supply and demand curves might shift. Let's look at each curve and list the main causes of changes in each.

Factors That Shift the Demand Curve

The demand for peanut butter will be affected by anything that changes consumers' desire for peanut butter. In this section, we consider four key factors.

Complements Goods that buyers like to consume together.

The Price of Complements Many consumers like to eat peanut butter and jelly together. So, a change in the price of jelly will change consumer demand for peanut butter. Goods that buyers like to consume together are called **complements**.

Think about how an increase in the price of jelly might affect consumers' demand for peanut butter. Because jelly is more expensive, consumers will buy less jelly, and because they consume peanut butter with their jelly, consumers will consume less peanut butter, too. So, holding everything else that might change the position of the demand curve constant (which economists often refer to as the *ceteris paribus* assumption), an increase in the price of jelly will cause the demand for peanut butter to decrease.[1] (Exactly the opposite occurs if the price of jelly decreases: Consumers will want more jelly and will demand more peanut butter to go with it.)

Substitutes Goods that can serve in place of one another.

The Price of Substitutes Another factor that might affect the price of peanut butter is a change in the price of ham. Consumers don't generally eat peanut butter and ham together; instead, they choose one or the other. Peanut butter and ham are called **substitutes** —goods that can serve in place of one another (as sandwich filling, in this case). If the price of ham decreases, consumers might say, "I was eating peanut butter because I couldn't afford ham. But now ham is cheaper, so I'm going to buy more of it and buy less peanut butter." So a decrease in the price of a substitute good (ham) causes the demand for the good we're interested in (peanut butter) to decrease.

A Change in Income A third factor that might affect peanut butter buying behavior is a change in consumers' income. Unfortunately, there isn't a theory that gives economists tremendous guidance as to *how* such a change might affect demand. Suppose

---

[1]*Ceteris paribus* is a Latin phrase meaning "other things equal."

that peanut butter buyers experience rising incomes. It's possible that they could say, "Wow, I got a nice raise at work. Now I can afford to buy more peanut butter!" In other words, the increase in income *might* cause the demand for peanut butter to increase. If that's the case, economists classify peanut butter as a **normal good**.

But it's possible instead that consumers might say, "Wow, I got a nice raise at work. Now I can stop eating peanut butter and start eating chicken!" Here, the increase in income causes the demand for peanut butter to decrease. If that's the case, peanut butter is referred to as an **inferior good**.

Changing Tastes and Preferences Finally, the demand for peanut butter may be affected by changing tastes, preferences, or information. For example, if the FDA suddenly reveals that eating peanut butter prevents cancer, you could expect consumers to react to that good news by demanding more of it. On the other hand, if it were discovered that eating peanut butter leads to premature baldness, you might expect demand to decrease.

Table 1A.4 summarizes the demand shifters.

Normal good A good that consumers buy more of as their incomes rise.

Inferior good A good that consumers buy less of as their incomes rise.

Table 1A.4 Factors That Shift the Demand Curve		
An increase in	**Causes demand to**	**Example**
the price of a complementary good	decrease	An increase in the price of pretzels causes the demand for beer to decrease.
the price of a substitute good	increase	An increase in the price of Toyota cars causes the demand for Ford cars to increase.
income, with a normal good	increase	An increase in income causes the demand for silk neckties to increase.
income, with an inferior good	decrease	An increase in income causes the demand for ramen noodles to decrease.
taste for the good	increase	Consumers learn of the benefits of a high-protein diet, causing the demand for eggs to increase.

Factors That Shift the Supply Curve

Of course, not all changes begin on the demand side of the market. The supply relationship can shift, too. Generally speaking, anything that affects how much it costs to produce peanut butter will shift the supply curve.

The Price of Inputs One obvious factor that can change the cost of making peanut butter is the cost of the resources that go into peanut butter. Economists call those resources **inputs**, and they include labor, electricity, packaging, and, of course, peanuts. If the cost of raw peanuts rises, for example, peanut butter makers have to spend more to make each jar. Some sellers will find it more difficult to profitably produce peanut butter, and as a result, the supply of peanut butter will decrease. (On the other hand, if peanuts become less costly to obtain, you could expect the supply of peanut butter to increase.)

A Change in Production Technology A second factor that can change the cost of making peanut butter is how efficiently the firm converts its inputs into output. Economists call this **production technology**. A technological improvement means, essentially, that producers have discovered a way to squeeze more jars of peanut butter out of the same amount of inputs. As a result, each jar ends up costing less to produce, and the supply of peanut butter increases.

The Price of Substitutes in Production A third factor that can affect the supply of peanut butter is a change in the price of other products the producer could be making with

Inputs Resources that are used in the production of a good or service.

Production technology The efficiency with which firms convert inputs into outputs.

Substitutes in production Different goods that can be produced with the same inputs.

the same inputs. Economists call such goods **substitutes in production**. For example, suppose that the price of peanut brittle suddenly skyrockets. Producers might want to stop making peanut butter and make peanut brittle instead. Here, the increase in the price of peanut brittle raises the *opportunity cost* of making peanut butter. As a result, the supply of peanut butter decreases.

Changes in the Numbers of Producers Finally, the position of the supply curve depends on the number of producers in the industry. If people sense that there's lots of money to be made producing peanut butter, then they might quit their jobs and open peanut butter factories. As firms enter the industry, the supply of peanut butter increases. On the other hand, if firms leave the industry, then the supply of peanut butter will decrease.

Table 1A.5 summarizes the supply shifters.

Table 1A.5	Factors That Shift the Supply Curve	
An increase in	**Causes supply to**	**Example**
the price of an input	decrease	An increase in the price of steel causes the supply of automobiles to decrease.
production technology	increase	Improved drought resistance causes the supply of soybeans to increase.
the price of a substitute in production	decrease	An increase in the price of wheat causes the supply of corn to decrease.
the number of producers	increase	An increase in the number of smart phone app developers causes the number of available apps to increase.

Putting the Pieces Together

You are now prepared to use the supply and demand model to analyze how various events affect the market for peanut butter. This is a simple four-step process:

1. Draw a supply and demand graph to determine the original equilibrium price and quantity.
2. Determine whether the event affects the supply relationship or the demand relationship.
3. Determine *how* the event affects the supply or demand relationship. Does the event cause demand or supply to increase or decrease? Draw the new supply or demand curve.
4. Find the new equilibrium price and quantity and compare them to the original price and quantity.

Let's walk through an example. On your own, draw a supply and demand graph for peanut butter and find the initial equilibrium price and quantity (step 1). Now suppose that a bountiful peanut harvest causes the price of raw peanuts to decrease. How will this affect the market for peanut butter? Because peanuts are an input into the production of peanut butter, this event affects the supply relationship (step 2). Further, because the decrease in the cost of obtaining peanuts reduces the cost of making peanut butter, this event causes the supply of peanut butter to increase. On your graph, shift the supply curve to the right (step 3). Finally, determine the effect of the supply increase on price and quantity: As shown in the section above, an increase in supply causes the price of peanut butter to decrease and the equilibrium quantity to increase (step 4).

Congratulations—you've just used supply and demand to successfully analyze how falling peanut prices affect the market for peanut butter! With some practice and careful thought, you will be able to accurately apply this important tool of analysis to understand how other events affect other markets.

The Price Elasticity of Supply and Demand

1A.6 Learning Objective

Demonstrate how the effects on price and quantity of a change in demand or supply depend on the elasticity of demand and the elasticity of supply.

You now know the basics of supply and demand and can use the supply and demand model to predict the effects of various events on price and quantity. For example, you saw that if the supply of peanut butter increased, the equilibrium price would decrease and the equilibrium quantity would increase. But sometimes it's important to know not only the direction you can expect prices and quantities to move but the amount of the movement. For example, if you run a small convenience store that sells peanut butter, how much more will your customers want if the price of peanut butter suddenly decreases? As you will see, the *size* of those effects is determined by the *shape* of the supply and demand curves.

Economists often use a measure called *elasticity* to describe the shapes of the supply and demand curves. In general, elasticity indicates the ability to bend or stretch. That's true in economics, too, where elasticity represents the ability of consumers and producers to alter their behavior in response to a change in incentives. Economists are particularly interested in the **price elasticity of demand**, which measures how sensitive consumers' buying behaviors are to changes in prices. Consider, for example, what happens when the price of coffee jumps by 25% at the local Starbucks. Erin, who starts her morning with a cup of coffee each day, decides to go cold turkey on coffee and start drinking tea instead. She is sensitive to changes in the price of coffee, and she's flexible enough to change her drinking habits when the price of coffee changes. Because of that flexibility, Erin's demand for coffee is called *price elastic*. Erin's friend Jill, however, won't drink anything but coffee in the morning, and she will continue to purchase a cup each day, even if the price doubles. Jill is rigid, unwilling to change her behavior in response to a price change; her demand is *price inelastic*.

Price elasticity of demand The sensitivity of consumers' buying behaviors to changes in prices, measured as the percentage change in the quantity of a good demanded by consumers for each 1% change in price.

The price elasticity of demand has a more precise definition. Specifically, the price elasticity of demand measures the percentage change in the quantity of a good demanded by consumers for each 1% change in price:

$$\text{Price elasticity of demand} = \frac{\text{Percentage change in quantity demanded}}{\text{Percentage change in price}}$$

So, if the price of coffee decreases by 3%, and consumers purchase 12% more coffee in response, the price elasticity of demand for coffee is:

$$\text{Price elasticity of demand} = \frac{12\%}{-3\%} = -4$$

In this case, the demand for coffee is said to be highly elastic because a change in the price causes a disproportionately outsized (fourfold) change in consumer's buying behavior. In other words, a relatively small change in price causes a large change in quantity demanded.[2]

In contrast, consider the demand for gasoline: A 10% increase in the price of gasoline might cause consumers to cut their purchases by 2%, yielding a calculated demand elasticity of -0.2. In this case, a relatively large change in price causes a comparatively small change in quantity demanded: Consumers are unwilling or unable to respond to the change in price. Their demand for gasoline is said to be inelastic.

We mentioned earlier that elastic and inelastic demand curves look different. Those differences can be seen in Figure 1A.8, which depicts Erin's and Jill's coffee-buying behaviors.

Consider Erin, whose demand for coffee is elastic. Her demand curve is shown in panel (a) of Figure 1A.8. When the price of coffee increases even a little bit, she makes major cuts in her coffee consumption. In other words, small changes in price lead to

---

[2]In general, a calculated elasticity less than –1 (or greater than 1 in absolute value) denotes elastic demand. A calculated elasticity between 0 and –1 (or 0 and 1 in absolute value) denotes inelastic demand. If the calculated elasticity is exactly –1, demand is said to be unit elastic.

▶ **Figure 1A.8**

Depicting the Elasticity of Demand with Graphs

When demand is elastic, as in panel (a), the demand curve is relatively flat: A small change in price leads to a comparatively large change in quantity demanded. When demand is inelastic, as in panel (b), the demand curve is relatively steep: A large change in price causes a comparatively small change in quantity demanded.

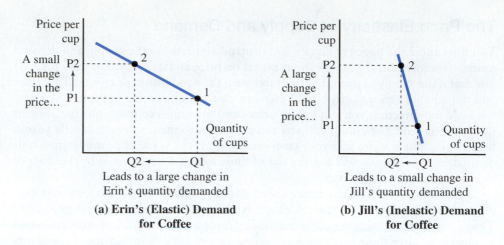

(a) Erin's (Elastic) Demand for Coffee

(b) Jill's (Inelastic) Demand for Coffee

big changes in quantity. Jill, whose coffee demand is inelastic, is shown on the right. For Jill, a large change in price causes only a small change in her coffee consumption, as shown in panel (b).[3]

The price elasticity of demand depends critically on the availability of substitutes. For consumers like Erin, tea is a good substitute for coffee, so her demand for coffee is elastic. For consumers like Jill, there *is* no good substitute for coffee; Jill's demand is inelastic. Substitutes are often easier to find over long time horizons: The demand for gasoline is inelastic in the short run but more elastic in the long run because, given enough time, consumers can alter their driving patterns and trade gas guzzlers for fuel sippers when the price of gas increases.

Supply, too, can be price elastic or price inelastic. Consider the supply of corn, which farmers plant in the spring and harvest in late autumn. If the price of corn increases by 50% between July and September, there is very little farmers can do to increase the amount of corn they're growing. So, at least during a growing season, the supply of corn is relatively inelastic. In other industries—retail coffee service, for example—it's easier to ramp up production when prices rise; supply in those industries is more elastic.

Supply elasticity is calculated just like demand elasticity. It is the percentage change in quantity *supplied* divided by the percentage change in price:

$$\text{Price elasticity of supply} = \frac{\text{Percentage change in quantity supplied}}{\text{Percentage change in price}}$$

We can depict elastic and inelastic supply graphically, as shown in Figure 1A.9. When supply is elastic (as shown in panel (a)), the supply curve is relatively flat:

▶ **Figure 1A.9**

Depicting the Elasticity of Supply with Graphs

When supply is elastic, as in panel (a), the supply curve is relatively flat: A small change in price leads to a comparatively large change in quantity supplied. When supply is inelastic, as in panel (b), the supply curve is relatively steep: A large change in price causes a comparatively small change in quantity supplied.

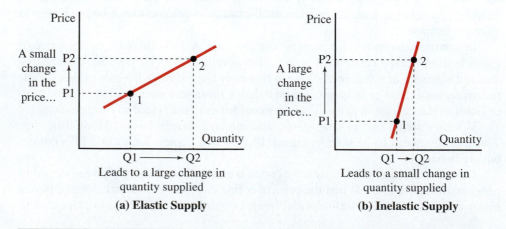

(a) Elastic Supply

(b) Inelastic Supply

---

[3]The slope of a demand curve, as shown here, is a good visual indicator of elasticity, but not a perfect one. Technically, the elasticity of demand depends on both the slope *and* position of the demand curve. You can find more information about elasticity and how it is calculated in almost any principles of microeconomics text.

Small changes in price lead to large changes in quantity supplied. When supply is inelastic (as shown in panel (b)), the supply curve is relatively steep: Large changes in price lead to relatively small changes in quantity supplied.

The elasticities of demand and supply have important implications for the way different markets function. For example, suppose the government wants to reduce illegal drug use and tries to achieve this goal by interrupting the supply of drugs. The effectiveness of such supply reductions depends on how elastic the demand for drugs is. If the demand for drugs is highly elastic, drug interdiction efforts will be highly successful in reducing drug use, as shown in Figure 1A.10.

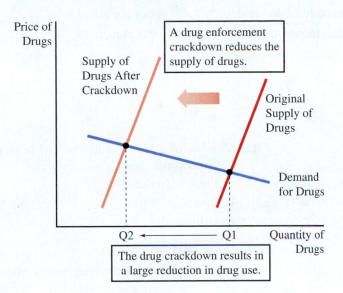

◀ **Figure 1A.10**
The Success of Drug Interdiction if Drug Demand Is Elastic
A drug interdiction reduces the supply of illegal drugs. If the demand for drugs is elastic, overall drug use will decline substantially, from Q1 to Q2.

On the other hand, if the demand for drugs is highly inelastic, reducing the supply of drugs will not cause much of a reduction in drug use; rather, it will drive up prices. Those price increases compensate smugglers and dealers for the increased risk of arrest and prosecution and may drive some users to crime in order to fund their habit. But, as shown in Figure 1A.11, overall drug use—the target of the program—will be relatively unaffected.

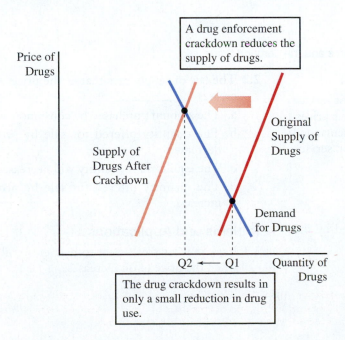

◀ **Figure 1A.11**
The Success of Drug Interdiction if Drug Demand Is Inelastic
A drug interdiction reduces the supply of illegal drugs. If the demand for drugs is inelastic, a major drug interdiction will result in only a small reduction in overall drug use.

Appendix Summary and Problems

Key Terms

Complements, p. 26
Demand curve, p. 20
Increase in demand p. 23
Increase in supply, p. 25
Inferior good, p. 27
Inputs, p. 27

Law of demand, p. 21
Law of supply, p. 21
Market equilibrium, p. 22
Normal good, p. 27
Price elasticity of demand, p. 29
Production technology, p. 27

Shortage, p. 22
Substitutes, p. 26
Substitutes in production, p. 28
Supply and demand model, p. 20
Supply curve, p. 21
Surplus, p. 22

1A.1 Demand, pages 20–21

Define the *law of demand*.

Summary

The demand curve indicates the quantity of a good or service that consumers are willing to buy at various prices. The law of demand states that price and quantity demanded are inversely related: As the price of a good or service increases, the quantity demanded by buyers decreases.

Review Questions

All problems are assignable in MyEconLab.

1.1 In the supply and demand model, the buyers' side of the market is depicted by the _____.

1.2 The law of demand indicates that price and quantity demanded are _____.
   a. Positively related
   b. Inversely related
   c. Unrelated

Problems and Applications

1.3 Explain why retail clothing stores often reduce the price of sweaters and coats after the holidays.

1.4 Explain the rationale behind taxing cigarettes to discourage smoking.

1A.2 Supply, page 21

Explain the difference between the supply curve and the demand curve.

Summary

The supply curve indicates the quantity of a good or service that producers are willing to offer for sale at various prices. The law of supply states that price and quantity demanded are positively related: As the price of a good or service increases, the quantity supplied by sellers increases.

Review Questions

All problems are assignable in MyEconLab.

2.1 The seller's side of the market is represented by the

_____.
   a. Demand curve
   b. Supply curve
   c. Price elasticity of supply
   d. Equilibrium price and quantity

2.2 The law of supply says that as the price of a good increases, _____.
   a. The amount purchased by consumers will decrease.
   b. The quantity offered for sale by producers will decrease.
   c. The equilibrium quantity will decrease.
   d. The quantity offered for sale by producers will increase.

Problems and Applications

2.3 Explain what you expect to happen to oil exploration when the price of oil increases.

Equilibrium, pages 21–22

Use the supply and demand model to find an equilibrium price and quantity.

Summary

The market for a good or service can be represented by drawing the supply and demand curves on the same graph. The market equilibrium occurs at the price where the quantity consumers demand equals the quantity sellers supply. If the price is higher than the equilibrium price, a surplus exists that will place downward pressure on prices. If the price is lower than the equilibrium price, a shortage exists that will place upward pressure on prices. Therefore, market forces tend to push the price to its equilibrium value.

Review Questions

All problems are assignable in MyEconLab.

3.1 When the quantity of a good demanded exceeds the quantity supplied, a _____ exists.

3.2 A surplus of a good is likely to put _____ pressure on the price of that good.
  a. Upward
  b. Downward
  c. Neither upward nor downward

Problems and Applications

3.3 The table below shows the supply and demand relationships in the market for cars. Graph the demand for and supply of cars and find the equilibrium price and equilibrium quantity of cars sold.

Accompanies problem 3.3

Price	$10,000	$15,000	$20,000	$25,000	$30,000	$35,000	$40,000	$45,000
Quantity demanded per month	60,000	55,000	50,000	45,000	40,000	35,000	30,000	25,000
Quantity supplied per month	20,000	25,000	30,000	35,000	40,000	45,000	50,000	55,000

Changes in Supply and Demand, pages 23–26

Analyze the effects on equilibrium price and quantity of a change in demand or a change in supply.

Summary

Demand and supply relationships may change over time or in response to certain events. Demand increases when consumers want more of a good or service at any given price. When this occurs, the demand curve shifts to the right. Supply increases when sellers offer more units for sale at any given price. When this occurs, the supply curve shifts to the right. Changes in supply and demand cause changes in equilibrium prices and quantities. Demand increases cause equilibrium prices and quantities to increase; supply increases cause equilibrium prices to decrease but equilibrium quantities to increase.

Review Questions

All problems are assignable in MyEconLab.

4.1 When the demand for pickles decreases, the demand curve _____.
  a. Shifts to the right
  b. Shifts to the left
  c. Does not shift (you move downward along the existing demand curve)
  d. Does not shift (you move upward along the existing demand curve)

4.2 When the supply of chairs decreases, the equilibrium price of chairs will _____ and the equilibrium quantity of chairs sold will _____.
  a. Increase; increase

  b. Increase; decrease
  c. Decrease; increase
  d. Decrease; decrease

Problems and Applications

4.3 Using the information in problem 3.3, suppose that demand decreases by 10,000 units at each price. Construct a new table of supply and demand relationships. Then illustrate the change in demand by graphing the new demand curve.

4.4 Using the information from problems 3.3 and 4.3, graph the original supply and demand curves and indicate the equilibrium price and quantity. Then graph the new demand curve and determine the new equilibrium price and quantity. How does the decrease in demand affect the price and quantity of cars sold?

4.5 Refer to the table in problem 3.3. Suppose that, because of rising steel costs, sellers offer 10,000 fewer cars at each price. Create a new table that reflects that change in the supply relationship. Then, following methods similar to those you used in problem 4.4, use supply and demand analysis to construct a graph that shows the effect of rising steel prices on the equilibrium price and quantity of cars sold.

List four factors that can cause demand to increase and four factors that can cause supply to increase.

Summary

A demand increase can be caused by a decrease in the price of a complementary good, an increase in the price of a substitute good, an increase in income (if the good is a normal good) or a decrease in income (if the good is inferior), or a change in tastes and preferences. A supply increase can be caused by a decrease in the price of inputs, technological improvements, a decrease in the price of a substitute in production, or an increase in the number of producers.

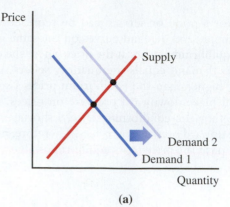
(a)

Review Questions

All problems are assignable in MyEconLab.

5.1 Coffee and doughnuts are probably considered _____ .

5.2 Flour is a(n) _____ into the production of cookies.

5.3 Which of the events will *not* cause the demand for pasta, an inferior good, to decrease?

  a. An increase in the price of marinara sauce

  b. An increase in the price of rice

  c. An increase in consumers' income

  d. The surgeon general's conclusion that eating pasta more than once a week dramatically increases the risk of diabetes

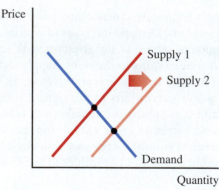
(b)

Problems and Applications

5.4 Determine the effects of the following events on the price and quantity of coffee sold. Assume that coffee is a normal good.

  a. The price of tea, a substitute for coffee, increases.

  b. The price of doughnuts, a complement to coffee, increases.

  c. Congress mandates a $20/hour minimum wage for baristas.

  d. Consumers' incomes fall as the economy sours.

  e. Coffee growers discover that they can make more money raising corn than they can growing coffee.

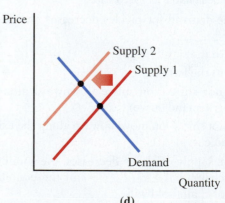
(c)

5.5 Consider the following graphs, labeled (a) through (d), which depict the effects of events in the corn market. Associate each of the following events with one, and only one, of the graphs.

Event 1: A 3-year drought strikes the Midwest.

Event 2: Drivers start fueling their cars with corn-based ethanol instead of petroleum-based gasoline.

Event 3: The latest low-carb diet fad recommends replacing corn with meat and eggs.

Event 4: CF Industries, a major fertilizer producer, invents a more effective fertilizer.

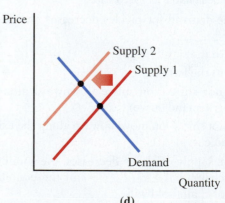
(d)

1A.6 The Price Elasticity of Supply and Demand, pages 29–31

Demonstrate how the effects on price and quantity of a change in demand or supply depend on the elasticity of demand and the elasticity of supply.

Summary

The price elasticity of demand measures buyers' sensitivity to changes in price. When a small change in price leads to a large change in quantity purchased, demand is price elastic. Elasticity generally is higher the larger the number of substitutes for a particular good. The price elasticity of supply measures sellers' sensitivity to changes in price. When a small change in price leads to a large change in quantity supplied, supply is price elastic. The elasticities of demand and supply are reflected in the slope and position of the demand and supply curves and have implications for the behavior of equilibrium prices and quantities when demand and supply change.

Review Questions

All problems are assignable in MyEconLab.

6.1 The sensitivity of buyers to changes in the price of a product is called _____.

6.2 If a large increase in the price of pickles causes only a small reduction in the quantity of pickles consumers buy, then the demand for pickles is said to be _____.

6.3 Sears has a 10% off sale on lawnmowers, and managers notice an 8% increase in lawnmower sales. This suggests that the demand for Sears lawnmowers is _____.

   a. Elastic
   b. Inelastic
   c. Unit elastic
   d. It is impossible to reach a conclusion about the elasticity of demand for Sears lawnmowers.

Problems and Applications

6.4 Use a supply and demand graph to show that if the supply of toothpicks is highly elastic, large increases in the demand for toothpicks will cause only small increases in the price of toothpicks.

6.5 Use supply and demand graphs to determine which of the cases below will lead to the largest increase in price.

   a. Demand is highly elastic; there is a large increase in supply.
   b. Supply is highly inelastic; there is a large decrease in demand.
   c. Supply is highly elastic; there is a small increase in demand.
   d. Demand is highly inelastic; there is a large decrease in supply.

Cost–Benefit Analysis and the Value of a Life

Chapter Outline and Learning Objectives

2.1 Cost–Benefit Analysis, page 37

Apply cost–benefit analysis to choose among alternative courses of action.

2.2 Applying Cost–Benefit Analysis to Life, page 40

Explain why decision makers cannot avoid placing a dollar value on a life when conducting a cost–benefit analysis.

2.3 Using Cost–Benefit Analysis to Determine an Appropriate Level of Safety, page 41

Use cost–benefit analysis to determine whether a safety precaution is cost-justified.

2.4 Problems and Pitfalls of Cost–Benefit Analysis When Life Is Involved, page 44

Explain how errors in assessing risks and valuing lives may affect cost–benefit analysis.

2.5 Approaches to Valuing a Life, page 47

Describe the two approaches economists use to value a life.

Experiment: The Dictator Game, page 55

MyEconLab
MyEconLab helps you master each objective and study more efficiently.

Because of scarcity, we all must make choices among competing alternatives. Should you buy a Honda or a Hyundai? Should you attend a community college or an Ivy League school? Should you install a new ceiling fan by yourself or hire an electrician to do it? Should you take up motocross as a hobby or enter crossword puzzle competitions instead? Good economic decision making requires us to evaluate such choices in a systematic way and then select the best course of action.

Cost–Benefit Analysis

2.1 Learning Objective

Apply cost–benefit analysis to choose among alternative courses of action.

The primary method that decision makers use to evaluate choices among competing alternatives is called **cost–benefit analysis**. Cost–benefit analysis means that before we decide to do something, we systematically compare the costs of doing it to its benefits. If the benefits outweigh the costs, then generally we should do it. If they don't, we should not do it.

Cost–benefit analysis A method that decision makers use to evaluate choices among competing alternatives.

Cost–Benefit Analysis: The Basics

Businesses regularly apply cost–benefit analysis to determine whether new ventures are worth undertaking. For example, suppose a small software engineering firm is considering developing an iPhone app that pinpoints the user's position and then locates the nearest pipe organ. The manager at the software firm determines that hiring a programmer to code the software will cost $70,000 and that 6,000 iPhone users will download the app at a price of $3. In this case, the costs of developing the app ($70,000) outweigh the benefits of selling the app ($18,000), and the software company should scrap the project.

In much the same fashion, governments often apply cost–benefit analysis to evaluate the cost-effectiveness of projects or regulations they are considering. For example, a government might use cost–benefit analysis to decide whether to adopt stricter air pollution guidelines. When it conducts such a cost–benefit analysis, its first job is to identify the relevant *stakeholders*—the parties who stand to gain or lose as a result of the policy. Then it must measure the benefits and costs faced by each of those stakeholders. Finally, the government nets out costs and benefits to determine an overall impact.

While the cost–benefit analysis the government performs is fundamentally the same as the cost–benefit analysis the software firm undertakes, it may be quite a bit more difficult to implement in practice. One reason is because the costs of such a regulation might be difficult to measure. When a government tells society to clean up its emissions, for example, the cost of doing so may be spread out across thousands and thousands of polluters—factories, power plants, and car drivers, for example. Accurately accounting for all those varying sources of pollution is more difficult than determining, as the software firm had to do, how much it would cost to write one computer program.

The government also might have a hard time measuring the benefits of reduced air pollution. The government might know that cleaner air will result in fewer illnesses. But how many fewer illnesses? How many dollars in health care costs will be saved? How many fewer sick days will workers take, and how much value do their employers lose when they call in sick? Determining the answers to these questions requires a mountain of data and the brainpower to process it. Nevertheless, despite the difficulties inherent in performing cost–benefit analysis on such a large scale, it continues to be a useful tool for policymakers.

Using Cost–Benefit Analysis to Select Among Competing Alternatives

Businesses and governments can also use cost–benefit analysis to select among competing alternatives. Suppose that BMW has room on its motorcycle assembly line to produce one new model in the coming year. It must choose between producing a new off-road motorcycle or a low-slung boulevard cruiser. BMW's number crunchers can use cost–benefit analysis to see which motorcycle will generate the greatest excess of benefits over costs.

Suppose the off-road motorcycle would generate benefits of $8 million at a cost of $5 million. Producing the off-road bike, then, would add $3 million to BMW's bottom line. Alternatively, the cruiser would generate benefits of $12 million at a cost of $10 million, which means that producing the cruiser would add $2 million to BMW's profits. If BMW can add only one motorcycle to its lineup, then its cost–benefit analysis suggests that producing the off-road motorcycle (which generates net benefits of $3 million) is a better choice than producing the cruiser, which generates only $2 million.

Notice that BMW ultimately must consider both the benefits *and* the costs of each project. The cruiser does generate greater benefits (sales revenue, generally) than the off-road motorcycle, and if BMW looked only at benefits, the cruiser would be its choice. But the cruiser is also much more expensive to produce—so that the extra cost of producing it instead of the off-road bike outweighs the extra revenue it generates. If BMW fails to consider how costly the cruiser is to build when it makes its decision, that failure will cost its shareholders $1 million in potential profits.

Evaluating Alternatives at the Margin

When conducting cost–benefit analysis, it is important to consider only costs and benefits over which you have control. Specifically, it is important to ignore both costs that you have already incurred and benefits you have already received.

Here's an example to help explain why. At the beginning of summer, Joan noticed that pumpkins were selling for $10 each, a price she considered pretty high. Excited about earning some money, she spent $4,000 plowing a garden in her backyard, preparing the soil with fertilizer, and purchasing enough seeds to grow 1,000 pumpkins. At the time she planted her pumpkins, she estimated it would cost her an extra $2,500 to pick the pumpkins at the end of the season and take them to market, making her overall profits for the year $3,500.

When November came and her pumpkins ripened, Joan discovered that pumpkins were selling for only $3 each. "My crop is worth only $3,000," Joan tells herself. "I've already spent $4,000 on this worthless crop of pumpkins," she reasons, "and it's going to cost me another $2,500 to harvest, so in the end I'd be spending $6,500 to make a crop that I can sell for only $3,000. Since the costs outweigh the benefits by $3,500, I think I'll just forget about taking the pumpkins to market and let them rot on the ground instead."

Joan has based her decision on a comparison of the total cost of growing the pumpkins ($6,500) and the total benefits of selling the pumpkins ($3,000). But she made that decision in November, when $4,000 of the cost of growing the pumpkins had already been incurred. That cost was out of her control; she couldn't get that $4,000 back by harvesting her pumpkins, and she couldn't avoid those costs by not harvesting. Since Joan can't change those costs, good decision making requires her, oddly enough, to ignore them.

Instead, Joan should consider only the marginal costs and benefits of bringing her pumpkins to market. In the context of decision making, the **marginal cost** of an activity is the additional cost you expect to incur if you undertake that activity, while the **marginal benefit** measures the additional benefit you expect to receive. Comparing marginal costs and marginal benefits in this way is called **marginal analysis**.

Let's see how cost–benefit analysis might proceed when Joan considers only marginal costs and benefits. Remember that it's late in the fall, the pumpkins were planted long ago, and the only decision Joan has to make is whether to harvest the pumpkins. If she harvests her 1,000 pumpkins, she can sell them for $3 each, which means that harvesting brings her $3,000 of benefits.

This part of Joan's cost–benefit analysis is easy. Evaluating Joan's marginal costs is trickier. Recall that the only choice Joan faces is whether to harvest the pumpkins. She can let them rot, which costs her nothing at the margin. Or she can harvest them, if she's willing to spend $2,500. That $2,500 is the marginal cost of bringing in her crop,

Marginal cost The additional cost you expect to incur if you undertake an activity.

Marginal benefit The additional benefit you expect to receive if you undertake an activity.

Marginal analysis Arriving at a decision by comparing marginal costs and marginal benefits.

and it is the only cost that matters. The $4,000 she spent earlier in the year is going to stay spent no matter what she chooses in November, and it is therefore irrelevant.

When Joan carefully compares the *marginal* benefit of harvesting ($3,000) to the *marginal* cost ($2,500), cost–benefit analysis indicates that she should go ahead and harvest the crop. That's a different conclusion than she reached when she compared *total* benefits to *total* costs. But is that conclusion correct? Note, as indicated earlier, that if she lets the crop rot on the ground, she will lose $4,000 in total—the $4,000 she spent in the spring. But if she harvests the crop, she will lose only $3,500. In other words, harvesting the crop won't make her pumpkin farm profitable, but it does reduce her losses by $500. Comparing costs and benefits at the margin leads her to exactly the right conclusion.

Application 2.1

Cost–Benefit Analysis and the Tobacco Settlement

In the early 1990s, state governments filed suit against the big four tobacco companies—R. J. Reynolds, Philip Morris, Brown and Williamson, and Lorillard. The states sought to recover some of the money they had spent treating smoking-related illnesses. Those suits were eventually settled to the tune of over $200 billion.

It is easy to paint the big tobacco companies as villains who hook smokers on their product and force the rest of society to bear the cost. But that presumes an answer to an all-important question: Do smokers really harm society financially?

A thorough cost–benefit analysis of smoking's impact should identify all the relevant stakeholders and accurately measure the magnitude of their stakes. Vanderbilt law and economics professor Kip Viscusi has done just that, and his conclusions are surprising. Viscusi says that far from being a drain on the rest of society, smokers actually provide a net public service.

Viscusi admits that smokers have higher medical costs than nonsmokers. He estimates those additional medical costs at about 72 cents per pack of cigarettes. And because smokers tend to die earlier than nonsmokers, they contribute about 43 cents per pack less to Social Security and Medicare programs.

But the fact that smokers pass away early isn't entirely a bad thing. One benefit is that smokers rack up fewer nursing home costs later in life, which generates a cost *savings* of about 24 cents per pack. And because smokers spend their working years contributing to retirement and pension programs but don't live long enough to pull all of their contributions back out, their early demise saves society $1.26 per pack. When all the costs and benefits of smoking have been accounted for, Viscusi says that smokers end up providing about 32 cents of net benefit to everybody else for each package of cigarettes smoked.

In 2009, smoking was back in the spotlight as the Food and Drug Administration sought congressional approval to regulate tobacco products. Based largely on the health care costs associated with smoking, the Tobacco Control Act easily passed through both houses of Congress, and the president signed it into law.

Viscusi remains critical of that decision, citing Congress's failure to impartially examine the impact on *all* of the relevant stakeholders. "It looks unpleasant or ghoulish to look at the cost savings as well as the cost increases and it's not a good thing that smoking kills people. But if you're going to follow this health-cost train all the way, you have to take into account all the effects, not just the ones you like in terms of getting your bill passed."[1]

See related problem 1.9 on page 51 at the end of this chapter.

Based on Kip Viscusi's "The New Cigarette Paternalism," *Regulation*, Winter 2002–2003; Viscusi's *Smoke-Filled Rooms: A Postmortem on the Tobacco Deal*, 2002; and "Do Smokers Cost Society Money?" *USA Today*, April 8, 2009.

---

[1]"Do Smokers Cost Society Money?" *USA Today*, April 8, 2009.

It is important to consider only marginal costs and benefits when conducting a cost–benefit analysis. But it is also important to ensure that those costs and benefits encompass *all* of the costs and benefits, both explicit and implicit. Suppose that Joan's neighbor Greg can spend $1,000 to harvest a cantaloupe crop that he can sell for $1,200. Comparing those explicit costs and benefits might lead you to conclude that Greg should complete the harvest. But suppose bringing in the harvest would require Greg to take a day off from work, where he would have earned $300. That lost opportunity must be accounted for: Greg's real cost of harvesting is $1,300, not $1,000; he'd be better off letting his melons rot in the field.

Applying Cost–Benefit Analysis to Life

When making decisions using cost–benefit analysis, you obviously need to weigh *all* the relevant costs and *all* the relevant benefits of a particular course of action. But, as mentioned earlier, sometimes doing so is complicated by the fact that not all costs and benefits can be easily measured. Nowhere is that more true than in the case in which costs and benefits are measured in human lives.

Corporations Do It: The Ford Pinto

Corporations conduct cost–benefit analyses all the time. Sometimes this involves measuring costs and benefits in terms of people's lives. Consider Ford Motor Company: In 1968, Lee Iacocca, Ford Motor Company's president, initiated the development of a new type of car that would weigh no more than 2,000 pounds and cost no more than $2,000. That car was the Ford Pinto. In 1970, the Pinto hit showroom floors. It was sporty, got 25 miles to the gallon (more than any other vehicle at the time), and was affordable. Initially sales of the car were brisk. They got even better in 1973, when gas prices spiked upward sharply. The sales of the economical little Pinto rose along with them. Television ads featured happy families that had each purchased multiple Pintos.

Nonetheless, Ford stopped producing the Pinto in 1980, and since then the car has appeared in virtually every "Worst Car Ever" list. Why? The design of the car's fuel tank meant that when the car was rear-ended, the collision sometimes resulted in fuel spills. Coupled with an errant spark, the spills could create deadly fireballs that caused injuries and deaths.

In 1977, *Mother Jones Magazine* published a report of the cost–benefit analysis Ford had done when debating whether to fix the defect. According to the report, Ford calculated that it would cost $11 per car to remedy the design flaw.[2] After weighing the $11 per-car cost against the cost of paying damages to the families of those killed or injured in rear-end fireball crashes, Ford determined that it would be cheaper simply to leave the Pinto as it was. "For seven years the Ford Motor Company sold cars in which it knew hundreds of people would needlessly burn to death," *Mother Jones* reported. "Ford waited [to fix the defect] . . . because its internal 'cost–benefit analysis,' *which places a dollar value on human life*, said it wasn't profitable to make the changes sooner."

In short, Ford weighed dollars against lives, and dollars won.

The public was outraged, and not surprisingly, Ford found itself on the receiving end of lawsuits. The courts ordered compensation for the families of the victims as well as enormous punitive damages. The state of Indiana went so far as to charge Ford with reckless homicide—a criminal offense—though the charge was eventually dropped. When the smoke cleared, Ford had paid millions of dollars in damages[3] and had corrected the defect in the Pinto.

---

[2] As it turns out, there were a number of factual errors in the *Mother Jones* article that, while significant, are not particularly pertinent to this discussion. A more accurate accounting of the Ford Pinto scandal can be found in Gary Schwartz's "The Myth of the Ford Pinto Case," 43 Rutgers L. Rev. 1013 (1991).

[3] In the oft-cited *Grimshaw v. Ford Motor Co.* (1981), Grimshaw was initially awarded $2.5 million in compensatory damages and $125 million in punitive damages. The punitive portion was reduced to $3.5 million on appeal.

However, the all-important question remained: Is a cost–benefit analysis appropriate in situations in which a defect in design or manufacturing could lead to death or serious bodily harm? If a reporter asked you this question, your answer might well echo that of the California Court of Appeals, which in rejecting Ford's appeal wrote, "The conduct of Ford's management was reprehensible in the extreme. It exhibited a conscious and callous disregard of public safety in order to maximize corporate profits."[4] In other words, human lives are too precious to be put at risk for the mere pursuit of personal gain.

You Do It: Exposing Yourself and Others to Risk

It's one thing to *say* that life is priceless, but it's another thing entirely to *demonstrate* it. Valuing life is one case in which actions really do speak louder than words because despite claims that life is priceless, people regularly make potentially life-changing cost–benefit decisions. Did you ride a bike to class today or walk down a flight of stairs? Each of these choices exposes you to some risk of death. The truth is that we do all kinds of things that stand to shorten our lives—we eat fatty foods, we smoke, we swim, we ski. And every time we do something risky, like drive to a movie theater on a Saturday night, we're implicitly making this cost–benefit calculation: "Wow, I'm really excited about this movie, and that prospect brings me so much joy that I'm willing to risk my life to see it." Those decisions tell us that our lives are not, in fact, priceless. After all, why would we risk losing something with infinite value over the chance to see a movie? If life were *truly* priceless, we would have stayed home, safe in bed, and eaten nothing but wheatgrass smoothies (making sure to be very, very careful using the blender).

"But wait," you may say, "it's one thing to risk your own life. But Ford put *other* people at risk to benefit itself and its stockholders. *That's* what's so awful about the whole thing." And so it is. However, you again have something in common with Ford. Each minute you delay shoveling snow from your sidewalk, you increase the chance that your postal carrier will slip and break a leg. Each time you take the wheel of a car, you put other drivers and pedestrians at risk. And when you glance away from the road to change radio stations, check your GPS, or make a phone call, you increase the chance that you will kill yourself *and others*. This problem gets worse if you become a parent: The minute you put your baby in the car for a trip to the supermarket, you're exposing your most precious asset to the possibility of injury and death. If you're willing to do that to your own child, you're *certainly* willing to do it to strangers!

The simple truth is that your actions indicate your willingness to expose others to risk and that you're doing it for your own benefit. You wait to shovel snow from your sidewalk because it's cold outside. You take one hand off the steering wheel to replace a CD with something you like better. You may think that Ford is different than you because Ford traded lives to fatten its bottom line, but economists consider benefits as benefits, whether they're measured in dollars or something else (see Chapter 1). The bottom line is that your actions are fundamentally no different than Ford's actions.

Using Cost–Benefit Analysis to Determine an Appropriate Level of Safety

2.3 Learning Objective

Use cost–benefit analysis to determine whether a safety precaution is cost-justified.

"Wait!" you may say. "Ford sold *millions* of Pintos, and put *millions* of lives at risk, and all for just $11 a car. Surely the magnitude of the offense puts Ford in a different league than me, right? Couldn't the company have just spent the $11 and saved society the trouble?"

It certainly seems that way, doesn't it? But it's important to remember that when Ford designed the Pinto, there were literally thousands of possible modifications that *could* have been made to improve safety. One of the easiest ways to make a car safer,

---

[4]*Grimshaw v. Ford Motor Co.* (1981).

for example, is to add weight to it. Ford could have made the Pinto longer and wider, and it could have added huge lead weights behind the bumpers and used extra-thick steel in the doors and roof. And Ford could have installed a pressurized system that would have filled the cabin with soft, shock-absorbent foam in the event of a crash. Some of these safety features would have cost $11, some $111, and some $1,111. And some of them would have saved one life, and some a hundred lives, and some a thousand lives. So out of all the possible safety improvements available to Ford, which ones should Ford have chosen?

Application 2.2

What Is the Value of a Child Safety Seat?

One day, some of you are probably going to *consider* acquiring one of life's most costly possessions: a baby. Babies, and kids in general, are expensive. As infants, they require around-the-clock care, use lots of diapers, and blow through clothes quickly.

Then there are the car seats. You start with a rear-facing car seat, which is soon replaced by a slightly larger rear-facing car seat, which is followed by a forward-facing car seat. Then the law requires booster seats until your child is well on his way to adolescence. No wonder Americans spend a few hundred *million* dollars on car seats each year!

Why buy this series of costly seats for your child? If your answer is, "Safety, of course!" then count yourself among the many who understand that several hundred dollars is a small price to pay to reduce the risk of a child dying. The National Highway Traffic Safety Administration (NHTSA) tells us that car seats reduce by 54% the accident death rate of children ages one to four. You can't argue with data like that. Or can you?

That's the question economist Steven Levitt asked. The NHTSA data shows only that it's better to use a car seat than to use nothing. But Levitt was curious: Do costly car seats outperform ordinary seat belts? To figure that out, he examined the information recorded in the Fatality Analysis Reporting System (FARS), which contains data on every fatal collision in the United States. That data includes information on what kind of restraint the occupants were wearing, if any. What Levitt found was amazing: For children under age two, car seats are undoubtedly safer than any alternative. But beyond age two, they provide no appreciable benefit over simply buckling a child into a seat belt.

That real-world finding was so unexpected that Levitt felt compelled to verify it in the controlled environment of a lab. He enlisted two child-sized crash-test dummies and subjected each to two 30 mph crashes: one in a properly installed car seat, and one in which the dummy was wearing a standard lap and shoulder belt. And again, seat belts did just as good a job of preventing injury and death as properly installed car seats.

Both the FARS data and Levitt's own crash tests indicate that spending money on child safety seats beyond the age of two is tantamount to throwing away money. The important thing is not *how* your child is restrained but *that* your child is restrained! To their credit, this is where car seats excel: They do a much better job of keeping children immobilized than seat belts, so if your child is likely to squirm out of his seat belt, the car seat may be worth the money. That is, unless there's a cheaper way to keep your child immobilized. Levitt claims there is—a device that can keep children glued to their seats and into their seat belts: an ordinary backseat DVD player.

See related problems 3.10 and 3.11 on page 53 at the end of this chapter.

Based on Steven Levitt and Joseph Doyle, "Evaluating the Effectiveness of Child Safety Seats and Seat Belts in Protecting Children from Injury," *Economic Inquiry*, 2010; and Steven Levitt and Stephen Dubner, "The Car Seat Solution," *New York Times Magazine*, July 10, 2005.

If cost were no object, then Ford should have incorporated all of the safety improvements. However, cost does matter; remember that there are no free lunches. And if cost matters to Ford, as it matters everywhere else in society, then Ford is going to have to make some tough choices about which improvements to make and which to forgo. If Ford refuses to make these choices, then it will spend tons of money to manufacture super-safe, huge cars, and then it will pass those costs on to the consumer. The only cars the company will produce will be expensive ones that drive like armored tanks and that only rich people are able to afford.

So, Ford has to pick and choose, and it needs some objective basis for choosing which modifications to adopt and which not to adopt. Comparing the cost of the modification with the lives it would save is the best way Ford can save the greatest number of lives at the lowest possible cost.

Suppose that fixing the gas tank would have saved 1 life for every 100,000 Pintos on the road in the 1970s. Should Ford have spent $11 per Pinto to do so? Should Ford have spent $1,100 per car? How about $11,000? What about $1 million? If you ask your friends, you're likely to find that even the most soft-hearted among them will generally agree that adding $1 million worth of safety improvements to a $2,000 car in order to save 1 life out of 100,000 is just too much.

Remember the issue that we started with: Ford made an unprincipled decision to sacrifice human lives in order to save a few dollars. But now almost everybody agrees that there is *some* amount of money that is too much to spend to save one very important life. The principle has been abandoned, and now the only thing to determine is how much is too much.

So how much *should* Ford spend on any given modification? Here's the basic process Ford and other automakers go through when they make these calculations. Suppose Ford knows that the gas tank is a potential area of weakness. It conducts some crash tests and simulations and determines that for every 100,000 Pintos on the road, on average, 1 will blow up and kill someone. Because Ford is doing cost–benefit analysis, it needs to figure out what that person's life is worth. In the case of the Pinto, Ford turned to guidelines set by the National Highway Traffic Safety Administration (NHTSA), which suggested that each life lost was worth about $200,000 (more on this later).

Of course, if Ford knew *which* car was going to explode, it would spend the $11 to fix that car and avoid exposing the company to $200,000 of liability. However, because Ford does not know which one will explode, the most basic way to figure out what to spend on each car is for Ford to divide the $200,000 of liability by the 100,000 cars produced and assign a $2 "death cost" to each car.[5]

If a failure to fix the defect will result in each car being $2 more expensive to produce, then fixing the defect will allow Ford to avoid those costs. Should Ford fix the defect if it can be done for $1.50? Yes. Spending $1.50 per car prevents Ford from having to pay $2 per car in damages and improves the company's bottom line by 50 cents per car. In other words, fixing the defect is a **cost-justified precaution**, a safety measure whose benefits outweigh its costs.

Cost-justified precaution A safety measure whose benefits outweigh its costs.

But what if the repair costs more? Some of you might say that Ford should repair the defect if it can be done for less than $10 per car, some might say $20, and some $200. While it might be easy to legislate a standard such as "Ford should spend up to $20 to save $2 worth of life," it's much harder to *choose* that standard because it will depend on who you ask. That's because individuals' preferences can be both arbitrary and subjective. After all, if you're willing to say that Ford should spend $20 to save $2 of life, then why not $21? If $21, why not $22? Out of all the arbitrary and subjective guidelines society might choose, the only one that really makes sense is this: "Ford should spend up to $2 to save $2 worth of life." You might not agree with that

---

[5]This may be easier to understand if you work backward. Note that for every 100,000 cars Ford produces, it expects 1 fatality. If you multiply the $2 death cost per car by 100,000 cars, you end up with $200,000. That amount is just sufficient to cover damages for the 1 fatality Ford expects.

amount, but it is easy to conclude that it's the least arbitrary and most objective of all possible standards.

That standard—that Ford should spend up to, but not more than, $2 to save $2 worth of life—is a clear and unambiguous rule that Ford can apply to any potential safety modification it might consider. It's a rule that makes sense to the company and its bottom line. But the standard also makes sense to the benevolent social planner, who really does *not* want society (a society that includes Ford) to spend, say, $6 to save $2 worth of life. Simply put, that money can be put to better use elsewhere. We could, for example, spend the $6 to buy a movie ticket. You may say to yourself, "A movie? Really? C'mon, we're talking about *lives* here!" But remember that you put your life *and* the lives of others at risk for things that appear just as trivial as going to the movies. So why should Ford be held to a different standard?[6]

This type of cost–benefit analysis makes a great deal of sense to economists, even if it does appear to be a bit hard-hearted. The truth is that in a world of scarcity, we can't save everybody from everything, so we have to make hard choices. Cost–benefit analysis helps us make those choices in the least arbitrary way possible. This is why the American legal system generally uses this method when deciding product liability and negligence cases. It may not be perfect, but in an imperfect world, it's the best we can do.

2.4 Learning Objective

Explain how errors in assessing risks and valuing lives may affect cost-benefit analysis.

Problems and Pitfalls of Cost–Benefit Analysis When Life Is Involved

While cost–benefit analysis may be the least arbitrary method to determine how to use scarce resources, it is far from perfect. If the numbers used in the cost–benefit analysis aren't accurate, then the conclusions you draw from your analysis may well be flawed. In other words, garbage in, garbage out. That is particularly likely to occur when cost–benefit analysis is applied to random or uncertain events. If you use inaccurate measures of how likely an event is to occur in your cost–benefit analysis, or if you don't properly estimate the consequences of a particular outcome, then your analysis may lead you to an incorrect conclusion.

Mistakes in Estimating Risk

When applying cost–benefit analysis to an uncertain event, you must, as Ford did, include some probability that the event will occur. Sometimes that probability can be fairly accurately measured. A light bulb company, for example, can estimate the probability of one of its bulbs burning out early by analyzing data from its quality control tests. But sometimes the probability of an unlikely event is tougher to measure because a company lacks resources for extensive product testing or because the event in question happens so infrequently.

When the probability of an event we want to include in a cost–benefit analysis is tough or impossible to measure accurately, we often rely on guesswork. Unfortunately, human beings are often poor guessers. One reason is that most people don't have a very good understanding of probability. Suppose your roommate is idly flipping a coin and manages to flip 9 heads in a row. What is the probability of him flipping a head on the 10th toss? Most people, recognizing that flipping 10 heads in a row is extremely unlikely, generally respond that the probability of flipping a head on the 10th toss must be very small: "He's flipped 9 heads in a row—the next one's just got to be a tail!" In fact, the chance of flipping a head on the 10th toss is exactly 50%, just as it was exactly 50% for each of the first 9 throws![7]

---

[6]It is also possible that we could take that $6 and save more lives by spending it on police officers or firefighters or lifeguards than we could by spending it on making the Pinto safer.

[7]This is another example of confusing a total quantity (the probability of flipping 10 heads, which is very small, around 1/1,000) with a marginal quantity (the probability of flipping a head on the 10th toss, which is 1/2).

There is a second reason that simply guessing the probability of an event is likely to introduce error into cost–benefit analysis. It turns out that even human beings who understand the laws of probability are generally not very good at actually estimating probabilities, and the more remote and spectacular an event is, the bigger the error is likely to be. That is partly because truly remote and spectacular events tend to generate a lot of media coverage, which makes them seem more familiar to us and therefore more likely to occur. And it's partly due to our inability to separate our fears from our assessments of risk. After terrorists flew hijacked aircraft into New York's World Trade Center and the Pentagon in 2001, for example, millions of people altered travel plans to avoid flying and drove instead; they vastly overestimated the probability of a repeat attack and felt safer in their cars.[8] But in reality, driving is far more dangerous than flying, and it's estimated that in the year following those attacks, as a result of those decisions, more than 1,500 extra people died in traffic accidents.[9]

Let's return to Ford' cost–benefit analysis. What if Ford's calculations are wrong? If Ford makes an error when calculating the true death cost per car, it will build the wrong amount of safety into its cars. Suppose Ford mistakenly estimates that there will be only 1 death for every 200,000 Pintos on the road. Then Ford will mistakenly estimate the death cost per car to be just $1, even though the real death cost per car is $2. Based on the mistaken estimate, Ford will reject the $1.50 repair, and as a result, people will die unnecessarily.

That ill-informed decision makes Ford poorer: Making the repair would have cost the company $1.50 per car. Instead, compensating the victims' families costs the company $2 per car. From society's standpoint, the world is poorer, too: It would have been worth spending $1.50 worth of scarce resources to save $2 of life. Because Ford rejects the repair, each time a Pinto rolls off the assembly line, both Ford and society are made 50 cents poorer.

Let's summarize the effect of that miscalculation by comparing Ford's decision making to society's ideal in the presence of inaccurate information:

- True probability of a death $= 1/100,000$
- True death cost per car $= (1/100,000) \times \$200,000 = \$2$
- Cost of repair $= \$1.50$
- True cost–benefit recommendation: Ford should repair the Pinto.
- Ford's estimate of the probability of a death $= 1/200,000$
- Ford's estimated death cost per car $= (1/200,000) \times \$200,000 = \$1$
- Cost of repair $= \$1.50$
- Ford's cost–benefit recommendation: Don't repair the Pinto.

Oddly, the same process works in reverse. If Ford estimates that the likelihood of injury is higher than it actually is, then the company may spend more money trying to save lives than the lives are really worth. If Ford mistakenly estimates the deaths per 100,000 cars produced to be 3, it will end up using an artificially high death cost of $6 in its cost–benefit calculations. As a result, Ford will spend more on safety improvements per car than it should, and both Ford and society end up poorer for every Pinto produced.

Because small errors in estimating the likelihood of death can result in disastrous decision making and reduced profits for companies, products like the Pinto undergo

---

[8]In addition, even when people have perfectly accurate estimates of probabilities, sometimes their decisions vary depending on whether those probabilities are framed as positives or negatives. If your doctor tells you that a semi-elective surgery has an 80% survival rate (a positive frame), you may be more likely to elect that surgery than if the doctor tells you that the surgery has a 20% fatality rate (a negative frame). For more on framing effects, see Daniel Kahneman and Amos Tversky, "The Framing of Decisions and the Psychology of Choice," *Science*, 1981.

[9]See "September 11's Indirect Toll: Road Deaths Linked to Fearful Flyers," *The Guardian*, September 5, 2011. Also see "10 Ways We Get the Odds Wrong," *Psychology Today*, January 1, 2008.

Application 2.3

Better Safe Than Sorry?

It's possible to be too reckless. When large and likely losses can be prevented with little effort, it is foolish to neglect safety. Yet it is just as foolish to spend resources trying to prevent accidents that are unlikely to occur anyway.

Corporations and governments often have the resources to determine how much precaution is cost-justified. But individuals often lack the resources and training to perform accurate cost–benefit analysis. And individuals are incredibly poor at assessing risks, which may lead them to take too little care when care is justified or too much care when it is not.

For example, do you:

- Text while driving?
- Wear your seat belt?
- Know the location of the nearest tornado shelter?
- Avoid stinging insects?
- Hold the handrail when using stairs?
- Wear your walking helmet?

Your *what*? Walking helmets are a pet project of the Danish Road Safety Council. To avoid injury, the council encourages pedestrians in Denmark to use special walking helmets, although the council concedes that a bike helmet probably does just as well, so bicycle commuters might consider simply keeping their helmets on through the day.

But really, how dangerous could walking be?

More dangerous than you realize. According to the U.S. National Safety Council, you're more than 6 times more likely to be killed while walking than you are while biking. And you're 10 times as likely to die walking than in an aircraft accident; you're also 17 times more likely to die walking than by being electrocuted, and you're 40 times more likely to die walking than to fall victim to thunderstorms, tornadoes, and hurricanes combined. Yet, many people buckle up while flying, are super-careful around electricity, and seek shelter in their basements when Mother Nature threatens a heavy dew. Probably no one you know wears a walking helmet.

People's failure to wear walking helmets may be a result of poor cost–benefit analyses based on inaccurate guesses about the likelihood of being killed while walking. After all, if biking is safer than walking and bikers wear helmets, surely walkers should, too.

According to the National Safety Council, the most effective precautionary measure might be to choose a healthy lifestyle. The National Safety Council's data indicates that America's number-one killer is heart disease, which is 6 times more fatal than driving, 50 times more deadly than firearms, and 100 times more dangerous than walking. The experts aren't kidding when they tell you to eat less and exercise more. But if you choose to walk for that exercise, be sure to wear your walking helmet.

See related problem 4.6 on page 54 at the end of this chapter.

Based on the National Safety Council's *Injury Facts 2013*, "A Walking Helmet Is a Good Helmet," Copenhagenize.com, August 5, 2009, and A. J. Jacobs's *Drop Dead Healthy: One Man's Humble Quest for Bodily Perfection*, 2012.

extensive safety testing and detailed statistical analyses before they ever go into mass production. Truth be told, Ford's analysis probably wasn't too bad: Long after the Pinto scandal was over, the NHTSA determined that fires from rear-end collisions involving Pintos resulted in only 27 deaths. This was far fewer than the 900-plus deaths reported by *Mother Jones*. Considering that Ford sold about 2.5 million Pintos, that number isn't particularly startling; in fact, it's consistent with the fatality rate for other subcompact cars on the market at the time.[10]

Cost–benefit analysis helps companies make good decisions about how much safety to build into their products. But because the kind of testing and analysis big corporations do is both costly and time-consuming, it is much more difficult for individuals like you and me to decide how much precaution we should take in our everyday lives. When we do our own mental cost–benefit analysis, we are forced to *guess* about how likely it is that our actions will cause harm to ourselves and to others.

Suppose, for example, that you want to have one glass of wine while eating dinner at a restaurant. How much does this raise the probability of you having an accident and killing someone on the way home? Or perhaps you want to make a call while driving. How much does this elevate the risk of being in an accident? Maybe you want to go for a walk in the woods. How likely are you to be hit by lightning while walking under an oak tree? The truth is that individuals are simply terrible at estimating the probabilities of unlikely events. We systematically make large errors when assessing risks. As a result, we often take too much or too little precaution as we go about our everyday lives.

Mistakes in Estimating the True Value of a Life

Another way that Ford's cost–benefit calculations can go awry is if the company uses an inappropriate value for what a life is worth. If the value of those killed were really $600,000, while Ford continued to (inaccurately) use a $200,000 figure, then the "death cost per car" figure that Ford used in its comparison would be artificially low. Consequently, Ford might fail to adopt safety measures that were truly cost-justified. On the other hand, if human life were really only worth $100,000, then Ford might be convinced to make cars that, as odd as it sounds, were *too* safe!

Approaches to Valuing a Life

2.5 Learning Objective
Describe the two approaches economists use to value a life.

To perform the cost–benefit analysis on the Pinto, Ford relied on a $200,000 figure supplied by the NHTSA. That figure was, in fact, the very one that the NHTSA used in conducting its own cost–benefit analyses of highway safety measures. If that figure were too low, it might have led Ford to make a poor decision regarding the safety of its fuel system. This raises the question: How much *is* a human life worth?

The Lost-Income Approach

Forensic economists attempt to answer the question of how much a life is worth. Attorneys hire forensic economists to assess economic damages in wrongful death and injury lawsuits. Most often, this involves estimating what the injured or deceased person would have earned over the remainder of his or her life. Such an approach is called the **lost-income approach**. This is a complex calculation because the typical person might change jobs or even careers, get raises or bonuses, or might see earnings eroded by the effects of rising prices.

Lost-income approach Estimating the value of an injured or deceased person's life by adding up that person's lost future earnings.

---

[10]Many people wonder why Ford's cost–benefit analysis didn't account for the incredible adverse publicity the Pinto generated. This figure helps explain why: The Pinto was actually about as safe as other cars on the market, and the disastrous publicity was the result of the wildly inflated numbers published by *Mother Jones*. Ford simply could not have anticipated such a media disaster.

Because the court needs objective and measurable criteria for awarding damages, whether you like it or not, money is what matters. Someone who is young will be worth more than someone who is old, simply because she has more of her working life ahead of her, and her family will suffer more for her loss. A computer programmer will be worth more than a cashier because the programmer earns a higher salary. A person with a college degree (an investment in what economists call *human capital*) will be worth more than someone with just a high school diploma because a college degree opens access to a higher earnings profile. Someone who is healthy will be worth more than someone with a chronic illness for no other reason than the healthy person will likely have more productive work time ahead of him.

The court does *not* consider the victim's character or personality or the number of relatives who loved her. Admittedly, someone who is loved by many people probably brings more joy to the world than someone whom everyone dislikes. However, it's difficult for the courts to assess how much love and joy a deceased person might have brought to the world around her. It's even more difficult to determine how much that was worth in dollars.

Have you ever seen an obituary that read something like this: "The deceased was a genuine rat, reviled by his co-workers and barely tolerated by his family. Even his priest asked him to please join another church." Of course you haven't, even though we all know that some people really are like that. The point is that if people's families are willing to shade the truth about their nature in their obituaries, then surely they would be willing to shade the truth when many thousands of dollars are at stake. Were the courts to incorporate love and joy into damage awards, you can be sure that only absolute angels would die.

The Compensating Differential Approach

For the reasons just discussed, courts generally make a practice of awarding only economic damages in cases of wrongful death and injury. But we know that a person is the product of his work and his family and his life and his passions and his loves. Because those things have genuine value, people who make public policy—for example, the ones who determine how many police officers to put on the streets or how strong to build a bridge—should consider those things, even if the courts cannot.

The problem, of course, is that when society makes public policy decisions, cost–benefit calculations must be done. Those calculations are measured in dollars, not smiles or hugs. We need a way to incorporate those things into our decisions, and who knows better how much a person's life is worth than the person himself?

Of course, just asking won't get you anywhere. Ask a man what his life is worth and, despite the fact that he routinely jaywalks or jumps out of perfectly good airplanes just for sport, he'll tell you that his life is priceless. But talk is cheap, so instead of relying on his word, economists interested in studying how much a life is worth have developed methods to determine how much a person's life is worth by observing that person's *actions*. Those economists look at the risks the person takes and the reward he gets for taking those risks, and with that data, they determine how much the man thinks his life is worth. Of course, the reward someone gets from skydiving is hard to measure, so economists generally tend to look for places where risk is rewarded with dollars—in the workplace.

All else equal, people with risky jobs make more money than people with safe jobs. For example, CNN reports that garbage-truck workers, who earn an average of $34,000 per year, have the fourth-most-dangerous job in America.[11] In contrast, janitors, who do similar work in a much safer environment, earn only about $19,000 per year. The extra pay people earn in exchange for undertaking risky or otherwise

---

[11]In the sanitation industry, about 41 out of 100,000 workers die on the job annually. The most dangerous job is fishing, with 121 workers being killed for every 100,000 employed annually. Fishermen earn about $30,000 but typically make that money in a short fishing season. On an hourly basis, fishermen often fare quite well.

undesirable work is called a **compensating differential**. By observing the size of the compensating differential, we can estimate how much money it takes to get the typical person to bear an additional risk of death that would strip the person not only of her earnings but also of love, joy, and all the other things the individual values. This method of valuing a life is called the **compensating differential approach**.

So how do we apply the method of compensating differentials? Suppose that you and 9,999 of your closest friends are all employed at a certain company. You're a keen observer of the world around you, and based on your experience, you know that the probability of being killed in a work-related accident is 2/10,000. In other words, odds are that 2 of you will die in a work-related accident this year. You don't know *which* 2, but you've built enough into your salary demands to compensate for the chance that it might be you.

Then your company introduces a new production process that increases the number of workers that will die each year from 2 to 3. (In other words, the probability of being killed in a work-related accident rises to 3/10,000.) Two of you were going to die anyway. Now 1 more of you (out of the 10,000 workers at the company) is going to die. You just don't know which person! So to compensate you for the very, very slight chance it might be you, you and each of your 9,999 co-workers ask for an extra $500 per year. When all is said and done, your employer collectively pays $5 million in exchange for killing 1 more worker, and you and your co-workers collectively agree that $5 million is a sufficient price to pay. It's as if you've each agreed that if you are the one to go, $5 million is what you're worth!

This means that you can infer how much people value their lives by how risky the jobs they select are and by how much they demand in compensation. Mathematically, that value can be calculated as:

$$\text{Value of a life} = \frac{\text{Compensating differential}}{\text{Increased chance of death}}$$

which, in turn, looks like this:

$$\text{Value of a life} = \frac{(\text{Salary in risky job} - \text{Salary in safer job})}{(\text{Probability of death in risky job} - \text{Probability of death in safer job})}$$

Let's verify that this formula produces a result consistent with the story we told above. In exchange for an extra $500 annually, you were willing to accept an increase in your likelihood of dying on the job from 2 per 10,000 to 3 per 10,000. Plugging those figures into our formula, we get exactly the same $5 million as before:

$$\text{Value of a life} = \frac{\$500}{\left(\dfrac{3}{10,000} - \dfrac{2}{10,000}\right)}$$

$$\text{Value of a life} = \frac{\$500}{\dfrac{1}{10,000}} = \$5 \text{ million}$$

When we use this method in the real world, what numbers do we come up with? As it turns out, lots of studies have used this method, and though a consensus hasn't been achieved, most of them have estimated the value of a life to be between $3 million and $7 million. Even at the low end of this range, estimates developed using this method are substantially higher than what we get just by adding up a person's lost income, which, you'll remember, is the approach the courts take.

The compensating differential method, though imperfect, is the best method available to value the intangible, but important, parts of life that are not measurable in dollars. These are the amounts the benevolent social planner cares about, and these are also the amounts that public policymakers (such as the NHTSA, the Environmental Protection Agency, and your local county commission) should care about if they are truly interested in taking measures that bring the greatest possible net benefits to society.

Compensating differential The extra pay people earn in exchange for undertaking risky or otherwise undesirable work.

Compensating differential approach A method of valuing a life that estimates how much money it takes to get the typical person to bear an additional risk of death.

And government policies do often result in lives lost or lives saved—more often than you'd think. For example,

- Government-imposed fuel economy standards encourage automakers to shave weight from their cars. With less protection in a crash, more people die.
- Clean water regulations save lives, but how many lives and at what cost? Could the dollars spent cleaning water that is already nearly pure have saved more lives if spent on cancer research?
- Lengthy drug testing procedures required by the Food and Drug Administration help keep unsafe drugs off pharmacy shelves but also create delays in bringing safe and effective drugs to market. In the meantime, people die.

If the government wants to appropriately evaluate these policies to squeeze the greatest possible social benefits out of your hard-earned tax dollars, it needs the best possible measure of the value of the lives it saves or sacrifices. Consequently, it uses the compensating differential method.

It makes sense for policymakers to use the compensating differential method when designing laws and regulations. It makes just as much sense for you to use the method when deciding how much care to exercise in your own behavior. The danger, however, is this: If you're a cold and unfeeling person who is thinking about engaging in a behavior that exposes others to the risk of death, you might conduct your cost–benefit analysis by asking yourself, "If my behavior ends up killing someone, how much will I be on the hook for when the victim's family sues me?" But remember that the courts (for good reason) generally follow procedures that only add up lost income rather than account for the full value of a life. By considering only the costs that the courts might assess you, rather than the full costs to society (which include love, joy, happiness, and other intangibles), you might be led to engage in behavior that exposes others to risks that are not justifiable on a cost–benefit basis. That difference—the difference between what is best for the individual and what is best for society—is the key feature of collective action problems and will be a recurring theme throughout the rest of this book.

Conclusion

The first chapter of this book is devoted to the idea that there is no free lunch—that everything comes at some cost. This chapter is devoted to the intriguing notion that sometimes those costs are measured in human lives. Every day, our actions unavoidably expose ourselves and others to the risk of death. Learning how to incorporate that risk into the choices we make is an important step in making better decisions about how much precaution to exercise in our daily lives. Perhaps more importantly, many of the social problems discussed later in the book have real human costs. Understanding how policymakers can incorporate those costs into their decision making is one key to crafting more effective policy.

Chapter Summary and Problems

Key Terms

Compensating differential, p. 49

Compensating differential approach, p. 49

Cost–benefit analysis, p. 37

Cost-justified precaution, p. 43

Lost-income approach, p. 47

Marginal analysis, p. 38

Marginal benefit, p. 38

Marginal cost, p. 38

2.1 Cost–Benefit Analysis, pages 37–40

Apply cost–benefit analysis to choose among alternative courses of action.

Summary

Economic decision makers often use cost–benefit analysis to help guide their choices. Good cost–benefit analysis identifies the relevant stakeholders and measures how much they stand to gain or lose. An alternative is good if benefits are greater than costs; it should be avoided if costs are greater than benefits. Good cost–benefit analysis is based on marginal costs and benefits—costs and benefits looking forward—not total costs and benefits, which may include costs already incurred.

Review Questions

All problems are assignable in MyEconLab.

1.1 The additional cost you will incur when you choose a particular action is called the _____ cost.

1.2 You are trying to decide whether you should go to college. To help decide, you compare what you would sacrifice to go to college with the higher earnings you will generate with a college degree. The analysis you have just conducted is called _____.

1.3 You are wondering whether to buy a new Jeep. Your cost–benefit analysis indicates that the costs exceed the benefits. You should _____.
   a. Buy the jeep
   b. Not buy the jeep
   c. There is not enough information to determine whether you should buy the Jeep.

1.4 Cost–benefit analysis is a tool that is used _____.
   a. Only by businesses
   b. Only by governments
   c. Only by individuals
   d. By all of the above

1.5 You are deciding where to study abroad—England or Spain. A year's study in England costs $15,000, and a year's study in Spain costs $20,000. You estimate that the benefits of studying in England are $30,000, and the benefits of studying in Spain are $36,000. Based on those numbers, you should _____.
   a. Study in England because it is cheaper
   b. Study in Spain because it creates greater benefit
   c. Study in Spain because it creates the greater net benefit
   d. Study in England because it creates the greater net benefit

1.6 When conducting cost–benefit analysis, you should consider _____.
   a. Only marginal costs and marginal benefits
   b. Total costs and benefits
   c. Only costs and benefits that have already been incurred
   d. Every cost, whether it has been incurred yet or not

Problems and Applications

1.7 Jessie is considering breaking up with Taylor. Taylor is becoming withdrawn and sullen, and their relationship is deteriorating. When her friends encourage her to make the break, Jessie replies, "Taylor's a lot of work right now—more than I'm getting out of the relationship. But we've been together for five years, and we have a lot of really good history. It'd be a shame to throw those good years away. I'm just going to have to stick it out." Critique Jessie's cost–benefit analysis. Should she make the break?

1.8 At the beginning of the growing season, Cecil planted 10 acres of wheat at a cost of $5,000. Now it is harvest time. Each acre will produce 40 bushels of wheat, and wheat sells for $3 per bushel. Harvesting the wheat will cost Cecil $1,500. What does cost–benefit analysis suggest that Cecil do? Most importantly, why?

1.9 [Related to Application 2.1 on page 39] Suppose that the government of Nebraska is considering siphoning off as much water as it can from the Republican River before it flows into Kansas. Siphoning off water is expensive but provides great benefits when the water is used to irrigate crops. Who are the relevant stakeholders Nebraska should consider in its own cost–benefit analysis? If the decision were up to the federal government, and not the Nebraska government, would the answer change?

2.2 Applying Cost–Benefit Analysis to Life, pages 40–41

Explain why decision makers cannot avoid placing a dollar value on a life when conducting a cost–benefit analysis.

Summary

Cost–benefit analysis is hard to do when costs and benefits cannot be easily measured. This is particularly true when the costs and benefits are measured in terms of human lives. Nevertheless, everybody—corporations, governments, and you—incorporates the value of human life into their implicit and explicit cost–benefit analyses.

Review Questions

2.1 Who regularly trades their own gain against others' lives?

   a. Corporations

   b. Governments

   c. Ordinary people

   d. All of the above

2.2 Which of the following statements is true?

   a. It is possible for corporations to avoid trading their own gain against others' lives.

   b. It is possible for governments to avoid placing a value on peoples' lives when designing policy.

   c. There is a fundamental difference between a government that places a value on life and a corporation that places a value on life.

   d. There is no fundamental difference between the risks individuals expose one another to and the risk corporations expose their customers to.

Problems and Applications

2.3 "There is no difference between you driving your car on public streets and Ford selling a product that it knows will sometimes explode." Is this statement true or false? What unmentioned factor might your answer depend on?

2.3   **Using Cost–Benefit Analysis to Determine an Appropriate Level of Safety, pages 41–44**

   Use cost–benefit analysis to determine whether a safety precaution is cost-justified.

Summary

Scarcity demands that people accept some degree of risk in their lives. Too much precaution causes people to forgo too many opportunities. But too little precaution may expose them to risks that could have been easily avoided. Cost–benefit analysis can be used to determine which precautions are cost-justified and which are not. For any given precaution, if the cost of the precaution outweighs the value of lives saved, the precaution is not cost-justified. If the cost of the precaution is less than the value of lives saved, the precaution is cost-justified.

Review Questions

3.1 When a safety measure produces benefits in excess of its costs, that safety measure is called a _____ precaution.

3.2 A corporation is considering producing a product that it knows will probably result in some people, somewhere, dying. That corporation _____.

   a. Must, under no circumstances, produce that product

   b. Cannot include the value of the lost lives in its cost–benefit analysis

   c. Has little choice but to include the value of the lost lives in its cost–benefit analysis

   d. Must design and incorporate every available precaution into its product until it is sure no lives will be lost

3.3 A ladder manufacturer can make a ladder more stable by adding wider feet to the product. Adding wider feet costs $6 per ladder. The manufacturer estimates that this will prevent 4 injury-causing falls for every 1,000 ladders sold and that, on average, each injury causes $1,800 of harm. The injury cost per ladder is _____.

   a. $6

   b. $1,800

   c. $7,200

   d. $7.20

3.4 A ladder manufacturer can make a ladder more stable by adding wider feet to the product. Adding wider feet costs $6 per ladder. The manufacturer estimates that this will prevent 4 injury-causing falls for every 1,000 ladders sold and that, on average, each injury causes $1,800 of harm. The manufacturer _____.

   a. Should add the wider feet because they are cost-justified

   b. Should add the wider feet even though they are not cost-justified

   c. Should not add the wider feet because they are not cost-justified

   d. Should not add the wider feet because doing so will harm its profits

3.5 Regarding safety, cost–benefit analysis tells us that _____.

   a. It is possible to be too unsafe

   b. It is possible to be too safe

   c. It is possible to be just safe enough

   d. All of the above are possible.

3.6 The benevolent social planner would like to see people _____.

   a. Take all possible precautions

   b. Take all cost-justified precautions

   c. Take only cost-justified precautions

   d. Take all cost-justified precautions, and only cost-justified precautions

3.7 Suppose that a chemist detects trace amounts of insecticide in food from your student union. Which statement below best captures what an economist might say about this?

    a. "Goodness! We must find a way to remove all the insecticide!"

    b. "Greedy people—always willing to sacrifice students in pursuit of the bottom line."

    c. "We could clean up the food, but it might be very costly and bring very little benefit."

    d. "If it will save a human life, we should spend the resources necessary to clean up the food."

Problems and Applications

3.8 There are lots of things homebuilders could do to make homes safer—install rubber floors, handrails on every wall, elevators instead of stairs, and so on. Should we require contractors to incorporate every possible safety feature into the homes they build? Should we let contractors build homes with absolutely no regard to safety? If we are to require some safety considerations but not others, how will we pick which ones to incorporate and which to discard?

3.9 Suppose that the government is considering a policy that will result in cleaner, safer drinking water. Specifically, the policy targets the amount of arsenic in drinking water supplies. Arsenic is a naturally occurring element that also happens to be the active ingredient in rat poison. Most drinking water has a bit of arsenic in it. Sometimes, that arsenic kills people. Current standards mandate that no supply of drinking water may have greater than 50 parts per billion (ppb) arsenic. The proposed standard would remove 80% of that arsenic, reducing tolerance levels to 10 ppb arsenic. You are an economist who has been called in to help decide whether this policy is a good idea. Explain the process you will use. What questions will you need to ask to reach a conclusion?

3.10 [**Related to Application 2.2 on page 42**] Every state requires car seats for children beyond age two. Application 2.2 suggests that such a requirement beyond age two does no good—that car seats provide no measurable safety difference. If most people eventually become parents, and all those parents are throwing significant money down the drain, why do you suppose there is no outcry to get rid of child safety seats? Is there a collective action problem at work? Explain.

3.11 [**Related to Application 2.2 on page 42**] Almost every state requires car seats for children beyond age two and mandates safety belt use beyond that. Yet only five states require seat belts of any kind in school buses. Can you justify this seemingly contradictory message about child safety? Explain.

3.12 Visit www.livingto100.com and complete the life expectancy calculator. The results you receive will present the trade-offs between your behaviors and your life expectancy. Survey your results and think about questions like this: Is the extra cup of coffee every day worth losing a year of life expectancy? Create a short list of the livingto100.com recommendations and then indicate which behaviors bring you enough happiness that you might consider them cost-justified in terms of reduced life expectancy. By the same criterion, which of your behaviors aren't cost-justified?

2.4   **Problems and Pitfalls of Cost–Benefit Analysis When Life Is Involved, pages 44–47**

Explain how errors in assessing risks and valuing lives may affect cost–benefit analysis.

Summary

Good cost–benefit analysis requires accurate assessment of the risks involved and accurate assessment of the value of the outcomes. If the risk associated with a particular outcome is underestimated, or if the value of that outcome is overestimated, then cost–benefit analysis might lead people to indulge in too much risk or take too few precautions. If the risk of a particular outcome is overestimated, or the value of a particular outcome is underestimated, then people may accept too little risk or take precautions that are not cost-justified.

Review Questions

All problems are assignable in MyEconLab.

4.1 If a conscientious manufacturer overestimates the probability of its product killing someone, that manufacturer _____.

    a. Will likely fail to take all cost-justified precautions

    b. Will likely take precautions that are not cost-justified

    c. Will likely take the ideal amount of precautions

    d. We cannot predict the level of precaution the manufacturer will take.

4.2 If a conscientious manufacturer overestimates the true value of life, that manufacturer _____.

    a. Will likely fail to take all cost-justified precautions

    b. Will likely take precautions that are not cost-justified

    c. Will likely take the ideal amount of precautions

    d. We cannot predict the level of precaution the manufacturer will take.

4.3 When it comes to unlikely but potentially deadly events, _____.

    a. Individuals are very good at estimating risks

    b. Individuals are very poor at estimating risks

    c. Individuals are better at estimating risks than large corporations

    d. Individuals' cost-benefit analysis does not depend on properly estimating risks

Problems and Applications

4.4 A lawnmower manufacturer estimates that the probability of a fatal accident caused by the design of its product is 1/10,000 and that the value of a life lost is $1 million. The manufacturer can change the design to eliminate that chance for $80 per mower and stands ready to incorporate all cost-justified precautions. Will the manufacturer change the design? What would the benevolent social planner think about the manufacturer's decision if the true probability of a fatal accident is not 1/10,000 but 1/15,000?

4.5 A tire manufacturer estimates that the probability of a fatal accident caused by the design of its product is 1/90,000 and further estimates that the value of a life lost is $3 million. The manufacturer can change the design to eliminate that chance for $40 per tire, and it stands ready to incorporate all cost-justified precautions. Will the manufacturer change the design? What would the benevolent social planner think about the manufacturer's decision if the true value of a life is not $3 million but $5 million?

4.6 **[Related to Application 2.3 on page 46]** Everybody dies of something, but what will it be? Estimate the probability that your demise will be caused by a bee sting, by lightning, by electricity, by drowning, or by a bicycle accident. Write down your numbers. Then refer to the National Safety Council's "Odds of Dying From" graphic (which can be found with a quick search at www.nsc.gov) and see how close your estimates were. Were your answers accurate? Were they off by more than a factor of 10 in either direction? Assuming that you take only what you believe to be cost-justified precautions, are you devoting too much care and worry to dying in any particular way? Too little?

2.5   ## Approaches to Valuing a Life, pages 47–50

Describe the two approaches economists use to value a life.

Summary

To use cost–benefit analysis in situations that may put lives at risk, it's important to incorporate the monetary value of a human life. One way to place a value on a person's life is to add up the income that the person would likely earn from the time the action is taken until his or her retirement. This is called the lost-income approach. A second method, the compensating differential approach, uses data on how much risk a person accepts in his employment in exchange for a higher wage to impute how much that person values his or her life.

Review Questions

All problems are assignable in MyEconLab.

5.1 The extra pay that people earn for taking risks in their jobs is known as a _____.

5.2 Valuing a person's life by adding up what that person would probably have earned over the remainder of his working life is known as the _____ approach.

5.3 Valuing a person's life by seeing how dangerous a job that person takes in exchange for higher pay is called the _____ approach.

5.4 When determining the value of human life in wrongful death suits, the courts generally use the _____.

    a. Lost-income method

    b. Contingent valuation method

    c. Compensating differential method

    d. Generalized method of moments

Problems and Applications

5.5 Suppose that Bill is currently working as a high school math teacher, where his likelihood of dying on the job is 5 in 100,000. (In other words, the probability that he will be killed on the job this year is 0.00005.) Bill leaves his school job for a career as a professional magician, where his likelihood of dying on the job is 50 in 100,000 (or 0.00050). Bill earned $30,000 per year as a teacher, and he earns $40,000 as a magician. Use the compensating differential method to determine how much Bill implicitly values his life.

5.6 Two innocent victims are killed in a tragic roller-derby accident. One is a 26-year-old college graduate who sells insurance for a living. She's not very good at it but manages to eke out a living. She is mean to her neighbors, cheats on her husband, and has three misdemeanor convictions for taking candy from small babies. The other is a 45-year-old nun who was recently nominated for the Nobel Peace Prize after years of volunteer service building schools for children in central Africa. In a joint wrongful death suit, whose life will be worth more in the eyes of the court? Why?

The Dictator Game

This chapter introduced cost-benefit analysis as an aid to decision making. In this chapter's experiment, you'll have a chance to apply cost-benefit analysis and you'll explore once again the power of incentives.

Your instructor will pair you with a classmate. The pairings will be anonymous; no player will know who his or her partner is.

One person in each pair will be designated the "allocator." The other will be designated the "receiver." You will get the chance to play both roles during today's game.

At the beginning of game, the allocator receives $1,000. However, there is a condition: The allocator must offer some portion of those dollars to the receiver. The allocator may offer as little as $0 or as much as $1,000.

The receiver has no choice but to accept the offer of the allocator. After all, this is a dictatorship! The receiver will earn the amount offered, and the allocator will earn whatever is left over ($1,000 minus the amount offered).

Your instructor will outline the procedures for submitting offers.

MyEconLab

Please visit http://www.myeconlab.com for support material to conduct this experiment if assigned by your instructor.

Basic Game Theory: Games Between Two Players

Chapter Outline and Learning Objectives

3.1 What Is Game Theory? page 57

Explain the concepts of strategic interaction and mutual interdependence.

3.2 The Basic Structure of Games, page 58

Learn and apply the basic elements of games.

3.3 The Basic Types of Games, page 63

Compare and contrast the key characteristics of five basic types of games.

Experiment: The Push–Pull Game, page 78

MyEconLab

MyEconLab helps you master each objective and study more efficiently.

I t's obviously not possible to address all of the world's problems by reading one book. However, applying the economic ideas in this book to social issues provides two benefits. First, you'll learn that problems that *appear* to be different are often actually quite similar.

For example, the problem of pollution, which is the process of putting unwanted substances into our air, soil, and water, and the problem of depletion, which is the process of taking desired substances out of our air, soil, and water, appear to be opposites. However, when we view these problems through the economist's lens, we'll find that they're virtually identical.[1] Throughout the book, we will apply the tools developed in this chapter to find similar parallels. This will give us a great deal of intellectual power.

Second, economics provides an important tool for understanding the causes of, consequences of, and potential solutions to many of the problems society faces— problems that range from whooping cough epidemics to the best way for police detectives to elicit confessions from suspected criminals. Applying the economic ideas in this book will help prepare you to analyze new situations that don't necessarily resemble others you've seen before.

What Is Game Theory?

If you have already taken an economics course in high school or college, you may have been bewildered by complex math and graphs. Here's some good news: You don't need a deep understanding of math or graphs to use economics to analyze social problems. In fact, in this text we'll use very little math and few graphs.

We will, however, draw repeatedly on a subdiscipline of both economics and mathematics called game theory. **Game theory** is a method of analyzing the strategic interaction that occurs between small numbers of people, firms, organizations, and even countries. **Strategic interaction** simply means anticipating the decisions others will make in response to your decisions, knowing all the while that they are anticipating your response.

A thorough understanding of game theory can make you deadly at games like chess and a force to behold in the rock–paper–scissors game. But there is much more value to game theory than simply understanding games. Strategic interactions encompass a large variety of situations that may include, for example, two countries threatening each other with nuclear war, executives at two different companies deciding what price to charge for their competing products, and city councilors deciding whether to grant a restaurant a liquor license, among others. Each of these situations can be depicted as an economic game, even though the players may not be having much fun. We will call them games nonetheless.

The characteristic that defines these situations as games is called **mutual interdependence**. Mutual interdependence simply means that the outcome of the game depends not only on what you do but what the other players do in response. Those other players might be trying to help you, or they might be trying to hurt you, but in either case their actions affect your outcomes. In contrast, a different method of analysis called *decision theory* is used to analyze your best strategy in situations where no mutual interdependence exists.

Choosing what analytical framework to use requires you to evaluate whether mutual interdependence exists and, if so, whether it is significant enough to affect your choices. For example, if North Korea is thinking about launching a missile at South Korea, it should probably anticipate the likelihood that South Korea will respond in kind. That mutual interdependence suggests that game theory is an appropriate analytical framework for both South Korea and North Korea to use in evaluating their options.

3.1 Learning Objective

Explain the concepts of strategic interaction and mutual interdependence.

Game theory A method of analyzing the strategic interaction that occurs between small numbers of people, firms, organizations, and even countries.

Strategic interaction Anticipating the decisions others will make in response to your decisions, knowing all the while that they are anticipating your response.

Mutual interdependence The characteristic of games whereby the outcome of the game depends not only on what you do but on what the other players do in response.

---

[1]Pollution and depletion are given extensive coverage in the text (in Chapters 7, 8, and 9).

In contrast, suppose that you are using an Amazon.com gift card to buy a new television. There are all kinds of considerations that go into such a purchase, including size, price, resolution, and reliability. But there is little or no mutual interdependence. The only interaction is between you and the computer on the other end, and that computer isn't trying to hinder you or help you; it's simply there to process your order. Choosing the right TV might require carefully evaluating competing alternatives, but it doesn't require you, for example, to outwit anybody. So this situation describes a decision but not a game.

When you're playing a game (as opposed to making a decision), you need to:

1. Anticipate the move that others might be making.
2. Choose a strategy based on the move you anticipate from your rival.

The Basic Structure of Games

The practical application of game theory involves creating economic models of human behavior. An **economic model** is a structured and simplified version of reality that we can use to explain real-world behavior. It's a lot like a map, in that it filters out a lot of extraneous detail but retains a few key features. If you want to get from your home to Beatrice, Nebraska, a map that shows every house, barn, haystack, and tree would be useless; it would be both huge and too cluttered to read. So a map shows only the biggest and most important features of the landscape it describes: roads, major rivers, a particularly large mountain or two. And because it leaves out so much detail and allows you to focus more clearly, the map enables almost anyone to make it to Beatrice without difficulty. In the same way, our economic models will prove useful in explaining the economic landscape.

Let's begin our discussion of game theory with a classic example that we will return to frequently in this book. Dick and Jane support their lavish lifestyle by robbing people. Arrested by the police following a bungled holdup at a local IHOP, Dick and Jane are immediately separated and taken to different interrogation rooms. An investigating officer goes to one room, and then the other room, with the same proposal: "We know you committed armed robbery, which carries a maximum penalty of 25 years in prison. But we're not sure how well our eyewitness will hold up on the stand. We're sure that we've got enough to put you both away on a weapons charge even without the eyewitness. Each of you will receive 3 years for that. So I'll make you the following deal: If you confess to the crime and testify against your partner, we'll let you walk after 1 year and use your testimony to put your partner away for 25 years. But if you deny the crime and your partner testifies against you, you'll go away for 25 years, and your partner will get only 1 year. If you both confess, we'll have you both nailed for the serious offense, but because your confessions save society the cost of a trial, we'll only put you away for 10 years each."

Suppose that you're Dick. What should you do when the police offer you this deal? Should you be loyal to Jane and deny the crime? Should you leap at the chance to rat out your partner? The information you've received is complex. Organizing the information would make the choices and consequences facing Dick and Jane easier to understand and analyze.

Setting Up a Game

The organizational tool that we'll use is a **payoff matrix**, which is a table with numbers that summarizes:

- Who the players are
- The actions available to each player
- The payoffs available to each player for each action that he or she might choose, given the action chosen by his or her rival

So let's put our Dick and Jane example into a payoff matrix. We know the following:

- There are two players: Dick and Jane.
- Each player has two possible moves: confess to the crime (confess) or deny the crime (deny).
- The payoff each person receives depends on the action he or she chooses and the action the partner chooses.

Let's examine this information by beginning with one player, Jane. Jane has two options: confess or deny. Figure 3.1 shows a blank payoff matrix.

	Jane	
	Confess	Deny

◀ Figure 3.1
A Payoff Matrix: Jane's Options
Each column of a payoff matrix corresponds to a strategy available to the column player.

Don't worry about all the blank spaces in the table; we'll fill those in soon. Instead, notice that Jane, in deciding whether to confess or deny, chooses the column of the table that she'll end up in. For this reason, Jane is often called the *column player*.

Now let's add Dick and his choices to the table, recognizing that his choices in this case are identical to Jane's (Figure 3.2). Because Jane has already chosen what column we'll end up in, let's let Dick choose the row (so we might refer to Dick as the *row player*).

		Jane	
		Confess	Deny
Dick	Confess	*A*	*B*
	Deny	*C*	*D*

◀ Figure 3.2
A Payoff Matrix: Dick's and Jane's Options and the Associated Outcomes
Each row of a payoff matrix corresponds to a strategy available to the row player. Each possible outcome of the game can be found at the intersection of various row and column strategies.

Figure 3.2 includes letters to help clarify the discussion. Note that if Dick and Jane both choose to confess, we end up at outcome *A*, where Dick's row and Jane's column intersect. If Dick confesses but Jane does not, we end up in cell *B*. If Jane confesses and Dick does not, we end up in cell *C*, and if Dick and Jane both deny the crime, we end up in cell *D*.

So our payoff matrix incorporates all the players, all their choices, and all the possible outcomes. All that is left to include in the matrix are the payoffs to each player. Let's pick an outcome and see what information we can fill in. Just for fun, let's choose cell *B*, where Dick confesses and Jane does not. According to the original story, this outcome will result in Dick serving 1 year in prison and Jane serving 25 years. It's standard in game theory to present both of these payoffs in the same cell, but sometimes it's confusing to remember which payoff goes to which player. If we can't keep that straight, we may end up reaching the wrong conclusions about how the game will turn out. So to clarify things, let's adopt a rule of thumb: *The payoff on the left goes to the player on the left. The other payoff goes to the other player.*

Applying that rule, our payoff matrix now looks like the one in Figure 3.3.

		Jane	
		Confess	Deny
Dick	Confess	*A*	**1 year** **25 years** (for Dick) ' (for Jane)
	Deny	*C*	*D*

◀ Figure 3.3
Determining Payoffs
A payoff matrix presents payoffs corresponding to each possible outcome. Here, when Dick confesses and Jane denies, Dick receives 1 year in prison, and Jane receives 25.

▶ **Figure 3.4**
Completing the Payoff Matrix
This complete payoff matrix presents the players, their strategies, each possible outcome, and the payoffs associated with each outcome.

		Jane	
		Confess	Deny
Dick	Confess	**10 years** **10 years** (for Dick) ' (for Jane)	**1 year** **25 years** (for Dick) ' (for Jane)
	Deny	**25 years** **1 year** (for Dick) ' (for Jane)	**3 years** **3 years** (for Dick) ' (for Jane)

Filling in the payoffs associated with the other outcomes, we can replace A with 10 years for Dick and 10 years for Jane, C with 25 years for Dick and 1 year for Jane, and D with 3 years for Dick and 3 years for Jane. Figure 3.4 reflects these changes.

Finally, implementing our rule that the payoff on the left goes to the player on the left, we can eliminate the parentheses in each cell to give us the final form of our payoff matrix, as shown in Figure 3.5.

▶ **Figure 3.5**
Dick's and Jane's Game in Final Form
This complete payoff matrix expresses the payoffs to the players in compact form. Remember that for each outcome, the payoff on the left goes to the player on the left. For example, when Dick denies and Jane confesses, Dick receives 25 years, and Jane receives 1 year.

		Jane	
		Confess	Deny
Dick	Confess	**10 years, 10 years**	**1 year, 25 years**
	Deny	**25 years, 1 year**	**3 years, 3 years**

Nash equilibrium An outcome where both players are playing their best strategy, given the strategy chosen by the opponent.

Nash Equilibrium

We can use the matrix we constructed to predict the outcome of Dick's and Jane's game. We will do this by using the numbers in the cells to find a **Nash equilibrium**, which is an outcome where both players are playing their best strategy, given the strategy chosen by the opponent. In a Nash equilibrium, neither player wishes to unilaterally change his or her mind.

Let's shed some light on the concept of a Nash equilibrium by walking through our Dick and Jane example. In particular, let's look at the outcome in Figure 3.5 where both Dick and Jane rat one another out and see if it is a Nash equilibrium. First, look from Dick's perspective: Given that Jane has chosen to confess, if Dick recants his confession, his sentence will rise from 10 to 25 years. So clearly, Dick is satisfied that he's made the right move, given Jane's choice to confess. Now look at the problem from Jane's point of view: Dick has chosen to confess, and if Jane switches her strategy from confess to deny, her sentence will increase from 10 to 25 years. So Jane is satisfied that, given Dick's choice of confession, she has chosen the best strategy for herself. Therefore, when both players confess, each is making his or her best response to the strategy chosen by the other player. This matches our official definition of a Nash equilibrium: an outcome where each player is playing his or her best strategy, given the play of the other.

From a player's perspective, the Nash equilibrium is a "no regrets" outcome. One can envision a player in a Nash equilibrium saying to himself, "Well, I don't have the power to change the move my opponent made, so given the move that she *did* make, I couldn't have done any better by choosing any other strategy." On the other hand, envision a player who is *not* in a Nash equilibrium. That player might say to himself, "Darn it! If I'd known that she was going to make that move, I would have chosen a different strategy. Can I have a do-over, please?"

Strategies for Finding Equilibria

Many of the games we'll examine in this book have more than one Nash equilibrium. We need to be sure that we've found them all if we want to declare the Dick and Jane game solved.

The People Behind the Theory

John Nash

Throughout this book, we're going to be solving games and looking for Nash equilibria, so you're probably curious about where the name Nash came from. The Nash equilibrium is named in honor of the game theory pioneer who discovered it, John F. Nash, Jr. In the late 1940s, Nash was a graduate student in mathematics at Princeton University. At that time, Princeton's Institute for Advanced Study was the academic home of some of the most brilliant scientists and mathematicians in the world, including Albert Einstein. Among those scientists was a mathematician named John von Neumann, who is often credited with inventing modern game theory.

In addition to being a key member of the Manhattan Project, a World War II–related research and development effort that resulted in the world's first atomic bomb, von Neumann is considered one of the last great mathematicians. He is lumped into the same group of mathematical geniuses Isaac Newton belongs to. Von Neumann had developed game theory to provide insight into the game of poker. His work primarily focused on what economists now call *zero-sum games*. In a zero-sum game, a gain to one player means an equal and opposite loss to the other player.

Nash's inspiration, developed as a graduate student, was that equilibria might exist even in non-zero-sum games. Building on the work of von Neumann, a young Nash provided the foundation for an entirely new branch of game theory. In the process, he proved a result that had eluded even the brilliant von Neumann: Under certain conditions, every non-zero-sum game has at least one equilibrium, although sometimes that equilibrium may be hidden.

Less than a decade after receiving his doctorate from Princeton, Nash began to suffer from paranoid schizophrenia. He spent much of the 1960s involuntarily committed to various mental hospitals, where he received antipsychotic medications and insulin shock therapy. Both types of treatment were ineffective. Released in 1970, Nash refused all medications and treatment. Over the next 25 years, through patience and sheer force of will, Nash recovered and gradually resumed life as an academic and scientist. In 1994, he received the Nobel Prize in Economics for his pioneering work in game theory, and in 2001, a semi-fictional account of his life was made into a major motion picture, *A Beautiful Mind*. Starring Russell Crowe as Nash, the film—a biography about an *economist*, mind you—won four Oscars. And you thought economists were boring!

Based on Sylvia Nasar's *A Beautiful Mind*, 1998, and autobiographical information published at nobelprize.org.

Cell-by-Cell Inspection One way to go about finding all the equilibria in a game is to look at each possible outcome of the game and check to see if it is a Nash equilibrium. This method of looking for equilibria is appropriately called *cell-by-cell inspection*. Let's return to Figure 3.5 and start with the outcome that results when Dick confesses but Jane does not. In that case, Dick faces 1 year in prison, and Jane faces 25. If Dick alters his strategy by recanting his confession, his penalty will increase to 3 years. So, clearly, Dick is happy with his choice of strategy, given that Jane has chosen to deny the crime. But Jane should be unhappy with her choice: Given Dick's choice of strategy, if Jane changes her mind and confesses, she'll reduce her sentence from 25 years to 10. Because Jane can improve her payoff by altering her strategy, the (Dick, Jane) = (confess, deny) outcome is *not* a Nash equilibrium.

In this game (but not in all games), the penalties and rewards are symmetric. In other words, the payoffs facing Dick for playing various strategies are identical to the payoffs facing Jane when she plays in a similar fashion. We can therefore reach the same conclusion about the outcome where Dick denies the crime and Jane confesses. In that case, it's Dick who has the incentive to change his mind, switching his steadfast denial of involvement in the crime to a last-minute confession. So (Dick, Jane) = (deny, confess) is not a Nash equilibrium.

Let's now examine the remaining outcome, where both Dick and Jane choose to deny the crime. In that case, both face penalties of 3 years in prison. Is either player satisfied with his or her choice of strategy in this case? Or does one or the other or both wish to change strategies? Given that Jane has decided to deny the crime, Dick can reduce his sentence from 3 years to 1 by switching strategies. And given that Dick has chosen to deny the crime, Jane can reduce her sentence from 3 years to 1 by switching strategies. So the (deny, deny) outcome is one where both parties say to themselves, "Darn it! I wish I had a second chance. I would have chosen a different strategy." (Deny, deny), then, is not a Nash equilibrium.

You're probably wondering why we're spending so much time looking for Nash equilibria. The Nash equilibrium is important to our understanding of economics because it's the outcome that the game is likely to gravitate toward. It's not foolproof because game theory deals with individuals and small groups of people, and although a great deal of predictability exists when you're dealing with a large group of people, trying to figure out what any *individual* will do in a given situation is tough. But the Nash solution, as you will see, is pretty likely to occur most of the time, and it gets more and more likely to occur the more often players play the game.

We've come a long way. We've told a story, we've represented that story in a compact and usable form, and we've looked for the likely outcome of that story by using cell-by-cell inspection. However, cell-by-cell inspection is tedious and time-consuming. You might be wondering if there are shortcuts to solving these games. Luckily for you, the answer is yes: There are easier ways to find Nash equilibria in a game. Let's look at them.

Dominant Strategies   One method we can use to simplify the search for a Nash equilibrium is to look for situations where players always have an incentive to play the same strategy, no matter what the other player does. In that case, the strategy that is universally best, regardless of the strategy chosen by others, is called a **dominant strategy**.

Dominant strategy A strategy that is universally best, regardless of the strategy chosen by others.

Looking for dominant strategies will help us predict the outcomes of games and will also help us understand the underlying incentives facing the players. In other words, not only will we be able to predict the outcome, we will also be able to explain *why* that outcome is likely.

Although we can't predict the outcome of every game by looking for dominant strategies, dominance crops up in many of the social problems we'll examine in this book. It is critical, for example, in understanding the depletion of natural resources (see Chapter 9). Consequently, it's important that you understand what it is, how to look for it, and how to use it to find a Nash equilibrium. Let's apply the idea of dominance to predict the outcome of the game Dick and Jane are playing.

Does Dick have a dominant strategy? Return to Figure 3.5 and consider a series of if–then statements about each of the strategies Jane could play and Dick's best response to them:

- If Jane denies the crime, then Dick should confess: Confessing lowers Dick's penalty from 3 years to 1.
- If Jane confesses to the crime, then Dick should also confess: Confessing lowers Dick's penalty from 25 years to 10.

So no matter what Jane does, Dick is best off confessing. Therefore, confessing is a dominant strategy for Dick.

We can perform a similar analysis for Jane by creating the same series of statements regarding her best response to the strategies available to Dick:

- If Dick chooses deny, then Jane should choose confess.
- If Dick chooses confess, then Jane should also choose confess.

So no matter what Dick does, Jane is best off confessing. Therefore, confessing is a dominant strategy for Jane.

The power of solving games using dominance becomes apparent when we think about what it really means in terms of the mechanics of the game. The fact that confessing is a dominant strategy for Dick means that he is unlikely to deny the crime. So we can remove the Deny row from Dick's choices, as shown in Figure 3.6.

		Jane	
		Confess	Deny
Dick	Confess	**10 years, 10 years**	**1 year, 25 years**

◄ **Figure 3.6**
Eliminating Dick's Non-dominant Strategy
If confessing is a dominant strategy for Dick, you can simply remove any non-dominant strategies from the payoff matrix.

And because confessing is a dominant strategy for Jane, we can remove the Deny column from her choices, as shown in Figure 3.7.

		Jane	
		Confess	
Dick	Confess	**10 years, 10 years**	

◄ **Figure 3.7**
Solving the Game Using Dominant Strategies
The Nash equilibrium is found where Dick's and Jane's dominant strategies intersect.

As Figure 3.7 shows, we are left with only one outcome: the outcome where the dominant strategies for both Dick and Jane intersect. That is the (confess, confess) outcome that we already know is a Nash equilibrium. And dominance has led us to that outcome.

The nicest thing about trying to predict the outcome of this game by looking at dominant strategies is that we now have a better understanding of the incentives facing Dick and Jane. The police have done a clever job in crafting the penalties so that Dick will always benefit by ratting out Jane, and Jane will always benefit by ratting out Dick. The police ensure that they will get a confession and that both Dick and Jane will spend a good long time off the streets and behind bars.

The Basic Types of Games

The game we've been analyzing is a special type of game that crops up often in game theory, and as crazy as it sounds, it often appears in your life. In fact, much of the rest of this book is devoted to examining the numerous places where you might find yourself playing a game similar in structure to the one that Dick and Jane were playing. Because the Dick and Jane example is going to be such an important prototype for us, let's dig a bit deeper into the game and see what else we can learn from it.

Prisoner's Dilemma Games

First, it's important to note that Dick and Jane are simply the members of a small group. In this case, it's a group of criminals. But it's a group nonetheless, and as members of that group, Dick and Jane can either *cooperate* with one another to produce the best outcome for the group, or they can *defect* from the group and pursue their own interests.

In this case, the best outcome for the group is the one that minimizes the *total time* that the members of the group spend in prison. That is the outcome where both Dick and Jane deny involvement in the crime. Each will then serve 3 years, for a total of 6 years behind bars. All other outcomes are worse for the group: If both confess, the total sentence is 20 years (10 years apiece), and if one confesses and the other denies,

3.3 Learning Objective
Compare and contrast the key characteristics of five basic types of games.

the total sentence is 26 years. So let's call deny the *cooperative strategy* because it is best for the group. The cooperative outcome is likely to be an outcome that the players would agree to in advance: "Hey, Jane, if we get caught, let's make a pact not to rat the other one out. Here—let's raise our glasses and toast our agreement."

But notice that once captured, neither player has an incentive to abide by that agreement. Instead, each has an incentive to defect—that is, to pursue individual interests that are counter to the interests of the group. Namely, each player has a dominant strategy of confessing to the crime. So we'll say that when a player confesses, she has defected from the group.

Therein lies the beauty of the game we've just created: If the prisoners cooperate with one another, they will each serve 3 years in prison. But, because of the way the payoffs are constructed, the players each defect from the group in pursuit of individual gain and end up serving 10 years instead. Each player ends up worse off than he or she would have been if they had both cooperated. The group as a whole ends up worse off as well. The most amazing thing is that because of the structure of the payoffs, Dick and Jane both have an incentive to confess—*even if they did not commit the crime.*

This game is an example of what game theorists call a **prisoner's dilemma** game. It is easy to see where that name comes from: The prisoners are torn between cooperating and doing what's best for the group and pursuing their own interests and making everyone worse off. Let's summarize the key features of the prisoner's dilemma game:

> ### Characteristics of the Prisoner's Dilemma Game
> - Each player has two strategies: cooperate or defect.
> - Defecting is a dominant strategy for each player.
> - There is a single Nash equilibrium at (defect, defect).
> - The Nash equilibrium is worse for each individual and for the group than the cooperative solution (cooperate, cooperate).

The prisoner's dilemma is an *archetype*: an example of a frequently appearing game with particular characteristics. In addition to prisoner's dilemma–type games, we will encounter a host of others in this book. So let's familiarize ourselves with a few different archetypes and also consider another way to predict the outcomes of games.

Pure Coordination Games

Jen and Ben are young college students in the beginning stages of a relationship. In the middle of Ben's 11:30 Comparative Astrology class, he decides that he needs to see Jen desperately and sends her the following text message: "Lunch?"

Jen, halfway through her Applied Numerology lecture, is startled awake by the vibration of her cell phone. She reads Ben's text and texts back, "Where?" At this point, her tyrannical professor seizes her cell phone and tosses it out the window and into the campus pond.

Luckily for Jen, the college is small, and there are only two places where Ben might go. The first place is Porubsky's, a deli known for its spicy dill pickles and outstanding chili. The second place is Hog Wild, a barbeque joint famous for smoky pulled pork. Jen knows Ben will go to one of these two restaurants; the only question in her mind is which one.

Ben sends numerous text messages to Jen but receives no replies. He realizes that she may not have received his original reply to her question of where to meet for lunch. He knows that Jen will go to one of the town's two restaurants, but just like Jen, he doesn't know which one. It's just plain bad luck that the restaurants are at opposite ends of town because Jen and Ben will only have enough time to check one restaurant each before their 1:30 classes.

Jen and Ben need a way to coordinate their actions to produce the best outcome—in this case, a meeting. Each needs to get inside the other's head in order for both to end up at the same place. Jen must predict where Ben will go, and Ben, in turn, must

Prisoner's dilemma A game in which each player has a dominant strategy of defecting, and each ends up worse off than if they had both cooperated.

Application 3.1

Game Theory and the Tobacco Advertising Ban

Throughout the 1950s and 1960s, tobacco companies advertised heavily on television. That ended in 1970, when the Public Health Cigarette Smoking Act banned smoking-related television advertising. Oddly, tobacco companies raised little objection to the act, despite its draconian nature. Game theory can help explain why.

Suppose that there are only two tobacco companies, Brown and Black, that split a $1 billion tobacco market. Each firm has a choice of advertising on TV or not advertising at all. One reason to advertise is to lure new smokers: If one firm advertises on TV, the market will grow to $1.05 billion, and if both firms advertise, the market will grow to $1.1 billion. The firms also advertise to steal customers from one another. If neither advertises, or if both advertise, they will split the market 50–50. But if one advertises while the other does not, the firm that advertises will capture 75% of the market, and the other will be left with 25%. Finally, assume that advertising on television costs $100 million.

We can use these numbers to generate payoffs for each firm:

- If neither firm advertises, each firm will capture $500 million of the market.
- If both firms advertise, they will split $1.1 billion. Each firm will capture $550 million but will spend $100 million to do it, for a net of $450 million.
- If one firm advertises and the other does not, the market will be $1.05 billion. The firm that doesn't advertise will get $262.5 million. The firm that advertises will get $787.5 million but will spend $100 million in advertising, for a net of $687.5 million.

This information can be easily represented in a payoff matrix:

		Brown Tobacco	
		Advertise	Don't Advertise
Black Tobacco	Advertise	$450m, $450m	$687.5m, $262.5m
	Don't Advertise	$262.5m, $687.5m	$500m, $500m

Organizing the information in this way makes two things apparent. First, each firm has a dominant strategy of advertising. Second, there is an equilibrium outcome where both firms advertise. Unfortunately, that outcome is a poor one: Both firms would be $50 million better off if they could agree *not* to advertise.

But such an agreement would not be upheld for long. Both firms have an incentive to cheat: Reneging on the agreement raises the cheater's payoff by $187.5 million. And, unfortunately, there is no way to punish cheaters. If only there were someone around with the power to enforce the agreement. . . .

And that is exactly what the advertising ban does. It removes each firm's dominant strategy from the board and forces the game to the cooperative outcome. And now we know why tobacco companies didn't resist the advertising ban: It benefited tobacco companies by helping them escape a costly prisoner's dilemma!

See related problem 3.14 on page 77 at the end of this chapter.

---

predict where Jen will go, which, crazily, means predicting where Jen will predict that Ben will go. Or perhaps we can stack on another layer of complexity and say that it means predicting where Jen will predict where Ben will predict where Jen will go, or. . . . As you can tell, this is a confusing and difficult task.

You may have experienced something similar if you've ever been separated from someone at Disney World, at an airport, or in a shopping mall. The sage advice in situations like that is for you to stay still and let the other party come to you. But if you both follow that advice, you might both be sitting still for a very long time and, potentially, a very short distance from one another. And if you're both moving, there is no guarantee that you'll find one another. The optimal solution in such a case is for one of you to sit still and the other to move around. But without the ability to communicate, how do you know if you're the sitter or the mover?

Let's apply the tools of game theory to Jen's and Ben's situation and see what insights they offer. We will make three changes to the analysis we used in the Dick and Jane situation:

1. **Measuring payoffs.** Recall that in the Dick and Jane prisoner's dilemma, higher numbers meant longer terms in jail, which is clearly a bad thing. But from now on, unless we specify otherwise, let's reverse that: Higher numbers now represent *better* payoffs rather than worse payoffs. This is a conventional assumption in game theory. In the Ben and Jen example, you can think of the payoffs as representing units of happiness—perhaps measured in smiles or kisses.

2. **How numbers relate to each other.** In the Dick and Jane prisoner's dilemma game, we used years in prison to represent payoffs. But we could just as easily have assigned ranks to the outcomes: The best outcome is 1 year in prison, so we'll give it 4 points; the second-best outcome is 3 years, so we'll give it 3 points; the third-best outcome is 10 years, so we'll give it 2 points; and the worst outcome is 25 years, so we'll give it only 1 point. Even if we change from years to points, however, the incentives and outcome remain the same: Confessing is a dominant strategy for each player, and the Nash equilibrium is found where both players confess. That would be just as true if we used 300, 200, 100, and 0 instead of 4, 3, 2, and 1. What really tells the story in the game is not the magnitude of the numbers we use but how those numbers relate to one another.

3. **What players care about.** In the Dick and Jane example, we ignored the possibility that Dick might love Jane and would therefore be reluctant to rat her out for a small reduction in his own jail sentence. We also ignored the possibility that if Dick rats out Jane, she will have her minions break his kneecaps. In the context of the game we presented, we could have done that by adjusting the actual jail terms upward or downward to represent those additional complicating factors.

   The bad news is that these adjustments are tough to make because we would have to know, for example, how many extra years in jail Dick would be willing to serve to keep his kneecaps intact. The good news is that often, making these adjustments won't alter the game or its outcome in any significant way. So in the Ben and Jen game and later games, let's assume that these kinds of adjustments have already been made. If we need to consider additional complicating factors, we'll address them explicitly and on a case-by-case basis. In other words, *we assume that the payoffs capture everything that the players care about.*

Because we're now operating under the assumption that the payoffs reflect everything that the players care about, we're going to further assume that, given the strategy chosen by the other participant, a player will always choose the strategy that brings him or her the best payoff. Economists call this the **rationality assumption**, and it seems like a reasonable one to make: We don't systematically do things that make us worse off, like flushing money down the toilet or telling our work supervisor that he smells like rotting tuna. Of course, such things *do* happen from time to time. But one of the purposes of game theory is modeling how the world works in order to predict how people will behave—and people *generally* behave in pretty reasonable and rational ways. Assuming rationality, then, means that we assume that most people will act in a predictable way: They compare the costs and benefits of various actions and then choose the action that brings them the greatest reward. With that general discussion behind us, let's model the game being played by Jen and Ben. The payoff matrix needs to account for all the players (Jen and Ben), all their options (Porubsky's and Hog Wild), and the payoffs associated with each outcome.

Rationality assumption The assumption that given the strategy chosen by the other participant, a player will always choose the strategy that brings him or her the best payoff.

	Jen	
Ben	Porubsky's	Hog Wild
Porubsky's	**10, 10**	**0, 0**
Hog Wild	**0, 0**	**10, 10**

◄ **Figure 3.8**
The Pure Coordination Game
In the pure coordination game, the only thing that matters is that the players coordinate their actions. If Ben and Jen successfully meet, they will get a better payoff than if they fail to meet.

Notice in Figure 3.8 that Jen and Ben both get the best possible payoff when both happen to go to the same place. If Ben chooses Porubsky's and Jen chooses Porubsky's, then both get a payoff of 10. However, if Ben is at Porubsky's and Jen is at Hog Wild, each gets a payoff of 0. Similarly, if Ben and Jen both go to Hog Wild, each will get a payoff of 10. However, if Ben goes to Hog Wild and Jen goes to Porubsky's, each will receive 0.

This is a simple game, but it's a game that tells a nice story—a story of a young couple in love. The payoff matrix shows us that Jen and Ben really don't care *where* they meet; they only care *that* they meet. The payoffs are identical whether they meet at Porubsky's or at Hog Wild. For this reason, this type of game is called a **pure coordination game**—it only matters that the players coordinate on an outcome; it does not matter which outcome they coordinate on. It shouldn't be too much of a surprise that there are two Nash equilibria in this game—one where Jen and Ben meet at Porubsky's and the other where Jen and Ben meet at Hog Wild. In both cases, neither Jen nor Ben wishes to unilaterally stand up and walk out, leaving the restaurant and his or her one true love behind.

You can verify that these two outcomes are Nash equilibria by using cell-by-cell inspection; you can just as easily check the other two outcomes to ensure that they are not Nash equilibria. For example, if Jen goes to Porubsky's and Ben goes to Hog Wild, Jen will likely say to herself, "Oh, no! Ben has gone to Hog Wild, and here I'm at Porubsky's. If only I could change my mind, I would be much happier." And Ben, we're sure, is saying exactly the same thing. Because each player would like a do-over, we know that the two outcomes where Ben and Jen fail to coordinate are not Nash equilibria.

We do want to find Nash equilibria, but as we mentioned earlier, cell-by-cell inspection can be slow. This is especially true when each player has more than two possible choices. If there were three restaurants in town instead of two, we'd have to examine 9 outcomes instead of 4; if there were four restaurants, we'd have to look at 16. And, unfortunately, you'll find that neither Ben nor Jen has a dominant strategy in this game; each player's best choice depends on what the other player does. So dominance can't lead us to the Nash equilibria.

But there is another method we can use to find Nash equilibria, and although it doesn't tell us as much about the incentives facing Jen and Ben as would looking for dominant strategies, it's a quick and easy way to find the solution to any game of any size, as long as that game can be illustrated in the form of a payoff matrix. That solution method is called best-response analysis. **Best-response analysis** is a technique for locating equilibria by marking the best strategy a player can use to counter each of his or her rival's possible moves. A best-response analysis simply requires you to create a general if–then statement: "If Jen does *this*, then Ben should do *that*." For example, if Jen goes to Porubsky's, then clearly Ben is best off if he goes to Porubsky's, too. We know that because the 10 Ben receives when he goes to Porubsky's is bigger than the 0 he receives when he goes to Hog Wild. So, noting that we're in the Porubsky's column of the payoff matrix shown in Figure 3.9, let's underline that payoff to Ben, remembering the rule that the payoff on the left goes to the player on the left.

Pure coordination game A game where it only matters that the players coordinate on an outcome, not which outcome they coordinate on.

Best-response analysis A technique for locating equilibria by marking the best strategy a player can use to counter each of his or her rival's possible moves.

◄ **Figure 3.9**
Ben's Best Response to Jen's Porubsky's
Ben's best response to Jen's Porubsky's is to go to Porubsky's as well. To begin best-response analysis, underline Ben's payoff (10) in the cell corresponding to that outcome.

	Jen	
Ben	Porubsky's	Hog Wild
Porubsky's	**<u>10</u>, 10**	**0, 0**
Hog Wild	**0, 0**	**10, 10**

Now let's look at Jen's Hog Wild column. If Jen goes to Hog Wild, then Ben's best response is to go to Hog Wild, too. So let's underline the payoff (10) he receives when he plays his best response, as shown in Figure 3.10:

▶ **Figure 3.10**

Ben's Best Response to Jen's Hog Wild

Ben's best response to Jen's Hog Wild is to go to Hog Wild. Underline Ben's payoff (10) in the cell corresponding to that outcome.

		Jen	
		Porubsky's	Hog Wild
Ben	Porubsky's	**<u>10</u>, 10**	**0, 0**
	Hog Wild	**0, 0**	**<u>10</u>, 10**

We've considered Ben's best response to each of Jen's possible strategies; now let's consider Jen's best response to each of *Ben's* possible strategies. Given that Ben has gone to Porubsky's, Jen's best response is to go to Porubsky's, too. So, we'll underline her payoff (the second number in the cell) from playing her best response, as shown in Figure 3.11:

▶ **Figure 3.11**

Jen's Best Response to Ben's Porubsky's

Jen's best response to Ben's Porubsky's is to go to Porubsky's. Underline Jen's payoff (the right-hand 10) in the cell corresponding to that outcome.

		Jen	
		Porubsky's	Hog Wild
Ben	Porubsky's	**<u>10</u>, <u>10</u>**	**0, 0**
	Hog Wild	**0, 0**	**<u>10</u>, 10**

Finally, if Ben goes to Hog Wild, Jen's best response is to go to Hog Wild, too. So let's underline that to complete the payoff matrix, which is shown in Figure 3.12.

▶ **Figure 3.12**

Completing Best-Response Analysis and Finding Nash Equilibria

Jen's best response to Ben's Hog Wild is to go to Hog Wild, too. Once best-response analysis is complete, any Nash equilibria can be found by looking for cells that have both payoffs underlined. Here, two equilibria exist—one where Ben and Jen both go to Porubsky's, and one where they both go to Hog Wild.

		Jen	
		Porubsky's	Hog Wild
Ben	Porubsky's	**<u>10</u>, <u>10</u>**	**0, 0**
	Hog Wild	**0, 0**	**<u>10</u>, <u>10</u>**

Notice in Figure 3.12 that each cell that represents a Nash equilibrium has two underlined numbers in it. This suggests, correctly, that any Nash equilibrium can be found where both players are playing their best response to the play of the other. In fact, whenever you find a cell with all the payoffs underlined, that outcome must be a Nash equilibrium.

Let's review the characteristics of the pure coordination game:

Characteristics of the Pure Coordination Game

- Neither player has a dominant strategy.
- There are two general outcomes: The players either coordinate with one another or fail to coordinate.
- Nash equilibria exist at every outcome where the players successfully coordinate.
- The payoff for coordinating is higher than the payoff for not coordinating.
- Each of the Nash equilibria offers identical payoffs to any particular player.

Jen and Ben are stuck in a tough situation because there is no guarantee that they will successfully coordinate. The odds of them meeting randomly are 50%. But Jen and Ben could potentially improve these odds if the game they're playing is characterized by a *focal point* (often called a *Schelling point*, after Nobel Prize–winning game theorist Thomas Schelling). A focal point is a commonly held piece of knowledge, culture, or convention that helps people successfully coordinate their actions.

One example of a focal point is this: Suppose you get a great job offer to work for a startup company in Paris. Your contact tells you to meet him in Paris on March 7, but he doesn't tell you anything else. What would you do? Chances are, you'd go to a prominent landmark in Paris and try to meet your instructor at some notable time of day. There are several landmarks in Paris, but when asked to name one such landmark, Americans generally name the Eiffel Tower. And asked what time would be a good meeting time, most will pick noon.

So you can improve your odds of successfully meeting in Paris if everybody zooms in on what is commonly considered to be a focal point. In a recent ABC News special, 12 strangers who had never met were asked to go to New York and find one another without any knowledge of where they should go, when they should meet, or even who they were looking for. A tough job, but all 12 quickly found each other by relying on focal points!

Unfortunately, focal points are not foolproof because they vary based on the culture that defines them. For example, when people are asked to choose a focal location in New York City, people raised on the east coast often lean toward Penn Station; Midwesterners generally choose the Empire State Building. So when you try to meet your job contact in Paris, although it's likely that he will be waiting at the Eiffel Tower, the family or culture he was raised in might have a deep and abiding love for the arts, which might put the Louvre foremost in his mind as a meeting spot. In that case, you'll find yourself out of luck—and a job. Focal points can help, but they don't guarantee success.

Assurance Games

What might serve as a focal point for Jen and Ben? Perhaps Jen and Ben have developed a pattern of alternating restaurants. Then both can say, "Well, yesterday we ate at Porubsky's, so today we'll probably go to Hog Wild." Or perhaps they can coordinate based on the weather: If it's raining, we go to Porubsky's for a warm klobasa, but if it's sunny, we go to Hog Wild for pulled pork and lemonade. Whatever pattern they choose, that pattern can help them improve their chances of a successful meeting—but it's no guarantee.

Now that you understand how the pure coordination game works, let's modify the game slightly. Suppose the story remains the same but that we let Jen and Ben's relationship progress a bit so that they're beyond the sugary "I only have eyes for you" stage.

The game shown in Figure 3.13 is still a game of coordination, and just like the game of pure coordination we played, there are two Nash equilibria at the two outcomes where Jen and Ben successfully meet. And as before, any meeting between Jen and Ben is preferred to no meeting at all. The difference in this version of the game is that both prefer the Nash equilibrium in which they meet at Hog Wild for pulled pork to the Nash equilibrium in which they meet at Porubsky's. In other words, they are still interested in each other, but they're also interested in more practical matters like food.

		Jen	
		Porubsky's	Hog Wild
Ben	Porubsky's	**10, 10**	0, 0
	Hog Wild	0, 0	**20, 20**

◀ **Figure 3.13**

The Assurance Game

In assurance games, successfully coordinating is important, but where the players coordinate matters, too. Both Ben and Jen agree that meeting at Hog Wild is better than meeting at Porubsky's.

So our players, cut off from communication, both recognize that the best outcome is meeting at Hog Wild. However, Ben may suffer from uncertainty: "Well, I know I like the food at Hog Wild better, and I definitely want to meet Jen, but maybe she thinks I like the food at Porubsky's better, in which case I'm better off going to Porubsky's than Hog Wild." We can see that Jen and Ben are stuck in the same trap as before. What each needs is assurance that the other will choose the preferred alternative—that they'll establish that alternative as a fallback or focal point that will improve their chances of coordinating—and coordinating on the best outcome.

Assurance game A game in which players want to coordinate on an outcome and in which both agree that coordinating on one particular outcome is preferred to coordinating on the other.

For that reason, a game with the payoff structure like the game we've just examined is called an **assurance game**, and here are its characteristics:

Characteristics of Assurance Games

- Neither player has a dominant strategy.
- There are two general outcomes: The players either coordinate with one another or fail to coordinate.
- The payoff for coordinating is higher than the payoff for not coordinating.
- Nash equilibria exist at every outcome where the players successfully coordinate.
- One of the Nash equilibria offers both of the players a better payoff than the others.

Battle of the Sexes Games

Time passes, and Jen's and Ben's preferences begin to change. Let's modify the game to reflect these changes.

The game shown in Figure 3.14 still has the same underlying feel as the pure coordination game we looked at first: There are two Nash equilibria where the players successfully coordinate, and when the players don't coordinate successfully, neither gets a payoff. But in this case, we can see that Ben prefers the Nash equilibrium where they successfully coordinate on Hog Wild, and Jen prefers the Nash equilibrium where they coordinate on Porubsky's.

▶ **Figure 3.14**

The Battle of the Sexes Game
In the battle of the sexes game, Jen and Ben still want to coordinate. But Jen would like to coordinate at Porubsky's, and Ben would prefer to coordinate at Hog Wild.

		Jen	
		Porubsky's	Hog Wild
Ben	Porubsky's	**10, 20**	**0, 0**
	Hog Wild	**0, 0**	**20, 10**

So now we've really got a story to tell because Ben and Jen are no longer perfectly united. In this game, there are elements of cooperation (neither gets any payoff if they fail to coordinate), but there is also an element of conflict. You can practically see the wheels turning in Jen's head: "I really want to meet Ben for lunch, but I also want klobasa pretty badly." And Ben is saying, "Wow, it'd be nice to have lunch with Jen, but it would be *really* nice to have lunch with Jen and have pulled pork, too."

In pure coordination and assurance games, the players are only interested in coordination. In other words, they fully want to cooperate with one another. This game is different: The players want to cooperate with one another, but they also, in part, want to get their own way. So how do the players do what's in the best interest of the group and simultaneously do what's best for themselves?

In the language of game theory, we say that each player has a *tough strategy* that leads to his or her preferred Nash equilibrium and a *weak strategy* that leads him or her to the other Nash equilibrium. In this example, Jen's tough strategy is to go to Porubsky's, and Ben's is to go to Hog Wild. Clearly, if both adopt their tough strategy, they will fail to coordinate. The key to "winning" this game is to artfully manipulate the other player into choosing your preferred alternative, which can be a difficult job that can potentially jeopardize your relationship.

Battle of the sexes game A game in which both players want to coordinate, but each player prefers coordinating on a different outcome.

This type of game, which highlights the tension between cooperation and conflict, is called a **battle of the sexes game**. The name of the game dates back to 1973, when female tennis star Billie Jean King bested male tennis star Bobby Riggs in a widely publicized match. Despite its gender-oriented name, the game crops up in many gender-neutral places in real life; we'll be sure to look at a few later in the book. It also appears often in our interpersonal relationships in various forms. Sometimes the game is small, such as when you and your significant other decide to go out for a movie—but one of you wants to see a drama and the other wants to see a comedy. Sometimes the game is large, such as when you and your significant other are deciding what city

Application 3.2

Meeting Your Problems Head On

What's the best side of the road to drive on? Ask an American, and he'll tell you the right. Ask a Brit, and he'll tell you the left. So who's right? Maybe you should ask a Samoan because Samoa has had it both ways. In 2009, Samoa switched from the right to the left.

Why would a country do that? Let's draw on game theory to find out. Game theory can be a useful tool for describing human interactions, but remember that it is important to build everything players care about into the payoffs. To illustrate, imagine a small island with only two inhabitants. In such a place, the answer to the question "What's the best side to drive on?" is simply "The side the other guy drives on" because that reduces the chances of a head-on collision. Left or right doesn't matter, as long as both people choose the same side. This describes a game of pure coordination with two Nash equilibria: one where both drive on the left, and another where they drive on the right.

But if the choice of driving side truly is a game of pure coordination in which both equilibria offer identical payoffs, then why did Samoa bother to jump from one equilibrium to the other? Perhaps the payoffs at one of the equilibria really *were* better. Samoa, a nation of about 200,000 people, doesn't have many cars. There are plenty of inexpensive used cars in nearby Australia, but everyone there drives on the left. Those cars' steering wheels are on the wrong side for right-driving Samoa!

This added reality makes Samoa's reason for switching sides apparent. The right-hand equilibrium required cars to be shipped at great expense from America. The left-hand equilibrium was a *better* equilibrium, one that gave Samoans access to cheap and dependable cars from Australia. In other words, Samoans were really playing a game of assurance.

But wait! If Samoans were playing an assurance game, everyone should have been happy about the switch. Yet there was fierce resistance to the proposal. That resistance came from the few Samoans who already owned cars, most of which were equipped for driving on the right. The switch made those cars harder to drive and eroded their resale value.

Make no mistake: Everybody agreed that it was important to drive on the same side. But those who already owned cars preferred the right, and those who wanted access to less expensive cars preferred the left. Because of the disagreement about which Nash equilibrium was the best equilibrium, this final version of the story, in which we consider everything the players care about, describes the real game Samoans were playing: a battle of the sexes.

On balance, the switch turned out well. Changing equilibria made about 15,000 existing car owners substantially poorer but made driving both possible and affordable for hundreds of thousands of others, for generations to come. In the end, the gains to the winners far outweighed the losses to the losers, and the country as a whole emerged better off.

See related problem 3.15 on page 77 at the end of this chapter.

Based on "Shifting the Right of Way to the Left Leaves Some Samoans Feeling Wronged," *Wall Street Journal*, August 24, 2009, and "Whose Side of the Road Are You On?" Salon.com, August 14, 2009.

you'd like to settle down in or which house to buy—and you can't quite agree. Hence, the game begins. Here are the basic characteristics of a battle of the sexes game:

Characteristics of Battle of the Sexes Games

- Neither player has a dominant strategy.
- There are two general outcomes: The players either coordinate with one another or fail to coordinate.
- Nash equilibria exist at every outcome where the players successfully coordinate.
- The payoff for coordinating is higher than the payoff for not coordinating.
- Each player has a tough strategy and a weak strategy. These strategies differ for each player.
- Each player prefers a different Nash equilibrium: For a particular player, the Nash equilibrium corresponding to that player's tough strategy is preferred to the Nash equilibrium corresponding to that player's weak strategy.

Games of Chicken

Chicken game A version of the battle of the sexes game that results in disaster if each player plays his or her tough strategy.

Let's modify this last game a bit more and develop our last archetype. Suppose that the struggle for dominance in Jen and Ben's relationship has progressed to the point of out-right hostility. They decide to settle the question of who is the alpha dog once and for all. On a dark and stormy night, they each steal a car and drive to an abandoned airstrip, where they engage in a game of chicken. In a **chicken game**, Jen and Ben drive the cars directly toward one another at a high rate of speed until one of them chickens out and swerves off the runway. Such a game might be represented as shown in Figure 3.15.

▶ **Figure 3.15**
The Chicken Game
In the chicken game, when both players play their tough strategy, the outcome is disastrous. Each player receives the lowest possible payoff.

		Jen	
		Go Straight	Swerve
Ben	Go Straight	−100, −100	**20**, **0**
	Swerve	**0**, **20**	10, 10

The payoff matrix tells an interesting story. Our game has two players, each of whom has the option of going straight (the tough strategy) or swerving (the weak strategy). It's disgraceful to be a chicken when the other player is tough (a payoff of 0 to the chicken); it's less disgraceful if both players chicken out, so in that case we'll give each a token payoff of 10. The player who remains tough and goes straight while the other player swerves earns the highest payout, which is 20. But if both players remain tough and refuse to swerve, certain death results for both. In that case, we'll arbitrarily make the lowest payout −100.

Several similarities exist between the chicken game and the battle of the sexes game. For example, as in the battle of the sexes game, best-response analysis will uncover two Nash equilibria. One of these is where Jen swerves and Ben goes straight, and the other is where Ben swerves and Jen goes straight. And, as in the battle of the sexes game, there is conflict between the two players. Jen likes the equilibrium where she remains tough and Ben swerves; Ben likes the equilibrium where he remains tough and Jen swerves.

The crucial difference that distinguishes the chicken game from the battle of the sexes game is what happens when both players remain tough. In the battle of the sexes game, the outcome is a simple failure to coordinate, and the payoffs are identical to what happens when the players fail to coordinate by playing their weak strategies. But in the chicken game, if both play their tough strategy, disaster (defined as the worst possible outcome for all parties) results. With that in mind, let's summarize the primary characteristics of chicken games:

Characteristics of Chicken Games

- Neither player has a dominant strategy.
- Each player has a tough strategy and a weak strategy.

- There are two general outcomes: The players either coordinate with one another or fail to coordinate. Coordination occurs when one player plays a tough strategy and the other plays a weak strategy.
- Nash equilibria exist at every outcome where the players successfully coordinate.
- Each player prefers a different Nash equilibrium: The Nash equilibrium where the players coordinate on a player's tough strategy is preferred to the Nash equilibrium where the players coordinate on a player's weak strategy.
- When both players play their tough strategy, both experience a disastrous outcome (represented by the worst possible payout in the game).

Generally, as the Nash equilibrium predicts, one player or the other chickens out. But sometimes the players fail to coordinate their choices. A quick search for "game of chicken" in a major newspaper database such as Lexis-Nexis will almost invariably bring up a recent article about two players who played chicken, stood tough, and failed to live to tell the tale. The ready availability of such deadly examples tells us that these games do happen in real life and that the mere existence of a Nash equilibrium is no guarantee that we'll end up there. Nash equilibrium is a tendency, not a surety.

We've completed our survey of the major game archetypes. Table 3.1 recaps their essential features.

Table 3.1   Summary Characteristics of Five Important Game Archetypes

This table summarizes some essential features of two-player game archetypes.
Use this table to help identify game types.

Game Type	Dominant Strategies	Number of Equilibria in Two-Player Game	Tension Between Cooperation and Individual Self-Interest	Other Features
Prisoner's dilemma	Each player has a dominant strategy of pursuing individual interest at the expense of the group.	One equilibrium, found where both players play dominant strategies.	Great tension. Pursuit of self-interest dominates cooperation.	Equilibrium outcome is a poor outcome—poorer than if both players had played their non-dominant strategy. However, each player *could* do worse than the equilibrium outcome.
Pure coordination	None.	Two equilibria. Each player receives the same payoff at each equilibrium. Payoffs at equilibria are greater than payoffs at non-equilibrium outcomes.	None. What is in the best interest of the group is in the best interest of the individual.	It doesn't matter where players coordinate; it matters only that they do coordinate.
Assurance	None.	Two equilibria. Both players receive a higher payoff at one equilibrium than they do at the other. Payoffs at equilibria are greater than payoffs at non-equilibrium outcomes.	None. What is in the best interest of the group is in the best interest of the individual.	Both players want to coordinate on an equilibrium. Both agree that one particular equilibrium is the best equilibrium.
Battle of sexes	None.	Two equilibria. Each player receives a higher payoff at one equilibrium than at the other. Payoffs at equilibria are greater than payoffs at non-equilibrium outcomes.	Some. Both players agree on the importance of being at an equilibrium. But each player prefers (receives a higher payoff at) a different equilibrium.	Each player's "tough" strategy is the one that might result in his or her preferred equilibrium. Equilibria are found at (tough, weak) and (weak, tough).
Chicken	None.	Two equilibria. Each player receives a higher payoff at one equilibrium than at the other.	Great tension. Each player prefers a different equilibrium. Preferences for the preferred equilibrium are very strong.	As in a battle of sexes game, each player has tough and weak strategies, with equilibria at (tough, weak) and (weak, tough). (Tough, tough) gives each player the worst possible payoff in the matrix.

Conclusion

All the archetypes we've studied—the various types of coordination games and the prisoner's dilemma—appear in other contexts. Many real-world problems have the "feel" of strategic games, and you will see examples of each archetype throughout this text. Learning to filter out the noise in the real-world scenarios and represent the essence of a problem as a game is an important and useful skill that you will develop as the book progresses. For now, let's review what you have learned:

1. We can represent stories using a payoff matrix.
2. We can interpret the payoff matrix and uncover the incentives facing the players.
3. We can solve games by finding the Nash equilibrium.
4. We can identify the fundamental game types that arise over and over in real life.

Chapter Summary and Problems

Key Terms

Assurance game, p. 70

Battle of the sexes game, p. 70

Best-response analysis, p. 67

Chicken game, p. 72

Dominant strategy, p. 62

Economic model, p. 58

Game theory, p. 57

Mutual interdependence, p. 57

Nash equilibrium, p. 60

Payoff matrix, p. 58

Prisoner's dilemma, p. 64

Pure coordination game, p. 67

Rationality assumption, p. 66

Strategic interaction, p. 57

3.1 What Is Game Theory? pages 57–58

Explain the concepts of strategic interaction and mutual interdependence.

Summary

Game theory is a tool economists use to describe interactions between small numbers of people, including individuals, businesses, and nations. Game theory models strategic interactions where the outcome depends on the choices made by all the participants. Those interactions are said to be characterized by mutual interdependence.

Review Questions

All problems are assignable in MyEconLab.

1.1 When the payoff you receive depends on what you choose *and* on what your opponent chooses, _____ is said to exist.

1.2 _____ is a modeling tool economists use to analyze strategic interactions.

Problems and Applications

1.3 Explain why choosing the Ivy League college you'd like to attend constitutes a game, while choosing which Netflix movie to stream is more likely just a decision.

1.4 You and your significant other are trying to decide what movie to watch on Friday night. You like action; your significant other likes comedy. Is deciding what movie you should both watch really a decision? What elements of strategic interaction might be at work?

1.5 Describe a situation in which you have had to account for the reaction of somebody else when deciding what action to take for yourself.

3.2 The Basic Structure of Games, pages 58–63

Learn and apply the basic elements of games.

Summary

The primary tool of game theory is the payoff matrix, which summarizes the players, their available strategies, and the payoffs associated with each outcome. Some (but generally not all) outcomes are special in that no player wishes to change strategy, given what the other players have chosen. Those outcomes are called Nash equilibria. Nash equilibria can be found by the method of cell-by-cell inspection.

They can also be easily located, in cases where players have a dominant strategy, at the intersection of the players' dominant strategies.

Review Questions

All problems are assignable in MyEconLab.

2.1 Analyzing each possible outcome in a game one-by-one to locate Nash equilibria is called _____.

2.2 When barking like a dog is Woody's best strategy, no matter what action Barney chooses, barking is said to be a _____ strategy.

2.3 A _____ exists if both players in a game are satisfied that they can't do any better, given the way the opponent played.

2.4 The _____ summarizes the players, their strategies, and the results of their choices in a compact table.

For questions 2.5–2.9, refer to the following payoff matrix:

		Jerry	
		Left	Right
	Up	1, 6	4, 8
Tom	Down	5, 7	3, 10

2.5 If Tom plays Up and Jerry plays Left, what is Tom's payout?
   a. 1
   b. 6
   c. 4
   d. 5

2.6 If Tom plays Down and Jerry plays Left, what is Jerry's payout?
   a. 1
   b. 3
   c. 7
   d. 5

2.7 Tom's dominant strategy is _____.
   a. Up
   b. Down
   c. Left
   d. Tom has no dominant strategy.

2.8 Jerry's dominant strategy is _____.
   a. Right
   b. Down
   c. Left
   d. Jerry has no dominant strategy.

2.9 A Nash equilibrium occurs where _____.
   a. Tom goes up and Jerry goes right
   b. Tom goes down and Jerry goes left
   c. Tom goes down and Jerry goes right
   d. Both a and b

2.10 If both players in a game have a dominant strategy, then the game they are playing _____.
   a. Must not have a Nash equilibrium
   b. Must have one Nash equilibrium
   c. Must have two Nash equilibria
   d. We cannot determine how many equilibria exist without seeing a payoff matrix.

Problems and Applications

2.11 For each of the following games, indicate Tom's dominant strategy (if any) and Jerry's dominant strategy (if any):

Game A.

		Jerry	
		Left	Right
	Up	1, 6	4, 8
Tom	Down	5, 7	8, 10

Game B.

		Jerry	
		Left	Right
	Up	10, 16	14, 8
Tom	Down	5, 7	8, 12

Game C.

		Jerry	
		Left	Right
	Up	–1, 8	4, 6
Tom	Down	5, 7	–8, 3

Game D.

		Jerry	
		Left	Right
	Up	4, 6	2, 80
Tom	Down	50, 1	3, 2

2.12 In each of the games in problem 2.11, there is a single Nash equilibrium. Identify the location of that Nash equilibrium.

3.3 The Basic Types of Games, pages 63–73

Compare and contrast the key characteristics of five basic types of games.

Summary

Not all games look exactly alike, but many games share critical features. Games that share common features may be archetypes. Five major archetypes are the prisoner's dilemma, the pure coordination game, the assurance game, the battle of the sexes game, and the chicken game. These games differ in the amount of tension between individual interest and group interest. Best-response analysis, a third technique that can be used to locate Nash equilibria, can help determine whether any particular game fits one of these archetypes.

Review Questions

All problems are assignable in MyEconLab.

3.1 The _____ game has two equilibria, and the players earn the same payoff no matter which equilibrium they happen to be at.

3.2 The _____ game archetype has a single Nash equilibrium, and each player receives a lower payoff at that outcome than if they both switched strategies.

3.3 In battle of the sexes and chicken games, the strategy a player must take to get to his or her preferred equilibrium is that player's _____ strategy.

3.4 The only game archetype you studied in which players have dominant strategies is the _____ game.

3.5 In the chicken game described in the text, going straight is a _____ strategy.

  a. Dominant

  b. Deadly

  c. Tough

  d. Weak

3.6 Which of the following is a true statement regarding chicken games and prisoner's dilemma games?

  a. In chicken, players have a dominant strategy; in prisoner's dilemma games, they don't.

  b. Both chicken games and prisoner's dilemma games have a single Nash equilibrium.

  c. Both chicken games and prisoner's dilemma games have a disastrous outcome.

  d. In chicken, the disastrous outcome is not a Nash equilibrium.

3.7 Which game displays no tension between individual interest and group interest?

  a. Prisoner's dilemma

  b. Battle of the sexes

  c. Assurance

  d. Chicken

Problems and Applications

3.8 Find all Nash equilibria in games E through I. Circle the cell or cells that are equilibrium outcomes.

Game E.

		Jerry	
		Left	Right
Tom	Up	1, 1	3, 3
	Down	3, 3	1, 1

Game F.

		Jerry	
		Left	Right
Tom	Up	4, 4	2, 2
	Down	1, 1	3, 3

Game G.

		Jerry	
		Left	Right
Tom	Up	2, 2	4, 6
	Down	5, 3	2, 2

Game H.

		Jerry	
		Left	Right
Tom	Up	10, 10	5, 50
	Down	50, 5	0, 0

Game I.

		Jerry	
		Left	Right
Tom	Up	10, 10	5, 50
	Down	50, 5	7, 7

3.9 Each of the games in problem 3.8 is one of the five archetypes described in the chapter. Name the archetype for each game.

3.10 Consider the following games:

Game J.

		Sheldon	
		Bump	Grind
Penny	Rock	8, 8	1, 12
	Roll	10, 2	2, 3

Game K.

		Sheldon	
		Bump	Grind
Penny	Rock	4, 4	2, 7
	Roll	7, 2	20, 20

Game L.

		Sheldon	
		Bump	Grind
Penny	Rock	8, 8	1, 12
	Roll	10, 4	2, 3

For each game, answer the following four questions:

a. Is the game a prisoner's dilemma game?

b. If your answer to part (a) is "yes," then what is each player's "cooperate" strategy?

c. If your answer to part (a) is "yes," then what is each player's "defect" strategy?

d. If your answer to part (a) is "no," explain why the game is *not* a prisoner's dilemma.

3.11 Game M is a battle of the sexes game:

Game M.

		Sheldon	
		Bump	Grind
Penny	Rock	2, 3	3, 12
	Roll	10, 4	2, 3

For this game, do the following:

a. Find and circle the Nash equilibria in the game. There are two.

b. Indicate Penny's tough strategy.

c. Indicate Sheldon's tough strategy.

d. Change the payouts in *one cell* to turn it into a game of chicken.

3.12 Game N is a game of pure coordination:

Game N.

		Sheldon	
		Bump	Grind
Penny	Rock	5, 5	2, 2
	Roll	2, 2	5, 5

For this game, do the following:

a. Find the Nash equilibria in the game. There are two.

b. Indicate whether either player has a preference as to which equilibrium he or she ends up at. Explain.

c. If you indicated that players had preferences about which equilibrium they ended up at, then indicate whether those preferences agree.

d. Change the payouts in *one cell* to turn it into a game of assurance.

3.13 Consider the following story:

- Woody loves bowling, and he also loves Beth.
- Woody does not particularly like the beach.
- The best outcome for Woody is to be at the bowling alley with Beth.
- Given the choice of going bowling alone or being at the beach with Beth, Woody would choose to be with Beth.
- The worst outcome for Woody is to be at the beach alone.
- Beth loves the beach, and she also loves Woody.
- Beth does not particularly like bowling.
- The best outcome for Beth is to be at the beach with Woody.
- Given the choice of going to the beach alone or bowling with Woody, Beth would choose to be with Woody.
- The worst outcome for Beth is to be at the bowling alley alone.

Woody and Beth plan to meet after work, but each has forgotten where. Add payoffs to the following matrix to tell the story, given Woody and Beth's preferences:

		Beth	
		Bowling	Beach
Woody	Bowling		
	Beach		

a. Find all Nash equilibria in this game, if any.

b. Is this game an archetype? If yes, identify the archetype and explain your selection.

3.14 [**Related to Application 3.1 on page 65**] During the height of the Cold War, the United States and the U.S.S.R. each possessed enough nuclear weapons to destroy the world many times over. Draw a parallel between the arms race and the tobacco advertising problem presented in Application 3.1. Then model the arms race as a game, choosing players, strategies, and payoffs. Explain your choices carefully.

3.15 [**Related to Application 3.2 on page 71**] Read Application 3.2. Referring to the key characteristics of each game type, explain why the battle of the sexes does a better job than chicken of describing Samoa's decision about which side to drive on.

The Push–Pull Game

This chapter introduced you to economic games and explained the concepts of equilibria and dominance. This chapter's game is designed to help you apply these concepts to real-world behavior.

Imagine that you are seated across a table from someone you don't know who is now your partner in this game. There is a large pile of cash in the middle of the table. You and your partner receive a signal to take one of the following actions:

1. Push $400 from the pile toward the other player.

Or

2. Pull $300 from the pile toward yourself.

When the game is over, you will take home whatever cash is immediately in front of you. You and your partner are forbidden to communicate.

The signal comes. What will you do?

MyEconLab

Please visit http://www.myeconlab.com for support material to conduct this experiment if assigned by your instructor.

Game Theory: Games Between Three or More Players

Chapter Outline and Learning Objectives

4.1 Introduction to Three-Player Games, page 80

Illustrate three-player games using payoff matrixes.

4.2 Finding Nash Equilibria in Three-Player Games, page 82

Locate Nash equilibria in three-player games.

4.3 Depicting Games with More Than Three Players, page 87

Use graphs to illustrate games with more than three players.

4.4 Finding Equilibria in Games with More Than Three Players, page 88

Locate equilibria in n-player games.

Experiment: The Red–Green Game, page 97

MyEconLab
MyEconLab helps you master each objective and study more efficiently.

This book is about social problems—problems that affect an entire society. And our society is composed of lots and lots of people. So, although the previous chapter talked a lot about games played by two players, society has bigger concerns to address than whether you'll be able to meet up with your best friend at the local rib joint. Those concerns—issues like global warming, the depletion of the world's oil reserves, clean air, and the rising cost of health care—result from the collective decisions made by thousands, millions, and even billions of people. To fully understand the nature of those problems, we need to extend the game theory we developed in the previous chapter to games with more than two players. This chapter presents that theory, and the chapters that follow use that theory to discuss those very important problems.

4.1 Learning Objective

Illustrate three-player games using payoff matrixes.

Introduction to Three-Player Games

Let's look at adding a third player to a game. Mary, Jose, and Chris are college students disgruntled by budget cuts at their university. They plan to stage a sit-in at the college's administration building. Prior to the sit-in, they decide to meet so they can brainstorm and outline the logistics. Tentatively, Mary will be in charge of mobilizing supporters. Jose will be in charge of creating a list of demands. And Chris will be in charge of snacks for the protesters. Mary, the unofficial leader of the trio, sends a cryptic email: "Meet tomorrow at noon to discuss the insurrection."

But Mary has forgotten to tell her partners where to meet. And before they can hit the reply button, the university administration's failure to pay its Internet service bill results in a shutdown that halts all communication among the members of the group. Luckily, the group has always held its meetings in one of two places: the back room of the car-repair shop or the basement at Pepe's, the local coffee shop. As you might guess from your work on two-player games, the problem facing the trio is one of coordination; it doesn't matter *where* they meet, it simply matters *that* they meet.

Each player has two options: Go to the auto shop or go to Pepe's. If they all happen to end up in the same place, they'll have a successful brainstorming session, the sit-in will go off without a hitch, and the administration will accede to their demands. On the other hand, if only two players manage to meet, the group will lack synergy, some important elements of the protest will be neglected, and the sit-in will fail. Let's give each group member a payoff of 1 if the sit-in is a success and a payoff of 0 if it's a failure.

There's nothing particularly novel here; this is really exactly the same pure coordination problem Jen and Ben faced in the previous chapter. The hard part is incorporating the third player into the payoff matrix. The way to approach this problem is to pick one of the players (it doesn't matter which one) and temporarily lock that player into a particular choice. Let's pick Mary and lock her into going to the auto shop. Now the problem is for Jose and Chris to choose where to go. If they both go to the auto shop, the sit-in will be a success. If either one chooses to go to the coffee shop, the sit-in will fail. We can incorporate that information into a payoff matrix as shown in Figure 4.1.

Notice in Figure 4.1 that there are three payoffs in each cell instead of two. You've probably guessed that each of the payoffs can be assigned to one of the three players. Our rule of thumb will be the same as with two-player games: The payoff on the left

▶ **Figure 4.1**

The First Half of a Three-Player Sit-in Game

This payoff matrix shows the possibilities available to Jose and Chris, once Mary has decided to go to the auto shop. Payoffs in each cell go to Jose (in black), Chris (in blue), and Mary (in red).

Mary
Chooses the Auto Shop

		Chris	
		Auto Shop	Coffee Shop
Jose	Auto Shop	**1, 1, 1**	**0, 0, 0**
	Coffee Shop	**0, 0, 0**	**0, 0, 0**

goes to the player on the left. This means that the first number in each cell represents Jose's payoff, and it is color-coded black here for convenience. Let's assign the second payoff in each cell to the other player in the table, Chris (color-coded blue), and the third payoff to the player outside the table, Mary (color-coded red).

Now we know what needs to happen if our group is to stage a successful sit-in and achieve a payout of 1 each: Given that Mary is locked into going to the auto shop, Jose and Chris must also choose the auto shop. If either of them goes to the coffee shop, the sit-in will fail, and everyone will get a payoff of 0.

It's important to note that, in reality, Mary isn't locked into going to the auto shop. In fact, in this game, Mary faces the same choices the other group members face. So what happens if Mary goes to the coffee shop instead? The key to answering this question is to create a new matrix. Once again, we temporarily lock Mary into a particular option and then see, given that option, what Jose's and Chris's best choices are. The payoff matrix that represents those choices and the associated outcomes is shown in Figure 4.2:

Mary
Chooses the Coffee Shop

		Chris	
		Auto Shop	Coffee Shop
Jose	Auto Shop	0, 0, 0	0, 0, 0
	Coffee Shop	0, 0, 0	1, 1, 1

◄ **Figure 4.2**
The Second Half of the Three-Player Sit-in Game
This payoff matrix shows the possibilities available to Jose and Chris, given that Mary has chosen to go to the coffee shop.

Notice that, given Mary's choice of going to the coffee shop, the only choices Jose and Chris can make that will produce a successful sit-in are to both go to the coffee shop, too. Most importantly for our purposes, we have every possible combination of Mary's, Jose's, and Chris's choices represented in one payoff matrix or the other. But the matrixes are spread apart, and that makes determining the outcome of this game difficult. So, let's group them together so that all the information is in one place, as shown in Figure 4.3:

Mary
Chooses the Auto Shop

		Chris	
		Auto Shop	Coffee Shop
Jose	Auto Shop	1, 1, 1	0, 0, 0
	Coffee Shop	0, 0, 0	0, 0, 0

◄ **Figure 4.3**
The Complete Three-Player Sit-in Game
These two payoff matrixes summarize all the options, outcomes, and associated payoffs in the sit-in game. Each matrix is called a "page" of the game.

Mary
Chooses the Coffee Shop

		Chris	
		Auto Shop	Coffee Shop
Jose	Auto Shop	0, 0, 0	0, 0, 0
	Coffee Shop	0, 0, 0	1, 1, 1

Remember that each player has exactly two choices. Although all the players are making their choices at the same time, for simplicity, let's look at the players and their choices one by one. Doing so allows us to say that Mary "starts" the game by choosing which payoff matrix in Figure 4.3 the group will be in: Either the players will find themselves in the "Mary Chooses the Auto Shop" matrix, or they will find themselves in the "Mary Chooses the Coffee Shop" matrix. In the language of game theory, we say that Mary determines the *page* that the group will end up on, as if the payoff matrix corresponding to each of Mary's possible choices were printed on a separate page in a book.

After Mary makes her choice of auto shop or coffee shop, Jose gets to make his choice. His selection of the auto shop or the coffee shop determines which row of Mary's payoff matrix the group will end up in. If Jose picks the auto shop, we'll be in the top row. If he picks the coffee shop, we'll be in the bottom row.

With Mary having decided which payoff matrix we'll use, and with Jose having selected our row, the only thing left to determine is which column of the payoff matrix we'll end up in. That is determined by what Chris picks. If Chris picks the auto shop, we'll end up in the left-hand column of whatever matrix Mary picked. If Chris picks the coffee shop, we'll end up on the right. And once Chris's choice has been registered, we know exactly which of the eight possible cells we'll be in.

Finding Nash Equilibria in Three-Player Games

You may be thinking: "That's all well and good. But how do we determine the outcome of this game? Surely it's tougher than it is with only two players." Well, you're right. But although the game has gotten a bit larger, the basic ideas behind our two-person solution methods—dominance and best-response analysis—remain.

Dominance in Three-Player Games

Let's start by thinking about dominance. In a two-person game, dominance can be established by creating a set of if–then statements about a player's ideal strategies. Specifically, for each strategy that could be chosen by a player's rival, the player should say, "If my rival does *X*, then I should do _____. But if my rival does *Y*, then I should do _____." A dominant strategy exists if the strategies in the blank spaces turn out to be the same.

We need to jump through exactly the same hoops for a three-person game. The only difference is that the three-person game has more hoops. So let's put ourselves in Jose's shoes for a moment to see if he has a dominant strategy:

- "If Mary chooses Auto Shop and Chris chooses Auto Shop, then I should choose **Auto Shop**."

- "If Mary chooses Auto Shop and Chris chooses Coffee Shop, then I should choose either **Auto Shop or Coffee Shop**."

- "If Mary chooses Coffee Shop and Chris chooses Auto Shop, then I should choose either **Auto Shop or Coffee Shop**."

- "If Mary chooses Coffee Shop and Chris chooses Coffee Shop, then I should choose **Coffee Shop**."

There are three things worth mentioning about these if–then statements. First, notice that in each case, Mary is choosing the page and Chris is choosing the column; it is up to Jose to pick the best row, given those choices. Second, in some cases, it doesn't matter which row Jose picks. Why? Because Mary has gone to one place and Chris another, so no matter what Jose does, the group will end up with two members in one place and one in another. So in those cases, the sit-in is doomed to fail.

Most importantly, though, is the fact that Jose's strategies are not the same in each statement. If Mary and Chris are at the coffee shop, then Jose should also be at the coffee shop. If Mary and Chris are at the auto shop, then Jose should be at the auto shop, too. In other words, Jose's best choice depends on the choices made by the other players, and therefore Jose does not have a dominant strategy. Further, because this game is symmetric (in that all the players have the same choices and receive the same payoffs in similar situations), neither Mary nor Chris has a dominant strategy, either.

Best-Response Analysis in Three-Player Games

If dominance cannot lead us to the outcome of this game, we're going to have to rely on best-response analysis instead. Luckily, this method works every time and is easy to use. Plus, we already have a head start because when we asked the questions necessary to look for dominance, we essentially performed the best-response analysis for Jose.

Let's revisit those questions for a moment and make Jose's analysis more explicit. The first two questions asked about different situations that might arise when Mary's choice placed us on the auto shop page. The first question asked what Jose should do if he finds himself in the left-hand column of Mary's auto shop page. Because the answer was "Go to the auto shop," we'll underline Jose's payout, as shown in the first page of Figure 4.4. The second question asked what Jose should do if he finds himself in the right-hand column of Mary's auto shop page, and the answer was that it doesn't matter. No matter where he goes, the players won't end up at the same place. Consequently, Jose will get a payout of 0, regardless of where he goes. So in Figure 4.4, let's underline each of those zeros because both responses are best responses for Jose.

The next two questions dealt with what Jose might do if Mary has chosen the coffee shop. One asked what Jose should do if Mary is at the coffee shop, and Chris chooses the left-hand column (which, of course, represents the auto shop). Again, the answer is that it doesn't matter: No matter where Jose goes, the group will fail to coordinate, and Jose will get a payout of 0. So let's underline both of Jose's zeros in the left-hand column of the second page in Figure 4.4. The final question asked what Jose should do if Mary chooses the second (coffee shop) page and Chris chooses the right-hand (coffee shop) column. Of course, Jose's best response is to choose the coffee shop row, as his payout in that case is 1, but he gets 0 if he goes to the auto shop. So let's underline the 1 in the lower row of the right-hand column of the second page.

You're probably thinking that at least so far, best-response analysis in our three-person game is done just like best-response analysis in two-person games. And that's

Mary
Chooses the Auto Shop

		Chris	
		Auto Shop	Coffee Shop
Jose	Auto Shop	**1, 1, 1**	**0**, 0, 0
	Coffee Shop	0, 0, 0	**0**, 0, 0

Mary
Chooses the Coffee Shop

		Chris	
		Auto Shop	Coffee Shop
Jose	Auto Shop	**0**, 0, 0	0, 0, 0
	Coffee Shop	**0**, 0, 0	**1, 1, 1**

◄ Figure 4.4
Jose's Best Responses in the Three-Player Sit-in Game
Payoffs for Jose's best response to the strategies chosen by Mary and Chris are shown underlined.

exactly right: In an abstract sense, by choosing the page, Mary is essentially choosing which game Jose and Chris will play. Once that page has been chosen, best-response analyses for Jose and Chris are done exactly as they would be done in two-person games. Given that, Figure 4.5 shows Chris's best responses in each of the two games he might find himself playing underlined, remembering that (1) the value in the *middle* of each cell represents Chris's payoffs, and (2) while Jose compared the first values in the top and bottom row of each payoff matrix, Chris compares the middle values in the left and right columns.

▶ **Figure 4.5**

Jose's and Chris's Best Responses in the Three-Player Sit-in Game
Payoffs for Chris's best responses to the strategies chosen by Mary and Jose are shown underlined in blue. Jose's best responses are underlined in black.

Mary
Chooses the Auto Shop

		Chris	
		Auto Shop	Coffee Shop
Jose	Auto Shop	**1**, **1**, 1	**0**, 0, 0
	Coffee Shop	0, **0**, 0	**0**, 0, 0

Mary
Chooses the Coffee Shop

		Chris	
		Auto Shop	Coffee Shop
Jose	Auto Shop	**0**, 0, 0	0, **0**, 0
	Coffee Shop	**0**, 0, 0	**1**, 1, 1

Finally, we need to perform best-response analysis for Mary. Remember that (1) Mary chooses the page, holding fixed the choices made by Jose and Chris, and (2) Mary's payouts are given by the third number in each cell. So we need to compare Mary's payoffs from the same cells but on different pages. That process is illustrated in Figure 4.6.

▶ **Figure 4.6**

Mary's Best Response in the Three-Player Sit-in Game
To conduct best-response analysis for Mary, compare her payoffs from corresponding cells on different pages of the game.

Mary
Chooses the Auto Shop

		Chris	
		Auto Shop	Coffee Shop
Jose	Auto Shop	1, 1, **1**	0, 0, **0**
	Coffee Shop	0, 0, **0**	0, 0, 0

Mary
Chooses the Coffee Shop

		Chris	
		Auto Shop	Coffee Shop
Jose	Auto Shop	0, 0, 0	0, 0, **0**
	Coffee Shop	0, 0, **0**	1, 1, **1**

Let's start by assuming that both Jose and Chris have chosen the auto shop. Then Jose and Chris have essentially told Mary, "Hey, Mary. We've chosen to be in the upper-left cell of whatever payoff matrix you pick. So . . . which payoff matrix is that gonna be?" Mary compares the 1 that she would get from choosing the auto shop to the 0 that she would get if she chose the coffee shop and decides that she'd rather have 1 than nothing. So let's underline the red 1, as shown in Figure 4.6.

Doing the same type of comparison for each of the remaining relative cell positions (upper right, lower left, and lower right) gives us the final version of our payoff matrix, as shown in Figure 4.7:

Mary
Chooses the Auto Shop

Chris

		Auto Shop	Coffee Shop
Jose	Auto Shop	**1**, **1**, **1**	**0**, 0, **0**
	Coffee Shop	0, **0**, **0**	**0**, **0**, **0**

Mary
Chooses the Coffee Shop

Chris

		Auto Shop	Coffee Shop
Jose	Auto Shop	**0**, **0**, 0	0, **0**, **0**
	Coffee Shop	**0**, 0, **0**	**1**, **1**, **1**

As you may remember, a Nash equilibrium exists when all the players are playing their best response to one another. This means that all the numbers in a cell must be underlined in order for that cell to represent a Nash equilibrium. Not surprisingly, there are two Nash equilibria in this game: One exists where all the players go to the coffee shop; the other exists where all the players go to the auto shop. And because the numerical values are the same at both of those equilibria, the game our three students are playing is, in fact, a game of pure coordination.

◄ **Figure 4.7**
Complete Best-Response Analysis for the Three-Player Sit-in Game
Best-response analysis reveals two outcomes where all payoffs are underlined. Those two outcomes are Nash equilibria.

Application 4.1

Blondes Have Less Fun: Game Theory in *A Beautiful Mind*

Not many economists inspire movies. One exception is John Nash, who won the 1994 Nobel Prize in Economics for his pioneering work in game theory. The Oscar-winning *A Beautiful Mind* was based on Nash's life, but the movie stretched some truths—about both his life and his theories.

The critical game theory scene in *A Beautiful Mind* is Nash's "Eureka!" moment in which he discovers the equilibrium now named after him. He and several friends are at a bar when a beautiful blonde woman enters, accompanied by several brunettes. In the movie, Nash's character explains to his friends: "If we all go for the

(Continued)

(Continued)

blonde, we block each other, and not a single one of us is going to get her. So then we go for her friends, but they will all give us the cold shoulder because nobody likes to be second choice. But what if no one goes for the blonde? We don't get in each other's way, and we don't insult the other girls. It's the only way we win."

But was this analysis in the movie correct? Let's model this scene as a game between Nash and his friends, Sol and Bender. Four women enter: one stunning blonde and three above-average brunettes. Let's assign payoffs as follows:

- The payoff for attracting the blonde is a 2.
- The payoff for attracting a brunette is a 1.
- If more than one player approaches the blonde, she and her brunette friends reject them for a payoff of 0.

In payoff matrixes, the game looks like this:

Nash
Go for the Blonde

		Sol	
		Go for the Blonde	Go for a Brunette
Bender	Go for the Blonde	0, 0, 0	0, 1, 0
	Go for a Brunette	1, 0, 0	<u>1</u>, <u>1</u>, <u>2</u>

Nash
Go for a Brunette

		Sol	
		Go for the Blonde	Go for a Brunette
Bender	Go for the Blonde	0, 0, 1	<u>2</u>, <u>1</u>, <u>1</u>
	Go for a Brunette	<u>1</u>, <u>2</u>, <u>1</u>	1, 1, 1

This game has three equilibria (shown with payoffs underlined), each with one player going for the blonde and the other two going for brunettes. The problem, of course, is deciding who gets the blonde.

In the scene's closing moments, Nash's character says, "Adam Smith [the father of modern economics] said that the best result comes from everyone . . . doing what's best for himself . . . Incomplete. The best result would come from everyone . . . doing what's best for himself *and* the group."

Is that, as the movie suggests, a no-blonde result? Absolutely not: If everyone goes for a brunette (a combined payoff of 3), the group leaves the reward for approaching the more-valued blonde unclaimed. If just one goes for the blonde, the combined payoff rises to 4.

"Adam Smith was wrong," Nash's character concludes. But now we know the movie was also wrong—and on two accounts: A no-blonde strategy was *not* best for the group. And in the scene in which Nash was to have made his Nobel-winning discovery, his breakthrough solution wasn't even a Nash equilibrium!

See related problems 2.6 and 2.7 on page 94 at the end of this chapter.

Depicting Games with More Than Three Players

You learned about two-person games in the previous chapter, and now you've learned the mechanics of representing and predicting the outcomes of three-person games. You'll see several three-person games over the course of the remainder of the book. But you may be thinking that three people don't constitute much of a *society*. So, how are we going to apply game theory to learn about social problems if we don't even have enough players to explain a hand of bridge?

Our two- and three-person games have given us a decent understanding of the nature of games, and it's on that foundation that we're ready to do some heavy construction. The framework we build will allow us to understand games with 4 or 400 or even 4 *billion* players. Economists often call these larger games **n-player games**, where *n* is an algebraic variable that can assume any value between, in this case, 4 and infinity. The method of analysis this framework incorporates is predominantly a graphical method, although once in a while a bit of basic algebra can be useful. Neither the graphing nor the algebra is anything to be scared of, however.

So let's dig right in with a real-world problem. On the final exam in my Game Theory course, here's what I ask students:

***n*-player game** A game that helps us evaluate the interaction of four or more players, where *n* is an algebraic variable that can assume any value between four and infinity.

Dear Students,

I'm sure you did a great job on your final exam, but if you're worried you didn't, I'd like to give you the chance to **earn two extra-credit points**. You'll notice that there is a blank space below. If you leave that blank space empty, your score will stay the same. But if you would like to try for two extra-credit points, simply fill in the blank with the following: 'Yes, I would like to try for two extra-credit points, please!'

   Here's the catch: If less than half the class tries for extra credit, those who did try will receive the two points they asked for. However, if *over* half the class tries for extra credit, I will deduct two points from the score of everyone who requested extra credit.

   Good luck, and congratulations on completing your course in Game Theory!

Sincerely,

Your Professor

This problem presents you with a real conundrum. "Do I respond or not? I wonder how many other students have responded already. I wonder if my professor is tenured. . . . Surely he'd get fired for this if he weren't."

Let's suppose that you are one of seven students in a Game Theory course, and you've just read this problem. What would *you* do? It's clear that the best answer for you depends on the actions of your six classmates. As is true with two- and three-player games, you need to develop a framework that helps you make decisions based on your choice and the choices of the other players.

So let's think about your payoffs and how they depend on what your classmates are doing. If a sufficiently small number of your classmates choose to respond, you will receive two points of extra credit if you respond but nothing if you do not. The question, then, is what constitutes "sufficiently small."

The easy way to answer this is to start with zero: If nobody else asks for points, then you'll earn a payoff of 2 if you ask. And then we ratchet up the number of respondents to one: If one other classmate asks for points, and you ask, too, then you'll receive a payoff of 2. Continue by adding another greedy classmate: If two of your classmates ask for points, and you do, too, then the total number of students asking for points will be three, and you'll still get your 2 points. But what happens if three of your classmates ask for points? If you ask, too, you'll be the one that tips the balance; four of the seven students will have asked for points, and everyone who asked will receive −2, whereas those who left the space blank will receive 0. Finally, it should be obvious that if four, five, or all six of your classmates ask for points, you'll lose 2 if you ask also, but you'll get 0 if you leave the space blank.

Figure 4.8 depicts these payoffs graphically. Across the bottom of the graph, which is the horizontal axis, we have the number of your classmates who choose to ask for points. This number ranges from zero to six (because, of course, you are the class's seventh and final student). The vertical axes, those along the sides of the graph, measure your payoffs for choosing various strategies, given the number of your classmates who ask for points. In our simple example, there are only three possible payoffs: Either you receive two points, lose two points, or receive nothing.

Let's begin graphing in Figure 4.8 by plotting your payoff from doing nothing—in other words, you decided to leave the space blank. In that case, no matter how many of your classmates ask for points, you will receive nothing. We'll plot that choice in green, just to help keep track of what's going on. In our simple seven-student example, we could use green dots to do this, but as our games get bigger (that is, as we add more and more students), we'll have to plot more and more dots, and sooner or later those dots will begin to form a line. So let's just use a solid green line rather than individual dots.

And now let's plot your payoff from asking for points. If zero, one, or two of your classmates ask for points, then you'll get a payoff of 2. But if three, four, five, or six of your classmates ask for points, you'll get a payoff of −2. In Figure 4.8 we plot these values in red, again using a solid line rather than discrete points.

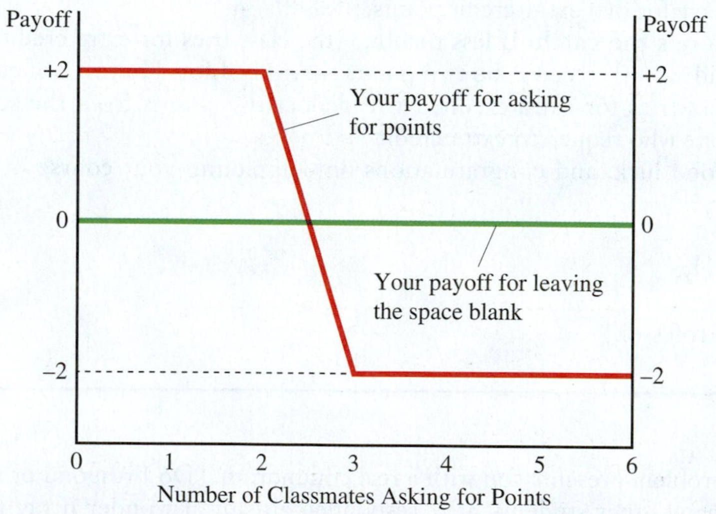

▶ **Figure 4.8**

The Extra Credit Game

N-player games depict the payoffs available to you, given the number of other participants who have chosen a particular action. In the extra credit game, the red line shows the payoff you might receive if you ask for points. The green line shows your payoff if you don't ask for points.

Figure 4.8 shows that if a lot of your classmates choose to respond, you should not. By contrast, if only a few of your classmates respond, you should. In other words, this graph describes a seven-player version of chicken!

Finding Equilibria in Games with More Than Three Players

We can gain insight into how the class as a whole might end up playing the extra credit game by looking for a multiplayer version of the Nash equilibrium. Remember that every player in the game faces the same set of incentives—in other words, everyone is looking at a graph exactly like yours. Refer to Figure 4.8 and suppose that none of your classmates has chosen to respond. At zero, the red line is above the green line, which tells you that you're better off responding to the question than leaving it blank. If your classmates have any idea how few people have responded, some of them may decide to switch their strategy and respond, too. So if there are very few respondents, we can expect the number of respondents to increase. This is shown by the rightward-pointing black arrows along the horizontal axis in Figure 4.9.

Similarly, if everyone in the class except you has responded to the question, it's in your best interest to leave the question blank. (The fact that the green line is above the red line tells you this.) If your classmates have an inkling that quite a few of you have responded, some of them will be digging in their backpacks for their erasers so they can switch from responding to leaving the space blank. In other words, if there are a lot of respondents, we can expect people to switch strategies and the number of responses to decrease. This is indicated by the leftward-pointing black arrows in Figure 4.9.

It's unclear exactly where this game will end up, but we do know that there comes a point where no one has an incentive to switch.[1] That point is where the two lines in Figure 4.9 cross—where the payoffs for responding and the payoffs for not respond-ing are identical. In our game of chicken, we'll tend to gravitate to that point: It's the point at which just less than half the class ends up asking for points and the rest doesn't. Why do we gravitate to that point? Because, again, if less than half the class responds, we can expect blank-leaving students to switch until it no longer pays to do so. On the other hand, if more than half the class has responded, some of those stu-dents will switch until it no longer pays to switch. The place where it doesn't pay to switch is the same in both cases—right where the payoffs to the two actions are equal.

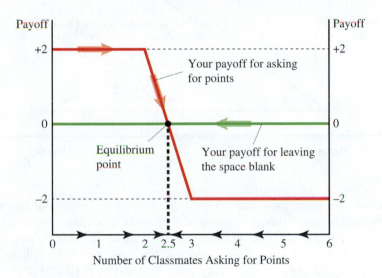

◄ Figure 4.9
Equilibrium in the Extra Credit Game
In the extra credit game, an equilibrium can be found where the payoffs to the two strategies are identical. This occurs where the red and green lines cross. Natural incentives tend to push the out-come toward that equilibrium.

Not every *n*-player game has the same solution. There are types of *n*-player games other than chicken. Learning to identify equilibria and classify a game as a multiplayer version of our two-player archetypes are useful skills. With that in mind, let's walk through a simple example that extends the ideas presented so far. But this time, let's let the number of players be 301, with the final one being you. (You are the 301st player, in other words.) And instead of thinking about secret meetings to plan a protest or extra credit problems, let's think about something fun: going clubbing.

The more people you find at the club, the more fun it is, and the more chances you have to find a suitable dance partner. There are two clubs in your town: Mercury and Gravity. Your payoff depends on the number of people that show up at the club you choose. Specifically, you will receive a payoff of 10 points for each person at the club besides yourself. So if you find yourself at either club alone, you'll receive 0 points.

---

[1]This lack of clarity stems from the fact that half a student can't respond to the question while her other half leaves it blank. As a result, the equilibrium will be accurate only within a student or so.

But if you find all 300 of your closest friends at either club, you'll receive 3,000 points. Assume, too, that everybody else's payoff is determined the same way—10 points for each person they find at the club they choose.

Figure 4.10 shows these payoffs in the same type of graph we used to analyze the extra credit problem. Across the bottom, on the horizontal axis, let's put the number of your friends who have decided to go to Gravity. That number will range between 0 and 300. (Of course, if we wanted, we could make the horizontal axis represent the number of your friends at Mercury. Because your friends will be at one club or the other, it doesn't particularly matter which label we choose—we'll get the same answer either way.)

In green, let's plot your payoff from going to Gravity. If none of your friends are at Gravity, you get 0 points. If 100 are at Gravity, you'll get 1,000 points. And if 300 are at Gravity, you'll get 3,000 points. If you connect these points, you'll get a line that starts at 0 on the left and slopes upward to 3,000 at the far right.

▶ **Figure 4.10**

Payoffs in a Clubbing Game
In the clubbing game, you get a better payoff by going where others go.

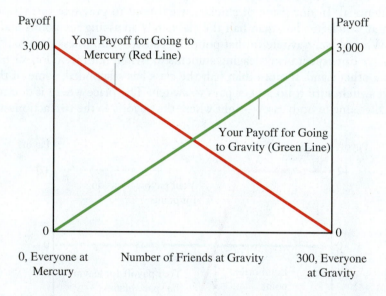

How will this game turn out? Graphically, this game looks a lot like the game of chicken that my game theory students play on their final exam. But this game differs in one very important way: In an extra credit game of chicken, you *don't* want the others to do what you are doing (which is also true in the two-player game of chicken). But in this game, you do. As Figure 4.10 shows, if all 300 of your friends are at Gravity, you get a much better payoff from going to Gravity than you would if you went to Mercury. So you'll choose Gravity, and none of your clubbing pals has any incentive to leave Gravity because that's where they find the most people to dance with. (In other words, it's where they find their highest payoff, too.) Once everyone is at Gravity, they stay there, which means that "everyone at Gravity" is a Nash equilibrium in this multiplayer game.

But what if everyone goes to Mercury instead? In that case, you'll get your highest payoff by going to Mercury. If anyone leaves Mercury, they'll find themselves at Gravity all alone, with nobody to dance with when the DJ puts on the Harlem Shake. So once everyone is at Mercury, they stay there, which means that "everyone at Mercury" is also a Nash equilibrium in this multiplayer game.

So, we've found two Nash equilibria. But there is a third equilibrium in this game, and you can find it right where the lines cross. At that point, your payoff from going to either club is identical—1,500 points if you go to Gravity, or 1,500 points if you go to Mercury. Consequently, where you go is really immaterial: You have to pick one club, and it doesn't matter which one in terms of the points you get.

What's really interesting about this third equilibrium is that it's not a stable equilibrium that we tend to return to when something unexpected happens to push us away from it. If an equilibrium is unstable, we can't expect to remain there long because a slight bit of randomness coupled with natural forces will tend to push us away from that equilibrium. To illustrate that point, consider what happens when you make your choice. There are 150 friends at Mercury and 150 at Gravity, which means that whichever club you choose, you'll be getting 1,500 points. But you can't decide, so you toss a coin, and the next thing you know, you're in the mosh pit at Mercury.

But now there are 151 people at Mercury and only 150 at Gravity. And somebody at Gravity who snuck out on the fire escape to smoke peeks through the window of the across-the-alley Mercury and says to herself, "I'm here at Gravity with 149 of my friends, which gives me 1,490 points. But if I leave here and go to Mercury, where there are 151 people, I will increase my points to 1,510. Hand me my sunglasses; I'm headed for Mercury."

Once that person heads for Mercury, Gravity becomes even less attractive, so another person leaves, and another, and before you know it, everyone's at Mercury, and Gravity is empty. That process is illustrated by the leftward-pointing black arrows in Figure 4.11. The equilibrium at the 50–50 point exists, but the minute that equilibrium is disturbed, we leave it, and nothing tends to make us return to it.

Recall that it was sheer chance—literally your toss of a coin—that led you to Mercury. If you had gone to Gravity instead, that choice would have tipped the balance toward Gravity. One by one, people from Mercury would have joined you, and you would end up at the all-Gravity Nash equilibrium. Unlike the half-and-half equilibrium, both the all-Gravity and all-Mercury equilibria are stable. Natural incentives tend to push us toward one club or the other, and once we are at one, we tend to remain at that one.

The key point in our clubbing game is that we're not going to end up in the middle, as we did when we played chicken. Instead, we're going to end up at one of the ends, with everyone at Gravity or everyone at Mercury. Because your payoff is identical (3,000) at each of those equilibria, you might suspect that this is a game of pure coordination, just like the three-player game we began the chapter with. If you did, you are right.

We'll use this framework repeatedly throughout the book, so it's worth some study. As we use it, we'll also explore other archetypes, including multiplayer games of assurance, multiplayer battles of the sexes, and even a multiplayer prisoner's dilemma.

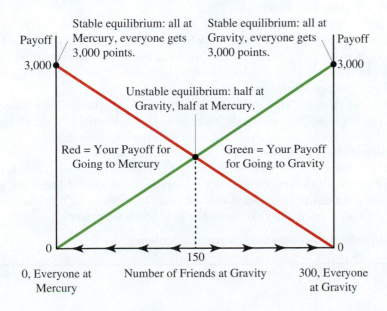

◄ **Figure 4.11**

Equilibria in the Clubbing Game
Natural incentives tend to push the clubbing game toward one of two equilibria—one where everyone is at Mercury or one where everyone is at Gravity.

Application 4.2

Breaking Facebook's Stranglehold

In the fall of 2012, Facebook logged its one-billionth account. Facebook dominates social networking, single-handedly accounting for one-fifth of all Internet page views. The company has reunited friends, kindled romances, and even ignited revolutions, beginning in 2010 with the Arab Spring uprisings in the Middle East.

Yet it seems that everybody hates Facebook. Some hate the website's Timeline feature. Some worry about privacy. Some can't stand seeing advertisements in their newsfeeds. So disgruntled are Facebook users that a Google search for "I hate Facebook" generates 700 *million* results.

There *are* alternatives to Facebook, including Google+, Google's third attempt to derail the Facebook juggernaut. Google+ went live to rave reviews, comparing favorably to Facebook in terms of its technical execution and overall user experience. Yet Google+ has gone nowhere. Why do people continue to use a product they hate when there's a better one available? That wouldn't happen with microwave ovens!

The reason is that social media sites, unlike microwave ovens, grow in value as more people use them. When the number of Facebook users increases, the number of potential connections *you* can make with it increases, too. This makes Facebook more valuable to you. Economists call such goods *network goods*.

But Google+ is a network good, too, and it's one that's arguably better than Facebook. So why don't people switch? Thinking of social networks as a game theorist might can help answer that question. Suppose your friends have a choice of using Facebook or Google+. If nobody uses Facebook, it holds zero value to you. The more people who sign up for Facebook, the greater the number of connections you can make: You'll see more status updates, and more people will see yours.

The point of social networks is connectedness, so there are payoffs to using Google+, too. If no one is using Google+, your payoff for using it is zero. The more people who use it, the greater your payoff. But because Google+ creates a better user experience, your payoff when everyone uses it is higher than the potential payoff when everyone uses Facebook.

As is the case in the clubbing game, you'll find two stable equilibria here: one where everyone uses Facebook and one where everyone uses Google+. But because Google+ offers a better platform than Facebook, everyone agrees that the Google+ equilibrium is better than the Facebook equilibrium. This situation describes a multiplayer game of assurance.

Today, we're at an "all Facebook" equilibrium simply because Facebook came along first. But equilibria, even inferior equilibria, can be sticky. We'd all be better off if everyone would *collectively* switch from Facebook to Google+. But if you as an *individual* switch on your own, you don't gain. You lose.

We use Facebook because we literally can't help ourselves! Google+ won't replace Facebook unless it can convince hundreds of millions of Facebook users to switch simultaneously. This means that 10 years from now, we'll probably still be using Facebook—and telling everyone just how much we hate it.

See related problem 4.5 on page 96 at the end of this chapter.

Conclusion

Chapter 3's introduction to two-player games laid the groundwork for your study of social problems. But while many of society's biggest social problems can be modeled as games, very few of them are actually two-player games. Instead, they result from the strategic interaction of thousands, millions, or even billions of people. This chapter developed the tools needed to model these large-scale interactions.

Despite the more complicated nature of these games, you'll find that they retain the basic flavor of the two-player games from the previous chapter. As the book progresses, you will see multiplayer versions of each of the two-player archetypes, and you'll see them in the context of social problems that are both very real and very difficult to solve. Understanding the theory that underlies those problems will help explain why it's so hard to come up with good solutions to those problems.

Chapter Summary and Problems

Key Term

N-player game, p. 87

4.1   **Introduction to Three-Player Games, pages 80–82**

Illustrate three-player games using payoff matrixes.

Summary

To model a game with three players, economists use a special version of a payoff matrix that contains a separate page for each possible strategy available to one player. On each page, an ordinary payoff matrix summarizes the choices available to the remaining two players, given the strategy chosen by the first player. Each cell in this special version of a payoff matrix shows three payoffs. The first goes to the row player, the second goes to the column player, and the third goes to the page player.

Review Questions

All problems are assignable in MyEconLab.

1.1 In a payoff matrix for a three-player game, one player picks the row, another picks the column, and the third player picks the _____.

1.2 In a payoff matrix for a three-player game, there are three payoffs in each cell. The second payoff goes to the _____ player.

Refer to the following payoff matrixes to answer questions 1.3 and 1.4.

1.3 Hugo's available strategies include _____.
  a. Top and bottom
  b. Left and right
  c. Up and down
  d. None of the above

1.4 Suppose Hugo chooses top, while Larry chooses down, and Serena chooses left. Then Hugo will receive a payoff of _____.
  a. 7
  b. 3
  c. 2
  d. Some other number

Hugo
Chooses Top

		Serena	
		Left	Right
Larry	Up	6, 6, 6	3, 7, 3
	Down	7, 3, 2	4, 4, 1

Hugo
Chooses Bottom

		Serena	
		Left	Right
Larry	Up	2, 2, 7	1, 3, 4
	Down	3, 1, 3	2, 2, 2

Problems and Applications

1.5 Consider a modified version of the sit-in game played by Mary, Jose, and Chris. If all three meet in the auto shop, a decent sit-in will be organized. But if they all meet in the coffee shop, the access to caffeine will help them organize an even better sit-in. If they fail to all meet in the same place, the sit-in will fail. Create the payoff matrix for this game.

1.6 Modify the original sit-in problem described in the text to incorporate the following changes. There are three places to meet: the coffee shop, the auto shop, or the library. If all three players meet in the same place, an excellent sit-in will be organized, and everyone will receive a payoff of 2. If two of the three meet in the same place, a decent sit-in will be organized, and everyone will receive a payoff of 1. If nobody meets in the same place, the sit-in will fail, and everybody will receive a payoff of 0. Create a payoff matrix that incorporates these changes.

4.2 | **Finding Nash Equilibria in Three-Player Games, pages 82–86**

Locate Nash equilibria in three-player games.

Summary

There are two ways to find equilibria in three-player games. If the players have dominant strategies, there will be an equilibrium where those dominant strategies intersect. If the players don't have dominant strategies, best-response analysis can be used. Best-response analysis is done in the usual way for the row and column players. However, to find the page player's best responses, you must compare the page player's payoffs from cells that are in the same position but on different pages of the game.

Review Questions

All problems are assignable in MyEconLab.

Use the payoff matrix that accompanies questions 1.3 and 1.4 to answer questions 2.1 to 2.4.

2.1 What is Larry's dominant strategy?

  a. Up

  b. Down

  c. Both up and down are his dominant strategies.

  d. Larry does not have a dominant strategy.

2.2 What is Hugo's dominant strategy?

  a. Top

  b. Bottom

  c. Up

  d. Hugo does not have a dominant strategy.

2.3 A Nash equilibrium can be found where Hugo plays _____, Larry plays _____, and Serena plays _____.

  a. Top; up; right

  b. Left; top; down

  c. Bottom; down; right

  d. There is a Nash equilibrium in this game, but it is not listed in a–c.

2.4 The game described here has the characteristics of a(n) _____ game.

  a. Assurance

  b. Battle of the sexes

  c. Chicken

  d. Prisoner's dilemma

Problems and Applications

2.5 Consider the modified sit-in game in problem 1.5. Use cell-by-cell inspection to locate all equilibria. Then classify the game as a three-player version of one of the two-player archetypes.

2.6 [Related to Application 4.1 on page 85] Consider the three-player game played by Nash, Bender, and Sol in Application 4.1. Reproduce the payoff matrix and then perform best-response analysis. Do you find the same equilibria as are indicated in the application?

2.7 [Related to Application 4.1 on page 85] Read Application 4.1 carefully. Then classify the game played by Nash, Bender, and Sol as one of the game archetypes.

4.3 | **Depicting Games with More Than Three Players, pages 87–88**

Use graphs to illustrate games with more than three players.

Summary

Games with more than three players, known as *n*-player games, can be represented graphically. In an *n*-player game, you put yourself in the position of the last player. The horizontal axis of the graph measures the number of players minus one (you) who have chosen a particular strategy. The vertical axes measure your payoffs. Different lines in the graph indicate your payoffs from choosing various strategies, given the choices made by the other players.

Review Questions

3.1 A game with more than three players is called a(n) _____ game.

3.2 Games with more than three players are generally analyzed using a _____.

3.3 In an *n*-player game, the vertical axes measure _____.

For questions 3.4–3.7, consider the following game. There are 13 students in the class, including you. Each student must choose either solid or dash. Payouts to solid and dash are indicated by the appropriate lines in the graph below:

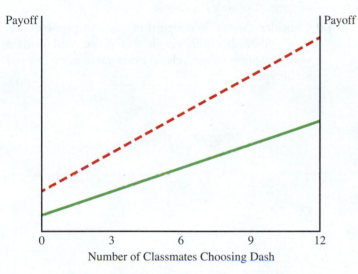

3.4 If all of your classmates choose dash, what should you choose?

a. Solid

b. Dash

c. Both solid and dash give you the same payoff, so it doesn't matter which you choose.

3.5 If all of your classmates choose solid, what should you choose?

a. Solid

b. Dash

c. Both solid and dash give you the same payoff, so it doesn't matter which you choose.

3.6 Suppose that exactly half (six) of your classmates have chosen dash. What should you choose?

a. Solid

b. Dash

c. Both solid and dash give you the same payoff, so it doesn't matter which you choose.

3.7 Suppose that exactly half (six) of your classmates have chosen dash. Who among your classmates will wish to change their minds?

a. The ones who chose solid

b. The ones who chose dash

c. Nobody wishes to change their mind.

d. Everybody wishes to change their mind.

Problems and Applications

3.8 Commuting to work can be difficult in big cities. Suppose you and 1 million other commuters are driving downtown to work. You can either take the freeway or take surface streets. Your payoff depends on how quickly you get downtown. All else equal, the freeway is faster than surface streets. But both get slower the more people there are driving on them; if every commuter chooses the same option, traffic will come to a standstill and commuters will get a payoff of zero. Draw the graph that represents this million-player game. Let the horizontal axis represent the number of commuters on the freeway, and the vertical axes represent the payoffs to choosing a particular roadway.

3.9 Redraw the multiplayer game from problem 3.8, but let the horizontal axis represent the number of commuters on surface streets.

4.4 **Finding Equilibria in Games with More Than Three Players, pages 88–92**

Locate equilibria in *n*-player games.

Summary

N-player games have equilibria just like two- and three-player games. Generally, equilibria can be found either at the endpoints of the game or where your payoffs from choosing either available strategy are equal. A stable equilibrium exists at a point if natural forces cause the game to gravitate toward that point. To determine whether a point is an equilibrium, you must analyze whether incentives tend to push the outcome toward that point or away from that point.

Review Questions

Consider the game played by 13 students in questions 3.4 to 3.7. Use that information to answer the following two questions:

4.1 Which of the following are equilibrium outcomes in this game?

    a. All solid

    b. All dash

    c. Half solid and half dash

    d. Both a and b are equilibrium outcomes.

4.2 What two-player game does this game most resemble?

    a. Assurance

    b. Battle of the sexes

    c. Prisoner's dilemma

    d. This game is not similar to any of the two-player archetypes.

Problems and Applications

4.3 Carefully inspect the game shown below, where players have a choice of playing solid or dash:

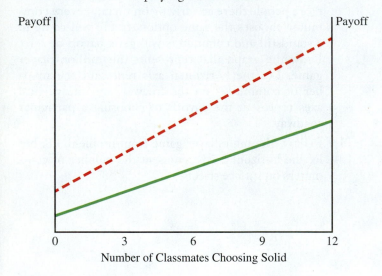

Payoffs for playing solid and dash are indicated by the appropriate lines in the figure. If you were playing this game, what would you choose if you thought everybody were playing solid? What would you choose if you thought everybody were playing dash? What is the equilibrium outcome in this game?

4.4 Consider the game illustrated in problem 4.3. Can you classify this game as one of the game archetypes?

4.5 **[Related to Application 4.2 on page 92]** Read Application 4.2 carefully. Then depict the game played by users of social media graphically. Remember that users have a choice of using either Facebook or Google+. Let the horizontal axis measure the number of users choosing Facebook.

4.6 Consider the traffic congestion game in problem 3.8. Find all Nash equilibria in this game, and explain your reasoning. Then, classify this game as one of our archetypes.

Experiment

The Red–Green Game

This chapter introduced you to the mechanics of multi-player games, games with more than two players. Today, you'll play a multiplayer game that highlights a tension between individual incentives and collective well-being. In this game, each student in your class is asked to choose a color for himself or herself: red or green. The government will pay each student a cash reward based on his or her choice. Holding the choices of your classmates constant, choosing green will always pay you more than choosing red. However, the more students in your class who choose red, the more money the government will pay the class as a whole; your potential reward will increase as a result. What color will you choose—red or green?

MyEconLab

Please visit http://www.myeconlab.com for support material to conduct this experiment if assigned by your instructor.

Free Exchange: Individual and International Trade

Chapter Outline and Learning Objectives

5.1 Comparative Advantage, Exchange, and Wealth Creation, page 99

Illustrate the process by which exchange creates wealth.

5.2 Restrictions on Free Exchange, page 105

Explain how restricting free exchange creates deadweight losses.

5.3 International Trade and Not-So-Free Exchange, page 109

Describe the direct and indirect consequences of restricting international trade.

Experiment: The Gains-from-Trade Game, page 118

MyEconLab
MyEconLab helps you master each objective and study more efficiently.

Have you ever found yourself waiting in an agonizingly slow-moving line for beer at a crowded club? Part of the reason for "beer bottlenecks" such as this is because beer-pouring technology and techniques have been rather primitive until recently. You probably know how the beer-pouring process goes: The bartender fetches a glass and tilts it under the tap at a 45-degree angle, and with a quick slap of the paddle, beer starts to flow into the glass. By the time fluid reaches the rim, about 3 inches of foam has accumulated in the glass. So the bartender stops the tap, pours off the foam into a nearby sink, and repeats the process until the beer has a perfect, 1-inch head of foam. Consequently, it takes a while to pour a single serving. Worse yet, the bartender pours perfectly good beer down the drain!

Enter Matt Younkle, an enterprising engineering student and beer aficionado from the University of Wisconsin. Tired of waiting in line for beer, Younkle put a substantial amount of effort into improving beer-pouring technology. The end result was the Turbo Tap, a device that allows a bartender to pour a perfect glass of beer in 3 seconds flat. The Turbo Tap has saved society hundreds of thousands of hours by reducing the amount of time people spend in line, waiting for beer.

Bar owners love the Turbo Tap, too. They can serve more customers, and because the customers don't have to wait in line as long for the beer, they're willing to pay a bit more for it. Moreover, because the tap eliminates the need to pour off foam, bartenders get 8 to 10 extra glasses of beer from every keg. You can think of the extra glasses as "found beer," which, from an economic perspective, is a terrific thing. Due to one little piece of technology, the world now has more of something it values and therefore is a richer place.

Comparative Advantage, Exchange, and Wealth Creation

5.1 Learning Objective

Illustrate the process by which exchange creates wealth.

In this chapter, we're going to discover that there are many parallels between Turbo Tap and the market system of organizing an economy. The market system is based on the freedom to buy and sell, or *exchange*, goods and services. The desire to exchange goods and services is necessarily intertwined with the notion of scarcity. If we had unlimited resources, we could produce everything we want for ourselves. But because our resources are limited, we must make the best use of the resources we have. That means spending our time doing the things we are best at and hiring other people to do the things we're not particularly good at. Allocating resources in this way is called **specialization**.

Specialization The process of making the best use of our limited resources by doing the things we are best at and hiring other people to do the things we're not particularly good at.

Comparative Advantage and Specialization: Catalysts for Exchange

The idea of specializing in something you are good at is intuitively appealing. Suppose that you and your roommate want nothing more than to eat as much pizza and pie as possible. If you can make pizzas faster than your roommate, and your roommate can make pies faster than you, then it probably makes complete sense that you and your roommate can both gain by specializing in making the item you're good at and then trading with one another for the item you're not.

What is not intuitively obvious is how specialization can create material gains for everybody, even if one person is better than the other at *everything*. To illustrate, consider the following example:

- Pat and Martha are each capable of making both pizzas and pies. They both spend 60 hours each week cooking for themselves.
- It takes Pat 12 hours to make a pizza and 12 hours to make a pie. So if Pat devotes all his efforts to making pizzas, he can make 5 pizzas in a week. On the other hand, if he devotes all his efforts to producing pies, he can produce 5 pies in a week. Typically, Pat spends 36 hours making pizza and 24 hours making pies each week. That allows him to consume 3 pizzas and 2 pies.

Absolute advantage The ability to produce a good using fewer resources than someone else.

- It takes Martha 10 hours to make a pizza and 5 hours to make a pie. If she devotes all her efforts to pizza making, she can make 6 pizzas in a week. If, instead, she devotes all her efforts to pie baking, she can make 12 pies. In a typical week, Martha divides her workweek so that she ends up consuming 2 pizzas and 8 pies.

Based on how long it takes each to make pizza and pie, it's clear that Martha is better than Pat at producing both pizzas and pies. Economists say that Martha has an **absolute advantage** in producing both goods. That might suggest to you that she has nothing to gain from specializing and trading with Pat. It is fairly easy to show, however, that even in this case, both Martha and Pat can gain from specializing in the production of one good and then trading for the other.

Measuring the Gains from Specialization and Exchange Suppose that Pat specializes in making pizza, and Martha specializes in making pie. At the end of the week, Pat is sitting on a stack of 5 pizzas, and Martha has a dozen pies. Now, let Pat trade 2 of his pizzas for 3 of Martha's pies.

Does this trade benefit Pat? Let's find out. First, figure out what Pat ends up eating when he specializes and trades with Martha. He ends his workweek with 5 pizzas. He trades 2 of his pizzas away for 3 of Martha's pies. In the end, Pat ends up consuming 3 pies and the 3 remaining pizzas. But recall that when Pat did all his own cooking, he could only consume 2 pies and 3 pizzas. So, trading with Martha has made Pat exactly 1 pie better off!

Do Pat's gains come at Martha's expense? Let's calculate what Martha will end up eating if she trades with Pat. At the end of the week, she has 12 pies and no pizza. She trades away 3 pies to Pat in exchange for 2 pizzas. That leaves her with 9 pies and 2 pizzas. But recall that when Martha cooked for herself, she could only consume 8 pies and 2 pizzas. Because of trade with Pat, Martha, too, can consume 1 extra pie!

Opportunity Cost and Comparative Advantage Trade between Pat and Martha doesn't result in one person getting richer at the other's expense. Rather, both Pat *and* Martha get to enjoy extra pie. And just where did that extra pie come from? It came from making better use of Pat's and Martha's *relative* talents. Here's a thought experiment to help explain why: Suppose Pat and Martha are making nothing but pies—17 of them, to be exact—that they will share. Then one day they decide it might be nice to have just one pizza to split between them. Who should make that pizza? It's tempting to say that Martha should make the pizza because she is faster. But is that certain?

No matter who does the work, both Pat and Martha will get to enjoy more pizza. But there's a trade-off: They'll end up consuming less pie. Let's see exactly how much pie they'll have to sacrifice. Suppose Martha makes the pizza. In the 10 hours it takes her to make that pizza, she could have made exactly 2 pies. So, at the end of the week, Martha and Pat end up splitting 15 pies and 1 pizza.

But what if Pat makes the pizza? It takes him 12 hours to make a pizza, which is longer than it takes Martha. Alternatively, in that amount of time, Pat could make 1 pie. This means that if Pat makes the pizza, at the end of the week, he and Martha can split *16* pies and 1 pizza. This is pretty amazing: Even though Martha is a faster pizza maker, Pat and Martha are better off if Pat makes the pizza! This happens simply because the opportunity cost of Pat making pizza (1 pie) is lower than the opportunity cost of Martha making a pizza (2 pies). On that basis, we say that Pat has a **comparative advantage** in making pizza.

Comparative advantage The ability to produce a good at a lower opportunity cost than another producer.

In other words, if your goal is to produce the greatest possible material wealth for society, the right measuring stick to use when calculating the cost of a pizza is not how much *time* gets sacrificed but rather how much *pie* gets sacrificed. It is true that Martha is a little bit faster than Pat at pizza making. But she is *so much faster* at making pies that drawing her away from pie production to make pizza is exceptionally costly.

Pat may have a comparative advantage in making pizza, but Martha has a comparative advantage in making pie. Note that every pie Martha makes costs her only half a pizza, but every pie Pat makes costs him a full pizza. It makes little sense to have

Pat produce pies when Martha can make the same pie with less material sacrifice. Ultimately, society creates the greatest material wealth when participants in the economy specialize in the good they have a comparative advantage in producing and trade for the other good. Pat should specialize in making pizzas, and Martha should specialize in making pies.

In the highly simplified pizza-and-pie example above, specialization helped Pat and Martha enjoy greater material wealth. But in the real world, specialization can help you live a richer life, too. How difficult would your life be if you had to grow all your own food, draw your own water, cut wood to heat your own home, make your own clothes from fabric you had woven from fibers you had grown, and wash those clothes by hand every week? That kind of lifestyle can be managed, but it requires a tremendous amount of work to produce a bare minimum of material comfort.

Few people choose to live in such a self-sufficient way. Instead, specialization and exchange allow people to work less and enjoy more. For example, you are probably looking forward to graduating from college and getting a job in your chosen field—in other words, specializing—and exchanging your paycheck for the food, clothing, shelter, and other things that you want. That will allow you to focus on something you are relatively good at and achieve a standard of living much higher than you could if you tried to do everything for yourself.

The same general principles apply to countries. Most countries specialize to a greater or lesser extent in producing various goods and services. The United States specializes in producing agricultural commodities like wheat and services like financial services; it exchanges those products and services with other countries such as Bangladesh that have specialized in producing things like clothing and consumer goods. Specialization in the United States is driven by high productivity in agriculture and financial services, which in turn stems from the country's comparatively abundant and fertile land and the relatively high educational attainment and skills of its workers.

You might be led to believe that the United States would be better off if it were self-sufficient. After all, it is undoubtedly true that if it wanted to, the country *could* clothe its own people. But doing so would draw resources from its farms and its financial centers—places where those resources are highly productive—and employ them in places like clothing factories where they are comparatively less productive. At the same time, resources in Bangladesh would be diverted from clothing factories, where they are relatively highly productive, to activities like growing wheat, where they are less productive. Both the United States and Bangladesh, in trying to produce something that their resources are not well suited to, end up throwing away their comparative talents: Output falls, and both nations get poorer. As economist Russell Roberts of Stanford University asserts, "Self-sufficiency is the road to poverty."

Exchange and Cooperative Surplus

You now understand how specialization can create greater wealth for society to enjoy. It is less obvious, but equally true, that the process of exchange creates wealth, too. To understand why, consider the following example: Sam is a buffalo rancher. He produces buffalo steaks and values a 20-pound package of steak at $100. His neighbor Erica runs an upscale restaurant that serves buffalo steaks. She would be willing to pay up to $200 for a 20-pound package of buffalo steaks.

So what happens if we put Sam and Erica in a room together? Will they be able to work out a deal by which buffalo steaks trade hands? Will their negotiations be contentious as each tries to get the better of the other? To answer these questions, let's impose a couple of rules on the exchange. First, let's stipulate that the buyer gets to make one and only one offer. Second, let's stipulate that the seller must either accept or reject the buyer's offer. In other words, the seller cannot make any kind of counteroffer. Given these rules, will Sam and Erica be able to strike a deal?

It seems like they probably could. Suppose Erica offers Sam $150 for a package of steaks. If Sam accepts the offer, then Erica gets the steaks for the low price of $150, even though she was willing to pay $200. She can then use the $50 she didn't have to spend on steaks to buy barbeque sauce, charcoal, or anything else her heart desires. Sam gains as well. As a result of the trade, he receives $150 for steaks that he values at only $100. He, too, walks away with a gain of $50. In other words, when the steaks trade hands, everyone benefits, which is why such a transaction is often called a *mutually beneficial exchange*. This is why both Sam and Erica are likely to conclude this transaction with a polite "thank you."

Figure 5.1 shows the payoff matrix for this game, in which Erica makes an offer and Sam has the choice of accepting or rejecting it.

► **Figure 5.1**

Payoff Matrix for a Simple Bargaining Game
In this game, Erica (payoffs shown in black) makes an offer, and Sam (payoffs shown in blue) can either accept or reject it. In this example, the equilibrium outcome is for Sam to accept Erica's offer.

		Sam	
		Accepts Offer	Rejects Offer
Erica	Offers $150	+$50, +$50	$0, $0

The matrix shows the players, their options, and possible gains for each of them. If Sam rejects Erica's offer, no trade occurs. Both parties leave no better off than they were before, and each gains nothing. But if Sam accepts the offer, which is the equilibrium outcome, a trade occurs, and both Sam and Erica find themselves better off by $50. Economists have special terminology for the gains that both Sam and Erica receive. Because Sam is the producer of buffalo steak, his $50 gain is called **producer surplus**. Because Erica is the buyer, or *consumer*, of buffalo steak, her $50 is called **consumer surplus**. Adding Sam's and Erica's gains, we say that the transaction creates $100 of **cooperative surplus**, which is simply the sum of all the net benefits received by the parties to a transaction. Cooperative surplus is sometimes called *surplus value*, or simply *surplus*.

But what if Erica makes a lower offer? Suppose she says, "Hey, Sam. I've got $110 right here that I'll give you for your steaks. But I don't have time to haggle, so is it a deal?" Erica's revised offer changes the game's payoff matrix, as shown in Figure 5.2:

Producer surplus The amount a seller receives for a good or service beyond the minimum he or she would be willing to sell the good for.

Consumer surplus The maximum amount a buyer would be willing to pay for a good or service less the price he or she actually pays.

Cooperative surplus The sum of all the net benefits received by the parties to a transaction.

► **Figure 5.2**

A Revised Bargaining Game
In this version of the bargaining game, Erica makes a lower offer. If Sam accepts the offer, the size of the cooperative surplus is unaltered, but the distribution of that surplus changes.

		Sam	
		Accepts Offer	Rejects Offer
Erica	Offers $110	+$90, +$10	$0, $0

Revising the offer downward increases Erica's gain and reduces Sam's, assuming that Sam accepts the deal. But the amazing thing that might escape the casual observer is the following: Although the offer alters the *distribution* of the cooperative surplus, it does not alter the total *amount* of it. As long as a transaction takes place, society gets richer by exactly $100!

Cooperative Surplus as a Measure of Wealth Creation

In Sam and Erica's situation, where exactly does the $100 surplus come from? Fundamentally, it comes from the process of moving steaks from a place where they are less highly valued (Sam's ranch) to a place where they're more highly valued (Erica's restaurant). You might notice that Erica values the steaks by exactly $100 more than Sam does, and when the steaks move from the ranch to the restaurant, it's that extra $100 that is captured in the form of surplus value. Some of it goes to Sam as his reward for raising the buffalo, and some of it goes to Erica. However, neither person gets richer at the other's expense. The exchange *creates* wealth for both. That's true whether we're talking about buffalo steaks, or hairbrushes, or a gallon of milk, or even economics lectures.

Application 5.1

The Globalization of Wine—Our Cups Runneth Over

A large group of economists agree that "beer is made by men, wine by God."[1] Many of these economists belong to the Association of Wine Economists (AWE), which publishes its own academic journal, the *Journal of Wine Economics*, and holds an annual conference where wine is tasted and new research is presented.

In a paper presented at the 2007 AWE conference in Trier, Germany, economists Omer Gokcekus and Andrew Fargnoli asked a key question: Is increasing world trade, or globalization, good for wine drinkers? The data they used to answer this question is interesting, and it helps us understand how an abstract notion like cooperative surplus creates real benefits for society.

In the past few decades, many governments have reduced restrictions on the sale of wine. One result of this greater freedom is that an increasing share of global wine production is being consumed in places other than its country of origin. The impact of this globalization is apparent when one examines *Wine Spectator* magazine's annual top 100 list. The list contains the year's best wines, the release price of each wine, and an assessment of each wine's quality. Gokcekus and Fargnoli's research explored how each of those factors changed over the span of nearly two decades.

For years, the list was dominated by wines from France, Australia, Italy, and the United States. In 1988, there were only 6 countries represented in the top 100, and only 5 of the 100 wines were from countries other than the "Big Four." But wines from other countries have recently begun to penetrate the list: Eighteen years later, 11 countries were represented, and 24 wines were from countries other than the Big Four.

Not only do consumers have access to a greater variety of wines, they also have begun paying less for them. In 1988, buying one bottle each of the top 100 wines would have cost a whopping $4,313. By 2005, filling your cart with them would have cost a mere $2,622.[2] That's a 40% discount!

Are those lower prices due to a flood of low-quality imports? Gokcekus and Fargnoli say no. Each wine on the top 100 list is graded on a 100-point scale, the same rating you might find posted beneath the wines at your local wine shop. The top 100 wines in 1988 averaged about 93 on a 100-point scale—an average that did not drop measurably over the years, even as prices plummeted.

Falling prices encourage consumers to buy more, with wine as with other goods. Over the two decades that Gokcekus and Fargnoli examined, total wine sales in the United States rose from 182 million cases in 1988 to 271 million cases in 2005, spurred in part by falling prices and increasing globalization. Those exchanges created more cooperative surplus for buyers and sellers of wine to share: lower prices, more choice, greater value. That's something worth toasting!

See related problem 1.10 on page 115 at the end of this chapter.

Based on Omer Gokcekus and Andrew Fargnoli, "Is Globalization Good for Wine Drinkers in the United States?" *Journal of Wine Economics*, 2007; Michael Veseth's *Wine Wars: The Curse of the Blue Nun, the Miracle of Two Buck Chuck, and the Revenge of the Terroirists*; and M. Hussain, S. Cholette, and R. M. Castaldi, "An Analysis of Globalization Forces in the Wine Industry: Implications and Recommendations for Wineries," *Journal of Global Marketing*, 2007.

---

[1] This quote is attributed to Martin Luther (1483–1546), the German monk on whose teachings the Lutheran church was founded.

[2] The prices quoted are in constant 1988 dollars, which means that our wine prices have been adjusted for a general decrease in the purchasing power of a dollar, or *inflation*. Gokcekus and Fargnoli show that even if you don't adjust wine prices for inflation, the top 100 wines got cheaper while wages and the price of most other goods sold in the United States rose.

The People Behind the Theory

Adam Smith

What was the most important event of 1776? Many people might think it was the signing of the Declaration of Independence. But others might argue that an even bigger event was the publication of an economics book by Adam Smith, an absent-minded Scottish philosophy professor.

Born in 1723 and raised by his widowed mother, Smith eventually studied philosophy at the University of Glasgow. There, he developed a passion for liberty, reason, and free speech. Later Smith started a teaching career at Glasgow, where he began to develop an interest in economics.

It was an interesting time to be studying economics: Global economic production, largely stagnant for almost two millennia, was beginning to skyrocket. But this new-found prosperity wasn't shared by all countries, and Smith devoted himself to figuring out why. In his studies, Smith observed, for the first time, several key factors that were critical in generating economic prosperity:

1. Smith observed the division of labor, or specialization. Smith drew on his personal study of a pin factory to illustrate the increase in material well-being that specialization generates:

   One man draws out the wire, another straights it, a third cuts it, a fourth points it, a fifth grinds it at the top for receiving the head. . . . Those ten persons, therefore, could make among them upwards of forty-eight thousand pins in a day. But if they had all wrought separately and independently . . . they certainly could not each of them have made twenty, perhaps not one pin in a day.

2. Smith established the link between specialization and exchange, and he pointed out the inherent nature of humans to further their own self-interest through exchange:

   This division of labour . . . is the necessary, though very slow and gradual, consequence of a certain propensity in human nature which has in view no such extensive utility; the propensity to truck, barter, and exchange one thing for another.

3. Finally, Smith observed that generally, the pursuit of self-interest caused people to behave in ways that were good for society as a whole:

   It is not from the benevolence of the butcher, the brewer, or the baker that we expect our dinner, but from their regard to their own interest.

Smith published his observations in his 1776 magnum opus, *An Inquiry Into the Nature and Causes of the Wealth of Nations*. That book laid the groundwork for the modern study of economics. *The Wealth of Nations* makes a general case for free-market principles and limited government involvement in the economy. Those ideas were revolutionary at the time but have since spread around the globe, and today the market system is the primary means of organizing the world's economies.

The Declaration of Independence laid down the guiding principles for what would become the greatest country in world history. But Adam Smith's economic principles have made meaningful differences in billions of people's lives and will continue to do so for centuries to come. The enormity of Smith's impact makes it easy to argue that the publication of *The Wealth of Nations* was, in fact, the most important event of 1776.

Based on Adam Smith's *An Inquiry Into the Nature and Causes of the Wealth of Nations*, 1776.

Our Sam and Erica example was encumbered by a fairly rigid set of rules. One of the obvious restrictions was the take-it-or-leave-it nature of Erica's offer. What if Sam doesn't like Erica's offer and tries to get her to pay a bit more? Sam certainly could do this, but that doesn't mean the rules are completely unrealistic. Many market transactions involve no haggling. Do you haggle with a clerk at a grocery store over the price of a can of tuna? Probably not. The store makes an offer in the form of a price tag, and you're free to accept the offer (by buying the tuna) or reject it (by leaving it on the shelf).

Regardless of whether we relax the no-haggling rule, if a deal is made, nothing will fundamentally change as far as the cooperative surplus goes. Depending on the relative bargaining strength and negotiating prowess of Sam and Erica, the price might move up or down a bit. We don't have any way to predict where it will end up, although we know for sure that it will settle somewhere between $100 and $200 because a price lower than $100 will make Sam worse off, and a price higher than $200 will make Erica worse off. The good news for us is that no matter where the price ends up, just the process of completing the transaction creates the same $100 of cooperative surplus, and in this course, that's what matters most.

At this point, you might be wondering what the invention of the Turbo Tap, which we opened the chapter with, has to do with an exchange of buffalo steaks. To an economist, a free exchange like Erica and Sam's looks an awful lot like the invention of the Turbo Tap: Both are innovations that help us extract more value from the same quantity of resources. Both are innovations that make our lives easier and richer. Even though one is a mechanical innovation and the other is a commerce-related innovation, fundamentally, there's little difference in the result. Both make buyers and sellers better off.

Restrictions on Free Exchange

5.2 Learning Objective
Explain how restricting free exchange creates deadweight losses.

Although we tend to view today's marketplace as one of free exchange, governments around the globe regularly enact policies that inhibit rather than encourage free exchange. For example, in some U.S. states, it is illegal to buy liquor on Sundays. Similarly, the federal government prohibits people who need kidney transplants from buying the perfectly good spare kidneys of other people. Policies such as these are obvious barriers to exchange, and most economists (as well as the benevolent social planner) would agree that they make the world poorer, not richer.

Taxes

Many of the policies that adversely affect free exchange are more subtle than the ones we just discussed, and for that reason, they deserve special attention. Of these policies, the most prominent are taxes. A **tax** is a compulsory payment to the government that is generally linked to engaging in some activity. For example, when you earn income, the government requires you to pay a tax linked to how much you made. When you buy gum, your state and local governments will collect sales tax based on the amount you spent. If you own a house, the state and local governments often collect an annual tax called a property tax that is proportionate to the value of your home.

Tax A compulsory payment to the government that is generally linked to engaging in some activity.

Let's return to Sam and Erica to see what happens when the government imposes a $50 tax on the sale of buffalo steaks and makes sellers legally responsible for collecting the tax. Erica strolls into the marketplace, where she spies Sam selling buffalo steaks. Because Erica is an astute buyer, she realizes that Sam will have to send the government $50 if he sells her a package of steaks. Erica knows that in order to convince Sam to sell her buffalo steaks, she needs to offer at least $150 for them. To encourage him to deal with her, she offers Sam $175.

If Sam rejects Erica's offer, he won't owe the government anything, but neither will either of our parties gain anything. On the other hand, if Sam accepts Erica's offer, he will bring in $175, of which $50 will immediately be sent to the government,

► Figure 5.3
The Effect of a Tax in the Bargaining Game
Imposing a $50 tax on the sale of buffalo steak reduces the cooperative surplus that Sam and Erica receive from reaching a deal.

		Sam	
		Accepts Offer	Rejects Offer
Erica	Offers $175	+$25, +$25	$0, $0

leaving Sam with a gain of $25 (the $125 Sam has left minus the $100 he valued the steaks at), and Erica with a $25 gain as well. The payoff matrix that reflects the effects of the tax is shown in Figure 5.3.

Because imposing a tax reduces Sam's and Erica's cooperative surplus from $100 to $50, you might be tempted to say that the tax is a bad thing. But keep in mind that the $50 that was lost didn't just disappear. The government will, of course, return that $50 to the public in the form of education, roads and bridges, and other things people value. (Or at least we hope so. In later chapters, we will discuss whether that really happens. For now, assume that it does.) And so, once we account for the benefits the public receives, we still get $100 of surplus:

- $25 goes to Sam.
- $25 goes to Eric.
- $50 goes to the rest of society.

"So what's the problem?" you're probably asking. "You went to great lengths in earlier chapters to say that in this course, we don't pick sides—a gain is a gain is a gain, no matter who gets it. And in this case, Sam lost a little, and Erica lost a little, but the rest of society gained back everything that Sam and Erica lost. So if we're not going to take sides, where's the harm? And if there's no harm, why are we wasting paper and killing trees talking about the tax?"

Deadweight Losses

The questions you just asked are worthy ones. If the steak market consisted of just Sam and Erica, the tax wouldn't be meaningful in any way whatsoever. Markets, however, often consist of multiple buyers and multiple sellers. So we need to consider the impact of the tax on *all* the market's participants, not just Sam and Erica.

With that in mind, let's carefully choose another pair of parties with an interest in swapping steaks. Ralph wants to buy some buffalo steaks, and he'd be willing to pay $170. Jackie has some steaks she's willing to sell, but only if she can get at least $130 for them. In a free market, with no governmental intervention, Jackie and Ralph would work out an exchange for a price of somewhere between $130 and $170 and split the $40 of cooperative surplus between them. The world would be a richer place, and the benevolent social planner would rejoice.

But what happens if government imposes the $50 tax we discussed previously? Although the tax had no fundamental effect on the trade between Sam and Erica, we can't say the same thing in this case. To convince Jackie to sell her steaks, she'll need to receive $130 for herself and another $50 that she'll immediately turn around and send to the government, for a total of $180. But Ralph is willing to spend only $170, so no deal will be struck. The tax has prevented a surplus-creating transaction from occurring, and there's a $40 opportunity loss associated with it. That loss has a special name: Economists call it a deadweight loss. A **deadweight loss** is simply surplus value that is lost because something is keeping the market from functioning as well as it can.

Deadweight loss Surplus value that is lost because something is keeping the market from functioning as well as it can.

A deadweight loss is a sad, sad thing indeed. Ralph, who really wants to eat buffalo steak (and who *would* eat buffalo steak in a free market) goes home to less-desirable Brussels sprouts instead. And Jackie, who was planning to use the proceeds of the steak sale to finance her dear aunt's kidney-transplant operation, must tell her aunt she'll have to endure another few months of painful dialysis instead.

For governments, fewer trades are a problem because the tax revenue trades generate pays for public programs. You might find it paradoxical that state and local governments devote a tremendous amount of resources to bolster local commerce and at the same time impose taxes that tend to discourage local commerce. Similarly, the federal government spends billions of dollars on programs designed to stimulate consumer spending, encourage production, and create jobs yet funds its operations, including these programs, with an income tax that encourages people to work and earn less rather than more!

Given the tax-revenue paradox we just discussed, you might wonder if governments impose taxes for purposes *other* than raising revenue. The answer is yes. Legislators frequently levy taxes to discourage behaviors their constituents view as immoral or sinful and to protect people from themselves. Taxes on cigarettes, alcohol, striptease clubs, tanning salons, and the purchase of gas-guzzling automobiles are examples.

Another reason that legislators impose taxes is to cater to special-interest groups. For example, domestic producers regularly—and successfully—lobby their governments to protect them from foreign competition. Attempting to influence the law for your own private economic advantage is a tactic economists call **rent seeking**.

Rent seeking Attempting to influence the law for your own private economic advantage.

Rent seeking is rampant, even in the domestic economy. It appears in many forms. As mentioned earlier, many businesses lobby their governments to protect them from foreign competition. But there are other ways businesses seek to use the power of government to fill their own pockets. For example, limousine companies in New York City push for laws that prohibit taxis from accepting prearranged rides. Licensed cosmetologists in 28 states have lobbied for laws that require anyone braiding hair for money to graduate from cosmetology school and obtain a cosmetologist license. These types of restrictions reduce competition, which allows existing sellers to raise prices. Unfortunately, when prices rise, some buyers are priced out of the market, and cooperative surplus falls.

When government policies disrupt the process of free exchange, it is natural for some people to try to circumvent the policies. When a tax on buffalo steak prevents Jackie and Ralph from closing a deal, they might simply conduct the sale in cash and not report the transaction to the government. If government were to ban the sale of buffalo steak altogether, you can bet that some enterprising rancher would find a way to raise buffalo in secret and then sell the steaks to willing buyers. Those deals take place in what is called the **black market**, a market where goods are sold in violation of governmentally imposed restrictions.

Black market A market where goods are sold in violation of governmentally imposed restrictions.

Lots of items are sold in the black market. Some may be viewed as good things: There is a black market in breast milk for mothers who can't nurse their own children and who don't want to use formula. Other black markets might be regarded as bad things: The markets for sex and crystal meth spring to many peoples' minds as examples. In both cases, however, it is important to note that black markets spring to life because somebody, somewhere, has a need, and somehow government policy is preventing him or her from meeting that need. Of course, not everybody who is affected by a government policy will choose to break the law and participate in black market activity. But some will, and by helping those people meet their needs, black markets may reduce the deadweight losses that restrictive government policies create.

Subsidies

Another interesting government policy is a subsidy. A **subsidy** is a payment that a person receives from the government for engaging in a particular activity. In other words, a subsidy is a negative tax! And if taxes and other restrictive measures *reduce* cooperative surplus, that suggests that subsidies might *increase* the cooperative surplus.

Subsidy A payment that a person receives from the government for engaging in a particular activity.

Let's find out whether, in the case of ordinary products like buffalo steaks, a subsidy might help create wealth. Let's suppose that the government offers a $40 subsidy to buyers of buffalo steaks. In other words, every time Erica buys a box of steaks, the government will give her a $40 check. Does that subsidy make society richer?

Application 5.2

Something Stinks in Louisiana's Floral-Arranging Industry

Jill Jackson, the owner of Lady Bug Flowers, in Baldwin City, Kansas, has an amazing green thumb. At the local farmers' market, she sells stunning bouquets of flowers she's grown, harvested, and arranged.

It's a good thing she doesn't live in Louisiana. It's the only state where florists have to pass a licensing exam. That exam is tough: In a good year, the failure rate is 50%. In Louisiana, it's quite possible that Jackson's beautiful flowers might never grace a dining room table or be received in apology for boundaries transgressed. Any surplus her flowers might have created would simply disappear.

"What's the big deal?" you might be wondering. "Lawyers and nurses have to pass exams. Why not florists?"

You want your lawyer to know the law because you want effective counsel. You want your nurse to know about nursing because your life might hang in the balance. In these cases, the state has a *compelling interest* in ensuring that practitioners meet some minimum standard of competence.

What is Louisiana's compelling interest in ensuring competent florists? Bob Odom, who administered the licensing exam between 1980 and 2008, claims it protects consumers. "If [flower arrangers] can't … pass the exam, how can they do an arrangement that you and I want to buy?"

Economists are skeptical of that argument. Suppose you ask a florist to deliver a stunning bouquet to your girlfriend. If that florist delivers a very costly bunch of wilted flowers, will you ever use him again? No! In fact, you might use Facebook and Twitter to tell everyone you know not to use that florist. In a competitive marketplace, it won't be long before the florist is forced to improve his services or go out of business. You don't need Bob Odom to protect you; all you need is the stern discipline of the market.

Why, then, does Louisiana insist on licensing florists? Licensing requirements make it difficult for some people to participate in the market. Louisiana's exam is supported *and* administered by licensed florists, who have a financial interest in limiting their competition. Why not fail the most promising new florists—people like Jill Jackson—who threaten your business because they are so good at what they do?

Attorney Clark Neilly filed suit against Louisiana on behalf of Shamille Peters, who failed the exam five times. Neilly challenged Odom's claim that the exam improves quality by asking florists from Louisiana and Texas (where no license is required) to prepare floral arrangements according to specific guidelines. A panel of florists from both Texas and Louisiana evaluated the arrangements and could find no discernible differences between Louisiana and Texas arrangements.

Largely on the strength of Neilly's arguments, the Louisiana legislature voted to eliminate part, but not all, of the exam. In other words, in Louisiana, you still need a license to arrange flowers. As Peters puts it, "You don't have to take any kind of test to get a gun in Louisiana, but you can't put a flower in a vase and sell it unless the state says it's okay."

See related problems 2.9 and 2.10 on page 116 at the end of this chapter.

Based on "Florist Licensing Under Attack; Lawsuit Says Test Is Unconstitutional," *Times-Picayune*, January 5, 2004; Dick Carpenter's *Blooming Nonsense: Experiment Reveals Louisiana's Florist Licensing Scheme as Pointless and Anti-Competitive*, published by the Institute for Justice in 2010; and National Public Radio's "Louisiana Sued over Florist License Test," 2004.

In the case of Sam and Erica, the answer is no. Because she knows she'll be receiving $40 from the government every time she buys a box of steaks, Erica can now offer up to $240 without spending more than $200 of her own money. If she and Sam reach a deal at, say, $170, then Sam walks away with $70 of producer surplus, and Erica walks away with $70 of consumer surplus ($30 of which comes from her desire not to pay more than $200 out of her *own* pocket for steaks, and $40 of which comes from the government check). The cooperative surplus appears to have grown from $100 to $140.

But remember that the $40 Erica receives has to come from somewhere, and in this case, it comes from taxpayers who sent their money to the government, only to see the government turn right around and mail it to Erica. When you net out the gains and losses to all parties ($70 gain to Sam, $70 gain to Erica, $40 loss to taxpayers), you end up with exactly the same $100 of cooperative surplus that Sam and Erica would have generated on their own without the subsidy. In other words, for this transaction, the subsidy does not produce any wealth.

But what about transactions that wouldn't have occurred on their own? Does the subsidy create wealth in those cases? Suppose that another buyer, Ted, is willing to pay up to $80 for a box of buffalo steaks. Ordinarily, he and Sam wouldn't be able to work out a deal because Sam isn't willing to settle for a price less than $100. However, with the subsidy, Ted knows he can now spend up to $120 because once he receives his check from the government, he won't be spending more than $80 of his own money. He and Sam quickly agree to a price of $110.

That new transaction makes Sam $10 better off because he receives $110 for something he valued at $100. The transaction also makes Ted $10 better off: He spends $70 of his own money to get something he values at $80. But the $20 of cooperative surplus those two receive is more than offset by the $40 taxpayers spent encouraging Ted and Sam to complete a deal. In the end, this subsidy creates a deadweight loss of $20. Fundamentally, that loss occurs because Sam devoted $100 of resources to producing something that Ted valued at only $80. The world doesn't get richer when goods are transferred from places where they're highly valued to places where they're less valued.

This section has shown that for ordinary products where the market functions well, there is little the government can do to create wealth. Taxing the market makes society poorer; subsidizing the market also makes society poorer. Intervening in other ways is just as damaging. If our goal is to produce the largest possible economic pie, the best recipe is generally for governments to avoid policies that disrupt the process of free exchange.[3]

International Trade and Not-So-Free Exchange

5.3 Learning Objective

Describe the direct and indirect consequences of restricting international trade.

One can imagine rent-seeking buffalo steak producers lobbying their representatives in Congress for direct subsidies. But such subsidies may be politically unpopular: Subsidies are very visible, and taxpayers often get angry when their representatives pass laws that transfer taxpayers' money directly to someone else's pockets.

There is another way for lawmakers to confer economic favors on businesses. Governments routinely offer to protect domestic producers from foreign competition by restricting the ability of foreigners to sell their products in domestic markets. Such restrictions, commonly known as **protectionism**, are often regarded not as intrusions into free markets but rather as patriotic gestures that create or preserve jobs at home.[4]

One example of such reasoning is found in the *infant industry rationale* for restricting trade. Sometimes it is argued that new and developing industries can't be

Protectionism The process of governments protecting domestic producers from foreign competition by restricting the ability of foreigners to sell their products in domestic markets.

---

[3]There are, however, markets that don't function as well as the market for buffalo steak. In those cases, which are discussed extensively in later chapters, taxes and subsidies may indeed have the power to make the world a better place.

[4]Whether those perceptions are accurate is a big question. At least part of that question is addressed in the sections that follow.

competitive in world markets unless they can operate at a sufficiently large scale. By restricting the ability of domestic consumers to buy imported goods, the government can create a large captive market for the developing industry. Then, once that domestic industry becomes competitive, the restrictions can be lifted, and the domestic industry can be set free to compete globally.

The infant industry argument is just one rationale that is advanced in support of restricted trade. A complete discussion of the various rationales used to justify protectionist measures could easily fill a book.[5] The infant industry rationale is described here because it highlights a popular tendency to look favorably on restricting the ability of foreign producers to sell in the domestic market. It is precisely because protectionist measures are able to garner such popular approval that rent seeking is so commonplace in the international economy.

Tariffs

The most common method government uses to discourage domestic consumers from buying imported goods is to apply a tax to products purchased from foreign producers. Such taxes are called **tariffs**.

Tariffs Taxes the government imposes on imported products.

How exactly does a tariff affect the buyers of products? As President Abraham Lincoln put it in 1843, "By the tariff system the whole revenue is paid by the consumers of foreign goods. . . . By this system the man who contents himself to live upon the products of his own country pays nothing at all."[6]

But Lincoln, for all his wisdom, got this one wrong. To explain why, let's revisit Sam and Erica. Suppose that, as before, Erica is willing to pay up to $200 for a box of buffalo steaks and that Sam is willing to sell a box of buffalo steaks for $100. However, this time, let's suppose that Erica is from Spokane, Washington, and that Sam is from Calgary, Canada. Should it matter that Erica is from one nation and Sam from another? The benevolent social planner's answer is clearly no: An arbitrary geographical boundary shouldn't keep these two from working out a gain-producing deal. After all, in so many ways, Spokane is closer to Calgary than it is to Cincinnati. Remember, too, that at the beginning of the book we decided that the concept of fairness is so abstract that it's best not to choose sides. So, like the benevolent social planner, we shouldn't make arbitrary distinctions between Americans and Canadians.

However, governments often aren't as impartial as you and the benevolent social planner. After all, tax revenues have to be raised and special-interest groups appeased. Suppose the U.S. government imposes a $40 tariff on imported Canadian buffalo steak. Clearly, if Erica wants to buy Sam's steaks, she's going to have to fork over at least $140, $100 of which is needed to meet Sam's minimum price and $40 that will be used to satisfy the U.S. Customs Service (the agency responsible for ensuring that all import duties are paid). So Abraham Lincoln is at least half right: If Erica buys the imported product, she has to pay the tax. But what if Erica buys steaks produced in the United States instead? Can't she, as Lincoln suggested, avoid paying the tax then?

The answer to this question is complex. Suppose Erica starts looking around for a good domestic source of buffalo steak, and the best producer she finds is Stephen, a Texas buffalo rancher. Recall that Sam can produce and sell a box of buffalo steaks for $100. Obviously, if Stephen were able to produce and sell steaks for $90, Erica wouldn't be interested in buying from Sam in the first place. But suppose that's not the case; suppose that Stephen is able to produce and sell steaks for $120 compared to Sam's $100. With free markets, of course, Erica would buy from Sam, and the two would split $100 of surplus. But when government imposes the $40 tax on Canadian buffalo steaks without levying a similar tax on U.S. steak, Erica is given an incentive to

---

[5]In fact, such a complete discussion can already be found in Douglas A. Irwin's magnificent nontechnical volume, *Against the Tide: An Intellectual History of Free Trade*, Princeton University Press, 1998.

[6]President Abraham Lincoln, in "Complete works of Abraham Lincoln."

buy from Stephen rather than Sam. And even though Erica is now buying American, note that the tariff forces her to pay a higher price.

Effects of a Tariff on Cooperative Surplus You might be wondering what's wrong with the picture painted in the preceding section. The problem is that exchange between Erica and Stephen creates less wealth than exchange between Erica and Sam. By purchasing steaks from Stephen instead of Sam, the cooperative surplus is reduced from $100 to $80. This lost surplus reflects the fact that for whatever reason, Sam is a more efficient buffalo producer than Stephen.

Recall that society's most basic economic problem is resolving the conflict between our unlimited wants and the limited resources available to fulfill those wants. Consequently, the best way to maximize our well-being is to produce the things that we want most by using the fewest inputs. Given this perspective, it's better for Sam to use $100 of resources to produce a carton of buffalo steaks than it is for Stephen to tie up $120 making essentially the same carton of steaks. It's the $20 difference between those two production costs that accounts for our lost surplus.

Tariffs and Deadweight Losses The $20 of lost surplus is really just the starting point when it comes to analyzing why the tariff makes the world a worse place rather than a better one. Suppose we add a second buyer, named Courtney, to our market. Courtney is willing to pay up to $115 to get a box of buffalo steaks. In a world where Courtney is free to trade with Sam, she walks away with some steaks, and the world gets $15 of surplus. But in a world with a tariff, the best price Courtney will be able to find will be $120. So instead of buying buffalo steaks, Courtney might buy a product she desires less, perhaps chicken. Of course, it's not because buffalo steak is so rare and delicious that Courtney can't afford it. Buffalo is entirely affordable to her, until the tariff pushes it out of reach. As a result, the total surplus generated in the world will be less than it could have been.

Courtney's dilemma should sound familiar to you because it is exactly the same type of problem you saw on page 106, when we discussed the deadweight loss of a tax. A tariff is simply a tax on imported goods, so it shouldn't surprise you that the lost surplus in Courtney's case is called the *deadweight loss of a tariff*.

So now we know two reasons a tariff on Canadian buffalo steak might be a bad thing:

1. The tariff encourages the less efficient domestic production of a product that can be produced more cost-effectively north of the border. The resources devoted to producing buffalo steak in the United States would be better employed producing a product more in line with America's comparative advantage.

2. The tariff encourages domestic consumers to substitute away from the now-more-expensive buffalo steak to second-best sources of protein, like chicken or fish.

For both of these reasons, the scarce and valued cooperative surplus that might have been never materializes.

Some Hidden Costs of a Tariff "But wait!" you might be saying. "You've been railing about how we shouldn't make arbitrary distinctions between Americans and Canadians, but that's how the world works. And the good news is that once we start identifying ourselves as U.S. citizens instead of global citizens, the tariff makes really good sense." Then you point out, in between waving the American flag and reciting the Pledge of Allegiance, that with free trade, the world gets $100 of surplus, but part of that surplus (let's say $50, if we're splitting it down the middle) is captured by Sam, a Canadian, who frankly you don't really care much about. But with restricted trade, Erica trades with Stephen, an American, and all $80 of the surplus is captured by Americans. Because it's better to get all of $80 than half of $100, America wins!

That reasoning sounds solid, right up to the moment when you remember that there are people in the economy besides just Sam, Erica, Stephen, and Courtney.

And those people are most definitely *not* helped by the tariff. They are unequivocally made worse off by it.

Who are these people we've forgotten to consider? Let's think about how trading across international borders works. In a world without money, products would be traded for other products. So, if we wanted to bring products in from a foreign country (we call those products **imports**), we would also have to send some products out to the foreign country in exchange (we call those products **exports**). In other words, we pay for our imports with our exports.

Adding money back into the picture does little to change the analysis. If Sam accepts U.S. dollars for his steaks, he's not going to be able to spend them in Calgary because Canada has its own currency. So if Sam is willing to accept U.S. dollars, it must be because he has some intention of spending those dollars in the United States—on U.S. goods. Perhaps Sam is planning to buy some U.S.-made replacement windows for his home. When he does, the U.S. window maker sees his exports to Canada increase. In other words, even when transactions are facilitated with money, we pay for our imports with our exports.

If we are paying for our imports with our exports, anything that reduces our imports, like tariffs do, reduces our exports, too. In other words, a tariff on buffalo steak might help domestic buffalo producers, but somewhere else in the economy, it has negative repercussions for, say, Americans who produce windows for installation in Canadian homes.

Ultimately, if we're going to account for the effects of a policy like the tariff, it's important to account for *all* the parties affected. It is fairly easy to measure the effect that a tariff on imported buffalo steak has on U.S. buffalo producers. It is much more difficult to measure the effect of the buffalo tariff on the exports of U.S. window makers and wheat farmers and software producers and all the other people who export products from the United States to Canada. Those effects are subtle and indirect: When a U.S. window maker sees his Canadian business evaporating, he has no way of discerning that the reason Canadians are not buying his windows is because the incomes of their buffalo producers are falling due to the U.S. buffalo tariff. Nevertheless, economists know that this damage exists, and with a little bit of advanced training, it's pretty easy to show that the losses to U.S. buffalo steak buyers and U.S. window makers outweigh the gains to the U.S. buffalo producer. In other words, the tariff unambiguously makes the United States worse off.

Accounting for those effects is difficult, but it's even harder when we consider the fact that the Canadians are unlikely to take the U.S. buffalo tariff lying down. The history of international trade relations tells us that the Canadians are likely to retaliate by imposing tariffs on imports from the United States. Perhaps Canadians slap a tariff on imports of U.S. motorcycles. Once we've accounted for the losses to U.S. consumers of buffalo steak, U.S. window makers, and U.S. motorcycle manufacturers, the gains from the tariff on Canadian buffalo steak look pretty small indeed.

Quotas

A tariff works to discourage competition from imports by making those imports appear more costly. But there is a more direct way to limit foreign competition. The government can simply set a limit on how many imported goods it will allow into the country. Such a limit is called a **quota**.

A quota is a very specific tool for limiting trade because it is imposed on both a particular product and also on a particular country. For example, if the United States wanted to limit competition from Sam's buffalo steaks, it might pass a law that says, "We will allow only 100 boxes of steaks to be imported to the United States from Canada." By contrast, once a tariff is set, it generally applies equally to all countries.

The effects of a quota are similar to the effects of a tariff. First, both a quota and a tariff tend to drive up prices. A tariff does this by adding a tax to the existing price;

Imports Products produced in a foreign country and sold domestically.

Exports Products produced domestically and sold in foreign countries.

Quota A limit on the number of imported goods allowed into the country.

Application 5.3

Chickens, Turkey, and the Transit Connect

The Ford Transit Connect is a compact, economical commercial delivery vehicle with surprising cargo capacity, thanks to its distinctively high roof. These features make it a dandy commercial vehicle for negotiating tight urban neighborhoods. Consequently, it's been a strong seller.

The story behind the Transit Connect highlights some of the hidden costs of restricting free trade. That story begins in Europe, half a century ago. Still recovering from World War II, the continent's agricultural sector was struggling.

Postwar advances in U.S. chicken-producing technology had created an abundance of chicken in the United States, so U.S. farmers began exporting chicken to Europe. Oddly, the European governments tried to stop them: After decades of wars, European nations had discovered that being dependent on imported food can backfire if your supplier decides to cut you off.

So, in the interest of maintaining their agricultural self-sufficiency, European nations encouraged their citizens to buy domestic chicken by levying high tariffs on chicken imports. As a result, U.S. chicken exports to Europe fell by 25%. How did the United States respond? With tariffs of its own, of course—on potato starch, dextrin, brandy, and light trucks—four products that came predominantly from the European nations that had taxed U.S. chicken. Those retaliatory tariffs became known as the "chicken tax."

Fifty years later, the European Union continues to restrict imports of U.S. agricultural products, and 50 years later, the United States continues to tax imported light trucks. This takes us to Turkey, where Transit Connects are made. The Transit Connects you see in the United States look very different than the ones that leave the factory in Turkey. *Those* Transit Connects have rear side windows and back seats. Once they arrive in the United States, their rear windows are removed and replaced with steel panels. Then the rear seats are removed and broken down for recycling.

Why would Ford do that? Because a vehicle designed to move cargo is subject to the 25% chicken tax. A vehicle designed to move people is not. So, when Transit Connects arrive with seats and windows, they are categorized as cars rather than light trucks, which reduces the tariff to a paltry 2.5%. It costs Ford hundreds of dollars to equip each vehicle with unneeded equipment, but it saves the company thousands of dollars in taxes.

So Ford buys raw materials and uses labor and energy to convert those materials into seats and windows. Then Ford hires more laborers to install those seats and windows, and it hires still more laborers to uninstall those seats and windows. Still other laborers convert the seats and windows back to raw materials. All that activity creates absolutely zero value: windows no one will look out of and seats no one will sit in. Every bit of that time, energy, equipment, and material is nothing but a pure cost to society—a cost that is hidden, but just as big, dollar for dollar, as what economists generally measure as deadweight loss.

See related problems 3.14 and 3.15 on page 117 at the end of this chapter.

Based on Matthew Dolan's "To Outfox the Chicken Tax, Ford Strips Its Own Vans," *Wall Street Journal Online*, September 23, 2009, and "Feds Watching: Ford's Run Around on 'Chicken Tax' Riles U.S. Customs Officials," *Car and Driver Online*, September 26, 2013.

a quota drives up prices by creating an artificial condition of scarcity. When prices increase because of a quota, some buyers forgo their purchases of buffalo steak in favor of less-desired alternatives. That creates deadweight loss. In this case, it's called the *deadweight loss of the quota*.

But quotas and tariffs differ in one key respect. Suppose a local college senior has asked Erica to cater a barbeque to celebrate his graduation. Erica knows that Sam's buffalo is the tastiest buffalo on the planet, and she vows never to settle for second best. If the United States protects its domestic buffalo ranchers by imposing a tariff, Sam's buffalo will always be available to Erica, as long as she is willing to pay the tax. But if the United States protects its domestic buffalo ranchers by establishing a quota, Erica might find herself out of luck. "I'm sorry, ma'am," the customs agent might tell her, "but we've already hit the quota limit on imported buffalo steak this year. No more steaks until January 1."

With a quota, no matter how much Erica is willing to pay, she will be unable to obtain Canadian buffalo steak. In that sense, quotas are more restrictive than tariffs. For exactly that reason, the **World Trade Organization (WTO)**, an international organization dedicated to reducing trade barriers between its 159 member nations, encourages those nations to replace quotas with tariffs wherever possible.

World Trade Organization (WTO) An international organization dedicated to reducing trade barriers between its member nations.

Conclusion

We began this chapter by discussing the Turbo Tap beer-pouring device. Let's end the chapter with it also. You might imagine that there are some people who simply won't like the Turbo Tap. An old-school bar owner who doesn't want to bear the expense of installing the Turbo Tap, for example, might be quite upset to see his customers leaving for other bars where the service is faster. It's not hard to picture him lobbying senators and representatives to pass laws to protect his business from the competition the new technology poses. Such laws would benefit old-school bar owners at the greater expense of everybody else.

Other businesses have a similar incentive to push for laws that limit competition, the most obvious of which are tariffs and quotas. Now that you understand how laws against Turbo Tap can make society a poorer place, you can see how laws that limit the free exchange of other products can make society a poorer place as well. Those laws are, in a sense, laws against found beer.

This chapter has shown how the pursuit of self-interest can create wealth for society and how government intervention into the process of free exchange can destroy wealth. There are, however, instances in which the pursuit of self-interest can destroy wealth. In those instances, well-crafted government policies have the potential to restore some of that wealth and make our world a better place. Much of the rest of this book is devoted to exploring those cases.

Chapter Summary and Problems

Key Terms

Absolute advantage, p. 100

Black market, p. 107

Comparative advantage, p. 100

Consumer surplus, p. 102

Cooperative surplus, p. 102

Deadweight loss, p. 106

Exports, p. 112

Imports, p. 112

Producer surplus, p. 102

Protectionism, p. 109

Quota, p. 112

Rent seeking, p. 107

Specialization, p. 99

Subsidy, p. 107

Tariffs, p. 110

Tax, p. 105

World Trade Organization (WTO), p. 114

Comparative Advantage, Exchange, and Wealth Creation, pages 99–105

Illustrate the process by which exchange creates wealth.

Summary

Specialization and trade help society to make the best use of its scarce resources. When people or countries direct effort toward producing things in which they have a comparative advantage, greater material wealth is created. The process of exchanging goods and services also creates wealth for both buyer and seller. The wealth that is created is called the cooperative surplus, and it is divided between consumer surplus (which is captured by buyers) and producer surplus (which is captured by sellers). The size of the cooperative surplus does not depend on the price buyers and sellers agree on but only the difference between how much the buyer values the item and how much the seller values the item.

Review Questions

All problems are assignable in MyEconLab.

1.1 If your opportunity cost of making ice cream is lower than your roommate's, you have a(n) _____ advantage in making ice cream.

1.2 If Richard can produce clocks in less time than Yvonne, then Richard has a(n) _____ advantage in clock-making.

1.3 _____ is the sum of all the net benefits received by the parties to a transaction.

1.4 Luke has a droid that he values at $500. Leia values the same droid at $750. Luke decides to sell the droid to Leia for $650. What is the total cooperative surplus gained as a result of this trade?
a. $250
b. $150
c. $100
d. $50

1.5 In problem 1.4, the amount Leia gains from the transaction is called _____.
a. Producer surplus
b. Consumer surplus
c. Cooperative surplus
d. Deadweight loss

1.6 In problem 1.4, if the price Luke and Leia set had been $50 higher ($700 instead of $650), the cooperative surplus would _____.
a. Increase by $50
b. Decrease by $50
c. Remain unchanged
d. Disappear

1.7 If you have an absolute advantage in making violins, _____.
a. You must also have a comparative advantage in making violins
b. You cannot have a comparative advantage in making violins
c. You may or may not have a comparative advantage in making violins

Problems and Applications

1.8 Why is specialization an essential ingredient in the process of exchange? How do specialization and exchange work together to make society wealthier?

1.9 Will a trade occur if one party believes that the trade will make him or her worse off? If a trade occurs, and later one party believes that he or she has become worse off, what might have happened?

1.10 [Related to Application 5.1 on page 103] Some U.S. wine producers might be very concerned about falling wine prices. If U.S. wine producers were to lobby the government for a law that would restrict imports of wine, what arguments against the law should politicians consider?

1.11 It takes Bill 3 hours to write an essay and 6 hours to compose a song. It takes Susie 1 hour to write an essay and 3 hours to compose a song. Determine who has a comparative advantage in writing songs. Then verify that the other person has a comparative advantage in writing essays. If Bill and Susie were to specialize and exchange with one another, who should write songs?

Restrictions on Free Exchange, pages 105–109

Explain how restricting free exchange creates deadweight losses.

Summary

Various government policies disrupt the free exchange of goods and services. Adding a tax to the sale of a product may raise the price and discourage some buyers. The opportunity loss the tax creates is called a deadweight loss. Subsidizing the purchase of a product may also cause deadweight losses by convincing buyers who don't value the product as highly as sellers to purchase it anyway. Other governmental barriers to completing transactions, such as restrictions on the number of people allowed to sell a product, reduce the number of exchanges and cause deadweight losses. Sometimes these policies are the political result of rent-seeking behavior by buyers or sellers in an industry.

Review Questions

All problems are assignable in MyEconLab.

2.1 _____ is surplus value that is lost because something is keeping the market from functioning as well as it could.

2.2 Attempting to influence the law for private economic advantage is a tactic economists call _____.

2.3 In problem 1.4, if government imposed a $200 tax on the sale of droids, _____.

 a. Luke and Leia would not be able to complete a bargain

 b. Luke and Leia would still be able to complete a bargain

 c. The tax would cause a deadweight loss of $250

 d. Both b and c are true.

2.4 In problem 1.4, if government imposed a $300 tax on the sale of droids, _____.

 a. Luke and Leia would not be able to complete a bargain

 b. Luke and Leia would still be able to complete a bargain

 c. The tax would cause a deadweight loss of $250

 d. Both (a) and (c) are true.

2.5 A subsidy is the opposite of a tax. When a government taxes the sale of avocados, cooperative surplus decreases, and society gets poorer. Therefore, when a government subsidizes the sale of avocados, _____.

 a. Cooperative surplus increases, and society gets richer

 b. Cooperative surplus decreases, and society gets poorer

 c. Cooperative surplus increases, but society gets poorer

 d. Cooperative surplus doesn't change, but society gets richer

Problems and Applications

2.6 Describe the potential negative effects of an additional tax on the sale of swords within the United States.

2.7 Harry has a decorative sword that he values at $150. Tom is looking for a similar sword but is interested in paying only up to $125. Will a trade between these two occur? Is there a policy government could implement that would encourage a trade to occur between Harry and Tom? If so, does that policy make society richer?

2.8 Suppose that the government decides to impose a heavy tax on the sale of milk. Explain why a black market in milk is likely to form. Is that black market bad for society? Explain your answer.

2.9 [Related to Application 5.2 on page 108] Read Application 5.2 carefully. Explain why one might be skeptical of Bob Odom's claim that "If [flower arrangers] can't . . . pass the exam, how can they do an arrangement that you and I want to buy?"

2.10 [Related to Application 5.2 on page 108] Do you believe that consumers benefit from the protection of the licensure for florists? What are some examples of licensures, besides those for doctors or lawyers, that you believe *do* benefit consumers? Why? Can you name a profession where you don't think licensing is necessary? Explain why.

2.11 After Hurricane Sandy ravaged the east coast, some New Jersey hardware stores doubled their prices on portable generators. That violated the state's anti-gouging laws, which prohibit raising prices more than 10% in an emergency. Why do you think prices rose so high? Were hardware stores exploiting buyers?

5.3 International Trade and Not-So-Free Exchange, pages 109–114

Describe the direct and indirect consequences of restricting international trade.

Summary

Governments often tax the sale of goods produced in other countries (a tariff) or limit the number of goods that can be imported (a quota). Both tariffs and quotas may appear to create wealth for the country that imposes them. But because tariffs and quotas raise prices for both imported and domestic goods, and because both tariffs and quotas end up reducing the ability of foreign countries to buy the domestic country's exports, they actually create deadweight losses and destroy wealth. Further, imposing tariffs or quotas may prompt retaliation by foreign countries, which further reduces the domestic country's ability to export.

Review Questions

All problems are assignable in MyEconLab.

3.1 A _____ is a tax on imported goods.

3.2 Goods brought into our country from a foreign country are called _____, and goods that are sent to foreign countries in exchange are called _____.

3.3 A limit set by a country on how many imported goods it will allow into the country is called a(n) _____.

3.4 Policies designed to help domestic producers by making imported goods more costly or difficult to obtain are commonly referred to as _____ policies.

3.5 In 2002, then-President George Bush placed a tax on imported steel, which was lifted in 2003. A tax on imported goods is called a(n) _____.
   a. Deadweight loss
   b. Tariff
   c. Quota
   d. Export

3.6 It is clear that to produce the maximum material comfort for its citizens, a nation needs to _____.
   a. Strive for self-sufficiency
   b. Specialize in producing something that it is relatively good at producing
   c. Limit competition from the products of foreign nations
   d. Subsidize the sale of lots of goods and services

3.7 In 2002, steel industry lobbyists and auto industry lobbyists pressured then-President George Bush and Congress for the highest possible tariffs on imported steel. In response, President Bush and Congress imposed stiff tariffs on steel. This type of behavior, in which individuals, industry lobbyists, or other special interest groups attempt to influence law for their own economic advantage, is called _____.
   a. Rent seeking
   b. Deadweight loss
   c. Quota renting
   d. Export enhancement

3.8 In problem 3.7, the loss that is associated with fewer transactions occurring because of the tariff is called the _____.
   a. Sunk cost of the tariff
   b. Quota rent
   c. Export opportunity cost
   d. Deadweight loss

3.9 An American painter sells to an individual in Italy one of his paintings of the Mississippi river at dusk. To Americans, the painting is a(n) _____.
   a. Deadweight loss
   b. Import
   c. Quota
   d. Export

3.10 If the same American painter as in problem 3.9 purchases his art supplies from an Italian wholesale art supply shop that ships supplies globally, those art supplies are _____.
   a. Deadweight losses
   b. Tariffs
   c. Exports
   d. None of the above

3.11 The U.S. government determines that the number of avocados imported to the United States from other countries is severely affecting California avocado farmers. It decides to limit the number of foreign-grown avocados. Such a restriction is called a(n) _____.
   a. Quota
   b. Negative surplus
   c. Import enhancement
   d. Tariff

3.12 The restriction in problem 3.11 prevents many transactions from occurring. The opportunity loss associated with this restriction is called _____.
   a. Deadweight loss
   b. Negative surplus
   c. Rent-seeking
   d. National surplus

Problems and Applications

3.13 Explain three ways in which imposing a tariff on imported goods may reduce a country's overall economic well-being.

3.14 **[Related to Application 5.3 on page 113]** Read Application 5.3 carefully. Why did Europe initially place a tariff on chickens? How did the United States respond? Do you suppose the original tariff on U.S. chicken was good or bad for Europe? Explain.

3.15 **[Related to Application 5.3 on page 113]** Describe the process that Ford undertakes to avoid paying the chicken tax. Offer one reason Ford's efforts might be good for society. Then give one reason that Ford's efforts are bad for society. Do you think Ford is doing something underhanded in the way it brings in Transit Connects? Explain.

3.16 Discuss an example of a good or service that you use that has been impacted by a tax, tariff, or quota. Why was the tax, tariff, or quota implemented?

The Gains-from-Trade Game

This chapter highlighted the potential for trade to make society richer and happier. Today, you'll get the chance to measure those gains for yourself.

At the beginning of this activity, your instructor will give you a brown paper bag containing a snack. The snack is yours to keep if you wish. Please rate how happy you are with your snack on a scale of 0 to 10, with 0 meaning "No happiness at all," and 10 meaning "Wow! This is perfect! I've been craving one of these for weeks!"

Other students in your class have different snacks. You have the option to trade your snack with any other student.

In fact, you may trade the snacks as many times as you wish. If you choose to trade, rate the snack you end up with on a scale of 0 to 10. Your instructor will help quantify the increase in happiness that your class experiences because of trade. Once that's done, your snack is yours to enjoy!

MyEconLab

Please visit http://www.myeconlab.com for support material to conduct this experiment if assigned by your instructor.

The Market System: Functions, Structure, and Institutions

Chapter Outline and Learning Objectives

6.1 The Market System: Its Functions and Structure, page 120

Define *market* and compare the four market structures.

6.2 The Four Functions of Prices in the Market System, page 122

Summarize the four key functions of prices.

6.3 The Foundations of Well-Functioning Markets: A Role for Government, page 124

Explain how government action can improve the functioning of markets.

6.4 Connecting Effort and Reward: An Illustration, page 132

Compare and contrast the incentives for productivity and creativity created by private property and by common property.

Experiment: Capitalism and Communism Games, page 140

MyEconLab

MyEconLab helps you master each objective and study more efficiently.

The free exchange of goods and services described in the previous chapter generally results in wealth creation. But those exchanges don't happen in a vacuum: They take place in the context of various markets—from your local farmers' market to the global food market to the electronic market in financial assets. In this chapter, you'll compare and contrast some of the key characteristics of different markets, and you'll learn about some of the subtle but important functions of markets. The chapter gives special attention to one key piece of information markets produce: prices.

Some markets move goods and services between buyers and sellers more easily and create more wealth for society than other markets. In this chapter, you'll explore some of the factors that contribute to well-functioning markets and learn some of the ways that individuals and governments can improve the performance of markets.

The Market System: Its Functions and Structure

When we talk about the people who want to buy and sell a particular item, we often refer to them collectively as *the market* for that item. The term **market** generally refers to a forum where buyers and sellers go to conduct transactions. Sometimes the market is centralized in a particular place; for example, most of the world's rough diamonds are sold in Antwerp, Belgium. Sometimes the market is not centralized; for example, although rough diamonds are primarily sold in Antwerp, you can buy polished diamonds at your local mall and thousands of other locations around the globe. Sometimes the market is a virtual space: If you want to buy a polished diamond from a reputable seller on the Internet, you can do that, too.

Markets Are More Than Places to Trade

In whatever form they appear, markets do much more than just facilitate trade. In modern market-based economies, they actually determine what is going to be produced and what is not. If music lovers want a little bit more of Justin Bieber and a little bit less of Britney Spears, they communicate their wishes to Justin and Britney via markets. Justin sees his music sales climb, so he spends more time in the studio recording new songs and less time playing video games. Britney, by contrast, gets a different message from the marketplace. Faced with the prospect of spending an enormous amount of time recording songs likely to face lackluster sales, Britney redirects her energy toward something society would rather see from its aging performing artists: She begins performing a live show at Las Vegas's Planet Hollywood. In other words, led by the lure of profits, producers devote their efforts to producing things consumers want most. Economists call this phenomenon the principle of **consumer sovereignty**, which literally means that buyers are king.

Consumer sovereignty The idea that in the market system, consumers ultimately decide which goods and services firms will produce.

Of course, even kings can't defy the laws of scarcity. If buyers want cars that perform like a Ferrari and are priced like a Kia, they are not going to find many, if any, to buy. Only when consumers are willing to pay for all the resources embodied in a product (and, producers hope, maybe a bit more besides) will sellers rise to the challenge of giving buyers what they want.

Market Structures

In the market system, the sellers' side of the market consists of one or more business firms. Each firm has to make two important decisions: what quantity to produce and what price to charge. If the firm can find the ideal answer to those questions, it will earn the greatest possible *profits*—the difference between what the firm receives for the products it sells and the cost of producing those products. Economists refer to identifying the ideal combination of price and quantity as *profit maximization*.

Economists often classify markets for various goods and services by their *market structure*, or *industry structure*, which accounts for how many sellers there are in the market and how those sellers compete with one another. The number of sellers and the degree of competition on the sellers' side of the market is interesting because the number of competitors in an industry greatly influences how the sellers behave—how much they offer for sale and the price they charge. So the market structure has implications for the amount of profit each firm in an industry can earn, and as you will see in Section 6.3, it also has implications for the overall economic well-being of society.

Monopoly At one extreme, some markets have only one seller, and there is no close substitute for the product being sold. Those markets are called **monopolies**. Suppose, for example, that you are desperate to buy a self-balancing two-wheeled electric personal transporter. You've really got only one option—the Segway—so that particular market is classified as a monopoly.

> **Monopoly** A market where there is only one seller, and there is no close substitute for the product being sold.

Perfect Competition There is an opposite extreme to the monopoly market. Consider the U.S. wheat market, where about 200,000 farms produce a virtually identical product. Those farmers operate in a market characterized by **perfect competition**, a market with many sellers who all sell an identical product.

> **Perfect competition** A market with many sellers who all sell an identical product.

Monopolistic Competition Monopoly and perfect competition lie at opposite extremes of a competitive spectrum—from no competition at all to lots of competition. But other market structures—more competitive than monopolies but less competitive than perfect competition—lie between them. Consider the market for shoes. Hundreds of companies produce shoes, so the industry is pretty competitive. Those shoe producers compete with one another on price, but they also compete by trying to offer styles, colors, and other features that their competitors do not. A market structured like this, with many sellers offering *differentiated products*, is called **monopolistic competition**.

> **Monopolistic competition** A market with many sellers offering differentiated products.

Oligopoly Further toward monopoly's end of the spectrum, there are some industries where only a few sellers compete with one another, offering identical or differentiated products. Industries that are dominated by a limited number of producers are called **oligopolies**. If you have a cellular phone, you've probably done business with an oligopolist because almost 90% of all wireless service in the United States comes from one of four big companies: Sprint, AT&T, T-Mobile, or Verizon.

> **Oligopoly** A market dominated by a few large sellers, offering identical or differentiated products.

The basic features of the four different market structures are summarized in Table 6.1:

Table 6.1 The Four Major Market Structures

This table summarizes the four basic types of market structure, ranging from the least competitive (monopoly) to the most competitive (perfect competition).

Market Structure	Number of Sellers	Type of Product	Examples
Monopoly	One	No close substitutes for the product	• Utilities like your local cable and power companies • Major League Baseball
Oligopoly	A few	Identical or differentiated products that are close substitutes	• Tobacco (3 companies: R.J. Reynolds, Philip Morris, Lorillard) • Car batteries (3 companies: Exide, Johnson Controls, Delphi) • Game consoles (3 companies: Sony, Nintendo, Microsoft)
Monopolistic competition	Many	Differentiated product	• Restaurants • Colleges and universities • Clothing
Perfect competition	Very many	Identical product	• Corn • Coal • Rice

6.2 Learning Objective

Summarize the four key functions of prices.

The Four Functions of Prices in the Market System

When you think about it, the implications of markets are astonishing. The decisions about what and how much society will produce are being made, simultaneously, by millions of buyers and millions of sellers around the world. Buyers are telling sellers what items they desire, and sellers are informing buyers about the scarcity of the resources needed to satisfy those desires. And all these messages are being sent through the subtle signals communicated by prices.

Measuring Desire

Prices, in part, reflect the desire buyers have for a product. If markets are left to their own devices, the more a good or service is desired by buyers, the higher its price will be. This is why bluefin tuna, which is used in the finest sashimi, sells for over $500 per pound but bottom-feeding carp sells for pennies. Of course, the prices for products change as our desires for them change. If the surgeon general suddenly announces that eating carp fillet once a week will prevent male-pattern baldness, you can bet that more people will be shopping for the lowly bottom-feeder—and you can watch carp's price rise in response.

Reflecting Scarcity

Prices also reflect scarcity. The more scarce or rare something is, the higher its price is likely to be. This is why pure carbon in the form of diamonds sells for a much higher price than pure carbon in the form of graphite used to make pencils. The high price of diamond engagement rings doesn't mean they are more useful than pencils. In fact, you might argue just the opposite—that far more use has been derived from pencils than will ever be derived from a diamond ring. In other words, the price difference between the two products isn't due to differences in their usefulness; it stems from the fact that graphite is plentiful, and diamonds are not.

Together, the forces of scarcity and consumer desire determine the prices of goods and services. Something that is quite rare but not particularly desired by anyone probably won't sell for much: Floppy disks for storing computer files are hard to find on store shelves, but they are also dirt cheap when you find them, simply because few people ever use them. And things that are incredibly useful and highly desired are likely to be cheap if they are also relatively abundant: Water isn't cheap because we don't want it; it's cheap because it's easy to come by. On the other hand, things that are both exceptionally hard to come by and strongly desired—like uranium, autographed Babe Ruth baseball cards, and the ability to throw a 98 mph fastball to a target the size of a teacup—are likely to command high prices in the marketplace.

A Means of Communication

Prices serve as the means of communication between buyers and sellers. Suppose that a new all-carb diet increases consumers' desire for bread. Producers, of course, are initially unaware of this increased desire and go on baking just as much bread as before. Because of that, buyers aren't finding as much bread as they want.

How can consumers tell producers that they need to bake more bread? Do they need to pick up the phone and call Wonder Bread's CEO? As it turns out, they don't. When markets function well, that message gets communicated automatically. With less bread on store shelves than consumers want, buyers fight to obtain the loaves that are available. They don't, however, generally fight with fists, guns, or knives; they fight with their wallets, trying to outbid one another to lay hands on a loaf. As competition among consumers heats up, Wonder's CEO sees bread prices rise and says to himself, "Wow! Bread prices are soaring. There's more money to be made now than there was last week. I'd better add a third shift." That, of course, is *exactly* what consumers wanted all along—more bread! And the price system delivered that message quickly and accurately.

The price system also helps sellers deliver messages to buyers. Suppose a bad wheat harvest makes flour difficult and costly to obtain. As a result, bread bakers can't produce bread as profitably. They'd like to tell their buyers, "Hey, I'm sorry, but the ingredients I need are getting harder to find. I can't give you as much as you want. Why don't you have some rice cakes instead?"

That very message gets communicated through the price system. As making bread becomes less profitable (because the cost of the ingredients has gone up), bakers cut production. Bread becomes more scarce, and that drives up its price. Consumers respond by buying less bread, perhaps eating rice or potatoes instead.

The price system, then, communicates information about consumers' desires to producers, and it communicates information about scarcity (how hard or costly it is to actually make a product) from producers to consumers. The outcome of this two-way communication is impressive: If there's not enough bread to satisfy consumers, they bid the price up, and producers respond by making more. If there's too much bread, and consumers don't want it all, producers cut prices until the day's production gets snapped up by consumers. In the end, producers end up delivering consumers as much bread as they want at a price sufficient to pay for the resources that go into every loaf.[1]

And consumers *do* get as much bread as they want. After all, how many times have you gone shopping for a loaf of bread in the United States and not found one? Probably not often, if ever. Yet nobody is in charge of deciding how much bread to make every week. Nobody tells producers where to send it. There is no bread czar or committee of people making these decisions. Instead, it happens automatically, with the help of messages communicated by prices.

Coordinating Production Decisions

Just as there is no bread czar who decides how much bread to make, there is no bread czar who helps ensure that all the necessary resources are in the right place when it's time to bake that bread. And bread production is enormously complicated. Think about it: To make bread, producers need the right amount of wheat. And to produce the right amount of wheat, farmers need the right amount of seed, land, fertilizer, and equipment to plant the wheat and harvest it. To make the equipment, the right set of engineering skills, steel, rubber, aluminum, glass, and a thousand other materials need to be produced. Once the wheat is grown, it has to be milled into flour, using even more specialized equipment, and then it has to be combined with other ingredients that are just as hard to make as the wheat was.

If you left it up to one person to make sure that all the things needed to make bread were in the right places at the right times and in the right amounts, you might have to eat your peanut butter straight out of the jar because you wouldn't have any bread to spread it on. Putting all those pieces together would be like completing a million-piece jigsaw puzzle. In the former communist economies of Eastern Europe, the government planned and coordinated the production of bread. The result was frequent shortages that often forced people to stand in line for hours to get bread. If they were too late to get in line, they found only empty shelves.

But markets are able to accomplish what individuals cannot. Prices communicated at each stage of production enable the right resources to be put in the right places at the right times. Farmers, by looking at the prices they can earn growing various crops, decide to plant more land in wheat and less in corn. Equipment manufacturers, by monitoring prices, know almost instinctively whether they should be producing wheat-harvesting equipment or whether they need to be ramping up production of soybean pickers. At every step in the process, prices coordinate production with an accuracy and efficiency that no individual could hope to duplicate.[2]

---

[1]The process by which this happens is described in greater detail in the appendix to Chapter 1.

[2]Leonard Read's essay "I, Pencil" is a delightful description of how the price system coordinates production. It can be found in its entirety at www.econlib.org.

Economic growth An increase in the total value of the goods and services an economy produces each year.

Institutions The ground rules, customs, and conventions that govern the behavior of market participants.

Competition A market condition in which buyers and sellers are free to choose with whom to complete their transactions.

The Foundations of Well-Functioning Markets: A Role for Government

To a greater or lesser extent, most societies have chosen to rely on the market system to help meet their material needs. The market system has proven to be remarkably effective at creating a great deal of material satisfaction from scarce resources. Further, the market system has done a remarkable job encouraging long-term economic growth. **Economic growth** means that the total value of goods and services that an economy produces each year rises over time. That can happen because the economy is producing more of the same things or because the economy is producing more valuable things. Economic growth is important because, in a world with a growing population, the only way to improve a nation's standard of living is for the economy to grow. (Measuring the productive capacity and growth of the economy as a whole is discussed in Chapter 16.)

Although the market system is capable of doing amazing things, markets work well only if they are well-structured. The ground rules, customs, and conventions that govern the behavior of market participants are often referred to as **institutions**. Without good institutions, the markets for many products would function poorly or wouldn't exist. Poor ground rules limit the ability of markets to create wealth for society and can stifle economic growth.

In settings where there are small numbers of market participants, or where the participants have repeated contact with one another, people are often able to establish functional ground rules for themselves. However, when markets get larger and more complex, and in cases where market participants don't come together often enough to establish long-term relationships, it may be harder to agree on and enforce the rules of acceptable market behavior. In those instances, government—be it the federal government, city hall, or tribal elders—can help provide a framework to improve the functioning of markets.

Exactly what ground rules can government establish to help markets function well?

Competition

Competition is the first ground rule for a well-functioning market. **Competition** simply means that buyers and sellers are free to choose with whom to complete their transactions. Let's consider the buyer's side of a transaction for a moment, to show why competition is such a vital component of a well-functioning market: A tornado has ripped through Gunnar's hometown, and he wants a chainsaw to clean up the damage to his trees. He's got $300 to spend, which he takes to Mac, a chainsaw maker. Mac is able to make a chainsaw for $200.

If Mac is the only chainsaw producer, Gunnar has little choice but to deal with him. They sit down and begin to bargain with one another, but Mac knows that he's got Gunnar over a barrel. "Your yard is a wreck, Gunnar. If you don't clean up those fallen trees, the city council is going to write you a citation. I've got a chainsaw to sell you, and I'm the only game in town. That'll be $300 please." In other words, Mac is trying to capture as much of the cooperative surplus as he can and leave little, if anything, for Gunnar.

Gunnar truly doesn't have much power in this situation. Gunnar and Mac may hem and haw and threaten and cajole one another, but in the end, the odds are in Mac's favor. The balance of power, however, gets tilted a bit if we simply add one more seller of chainsaws to the community. "I couldn't help but overhear your conversation," Andreas says, pulling up to the curb in a U-Haul van. "I'm just moving in, and as it turns out, I make chainsaws, too." Andreas, however, is not quite as efficient as Mac: It costs Andreas $220 to make a chainsaw.

"Ooooooh," Gunnar says. "Mac has offered to sell me a chainsaw for $300. Do you think you could do better than that?" And because all Andreas has to do is cover his cost of making the saw, he comes back with an offer of $280. Gunnar, of course,

Application 6.1

Enforcing Honesty in India: Justice Delayed and Justice Denied

A long time ago in a land far away, Abdul Waheed sued his neighbor, Mohammed Nanhe. The year was 1961, the land was India, and the dispute was over two drains Nanhe had built into a wall between their properties. The drains diverted rainwater over ground where Waheed planned to build an addition to his house. In monsoon-prone India, Nanhe's drains put an end to Waheed's plans.

In 1963, the courts decided in Waheed's favor. But Nanhe appealed, and while the case was under review, the drains remained. Hearing after hearing was delayed, and 36 years later, the case was still undecided. By 2000, Nanhe and Waheed were dead, but the case lived on, inherited by their children.

One key ingredient for markets to work well is honesty. The courts play a key role in the economy by making people live up to their promises. By most accounts, the Indian court system is reasonably fair—but it's very slow. In 2010, *The Times of India* reported that if no new cases were filed, the Indian judicial system would take 320 years to clear its backlog.

Part of the problem is a shortage of judges. The United States has five times the number of judges per capita as India. Indians also disproportionately request jury trials that can be maddeningly slow.

Poor-quality lawyers and antiquated administrative systems are another reason the Indian court system is so slow. In India, getting into law school is easy. If your test scores are too low to study business, you become a lawyer. Lawyers are poor, so they often operate out of open stalls and type legal forms on typewriters. They often fail to show up for hearings, so the petitioners attend out of fear that judges will dismiss their cases. Meanwhile, court clerks, low-level officials responsible for setting the schedule for hearings, actively solicit bribes from petitioners. If you don't pay, you remain at the back of the queue.

Without a justice system to keep people honest, without adequate legal recourse to resolve disputes and help establish trust, the wheels of commerce turn far more slowly than they should. That may help explain why economic growth in India was stagnant for much of the past half-century: India has a rich culture, amazing natural resources, and a disciplined and educated labor pool. Yet the typical Indian earns only $1,500 per year. Economists attribute much of this stagnation to a cumbersome bureaucracy that makes commerce difficult. That bureaucracy includes the courts: Doing business in a place where labor or contract disputes may take decades to resolve isn't very appealing.

One notable symptom of poor institutions is brain drain: Many of India's most talented people move to countries where doing business is easier. There they thrive. As Nobel Prize–winning economist Milton Friedman once observed, "Indians do well everywhere, except in India."

See related problem 3.24 on page 138 at the end of this chapter.

Based on "In India, the Wheels of Justice Hardly Move," *New York Times*, June 1, 2000; "Courts Will Take 320 Years to Clear Backlog Cases: Justice Rao," *The Times of India*, March 6, 2010; and NBCNews.com's "Report: India Court 466 Years Behind Schedule," February 12, 2009.

their payment obligations. In small communities, the threat of social ostracism may be sufficiently large to convince people to be honest. In larger and more complex markets, however, those measures may not be adequate.

The government can create formal institutions that encourage buyers and sellers to live up to their promises. Contract laws penalize people for failing to deliver on their end of a bargain. However, laws are only as good as the procedures by which they are enforced. To enforce them, the government also needs a well-functioning court system that allows injured parties to seek redress.

What's really interesting about contract laws and their enforcement via courts is that they discourage people from reneging on their promises in the first place. People don't make their house payment every month because it's fun. They do so because they know that if they don't, legal procedures exist by which their homes can be taken from them.

Similarly, people who sell products online could easily take your money and never send you what you've ordered. However, the threat of your suing them is sufficient to make such behavior unprofitable. It is because of this that you're willing to give them your money in the first place. Without a set of legal institutions to discourage dishonesty, far fewer people would risk exchanging goods and services with one another. Many transactions, and the wealth they create, would disappear. In other words, laws and courts make markets work more effectively and society richer.

Information

So now you know that both competition and honesty are key to the efficient functioning of markets and that government can help ensure that both of these exist. However, markets require more than just these two elements to function well. A third crucial element is information.

In a well-functioning market, information flows smoothly between market participants. Information helps grease the wheels of markets by letting buyers know the options available to them. Those people who remember the time B.I. (Before the Internet) are really in a terrific position to understand how valuable information is. If you were interested in building a collection of vintage lightning rods B.I., you had to resign yourself to an endless search of antique stores, architectural salvage firms, and flea markets to build your collection. Sometimes you'd get lucky and find what you were looking for, but most of the time, you'd strike out, and your time and efforts would be wasted.

If you want to buy a lightning rod today, rather than travel to 17 antiques dealers in Hartford, Connecticut, where you might be lucky to find one or two lightning rods for sale, you can search eBay and in 5 minutes find hundreds of lightning rods. Or you can visit hundreds of antiques dealers online that sell them. Likewise, the Internet has made it easy for someone who runs across an old lightning rod in the attic of her house to find people around the world who are interested in purchasing it. By reducing the time and effort buyers and sellers spend searching for one another, the Internet and other institutions that increase the information available to buyers and sellers have made completing transactions easier.

The contributions to our well-being that come as a result of the Internet and other information-enhancing devices like the phone and the television are fairly obvious. But information facilitates exchange in one other important way: Information fosters competition, which you'll remember is one of the key ingredients in a well-performing market. We saw this just a moment ago, when we talked about lightning rods. Increased information gives the buyers of lightning rods more options, which means they have more power when negotiating with sellers: "Hey, you, dealer in vintage lightning rods: Even though you have in your possession an extremely rare Electra Amber lightning rod, I think you're asking too much for it. I know of a guy in Uzbekistan who has one for sale, so I'll see if I can cut a deal with him. If he won't give me a better price, then I'll simply buy the really neat OLR Co. lightning rod that I saw for sale instead."

Likewise, increased information gives sellers more negotiating power by exposing their products to more potential buyers. A seller of a highly sought-after lightning rod doesn't have to accept the first offer that comes along. She can simply say, "Thanks to the power of the Internet, I know of dozens of people trying to buy this choice rod. So take your lowball offer and don't let the door hit you in the backside on your way out."

Sometimes there is a cost to obtaining information. When there is, even if competition exists, the market won't function as well. Economist John McMillan, formerly of Stanford University, offers the example of an open-air marketplace like you might find in Mexico. In the marketplace, sellers are lined up in stalls and trying to earn your business. Suppose you're looking for a carving of an eagle, and you're willing to pay up to $10 to get one. Let's further suppose that every seller happens to be selling identical eagle carvings. Finally, assume that the cost of the materials and labor needed to make each eagle is $5.

If there were only one vendor selling eagles, you would likely pay a high price, right up to $10, which is the most you are willing to pay. On the other hand, if there were lots of competition (if there were lots of eagle sellers), and you had perfect and free information about what every seller was charging, you would have a great deal of bargaining power. Each merchant, knowing she could earn your business by under-cutting her rivals, drops her price. Eventually, rival merchants cut prices until it is no longer profitable to cut them any further. In the end, every merchant would charge $5, an amount just sufficient to cover her costs.

But when obtaining information is costly, competition is less effective at forcing prices down. Suppose, for example, that it costs you 10 cents' worth of effort to stop at a merchant's stall to ascertain her price. If there are 100 merchants, then even if you know that one of them (but not *which* one of them) is charging only $5, whereas everyone else is charging $10, it doesn't pay for you to try to find the lowest-price merchant.[5] Knowing that nobody will seek out price cutters under those circumstances, each merchant decides not to lower her price. Competition disappears, and the economic pie shrinks as a consequence.

It is often in both buyers' and sellers' interests to make information easily available. In the example above, the one seller offering eagles for $5 can gain a competitive edge on her rivals if she can make her low price known to consumers. So that seller may advertise her prices, which benefits both her and eagle-buying consumers. Sellers may offer more than just information about prices; they may also offer information about quality. Of course, making that information credible can be challenging. One way to do it is to let buyers weigh in: People who purchase items from Amazon.com and eBay.com can rate both the product and their experience with the seller. Another way is for sellers to have an independent and neutral party evaluate the quality of their product: Manufacturers of electrical devices, for example, often voluntarily have their appliances evaluated for safety by Underwriters Laboratories (UL), an impartial and independent consulting firm.

What is the government's role when it comes to information? To increase the rewards of a market system, the government can take steps to reduce the cost of obtaining information. Sometimes the government takes steps to improve the technology by which information is dispersed. The government, for example, was instrumental in developing and supporting the technological framework that the Internet was built on. In other cases, the government intervenes to improve the availability of information by requiring sellers to make that information public. By requiring publicly traded corporations to file financial reports with the U.S. Securities and Exchange Commission, the government makes information about the financial condition of these corporations available to people who might want to lend the firms money or buy shares of their stock. Finally, government helps ensure the *quality* of the information consumers receive. It does this by enforcing truth-in-advertising standards, by requiring business firms to undergo routine audits of their financial condition, by publishing the academic performance of schools that parents might want their children to attend, and by using a thousand other tactics. The government, by lubricating the flow of

---

[5] On average, you will find the low-cost seller on the 50th try. By then, you will have spent $5 worth of effort (10 cents × 50 vendors) trying to find that seller. In the end, it's just as cheap for you to pay the $10 asked by the first vendor.

information between producers and buyers, helps society gain the benefits of a well-functioning market system.

Property Rights

The fourth key ingredient we need before the market can bake the biggest and best economic pie possible is private property. Markets rely on transactions that result in the transfer of property from one party to another. If it is illegal to own something, then it follows that it will be problematic to try to buy, possess, or sell it. This doesn't mean that a market for the product doesn't exist. There are markets—albeit black markets—for crack cocaine and sexual services. But those markets are stunted versions of the markets that would exist if the ownership of those products were legal.

"Fine," you are probably thinking. "So the government has outlawed crack and sex for hire. You're going to have a hard time convincing me that the world is worse off for it." You may be right. But there are lots of places in the world where people are not permitted to own, buy, or sell things much more mundane. Consider **communism**, a form of economic and social organization in which all property is held *in common*—that is, everything is owned by society as a whole, and nothing is owned by any individual.[6] In strict communist countries, people are forbidden to own their own homes; they have to live where the government tells them to live, even if they don't like it. People in communist countries are also generally forbidden to own their own productive resources; that is, they can't open a business or produce things for profit. Nor do they control their own labor; in China, for example, children who display talent in gymnastics are taken from their homes very early in life and sent to grueling government training camps. Under communism, everybody works for the government, doing whatever the government tells them to do—whether it matches their abilities or not. In other words, in communist societies, true markets don't exist.

Contrast communism to **capitalism**, a form of economic organization in which productive resources are privately owned by individuals (or by groups of individuals, such as partnerships and corporations). That private ownership gives people economic freedom: In capitalist systems, individuals are free to own factories, stores, and farms. They are free to produce and sell whatever they want, as long as they can find someone willing to buy it, and they are free to keep any profits they earn. Of course, most people don't own farms or stores or factories, but they still own and control a productive resource—their ability to work, which economists call *labor services*. In a capitalist system, they are free to sell those labor services to anyone who is willing to buy them. In other words, capitalism is based on a market system, with private property as its foundation.

A third system, **socialism**, is generally regarded as a hybrid of capitalism and communism. In a true socialist economy, individuals are allowed to own private property, but the government owns and operates the means of production (factories, farms, businesses, etc.).

Economists call the right to own or control a resource a **property right**. A property right to a resource generally allows a person to use and earn income from that resource. Further, property rights are generally transferrable: A person can give control of that property to someone else if he wishes. Property rights can be informal and implicit; for example, it is understood that you are not supposed to use your roommate's pillow. Often, however, property rights are explicitly defined by government through regulation or legislation.

Once established, property rights must be enforced in order to have value. Few people, for example, will want to buy cars if the government doesn't ever pursue or punish car thieves. Even worse is when the government changes its mind about

Communism A form of economic and social organization in which all property is held in common, and the government decides what to produce and how to distribute it.

Capitalism A form of economic organization in which productive resources are privately owned by individuals, who independently decide what to produce.

Socialism A form of economic organization in which individuals may own private property but in which the government owns and operates productive resources.

Property right The right to own or control a resource.

---

[6]Often, communism is described as a system where everyone works for the good of society rather than for the good of the individual and where everyone receives an equal share of society's output. That highly idealized version of communism is the basis of this chapter's communism game.

property rights: One day it's okay for you to own a farm in Zimbabwe; the next day the government seizes your farm and gives it to someone it likes better. In countries that have a history of doing that—and Zimbabwe is one of them—property rights may exist, but those rights are so insecure that any practical market for farmland disappears.

Private property rights are important to the functioning of markets, but they also ensure that productive resources are preserved. Someone who owns land can use it to grow food to sell well into the future. This encourages the owner of the land to maintain and improve it. We are far more likely to take care of things we own than things we do not.

Property rights aren't limited to just land and machinery. They also protect ideas that lead to inventions—inventions that often fuel a nation's economic progress. Consider Emma, whose biggest pet peeve is toilet noise. Emma slaves days, nights, and weekends in her garage workshop, developing a completely soundproof toilet. And finally she hits pay dirt: She incorporates noise-canceling technology into her toilet and achieves completely silent elimination.

The public embraces this technology, and toilets begin flying off the shelves. Emma is raking in money like crazy, until her next-door neighbor Sue sees her driving a brand-new Maserati. "I thought this toilet thing was silly," Sue thinks to herself. "But look at how rich Emma is getting. I think I'll buy one of her toilets and take it apart to see what makes it tick. Then I'll make a silent toilet of my own, undercut Sue's prices, steal all her customers, and capture that wealth for myself!"

In a world without property rights in ideas, Sue is free to reverse-engineer Emma's toilet and make a version of her own. And if the silent toilet is really that terrific, you can bet that it won't be just Sue who does it. People coast to coast will be doing exactly the same. As quickly as Emma got rich, she'll see her profits evaporate as competitors like Sue drive down prices to the point where they will barely cover the cost of making the toilet in the first place.

"But wait!" you may be thinking. "I thought competition was good for society? Doesn't everyone want a silent, yet inexpensive, toilet?" The answer to your question is yes. At some point we want everyone to enjoy the benefits of this marvelous technology. But there's a problem with trying to seize those benefits too soon. If we immediately allow Sue, Carl, Terri, or anyone else to copy Emma's invention, then Emma will never devote her time, energy, creativity, and talents to inventing the soundproof toilet in the first place. As a result, instead of some people getting silent toilets at a fairly high price, nobody gets a silent toilet at all. With no transactions in silent toilets, the cooperative surplus that might have been never materializes in the first place.

For this reason, governments routinely award people who come up with brilliant inventions the exclusive right to produce and/or market those inventions. We call the property rights that protect inventions **patents**. Patents generally last for about 20 years. The patent system, then, balances the goal of having a competitive marketplace with the goal of encouraging innovation. The innovation lasts forever, but the inventor's exclusive right to profit it from it does not. Once the patent expires, anyone who wants to can legally market a version of Emma's toilet, and buyers, not surprisingly, will see the prices of the toilets fall.

Patent An exclusive property right the government gives an inventor to produce and/or market an invention. A patent typically lasts for about 20 years.

Just as patents are designed to foster innovation, copyrights are designed to encourage creativity. A **copyright** is the exclusive property right the government gives the creator of an original work to produce and sell that work for a specified period of time. Copyrights cover books, song lyrics, cartoons, sculptures, and just about any other creative endeavor you might imagine; they generally last for the life of the creator plus 70 years.

Copyright An exclusive property right the government grants the creator of an original work to produce and sell that work. A copyright typically lasts for the life of the creator plus 70 years.

Patents and copyrights link effort and reward. People who devote themselves to writing bestselling novels, inventing cool products and services, and conquering new challenges are allowed to capture, in the form of cold, hard cash, some of the benefits consumers receive from their efforts. The better the invention, the larger those rewards are likely to be.

Private Property and the Pilgrims' Progress

It has been almost 400 years since the Pilgrims celebrated their very first Thanksgiving in the New World. However, their first few years as colonists were bleak. By the end of the first winter, half of them had died of disease or starvation.

Historians often blame the weather for the Pilgrims' starvation. But an economist's lens reveals at least one other source of the hardship: a lack of private property. Upon landing on the shores of North America, the Pilgrims quickly established communal ownership of all pastures and of all agricultural production. As you can predict, the result was underproduction and overconsumption, which in turn created a shortage of food.

How, then, did the Pilgrims achieve their first bountiful harvest? Plymouth Plantation Governor William Bradford, noting that communal ownership "was found to breed much confusion and discontent and retard much employment," assigned each family a parcel of land to do with as they pleased. Bradford writes in his diary that, "This had very good success, for it made all the hands very industrious so as much more corn was planted than otherwise would have been by any means the Governor or any other could use . . ."

Bradford's recipe worked, and it worked well. It was so successful that as abhorrent as private property was to 20th-century communist leaders, their countries relied on similar schemes to feed their people. For example, prior to the fall of the Soviet Union in the late 1980s, private garden plots accounted for less than 4% of arable land but were responsible for one-third of the country's agricultural production.

These leaders, like Bradford, discovered that it's the system of private property that contains the promise of ever richer and more bountiful Thanksgivings to come. So this Thanksgiving, raise a glass to private property. It's earned your appreciation.

See related problem 3.25 on page 138 at the end of this chapter.

Based on the diaries of William Bradford; Mises.org's "Property and the First Thanksgiving;" the *Wall Street Journal Online's* "Thankful for Private Property;" and the American Institute for Economic Research's "The Real Meaning of Thanksgiving," found at aier.org.

Connecting Effort and Reward: An Illustration

Property rights in any productive resource do exactly the same thing as patents and copyrights: They connect effort with reward. Having a right to the profits your labor generates is an example. Consider Mellors and Nero, who are neighbors and who own adjacent garden plots. Mellors and Nero can choose to work somewhat hard (expend $50 worth of effort) or to work extremely hard (expend $75 worth of effort) on their gardens. If a gardener works somewhat hard, his garden will produce orchids he can sell for $110 to a local florist. If a gardener works extremely hard, his garden will produce orchids he can sell for $150. Each person has to make his own decision about how hard to work.

Figure 6.1 models Mellors's and Nero's decisions about how hard to work in the form of a two-person game.

▶ **Figure 6.1**

Payoffs to Mellors and Nero Under Private Property

When Mellors (shown in black) and Nero (shown in blue) keep all the revenue they earn for themselves, each has an incentive to work extremely hard.

		Nero	
		Somewhat Hard	Extremely Hard
Mellors	Somewhat Hard	$60, $60	$60, $75
	Extremely Hard	$75, $60	$75, $75

If Mellors works somewhat hard, he will earn $110 but expend $50. So his net payoff will be $60. If he works extremely hard, he will earn $150 but expend $75 of effort. In this case, his net payoff will be $75. Because Mellors owns his own garden plot, his payoffs are unaffected by Nero's choice of effort. No matter what Nero does, Mellors is better off working extremely hard than working somewhat hard. This is shown in Figure 6.1.

Because he is as good a gardener as Mellors, Nero faces exactly the same incentives. In the end, as Figure 6.1 shows, working extremely hard is a dominant strategy for both of our players. A Nash equilibrium, therefore, is found where both work extremely hard. This equilibrium maximizes both the production of orchids and the payoffs received by the two players.

But what happens if the two neighbors are forced to combine their garden plots and share what they make? Will this change in property rights, a change that entitles each to one-half of the other's production, affect their efforts?

Let's model this revision to the game. The change in the structure of Mellors's and Nero's property rights alters the payoffs for each strategy. So let's empty out the old set of payoffs and compute the new ones.

Suppose Mellors and Nero both decide to work somewhat hard. They then sell their combined agricultural production to a florist for $220 and split that amount equally. That leaves each of them with $110. After each man subtracts the $50 cost of working somewhat hard, he walks away with $60. This outcome is identical to the one in the first version of the game.

What if Mellors and Nero both decide to work extremely hard? They then sell their combined agricultural production to a florist for $300 and split that amount. That leaves each of them with $150. After each man subtracts the $75 cost of working extremely hard, he walks away with $75. This outcome is also identical to the one we saw in the first version of the game.

Now let's look at the case in which one (let's choose Nero) works extremely hard and the other (Mellors) works somewhat hard. Their combined agricultural production will sell to the florist for $260 (Nero's for $150 plus Mellors's for $110). They will split that amount evenly, and each walks away with $130. After subtracting the $50 cost of his effort, Mellors walks away with $80; after Nero subtracts the $75 cost of his effort, he walks away with $55. Of course, if we have Mellors work extremely hard while Nero works somewhat hard, their payoffs get switched, too.

We can use these new payoffs to construct the matrix shown in Figure 6.2.

The best outcome is still for both players to work extremely hard. If they do, their joint earnings are maximized at $150, which is higher than the $135 they collectively generate when one of them works extremely hard and the other doesn't. If they both choose to work somewhat hard, they make only $120.

But unlike in the earlier version of the game, both of them working extremely hard is not a Nash equilibrium. Notice in Figure 6.2 that if Nero works extremely hard, Mellors can actually improve his outcome from $75 to $80 by working only somewhat hard. Even if Nero works only somewhat hard, Mellors does better for himself by just working somewhat hard, too. (By doing so, he earns $60. If he works extremely hard, he earns only $55.) In other words, no matter what Nero does, working somewhat hard is a dominant strategy for Mellors. Because the game is symmetric, working somewhat hard is a dominant strategy for Nero, too. The Nash equilibrium

		Nero	
		Somewhat Hard	Extremely Hard
Mellors	Somewhat Hard	$60, $60	$80, $55
	Extremely Hard	$55, $80	$75, $75

◄ **Figure 6.2**
Payoffs to Mellors and Nero Under Common Property
When Mellors and Nero combine their gardens and operate as one, the incentive structure changes. Both Mellors and Nero now have a dominant strategy of working somewhat hard.

Application 6.3

Property Rights and the Chinese Agricultural Revolution

Property rights are critical to help make both people and nations productive. Even communist governments have come to understand the importance of property rights and the incentives those rights create.

In 1958, China's leader, Mao Tse Tung, launched a new socioeconomic program called the "Great Leap Forward." That program accelerated the pace of initiatives begun in the early 1950s that abolished private property and private enterprise and accelerated the seizure of individual farms that were then merged into communal operations.

The Great Leap Forward was actually a great leap backward. Economic output declined, particularly agricultural output. An estimated 20 to 40 million people died due to famine. By 1961, Mao abandoned the program, but its underlying philosophies resurfaced during China's Cultural Revolution. The Cultural Revolution, which lasted from 1966 until Mao's death in 1976, was a campaign to reaffirm communism and rid the country of any remaining capitalistic, traditional, or cultural influences. The government punished dissent with seizure of property, imprisonment, torture, and death.

This environment set the stage for a scene that played out in 1978 in rural Xiaogang Village. Under the law, the commune had to meet a production quota set by the government. Each year the villagers struggled to meet the quota, with little left over to feed themselves and no excess to sell in the market. Xiaogang's 20 farmers were scared of starving, and they were scared of failing to meet their quota, an arrestable offense. Panicked, they held a secret meeting—a meeting in which they agreed to divide the communal land into individual plots. They would continue as a group to deliver their annual production quota. But anything a farmer produced beyond his share of the quota could be sold for his own profit, a profit that didn't have to be split 20 ways.

That agreement created a crucial link between effort and reward. Farmers were now working for themselves and had an incentive to make smart choices about what to grow, how much to plant, and how hard to work. Almost overnight, productivity improved, with vast increases in the amount of land under cultivation. Within a few seasons, the villagers were meeting the government's quota, feeding themselves, and producing a surplus to sell, for profit, to others.

Other villages saw what was happening and began implementing similar arrangements. As the movement grew, officials in Beijing began to notice. With Mao dead and the political climate changing, China quickly legalized individual farming. Agricultural output skyrocketed, and markets teemed with livestock, grains, fruits, and vegetables that had been difficult or impossible to find a decade before.

By 1984, communal farms ceased to exist, and approximately 170 million rural Chinese had been lifted above the poverty line. The movement was the single largest anti-poverty campaign the world has ever known, one that started with a group of poor farmers who had an intuitive understanding of the power of private property.

See related problem 4.3 on page 139 at the end of this chapter.

Based on Kate Xiao's *How the Farmers Changed China*, Westview Press, 1996; Ronald Coase and Ning Wang's *How China Became Capitalist*, Palgrave Macmillan, 2013; and John McMillan's *Reinventing the Bazaar: A Natural History of Markets*, W. W. Norton & Company, 2002.

is found at the intersection of these dominant strategies: Both players work somewhat hard, and society gets fewer flowers as a result.

Our players are just as good at gardening as they were before. The ground is just as fertile. But the change in their property rights results in a change in their incentives.

Giving each player ownership of half of the other's production while taking away half of their own separates their efforts from their rewards. Having been guaranteed half of the other's output regardless of whether he works extremely hard or not, each man chooses to work a bit less. The economic pie shrinks as a result.

Essentially, the players are trapped in a prisoner's dilemma from which they can't escape. Each is made poorer than he would be if both cooperated to work extremely hard, yet neither wishes to unilaterally increase his effort. And why should he? From an individual's perspective, the extra effort needed to achieve the cooperative outcome is not tied to any additional reward; it actually makes the player worse off. The outcome is no surprise: When you separate effort from reward, you get less effort.

It is for this reason that property rights matter a great deal if an economy is to realize its potential. And it is governments, through decree or legislation, that decide whether their citizens have a right to their own land, labor, technological inventions, or other productive resources and the profits from them.

Conclusion

Markets work best if they are well structured. Successful economies are successful largely because they have a number of institutions that enable markets to work smoothly. Good institutions help economies generate the greatest possible economic well-being out of their limited resources and provide an economic framework that encourages the innovation necessary for the economy to grow through time. Government can help markets realize their potential in two ways. First, by encouraging competition, upholding contracts, and assisting the flow of information between buyers and sellers, government can make it easier for buyers and sellers to arrange transactions with one another. Second, by establishing and enforcing property rights, government can create the incentives necessary for the hard work and innovation that productive and progressive economies depend on.

When property rights are both clear and enforced, and when transactions between buyer and seller are easy to arrange, additional government intervention in the marketplace generally makes society worse off. But transactions aren't always easy to arrange, and property rights aren't always well defined. We'll talk in much greater depth about those cases throughout the rest of this book, and we'll do it in the context of some major social problems. As the book unfolds, you'll be surprised at how often these social problems can be traced back either to the difficulty of arranging transactions or to insecure property rights. When this happens, the government, instead of making society poorer, has the potential to be a positive force that increases the size of the economic pie available to everyone.

Chapter Summary and Problems

Key Terms

Capitalism, p. 130

Communism, p. 130

Competition, p. 124

Consumer sovereignty, p. 120

Copyright, p. 131

Economic growth, p. 124

Institutions, p. 124

Market, p. 120

Monopolistic competition, p. 121

Monopoly, p. 121

Oligopoly, p. 121

Patent, p. 131

Perfect competition, p. 121

Property right, p. 130

Socialism, p. 130

6.1 The Market System: Its Functions and Structure, pages 120–121

Define *market* and compare the four market structures.

Summary

A market is a forum where buyers and sellers meet to conduct transactions. Markets may be centralized or decentralized. They may also be physical spaces or virtual spaces. In addition to facilitating trade, markets help buyers and sellers jointly decide what will be produced and in what quantities. Markets can be classified by the number of competitors and the extent of competition. The least competitive type of market, a monopoly, has only one seller. The most competitive market structure is perfect competition. Between those two extremes are oligopoly and monopolistic competition.

Review Questions

All problems are assignable in MyEconLab.

1.1 A forum where buyers and sellers go to conduct transactions is called a(n) _____.

1.2 Sellers are generally quite responsive to the desires of buyers and work hard to give them what they want. Economists call this the principle of _____.

1.3 A market with only one seller is referred to as a(n) _____.

1.4 Which of the following is *not* an example of a market?

   a. eBay

   b. Apple's App Store

   c. A mall food court

   d. All of the above are examples of markets.

1.5 The automobile industry is dominated by a small number of very large producers who sell a differentiated product. The market structure that best fits the auto industry is probably _____.

   a. Monopoly

   b. Oligopoly

   c. Monopolistic competition

   d. Perfect competition

Problems and Applications

1.6 Give an example of a market that exists for an intangible good or for a service. What is the purpose of a market? Is it necessary for a physical product to change hands for a market to exist?

1.7 "It's impossible to find a good broccoli cake," Peter says. "I can't find anyone who makes them!" Why do you suppose there is no active market in broccoli cake? What principle discussed in this chapter might be at work?

6.2 The Four Functions of Prices in the Market System, pages 122–123

Summarize the four key functions of prices.

Summary

One critical component of the market system is prices. The price of an item reflects, in part, how much consumers desire that item. It also reflects the scarcity of the resources needed to produce that item. Prices serve as the key means of communication between buyers and sellers, and they therefore help determine what will be produced and in what quantities. Prices also help coordinate all phases of production so that producers have the right quantities of the resources they need, in the right place, to operate.

Review Questions

All problems are assignable in MyEconLab.

2.1 Which of the following items is *not* one of the key functions of prices in the market system?

   a. Measuring scarcity

   b. Communication

   c. Profit

   d. Coordination

2.2 When consumers suddenly stop wanting cheese, the price of cheese will likely _____.

   a. Increase

   b. Decrease

   c. Not be affected

2.3 A sudden discovery of massive reserves of oil in Iowa will likely cause the price of oil to _____.

   a. Increase

   b. Decrease

   c. Not be affected

2.4 In the U.S. economy, the quantity of bread produced each week is determined by the _____.

   a. Department of Commerce

   b. Department of Agriculture

   c. Individual decisions of thousands of bread makers

   d. Bread czar

Problems and Applications

2.5 Steel is incredibly useful. Gold is mostly just pretty. Explain, then, why gold costs so much more than steel.

2.6 When the Atkins low-carb diet became popular in the late 1990s, the price of eggs skyrocketed. Explain why this happened and discuss the likely effect on egg production. Does your conclusion support or negate the principle of consumer sovereignty?

2.7 Go online and find a chocolate chip cookie recipe. Make a list of all the ingredients that go into that cookie. Then make a list of at least a dozen different parties that were involved in producing and distributing those ingredients. How must all their actions and decisions be coordinated to ensure that the baker has the right amounts of the right ingredients at the right time?

6.3 The Foundations of Well-Functioning Markets: A Role for Government, pages 124–132

Explain how government action can improve the functioning of markets.

Summary

Markets function best when there are enough buyers and sellers to make the market competitive, when market participants are honest with one another, when both buyers and sellers have access to complete and accurate information about the product in question and available alternatives, and when participants have well-established property rights. Governments can help markets function well by creating institutions that embody these characteristics. Antitrust legislation helps ensure that sellers compete with one another. The court system encourages honesty. The government can create measures that improve access to and the accuracy of market information. The government can establish and enforce property rights.

Review Questions

All problems are assignable in MyEconLab.

3.1 When buyers and sellers have a choice of whom to complete transactions with, _____ is said to exist.

3.2 A form of economic and social organization in which all property is owned by society as a whole is called _____.

3.3 A form of economic organization in which productive resources are privately owned by individuals (or by groups of individuals, such as partnerships or corporations) is called _____.

3.4 The right to own or control a resource is called a(n) _____.

3.5 The practice of businesses colluding with one another about what they will charge customers is called _____.

3.6 A(n) _____ is the exclusive right, provided by the government, to produce and/or market an invention.

3.7 The _____ makes it a felony for competing businesses to collude with one another on prices.

3.8 The rules that govern the behavior of market participants are often referred to as _____.

3.9 Which of the following acts prohibits two competitors from merging with one another for the purpose of reducing competition?
   a. Robinson-Patman Act
   b. Clayton Act
   c. Federal Trade Commission Act
   d. Sherman Act

3.10 In the late 1990s, Microsoft was sued for "tying" its Internet browser, Internet Explorer, to its operating system. A seller forcing you to buy a product that you don't want before you can purchase one that you do want, known as tying, is prohibited by what act?
   a. Robinson-Patman Act
   b. Federal Trade Commission Act
   c. Magnuson–Moss Warranty Act
   d. Clayton Act

3.11 In 2008, lawsuits were filed against three producers (LG Display Co., Chunghwa Picture Tubes, and Sharp Corporation) for conspiring to fix prices of LCD panels. What act prohibits conspiring with your competitors to fix prices?
   a. Sherman Act
   b. Robinson-Patman Act
   c. Clayton Act
   d. Federal Trade Commission Act

3.12 Which of the following are not covered by copyrights?
   a. Song lyrics
   b. Books
   c. Sculptures
   d. A new type of mousetrap

3.13 In the video game *Grand Theft Auto: San Andreas*, drug dealer CJ attempts to wipe out his competitors. If he is successful, the price of drugs will likely _____.
   a. Increase
   b. Decrease
   c. Remain unaffected

3.14 A form of economic organization in which individuals can own property but not businesses is called _____.

  a. Capitalism
  b. Communism
  c. Socialism
  d. Darwinism

3.15 An exclusive government-granted license to produce and market a new invention for a period of time is called a(n) _____.

  a. Patent
  b. Trademark
  c. Copyright
  d. Exclusive franchise

3.16 It is clear that the actions of governments _____.

  a. Interfere with the functioning of markets and make the world poorer
  b. Can help markets function more smoothly and make the world richer
  c. Both options (a) and (b) are true in various circumstances.
  d. Neither option (a) nor option (b) is true.

Problems and Applications

3.17 In some college towns, landlords are known to hold all of a renter's security deposit at the end of a lease, regardless of the condition that the apartment is in. While contract laws may prevent this situation in theory, why might this happen in the real world? What key component(s) of a well-functioning market might be missing?

3.18 The U.S. government has a large bureaucracy devoted to creating a competitive marketplace. Describe the negative consequences that a lack of competition creates. Be sure to discuss the effects of a lack of competition on prices, consumer well-being, and the overall size of the economic pie.

3.19 Before the Internet, for many people the idea of purchasing many goods without physically seeing the goods or the seller would have seemed foolish. Now many customers find that they prefer purchasing goods over the Internet to going to a store. What are some examples of privately created institutions that online merchants use to help ensure that customers are satisfied making purchases online?

3.20 Hyundai offers a 10-year, 100,000-mile warranty on its vehicles. Why do you suppose Hyundai does this? How does such a warranty help the car market function better? Would that warranty be useful in the absence of government?

3.21 Name two things government has done that help information flow freely between producers and buyers.

3.22 Many social critics disparage commercial advertising as a wasteful expense that drives up prices yet creates no value. Explain, in the context of this chapter's material, how advertising may help markets function more effectively.

3.23 Government works to create a competitive marketplace because it believes competition helps markets function well. Yet government also awards patents, which prevent competition. Why are both competition and the patent system, seemingly working at cross purposes, essential to creating a large economic pie?

3.24 [Related to Application 6.1 on page 127] The Republic of India is the most populous democracy in the world; however, it suffers from "brain drain." Why do you suppose so many of India's most talented people are eager to leave? How might government be responsible for this brain drain? What is the effect of the brain drain on India's material well-being?

3.25 [Related to Application 6.2 on page 132] The early settlers in the United States had a disastrous experience with communal agriculture. Carefully explain why communal farming represents an instance of poorly defined and enforced property rights.

6.4 Connecting Effort and Reward: An Illustration, pages 132–135

Compare and contrast the incentives for productivity and creativity created by private property and by common property.

Summary

Property rights create a key link between effort and reward. When the fruits of one's effort are shared by all—when property rights are not complete—the rewards to working hard are diminished. When people get to keep the full product of their labor, they tend to work harder, produce more, and create a wealthier society.

Review Questions

All problems are assignable in MyEconLab.

4.1 In the example of Mellors and Nero, property rights connect _____.

  a. Cost and production
  b. Inputs and outputs
  c. Honesty and information
  d. Effort and reward

4.2 In a society where it is mandatory to share the product of one's work with others, economics predicts that people will _____ than they would if they could keep the full product of their work.

   a. Work harder

   b. Work more

   c. Exert less effort

   d. People's work effort will not be affected by how their work product is distributed.

Problems and Applications

4.3 **[Related to Application 6.3 on page 134]** China's experience with communal agriculture was a disaster. Carefully explain the effects of communal farming on the incentive for individual farmers to expand their farms and gardens, relative to the incentives that exist in a market system.

4.4 Economist Arthur Okun's 1975 book *Equality and Efficiency: The Big Tradeoff* highlights the tension between equally distributing the economic pie (equality, or equity) and generating the greatest possible economic pie (efficiency). Explain how the game played by Mellors and Nero in Section 6.4 illustrates Okun's trade-off.

Capitalism and Communism Games

This chapter has highlighted how property rights create incentives for people to work hard and innovate. Now, it's time to get out of your chairs and see for yourself why incentives are so important in shaping our behavior.

Grocery stores are filled with food that is produced by various companies. These companies employ workers to operate machinery, bake, cook, package food into containers, and ship food to grocery stores. In these two games, you and your classmates will work at a large bakery that specializes in making pies. The amount of effort you expend each day is for you to decide: The harder you work, the more pies you'll produce, but because work is not fun, the harder you work, the more physical discomfort you will experience.

And just why would you be working so hard? Let's explore this question by playing two different games.

Game 1: In the capitalism game, you'll get to eat everything you produce, and nothing else. The more you work, the more you'll eat, and the happier you'll be.

Game 2: In the communism game, the pies that everyone produces will be collected and then they will be divided evenly among you and your classmates. Again, the more you work, the more you and your classmates will eat.

Your only job in these two games is to decide how hard to work. Will you work hard in an attempt to increase your consumption of pie? Or, will you expend less effort and avoid the displeasure that work creates?

MyEconLab

Please visit http://www.myeconlab.com **for support material to conduct this experiment if assigned by your instructor.**

7 The Nature of Pollution Problems

Chapter Outline and Learning Objectives

7.1 **Externalities,** page 142

Define *externality* and distinguish between a positive externality and a negative externality.

7.2 **Pollution Problems (Negative Externalities) and Disagreements over the Competing Uses of Scarce Resources,** page 144

Evaluate whether all polluters are villains and everyone affected by pollution is a victim.

7.3 **How Much Pollution Is the Right Amount of Pollution?** page 145

Identify cases in which pollution is in society's best interest and cases in which it is not.

7.4 **The Coase Theorem,** page 148

Explain how the exchange of property rights can bring about the socially ideal amount of pollution.

7.5 **Why the Coase Theorem May Not Work: Transactions Costs,** page 151

Define *transactions costs* and explain how these costs can impede the bargaining process.

Experiment: The Herd Immunity Game, page 158

MyEconLab
MyEconLab helps you master each objective and study more efficiently.

So far in this book, you have covered important ground. You have learned a new analytical framework called game theory, and you have learned that well-functioning markets can help society create the greatest possible wealth from its limited resources. Unfortunately, not all markets function well. When they don't, the result is often what people regard as a social problem.

Now it's time to apply the framework you've spent so much time learning. In this chapter, we'll begin by examining some important environmental issues. Lots of people are concerned about having clean air and water. Many people worry about climate change. Still others are alarmed at the rate at which the world's rain forests are shrinking. This chapter and the next two discuss the environment: the nature of pollution problems, the difficulties in solving those problems, and the depletion of natural resources. Let's begin by taking a closer look at pollution problems—in this case, noise pollution created by an exuberant accordion player—and why they arise.

Externalities

7.1 Learning Objective

Define *externality* and distinguish between a positive externality and a negative externality.

Roy loves to play the accordion. And fortunately for Roy, he's been able to leverage his love for the accordion into a decent living by playing polkas in his backyard for neighborhood kids and other accordion aficionados.

Phil is a psychotherapist. Ten years ago, he made a splash with a televised talk show. But after Phil was sued for making insensitive comments during a particularly heated episode, the network yanked his contract. Now, from his home, Phil runs a small but lucrative business dispensing advice to distraught clients who need psychotherapy.

As fate would have it, Phil lives next door to Roy, and Roy's accordion playing is affecting Phil's ability to counsel his clients. Not only has Phil lost several accordion-hating clients, but he can no longer always hear his other clients' problems correctly and respond with appropriate advice. Some of Phil's clients are leaving because of this. Others are asking for a reduced hourly rate. Phil is understandably upset that Roy's accordion concerts are affecting his ability to earn a living.

Externality A by-product of an activity that hurts or helps someone who is not involved in that activity.

The problem faced by Phil and Roy is a classic problem of what economists call an externality. An **externality** is a by-product of an activity that hurts or helps someone who is not involved in that activity. In the example we just discussed, the principal *product* of Roy's activity is providing accordion lovers with delightful music in exchange for cash. The *by-product* of Roy's activity is that he also provides Phil and Phil's clients with lots of music that they would rather not hear.

In a well-functioning marketplace, when we want something, we buy it—as long as the price is right. When we don't want something, we don't buy it. But in Phil's case, neither of these scenarios apply: He and his clients are receiving something that they don't want and that they wouldn't voluntarily purchase at any price. They're receiving this good, oddly, because the market for next-door accordion music doesn't function as well as it might. Much of the rest of this chapter discusses what a well-functioning market looks like and what a well-functioning market could potentially accomplish in this situation.

Negative Externalities

It should be fairly easy for you to come up with examples of externalities:

- Those of you who have tried to study for exams while your next-door neighbors played *Guitar Hero* are certainly familiar with noise pollution as an example of an externality.

- In the Midwest, most lakes have murky green water. The green is algae growth, fueled by fertilizer that has run off of farmers' fields into lakes and streams.

- In Denver and Los Angeles, sun-baked car exhaust turns into smog so thick that local governments issue health advisories on particularly nasty days.

Application 7.1

Property Values and Megan's Law

Many homeowners are quite concerned about the quality of their neighbors. You may not like it, for example, if your neighbors regularly throw loud parties or fail to take care of their yard. Even worse, if your neighbors' behavior is bad enough, it may adversely affect your ability to resell your home.

There may be no neighbor less desirable than a sex offender. It's pretty easy to hypothesize that having a sex offender nearby will make your home less attractive to potential buyers. But it's one thing to guess that a negative externality exists; it's another thing entirely to dig up numbers to prove that it does and figure out how bad the problem might be. In 1996, Congress passed Megan's Law, which requires all sex offenders to register their address with the state. This law gave economists Leigh Linden of the University of Texas–Austin and Jonah Rockoff of Columbia University exactly the data they needed to quantify the externality.

Linden and Rockoff merged data on the residences of registered sex offenders with data on the sales prices of similar homes at various distances from sex offenders. The evidence the research uncovered suggests that the effects of having a sex offender in the neighborhood are highly localized and diminish rapidly with distance. If you live more than one-tenth of a mile away from a registered sex offender (that's roughly a major city block), you will experience little or no decline in the value of your property. If you live within one-tenth of a mile of a sex offender, you can expect your home value to fall by about 4%.

What if you're unlucky enough to have a registered sex offender living next door? Linden and Rockoff's numbers show that you can expect your home to fetch 12% less than it otherwise would. Given a median home value of about $200,000, you'll suffer losses of about $24,000. Now *that's* a negative externality!

Linden and Rockoff's article tells us two important things about people. First, people pay attention to the world around them—they care about externalities enough to comb through sex offender registries before they buy houses. Second, despite many people's claims to the contrary, everyone has a price. All it takes to get the typical homebuyer to move in next door to a registered sex offender is the equivalent of a 12%-off coupon.

See related problem 1.8 on page 154 at the end of this chapter.

Based on Leigh Linden and Jonah Rockoff, "Estimates of the Impact of Crime Risk on Property Values from Megan's Laws," *American Economic Review*, 2008; Slate.com's "There Goes the Neighborhood," March 22, 2013; and Business-insider.com's "Nine Things That Will Trash Your Home's Value," May 13, 2013.

Each of these types of pollution—noise, water, and air—is a result of a particular type of by-product economists call a negative externality. A **negative externality** is simply an externality that imposes a burden or cost on others. A negative externality might be caused by production, such as a power plant's emissions of sulfur dioxide. Or a negative externality might be caused by consumption: An airplane passenger who uses too much perfume might impose costs on her seatmates. This chapter focuses on noise pollution (Roy's accordion playing), but the same principles you learn regarding noise pollution apply to the other types of pollution as well.

Negative externality An externality that imposes a burden or cost on others.

Positive Externalities

Here's a bit of good news: Not all externalities are negative. Suppose your next-door neighbor keeps an obsessively neat lawn. Each morning, she crawls on hands and knees through her grass, picking up any twigs that fell from her trees the night before.

In addition to having a front yard that puts golf greens to shame, she also maintains beautiful flower beds and regularly cleans her driveway and sidewalks with a vacuum cleaner.

Clearly, your neighbor must receive a lot of benefits from being so fastidious. But you, too, receive some of the benefits of her labors. You get to look at a lovely yard every day, and when it comes time to sell your house, having her beautifully maintained yard next door will likely cause your property value to rise a little bit. In this case, the externality your neighbor creates is a **positive externality**, which is a by-product of an activity that confers benefits on others.

Positive externalities, like negative externalities, are everywhere. People who live next to bakeries get to enjoy the smell of hot, fresh bread. Vaccines protect the person getting the shot, but by keeping him well, they also protect the people he comes in contact with. Education, too, creates positive externalities: Teach a college student to program computers, and who knows—he might create the next Facebook. The good news for you, as a student of economics, is that the same tools you use to analyze negative externalities are just as powerful when applied to positive externalities.

Positive externality An externality that confers benefits on others.

7.2 Learning Objective

Evaluate whether all polluters are villains and everyone affected by pollution is a victim.

Pollution Problems (Negative Externalities) and Disagreements over the Competing Uses of Scarce Resources

Now that you have a better understanding of the nature of externalities, let's revisit Roy and Phil. It would be easy for us to conclude that Roy is imposing some of the costs of his activity on Phil, making himself richer at Phil's expense. After all, Phil didn't *ask* Roy to play concerts next door.

But before we settle on that conclusion, let's think more critically about what is actually going on between Roy and Phil. To do this, let's first consider a couple of college students, Harry and Justine, who have a sociology class together. Outside their classroom is a delightful green space with several centuries-old shade trees. Harry loves this area. Each day after class he goes there to do homework and catch up with his friends.

Justine, on the other hand, drives to campus each day and always has trouble finding a place to park. Often, she has to walk many blocks to her sociology class. For the past 3 months, Justine has eyed the wooded area. She would love to see it turned into a parking lot. Recently she submitted a proposal to the college's zoning board that would accomplish just that if approved. What a ruckus Justine's proposal caused! Cutting down trees and replacing them with concrete—that's unconscionable!

Or is it? It's important to note that Justine's plan only reflects a preference for parking closer to her final destination. This is a natural desire. And Justine is not unlike many of us. For example, not all of us would be content to park our cars at home and walk to school or to work, no matter how close those destinations might be. In other words, it's perfectly legitimate for Harry to prefer trees to parking, but it's just as legitimate for Justine to prefer parking to trees. And although some people might be sad to see the trees felled and the grass paved over with concrete, many of those same people would be glad to have a parking lot near their classes on days when it's rainy and cold or when they have a heavy load of books and papers to carry from their cars.

Harry and Justine are not engaged in a battle of good versus evil. Nor are they in a fight between right and wrong. They simply disagree about how a resource should be used. Once we recognize that Harry's and Justine's actions reflect natural and morally neutral preferences, the debate becomes not so much a matter of parking or not parking but *how much* parking. Subjectively speaking, we might say that it would be selfish for Justine to demand that the last tree in the county be felled so she could park just a few inches closer to her building. We might also say that it's selfish of Harry to refuse to allow a single tree to be felled when he's surrounded by thousands of acres of forest and there's not a parking spot to be found. Somewhere between these extremes lies a middle ground—the blend of parking and trees that makes the best use of the space society has available. As economists, it's our job to find it.

How Much Pollution Is the Right Amount of Pollution?

Let's step back to the problem from the beginning of this chapter—the one in which Roy's accordion music was disturbing Phil's psychotherapy practice. The lesson we can draw from Harry and Justine is this: Roy and Phil are not engaged in a battle of right and wrong; Phil is not a victim, nor is Roy a villain. Roy and Phil basically have a disagreement over how a resource is to be used. Roy would like the airspace between their houses to be used to transmit beautiful sound waves to the ears of his adoring listeners. Phil would like the airspace between their houses to serve as a buffer zone between the comforting cocoon of the therapist's couch and the harsh reality of the outside world. And although it's clear that Roy's desire for music is hurting Phil's income, if we turn the tables, it also becomes apparent that if Phil were to have his way, his desire for silence would have a similar effect on *Roy's* ability to earn a living.

Both Roy and Phil have preferences, and as was the case with Harry and Justine, it seems fairly straightforward for us to conclude that it would be selfish for Phil to demand that all accordion music, everywhere, be banned in case there happened to be a psychotherapist nearby. It would be similarly selfish of Roy to demand that all accordionists have the right to play their accordions wherever and whenever they please. Somewhere between these extremes lies a world with what society considers to be the right amount of both accordion music and psychotherapy. Again, it's our job to find it.

To find the right balance between accordion music and psychotherapy, we need to put numbers to the problem. Let's suppose that by playing the accordion, Roy can earn profits of $400 per week. If he were forced to quit, his next-best alternative would be dunking fries at a local diner, an honorable profession for certain, but one in which he would earn a mere $100 per week. Suppose also that when Phil counsels clients in silence, Phil's profits are $600, but when Roy plays the accordion, Phil's profits fall to $400. Those numbers give us reasonable estimates of how much society values accordion playing, french fries, and therapy. These values will help us figure out the ideal blend of music and therapy from a social perspective.

The Benevolent Social Planner and the Socially Optimal Amount of Pollution

Let's call in the benevolent social planner (BSP) for advice on this problem. Remember that the benevolent social planner cares only about the size of the economic pie; her job is to determine what actions will lead to the largest possible pie for society to share. Remember also that she doesn't particularly care about the law: Laws are made by fallible humans, not by all-seeing, all-knowing entities like the benevolent social planner.

As a starting point, let's pretend that we have a world without laws, one in which all disputes are settled on a case-by-case basis by the benevolent social planner. One morning, Roy and Phil appear before the BSP and ask for her help in resolving their conflict. "Hmmmm . . .," the BSP says, "I see that when Roy doesn't play, society gets $100 of french fries and $600 of therapy, for a total economic pie of $700. But when Roy does play, society gets $400 of music and $400 of therapy, for a total pie of $800. Based on those numbers, I decree that music shall be played!" And, of course, the BSP is correct: By allowing music to be played, society loses a little bit of client counseling but gains a relatively large amount of happiness on the part of concertgoers.

The Law, Bargaining, and the Socially Optimal Amount of Pollution

There is just one problem with our previous analysis: We don't live in a world where all-seeing benevolent social planners solve our disputes. We live in a world of laws, and as a society, we have hired people to enforce those laws when requested. So what effect might the law have on the dispute between Roy and Phil? The surprising answer is that no matter what the law says about playing the accordion, the law will have both little effect and great effect.

The Socially Optimal Amount of Pollution When Concerts Are Legal Let's assume that it's perfectly legal for Roy to play his accordion in his backyard for concertgoers. Next, let's represent the choices available to him and Phil as a game in payoff matrix form. That game is shown in Figure 7.1. Roy can play concerts and earn a payoff of $400, or he can dunk fries and earn a payoff of $100. If Roy plays concerts, Phil can either choose to do nothing or call the police and ask them to shut down Roy's concert.

But because concerts are legal, the police will simply shrug and say, "There's nothing we can do." Calling the police, then, does nothing to alter Phil's payoffs. So, no matter what he does, he will earn $400. Finally, notice that there is an "N/A" in the lower-right cell of the payoff matrix. Because Phil will call the police only if Roy plays concerts, neither Roy nor Phil should ever find himself in that cell.

▶ **Figure 7.1**

Phil's and Roy's Payoffs When Accordion Concerts Are Legal
This payoff matrix summarizes payoffs available for Phil (in black) and Roy (in blue), depending on whether Roy plays the accordion or dunks fries. Overall social well-being can be calculated by adding together Roy's and Phil's payoffs.

		Roy	
		Play Concerts	Dunk Fries
Phil	Do Nothing	400, 400	600, 100
	If Roy Plays, Call Police	400, 400	N/A

We can calculate the size of the economic pie simply by adding the numbers in the appropriate cells. Notice that if Roy chooses to dunk fries, Phil will do nothing (not call the police), and the economic pie will be $700: $600 of value that Phil's patients receive from therapy, and $100 of value that Roy creates by dunking fries.

But knowing that the law is on his side, Roy should choose to play concerts rather than dunk fries. Doing so increases his income by $300. And even though Phil loses $200 when Roy plays concerts, society is richer as a result because the total amount of the economic pie is $800 ($400 + 400). In other words, when the law allows concert playing, society gets the outcome the benevolent social planner would have wanted.

The Socially Optimal Amount of Pollution When Concerts Are Illegal But what if the law changes, and accordion concerts are illegal? In this case, the payouts available to the players look different, as shown in Figure 7.2.

If Roy dunks fries, Phil has no reason to call the police. Phil will earn $600, and Roy will earn $100. As a result, the economic pie will be $700. (This outcome appears in the upper-right cell.) But if Roy plays concerts, Phil can immediately pick up the phone, request police backup, and shut down the concert. Unable to earn any money playing the accordion, Roy will have to go back to dunking fries for $100, and Phil will again earn $600. (This outcome appears in the lower-left cell.) The economic pie will be $700.

It appears as if the law is stacked against Roy in this case. He is not completely without alternatives, though. Let's say that Roy picks up his accordion and begins to play. Just as Phil reaches for the phone, Roy says, "Wait! Don't call the police!

▶ **Figure 7.2**

Phil's and Roy's Payoffs When Accordion Concerts Are Illegal
When concerts are illegal, Phil can call the police to make Roy stop playing the accordion. Roy will then be forced to dunk fries and receive a payoff of only $100.

		Roy	
		Play Concerts	Dunk Fries
Phil	Do Nothing	400, 400	600, 100
	If Roy Plays, Call Police	600, 100	N/A

Please, let me play!" The tricky part is for Roy to convince Phil not to make the call. However, Phil won't have much of an incentive to do that. If Phil phones the authorities, they will shut down the concert, and his income will increase by $200 (from $400 to $600).

Application 7.2

The Salk Vaccine Versus the Sabin Vaccine

Polio is a crippling disease—one that can be deadly. The polio virus causes nervous system inflammation that can result in paralysis of the limbs and diaphragm. Victims may suffer skeletal disfigurement and may have to breathe with the assistance of an iron lung.

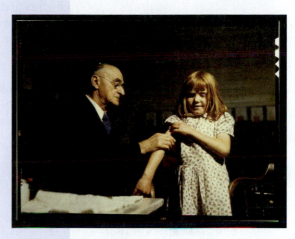

Although polio has not been eradicated around the globe, most of us have never seen a polio victim due to highly effective polio vaccines developed in the latter part of the twentieth century. Voluntary, and in many cases, compulsory, polio vaccination programs in Western countries have virtually eradicated the disease from these areas of the globe.

Jonas Salk developed the first polio vaccine in 1955. Salk's vaccine was a "killed-virus" vaccine: Doctors injected recipients with the dead virus, and after a series of shots, the vast majority of them became immune to the disease. Most importantly, Salk's vaccine did not cause anyone to get polio.

Unfortunately, some people chose to not get the vaccine because it entailed getting multiple shots. Others avoided it because of cost, or philosophical objections, or unfounded fears that the vaccine might give them the disease. As a result, many people had no immunity to polio, and the disease persisted.

In 1961, Albert Sabin developed a next-generation "live-virus" vaccine. Recipients received a highly weakened strain of the disease that was unlikely to develop into full-blown polio. The Sabin vaccine became the vaccine of choice for governments campaigning against polio for two reasons. First, the Sabin vaccine was an oral vaccine, so people afraid of needles were more likely to get vaccinated. Second, because the Sabin vaccine was a live-virus vaccine, recipients could pass along a highly weakened form of the disease to others. For example, just by kissing someone, you could give them the weakened form of the virus, and the person would develop some immunity to polio without ever getting seriously sick from it. However, because the Sabin vaccine consisted of a live virus, a very small number of people vaccinated with it each year developed polio as a result.

Imagine the trade-offs that policymakers faced. If they were to stick with the Salk vaccine, nobody who did the "right" thing by getting vaccinated would get polio. However, a sizable number who did not get vaccinated would contract the disease, including children whose parents decided not to have them vaccinated.

On the other hand, if policymakers opted for the Sabin vaccine, more people would end up being vaccinated. And because of the Sabin vaccine's positive externalities, even some people who rejected the vaccine would become immune to polio. Unfortunately, a handful of folks who did exactly the right thing by being vaccinated with the Sabin vaccine would come down with the disease. Now *that's* a tough trade-off!

That hard-fought debate is now in our past. The vaccination programs of the past half-century have virtually eradicated polio from the Western world, so unvaccinated individuals are highly unlikely to contract the disease through everyday contact. After accounting for the 8 to 10 lives lost each year because of the Sabin vaccine, the change in the cost–benefit comparison prompted the U.S. government to revert to a strengthened version of the original Salk vaccine.

See related problem 3.3 on page 156 at the end of this chapter.

In fact, the only way Roy can successfully convince Phil not to call the police is to promise to make it worth Phil's while not to do so. To get him to put down the phone, Roy must fully compensate Phil for the lost earnings that accordion concerts create. Where will Roy get the money to do this? Notice that playing concerts increases Roy's income by $300. Let's assume that Roy plays a concert, takes the $300 extra he earns from it, and gives $250 of it to Phil. That's enough to compensate Phil for his lost earnings ($200) with a little bit extra ($50) thrown in for good measure.

As Figure 7.3 shows, Roy's payment to Phil changes the game's payoffs. If Roy chooses to dunk fries, of course, nothing is different. But if he pays Phil to let him play concerts, his payoff becomes $150—the $400 he earns from playing a concert minus the $250 he pays to Phil. This change to Roy's payoffs is shown in the upper-left cell.

Phil's payoffs change, too. When Roy begins playing, if Phil calls the police to enforce the law, he'll get the same $600 as before. But if Phil accepts Roy's payment and lets him play, his total payoff becomes $650—the $400 he earns from counseling patients plus the $250 he receives from Roy. This change, again, is shown in the upper-left cell.

▶ Figure 7.3

Phil's and Roy's Payoffs After Bargaining Around the Law
When concerts are illegal, Roy can pay Phil for the right to play concerts. A payment of $250 makes both Phil and Roy $50 better off than they would be if Roy dunked fries.

		Roy	
		Play Concerts	Dunk Fries
Phil	Do Nothing	**650, 150**	**600, 100**
	If Roy Plays, Call Police	**600, 100**	N/A

So the equilibrium outcome is for Roy to play concerts and Phil to let him. Even after paying Phil what amounts to a bribe (economists call such deals *side bargains*, or *bargaining around the law*) not to call the authorities, Roy makes $150. That's $50 more than he would have made by working legally dunking fries. Phil benefits, too, taking home $650 instead of the $600 that he would have had Roy stayed out of the backyard concert-playing business.

The Coase Theorem

What has transpired between Phil and Roy is an odd case of mutually beneficial exchange. In this case, however, Phil and Roy are not trading tangible property. What they're trading is the **property right**—the right to own or control a resource—to the use of the air around their houses. The law against concerts gave that right to Phil, and Phil transferred that right to Roy for $250.

The voluntary exchange of property rights made both parties richer, and it made society richer, too. The economic pie grew from the $700 that it would have been if Phil had demanded that the law be enforced to $800 when he ignored it. Most surprisingly, regardless of the law, concerts are played, and we get the outcome that the benevolent social planner would have desired. This occurs in spite of the law, not because of it.

What we've just seen in action is an example of the Coase theorem, named for Nobel Prize winner Ronald Coase. The **Coase theorem** asserts that under certain conditions, the property right to an activity will be acquired by the party that values it most. (Those conditions are discussed more fully later in this chapter and in Chapter 8.)

The Coase theorem has two important implications. First, because the property right to an activity will be acquired by the party that values it most, the economic pie will be maximized. Second, legal constraints like those Roy and Phil faced will not affect this result. This version of the Coase theorem is slightly oversimplified, but for now it will serve us well. We'll make a few small modifications to the Coase theorem and present it in its final form in the last section of this chapter.

Application 7.3

The Nature Conservancy

Imagine a thousand-year-old redwood tree the size of a freight train. Now imagine a real estate developer ready to knock down this magnificent tree so the world can have yet another Costco, golf course, or suburb. Seems like a shame, doesn't it? But what can we do to stop it?

Not so long ago, a likely solution would have been for some trendy anti-capitalist to chain himself to the tree until the developer gave in. Or consider what Julia "Butterfly" Hill did. Hill, an environmental activist, lived in a redwood tree for 2 entire years, all to prevent a lumber company from turning it into a few hundred backyard decks.

But there are problems with relying on tactics like these to achieve your environmental goals. First, it's not respectful of property rights. But more fundamentally, it's important to recognize that we can't save every tree. We have other needs to satisfy, and sometimes trees stand in the way. There's no general shortage of trees, so we have to ask, "Which trees should stay, and which trees should go?"

Chaining yourself to a tree is easy, especially if your time isn't particularly valuable. So if we let tree-chainers answer our question for us, it's entirely possible to end up with somebody chained to a tree that nobody else values, standing in the way of something everybody else wants.

What would Coase say about tree-chaining? Maybe something like this: "Why don't you climb down out of that tree and put your money where your mouth is?"

In other words, if you really value the tree, don't take it by force or extortion. Either buy it from the developer or pay him not to destroy it. That encourages developers to axe the least-valued trees and save the most-valued trees. And it protects against the possibility that one person with nothing but time on her hands will stand in the way of something everybody else wants.

You might be thinking, "Sure. That may work for individual trees, but what if we're talking about an entire rain forest?" Getting together the big payments needed to prevent destruction of such large resources can be daunting. But it's not impossible. Consider The Nature Conservancy, a nonprofit environmental organization. The Nature Conservancy uses members' dues to purchase endangered habitats around the world. It then places those properties in trust with a university that will manage them for research purposes.

Since its inception in 1951, The Nature Conservancy has purchased hundreds of endangered habitats, ranging from rain forests to deserts. Those habitats are protected forever from any kind of commercial or residential development. Many habitats are open for the public to enjoy.

By putting its money where its mouth is, The Nature Conservancy embodies the essence of the Coase theorem. It doesn't achieve its goals by infringing on others' property rights. Rather, it relies on the power of bargaining to direct resources toward their most valued use. In other words, "We value this property more as wetlands than you do as a shopping mall. And that's not just cheap talk—we're willing to *pay* you to not develop it."

See related problem 4.6 on page 156 at the end of this chapter.

Based on Julia Hill's *Legacy of Luna: The Story of a Tree, a Woman and the Struggle to Save the Redwoods*, HarperCollins, 2001, and information obtained from nature.org.

The Coase Theorem, Applied

Before we modify the Coase theorem, let's apply it to the case of Roy and Phil. Being able to play concerts is worth $300 of extra income to Roy. Having silence is worth only $200 to Phil. So Roy values the airspace more than Phil. As the Coase theorem predicts:

1. Roy ends up playing concerts.
2. Playing concerts is the socially optimal (pie-maximizing) outcome.
3. Roy ends up playing concerts even when the law says he shouldn't.

The Coase theorem asserts that no matter what the law says about playing the accordion, the same outcome will occur. In the case of Roy and Phil, it *is* true that no matter who the law gives the property right to, we end up with concerts being played. However, it is *not* entirely true that the outcome is identical in both cases. The difference lies not in the overall size of the pie but in how that pie is split between Roy and Phil. Notice that when the law gives the property right to Roy by allowing accordion concerts to be played, both Roy and Phil end up with $400 at the end of the day. But when the law gives the property right to Phil (by outlawing accordion playing), Roy ends the day with only $150, whereas Phil ends the day with $650. In other words, the law makes no difference in terms of who ends up with the property right, but it makes a huge difference in the well-being of the parties involved.

The Coase Theorem: A Second Example

The Coase theorem delivers the socially desirable outcome when Roy values the air more than Phil. But would it work just as well if Phil valued the air more than Roy?

Let's explore that question. For simplicity, keep Phil's numbers the same: If no concerts are played, Phil earns $600; if concerts are played, he makes just $400. But let's change Roy's payouts so that when he plays concerts, he earns $200 instead of $400, and when he dunks fries, he still earns $100, just as he did before. What is the outcome likely to look like in this case?

The quick-and-dirty shortcut to answering this question is to note that Phil values silence at $200 (the difference in his earnings when he gets silence rather than the *Beer Barrel Polka*). Roy, however, values playing concerts at only $100. This is the *increase* in his earnings when he is allowed to play—the amount he makes over and above what he would earn dunking fries. So Phil values the property right to the air more than Roy. Consequently, we can use the Coase theorem to predict that no matter what the law says, we will end up with silence in the neighborhood.

The Socially Optimal Amount of Pollution When Concerts Are Illegal How exactly do we end up with silence, regardless of the law? Suppose first that concerts are illegal: In other words, Phil has the property right to use the airspace between their homes. If Roy were to begin playing and Phil were to do nothing, Phil's earnings would fall by $200, and Roy's would rise by $100. But Phil's best response is not to sit idly by; he can restore his lost income by picking up the phone and dialing the police. Because the property right belongs to Phil, Roy will quickly be admonished to stop playing the accordion, and he will end up dunking fries instead. In the end, Phil earns $600, and Roy earns $100.

In the previous example, Roy simply bribed Phil not to call the police. You might be wondering why that doesn't happen here. It is because Roy cannot afford to pay off Phil this time. To convince Phil not to call the police, Roy needs to fully compensate Phil for his losses. Phil is going to request at least $200. But Roy's additional earnings from playing versus dunking fries add up to only $100. So he doesn't have enough to cover Phil's losses. In this case, economists say that there is *no scope for a bargain* between Phil and Roy. The parties cannot reach an agreement, and Roy will end up dunking fries.

The Socially Optimal Amount of Pollution When Concerts Are Legal Suppose now that the law gives Roy the right to play concerts. This essentially dooms Phil to earnings of $400 and gives Roy the right to earn $200. Even if Phil calls the police, there is no way for the police to keep Roy from exercising his legal right, and concerts will be played.

You might be saying, "When Phil had the property right, we had silence, but when Roy has the property right, we have music. This violates the Coase theorem, doesn't it?" If that were where the story ended, you'd be right. But we have not yet considered the power of bargaining between Phil and Roy. Let's see what might happen if we put Roy and Phil in a room together with a pile of cash, a therapy couch, and an accordion. Will they be able to hash out some kind of agreement?

As a starting point, notice that Roy has the law on his side. So this time it's up to Phil to convince Roy to stop playing. In other words, to bargain around the law, Phil needs to pay Roy to *not* play the accordion. To fully compensate Roy for his losses, Phil needs to pay Roy at least $100 (the difference between what Roy can make playing music and what he can make dunking fries). Where does Phil get the money to do this? It comes from the fact that Roy's silence will increase Phil's earnings by $200. Out of that additional $200, Phil can give Roy his $100 of lost earnings and even a little more for good measure.

Let's suppose that Roy agrees to an offer of $150. Now when Roy chooses to dunk fries, his payoff becomes $250: $100 in earnings plus $150 he receives from Phil. Phil's payoff changes, too: He now earns $600 from his patients but gives $150 of that to Roy, for a net payoff of $450.

Notice that this exchange benefits both parties. By virtue of the law's structure, Phil can expect to earn only $400. However, by bargaining with Roy, he is able to increase that amount to $450. Similarly, by playing concerts (at the time, his best option) Roy could expect to make $200, but by bargaining for silence and then dunking fries, Roy ends his day with $250.

From a social perspective, Phil and Roy have bargained once again to the outcome the benevolent social planner would have wanted: When no bargain is struck, the economic pie is $600 ($400 + $200), but when Roy and Phil bargain around the law, the pie increases to $700 ($450 + $250). In this example, society has a preference for therapy over music, and the Coase theorem accurately predicts society's preferred outcome. Notice, too, that although the law does not affect the nature of the outcome, it once again has consequences for the distribution of that outcome. Roy much prefers a world in which the law allows concerts and earnings of $250 to a world in which the law does not and he makes only $100. Phil would like exactly the opposite. In either case, we end up with no concerts being played, but the well-being of the parties involved looks very different in the two situations.

Why the Coase Theorem May Not Work: Transactions Costs

7.5 Learning Objective
Define *transactions costs* and explain how these costs can impede the bargaining process.

If it's possible for polluters and victims to work out arrangements on their own, is it reasonable to conclude that we don't need to worry so much about regulating pollution? Can we infer that the pollution we currently have is pollution that society is willing to tolerate in exchange for the things that caused it? You might suspect that the answer is no, and it's quite likely that you're right. Let's shed a bit of light on the *why* of that answer by bringing in . . . the lawyers.

Let's revisit the example in which Roy could make $200 by playing the accordion. When the law demanded silence, Roy could not afford to pay off Phil, and silence prevailed. When the law permitted music, Phil paid off Roy, and silence prevailed. This socially optimal outcome came as a result of bargaining between the parties.

What we haven't done yet is talk about *how* that bargain was reached. In the back of your mind, you might have imagined that it went something like this:

Phil: I really like that music, Roy, but it's hurting my practice. Would you stop playing?

Roy: I understand your pain, Phil. But I've got to make a living, too.

Phil: What would it take to convince you not to play?

Roy: I'd lose at least $100 in earnings.

Phil: I'd be willing to pay you that.

Roy: Stealing my music would be like stealing my soul.

Phil: Okay, I'll throw in an extra $50.

Roy: Done.

This seems simple enough, but in the real world, such deals are often much more difficult to reach. For example, in the situation we're considering, suppose Phil would like to pay for Roy's silence, but he's worried Roy would take his money and play the accordion anyway. Creating an enforceable bargain often means calling in lawyers, and good lawyers aren't cheap. So let's modify the situation to include Phil's hiring an attorney at a cost of $125. Economists call the costs of arranging and enforcing bargains **transactions costs**. Transactions costs are the costs of making an exchange above and beyond the money that changes hands between Roy and Phil. Let's change our payoff matrix to reflect this new transactions cost. Figure 7.4 shows what it now looks like.

Transactions costs The costs of arranging and enforcing a transaction.

▶ **Figure 7.4**

Phil's and Roy's Payoffs When There Are Transactions Costs
Transactions costs unfavorably alter the payoffs available through bargaining. Here, concerts are legal, and the ideal outcome is for Roy to dunk fries. But because of $125 in transactions costs, Phil cannot afford to pay for Roy's silence. As a result, society gets a less-than-ideal outcome.

		Roy	
		Play Concerts	Dunk Fries
Phil	Do Nothing	**400, 200**	**325, 250**
	If Roy Plays, Call Police	**400, 200**	N/A

In this case, if Roy plays, Phil will make $400, and Roy will make $200. If Phil attempts to pay Roy $150 to stop playing, that agreement will need to be drawn up by an attorney, at a cost of $125. Phil will end up earning $600 from his patients but will spend $275 paying off Roy and the lawyer, leaving him with only $325. In this case, Phil would rather do nothing and let Roy play. That is true even if Roy simply asks to be compensated for his lost earnings. Phil would need to pay Roy $100 and the lawyer $125, for a total expenditure of $225, all in order to increase his earnings by $200. In other words, when transactions costs are sufficiently high, they interfere with the bargaining process that lies at the heart of the Coase theorem.

The implications of this are twofold. First, because of transactions costs, society cannot simply rely on arm's-length bargaining to resolve disputes about pollution. We might need to call in a higher authority, such as the government. Second, when transactions costs are high enough to preclude bargaining between polluter and victim, the law will not be irrelevant. Instead, it will be critical in determining the outcome society receives. With those thoughts in mind, we now present a final version of the Coase theorem, modified to reflect the nuances developed in this chapter: *When transactions costs are sufficiently low, the property right to an activity will be acquired by the party that values it most.* It is the purpose of the next chapter to discuss more fully what kinds of transactions costs might interfere with bargaining and what society can do to achieve the best outcome when transactions costs are high.

Conclusion

Our discussion of the Coase theorem highlights the notion that pollution represents a disagreement about how a resource is to be used. The Coase theorem tells us that it's possible for pollution problems to be resolved by bargaining between the interested parties, even if sometimes this means that the victims need to pay the polluters not to pollute. It also tells us that the outcome that polluters and victims reach will be the socially desirable outcome: When we're willing to tolerate pollution (a by-product) in exchange for the value created by the primary product, we end up with a good product and some pollution, too. But when the benefit we receive from the product

The People Behind the Theory

Ronald Coase

Few 20th-century economists have had as much of an impact on the discipline as Ronald Coase. His academic career began in his native England, and his first big research article, "The Nature of the Firm," introduced a new concept to economics: the idea of transactions costs. That 1937 article transformed economic thinking and gave rise to an entire branch of economic scholarship.

But Coase is even more famous for his namesake theorem, and the story behind that theorem is fascinating. Immigrating to the United States in 1951, Coase took an academic position at the University of Virginia. While there, he published a scholarly article, "The Federal Communications Commission," that contained an argument critical of prevailing economic wisdom. That criticism was the genesis of the Coase theorem.

Several economists at the University of Chicago (which arguably had the best economics program in the world) believed that Coase's argument was erroneous. They invited Coase to Chicago, where he insisted on having a chance to defend his position. That opportunity materialized at the home of professor Aaron Director. There, 20 intellectual powerhouses, including future Nobel Laureates Milton Friedman and George Stigler, debated the validity of Coase's reasoning. At the beginning of the evening, a vote was taken: 20 votes against Coase, and 1 (Coase himself) in favor.

Stigler recounts what transpired when Coase presented his controversial argument—the assertion that the law's assignment of property rights would have no effect on the way resources would end up being used:

> *As usual, Milton did much of the correct and deep and analytical thinking. [Ronald] refused to yield to all of our erroneous arguments. Milton would hit him from one side, then from another, then from another. Then, to our horror, Milton missed him and hit us. At the end of the evening the vote had changed. There were twenty-one votes for Ronald and [none against].*[1]

Coase was persuaded to write another scholarly article based on the evening's discussion. That article, "The Problem of Social Cost," became one of the most widely cited papers in all of economics, and it touched off an intellectual firestorm that transformed both economic thinking and legal scholarship. Coase went on to receive the 1991 Nobel Prize "for his discovery and clarification of the significance of transactions costs and property rights for the institutional structure and function of the economy."

Yet there is no greater testament to the power of Coase's intellect than Stigler's reflections on the meeting at Director's home. Stigler described it as one of the most exciting intellectual events of his life. In Stigler's words:

> *Scientific discoveries are usually the product of dozens upon dozens of tentative explorations. . . . An Archimedes who suddenly has a marvelous idea and shouts 'Eureka!' is the hero of the rarest of events. I have spent all of my professional life in the company of first-class scholars but only once have I encountered something like the sudden Archimedian revelation—as an observer.*[2]

Based on George J. Stigler's *Memoirs of an Unregulated Economist*, University of Chicago Press, 1988; the biographical entry on Coase in *The Concise Encyclopedia of Economics*, available online at the Library of Economics and Liberty (www .econlib.org); E.W. Kitch's "The Fire of Truth: A Remembrance of Law and Economics at Chicago, 1932–1970," *Journal of Law and Economics*, April 1983; and autobiographical information available at www.nobelprize.org.

---

[1] E.W. Kitch's "The Fire of Truth: A Remembrance of Law and Economics at Chicago, 1932-1970," *Journal of Law and Economics*, April 1983

[2] George J. Stigler, *Memoirs of an Unregulated Economist*, University of Chicago Press, 1988.

is overwhelmed by the damage of its by-products, we'll bargain with the polluter to either clean up his production process or not to produce at all.

Unfortunately, bargaining can deliver on those promises only if bargains are easy to arrange. When transactions costs are high, parties may be locked into a less-than-ideal outcome. In that case, it may be possible for government policy to improve on the outcome generated by individuals acting alone. The next chapter discusses more fully the nature of transactions costs, and it outlines in detail the types of policies the government uses to address pollution problems.

Chapter Summary and Problems

Key Terms

Coase theorem, p. 148

Externality, p. 142

Negative externality, p. 143

Positive externality, p. 144

Property right, p. 148

Transactions costs, p. 152

7.1 Externalities, pages 142–144

Define *externality* and distinguish between a positive externality and a negative externality.

Summary

An externality is the by-product of an activity that affects somebody else. A negative externality exists when bystanders are forced to bear part of the cost of someone else's activity. A positive externality exists when bystanders receive the benefits of someone else's activity.

Review Questions

All problems are assignable in MyEconLab.

1.1 A by-product of an activity that affects someone else is called a(n) _____.

1.2 A(n) _____ is a by-product of an activity that imposes a burden or cost on others.

1.3 If an externality makes a bystander better off than he was before the activity was undertaken, that externality is referred to as a(n) _____.

1.4 Sporting events are a source of income for some cities, but in 2011, following the defeat of the Vancouver Canucks by the Boston Bruins, a riot broke out in downtown Vancouver. In this instance, at least 140 people were reported injured. This type of violence would be considered a _____ of hockey games.
   a. Positive externality
   b. Transactions cost
   c. Negative externality
   d. Collective action

1.5 Since World War II, antibiotics have been available for use in treating bacterial infections. Increased antibiotic use has caused some antibiotic-resistant strains to evolve. Antibiotic resistance is a(n) _____ of antibiotic usage.
   a. Transactions Cost
   b. Negative Externality
   c. Explicit Cost
   d. Deadweight Loss

1.6 John lives in a second-floor apartment in Missoula, Montana. An elderly resident who prefers a very warm apartment lives directly beneath him. As a result, John rarely has to run the heat in his own apartment. The heat John receives from his downstairs neighbor could be considered a _____.
   a. Transactions cost
   b. Positive externality
   c. Negative externality
   d. Property right

Problems and Applications

1.7 A majority of the states have laws that ban smoking in enclosed public locations, including bars and restaurants. Can you think of a potential negative externality associated with these laws?

1.8 **[Related to Application 7.1 on page 143]** Read Application 7.1 carefully. Suppose that sex offenders move around often, rarely staying in the same place for more than a year or two. Under those circumstances, why might a person be interested in purchasing a house next door to a sex offender? Over a longer time horizon, does the sex offender confer a negative or positive externality on the homebuyer?

Pollution Problems (Negative Externalities) and Disagreements over the Competing Uses of Scarce Resources, pages 144–145

Evaluate whether all polluters are villains and everyone affected by pollution is a victim.

Summary

Pollution problems are generally not cases of good versus evil or villain versus victim. Instead, they represent morally neutral disagreements over competing uses for a scarce resource. From an economist's perspective, the problem is not necessarily to eliminate pollution; rather, it is to figure out the ideal amount of pollution.

Review Questions

All problems are assignable in MyEconLab.

2.1 When discussing problems of pollution, it is clear that _____.
   a. We can clearly delineate who is the victim and who is the villain
   b. Polluters must be made to stop polluting: they're harming other people
   c. Both a and b are true.
   d. Neither a nor b is true.

2.2 Economists generally assert the following about pollution: _____.
   a. The ideal amount of pollution is no pollution at all
   b. The problem we face in dealing with pollution is figuring out how much pollution is too much and how much pollution is not enough
   c. Because we like the products that polluters make, the best solution to pollution is to simply let polluters pollute as much as they wish
   d. Pollution is never a problem because polluters and victims can always bargain with one another

Problems and Applications

2.3 Jolie grows asparagus for a living. Her asparagus beds, fertilized with manure, are extraordinarily productive. When Jolie tends five beds, her profits are $3,000. When Jolie expands her operation to six beds, she earns $3,600. Next door, Maddox runs a tea shop. When Jolie tends five beds of asparagus, Maddox's customers can't detect the smell of manure from Jolie's beds, and Maddox earns $1,200. When Jolie tends six beds, the smell of manure is noticeable, and Maddox's profits fall to $800. Explain why it is probably unfair (though convenient) to characterize Jolie as the polluter and Maddox as the victim.

2.4 In 1992, the federal government mandated a switch to low-flow showerheads that only allowed 2.5 gallons of water to be used each minute. Prior to the measure, showerheads routinely allowed a flow of between 5 and 8 gallons per minute. The rationale for the measure was conservation: to reduce the wasteful use of water in the shower. Discuss this measure from the villain/victim standpoint. Who are the villains (and are they really villains)? Who are the victims the law is designed to protect (and are they really victims)?

How Much Pollution Is the Right Amount of Pollution? pages 145–148

Identify cases in which pollution is in society's best interest and cases in which it is not.

Summary

The socially ideal amount of pollution balances the cost imposed by an externality with the benefits created by the primary product. In some cases, it is possible for the interested parties to bargain over the existence or amount of pollution. If the one creating the externality values the right to pollute more than the people the pollution affects, he or she can, if necessary, acquire the right to pollute by paying those affected. That may occur even in instances when the law doesn't allow pollution.

Review Questions

All problems are assignable in MyEconLab.

3.1 Suppose that a brewer regularly dumps used yeast into a river and that a downstream water bottler must clean up the water before using it. Dumping the yeast into the river saves the brewer $500 in disposal costs each day. Cleaning up the water costs the bottler $600 each day. In this case, the benevolent social planner would _____.
   a. Like to see the brewer pollute
   b. Like to see the brewer dispose of the yeast somewhere other than the river

c. Strongly encourage the government to pass a law giving the brewer the right to pollute the river

d. We don't have enough information to determine what the benevolent social planner might want.

3.2 When it comes to pollution problems, Section 7.3 suggests that _____.

a. Whether we will have pollution or not depends on what the law allows

b. Polluter and victim can negotiate to the outcome that the benevolent social planner would want

c. Both a and b are true.

d. Neither a nor b is true.

Problems and Applications

3.3 **[Related to Application 7.2 on page 147]** According to the Centers for Disease Control and Prevention, the most common sexually transmitted infection is the genital human papilloma virus (HPV). It's so common that nearly all sexually active men and women get it at some point in their lives. In 2006, the Food and Drug Administration approved the first HPV vaccine.

What is the direct effect of the HPV vaccine? Does the HPV vaccine create an externality? If so, explain what that externality is and discuss whether it is positive or negative.

3.4 "I never get a flu shot . . . but I always make sure my wife does." Discuss this statement and link your discussion to recent outbreaks of measles, mumps, and whooping cough. Your discussion should be based on game theory and should also explicitly mention externalities.

3.5 Consider the case of Jolie and Maddox outlined in problem 2.3. Suppose that the law states that anyone using manure for fertilizer may not use so much that it bothers his or her neighbors.

a. If you were the benevolent social planner, would you like to see Jolie keep five beds or six? Why?

b. If bargaining between Jolie and Maddox is easy, how many beds will Jolie keep? Describe the bargain that results, if any, including the amount of money changing hands.

c. Is the outcome in (b) an outcome that the benevolent social planner would endorse? Why or why not?

7.4 ## The Coase Theorem, pages 148–151

Explain how the exchange of property rights can bring about the socially ideal amount of pollution.

Summary

The Coase theorem asserts that when bargaining is easy, the right to pollute will be acquired by the party that values it the most. That outcome will result no matter what the laws regarding pollution happen to say; if necessary, the parties will bargain around the law. Further, the outcome will result in the largest possible economic pie for society to enjoy.

Review Questions

4.1 When the law grants somebody control of a resource, that control is referred to as a(n) _____.

4.2 The _____ states that under certain conditions, the property right to an activity will be acquired by the party that values it most.

4.3 Suppose that in problem 3.1, the law gave the brewer the right to dump yeast in the stream. Assuming that the conditions of the Coase theorem are met, the Coase theorem suggests that _____.

a. The brewer will pay the water bottler for the right to dump yeast in the river

b. The brewer will dump yeast, and there's nothing the water bottler can do about it

c. The water bottler will have the police stop the brewer from dumping yeast

d. The water bottler will pay the brewer not to dump yeast in the river

Problems and Applications

4.4 Assuming sufficiently low transactions costs, the Coase theorem asserts that the property right to an activity will be acquired by the party that values it most. What are the two implications of the Coase theorem that are listed in the chapter?

4.5 Assuming that transactions costs are sufficiently low, the Coase theorem results in the economic pie being maximized, regardless of legal constraints. What impact, then, do legal constraints have?

4.6 **[Related to Application 7.3 on page 149]** The Nature Conservancy is one tool that consumers can use to put their money where their mouth is, but it's not the only one. Discuss how Internet technology is helping large groups of consumers raise money for causes they support. Does this technology make it more likely or less likely that the economic pie will be maximized?

4.7 Create the relevant payoff matrixes to illustrate the section "The Coase Theorem: A Second Example" on pages 150–151.

Define *transactions costs* and explain how these costs can impede the bargaining process.

Summary

The Coase theorem is valid only when bargains are easy to arrange. Unfortunately, bargains may not be easy to arrange. The difficulties and costs of arranging bargains are called transactions costs. If transactions costs are high enough, they may prevent people from bargaining with one another, and the predictions of the Coase theorem may not be realized. Society may be stuck with a less-than-ideal outcome.

Review Questions

All problems are assignable in MyEconLab.

5.1 The costs of arranging and enforcing bargains are called _____.

5.2 Fred lives in the United States and is interested in purchasing a crate of Trappist Westvleteren 12, a beer brewed by Belgian monks. The beer costs €40. In addition, the beer is sold only at the monastery gates, to customers who have made a reservation by telephone and who agree not to resell the beer to any third party. The costs of acquiring Westvleteren 12 above and beyond the €40 that would change hands for the purchase are called _____.

   a. Transactions costs

   b. Private costs

   c. External costs

   d. Side bargains

5.3 What implications do high transactions costs hold for the Coase theorem?

   a. Society cannot rely on arm's-length bargaining to resolve resource disputes.

   b. The economic pie may not be maximized.

   c. Legal constraints can affect whether the economic pie is maximized.

   d. All of the above are true.

5.4 Nobel Prize winner Ronald Coase's famous theorem suggests that _____.

   a. Pollution problems can't be solved without strong government

   b. Imposing taxes on polluters is the best way to solve pollution problems

   c. High transactions costs are good for society because they prevent polluters from buying the right to pollute

   d. Some pollution problems can be solved via negotiations between polluter and victim

Problems and Applications

5.5 A majority of the states have laws that ban smoking in enclosed public locations, including bars and restaurants. Do you suppose this law maximizes the economic pie? Why or why not? Why do you suppose state governments didn't leave this issue to be resolved by bargaining between smoking and nonsmoking restaurant patrons? Explain your reasoning.

5.6 Consider the case of Jolie and Maddox outlined in problems 2.3 and 3.5.

   a. Suppose that drawing up an enforceable contract costs $250. How many beds will Jolie end up keeping? Explain your answer carefully.

   b. Is the outcome Jolie and Maddox achieve in (a) an outcome that the benevolent social planner would endorse? Why or why not?

The Herd Immunity Game

This chapter focused on the analysis of externalities, which are by-products of an activity that hurt or help someone who is not involved in that activity. This game applies that analysis to the positive externalities that vaccinations create.

Suppose that a particularly potent strain of the flu virus has been discovered in your class. In an effort to avoid a pandemic, the government asked doctors and researchers from the Centers for Disease Control and Prevention to develop a vaccine. That vaccine is now on the market and is available at doctor's offices and pharmacies. You must decide whether to get the vaccination.

Receiving the vaccination is both painful and expensive, but it guarantees that you won't catch the virus. If you choose not to receive the vaccine, you stand some chance of contracting a costly illness. The greater the number of your classmates who choose to get the vaccine, however, the lower the chance you will get sick.

Do you get the expensive vaccine and guarantee your health? Or do you rely on so many of your classmates getting the vaccine that your odds of contracting the illness will be small?

MyEconLab

Please visit http://www.myeconlab.com for support material to conduct this experiment if assigned by your instructor.

Government Policies to Regulate Pollution

Chapter Outline and Learning Objectives

8.1 Four Major Types of Transactions Costs, page 160

Describe the four different types of transactions costs.

8.2 Regulating Pollution in an Ideal World, page 163

List the four basic principles that policymakers should consider when designing pollution regulations.

8.3 Tools Governments Use to Regulate Pollution, page 167

Explain how governments use taxes, subsidies, and cap-and-trade systems to reduce pollution.

Experiment: The Judge-Me-Not Game, page 178

MyEconLab

MyEconLab helps you master each objective and study more efficiently.

The previous chapter discussed scenarios where negotiation might be successful in eliminating pollution—be it noise pollution, water pollution, or air pollution—and scenarios where negotiation might not. When negotiation is unlikely to solve pollution problems, we might need government to help resolve conflicts about pollution. This chapter examines how the government might go about doing that. Before jumping into that material, let's briefly review the major points of the previous chapter:

- When people argue about pollution, they are really arguing about how society should use its scarce resources.

- Armed with the knowledge that environmental problems largely reflect differences in preferences, using the terms *polluter* and *victim* doesn't objectively characterize the problem.

- When the parties involved in a dispute about pollution can easily communicate with one another, the process of bargaining will reveal when pollution is in society's best interests and when it is not.

- When bargaining can easily occur, a higher authority will be less likely to have to step in to regulate pollution problems because the parties will reach the outcome the benevolent social planner would like to see, regardless of what the law says.

- Unfortunately, when transactions costs are high, the bargaining process breaks down. When that happens, society sometimes ends up locked into using resources in ways that are less desirable than other alternatives. This is when calling on a higher power for help is most reasonable.

This chapter looks more closely at the nature of transactions costs because the magnitude of transactions costs determines whether private individuals will be able to solve pollution problems for themselves. After examining different types of transactions costs, the chapter discusses what an ideal scheme for regulating pollution might look like. Finally, the chapter analyzes various regulations that governments use to help control pollution.

Four Major Types of Transactions Costs

8.1 Learning Objective

Describe the four different types of transactions costs.

Before bed, Nate Dodge poured himself a glass of water, drank half of it, and set the half-empty glass on his bedside stand. Awakened at 3 a.m. with a raging thirst, Nate reached for the glass on his nightstand and was surprised to find it glowing a phosphorescent green. Within a few months, Nate began to develop splitting migraine headaches, a problem he attributed to the glowing green stuff in his water. There was a polluter in town, and Nate took it upon himself to fix the problem.

Search Costs

In college, Nate had spent an entire semester studying the Coase theorem. So he immediately began looking for the polluter, with the hope of striking a bargain that would make his water once again drinkable. Midland City, Nate's hometown, draws its drinking water from Sugar Creek. Nate went down to the creek and, much to his dismay, discovered dozens of factories lining its banks.

Nate's first problem: Which one of the dozens of factories is emitting the harmful pollution? Without this critical piece of information, Nate does not know whom to bargain with.

The magnitude of this problem is daunting. Suppose that there are only two factories on Sugar Creek: one that belongs to a tire manufacturer and another that belongs to a breakfast cereal producer. Suppose further that the cereal maker is polluting the stream. If Nate mistakenly presumes that the tire manufacturer is the polluter and offers the owners of the firm a handsome sum of money to stop dumping the green gunk into the creek, they would be foolish to turn down the money. They'll take the cash, promise not to pollute, and never reveal to Nate that they were not polluting in the first place.

Nate needs a way to definitively pinpoint the source of the pollution. But doing that is likely to be quite costly because (1) there are many potential polluters and (2) the polluter could easily be tens or hundreds of miles upstream. Finding the source of the pollution might require sampling the emissions of dozens or hundreds of factories. These costs, which economists call *search costs*, could be so large that by the time Nate has figured out who the polluter is, he'll have no money left to bargain with.

Collectivization Costs

Suppose that Nate gets lucky: The first factory Nate happens upon, the cereal factory, is the one polluting Sugar Creek. Imagine what happens when Nate walks into the CEO's office:

> **Nate:** I've determined that you are the source of the glowing green goop in Sugar Creek.
>
> **CEO:** So?
>
> **Nate:** I'd like to pay you to stop polluting.
>
> **CEO:** What's it worth to you?
>
> **Nate:** I'd pay $200,000 to make these headaches stop.
>
> **CEO:** I'm sorry. Dumping my waste in the creek instead of disposing of it in a safer way is saving me $10 million. I reject your offer.

Because polluting is worth $10 million to the polluter, and clean water is worth only $200,000 to Nate, you might be tempted to conclude that Nate and the CEO have reached the socially ideal solution. The cereal company continues to pollute, and Nate either bears the health care costs related to the pollution or perhaps takes some other action to prevent drinking the water, such as moving to another town or drinking only bottled water. That would be an easy conclusion to reach, but in this case it might be wrong. Because Sugar Creek supplies the drinking water for everyone in Midland City, Nate is unlikely to be the only victim in town. So the cereal company may be creating far more than just the $200,000 of damage that Nate has incurred.

Fortunately, Nate has thought of this possibility. Within a few days, he finds 59 other people who are suffering just as much ($200,000 each) from the pollution as he is. And though the benefits to the polluter outweigh the cost to any *particular* individual, it's now clear that the *total* costs ($200,000 × 60 = $12 million) the polluter is imposing on the residents of Midland City outweigh the $10 million of benefits to the polluter. This is a case where pollution makes the world poorer, and where, in an ideal world, the victims and the polluter would negotiate it out of existence.

> **Nate's second problem:** How can Nate find, organize, and motivate his fellow victims to help him bargain with the polluter?

Nate needs to gather his fellow victims and convince them to contribute money to a fund used to pay the polluter not to pollute. For now, ignore the difficulties of getting people to contribute money to a worthy cause. That particular problem is addressed later in the text (see Chapter 10). Instead, think about the problem purely in terms of logistics. Have you ever done group work in college? If so, it's likely that you found organizing and motivating even a small group to be a challenge. Nate's challenge is tougher: He needs to find each of his 59 fellow victims, convince each of them to join in his effort, collect cash from them, and take it all to the cereal company. The cost of organizing such an effort might be substantial; he might have to run an ad on TV to let his fellow victims know what he's attempting. He might have to hold meetings and rallies. His job amounts to herding a very large group of cats. The costs of motivating and organizing a large group of people, which we might call *collectivization costs*, are likely to impede the bargaining that leads to an ideal social outcome.

Negotiation Costs

Nate is a marvel: He's ferreted out the polluter, he's inspired his fellow victims to action, and together they march on the cereal factory. With strength in numbers and a $12 million pile of cash contributed by all the victims of glowing green water, they offer to pay the CEO of the cereal company not to pollute. Here's how the conversation goes:

> **CEO:**   But wait. I want to call in my accountants and make sure that this $12 million will actually cover my costs. And we'll need to assemble negotiating teams to hash out all the legalities. Once that's done, I'll need to bring in some lawyers to look over the agreement to ensure that it says what you say it says. I'm assuming that you'll pick up the tab for all of that, right?

> **Nate:**   By my estimates, all the negotiators, accountants, and lawyers will cost $3 million. By the time we pay those costs, we'll have only $9 million left to pay you.

> **CEO:**   Sorry. That's not enough to cover my losses. I guess we're out of luck, and it's a shame because a bargain might have benefited both of us.

> **Nate:**   Nuts.

Nate's third problem: Negotiation is expensive. Will he be able to come up with enough cash to pay the polluter and his negotiating team?

Of course, you have already seen this problem—it appeared at the end of the previous chapter, when the costs of hiring lawyers prevented Roy and Phil from reaching a bargain. Lawyers are just one manifestation of *negotiation costs*, which are the costs associated with the process of hashing out the terms of an agreement. The costs of hiring accountants and professional negotiators are two other forms of negotiation costs. Plus, any process that requires a great deal of human power and paperwork probably requires a great deal of administrative overhead—clerks and secretaries and countless preparatory briefings from underlings and lackeys and middle managers about what bargains might benefit whom and what bargains would not.

Monitoring and Enforcement Costs

We now know that bargains can be used to resolve pollution problems but that search, collectivization, and negotiation costs can interfere with the bargaining process. There is still one more hurdle to clear to eliminate the cereal company's socially wasteful pollution, and it may well be the highest hurdle of all. Suppose the lawyers and accountants have agreed to volunteer their time, enabling Nate and the CEO to reach an agreement. Nate pays the CEO $11 million, and the CEO agrees to dispose of his toxic green sludge safely. Nate and his group thereby eliminate $12 million of medical costs by spending only $11 million. And because it costs the cereal company only $10 million to dispose of its waste, the company keeps an extra $1 million as a result of the deal. Does this mean that the residents of Midland City can breathe a sigh of relief?

Of course not! It's true that the CEO has made his company a bit better off in exchange for not polluting, but from his perspective, wouldn't it be nice if he could collect Nate's $11 million and continue to dump sludge in the river instead of disposing of it safely? That would increase his company's bottom line from a $1 million gain to a $21 million gain!

The incentive to cheat on the agreement is a problem that needs to be dealt with. In this case, Nate is likely to demand that the company be frequently monitored to ensure that it's complying with the agreement. Regardless of whether the CEO or Nate pays for the monitoring, if it is very costly (say, $2 million or more), then it is possible that these monitoring and enforcement costs may discourage the bargain from ever happening in the first place.

So what are we to do? We know that Nate and the citizens of Midland City value clean water more than the cereal company values the right to dump glowing green goop in the river. But because of all the types of transactions costs, it is quite possible that Nate and the CEO will not be able to reach a cease-polluting agreement.

You might be thinking that it makes sense for Nate to simply sue the cereal company for damages, and in a simpler context, that might work. But relying on a lawsuit to resolve this particular situation is unlikely to produce an ideal outcome largely for the same reasons that bargaining failed to do so. First, remember that Nate was initially unaware of the source of the glowing green water. So in order to sue for damages, Nate will still face substantial search costs. Second, hiring lawyers is expensive and may easily outweigh the $200,000 of damage that Nate suffered. Of course, Nate can spread the legal fees around by bringing in fellow victims to help bear the legal costs. In the legal world, a lawsuit like this is called a class-action lawsuit. Class-action lawsuits are designed to make it feasible and affordable for people who have suffered damages to get together with other damaged parties and sue for recovery. Class actions are fairly common and can be highly effective. When the Exxon *Valdez* ran aground and spilled oil over 1,300 miles of Alaska's coast, the victims brought a class-action suit against Exxon. Similarly, 46 states joined together to sue the major tobacco manufacturers for repayment of health care expenditures. (For more on the tobacco lawsuit, see Chapter 2.) But assembling a *class*—the group of people suing for damages—is not cheap. Once again, collectivization costs rear their ugly head. If they're high enough, they may prevent a lawsuit from being an effective way to resolve this dispute.[1]

Regulating Pollution in an Ideal World

8.2 Learning Objective

List the four basic principles that policymakers should consider when designing pollution regulations.

Because of transactions costs, Nate and the cereal company are unlikely to reach the agreement that the benevolent social planner would like them to reach. It's not their fault, and they're not being stubborn. It simply isn't in either party's interest to agree to a deal that, because of transactions costs, would make them worse off.

If Nate and the CEO are powerless to resolve their dispute, how can society ensure that the waters of Sugar Creek are put to their best use? One way is to call in someone with more power: the government. The government, unlike Nate, the CEO, or the benevolent social planner, has the power to resolve disputes by decree. The government can implement some sort of regulatory scheme oriented toward limiting the amount of pollution pumped into our rivers or air.

Before analyzing the various types of regulatory schemes governments use to fix real-world problems of pollution, let's think about what governmental regulation might look like in an ideal world. In other words, how would the benevolent social planner like to see governments intervene in environmental matters? In an ideal world, governments would follow four general principles. From an economist's standpoint, these principles should be generally agreeable and inoffensive to the ordinary person, regardless of the individual's political or environmental leanings. Let's look at each of them.

Principle 1: Regulation is Necessary Only When Transactions Costs Preclude Bargaining Between Polluter and Victim

In the previous chapter, Roy and Phil efficiently resolved their dispute by bargaining. They were able to do that because it was easy for them to negotiate with one another. This chapter, however, has shown how real-world complications might impede bargaining and leave society with an outcome that is less than desirable.

---

[1]For a closer look at how difficult and costly it is to deal with transactions costs and assemble a class, see Jonathan Harr's book *A Civil Action*, which was later made into a movie starring John Travolta.

It's tempting when you see smog in the air or oil in the streams to say, "There ought to be a law," and ask government to step in to regulate the amount of those things that is permissible. But Principle 1 says that government action is required only if transactions costs preclude bargaining between polluter and victim. It seems reasonable to suggest, then, that the *first* thing government regulators should do when confronted with a pollution problem is to ask themselves, "What transactions costs might be preventing the affected parties from bargaining to an ideal solution?" If regulators can't pinpoint substantial transactions costs, then perhaps the best thing government can do is to let the parties work out the matter for themselves.

Unfortunately, in environmental disputes, high transactions costs are probably the rule rather than the exception. Because of that, the parties are unlikely to bargain to a reasonable solution on their own. So if we're going to call in government to help us resolve these difficulties, what standard should the government set?

Principle 2: The Regulation Should Achieve the Outcome the Affected Parties Would Have Reached Had Transactions Costs Not Been So High

When dealing with pollution problems, government regulators often explicitly or implicitly assign the property right to one party. For example, most governments have banned the use of chlorofluorocarbon (CFC) gases in propellants and refrigerants because of the damage they cause to the ozone layer. That ban reassigned the property right to use CFCs from producers who wanted to incorporate CFCs in their products to the parties who were affected by the ozone damage.

Often, as is the case with CFCs, that property right is not an *absolute* property right. In other words, the government often forbids transferring a property right once it's been assigned. Even if a manufacturer wanted to make air conditioners that used CFCs, that manufacturer could not buy that right.

Unfortunately, sometimes government regulation may inhibit the bargaining that is necessary to achieve an ideal outcome. For example, a few decades ago, most countries around the world banned the use of DDT, an insecticide that also, unfortunately, damaged bird eggs. But DDT is highly effective and could be used to kill malaria-spreading mosquitoes. Potential malaria victims might be willing to pay for the right to use DDT, and society might be willing to trade a few birds for the chance to control a deadly disease. But even if the benefits of using DDT to control malaria outweigh the costs, the ban makes bargaining impossible. In this case, as well as others, the benevolent social planner hopes that the government assigns the right to the party that values it the most. If not, the regulation may leave society with too much or too little pollution.

One practical implication of Principles 1 and 2 combined is that one way for government to creatively regulate pollution problems may be to focus not on the pollution itself but on the transactions costs that impede bargaining. If the government can reduce the transactions costs, society will get the pie-maximizing outcome through the process of bargaining without government intervention.

Principle 3: The Regulation Should Be Designed to Make the Polluter Internalize the Cost of the Externality

Principle 3 simply states that if a polluter imposes $10 of costs on somebody else, a reasonable regulation should impose $10 of additional costs on the polluter. It's tempting (especially because we've used the slightly inflammatory *polluter* and *victim* language) to agree with Principle 3 simply on ethical grounds. If a polluter imposes costs on others, it's only fair that the polluter gets those costs thrown back at him.

But that is insufficient justification for Principle 3. One reason is because we've been working to deal *positively* with economic issues rather than *normatively*. Rather, from the standpoint of the benevolent social planner, the real problem of pollution is that polluters are able to force others to bear part of the cost of their activity. As a result, polluters tend to make decisions that shrink the economic pie rather than increase it.

As an example, suppose that Rachel, a barbeque pit master, produces delicious spareribs in a backyard smoke pit. Her customers get exactly $10 of value from eating her spareribs, and Rachel uses $8 worth of time and ingredients to create them.

Unfortunately, the smoke from Rachel's barbeque pit has the potential to aggravate her asthmatic neighbor. If Rachel were to produce her ribs in a nonpolluting way, she would spend $8 on the ribs themselves and $4 on a disposable filter that would remove the smoke from the air. If Rachel had to bear all $12 of those costs, she would decide that it wasn't worth making ribs for a living, and she'd get a different job instead. From society's point of view, that is exactly the right decision: It makes little sense to use $12 worth of resources to create $10 worth of value for customers.

But often, polluters like Rachel don't have to bear all the cost of their activity; they can force others to bear some of the costs. For the sake of argument, let's say that bargaining between Rachel and her asthmatic neighbor is prohibitively expensive due to transactions costs and that it's perfectly legal for Rachel to smoke ribs in her backyard pit. Then her neighbor will be forced to either (1) install a $4 filter on his own heating/air conditioning unit to remove the smoke or (2) suffer a debilitating asthma attack. Rachel, having shunted the cost of cleaning the air onto her neighbor, has no incentive to look for work elsewhere and will go on happily roasting ribs forever.

The problem is that Rachel makes decisions based only on the costs that *she* bears. Specifically, Rachel bears $8 of what economists call private costs. **Private costs** are costs that are borne by the producer of a good or service. In this case, the private costs might include the cost of the ingredients, the charcoal, and the value of Rachel's time. Unfortunately, Rachel also creates external costs of $4. **External costs** represent the value of a negative externality that someone imposes on others. Add the private and external costs, and in this example we get the full $12 social cost of ribs. The **social cost** of producing a product is the full cost of producing an item, including the producer's private costs and all the external costs. It's a reasonable jump to assert that the more costs Rachel can shunt to her neighbors, the more ribs she will produce. Although Rachel thinks that smoking ribs makes good sense, the benevolent social planner does not. She recognizes that every rib Rachel produces *still* costs $12 to make and that every rib Rachel makes shrinks the social pie by $2.

So the reason economists are interested in making polluters bear the costs they impose on others is not one of equity. Rather, economists are interested in imposing those costs on the polluter because the polluter will make better decisions for society if she has to consider all the costs of her activity. The government might accomplish this by requiring Rachel to install a $4 filter every time she makes an order of ribs. Or government might make Rachel pay a $4 fee for every plate of ribs she serves. Either way, absorbing the external costs Rachel imposes on her asthmatic neighbor changes Rachel's cost–benefit calculations. Absorbing, or paying for, an externality you create is what economists refer to as *internalizing* an externality. Internalizing the externality encourages Rachel to seek employment elsewhere. Society loses $10 of ribs but saves $12 of costs; the economic pie grows by $2, and the benevolent social planner rejoices.

Private costs Costs that are borne by the producer of a good or service.

External costs The value of a negative externality borne by those who do not produce the good or service.

Social cost The full cost of producing a good or service, including the producer's private costs and all the external costs.

Principle 4: Eliminating Pollution Entirely Should Not Be the Goal of Regulation

"Wouldn't it be nice," you might muse, "to live in a world free of pollution?" It's difficult to argue with the picture of pastoral serenity this statement paints. As a sentiment, it's terrific.

But as a policy, it's likely to be a disaster. The unfortunate reality is that virtually everything we do creates an externality; also, much, if not most, of the time,

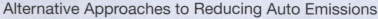

Application 8.1

Alternative Approaches to Reducing Auto Emissions

Many factors may contribute to climate change. But no single behavior attracts quite as much negative attention as our driving. So if we are to adopt policies that cause us to modify driving-related emissions of carbon dioxide (CO_2), what alternatives do we have?

To answer this question, one fact must be made plain: Every gallon of gasoline we burn produces about 19.5 pounds of CO_2. So if we are to reduce driving-related CO_2 emissions, we must reduce our fuel consumption.

Two mechanisms designed to reduce fuel consumption are already in force. One is a gasoline tax. The other is a mandate to automakers to make cars more fuel efficient. Which of these is most effective at reducing fuel consumption?

The fuel-economy mandate. Since the 1970s, the U.S. government has set Corporate Average Fuel Economy (CAFE) standards for automakers. For example, the standards set forth by President Obama's administration require an automaker's "typical" vehicle to achieve 34.1 miles per gallon of gasoline today, increasing to 54.5 miles per gallon by 2025.

You might think that increasing CAFE standards would reduce fuel consumption. But two important and offsetting forces are at work. First, if you increase fuel economy, you reduce the amount of fuel needed to drive a given distance. That lines up nicely with the goal of reducing emissions. The second effect of increasing CAFE standards is more subtle: Raising fuel efficiency reduces the *cost* of driving a particular distance. It makes driving cheaper, and when driving gets cheaper, people drive more. So on the one hand, we're sipping less fuel for each mile we drive; on the other, we're driving more miles. Those forces work in opposite directions, and the *Wall Street Journal* suggests that when it comes to total fuel consumption, they may largely cancel one another out: "Since 1970, the United States has made cars almost 50% more efficient; in that period of time, the average number of miles a person drives has doubled."[2]

The gas tax. A tax on fuel has no offsetting effect. It increases the cost of driving, and it increases it more for people who drive gas-guzzlers than it does for people who drive fuel-sipping vehicles. Furthermore, while increasing CAFE standards affects gas consumption only for those who buy new cars, a gas tax affects *all* drivers. This suggests that increasing the gas tax is likely to be more effective than increasing CAFE standards, which is exactly what economists Sarah West and Roberton Williams found when they researched the question.

West and Williams's results cast policymakers in an unfortunate light. For all the talk about reducing fuel consumption and carbon emissions, politicians have resisted raising taxes and instead have focused on increasing fuel economy standards. West and Williams imply that this is because voters view increased fuel economy as a good thing but high fuel prices (as might be caused by a fuel tax increase) as bad.

An economist's recommendation? If policymakers are really serious about reducing fuel consumption, they need to implement policies that make drivers think carefully about the costs and benefits of every mile. As unpopular as it may be, the best way to accomplish that is by ratcheting up the gasoline tax—perhaps by as much as $3 or $4 per gallon.

See related problem 2.7 on page 175 at the end of this chapter.

Based on Sarah West and Roberton C. Williams, "The Cost of Reducing Gasoline Consumption," *American Economic Review Papers and Proceedings*, 2005; Kimberley A. Strassel's "Conservation Wastes Energy," *The Wall Street Journal*, May 17, 2001; and Valerie Karplus, Sergey Paltsev, Mustafa Babiker, and John Reilly, "Should a Vehicle Fuel Economy Standard Be Combined with an Economy-wide Greenhouse Gas Emissions Constraint? Implications for Energy and Climate Policy in the United States," *Energy Economics*, 2013.

[2] Kimberley A. Strassel's "Conservation Wastes Energy," *The Wall Street Journal*, May 17, 2001.

we're willing to put up with the externality in exchange for the activity. The most extreme example of this is breathing. Every breath we take creates carbon dioxide, which is classified as a greenhouse gas and may be contributing to climate change. Unless we want to quit breathing, it would be foolish of us to outlaw carbon dioxide. What about driving cars, which also create pollution? Every gallon of gas we burn pumps carbon dioxide and other noxious gases and particulates into the atmosphere. The production of cars itself creates a great deal of pollution; it takes heat to smelt the iron to make the steel to make cars; it takes fuel to move cars from the factory to the dealer's showroom; it takes petroleum to make rubber to make tires, and in the process of melting the rubber into tire shapes, other pollutants are released into the atmosphere.

Yet even the most hardened environmentalists drive cars. The comfort, safety, and convenience they create are of such tremendous benefit that we're willing to bear the pollution costs they impose on the planet. Once we've accepted the fact that we're willing to trade some pollution for a great deal of convenience, the question becomes not whether we'll have pollution but "How much pollution will we have?"

Sometimes it is tempting to wrap oneself in normativism. For example, if someone drives a car that gets only 15 miles per gallon of gas, you might be tempted to claim that the person is environmentally irresponsible. But basically you make the same decision that person has made when you get behind the wheel, regardless of how many miles to the gallon your car gets. Essentially, you are making your life a bit easier by driving in exchange for making your fellow humans on the planet suffer. You might be making them suffer a bit less than the Hummer-driving, 90-mile-per-day commuter, but you're still making them suffer. Within the context of economics, that's okay, as long as the benefits received by the driver are greater than *all* of the costs, including the external costs. Put another way, it's unrealistic to get rid of pollution entirely; we are simply too attached to the comforts and conveniences (like cars and breathing) that create the pollution. Government's job, then, is to decide how much pollution we should tolerate in exchange for those comforts and conveniences and to design policies that guide polluters toward that amount. Unfortunately, governments frequently violate that principle in practice and base environmental policy on normative rather than positive concerns. The European Union, for example, has highly restricted the production and use of genetically modified organisms (GMOs) such as pest-resistant corn, despite a lack of compelling scientific evidence that they are harmful to humans. In the words of the Council on Foreign Relations, a bipartisan U.S. think tank, "European regulatory politics and policies [regarding GMOs] over the last fifteen years . . . are often politicized, highly contentious and characterized by a suspicion of science."[3]

Tools Governments Use to Regulate Pollution

8.3 Learning Objective

Explain how governments use taxes, subsidies, and cap-and-trade systems to reduce pollution.

What might government policies to reduce pollution look like? Traditionally, they have taken the form of fees or payments designed to steer polluters toward the correct (that is, pie-maximizing) amount of pollution. Let's revisit Rachel the pit master and see how such a solution might work.

Taxes

Recall that Rachel was able to produce ribs at a private cost of $8, ribs that she in turn sold to customers for $10. But in the process she imposed costs of $4 on her neighbors, which led to rib production being bad for society (but good for Rachel). Because Rachel considered only her private costs when deciding to produce ribs, she made a choice that was detrimental to society. One easy remedy to this problem is for

[3]See Diahanna Lynch and David Vogel's *The Regulation of GMOs in Europe and the United States: A Case-Study of Contemporary European Regulatory Politics*, CFR Press, 2001.

Application 8.2

Dealing with Climate Change

No environmental issue is more divisive, and none has us handcuffed more, than climate change. In short, scientists assert that the use of fossil fuels creates a negative externality—high concentrations of atmospheric carbon dioxide that holds Earth's heat. This greenhouse effect causes Earth's temperature to rise, changing weather patterns, raising sea levels, and bleaching coral reefs. Many fear that temperature increases will accelerate, with disastrous consequences.

Let's assume that it's 100% true: Climate change exists, and it exists because of us. What are we to do about it? Coase suggests that externality problems can potentially be resolved via bargaining. But the pollution is happening today, and the consequences won't materialize for decades. Many of the victims have yet to be born. So getting polluters and victims together to bargain seems pretty difficult.

This is why a solution to climate change must come from government. But that's not easy, either. Suppose you're a policymaker who has decided that imposing a gasoline tax is the way to curtail climate change. The ideal tax is set exactly at the value of the external costs. So you, the policymaker, must accurately answer the following questions:

1. *How much warming can we attribute to each gallon of gas?* Climate data is very volatile; in the short term, it jumps up and down a lot. That makes it hard to identify long-term trends and even harder to pinpoint the warming that is attributable to gasoline consumption. Even if we could, a gallon's worth of warming is likely to be measured in the trillionths of a degree Fahrenheit.

2. *If we know how much warming a gallon of gas causes, how much economic damage does that warming create?* The answer to this question determines the size of the tax. How much damage does one-trillionth of a degree do to the planet? Probably not much, especially considering that some people will be made *better* off by a warmer planet, particularly those who live in frigid, uncomfortable climates. Further, because problems of climate change will become apparent only through time, answering question 2 is exceptionally difficult.

   So these are questions policymakers need to answer if they are to implement a tax to control climate change. But good policymakers should also consider two more important questions:

3. *Controlling climate change will be expensive, if it can be done at all. Would it be more cost-effective to deal with the consequences of climate change rather than the causes?* In short, if it's cheaper to warm up the planet and deal with the problems it creates, then perhaps we shouldn't be devoting our resources to preventing climate change at all.

4. *We want to control climate change to improve lives. But controlling climate change will be expensive. Are there other things we could do that would improve more lives at the same cost?* We could save millions of lives today by distributing inexpensive mosquito netting and clean water. This suggests that maybe we've got our priorities wrong—that if we're really interested in bettering humanity, there may be better places to put our time, energy, and money than into climate control.

See related problem 3.10 on page 176 at the end of this chapter.

the government to impose a rib tax on Rachel. This will force her to consider the costs she imposes on others.

The key to designing good policy in this instance is choosing the appropriate tax level. If the tax is too low, say $1, then it will only raise Rachel's private costs to $9, and she will continue to produce ribs, even though it reduces the overall economic pie.

It's tempting to try to get rid of all rib-related pollution by imposing a very high tax—say, for example, a tax of $10 on every set of ribs Rachel smokes. But setting a tax too high will *also* lead to a smaller economic pie. Here's why: Suppose that another pit master in the neighborhood (call him Bryant) is also able to sell ribs for $10. But Bryant is more efficient than Rachel at producing ribs: Bryant's private costs are only $5. Even when Bryant imposes a $4 externality on his neighbors, the total value of the ribs to society ($10) outweighs the social cost of $9. Clearly, society values Bryant's ribs enough that it is willing to tolerate the pollution they bring.

Suppose that Bryant's city neighbors impose the aforementioned $10 tax on ribs. Now it costs Bryant $15 ($5 of private costs plus the $10 tax) to produce ribs he can sell for only $10. Consequently, Bryant quits the rib business and retires to his couch to watch daytime dramas, even though the benevolent social planner would like to see him smoking ribs.

From a social standpoint, we want to see Bryant's efficient (pie-increasing) ribs produced, and we want to discourage Rachel's inefficient (pie-shrinking) ribs. The implications for policy are as follows: Setting the tax below the external costs created may fail to discourage undesirable rib making. Setting the tax above the external costs created may discourage desired rib making. To maximize the social pie, the tax must equal the external costs the activity creates. That forces polluters to exactly internalize the externality they create, increasing their private costs of production to the full social cost of the ribs. As a result, they end up producing the ideal quantity of ribs for society.

Subsidies

Jackson and Max are the only inhabitants of a small tropical island. Each drives an old, smoke-belching Oldsmobile. Installing a pollution-control device on such a car costs $100, but each device installed would save Jackson and Max $70 apiece on their health care costs.

Let's model the problem that Jackson and Max face as a simple two-player game:

- Each has two options: Install a pollution-control device or don't install a pollution-control device.
- As a benchmark, if nobody installs a device, each will receive a payoff of 0.
- If only one person installs a device, that person will incur $100 of costs but save $70 on his health care costs, for a net loss of $30; the other person will gain $70 in reduced health care costs.
- If both install devices, each will incur $100 of costs but save $140 in health care expenses ($70 for each device installed), for a net gain of $40 per person.

The incentives Jackson and Max face are shown in Figure 8.1. The payoff matrix shows that Jackson and Max are playing an environmental version of a prisoner's dilemma game. Notice that "Don't Install" is a dominant strategy for both Jackson and Max and that the lower-right cell is a Nash equilibrium. There, neither installs a device, and each receives a payoff of zero. But that outcome is less than ideal; if Jackson and Max could cooperate with one another, they could each make themselves $40 better off, and the economic pie would grow by $80.

		Jackson	
		Install	Don't Install
Max	Install	+40, +40	−30, +70
	Don't Install	+70, −30	0, 0

◀ **Figure 8.1**
Jackson's and Max's Payoffs When They Make Independent Decisions to Install Pollution-Control Devices When Jackson and Max make independent decisions about whether to install pollution-control devices, neither has an incentive to do so.

Government could rearrange the incentives that Jackson and Max face by repeatedly taxing their pollution or perhaps by placing a tax on gas, but there may be an easier way for government to encourage Jackson and Max to install pollution-control devices.

To illustrate, assume that there is no government on the island. Nonetheless, Jackson realizes that it's in society's best interest for both cars to have pollution controls in place. But he also realizes that it's not in an individual's interest to be the sole person to install such a device. So he approaches Max with the following deal:

Jackson: Max, we'd both be better off if we would both install pollution-control devices on our cars. But neither of us has an individual incentive to do so. I don't want to go get one installed on my car if you're not going to.

Max: Oh, Jackson, you can trust me, really.

Jackson: No, I can't. So what I want to do is propose the following deal: You get a pollution-control device installed on your car, and I will pay you $50. And if I get a pollution-control device installed on my car, you pay me $50.

Max: That's silly. If we both install the pollution controls, we both pay each other $50, and it's like we never paid each other a dime.

Jackson: Precisely!

Jackson's scheme sounds silly, but when we represent it in a payoff matrix, it looks much more intelligent: Jackson's plan changes the payouts available to the players in a dramatic way. Let's run through the possible outcomes:

- If both install devices, they each spend $100 on a pollution-control device, save $140 each in health care costs, receive $50 from the other player, and spend $50 paying the other player. This nets out to a gain of $40 (−100 + 140 + 50 − 50). That is identical to the payout each player received in the previous version of the game.

- If neither installs a pollution-control device, each will receive 0.

- Suppose one player installs the pollution control device and the other does not:

  - The player who doesn't install a device sees his health care costs decline by $70 but is on the hook for a payment of $50 to the player who did install the device. These payoffs result in a $20 gain (+70 − 50) for the player.

  - The player who does install the device spends $100 on the device, sees his health care costs fall by $70, and receives a payment of $50 from the other player. Again, these payoffs net to a $20 gain (−100 + 70 + 50) for the player.

The payoff matrix that incorporates these new payoffs is shown in Figure 8.2. Close inspection reveals that Jackson and Max face a new set of incentives.

The game, which was originally a prisoner's dilemma, has turned into what some game theorists call a *prisoner's delight*. Each player still has a dominant strategy, but the payment scheme Jackson suggested changed the dominant strategy from "Don't Install" to "Install." There is still a single Nash equilibrium, but it is now found at the outcome where both players install the pollution-control device. That is exactly the outcome the benevolent social planner would like to see!

▶ **Figure 8.2**

Jackson's and Max's Payoffs When They Pay Each Other $50 for Installing Pollution-Control Devices
When Jackson and Max pay each other for installing pollution-control devices, the payment changes each player's dominant strategy to "Install." Individual incentives are now aligned with social goals.

		Jackson	
		Install	Don't Install
Max	Install	+40, +40	+20, +20
	Don't Install	+20, +20	0, 0

You might be thinking, "This is a nice blackboard exercise, but I don't live on a desert island, and I can't afford to pay all the people in our neighborhood to install a pollution-control device, much less all the people in my city, state, and country. And I wouldn't trust them to pay me for installing a device on my car. So where's the practical application?" It is true: If we tried, as individuals, to implement such a plan, it would be an administrative nightmare. But we don't have to attempt this as individuals. The government can step in and do the heavy lifting for us.

Suppose the government assumes a role in the process. Every time a person installs a pollution-control device, the government sends her a check for $50. You may remember that such a payment is called a *subsidy* and that it simply amounts to a tax in reverse. (See Chapter 5.) Where does the government get the money to pay subsidies? It taxes the general public. Now everyone has an incentive to install a pollution-control device, and as was the case in our simple two-person island world, the tax burden faced by each citizen is identical to the amount the individual receives in the form of the subsidy. This is truly a government program that can pay for itself and in the process make our lives richer rather than poorer.[4]

Subsidies are widely used by governments to promote environmental goals. For example, both the United States and China offer a subsidy (in the form of reduced income tax payments) to buyers of low-pollution electric vehicles. Many European nations (and many U.S. states) subsidize the installation of residential solar panels for power generation, and New Zealand subsidizes home insulation.

Cap-and-Trade Systems

Lisa and Maggie both operate factories in a small mountain town. Each of their businesses produces 20 tons of Prokrypton-B, a mild pollutant that is disposed of via the city's water treatment system. The local government is concerned that 40 tons of Prokrypton-B in the water might be too much and would like to reduce the total amount of pollution to 30 tons.

Government could, if it wished, try to set a tax that would give Lisa and Maggie an incentive to reduce their emissions by the desired 10 tons. But maybe that tax would be too small, leaving too much pollution in the water. Or maybe it would be too large and would remove too much pollution from the water. Government could also subsidize the installation of pollution-control equipment that would reduce the pollution to 30 tons total for the two factories. But taxing many citizens and sending all their hard-earned pennies to two wealthy businesspeople might be politically unpopular.

Both imposing taxes and offering subsidies are indirect ways of reducing pollution. Sometimes that's a nice way to approach policy, but sometimes it's nice to target a problem directly. What the government might do is simply pass a law that effectively limits the Prokrypton-B pollution in the city to only 30 tons.

The problem with such a law is that it is both blunt and ambiguous because it does not specify how the pollution reduction is to be achieved. Will Lisa be responsible for the full 10-ton reduction? Will Maggie? How might the government divide the pain between these two parties?

Perhaps the easiest way to implement this approach is to divide the responsibility for reducing the pollution equally between Maggie and Lisa. For example, the law might specify that every factory that emits Prokrypton-B must reduce its emissions by 25%, which in Maggie's and Lisa's cases is 5 tons each. This appears to be the equitable way to divide the job: Measured in tons of pollution reduction, both share an equal burden.

By now, however, you know that the concept of equity depends entirely on the system of measurement you happen to choose. To illustrate, suppose that Maggie has

---

[4]In this case, the private benefit of installing a pollution-control device is less than the total social benefit. Jackson and Max only consider their private benefits and costs, so without a subsidy, they choose not to install. The subsidy closes that gap, making what's best for society also best for Jackson and Max.

to spend $1,000 to clean 1 ton of pollutant from the water. But suppose Lisa runs a different type of business that lends itself more easily to pollution reduction; Lisa can clean up 1 ton of pollutant for only $600. In that case, the "equal burden" of 5 tons of pollution reduction apiece ends up imposing $5,000 of costs on Maggie and only $3,000 of costs on Lisa. That's hardly equal.

There are other points to consider, too. The first point is that government couldn't care less about who ends up actually cleaning up the water. It doesn't matter to the Prokrypton-B-ingesting public whether they end up drinking Lisa's Prokrypton-B or Maggie's. Furthermore, if society is determined to reduce emissions of Prokrypton-B, it would be nice if those reductions were achieved with the smallest possible impact on the economic pie. This is certainly what the benevolent social planner would desire, and there's no particular reason the government shouldn't agree. Adding together those two pieces of information, the surprising conclusion is that given the cleanup costs, Lisa should be made responsible for the entire cleanup, and Maggie should do none of it.

The problem is that the government will look capricious if it passes a law saying that Lisa has to reduce her emissions by 10 tons and Maggie doesn't have to reduce her emissions at all. The question the government faces, then, is, "How do we design a law that equitably distributes the burden of cleaning up the water but ends up giving Lisa the incentive to actually do the cleanup?" The answer to that question was elusive, but economists eventually found it about 30 years ago.

The answer, according to economists, is to create a structured program of pollution reductions that contains the following features:

1. The government sets an upper limit on the total amount of Prokrypton-B that it will tolerate. In our example, this is 30 tons.

2. For each ton of Prokrypton-B that it will allow, the government prints one certificate that says something along the lines of "This certificate allows the bearer to emit 1 ton of Prokrypton-B. This certificate will self-destruct once that ton has been emitted."

3. The government distributes the certificates to the emitters of Prokrypton-B according to some scheme. As it turns out, from society's standpoint, it doesn't really matter what scheme the government chooses; just assume that it gives 15 certificates to Lisa and 15 certificates to Maggie.

4. The government allows those holding the certificates to sell them back and forth in exchange for cash.

Cap-and-trade system A pollution-reduction scheme in which the government sets an overall limit (cap) on the amount of pollution that can be emitted and then allows polluters to negotiate about who will get to pollute via a system of tradable pollution permits.

Systems with this structure are called **cap-and-trade systems**. Let's examine the impact of a cap-and-trade system in our Prokrypton-B example. Both Maggie and Lisa have 15 certificates to start with, which means that each of the women is initially responsible for 5 tons of pollution reduction. But Maggie says to herself, "Dang . . . it's going to cost me $1,000 to reduce my emissions by a ton. Maybe I can get Lisa to sell me one of her certificates instead." So Maggie makes the following offer to Lisa: "Lisa, you've got some certificates that entitle you to pollute, and I know that you could choose not to pollute and it would cost you $600 per ton. It costs me $1,000 a ton to reduce my own emissions, so how about we split the difference? I'll pay you $800 to clean up a ton of your pollution, and you give me one of your certificates so I don't have to."

In the end, Maggie pays $4,000 to buy 5 certificates from Lisa and saves $1,000 by doing so. Lisa spends $6,000 cleaning up 10 tons of pollution (her 5 tons plus Maggie's 5 tons) but gets paid $4,000 to do it. She ends up spending a total of $2,000. That's a lot of money, but it is $1,000 less than the $3,000 she would have had to spend if she'd simply held on to her certificates and reduced her own emissions by 5 tons.

The trade of the certificates between Lisa and Maggie, like all other voluntary trades, is mutually beneficial. And the trade of the certificates makes society better off, too: We remove the full 10 tons, but we get the person who can most easily accomplish the reduction to shoulder the entire load. This makes the government happy, and it makes the benevolent social planner positively giddy.

The Prokrypton-B example is, of course, fictitious. However, systems such as these do exist in the real world. In the 1970s, sulfur dioxide emissions from coal-burning power plants began to cause problems. The sulfur dioxide would rise into the atmosphere, where it would eventually turn into sulfuric acid, only to return to Earth as acid rain. In an effort to reduce sulfur dioxide emissions, the U.S. government instituted a cap-and-trade system that was remarkably successful in reducing both emissions and acid rain. Many governments are now discussing using a cap-and-trade system to limit the amount of carbon dioxide emitted into the atmosphere in hopes of controlling climate change. This semi-market solution promises that whatever reductions are achieved come at the lowest possible cost and that everybody will share the burden of such reductions.

Let's spend a few final minutes thinking carefully about what such a system does for us. First, it forces both Lisa and Maggie to internalize the externalities they create. Every ton of pollution they emit either forces them to buy a pollution permit or use a pollution permit they already own that they could otherwise sell. Second, by making such permits tradable, the government has allowed the polluters to bargain about who will reduce emissions. This lowers transactions costs and allows society to accomplish its goals at the lowest possible cost. Third, the cap-and-trade system gives polluters an incentive to look for new, less-polluting ways to produce their goods: If Maggie finds a cleaner way to operate her factory, she will have to buy fewer permits; if Lisa finds a cleaner way to operate her factory, she will have more permits left over to sell. Fourth, the system makes future pollution reductions easy to implement: All the government needs to do is reduce the number of permits it prints.

Most interestingly, the system gives ordinary citizens a voice in the outcome. In our example, the government set a pollution cap of 30 tons. But let's suppose that the residents in town decide that 30 tons is too much—they'd rather have 25 tons. In a world without tradable permits, the citizens might have to wait for their elected officials to be voted out of office for that to happen. But in a world with tradable pollution permits, the residents simply need to purchase 5 of the certificates from Lisa, Maggie, or anyone else who has them for sale. And—*poof!*—that's 5 tons of Prokrypton-B that will never touch the waterways, forever. In other words, the cap-and-trade system reduces transactions costs by creating a forum for negotiation between polluters and the general public. That enhances the possibility of a Coasean bargain where citizens who value cleanliness more than polluters value the right to pollute simply purchase that right directly from the polluter.

Conclusion

Our discussion of pollution has come full circle, beginning in the previous chapter with Coase and ending with Coase in this chapter. Along the way, you've discovered when pollution should be regarded as a problem and when it shouldn't. You've discussed when government should try to fix pollution problems and when it shouldn't. And you've been introduced to some of the policies government can use when it wants to try controlling pollution. In the next chapter, you will revisit the environment one last time when you examine the problem of depletion.

You have already been exposed to the importance of property rights (see Chapter 6). But these two chapters have demonstrated the importance of property rights in a new context. They have also exposed you to the nature and importance of transactions costs. Throughout the remainder of this book, poorly defined property rights and transactions costs will reappear frequently as sources of social problems.

Key Terms

Cap-and-trade system, p. 172

External costs, p. 165

Private costs, p. 165

Social cost, p. 165

8.1 Four Major Types of Transactions Costs, pages 160–163

Describe the four different types of transactions costs.

Summary

Transactions costs can impede the bargaining that private individuals might do to resolve environmental disputes. Search costs are the costs of determining who to bargain with. Collectivization costs are the costs of organizing all the affected parties so that bargaining can take place. Negotiation costs are the costs of the actual bargaining process. Monitoring and enforcement costs are the costs of ensuring that the parties live up to the promises they made in bargaining. If any of these costs are sufficiently high, bargaining may not be an effective means of resolving environmental disputes.

Review Questions

All problems are assignable in MyEconLab.

1.1 _____ are the costs of finding, organizing, and motivating fellow victims so that bargaining can take place.

1.2 In the context of Coasean bargains between polluters and victims, the costs of determining who must be bargained with are referred to as _____.

1.3 The transactions costs represented by the lawyers, accountants, and other administrative overhead necessary to create enforceable bargains are examples of _____ costs.

1.4 The costs of ensuring that involved parties live up to promises made in bargaining are called _____.

1.5 A _____ is a civil action brought in a court of law that is designed to make it feasible for people who have suffered damages to come together to sue for recovery.

1.6 In the context of the environment, which type of transactions cost might include sampling the emissions of many companies (which may require expensive scientific equipment, laboratory time, and a great deal of staff power)?

   a. External cost

   b. Search cost

   c. Collectivization cost

   d. Negotiation cost

1.7 The costs of seeking out, uniting, and rallying pollution victims in order to bargain with a polluter are known as the _____.

   a. Collectivization costs

   b. Search costs

   c. External costs

   d. Negotiation costs

1.8 _____ are the costs of the actual process of hashing out the terms of an agreement between polluter and victim.

   a. Negotiation costs

   b. Search costs

   c. External costs

   d. Private costs

Problems and Applications

1.9 In 2012, the Department of Justice brought an antitrust lawsuit against Apple for conspiring to raise e-book prices (see https://ebooksagsettlements.com). The DOJ alleged that several publishers, together with Apple, planned an arrangement that raised e-book prices and then banded together to attempt to impose the pricing model on Amazon.com, which had been steeply discounting e-books. The settlement agreement resulted in $400 million in payments from Apple to individuals who paid high prices for e-books during the period in question. Explain why the government's action against Apple may be more effective at eliminating this anticompetitive behavior than relying on individuals to seek damages from Apple through a privately initiated lawsuit.

1.10 Are the costs of negotiating with polluters likely to be higher, lower, or equal to the costs of filing a class-action lawsuit against polluters on behalf of victims? Why do you suppose there are more class-action lawsuits filed against polluters than there are negotiations between polluters and victims?

Summary

When designing environmental regulations, regulators should pay attention to four principles. First, if transactions costs are low, parties can work out environmental disputes without the help of regulators. When transactions costs are high, regulators should strive to achieve the outcome that parties would have bargained to on their own. Whatever form regulation takes, it will be effective only if it makes the polluter internalize the cost that his pollution imposes on others. Finally, the goal of regulation should not be to eliminate pollution but to achieve the level of pollution that maximizes society's well-being.

Review Questions

All problems are assignable in MyEconLab.

2.1 The full cost of producing an item, including the producer's private costs and all the external costs, is referred to as the _____.

2.2 When a policy is created based on an ideal of what *should* be as opposed to what current data and research support, an economist would say that this policy is based on _____ concerns.

2.3 When a polluter is forced to account for the costs he imposes on others in his own cost–benefit analysis, we say that the polluter has been forced to _____.
a. Externalize the social cost
b. Subsidize social costs
c. Cap and trade
d. Internalize the externality

2.4 Costs that are directly borne by the producer of a good or services are called _____.
a. Social costs
b. External costs
c. Monitoring and enforcement costs
d. Private costs

2.5 The costs a polluter imposes on others are called _____.
a. Social costs
b. External costs
c. Negotiation costs
d. Private costs

2.6 Which of the following is *not* one of the principles for regulating pollution in an ideal world?
a. Regulations should be designed to make polluters internalize costs of externalities.
b. The goal of regulation should be to eliminate pollution.
c. Regulations are necessary only when transactions costs preclude bargaining between polluters and victims.
d. Ideally, regulations should achieve the outcomes that affected parties would have reached had transactions costs not been so high.
e. All of the above are goals that regulators should strive for in regulating pollution.

Problems and Applications

2.7 **[Related to Application 8.1 on page 166]** Read Application 8.1 carefully. One widely proclaimed government goal is to encourage the development and mainstream use of alternative-energy vehicles such as hydrogen fuel cell cars and electric cars. Moving toward these alternative fuel sources is viewed as a means to achieving long-term reductions in carbon emissions. Which of the policies discussed in the application—CAFE standards or gasoline taxes—is more likely to encourage consumers and producers to develop these alternative energy sources? Why?

2.8 Harry's neighbor Tom has recently installed a new floodlight on his porch. The floodlight has a sensor that turns the lights on at dusk and off at dawn. Unfortunately, the bright floodlight happens to shine right into Harry's bedroom. Harry tried to have a conversation with Tom about the light, but Tom says that the light is on a sensor, and so there is nothing he can do. Harry has determined that he has two options: (1) purchase blackout curtains or (2) file a complaint with the city that Harry and Tom live in. (Harry believes Tom may be violating a local ordinance.) What are some pros and cons of each of these solutions?

Tools Governments Use to Regulate Pollution, pages 167–173

Explain how governments use taxes, subsidies, and cap-and-trade systems to reduce pollution.

Summary

To reduce pollution problems, regulators must design policies that encourage polluters to act in socially desirable ways. Regulators can discourage pollution by imposing a tax on the activity that causes pollution. In that case, the ideal tax equals the damage caused by the externality. Regulators can encourage cleaner production by subsidizing pollution controls. The cap-and-trade system limits the total amount of allowable pollution but lets polluters bargain with one another about who will get to emit that pollution. Each of these policies forces polluters, in one way or another, to consider the externality they impose on others.

Review Questions

All problems are assignable in MyEconLab.

3.1 Three tools that a government might use to regulate pollution are _____, _____, and _____.

3.2 When government pays individuals to purchase pollution-reducing technology, that payment is called a(n) _____.

3.3 The market-based system developed by economists to help control pollution by allocating tradable pollution permits to companies is known as a _____.
  a. Subsidy
  b. Pollution tax
  c. Cap-and-trade system
  d. Class action lawsuit

3.4 A _____ is a payment or credit provided to producers or consumers by the government for behaving in a particular way.
  a. Quota
  b. Revenue
  c. Tax
  d. Subsidy

3.5 Suppose that John and Jacob both brew beer.
  • John can brew beer at a cost of materials and labor of $2.50 per bottle; Jacob can brew beer at a cost of $1.75 per bottle.
  • People who drink their beers get $5 of value from each beer.
  • Brewing beer is a messy and smelly process. Every bottle that is brewed causes $3 of damage to the people who live near the brewery.

The benevolent social planner would like to see _____.
  a. Both John and Jacob brew beer
  b. Only John brew beer

  c. Only Jacob brew beer
  d. Neither John nor Jacob brew beer

3.6 In problem 3.5, every time beer is brewed, pollution is created. Government can reduce this pollution to the *ideal* amount by taxing beer producers for each bottle they produce. The ideal tax to accomplish this is _____.
  a. $1.75
  b. $2.50
  c. $3.00
  d. $5

3.7 Drawing on problem 3.6, suppose that the government sets the tax at $6. From the benevolent social planner's standpoint, what is wrong with setting the tax this high?
  a. The tax discourages John from brewing beer.
  b. The tax discourages Jacob from brewing beer.
  c. The tax is not high enough to discourage John from brewing beer.
  d. The tax is not high enough to discourage Jacob from brewing beer.

3.8 Drawing on problem 3.6, suppose that the government sets the tax at $0.50. From the benevolent social planner's standpoint, what is wrong with setting the tax this low?
  a. The tax discourages John from brewing beer.
  b. The tax discourages Jacob from brewing beer.
  c. The tax is not high enough to discourage John from brewing beer.
  d. The tax is not high enough to discourage Jacob from brewing beer.

Problems and Applications

3.9 Describe how a cap-and-trade system of regulation works. How does such a system differ from the other tools that are used to regulate pollution?

3.10 [Related to Application 8.2 on page 168] Application 8.2 discusses some of the practical difficulties in dealing with climate change. Referring to each of the four types of transactions costs discussed in the chapter, explain why a solution to climate change is unlikely to stem from private bargaining between polluter and victims.

3.11 Consider the case of Jackson and Max, described in Section 8.3. Suppose that installing a pollution-control device costs $800. Suppose also that for each pollution-control device installed, both Jackson and Max will see their health care costs decrease by $600.

a. Recreate Figure 8.1, incorporating the new information given in this problem. What is the equilibrium outcome in the game Jackson and Max are playing? What type of game did you construct?

b. Suppose that government offers Jackson and Max a subsidy for installing a pollution-control device. What is the minimum subsidy necessary to induce Jackson and Max to do so? Incorporate that subsidy into a new payoff matrix that reflects the changed incentives. What is the equilibrium in this new game?

3.12 Fidelia and Ameenah are commercial chefs at neighboring restaurants. They both dump waste from their restaurants into the stream running through town. Currently, they are dumping 10 tons of waste apiece, for a total of 20 tons. The city council passes a law limiting dumping to 14 tons total, or a reduction of 6 tons. It costs Fidelia $5 to cut her dumping by 1 ton. It costs Ameenah $3 to cut her dumping by 1 ton.

a. If Ameenah reduces her dumping by 3 tons, and Fidelia reduces her dumping by 3 tons, what will the total cost of cleaning up the 6 tons of dumping be?

b. If Fidelia cleans up 6 tons and Ameenah cleans up nothing, what will the total cost of cleaning up the 6 tons be?

c. If Ameenah cleans up 6 tons and Fidelia cleans up nothing, what will the total cost of cleaning up the 6 tons be?

d. Of the options discussed in (a) through (c), which option results in the lowest total cleanup cost for society?

e. Suppose a pollution-reduction system is implemented under which both Ameenah and Fidelia are given 7 pollution permits (for a total of 14 tons, which is what the city council wants). If Ameenah and Fidelia are allowed to buy and sell permits from one another, will Ameenah buy some of Fidelia's permits? Will Fidelia buy some of Ameenah's permits? Or will each simply use up the permits she has been given? Explain your reasoning.

The Judge-Me-Not Game

You and your classmates all manage different firms producing tablet computers. Each of you has a choice of using clean technology or polluting technology when producing your computers. Clean technology avoids the use of hazardous substances such as lead, mercury, and toxic solvents in producing tablet computers. Clean technology is better for the environment, and the more producers who use clean technology, the lower society's health care costs will be. Polluting technology is less expensive and therefore more profitable for producers, but also imposes higher health care costs on society. You, as the chief executive officer (CEO) of your firm, have the choice of producing with clean or polluting technology. What will you choose? Play the "Judge-Me-Not" game and see what choices you and your classmates make.

MyEconLab

Please visit http://www.myeconlab.com **for support material to conduct this experiment if assigned by your instructor.**

Resource Depletion and Sustainability

Chapter Outline and Learning Objectives

9.1 Will the World Run Out of Oil? page 180

Explain how rising oil prices prevent the rapid depletion of world oil stocks.

9.2 What Resources Are in Danger of Depletion? page 184

Discuss the role property rights play in the depletion and sustainability of natural resources.

9.3 The Tragedy of the Commons, page 186

Compare and contrast depletion problems and pollution problems.

9.4 How Can Society Fix Depletion Problems? page 188

Describe the approaches governments use to try to solve depletion problems and promote sustainability.

Experiment: The "Gone Fishing" Game, page 196

MyEconLab
MyEconLab helps you master each objective and study more efficiently.

A disturbing report concludes that the world will run out of oil in about 40 years.[1] People accustomed to driving long distances and people with long commutes cringe in fear and wonder how they will cope in a world without oil. They have good reason to fear, for the report lays the facts bare: We guzzle oil like it's champagne, and every day is New Year's Eve. Yet the world's supply of oil is finite. Sooner or later, the oil will run out.

Will the World Run Out of Oil?

9.1 Learning Objective

Explain how rising oil prices prevent the rapid depletion of world oil stocks.

It doesn't take a degree in mathematics to figure out when the oil will run out. In fact, the report reduced the time frame to a simple calculation, one that even a fourth-grader could understand: Divide the world's *proven reserves* of oil (a measure of how much oil there is in the world that we'll talk more about later in this chapter) by the world's yearly consumption, and the result indicates how many years those reserves will last:

Proven reserves ÷ Annual consumption = Number of years to depletion

This method of calculating how long our oil supplies will last couldn't be more straightforward. It's like saying that if you start with a gallon bucket of water and take out a quart of water each day, by the end of the fourth day, your bucket will be empty.

A check of the numbers bears out this calculation. The U.S. Department of Energy estimated that the world's proven reserves of oil are about 1.2 trillion barrels. The Department of Energy also estimated that the world consumes about 31 billion barrels of oil each year. Based on these numbers, the number of years until the world's stock of oil runs out is:

1.2 trillion barrels ÷ 31 billion barrels per year = 38.7 years

Yikes!

Thank goodness this number is wrong. Believe it or not, it's so wrong that economists generally agree that the world will *never* run out of oil.

You might be thinking, "The math is right there, staring you in the face. The numbers are indisputable, the math flawlessly executed, the conclusion irrefutable. Are economists just in denial? Or are they apologists for Big Oil?"

It's true that the numbers on proven reserves and consumption are consistent with those published by many authorities. It's also true that when you plug those numbers into the formula, you'll get the same 38.7 years, each and every time. But the irrefutability of the conclusion is another story. Why? Because the formula is wrong. Read on to find out why.

▲ **Figure 9.1**

The World's Supply of Oil
For the discussion that follows, assume that this box contains every drop of the world's oil.

Depicting the World's Supply of Oil

Let's look at why the oil-depletion formula we discussed (and which gets used often in the popular press) is flawed. To demonstrate, consider Figure 9.1, which depicts every last drop of the world's supply of oil.

Now, let's split the world's supply of oil into two categories: oil that people know about and oil that has yet to be discovered. Once that's done, the figure looks something like Figure 9.2.

There is bound to be uncertainty about exactly where the dotted line falls because nobody really knows how much unknown oil there is. But given that about two-thirds of Earth's surface is covered by oceans, the vast bulk of which are largely unexplored, it's not such a stretch to say that there's a sizable amount of oil that simply hasn't been found yet.

Now, split the world's supply of oil in a different way, as shown in Figure 9.3. Split it by whether it's economical to extract, which simply means "Can we pump it

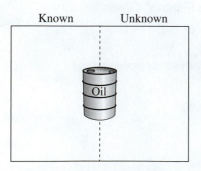

Known   Unknown

▲ **Figure 9.2**

Known Oil and Unknown Oil
Oil producers know where to find a lot of the world's oil. But some of the world's oil has yet to be discovered.

---

[1]See Donella H. Meadows, Dennis L. Meadows, Jørgen Randers, and William W. Behrens III, *The Limits to Growth*.

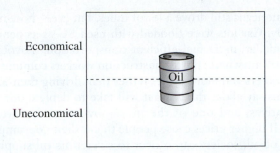

◄ **Figure 9.3**
Economical and Uneconomical Oil
Some of the world's oil is uneconomical:
At current prices, it is too costly to extract
and sell profitably.

out of the ground and sell it profitably at today's prices?" Some oil is really cheap to get to. It's estimated that the cost of bringing a barrel of oil to the surface in Saudi Arabia is only about $2. On the other hand, some oil is very costly to extract. For example, you can get oil from a rock called oil shale, but only after treating the rock chemically or heating it to high temperatures, both of which are expensive processes. If it costs $120 to get a barrel of oil from shale, and oil is selling in the marketplace for $75, producing shale oil is simply not economical at today's prices.

If we combine the two figures, as shown in Figure 9.4, we get the world's supply of oil divided into four categories: known and economical, unknown and economical, known and uneconomical, and unknown and uneconomical.

Dividing the world's oil supply in the way shown in Figure 9.4 is important because the proven-reserves figure used in most years-to-depletion calculations encompasses only *one* of the four categories of oil—the oil that is both known and economical to extract. Because the calculations don't account for all the oil in the world, we can tell that circumstances are not as dire as the formula indicates.

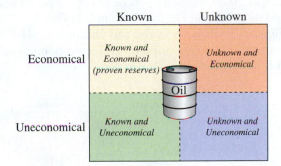

◄ **Figure 9.4**
The World's Oil Supply, Known
and Unknown, Economical and
Uneconomical
The world's supply of oil can be divided
into four categories: known and economical, unknown and economical, known
and uneconomical, and unknown and
uneconomical.

Depletion and the Role of Prices

The years-to-depletion formula doesn't take into account another important factor: that people are capable of changing their behaviors. To demonstrate, consider the world about 20 years from now, when oil is becoming more scarce. One of the first ways scarcity begins to manifest itself is in the form of higher prices (see Chapter 6). This is why diamonds are expensive and water is cheap, even though water is really quite useful and diamonds aren't.

Price Increases Encourage Conservation How will higher prices change our calculations? The first way is the most obvious: When oil and oil-derived products like gasoline increase in price, people tend to buy less of them. Of course, some people will continue to buy just as much of these products as before and make sacrifices elsewhere in their budgets. However, even fuel-hungry Americans seem willing to reduce their fuel consumption when prices rise. One way they do so is by driving less. When gas prices topped out at over $4.00 a gallon in 2008, American consumers cut by 53 billion miles the total vehicle miles they traveled that year. They thought twice about the miles they drove, cut back on vacations, carpooled, and, as time passed, began migrating from the suburbs closer to city centers to cut the lengths of their commutes.

Of course, Americans still drove a lot of miles, but even those miles were traveled more economically. Car lots were flooded with used SUVs as people traded in their gas guzzlers for smaller, more fuel-efficient transportation. Toyota couldn't keep its hybrid Prius in stock anywhere. Burly construction workers commuted to their jobsites on fuel-sipping scooters and motorcycles rather than driving their Ram trucks.

What does this say about the years it will take to deplete our oil stocks? People respond to incentives, and one of the most obvious and powerful incentives is increasing prices. If higher prices cause people to cut their consumption and conserve dwindling stocks of oil, society can expect to stretch its oil supply longer than the formula would predict. Using an arrow, we can graphically modify the years-to-depletion formula to show the effects of reduced consumption.

To illustrate, let's reduce our annual consumption by a "one-arrow" increment. Because annual consumption is in the denominator, the entire fraction (which measures the number of years to depletion) increases by a corresponding one-arrow increment. The corresponding increase in the years to depletion is shown on the right-hand side of the formula.

$$\text{Proven reserves} \div \text{Annual consumption}\downarrow = \text{Number of years to depletion}\uparrow$$

Price Increases Make Costly Sources of Oil More Economical A second effect of the price increase is that uneconomical sources of oil tend to become economical. Simply put, oil companies begin tapping into pools of oil that were too expensive to pump when oil was $10 a barrel but that are perfectly profitable when oil is $100 a barrel. There's no better example of this than Canada's Alberta Tar Sands. It is estimated that there's as much oil in the Tar Sands as there is in Saudi Arabia. But the oil is sludgy and difficult to extract. When oil was $25 a barrel, it wasn't economical to extract it from the Tar Sands. However, when oil prices rose from $25 to $75, and then to $150 a barrel (as they did in 2008), extracting those sludgy deposits became increasingly more profitable, and oil production in the Tar Sands boomed.

As shown in Figure 9.5, when prices rise and uneconomical oil becomes economical, the dotted line that divides economical oil and uneconomical oil shifts downward. As a result, proven reserves expand.

▶ **Figure 9.5**

The Effect of Rising Prices on Uneconomical Oil and Proven Reserves

When prices rise, some uneconomical oil becomes cost-effective to extract. When that happens, proven reserves expand.

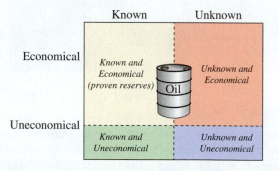

To represent the effects of this in the years-to-depletion formula, we can tick up proven reserves by one arrow. Combined with the previous change, this results in a second one-arrow increase in our overall years to depletion:

$$\uparrow\text{Proven reserves} \div \text{Annual consumption}\downarrow = \text{Number of years to depletion}\uparrow\uparrow$$

Now we know that the formula that generated the years-to-depletion number was based on data that is bound to change as time passes and that the data will change in a way that makes the problem less dire than it first appeared.

Price Increases Encourage Exploration Remember that oil companies aren't pumping oil because they love us and want us to have lots of it; they're pumping oil because it's profitable to sell. As the price of oil rises, potential profits from producing oil increase, too. That encourages oil companies to look for new sources of oil in places they previously hadn't and to conduct tests on the land where they have existing drilling leases to find where oil might lie. It also encourages them to look for oil in different ways: For example, rising oil prices spurred interest in horizontal drilling and hydraulic fracturing, a practice known as *fracking*. Development and widespread application of fracking technology over the past few years has unlocked large quantities of oil that are unavailable via conventional drilling techniques. As shown in Figure 9.6, those discoveries shift the vertical dotted line in our graph of the world's oil supply to the right.

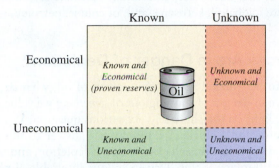

◄ **Figure 9.6**
The Effect of Oil Discoveries on Proven Reserves
Rising prices encourage exploration. As more of the world's oil is discovered, proven reserves expand.

Any economical oil that is found gets added to the world's proven reserves. As a result, we manage once again to stave off another arrow's worth of depletion:

↑↑Proven reserves ÷ Annual consumption↓ = Number of years to depletion↑↑↑

Price Increases Encourage the Development of Oil Substitutes Rising oil prices elicit even more behaviors that help stave off depletion of the world's oil by encouraging people to search for oil *substitutes*. The world still doesn't have a truly viable electric car, fuel cell automobiles are theoretically possible but not yet commercially viable, and wind and solar power still appear to be underutilized. Because for the past century we've been awash in a sea of cheap oil, there has not been much incentive to develop alternative energy sources or the infrastructure to support them.

But as oil prices increase, the incentive to look for good substitutes for oil increases with them. Rising oil prices, for example, fueled a fracking boom that resulted in huge discoveries of natural gas. As we start depleting our stocks of oil, and oil prices rise even further, the company that brings forth a viable alternative to oil-derived energy will have the world beating a path to its door. You can bet that power sources previously passed over in favor of cheap oil—wind, solar, hydrogen, and natural gas—will be researched, developed, and supported in a way that they're not today. Given those new alternatives, it's likely that consumers will buy less oil, further reducing annual consumption (by one more arrow, of course). Once again, the number of years left to depletion increases.

↑↑Proven reserves ÷ Annual consumption↓↓ = Number of years to depletion↑↑↑↑

The search for oil substitutes is another reason the claim that the world's oil will be gone in about 40 years is incorrect. In fact, it is easy to prove that the report is incorrect because the report mentioned at the beginning of the chapter wasn't from 2014; it was from 1973! More than 40 years ago, mainstream sources were predicting that we'd be out of oil in 40 years. Similar predictions were made in 1914, and 1939, and 1951. In 1970, the world's proven reserves were about 600 billion barrels of oil. Since that time, the world has extracted more than 800 billion barrels of oil, and our proven reserves have doubled in size. Despite that encouraging news, the 40-year figure continues to make waves in the press: As recently as 2010, the popular press reported that oil was likely to run out between 2041 and 2054.[2]

Despite the fact that most economists think it's unlikely that we will run out of oil, even if we do, by the time that happens, it's likely that nobody will really care.

---

[2]See, for example, the popular news item "Study: World Will Run Out of Oil in 2041," found on Minyanville Media's website. That article cites the following academic work, which predicts oil's rapid demise using a formula very similar to the one in this chapter: Nataliya Malyshkina and Debbie Niemeier, "Future Sustainability Forecasting by Exchange Markets: Basic Theory and an Application," *Environmental Science and Technology*, 44 (2010): 9134.

We'll have come up with new cheaper and cleaner alternatives, and we'll have been spurred to develop those alternatives by the rising prices that declining oil stocks create. After all, how many of you sit around the house bemoaning the passing of whale oil? Whale oil was a primary source of light and heat around the globe in the 1800s. It was only as stocks of the oil dwindled and prices rose that people began the search for substitutes. That search resulted in the discovery and development of a number of products that left society indifferent to whale oil's demise. Chief among those products were jojoba oil, kerosene, and, of course, petroleum.

9.2 Learning Objective

Discuss the role property rights play in the depletion and sustainability of natural resources.

What Resources Are in Danger of Depletion?

If we don't need to be worried about running out of oil, what *do* we need to worry about? Surely we're in danger of running out of *something* we value, right?

To shed some light on this, here's a very serious question: What is the difference between a rhinoceros and a chicken? The obvious answer to this question involves horns, feathers, and eggs. But this chapter is about depletion, and in that context, the more noteworthy difference is this: Driven by our insatiable appetite for succulent breasts and juicy thighs, we live in a world where chickens die by the millions each and every day. We just can't kill enough of them. Yet despite the wholesale slaughter, nobody is worried in the slightest that the world will run out of chickens. On the other hand, only a few dozen rhinos are killed every year, and people around the globe are frantic about the idea that the rhino will be driven to extinction.

What explains that paradox? It can't simply be greed: Chickens and rhinos are both commodities with market value (chickens largely for their meat and rhinos for their horns, which are reputed to have all kinds of curative and restorative properties). To an economist, the practical reason is this: The world's stock of chickens is privately owned and carefully managed to provide a sustained stream of sales and profits long into the future. Rhinos, on the other hand, run wild. They eat and trample villagers' crops and can be a nuisance to the people who cross paths with them.

Generally speaking, rhinos don't provide much benefit to the people who have to live with them—at least not until they're dead. When a rhino living in the wild is killed, crop-trampling stops, and the horn can be sold. In that case, the person killing the rhino generally receives some of the benefits its death creates. That is decidedly *not* the case with chickens: If you venture over your local farmer's fence and kill one of his hens, you're likely to end up in court or worse. That's because chickens are generally protected by property rights.

Resources like chickens that are privately owned tend to be carefully managed to provide profits not only tomorrow but well into the future. This ensures that the resources last a long time—maybe even indefinitely. This, incidentally, is why there is little danger of running out of oil: Many large oil-producing countries have nationalized their oil stocks, and their governments carefully plan and monitor their oil production. In those countries, national oil stocks are carefully managed, as if they were privately owned.

In addition, there is a second layer of oversight. The Organization of Petroleum Exporting Countries (OPEC) is a group of 12 large oil-producing nations, many of which have nationalized oil production. OPEC assigns its members production targets in an attempt to stabilize the world's oil supply. OPEC has a natural incentive to keep oil production on the low side: By making oil artificially scarce, it can keep oil prices high for its members. That's not good for oil importing nations, and anyone who drives a car probably doesn't love OPEC either. But OPEC's incentive to produce a stream of long-term profits for its member nations means that oil stocks will probably last a good while.

Unfortunately, it's harder to manage a stock of rhinos than it is to manage a stock of oil. Even though many governments have made rhino hunting illegal, those governments often lack sufficient resources to effectively enforce those laws; game officers are relatively few, and the African wilderness is vast. These factors essentially make the rhino, with its incredibly valuable horn, available to any poacher persistent enough to find one and daring enough to kill it. As a result, stocks dwindle.

Application 9.1

How to Turn a Rhino into a Chicken

Section 9.2 makes light of the differences between the rhino and the chicken. But make no mistake: Africa's black rhinoceros is in grave trouble. Between 1970 and 1992, Africa's black rhino population fell from 65,000 to fewer than 3,000. Most of them were killed for their horns, which are used as a homeopathic remedy in Asia. There, a pound of rhino horn can fetch more than $20,000 on the black market.

The black market is about the only place where rhino horn is traded: The multigovernmental Convention on International Trade in Endangered Species (CITES), in an attempt to protect the rhino from poaching, banned international trade in rhino horns. Many national governments have adopted measures to protect the rhino as well. In the 1970s, for example, Kenya completely banned hunting and ranching wildlife. Unfortunately, the measures have not worked: Following Kenya's ban, the number of black rhinos in Kenya plummeted from 20,000 to a meager 600, all of which survive only in protected areas.

This begs a serious question: If you can't save the rhino by protecting it, then how *can* you save it?

Some conservationists have come up with a brilliant solution: Legalize rhinoceros hunting. To support their idea, these people point out how Zimbabwe and Namibia have sustained their declining elephant populations: In both countries, a limited number of permits are sold to hunt elephants. The revenue from the permits is then shared with the locals. This gives them a financial incentive to tolerate the damage elephants do to their crops and an incentive to protect elephants from poachers and preserve elephant habitats. As a result, elephant populations have rebounded in those areas of the world.

But black rhino populations were much more fragile than elephant populations, and rhino hunting remained controversial. Bolstered by evidence that rhino herds grow fastest when the number of bulls in a herd is limited, South African officials asked CITES to allow limited trophy hunting of aged bull rhinos. In 2004, CITES issued five permits to South Africa.

The permits quickly sold for more than $150,000 each, much of which went to the people who owned the land the rhinos inhabited. Among the landowners was John Hume, on whose land the first black rhino was killed. For years, Hume has supported breeding populations of antelope, Cape buffalo, and black and white rhino on his 16,000-acre ranch. Revenue from the black rhino hunt was the first dividend he received on his investment.

Programs like South Africa's align the incentives of landowners like Hume with the larger goals of society. The South African government hopes that the limited trophy hunting will encourage landowners like Hume to manage, nurture, grow, and protect private herds—not out of their love for endangered animals but for ongoing profits. In other words, the government hopes to convince landowners to treat rhinos less like rhinos and more like chickens.

See related problems 2.4 and 2.5 on page 194 at the end of this chapter.

Based on "Saving the Rhino Through Sacrifice," *Bloomberg Businessweek*, June 21, 2013; Ross Tucker's "Hunt a Rare Rhino So You Can Save Rare Rhinos," *Yahoo News*, October 24, 2013; and John Pickrell's "Trophy Hunting Can Help African Conservation, Study Says," *National Geographic News*, March 15, 2007.

Resources that are not protected by well-defined property rights or resources whose property rights are not well enforced (as is the case with rhinos) are in the greatest danger of being depleted. In either case, individuals have an incentive to acquire as much of the resource as possible for themselves before someone else does.

The Tragedy of the Commons

In the previous few chapters, we spent a great deal of time discussing how the absence of well-defined property rights is the root of pollution problems. Now let's look more closely at how poorly defined property rights can lead to the overuse and depletion of natural resources. To do this, we'll draw on an example from *Science* magazine that's famous in the fields of economics, ecology, and biology.[3]

The Tragedy of the Commons: An Illustration

Ben and Jerry, both dairy farmers, share a pasture that is open to both. An open-access pasture like this is often referred to as a *commons* because it is common property: Everyone owns the right to graze his or her cattle on it. To keep the example simple, let's suppose for now that each farmer faces the choice of grazing either one or two cows on the commons.

The quality and quantity of grass available on the commons depends on how intensively it is grazed. With relatively few cattle on the commons, the grass will be rich and lush. But if too many cattle graze on the commons, the grass will get eaten down to the nub, exposing the soil to damaging heat and erosion, and slowing the regeneration of the grass. Of course, the worse the grazing conditions, the lower the milk production of the cows. The tendency of a society to overuse and deplete open-access resources like the commons (which economists often call *common pool resources*) is called the **tragedy of the commons**.

Tragedy of the commons The tendency of a society to overuse and deplete open-access (common pool) resources.

To see how the tragedy of the commons works, let's add some numbers to Ben and Jerry's story: With two cows on the commons, the grass will be plentiful, and each cow will produce 1,000 gallons of milk per year. With three cows on the commons, the grass will be sufficient, and each cow will produce 750 gallons of milk per year. Finally, with four cows on the commons, the grass will be sparse, and each cow will produce 400 gallons of milk per year.

Using these numbers, we can create a payoff matrix for Ben and Jerry:

- If Ben and Jerry each graze one cow, each cow will produce 1,000 gallons of milk during the year.

- If Ben and Jerry each graze two cows, then the four cows on the commons will each produce 400 gallons of milk. Ben's two cows will give him 800 gallons of milk in total; Jerry's two cows will do the same.

- Finally, if one of the farmers puts two cows on the commons and the other puts one on the commons, the farmer with two cows will get 1,500 gallons of milk; the farmer with one cow will get 750 gallons of milk.

The farmers' problem is shown in payoff matrix form in Figure 9.7.

► **Figure 9.7**
The Tragedy of the Commons
When a pasture is common property, farmers have an incentive to graze more cows than is socially optimal.

		Ben	
		One Cow	Two Cows
Jerry	One Cow	1,000, 1,000	750, 1,500
	Two Cows	1,500, 750	800, 800

[3]See Garrett Hardin, "The Tragedy of the Commons," *Science* 162 (1968): 1243.

Application 9.2

Good to the Last Drop

Here's a question: Who owns the water in a river?

Consider the Arkansas River, which flows through Colorado, Kansas, Oklahoma, and Arkansas. In Colorado, the Arkansas River is big—it carved out the Royal Gorge. In dry western Kansas, things are different. There, the fertile soil is ideal for growing thirsty crops like corn. But water is hard to come by. To irrigate thousands of acres of fruits and vegetables, Colorado does its best to drain the Arkansas River dry before it crosses into Kansas. This infuriates Kansans. "How dare those Coloradans suck the Arkansas River dry to grow melons when we want to suck it dry to grow corn," they lament.

So, in 1902, Kansas filed suit to force Colorado to use less water. *Kansas v. Colorado* went straight to the Supreme Court. The Court ruled that Colorado could use what it wanted, though later, the government intervened on behalf of Kansas, after the Arkansas River was dammed to create Colorado's John Martin Reservoir.

Filing lawsuits is one way that states establish property rights to water, but this isn't the only way. The six states in the Colorado River watershed (Colorado, Utah, Nevada, New Mexico, Arizona, and California) used bargaining to resolve their difficulties. The result was the Colorado River Compact, which carefully apportions the use of the river's abundant waters. Because it's the primary source of water for 30 to 40 million people, the Colorado River is so carefully managed that it is estimated that each drop from it is used and returned to the river 17 times.

Multistate compacts and lawsuits have largely settled the questions of property rights for rivers. That helps ensure that rivers continue to flow. But no such arrangements have been made for aquifers. The Ogallala Aquifer, an underground lake of fossil water that stretches from Wyoming to Texas, is an example. Residents of eight states access water from the aquifer to use in their homes and businesses and to irrigate farm land.

Because the aquifer is really just one big puddle, every gallon a Wyoming farmer pumps reduces the water level by the tiniest amount all the way to Texas. Although Texans might be angry about this, they know that trying to limit Wyoming's water usage might also result in limits on their own water usage. So Texans remain silent, content to pump everything they can before someone else does; the aquifer as a whole goes virtually unmanaged.

Further, the growing scarcity of the aquifer's water is not reflected in its price. Throughout its extent, it is tapped at no cost or low cost to the end user; prices, if they exist at all, are set by government and not by market forces. Consequently, the signals that market-determined prices would send to consumers about careful use and conservation disappear.

As a result, it is estimated that the aquifer, which took millions of years to create, might be depleted within the next 30 years. But it won't go alone: It will take with it the farms and the cities that depend on it, both victims and villains in the tragedy of the commons.

See related problem 3.5 on page 194 at the end of this chapter.

Based on "Southern Great Plains Could Run Out of Groundwater in 30 Years, Study Finds," *Christian Science Monitor*, May 30, 2012; "Tapping Unsustainable Groundwater Stores for Agricultural Production in the High Plains Aquifer of Kansas, Projections to 2110," *Proceedings of the National Academy of Sciences of the United States of America*, by David Steward, et al., August 26, 2013; and "Wells Dry, Fertile Plains Turn to Dust," *The New York Times*, May 19, 2013.

Notice in Figure 9.7 that no matter what Ben chooses to do, Jerry is always better off placing two cows on the commons rather than one. So two cows is a dominant strategy for Jerry. Notice further that two cows is also a dominant strategy for Ben. The intersection of those dominant strategies is the Nash equilibrium for the game: Both farmers place two of their own cows on the commons. Unfortunately, this creates such extensive overgrazing that the farmers end up worse off than if they had each chosen just one cow.

This problem contains all the elements of the classic prisoner's dilemma. Both Ben and Jerry are led by individual incentives to do something that is not in the best interest of the dairy farmers as a group or society as a whole. Overall milk production declines as a result. The incentives of this game trap Ben and Jerry into working more for less. If they could agree to each put just one cow on the commons, they could cut their milking chores by half and magically end up with more milk.

Depletion and Pollution: Mirror Images of the Same Problem

Think back to the previous chapter. Do you remember the problem Jackson and Max faced when they were each deciding whether to install pollution-control devices on their cars? If you compare that problem to the one we've just analyzed, you'll find that the game played by Jackson and Max is essentially the same as the game Ben and Jerry are playing. Both games are prisoner's dilemmas, even though one deals with the problem of putting too much bad stuff *into* the environment and the other deals with taking too much good stuff *out* of the environment. The two problems look like opposites on the outside, but underneath the packaging, they're members of the same structural family and occur due to similar circumstances. Pollution occurs because poorly defined property rights allow polluters to force others to share their costs. This is really the problem with depletion, too. Notice that when Ben puts another cow onto the commons, his payoff rises, but Jerry's falls. This is because Ben receives *all* of the benefits of that extra cow (namely, he gets the milk), but he forces Jerry to share the burden of the overgrazing that his extra cow causes.

9.4 Learning Objective

Describe the approaches governments use to try to solve depletion problems and promote sustainability.

How Can Society Fix Depletion Problems?

So how can depletion problems like Ben and Jerry's be fixed and our resources sustained? If poorly defined property rights lie at the root of the problem, then properly defining and assigning property rights is the solution. As is the case with pollution problems, individuals can sometimes work out suitable arrangements among themselves. Ben and Jerry, for example, might each agree to keep only one cow on the commons. And because Ben knows Jerry and Jerry knows Ben, and because they are the only two who share the commons, and because both of them can look out onto the commons and count how many cows each is grazing, such an arrangement might work out fine. But as the commons grows in size, and as the number of interested parties grows, working out equitable and enforceable arrangements becomes difficult, in part because of transactions costs. For example, how would several thousand fishermen, most of whom do not know one another, decide how many fish should be taken out of a very-large-and-difficult-to-monitor ocean? Negotiating a deal among the fishermen and monitoring compliance would be both expensive and difficult. We're going to need someone with a bit more reach and power to fix the problem. That someone is often the government.

Restricting the Access to Endangered Resources and Their Use

Just as governments have many ways to reduce pollution, they also have many ways to reduce depletion. One of the bluntest approaches is for a government simply to restrict access to the resource. This approach is often used when there is an interest in protecting fragile ecosystems as nature preserves. It's also the approach many states take to hunting big game. Alaska, for example, allows only a few hundred people to hunt brown or grizzly bears each hunting season. The state allocates the right to do so by lottery once each year.

A second, similar approach is for governments to leave open-access resources (oceans, forests, and so on) open to all but restrict the intensity of their use.

Measures such as this are often used to help manage stocks of wildlife. For example, in Kansas, people who wish to hunt ring-necked pheasant are welcome to do so, but they have to hunt between certain dates, are allowed to shoot only males, and can kill only four birds each day.

Both of these approaches—restricting the access to resources and restricting the intensity of their use—establish some form of property rights. The first approach makes the resource temporarily the property of those lucky enough to be given permission to use it; the second approach makes the resource everybody's property but dictates the manner in which that property can be used.

How Much Access Is the Right Amount of Access? As you can imagine, it's difficult for bureaucrats to manage a large resource from a distant seat of government in a way that maximizes society's well-being. If the first approach is used, for example, a government must accurately determine exactly how much access, or traffic, the resource can sustain. In terms of getting the most benefit from scarce resources, it's clear that sometimes the government gets the answer wrong: Palau's beautiful 70 Islands Marine Preserve, for example, is off limits to all visitors. This guarantees that the 70 Islands will be around forever. It also guarantees that nobody will be allowed to enjoy them. Consequently, the benevolent social planner, who loves underwater life, weeps in dismay. If access is granted, but the intensity of the use is limited, how likely is it that the right amount of usage will be allowed? Is the "right" number of Alaskan bear hunters 202, or 312, or 42? It's hard to say, although governments often employ reasonably well-trained individuals to come up with those numbers. Yet even if those number crunchers give perfect advice, it's important to remember that politicians don't serve the experts; they serve their constituents. Those constituents may lobby for more access or less access than is socially desirable, and if those efforts are persuasive enough, society as a whole may lose.

Is Access Being Granted in a Welfare-Maximizing Way? However many hunters Alaska happens to choose, a second very important concern is that permission be allocated to the right people. If Alaska gives a brown bear permit to Fred, who values a bear hunt at $1,200, instead of Yogi, who values a bear hunt at $2,000, it's made a bad decision from society's standpoint: It's left $800 of happiness unclaimed. That loss, just like the losses we talked about in Chapter 5, is a deadweight loss.

Society can, however, recapture that deadweight loss by making one simple modification to the procedures: Allow permits to be bought and sold in a secondary market. We can now imagine Fred and Yogi meeting in a waterfront bar in Anchorage and hashing out the terms of a bargain that would result in the transfer of Fred's permit (which he won in the Alaska Fish and Game Commission's annual bear-hunting lottery) to Yogi for a price somewhere between $1,200 and $2,000. No matter what price they settle on, the transaction results in society capturing an additional $800 of cooperative surplus because the same resource is now creating greater happiness (see Chapter 5).

If this scheme seems familiar to you, it should. It's really just a variation on the cap-and-trade system many governments have adopted to regulate pollution. Instead of deciding how much pollution to allow, a government decides how much depletion to allow and then lets the parties decide for themselves who gets the most value out of the resource. Systems like this, which were unheard of just 30 years ago, have become commonplace tools for resource management. The **individual transferable quota (ITQ) system**, discussed in Application 9.3 on the next page, is one such system.

Individual Transferable Quota (ITQ) system A system of controlling overfishing whereby the government decides how big the total fish catch will be and then lets fishermen negotiate to determine the share of the total catch each fisherman will be allowed.

Creating Absolute Property Rights

Governments have a third tool they can use in their war against depletion, and it's a tool that requires a lot less management, monitoring, and bureaucracy. All they need to do is assign some person an absolute property right to the commons. A government can do this by auctioning off the commons, conducting a lottery, or simply

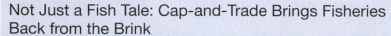

Application 9.3

Not Just a Fish Tale: Cap-and-Trade Brings Fisheries Back from the Brink

Perhaps the most visible example of the tragedy of the commons can be found in the world's fisheries. Over the past 100 years, global population growth has created more demand for seafood. Navigation and fishing methods have improved as well. The result? Chronic overfishing in most of the world's fishing grounds. Today, fishermen travel farther and work harder to catch fewer and smaller fish. Rhode Island lobsterer John Sorlien summed up the problem for the *New York Times* in August 2000: "Right now, my only incentive is to go out and kill as many fish as I can . . . because any fish I leave is just going to be picked up by the next guy."[4]

But as many fisheries falter, a few thrive due to a new management method: the individual transferable quota (ITQ). Under the ITQ, a government limits the number of fish that can be caught. It divides that quota among existing fishermen, who each receive a "catch share" that represents permanent ownership of part of the fishery.

The transferability of shares is the key to the system. A fisherman who wants to catch more than his or her share in a given year must purchase part of another fisherman's annual allocation. That's a lot like the cap-and-trade system used to control pollution.

More importantly from a conservation standpoint, fishermen can also sell their *permanent* shares in the fishery. In fact, someone who wants to become a fisherman must buy the right to fish by purchasing the permanent share of a fisherman who is leaving the industry. The more populated and productive the fishery is, the more an exiting fisherman will receive for his or her catch share. For just this reason, fishermen in Alaska's halibut fishery, which is governed by ITQs, have recently begun pushing for a 40% *reduction* in the overall quota.

Anecdotal evidence strongly supports ITQs: In Australia, where lobstering is governed by ITQs, lobsterers harvest as much with 60 traps as Americans do with 200—and they do it in half the time. Empirical evidence favors ITQs as well. Two economists (Christopher Costello and John Lynham) and a marine biologist (Steven Gaines), all of the University of California, Santa Barbara, recently surveyed each of the world's 11,135 fisheries and found that the 121 fisheries managed by ITQs were dramatically healthier. Costello, Lynham, and Gaines estimate that managing a fishery by ITQ cuts in half the risk of the fishery collapsing.

Resources that are carefully managed are more likely to last. The ITQ system encourages fishermen to view themselves as fish ranchers—careful managers who must balance this year's profits with the benefits of a growing fish population: bigger future harvests with less work required to bring them home. The work of Costello, Lynham, and Gaines suggests that those incentives may mean the difference between life and death for the world's fisheries.

See related problem 4.4 on page 195 at the end of this chapter.

Based on Christopher Costello, Steven D. Gaines, and John Lynham, "Can Catch Shares Prevent Fisheries Collapse?" *Science*, 2008; "Economies of Scales," *The Economist*, September 20, 2008; "A Rising Tide," *The Economist*, September 20, 2008; and "A Tale of Two Fisheries," *The New York Times*, August 27, 2000.

---

[4]"A Tale of Two Fisheries," *The New York Times*, August 27, 2000.

giving the commons to the first Ben or Jerry who wanders through the door and asks for it.[5] Once the commons is privatized, the person who owns it has an incentive to manage it carefully so that it will provide the greatest possible stream of income over the greatest stretch of time. In other words, privatizing the commons can turn a rhino into a chicken as well as maximize the economic pie. The benevolent social planner rejoices!

Privatization Encourages Efficient Management To show how privatization encourages efficient management, let's revisit Ben and Jerry, who are fussing with one another about the number of cows each is keeping on the commons. Up rides the king of the world, who taps Ben on the shoulder with his royal scepter and says, "Ben, I hereby decree this land to be land no longer held in common. From this day forward, it belongs to you. Carry on."

Ben now surveys the choices available to him (which are summarized in Figure 9.7) and says, "Well, I'm certainly not going to put just one cow on the commons. Maybe I'll try two. But without Jerry's cows out there eating all the grass, I'm sensing an opportunity to expand even more. Three cows it is!"

You may have already noticed that total milk production is at its peak (2,250 gallons per year) when there are three cows on the commons. This means Ben has correctly determined the best number of cows to graze in order to maximize milk production. Three cows is ideal for Ben, and it's also ideal for society because it creates the greatest possible value from the pasture, and it does so in a sustainable way.

Coase and the Case of Inefficient Resource Management Suppose that Ben isn't smart enough to figure out that putting three cows on the land is ideal. Or what if he's simply short-sighted or lazy, and instead of keeping three cows, he keeps four? Now society loses in two ways: Ben's not using the commons in the most efficient way, and he's depleting the stock of grass at the same time. At this point, you might be thinking that if the king hadn't given the commons to Ben, society might have been able to preserve the commons. Now all hope is lost: The commons belongs to a poor manager, and there's nothing anybody can do about it.

You might think that, but you'd be wrong. That's because if a government assigns the property to Ben, and he doesn't use it efficiently, then Ben's misuse creates the opportunity for someone who can use it better to simply purchase it from him. For example, if Ben keeps four cows on the commons, they will be producing only 1,600 gallons of milk. In addition, the poor production will be reflected in the land's market value: A chronically overgrazed pasture isn't worth very much. Along comes Jerry, who sees that with careful management, the grass can be regrown, and once that's done, cows on the pasture can capably produce 2,250 gallons of milk. So Jerry buys the land at a bargain price and turns it into something valuable again, and the benevolent social planner rejoices.

This, of course, is yet another application of the Coase theorem, which says that the property right to a resource will be acquired by the party (Jerry, in this case) that values it most. And where have you seen the Coase theorem before? In your study of pollution, of course. Now you know that depletion and pollution really are related—both in their causes and in their solutions.

Conclusion

This chapter highlights once again the role of property rights and transactions costs in creating difficult-to-solve social problems. The resources most likely to become endangered are resources that nobody has a clear claim to. Careful management of

---

[5]Of those alternative distribution mechanisms, the auction method immediately directs the resource to the party that values it most—the high bidder. However, as is shown in the discussion of Coase and inefficient resource management, that same outcome can be achieved no matter how the initial rights are assigned; it might just take a little longer.

The People Behind the Theory

Elinor Ostrom

The tragedy of the commons suggests that open-access resources are the ones most likely to be depleted—that individual incentives lead people into self-defeating behaviors. The standard policy prescription to prevent that from happening is to call in the government to regulate access to the commons.

Nobel Prize winner Elinor Ostrom, of the University of Indiana, disagreed with that recommendation. In 2009, she told NPR's *Planet Money* that while the potential for a society to overuse a shared resource is a problem, it doesn't necessarily have to be a tragedy. In Ostrom's judgment, economists are often too quick to label those problems unsolvable and too eager to recommend top-down government regulation or privatization.

Ostrom spent a lifetime studying how human beings living in community managed to prevent the overexploitation of commonly owned resources. She did her best work in the field, where she found that neighbors often established customs and conventions that regulated the use of common property—rules about how many cows to graze on a common meadow, or how much water to draw from a well. Common tasks like clearing irrigation canals were often done together, with monitors imposing penalties, including social exclusion, on rule-breakers. The Royal Swedish Academy, which awards the Nobel Prize in Economics, highlighted Ostrom's observation that customs and conventions that evolve over a long span of time are often far more effective than outsiders are willing to admit.

Ostrom argued that the institutions governing the commons had to work within the boundaries of cultural norms and had to be built from the ground up as a result of face-to-face discussion between the interested parties. She highlighted a few basic principles for effective resource management:

- Democratic processes should be used to establish the rules.
- The rules should delineate exactly how much of the resource everybody is entitled to.
- There must be an effective mechanism for resolving conflicts and disputes.
- Monitoring and sanctioning should be carried out by the users themselves, beginning with mild sanctions that escalate with repeated offenses.
- A person's duty to maintain a resource should be proportional to the benefit that person receives from the resource.

Ostrom admitted that such organic solutions are less capable of dealing with large-scale problems like global warming. "That doesn't mean we should just wait until the international agreement comes through. Instead, governments should encourage and aid people where they are trying to solve the problem, such as finding ways to make it easier for them to use solar energy or to bicycle to work."

For her groundbreaking work that showed how social institutions can sometimes outperform both markets and governments, Ostrom was awarded the Nobel Prize in Economics in 2009—the first woman to be so honored.

Based on *Planet Money*'s "Remembering Elinor Ostrom, Nobel Laureate," June 12, 2012; "Work of 2009 Economics Nobel Laureates Sheds Light on Regulation," *The Wall Street Journal*, October 12, 2009; Tim Harford's *The Undercover Economist*, Oxford University Press, 2006; "Nobel Looks Outside Markets," *The Wall Street Journal*, October 13, 2009; and "Elinor Ostrom," *The Economist*, June 30, 2012.

such a resource could potentially provide a long-lasting source of income, and it's possible that the members of society, on their own initiative, could come up with an agreement to limit their use of that resource in order to sustain those long-term profits. But transactions costs can make reaching and enforcing such agreements difficult. In those cases, careful government management can potentially produce a social outcome that is superior to what private individuals could produce on their own.

Chapter Summary and Problems

Key Terms

Individual Transferable Quota (ITQ) system, p. 189

Tragedy of the commons, p. 186

9.1 ## Will the World Run Out of Oil? pages 180–184

Explain how rising oil prices prevent the rapid depletion of world oil stocks.

Summary

Many mainstream sources predict that the world will run out of oil soon. But as oil becomes more scarce, its price will rise. In response, people will cut back their oil consumption, oil companies will search for new reserves of oil, society will tap into oil stocks that are more difficult to extract, and the search for oil substitutes will intensify. As a result, oil stocks will not deplete nearly as rapidly as predicted.

Review Questions

All problems are assignable in MyEconLab.

1.1 When the price of oil (and oil-derived products) increases, annual consumption tends to _____, and so the number of years to depletion _____.

1.2 When oil prices rise, some uneconomical oil becomes cost-effective to extract. That causes proven reserves to _____.

1.3 _____ consist of the supply of oil that is both known and economical to extract.

1.4 _____ oil prices encourage more oil exploration. When more oil is discovered, proven reserves _____.

1.5 If new substitutes for oil are found, the number of years remaining until oil is depleted will _____.

1.6 The world's oil supply can be divided in four ways: known, unknown, _____, and _____.
   a. Proven; reserved
   b. Economical; uneconomical
   c. Developed; undeveloped
   d. Conserved; reserved

1.7 Proven reserves of oil include oil that is _____ and _____.
   a. Known; unknown
   b. Unknown; economical
   c. Known and unknown; economical
   d. Known; economical

1.8 As the price of oil rises, oil exploration _____.
   a. Decreases
   b. Increases
   c. Remains the same
   d. Rising oil prices have an undetermined effect on exploration.

1.9 Which of the following is *not* true regarding increases in the price of oil?
   a. Oil price increases encourage conservation.
   b. Oil price increases make costly sources of oil less economical.
   c. Oil price increases encourage more oil exploration.
   d. a, b, and c are all true statements.

Problems and Applications

1.10 Explain why it is highly unlikely that the world's oil reserves will be depleted within the next 40 years.

1.11 Suppose that the U.S. government increases its federal excise tax on gasoline to $5 per gallon. Explain the likely impact of that tax, if any, on (a) conservation, (b) oil exploration, and (c) the development of substitutes for gasoline. Is such a tax likely to increase or decrease the number of years until oil is depleted?

9.2 What Resources Are in Danger of Depletion? pages 184–186

Discuss the role property rights play in the depletion and sustainability of natural resources.

Summary

Some resources are endangered, and others are not. Generally, what distinguishes them is property rights. Resources that have clearly assigned property rights are carefully managed and not likely to disappear. Resources that have no clear owner or manager but that are open to all are most likely to be depleted.

Review Questions

2.1 What is the world most likely to run out of?

 a. Gold
 b. Sharks
 c. Oil
 d. Beef

2.2 The key distinction that separates endangered resources from sustainable resources is the nature of _____.

 a. Transactions costs
 b. Coasean bargains
 c. Climate change
 d. Property rights

Problems and Applications

2.3 Explain why the world's stocks of tuna are more likely to be depleted than the world's stocks of cattle.

2.4 [Related to Application 9.1 on page 185] Carefully read Application 9.1, which describes the trophy hunting of endangered species. If such programs are to encourage conservation, explain why it is crucial that (a) governments share licensing fees with villagers and (b) governments allow the hunting of elderly males only.

2.5 [Related to Application 9.1 on page 185] In some African countries, wildlife officials have begun tranquilizing rhinos and sawing off their horns (a quick and painless procedure). Explain how programs like these may help prevent the extinction of the highly endangered rhino.

9.3 The Tragedy of the Commons, pages 186–188

Compare and contrast depletion problems and pollution problems.

Summary

The tendency of open-access resources to be depleted is called the tragedy of the commons. In the tragedy of the commons, incentives lead individual members of a society to extract more of a resource than is socially optimal. Society is trapped in an environmental version of a prisoner's dilemma. The incentive structure of depletion problems mirrors the incentive structure of pollution problems. At their source, both are problems of poorly defined property rights.

Review Questions

3.1 _____ is the tendency of a society to overuse and deplete open-access resources.

3.2 What type of game is the tragedy of the commons?

 a. Prisoner's dilemma
 b. Chicken
 c. Battle of the sexes
 d. Assurance

3.3 An open-access pasture is often referred to as a _____.

 a. Commons
 b. Reservation
 c. Property right
 d. Bureaucracy

Problems and Applications

3.4 Provide a modern, real-world example of the tragedy of the commons. (Your example should not be one referred to in the text.) Then explain how insecure property rights lie at the root of the tragedy you chose.

3.5 [Related to Application 9.2 on page 187] Application 9.2 describes how several southwestern states resolved their dispute over water rights to the Colorado River. The Colorado River eventually flows out of the United States and into Mexico, where it soon disappears, its waters exhausted. Explain why it is easier to keep the Colorado's waters flowing as it passes from state to state than it is to keep the Colorado's waters flowing as it passes from country to country.

How Can Society Fix Depletion Problems? pages 188–191

Describe the approaches governments use to try to solve depletion problems and promote sustainability.

Summary

When a resource becomes endangered, individuals could agree among themselves to cut back their use of that resource. But sometimes transactions costs make that difficult. In those cases, government intervention may more effectively prevent depletion. Government can restrict access to the resource, though care must be taken to prevent too little access. Or government can assign a clear property right to the resource so that it will be managed more carefully. If the party given the property right mismanages the resource, that mismanagement creates an opportunity for a more careful manager to earn a profit by purchasing it.

Review Questions

All problems are assignable in MyEconLab.

4.1 Some governments manage their fisheries by setting a limit on the total catch and dividing that total into shares for individual fishermen. Those fishermen can either catch their share or sell the right to their share to someone else. This type of fisheries management is called the _____ system.

4.2 What are ways that the government can reduce depletion of a resource?

a. Restrict access to the resource

b. Restrict how intensively the resource is used

c. Assign absolute property rights to a resource

d. All of the above

4.3 _____ property rights exist when one individual or entity has complete control over a resource, including the right to transfer that resource to someone else.

a. Complete

b. Flexible

c. Legal

d. Absolute

Problems and Applications

4.4 **[Related to Application 9.3 on page 190]** Read Application 9.3 carefully. It is certainly possible to manage fisheries by establishing a quota system in which catch shares are not transferrable. Why is a system where catch shares *are* transferrable likely to (a) be more efficient—enabling the same quantity of fish to be caught with fewer resources and (b) provide a stronger incentive for fishermen to collectively catch fewer fish?

4.5 Beginning in the late 1990s, growing wealth in Asia spurred strong demand for shark fin soup, which is a luxury food there. The unfortunate consequence of this demand is a practice called "shark finning," in which fishermen cut off sharks' fins and then return the still-living sharks to the sea to die. Despite the fact that several nations have banned shark finning, the practice continues to threaten shark populations, with an estimated 100 million sharks being finned annually. Why do you suppose the multination ban on shark finning has been unsuccessful in protecting sharks? Your answer should include some reference to property rights.

Experiment

The "Gone Fishing" Game

This chapter explained how difficult it is for societies to manage and sustain natural resources such as oil and water. The chapter highlighted the role that property rights play in achieving sustainability. Today, you and your classmates have the chance to see if *you* can manage and sustain a renewable resource.

You and your classmates all make your living catching fish that you sell at a local market. Fish are a renewable and potentially sustainable resource: Unharvested fish repopulate the waters at a predictable rate, potentially providing you with a stream of income that can last for years to come.

In this game, you are asked to manage a stock of fish over a large number of fishing seasons. There are two parts to this game:

1. In the first part of the game, you have a private lake where you, and only you, can fish. Each year, you have to decide how many fish to harvest. Unharvested fish will provide you with more fish to catch in years to come.

2. In the second part of the game, you and your classmates share a much larger lake where everyone fishes. You and your classmates have the opportunity to collectively manage the stock of fish to provide a sustainable stream of income that will last well into the future.

Do you think you and your classmates will be effective fish ranchers? This is your opportunity to find out!

MyEconLab

Please visit http://www.myeconlab.com for support material to conduct this experiment if assigned by your instructor.

Chapter Outline and Learning Objectives

10.1 Public Versus Private Goods, page 198

Describe the characteristics that make a good a public good.

10.2 How Nonexcludability Leads to Free Riding and the Public Goods Problem, page 200

Explain why private individuals tend to produce too few public goods.

10.3 Property Rights and the Public Goods Problem, page 204

Explain how poorly defined property rights and high transactions costs cause public goods to be underprovided.

10.4 How Governments Can Overcome the Public Goods Problem, page 205

List the pros and cons of governments providing public goods.

Experiment: The Garden Game, page 214

MyEconLab

MyEconLab helps you master each objective and study more efficiently.

Tuscola is a picturesque town of 4,000 in the plains of central Illinois. Brick streets pass between magnificent century-old homes, shaded by soaring oaks and maples. Tuscola boasts a Carnegie Library and a thriving downtown business district. The residents of the community are devoted to their town and think it is the finest place in the area to live.

Terrell, Grace, and Kalen each own restored Victorian-era houses at the intersection of Center Street and Sale Street in Tuscola. On summer evenings, the three neighbors sit on their wraparound porches, drink lemonade, and listen to mockingbirds sing. One evening, Grace suggested to the others that their intersection could be improved if a fountain were added to the existing traffic roundabout.

The three neighbors each agreed that it would be a lovely thing to fall asleep to the sound of falling water, and that it would be nice to open their curtains each day and see the beauty of a fountain. When Grace asked them how much they would value that fountain, each thought hard and then replied, "$150." Grace responded, "Terrific. I'd pay up to $150 to have a fountain in the intersection, too! I'll run some numbers and see what we can come up with."

A week later, Grace gathered the neighbors and shared what she had learned. "Installing the fountain will cost us $300. I've talked to the city, and they've agreed to pay for the water. So all we need to do now is come up with the money for the fountain, and we'll be set."

"Terrific," Terrell said. "Each of us needs to contribute only $100. That's less than each of us said we'd be willing to pay for the fountain. Give me a few days to get the money together, and then let's meet at the downtown diner next Tuesday to collect the cash."

On the appointed day, the neighbors met for lunch. Then Grace whipped off her hat and began passing it around the table. "Everybody put in their $100 for the fountain, please," she said. "Then I'll take the money and get the ball rolling."

The hat passed from Grace to Terrell to Kalen, and then back to Grace. She ceremoniously dumped it out on the table and began counting the bills and coins. "There's only $200 here," she announced. "Who didn't put in their money?"

She looked around the table. One after the other, Kalen and Terrell each said, "Well, it must have been one of you, because it wasn't me." When Grace asked again, Kalen left the diner saying, "I'm tired of this harassment. Figure it out yourselves."

"Well, I guess we can count Kalen out," Grace said. "But each of us was willing to spend $150 to see the fountain built, and each of us has put in only $100, so if we both just chip in the remaining $50, we can still get this project done. Pony up, Terrell."

Will Terrell chip in another $50? Will the fountain be built?

10.1 Learning Objective

Describe the characteristics that make a good a public good.

Public Versus Private Goods

Putting a fountain in an intersection presents a special type of economic problem. You have learned that allowing the free exchange of goods and services between individuals, states, and nations is generally the best way to maximize the size of the economic pie (see Chapter 5). But there are a few exceptions to that rule, and the fountain Grace longs for is one of them.

At this point, we don't know whether the fountain will be built. But we do know one important thing about the fountain: The benevolent social planner would like to see it built. Here's why: The fountain costs society $300 but creates $450 worth of benefits—$150 each to Grace, Terrell, and Kalen. By putting the fountain in the intersection, the economic pie grows by $150, and the benevolent social planner rejoices.

In a world of free exchange, if a person stands to receive $150 of value from something that costs only $100 (perhaps a new pair of Nikes), he or she will purchase that product, and the economic pie will grow. The potential problem in this case arises because a fountain is different from a pair of shoes.

Rival and Nonrival Goods

One reason a fountain is different from a pair of shoes is that many people can share the experience of viewing the fountain. Economists call goods that many people can use simultaneously **nonrival goods**. If you're viewing a fountain and your roommate steps up beside you to look, your experience probably isn't significantly diminished by the fact that she's there. You can't say that about shoes: If you buy a pair of Nikes and your roommate puts them on, you can't wear them, too. Goods like shoes that only one person at a time can enjoy are called **rival goods**. What's nice about nonrival goods from the benevolent social planner's perspective is that if society provides that good for one person, it is possible for society to make it available to everybody else with little additional trouble.

> **Nonrival good** A good that many people can use simultaneously.

> **Rival good** A good that only one person at a time can enjoy.

Despite the binary rival/nonrival distinction made here, it's useful to note that rivalry sometimes lies on a spectrum. For example, suppose you are driving on an interstate highway in far eastern Montana. If one more person hops on the highway, it probably won't bother you at all. That's very different than driving on an interstate highway through downtown Atlanta at rush hour: There, one more driver competes for space with everybody else.

Excludable and Nonexcludable Goods

The second reason a fountain is different than a pair of shoes is that once the fountain has been installed, it's difficult to keep people from viewing it. Everybody who walks or drives by gets to enjoy it. Economists say that the fountain is a **nonexcludable good**, which means that it is impossible, or at least quite costly, to prevent any passerby from receiving the benefits of the fountain once it's been built.

> **Nonexcludable good** A good that a producer finds difficult or costly to prevent people from consuming.

The fountain is different from, say, a movie: A theater that shows the latest James Bond film can easily lock out anybody who hasn't purchased a ticket. So movies are **excludable goods**—goods that a producer can prevent people from enjoying—but the fountain is not.

> **Excludable good** A good that a producer can prevent people from consuming.

Four Different Classes of Goods

Given the criteria—rival or nonrival and excludable or nonexcludable—it is possible to classify any good in one of four ways.

First, a good can be rival and excludable. These are goods that can't be simultaneously shared and that you can exclude others from using if you wish. Economists call these goods **pure private goods**. Most of the consumer goods you purchase—food and clothing, for example—are probably pure private goods.

> **Pure private good** A good that is rival and excludable.

Some goods are nonrival and nonexcludable. Those goods can be simultaneously shared by large numbers of people, and producers find it difficult to exclude anyone from enjoying the benefits of such a good: Provide it for one person, and you've provided it for everybody. Such goods are called **pure public goods**. A tornado siren is an example of a pure public good: You receive the same warning whether your neighbor is listening to it or not, and there is no easy way for the person operating the siren to alert you and at the same time keep your neighbor from hearing it.

> **Pure public good** A good that is nonrival and nonexcludable.

A third type of good is nonrival but excludable. If you provide it for one person, it's possible for others to enjoy it, too, but it's relatively easy to *keep* those others from enjoying it if you wish. Cable television is an example of this type of good: If you have cable TV, your service doesn't get any worse when someone new moves to town and signs up for cable, too. But it's not hard for the cable company to keep people from receiving the cable TV signal: If you've ever forgotten to pay your cable bill, you might know just how easy it is for the cable company to disconnect your service. Country club golf courses, too, have these characteristics: A lot of people can golf at the same time, but it's easy for the country club to keep nonmembers off the course. This explains why goods like this are often called **club goods**.

> **Club good** A good that is nonrival but excludable.

The fourth possible type of good is rival but nonexcludable. An ocean fishery is an example of this type of good. If you are fishing and catch a tuna, that tuna can't be

Common pool resource A good that is rival but nonexcludable.

caught by anyone else. At the same time, the size of the ocean makes it both difficult and costly to keep unwanted people out of the fishery. Goods like the fishery are called **common pool resources**. Common pool resources present particular challenges. You may have already spent some time studying those challenges in your study of depletion (see Chapter 9).

Figure 10.1 summarizes the four types of goods and lists some examples of each type.

▶ **Figure 10.1**

Four Types of Goods

Goods can be classified as pure private goods, pure public goods, club goods, or common pool resources.

	Excludable	Nonexcludable
Rival	**Pure private goods** Examples: 　Coffee 　iPhone 　Chair	**Common pool resources** Examples: 　Fisheries 　Fresh air 　Wildlife
Nonrival	**Club goods** Examples: 　Toll road 　Swimming pool 　Movie theater	**Pure public goods** Examples: 　Flood control 　Fireworks display 　National defense

10.2 Learning Objective

Explain why private individuals tend to produce too few public goods.

How Nonexcludability Leads to Free Riding and the Public Goods Problem

The fountain we've been considering is a pure public good: It is both nonrival and nonexcludable. Nonexcludability sounds like a good thing for society. It means that an unlimited number of people can receive the benefits of the fountain. This pleases the benevolent social planner. But nonexcludability also has a dark side, particularly when it comes to who should provide such goods.

The problem is that the nature of a nonexcludable good guarantees that everybody will receive the benefits of the good, even if they don't help bear the costs. In the case of the fountain, everyone suspects that Kalen didn't chip in a dime, but it's going to be difficult to keep him from viewing the fountain once it's been built.

Grace and Terrell might feel taken advantage of. Perhaps you, too, think that Kalen is a bit of a jerk. But that's irrelevant because in this course, it doesn't matter whether people are villains or saints. All that matters is the size of the economic pie. And in the example we're discussing, if Kalen does not contribute, Grace and Terrell should still be willing to pitch in the extra $50 each that building the fountain requires. Recall that they originally valued the fountain at $150, so chipping in an extra $50 is a break-even proposition for them.

Kalen, on the other hand, will get $150 of fountain viewing for nothing. Economists have a special name for people like Kalen. They call people who enjoy the benefits of a good without bearing a proportionate share of the cost **free riders**. But as we've mentioned, we don't care who gets the gains; we only care that somebody gets the gains. So what's the problem with nonexcludability and free ridership?

The answer to that question becomes apparent if we alter the scenario just a bit. Suppose the fountain doesn't cost $300; instead, it costs $310. The benevolent social planner would love for it to be built because its benefits ($450) exceed its costs ($310). But if Kalen walks out without contributing, the others do not value the fountain enough to build it. Because it isn't built, the economic pie shrinks.

Free rider A person who enjoys the benefits of a good without bearing a proportionate share of the cost.

The Not-So-Friendly Confines of Wrigley Field

If you ever get the chance to watch the Chicago Cubs play at Wrigley Field, take it. After all, everybody adores the humble and lovable Cubs, and seeing them play at Wrigley is like stepping back in time. The ancient stadium drips with character, from its steel-girder construction to the ivy-covered outfield fence.

A handful of apartment buildings sit across Waveland Boulevard from Wrigley Field. The buildings are tall enough that residents can watch the games from over the outfield wall. Not long ago, the buildings' owners realized that if people would pay money to watch the game from the stadium, they'd pay to watch from the tops of their apartment buildings. Quicker than you can say "Ernie Banks," bleachers sprang up on the rooftops. There, people could watch the game while enjoying catered food and drinks. "When they were up there with Weber grills and lawn chairs, it was a romantic thing that we really didn't have a whole lot of interest in," says Mark McGuire, the Cubs vice president. "The reality now is that [people] are paying more than $100 a person to be up there today and enjoy our product. And we are getting nothing out of it."

If you're the Cubs, you've got a problem: You've got one of the smallest ballparks in the majors, you're fighting for every dollar of revenue you can lay your hands on . . . and your game is nonexcludable. Apartment owners not only get to enjoy your games, they also get to sell your product to others!

The managers of the Cubs decided they didn't want to prevent people in apartments from watching the game. Instead, they wanted a piece of the revenue—essentially expanding their small stadium at someone else's expense! But how could they convince building owners to share their revenue? After all, they couldn't wall off the field, could they?

They could, and they did! On opening day 2002, fans were greeted by large mesh screens behind the outfield bleachers. Despite being quite costly, the screens could not be made tall enough to block the views from the rooftops where building owners were selling tickets. They were, however, tall enough to obstruct the views of apartment residents. Those residents complained to their landlords, and after the Cubs filed a federal lawsuit and threatened to build an even taller screen made of helium balloons, the building owners relented. Twelve of the 13 owners agreed to give the Cubs 17% of their revenues, totaling some $2 million each year.

But the 13th refused to pay. The Cubs were then faced with a dilemma—it's hard to block the view entirely, but it's almost impossible to block the view from 1 building while allowing the view from 12 others. Before opening day in 2004, the managers of the Cubs tested a number of alternatives until they found a successful one: attaching a large helium balloon to the left-field foul pole. Faced with large potential revenue losses, the owners of the 13th building settled with the Cubs just 4 days before the season opened.

See related problem 2.8 on page 211 at the end of this chapter.

Based on "Rooftop Owners and Cubs OK Deal but 3 Still Plan for March Trial," *Chicago Tribune*, January 30, 2004; "Owners to Pay 17 Percent of Revenue, *Associated Press*, January 30, 2004; "Skybox: We'll 'Never Pay Anything' to Cubs," *Associated Press*, March 21, 2004; and "Cubs, Holdout Rooftop Business Reach Deal," *Associated Press*, April 8, 2004.

The Free Ridership "Game"

You may have detected some elements of strategic behavior on Kalen's part. But truthfully, we don't know for sure that it was Kalen who didn't put the money in the hat. That's because whatever incentive Kalen had to free ride, Grace and Terrell did, too.

Consider a richer version of the game we just discussed: Players have the option of contributing or not contributing to the fountain. Their contributions may be in the form of effort, time, or money—it doesn't particularly change the analysis. To keep things simple, we'll eliminate the possibility that players can make partial contributions: A player can contribute either a full share or nothing at all.

When all the contributions come in, the fountain is built. Its size and splendor depend on the number of contributors. Any individual's decision to contribute makes the fountain bigger, better, and more enjoyable. But contributing also costs the contributor in terms of time, money, or effort. When these costs and benefits are accounted for, the individuals rank the potential outcomes as follows, from worst to best[1]:

- Build a small fountain all by yourself; payoff = 1
- Nobody builds a fountain; payoff = 2
- You contribute with one other person toward a medium-sized fountain; payoff = 3
- Somebody else builds a small fountain; payoff = 4
- You contribute with two others to make a large fountain; payoff = 5
- You do nothing while two others build a medium-sized fountain; payoff = 6

This scenario can be easily represented by using the three-player version of a game developed in your study of game theory (see Chapter 4). Let Grace choose the page, Terrell choose the column, and Kalen choose the row. Each player can either contribute to the project or not contribute. Using the payoffs we outlined, the game appears as shown in Figure 10.2, with payoffs in the cells going to Kalen, Terrell, and Grace, respectively.

▶ **Figure 10.2**

Building a Fountain

In this game, players may contribute to building a fountain, or they may attempt to free ride on the fountain provided by the other players. Payoffs in each cell go to Kalen (in black), Terrell (in blue), and Grace (in red). Society's best outcome is achieved when all players contribute.

Grace
Contribute

		Terrell	
		Contribute	Don't Contribute
Kalen	Contribute	**5, 5, 5**	**3, 6, 3**
	Don't Contribute	**6, 3, 3**	**4, 4, 1**

Grace
Don't Contribute

		Terrell	
		Contribute	Don't Contribute
Kalen	Contribute	**3, 3, 6**	**1, 4, 4**
	Don't Contribute	**4, 1, 4**	**2, 2, 2**

---

[1]These payoffs are based on the following underlying numbers: A small fountain provides 4 units of viewer benefit; a medium fountain provides 6 units of viewer benefit; a large fountain provides 8 units of viewer benefit. Contributing to the building of a fountain of any size costs the contributor 3 units of happiness.

A brief refresher of three-player game skills is in order. Remember that this is simply a two-player game with another layer added. So we can interpret this as a game played between Terrell and Kalen, once Grace has chosen her best action.

For example, suppose that Grace doesn't contribute, but Kalen and Terrell do. In this case, the game ends up in the second matrix (because Grace didn't contribute) and in the upper-left cell of the table (because Kalen and Terrell both contributed). Kalen receives the first number in the cell as his payoff (3), Terrell receives the second number in the cell as his payoff (3), and Grace receives the third number in the cell as her payoff (6).

You can use best-response analysis to find the likely outcome of this game, but it's even more telling to apply the concept of dominance. For simplicity, look only at Kalen's choices. Assuming that Grace has contributed to the fountain (which puts the game in the first matrix), note that if Terrell contributes, Kalen should not because it's better to receive a payoff of 6 than a payoff of 5. Even if Terrell doesn't contribute, Kalen should not because he prefers a payoff of 4 to a payoff of 3. So far, there is no instance in which Kalen should contribute.

To establish dominance, however, we also need to examine the incentives Kalen faces when Grace chooses *not* to contribute to the fountain. This puts the game in the second matrix. Now, if Terrell contributes, Kalen can get a payoff of 4 by not contributing but only 3 if he contributes. So Kalen should not contribute. If Terrell doesn't contribute, Kalen can get a payoff of 2 by not contributing, compared to a payoff of 1 if he does contribute. So, again, Kalen should not contribute.

This analysis confirms that not contributing is a dominant strategy for Kalen. No matter what Grace does and no matter what Terrell does, Kalen can always get a higher payoff by not contributing than he can by contributing. In other words, Kalen has every incentive to free ride on the efforts of the others.

Of course, because the game is symmetric, not contributing is also a dominant strategy for both Terrell and Grace. They are no different from Kalen in this regard. Consequently, dominance leads us to a Nash equilibrium where nobody contributes. Each player receives a payout of only 2 in this case because the fountain will not be built. (Recall from our original payoff list that when nobody builds a fountain, the payoff is 2.)

This is a poor outcome. If you inspect the matrixes closely, you'll find that the highest payout to the group occurs when each player contributes to make a large fountain: The total group outcome is 15, and each player receives a payoff of 5. Compare that to the Nash equilibrium outcome: In this case, each player receives a payout of 2, and the group payout is only 6. This is a less-than-ideal outcome from both an individual perspective and a group perspective. If Grace, Terrell, and Kalen could cooperate with one another, they could build a fountain that would make them all better off. But each player knows that if he can get the others to build a fountain, the nonexcludable nature of the fountain ensures that he or she will be able to enjoy the benefits with no costs. So each player tries to free ride, and as a result, society is poorer than it could be.

Let's see what type of game Grace, Terrell, and Kalen have been playing:

- Each player can contribute to produce a cooperative outcome or can choose not to contribute (defect) and attempt to free ride on the contributions of the others.

- Not contributing is a dominant strategy for each player.

- The Nash equilibrium, where no fountain is built, is worse for the group and for the individual players than the outcome that would be obtained if everybody cooperated.

These are the essential characteristics of a prisoner's dilemma game. The context is different than you've seen before, and there's an extra player, but the basic structure of the game is exactly the same as the prisoner's dilemma Dick and Jane faced earlier in the book (see Chapter 3).

The Public Goods Problem

The incentive to defect in the fountain-building dilemma stems entirely from the nonexcludable nature of the good. If we were talking about shoes instead of fountains, Kalen would buy new shoes if their benefits outweighed their cost or not buy them if the cost outweighed their benefits. Either way, Kalen's actions would produce the outcome that the benevolent social planner desires. But in the case of the fountain, Kalen tries to avoid buying the fountain even though the benefits he receives outweigh the cost he would incur by contributing. He fails to put money in a hat and storms off when he's accused of not contributing. Or maybe he cruelly says to the others, "Well, I'd like to have a fountain, but I think the rest of you want one bad enough that you'll put it up even if I don't contribute. So long, suckers!"

More realistically, when someone comes around asking for contributions for the fountain, Kalen, who really does want a fountain, will simply tell a little white lie such as, "I'm really not interested. I think a fountain in the intersection will disrupt traffic flow, and the sound of running water makes me want to potty all the time. I'm sorry, but you'll have to look elsewhere." Kalen does this because he hopes that the others will cough up the money to provide the fountain anyway, which he can then enjoy free of charge. But the others, feeling the same way, defect, too. As a result, a fountain that should be built is not built.

When a good that should be produced is not produced because everybody attempts to free ride, economists call it a **public goods problem**. Specifically, the public goods problem asserts that nonrival and nonexcludable goods are provided in less-than-ideal amounts if their provision is left to private individuals.

You may not have much experience with fountain-building, but you've probably run into the public goods problem in other places. This problem often rears its ugly head when college students are asked to work in groups. Group projects often bear the essential characteristics of a public good. First, the benefits are nonexcludable: Once you've been assigned to a group, you receive a grade whether you contribute to the group or not. Second, the benefits are nonrival: The professor can give as many A grades as he or she desires; just because you get an A doesn't mean that someone else in your group must be marked down to a C.

It's not uncommon for one or two members of the group to try to free ride on the efforts of others. They'll claim to have to work during group meetings, or they'll call in sick. Or maybe they'll turn in substandard work that required little effort, while hoping the others' work was better. Because the members of the group all receive the same grade, everyone has an incentive to work a bit less than they otherwise would, so the performance of the group suffers. Given that the free-rider problem produces a less-than-ideal outcome for the individuals in a group, it is no surprise that often all of the group members walk away saying, "I could have done a better job by myself." They are probably right.

Public goods problem The tendency for private individuals to provide pure public goods in less-than-ideal amounts because of free riding.

10.3 Learning Objective

Explain how poorly defined property rights and high transactions costs cause public goods to be underprovided.

Property Rights and the Public Goods Problem

Prior chapters talked a great deal about the importance of property rights. They motivate individuals to work harder and produce more economic pie than they would if property rights were not well defined (see Chapter 6). In addition, when the property rights to air and water are not well defined, too much pollution results (see Chapter 7).

It's probably no surprise that the lack of well-defined property rights in the example we're discussing stems from the nonexcludable nature of the fountain. If Grace had a way to secure the fountain for herself, she could build it with her own money and then charge Terrell and Kalen up to $150 to view it—and both Terrell and Kalen would gladly pay to see it because its benefits outweigh its cost. But because the benefits of the fountain belong to anybody and everybody who happens to pass by, neither Terrell nor Kalen will pay to build it because they can view it for free.

The fountain problem also stems from the existence of transactions costs, which were discussed in depth earlier in the context of the environment (see Chapter 8). If there were some way to accurately gauge how much Grace, Terrell, and Kalen valued the fountain and then bind them to an agreement with an inexpensive but enforceable contract, the fountain would be built. But nobody wants to tell the truth about how much they value the fountain, nor will they oblige themselves to help pay for the fountain if they're going to be able to view it for free.

How Governments Can Overcome the Public Goods Problem

10.4 Learning Objective
List the pros and cons of governments providing public goods.

How can society solve the free-rider problem and ensure that things like fountains get built when nobody wants to contribute to them? The easiest answer is to call in the government. We can simply go to the government and say, "We've got a fountain project that brings positive net benefits to society. But we're having trouble getting people to pay what they've promised. Can you build the fountain for us?" If enough people make this appeal to the government, it is likely to comply.

Government's Tax Powers and Free Ridership

And how does government pay for the fountain? It could assess a tax of $100 each on Grace, Terrell, and Kalen, who are the primary viewers of the fountain. In this way, government overcomes the free-rider problem by forcing the people who want the fountain to pay for it. With one stroke of the pen, government has changed the payout for not contributing: Terrell, Grace, and Kalen will face some sanction if they try to enjoy the fountain without paying taxes. Government has overcome almost insurmountable transactions costs by putting teeth in the implicit agreement that Grace, Terrell, and Kalen would have reached if property rights had been more well defined.

Of course, government might choose to tax the general public for the fountain, including individuals who might never see the fountain at all. In that case, the policy redistributes well-being from all of the taxpayers to Grace, Terrell, and Kalen. From an economist's perspective, that's not a problem. Remember that the benevolent social planner cares only about the size of the pie, not who gets the slices. But it is worth reiterating that redistributing well-being may create perverse incentives for the *creation* of economic pie. Earlier, for example, we found that people worked and created less when what they produced was to be shared with others (see Chapter 6). In the case of government-provided public goods, redistribution may create an incentive for society to create *more* things but perhaps the *wrong* things—at least from the benevolent social planner's perspective.

Suppose, for example, that the fountain brings Grace, Terrell, and Kalen $150 of benefits each but costs $600 to build. If the government promises to build the fountain and tax Grace, Terrell, and Kalen for the entire tab ($200 each), the trio would likely do everything in their power to stop construction (or at least they would complain loudly). But if government distributes the costs among all of the taxpayers in town, Grace, Terrell, and Kalen will receive large benefits at little cost to themselves.

Even if government chooses to tax everyone for the fountain, it is unlikely to generate much opposition from taxpayers. That's because the cost of the fountain is spread among so many people that the impact on any individual taxpayer is tiny; each of Tuscola's 4,000 residents would get a bill for a penny and a half. That's small enough that it's probably not worth the time it takes to call the mayor to complain. Once again, the separation of effort and reward has created a less-than-desirable social outcome: A fountain is built that really shouldn't be built.[2]

---

[2]Public choice economists refer to a case in which the government provides a good whose costs outweigh its benefits as a *government failure*.

Paying for Big Sugar's Sweet Deal

If you have a sweet tooth, you may be angry to discover that you pay twice as much for sugar in the United States than you would in most other countries. You might be even angrier to discover that the U.S. government is responsible for this inequity.

The government has established a quota that limits the quantity of foreign-produced sugar that can cross U.S. borders. That quota creates an artificial scarcity of sugar that is not felt elsewhere on the planet. That scarcity drives up sugar prices but also drives up the prices of ice cream and soda and any other sweetened food.

The quota is the product of strong lobbying efforts by a small group of major domestic sugar producers. To sugar producers, the quota is a public good: When sugar prices rise, every producer shares in the benefits. Economists Michael Wohlgenant and Vincent Smith estimated that the quota fattens producers' annual bottom line by a staggering $1.7 billion.

The money to pay for that public good doesn't come from sugar producers, however. It comes out of consumers' pockets. Wohlgenant and Smith estimated the total cost to consumers at $3 billion annually. Some of that cost shows up at the cash register. That money goes directly to sugar producers. But artificially high prices also encourage consumers to eat less sugar than they want, which creates a $1.3 billion deadweight loss. That money just disappears.

If that kind of waste angers you, you're not alone. Consumers have a $3 billion collective interest in repealing the quota. So why don't they appeal to their representatives to abandon the sugar program?

Because, as Mancur Olson suggested, while consumers might have a strong *collective* interest in repealing the quota, their *individual* stakes are much lower. $3 billion is huge, but divided among 315 million Americans, it's only about $9 per person. No matter how much the sugar quota angers you, with only $9 to gain, it's not cost-effective to drive to Washington to wine and dine your congressperson: After all, $9 barely gets you to the McDonald's across town.

Of course, consumers could all chip in something less—say, $8—to hire someone to lobby on their behalf. They could spend $2.5 billion on a lobbyist and *still* every man, woman, and child in society would be $1 better off. The problem with doing that, of course, is transactions costs: Somebody has to round up all the consumers and collect the money, a problem so daunting that an organized anti-sugar-program lobby will likely never materialize.

As Olson hypothesizes, the political outcome is a program that confers great rewards on a small, organized group of rent seekers while imposing small individual costs on a large and disorganized public. Ultimately, because the cost of the sugar program is not paid by the beneficiaries of that program, society is stuck with a quota that makes virtually everyone worse off—something to remember next time you feel like complaining about the price of your Ben & Jerry's.

See related problems 4.7 and 4.8 on page 213 at the end of this chapter.

Based on Michael Wohlgenant and Vincent Smith's "Bitter Sweet: How Big Sugar Robs You," *The American Online*, February 14, 2012; "The Insanity of U.S. Farm Policies," *National Review Online*, June 18, 2013; and Bryan Riley's "The U.S. Sugar Program: Bad for Consumers, Bad for Agriculture, and Bad for America," *The Heritage Foundation Issue Brief No. 3569*, April 18, 2012.

Economist Mancur Olson pointed out that less-than-desirable outcomes like this one are really collective action problems of a different sort. Because the benefits of projects like the fountain are concentrated, interest groups have an incentive to spend a lot of time and political energy fighting for them, even when they are welfare-destroying on the whole. But because the costs are diffuse, taxpayers rarely find complaining worth their while. If there were an easy way to get taxpayers together to speak with one voice, they could easily defeat such projects. But because of transactions costs, organizing taxpayers is difficult. As a result, such projects often go forward even when they make everyone collectively poorer. One solution to the problem is to tax only the people who receive the benefits of a particular project or to fund the project through user fees, such as the fees people pay for using toll roads. This makes it less likely that society will devote its scarce resources to projects in which the costs outweigh the benefits.

Some General Guidelines for the Government Provision of Public Goods

As we did with environmental regulation (see Chapter 8), let's set some guidelines governments might follow when they're asked to provide public goods. The guidelines should be fairly unobjectionable, no matter what one's political or philosophical leanings might be; keep in mind that from a purely economic standpoint, the ideal outcome is the one that produces the biggest economic pie.

Principle 1 simply reiterates the assertion made in the discussion of free exchange (see Chapter 5):

> Principle 1: Markets are generally more effective at providing pure private goods. The goods governments provide most effectively are pure public goods.

When a good is a pure private good—that is, when it is both rival in consumption and excludable—people can decide for themselves whether to purchase it, produce it, or sell it. Those decisions lead society toward the largest possible economic pie. From the standpoint of maximizing society's wealth, government can't improve on those decisions.

However, when the good is a public good—that is, when it is nonrival and non-excludable—individual incentives lead society to provide too little of it. In this case, a government can potentially increase the size of the economic pie for everyone by providing the good directly.

What if a good is neither a pure private good nor a pure public good? Remember that the public goods problem stems from nonexcludability. This suggests that in general, club goods—which are largely nonrival but still excludable—are likely to be more effectively provided by private producers rather than government. The private sector, for example, does a great job of providing golf courses and movie theaters, and it's hard to argue that government could provide them more effectively.

The private sector, on the other hand, often performs poorly when the good in question is rival but nonexcludable—a common pool resource. In that case, individual incentives may lead to overuse and eventual depletion. It may be possible in those cases for government to do a better job of providing the good in a sustainable way. Suppose, for example, that a fishery is being depleted. Government could ban private fishing and launch its own government fishing fleet, being careful not to overfish the waters. The government might be successful at doing this: Its size and resources make it more capable of monitoring and enforcing the fishing ban than a private party. And because it's the only party fishing, it doesn't have to compete with others for its catch.

But just because it's possible for a government to improve on the private sector by providing common pool resources doesn't mean that it necessarily should. In the case of the fishery, it is possible for government regulation to alter the incentives facing private individuals in such a way that depletion becomes less likely. (Such regulations are described in detail in Chapter 9.) In other words, the government has a choice: If the private provision of a common pool resource is endangering that resource, the government can (1) ban private production and replace it with government production or (2) regulate the private producers. Because businesses have to be accountable to their customers and conscious of their costs, while government is less so, many economists would argue that regulating private producers might be a less costly way to achieve the same outcome.

It is important to recognize, too, that there are other reasons government might want to provide a good besides simply maximizing the size of the economic pie. For example, a government that is interested in promoting equity may want to ensure that every child has access to a swimming pool (generally considered a club good) in the summer. One way to guarantee that equal access is for government to simply build and operate swimming pools rather than leave their construction up to private individuals.[3]

One good that governments are heavily involved in providing is education. Is education a public good? A private good? Clearly, the person who gets the most benefit from going to school is the student. But education creates other benefits—positive externalities—that are good for the people around the students and society as a whole. Educated people produce innovative ideas, may make better employees, and are less likely to engage in criminal activity. Because these spillover benefits are nonrival and nonexcludable, they are public goods. In other words, education is partly a private good and partly a public good! So if education were left solely to private providers, there would likely be fewer schools than is socially ideal because students would only be willing to pay for the benefits they, themselves, receive.

Further, government not only wants to make sure everyone has equal access to education, it actually *mandates* a certain level of education. But some people don't value education highly and wouldn't be willing to pay private school prices. And so, to correct for the private underprovision of schools, and to help people comply with the mandate, the government operates public schools.

We can conclude, then, that when the market for a purely private good is functioning well, social welfare is biggest when providing that good is left to private producers. However, when markets for a good aren't working well, the case for government provision is stronger, recognizing that sometimes the same result could be achieved through careful regulation.[4] Finally, when a good is a pure public good, government may well do a better job of providing that good than the private sector.

If a good is nonrival and nonexcludable, we don't want to leave its provision to private individuals. Principle 2 suggests that we may not want government to provide that good, either:

> Principle 2: Governments should provide nonrival, nonexcludable goods only if the social benefits of the goods outweigh the cost of providing those goods.

To illustrate, let's return to the fountain example. Grace, Terrell, and Kalen discovered that they wouldn't be able to put the fountain project into place because of the free-rider problem. So they asked their local government to do it for them, and in that case, it turned out to be a good thing—the government was able to tax and spend $300 to create a $450 benefit.

But what if, as we discussed earlier in this chapter, the fountain had cost $600 instead of $300? If the government builds the fountain, it creates a $450 benefit that costs $600. So society will be $150 poorer as a result. In other words, if the government does not carefully evaluate the fountain beforehand, it is possible that it will provide a good that costs more than it's worth to the residents of Tuscola on the whole.

Unfortunately, when a government spends lots of money providing goods with little benefit to citizens, the citizens often find themselves with little recourse. It would be nice if pie-reducing politicians were voted out of office for wasteful spending such as this, but the truth is that money is only one of many considerations that we account for in our voting. For example, we may tolerate politicians such as this simply because they happen to agree with us on other issues. This and other issues about voting are discussed later in the text (see Chapter 13).

---

[3]Here, again, government has a choice. If it wants to guarantee equal access to swimming pools, it can choose to build and run swimming pools or, alternatively, it can subsidize the cost of admission to a privately run pool.

[4]The externality discussed in the education example is just one example of what economists call a *market failure*. There are several other types of market failure. You will be exposed to more of them, and more instances where government can potentially improve social well-being, as the book progresses.

Application 10.3

Government-Provided Salt in Turkmenistan

Governments around the globe do lots of unusual things for their constituents, and the government of Turkmenistan is no exception. Turkmenistan is a relatively undeveloped country where both production and incomes are low. Turkmenistan's government, being relatively poor also, does little for its people by Western standards. But it does provide its citizens with a few key essentials for free. Those essentials include electricity, natural gas, water, and salt.

Why salt? Salt is both rival in consumption and wholly excludable. In other words, salt is a private good. Salt is also cheap. You can get top-quality table salt for about 50 cents per pound.

Just as strange is the *amount* of salt supplied to the citizens of Turkmenistan. Even if you're not a cardiac patient, a 26-ounce container of Morton salt, about the size of a quart jar, is likely to last several years. In other words, a little salt goes a long way. Yet the government of Turkmenistan gives the typical Turkmenistani household about *3 pounds* of salt monthly.

So why would the government of Turkmenistan provide salt—and so much of it—to its citizens for free? Part of the reason is health related: The government wants to be sure its citizens are getting enough iodine, a nutrient that helps ensure proper development and growth. The government accomplishes this by fortifying the salt ration with iodine. Almost certainly, another reason to give away so many essentials for free is to engender support for the political administration. "This decision would help ensure a carefree life for our people," President Saparmurat Niyazov stated as he extended the program through the year 2030.

The problem is that markets generally do a better job of providing private goods like salt than governments do. This is largely because governments don't have to worry about profits or about weighing costs and benefits very carefully. If the salt program operates "in the red," it can be supplemented with tax revenues. So when the government provides salt for free, it's likely that it will spend more than $1 in tax revenues to provide $1 of salt.

To make matters worse, it turns out that the salt provided by the government of Turkmenistan is of low quality. Consequently, many Turkmenistanis simply throw away the salt and buy higher-quality salt in the marketplace. So, essentially, people pay taxes the government uses to dig vast quantities of salt out of a big hole in the ground, package the salt, and distribute it to citizens for free. The citizens then discard the salt in the trash, which is collected by the government's sanitation workers... who subsequently throw it into a big hole in the ground.

See related problem 4.9 on page 213 at the end of this chapter.

Based on "Iodized Salt for Bright Schoolchildren: Turkmenistan Keeps Promise to Eliminate Iodine Deficiency," available at ceegis.org, *The Ashgabat Gazette*, Issue 43, January 16, 1999; "Turkmenistan's Leader Promises Citizens Free Gas, Electricity and Water Through 2030," Associated Press, October 25, 2006; and personal conversation with Turkmenistan native Dilyara Jepbarova.

Conclusion

This chapter has explored the unique characteristics of public goods: nonrivalry and nonexcludability. Because nonexcludability separates effort and reward by making it easy for people to capture the benefits of public goods without bearing a full share of the costs, private individuals tend to produce public goods in less-than-ideal amounts. This problem, like the environmental issues discussed in previous chapters, stems from a lack of well-defined property rights: Once a public good is provided, it is provided for everybody, whether the provider likes it or not. Here, as in environmental issues, government can potentially make the world richer. By providing the public good itself and then forcing potential free riders to pay through the tax system, government can increase the size of the economic pie.

In the next chapter we'll apply some of what we've learned to a special problem: Given a long commute, how does an economics professor make it home from work in time to fight in the local mixed martial arts competition?

Chapter Summary and Problems

Key Terms

Club good, p. 199

Common pool resource, p. 200

Excludable good, p. 199

Free rider, p. 200

Nonexcludable good, p. 199

Nonrival good, p. 199

Public goods problem, p. 204

Pure private good, p. 199

Pure public good, p. 199

Rival good, p. 199

10.1 Public Versus Private Goods, pages 198–200

Describe the characteristics that make a good a public good.

Summary

Goods can be classified by their ability to be simultaneously enjoyed. A rival good cannot be simultaneously enjoyed; a nonrival good can. Goods can also be classified by whether people can be prevented from enjoying the good's benefits. It is easy to keep people from enjoying an excludable good, and it's difficult to keep people from enjoying a nonexcludable good. A good that is both rival and excludable is a pure private good. A good that is nonrival and nonexcludable is a pure public good. A good that is rival but nonexcludable is a common pool resource. A good that is nonrival but excludable is a club good.

Review Questions

All problems are assignable in MyEconLab.

1.1 A good that is rival and excludable is known as a(n) _____.

1.2 If it's hard to prevent people from enjoying the benefits of a particular good, that good is said to be _____.

1.3 Because the enjoyment you get from watching a lunar eclipse doesn't diminish when others watch, too, the lunar eclipse is said to be _____.

1.4 A club good is a good that is nonrival and _____.

1.5 A pure public good is both _____ and _____.

1.6 Consider this copy of your textbook: It is difficult for more than one person at a time to read it. This means that your textbook is a(n) _____ good.
   a. Rival
   b. Nonrival
   c. Excludable
   d. Nonexcludable

1.7 Consider this copy of your textbook: If your annoying roommate, who didn't buy the book, keeps trying to read your copy, you can prevent it by hiding it or locking it away. This means your textbook is a(n) _____ good.
   a. Rival
   b. Nonrival
   c. Excludable
   d. Nonexcludable

1.8 Based on your answers to problems 1.6 and 1.7, it is likely that your textbook is a _____.
   a. Pure private good
   b. Pure public good
   c. Common pool resource
   d. Club good

1.9 If you wish, you can subscribe to the Netflix streaming service. Netflix streaming can be characterized as _____.
   a. Rival and excludable
   b. Nonrival and nonexcludable
   c. Rival and nonexcludable
   d. Nonrival and excludable

1.10 Based on your answer to problem 1.9, Netflix streaming can best be categorized as a _____.
   a. Pure private good
   b. Pure public good
   c. Common pool resource
   d. Club good

1.11 Which of the following best meets the criteria for being a pure public good?

    a. A city swimming pool

    b. A fireworks show

    c. A theatre performance of *Rent*

    d. An iPod

Problems and Applications

1.12 Explain, using the terminology developed in this section, why the aurora borealis (the Northern Lights) is different from a city swimming pool. Which best meets the criteria of a pure public good? What type of good is the other good?

1.13 Come up with one fresh example of each of the four types of goods discussed in this section: pure private goods, pure public goods, club goods, and common pool resources. Explain your reasoning, being sure to discuss for each good the criteria of rivalry and excludability.

10.2 **How Nonexcludability Leads to Free Riding and the Public Goods Problem, pages 200–204**

    Explain why private individuals tend to produce too few public goods.

Summary

The nonexcludability of pure public goods leads to the free-rider problem. Because people cannot be prevented from enjoying the benefits of the good, they have little incentive to help pay for that good. If enough people behave in such a strategic fashion, free riding can result in too little of the good being provided. This public goods problem decreases overall social well-being.

		Rafe	
		Contribute	Don't Contribute
Mai	Contribute	6, 6	4, 5
	Don't Contribute	5, 4	3, 3

Review Questions

All problems are assignable in MyEconLab.

2.1 A person who receives the benefits of a public good without bearing a proportional share of the costs is known as a(n) _____ .

2.2 If private individuals are the only producers of a pure public good, those individuals are likely to produce less of it than is socially desirable. This outcome is known as _____ .

2.3 The free-rider problem arises because pure public goods are _____ .

    a. Rival

    b. Nonrival

    c. Excludable

    d. Nonexcludable

2.4 Because of the opportunity for free ridership that pure public goods present, private individuals probably _____ .

    a. Provide the right amount of pure public goods

    b. Provide fewer public goods than the benevolent social planner would like to see

    c. Provide more public goods than the benevolent social planner would like to see

Problems and Applications

2.5 Mai and Rafe are considering contributing to a project. Their payoffs are shown in the following payoff matrix:

Will the public goods problem prevent this project from being completed? Explain why or why not.

2.6 Do you agree or disagree with the following statement: "The real problem with pure public goods is that they're nonrival." Explain your reasoning.

2.7 Homeowners in many rural areas obtain fire protection by voluntarily enrolling in, and paying a fee for, a rural fire service. In 2010, Gene Cranick's rural Tennessee home caught fire. The fire service sent its trucks to Cranick's neighborhood, but because Cranick had not paid his $75 annual fee, firefighters simply watched his home burn to the ground. When the desperate Cranick offered to enroll in the fire service on the spot, he was turned away. Would the benevolent social planner have approved of the fire service's decision to let Cranick's home burn? Was the fire department's refusal to extinguish the fire and accept Cranick's enrollment a good decision for society? Does your answer depend on whether you consider the short run or the long run? Explain.

2.8 [Related to Application 10.1 on page 201] Read Application 10.1 carefully. Many Cubs games are broadcast for free on television. Why, then, do you suppose the Cubs were so concerned about people watching their games for free from nearby apartment buildings? Would the Cubs's strategy have been as successful if the neighboring buildings were 10 stories taller?

Property Rights and the Public Goods Problem, pages 204–205

Explain how poorly defined property rights and high transactions costs cause public goods to be underprovided.

Summary

The public goods problem stems from poorly defined property rights. The individual who privately provides a public good is unable to capture all the benefits of that good. Instead, free riders capture a meaningful portion of those benefits, and those people cannot be compelled to pay for the value they receive. This problem would disappear if there were a way to bind free riders to a pledge to help pay for the good, but often high transactions costs prevent producers and free riders from reaching such agreements.

Review Questions

All problems are assignable in MyEconLab.

3.1 Four people want to commission a beautiful statue to grace their neighborhood. The difficulties they experience in getting one another to commit to paying for the statue are best described as _____.

a. Property rights

b. Transactions costs

c. Incongruent incentives

d. Eminent domain

3.2 In the case of public goods, the ability to free ride on the efforts of others is an example of _____.

a. low transactions costs

b. insecure property rights

c. the taxing power of government

d. poor cost–benefit analysis

Problems and Applications

3.3 Explain the role that transactions costs play in public goods problems.

3.4 Which characteristic of a pure public good is linked to poorly defined property rights? Which is not? Explain both of your answers.

3.5 Explain, referring to poorly defined property rights, the parallels between pollution problems and the public goods problem.

How Governments Can Overcome the Public Goods Problem, pages 205–209

List the pros and cons of governments providing public goods.

Summary

Governments can overcome public goods problems by providing the goods and then forcing everyone to contribute through their taxes. That power is most useful to society in the case of pure public goods; it is least helpful in the case of pure private goods. It is possible for government to provide goods whose costs exceed the benefits they provide to society. One reasonable check to prevent that is to charge users a tax that is proportional to the benefits the users receive.

Review Questions

All problems are assignable in MyEconLab.

4.1 A pure public good _____.

a. Is *any* good that is provided by government

b. Will *never* be provided by individuals acting on their own initiative

c. Both (a) and (b) are true.

d. Neither (a) nor (b) is true.

4.2 Government typically solves the free rider issue by using its _____.

a. Power of eminent domain

b. Ability to print money

c. Power of taxation

d. Ability to borrow money without paying interest

4.3 To maximize the economic pie, government _____.

a. Should provide all possible pure public goods

b. Should provide only public goods whose benefits outweigh their costs

c. Should provide only public goods whose costs outweigh their benefits

d. Should not provide any public goods

Problems and Applications

4.4 Club goods and common pool resources are neither purely private goods nor purely public goods. Explain why the government may have a more compelling economic interest in intervening in the market for common pool resources than in the market for club goods.

4.5 The federal government created the interstate highway system. That road network is largely nonrival, and the government has chosen to make it available to all. Suppose the government has the choice of paying for the maintenance and upkeep of the highway system with a tax on gasoline or, alternatively, with income tax. Which source would you recommend? Why?

4.6 Stephanie was shocked to discover that the federal government charges an entry fee to view the Grand Canyon. "It's everyone's property. I ought to be able to view it for free. The government should pay for it like it pays for everything else—with tax dollars!" Argue in favor of using an entry fee to pay for the upkeep and personnel needed to maintain the Grand Canyon.

4.7 **[Related to Application 10.2 on page 206]** The current farm bill includes a number of different subsidies for producers of mohair, a yarn made from the wool of the Angora goat, amounting to some $20 million each year. Taxpayers fund those subsidies. Economists know that the mohair subsidy makes Americans poorer on the whole. Apply Mancur Olson's explanation of the power of organized interests to explain why it is so difficult for U.S. taxpayers to end the mohair subsidy. Your explanation should incorporate the term *transactions costs*.

4.8 **[Related to Application 10.2 on page 206]** Read Application 10.2 carefully. Then describe a bargain between consumers/taxpayers and sugar producers that would (a) end the quota and (b) be mutually beneficial to both parties. The bargain you describe should incorporate numbers from the application. Why is such a bargain unlikely to be reached in real life?

4.9 **[Related to Application 10.3 on page 209]** Read Application 10.3 carefully. Can you come up with an example of a pure private good that your government provides? Or perhaps a club good? Hypothesize a likely rationale for the government provision of the good you list.

4.10 Consider the case of fire protection discussed in problem 2.7. To what extent is fire protection a public good? To what extent is it a private good? Can you make a case for the public provision of fire protection? Can you make a case for private fire protection? Does your answer depend on whether the people being served are rural or urban? Explain.

The Garden Game

This chapter highlighted the idea that when people work together, they can accomplish tasks that benefit themselves and society as a whole. Today, you get the chance to work with your classmates to create a flower garden. The greater the number of classmates who contribute to the garden, the more beautiful it will be. The more beautiful the garden is, the more pleasure you and your classmates will receive from viewing it. If everyone contributes, your class will create a truly awe-inspiring garden.

Contributing to the garden is voluntary. Will you be successful in convincing your classmates to work alongside you to create something wonderful?

MyEconLab

Please visit http://www.myeconlab.com for support material to conduct this experiment if assigned by your instructor.

CHAPTER

11

Public Goods: Tackling Large Projects and Eminent Domain

Chapter Outline and Learning Objectives

11.1 The Role of Individuals in Large Projects, page 216

List the difficulties private individuals may face when acquiring property from multiple owners.

11.2 The Role of Government in Large Projects, page 219

Describe how the government implements eminent domain and the conditions for its use.

Experiment: The "Ask and You Might Receive" Game, page 229

MyEconLab

MyEconLab helps you master each objective and study more efficiently.

Eastern Illinois University is located in Charleston, Illinois. Bill Duncan is a professor in the economics department at Eastern, but he lives 26 miles away, in the quaint town of Tuscola.

Each Friday evening, Proud Mary's, a bar near Tuscola's city limits, hosts a local mixed martial arts (MMA) competition. Bill, who is known to Eastern students as "that scrawny dude who's always talking about unemployment," regularly fights in these contests. Despite his lean physique, Bill has amassed quite a string of wins. "I'm wiry but vicious," he says.

Last spring, Bill was assigned to teach a late afternoon course about the U.S. Federal Reserve. The course ran from 3:30 to 4:30 on Mondays, Wednesdays, and, most crucially, Fridays. Because the course ended so late, Bill found it difficult to drive to Tuscola, change into his fighting clothes and still be on time for the 5 p.m. preliminary bouts.

You can imagine Bill's anguish on gloomy winter afternoons: He leaves his classroom right on time, tosses his briefcase in the back of his sensible subcompact, and hits the highway, hoping to make it in time for the weigh-in. Just as he heads out of town, he sees the lights of Tuscola far in the distance. As he motors northward, those lights never seem to get even the slightest bit closer. He's late, he's antsy, and he knows that the 26-mile drive is too long to cram into a short half-hour. He's right: Two times out of three, he arrives too late to fight.

11.1 Learning Objective

List the difficulties private individuals may face when acquiring property from multiple owners.

The Role of Individuals in Large Projects

After a semester of frustration, Bill receives a phone call from his brother, Parker, a math professor and world-renowned expert on the Pythagorean theorem. It's a watershed moment for Bill: "All this time, I've been driving 20 miles straight north, then 6 miles straight west. If I could cut the diagonal, I'd save myself precious minutes and make the Friday night fights!" Bill cranks through the math, and as shown in Figure 11.1, the as-the-crow-flies route from Charleston to Tuscola is slightly less than 21 miles, which shaves 5 crucial minutes from Bill's commute.

"Sadly," says Bill, "there's no road between Tuscola and Charleston. There are only cornfields as far as the eye can see. Unless I purchase a monster truck and trample all over other people's fields (and their property rights, which, being an economist, I am loathe to do), I'll never be able to use this amazing mathematical discovery to my own advantage."

But then Bill has an epiphany: "Surely there are other people who want to be able to drive straight from Charleston to Tuscola or vice versa. I've got a feeling that there's a way to get this road built *and* turn a quick buck doing it!"

▶ **Figure 11.1**

Commuting Distance from Charleston to Tuscola
Bill's evening commute is 26 miles. But the as-the-crow-flies route is only 21 miles.

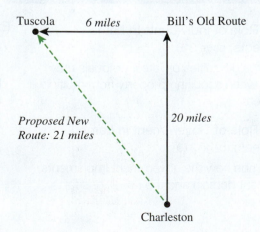

So Bill, being an entrepreneurial sort of fellow, committed to the principles of free enterprise, gets busy. He carefully researches the cost of building and maintaining such a road. Then he goes door to door throughout Charleston, Tuscola, and other towns in the area, surveying residents about whether they would like to see such a road built and, if so, how much they might be willing to pay to use it.

Once the numbers are crunched, Bill discovers that people would get a great deal of value from having a more direct route between Tuscola and Charleston. In fact, Bill estimates that if he were to build a private road and charge a toll for using it, the tolls would be more than sufficient to cover the cost of building and maintaining the road, with $800,000 left over to buy the land the road would run on. "I'm sensing that there's a profit to be made," Bill tells himself. "Let's see what that land is worth and find out what the bottom line is going to be."

So Bill estimates how much land he will need (a narrow strip of land 21 miles long). Then Bill estimates how much profit the land would generate if it were used solely to produce an agricultural product such as corn. Finally, he heads to the courthouse to verify his figures by looking at recent land sales and comparing the cost per acre to his figures. When all is said and done, Bill figures that the land needed to build the road is worth $600,000. "Amazing!" he tells himself. "I can build the road I need, run it as a toll road, earn myself a cool $200,000, and make every mixed martial arts competition with time to spare. Let's go buy some land!"

The Holdout Problem

While Bill is at the courthouse, he looks in the public records and discovers that the land he needs is owned by four farmers—Erin, Jim Bob, Mary Ellen, and Ben—whose landholdings look something like what is shown in Figure 11.2.

"Fantastic," Bill tells himself. "They're each sitting on $150,000 of land. I'll buy it from them, build the road, and laugh all the way to the bank." So Bill approaches Erin, Jim Bob, and Mary Ellen, and purchases the land he needs for the price he expected.

And then he comes to Ben. Ben says to himself, "This guy has to have my land to complete this road. No other land will do. And if he's offering $150,000 for it, it must be worth more than that to him. A *lot* more." Ben crunches some numbers of his own and comes back with a counteroffer for Bill: "The land you've already bought is worthless without mine. If I refuse to sell, you'll have nothing. But if I do sell, you'll build a road worth $800,000. So, my land must be worth $800,000. I'm a nice guy, though; you can have it for $750,000."

The fact that Ben's land is needed to complete the project gives him a great deal of leverage over Bill. Ben exploits that leverage by asking for a sum of money far beyond what his land is worth for any other use. Economists call Ben a **holdout**, a negotiator who hopes to get an unusually large amount of money for the land by refusing to come to terms.

Holdout A negotiator who hopes to get an unusually large amount of money for land by refusing to come to terms.

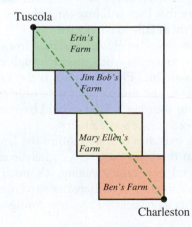

◄ **Figure 11.2**
Landowners Along Bill's Proposed Route
To build a new road, Bill will have to acquire land from Erin, Jim Bob, Mary Ellen, and Ben.

What happens next? Because Bill has already spent $450,000 on land, he knows he can only offer up to $350,000 for Ben's land. At Ben's mercy, Bill keeps raising the bid, and yet Ben refuses to yield. Every time Bill raises the offer, his profits dwindle, and pretty soon Bill has to walk away from his dream of paving the road.

Of course, Bill could show Ben his numbers and convince him that the very most he could possibly pay would be $350,000. And since Ben's land is really only worth $150,000 in its next best use, it is possible that Bill and Ben could work something out. But that might not prevent the holdout problem from standing in the way of Bill's progress. Here's why: Put yourself in the shoes of any one of the landowners, and assume that no deal has yet been struck. Let's pretend, for example, that you're Mary Ellen. Let's further suppose that you and everybody else knows Bill's expenditures for the land can't top $800,000. You might feel that your land is worth one-fourth of that, or $200,000, and establish that as the least you're willing to accept.

Yet you know that each landowner's land is really worth only $150,000 per parcel in its next-best use. So you say to yourself, "Hmmmm . . . if any of the others end up selling for less than $200,000, then there'll be money left on the table. And if I don't grab it, someone else will. If Bill can negotiate down the price for the others' land only modestly, say, to $175,000 each, then he should be able to spend $275,000 to get mine. I think that's how much I'll ask for it."

So Mary Ellen asks for $275,000. And because Erin and Jim Bob and Ben all reason through the problem in exactly the way Mary Ellen did, each asks for $275,000 for his or her land, too. Bill, who thought he could buy the land for $600,000, and who was willing to pay up to $800,000, finds himself facing four very stubborn farmers who have put a collective price tag of $1.1 million on the land—which is far beyond its value for any current alternative use. Demoralized, Bill walks away, his road unbuilt and his dreams of martial-arts glory unfulfilled.

This outcome leaves the benevolent social planner, who desires only the greatest possible economic pie for society, in tears. Bill had a chance to turn $600,000 worth of land into $800,000 worth of happiness for drivers, but that chance was spoiled by a few holdouts who set a price beyond their opportunity cost and refused to budge.

Bill's problem is this: He's not doing something like opening a blueberry farm, where any old land will do. If any old land would have worked, he could have used that as leverage to get the four landowners to reduce their prices: "Oh, you want $275,000, Erin? Well, I'll just go ask Jason, who lives three counties over and is asking $150,000, which is what his land is actually worth." But Bill is not building a blueberry patch. He's building a road. And for his road to be useful to anyone, it needs to connect two destinations and follow a reasonably straight path. In other words, Bill isn't just in the market for land, he's in the market for *contiguous* land, which is a different thing altogether. The contiguity requirement gives our four landowners a great deal of power to hold up the entire process.

You might be thinking that surely these four farmers aren't going to let an opportunity like this get away. They all have neighboring farms, so they probably all know one another. If they would just meet at the local cafe and talk about the proposal over coffee, they would recognize that they will lose their chance to turn $150,000 of land into $200,000 if any one of them fails to cooperate.

You may be right, although you might have learned from experience this semester that you shouldn't expect cooperation when playing tough can help a player capture a larger share of the economic pie. Playing tough is the foundation for games like battle of the sexes and chicken, and those games have only *two* players. Nevertheless, it's certainly possible that our four landowners would have enough common sense to cooperate so that they will each make some money.

But how many 21-mile stretches of road require the land of only four landowners? It is far more likely that there are 20, or 30, or maybe even 100 landowners that Bill will have to deal with, and, generally speaking, it's much easier to get 4 people to agree on how to split up a pie than it is to achieve an agreement with 40. Don't forget: When you're putting together a project that requires contiguous land like a road does, it takes only one holdout to ruin the project completely. Truly, this is a case where one bad apple can spoil the whole barrel.

Transactions Costs

Even if all the landowners in our example behave cooperatively and nobody tries to hold out for more money, the road still might not be built. Why? Because building the road requires striking deals with many landowners, and striking deals can be a time-consuming and costly process. It's not hard to imagine a situation in which hiring the attorneys and bankers and appraisers necessary to complete such a deal might well chew up the $200,000 difference between what the ground is worth for growing corn and what it is worth as a road. That's right: Transactions costs have reared their ugly heads once again. The moment those transactions costs eclipse that difference is the moment that a project everyone wants to see completed dies.

The Role of Government in Large Projects

So what is Bill to do? If he fails to build the road, society leaves $200,000 of cooperative surplus on the table. Unfortunately, failure is a likely outcome if we leave the building of roads to individuals like Bill. The answer lies with government, which has the power to simultaneously overcome the holdout problem and the transactions costs that result when multiple parcels of land must be joined in order for a project to be completed.

11.2 Learning Objective

Describe how the government implements eminent domain and the conditions for its use.

Takings Power and the Fifth Amendment

How does government bring order to situations like Bill's? It uses a special power given to it in the Fifth Amendment to the Constitution. The Fifth Amendment is the one that gives you the right to remain silent rather than incriminate yourself: Perhaps you have heard an arrestee say "I'll take the Fifth" on a rerun of the TV show *Law and Order*. But the Fifth Amendment also gives government the power to compel people to sell their land for a project like Bill's road. Here's the relevant language: " . . . nor shall private property be taken for public use, without just compensation." This says several important things. First, it indicates that even when we're talking about something as sacred as our homes, property rights are not absolute; the government has an overriding authority to *take* property from its owners. For that reason, this power is called *takings power* or, more commonly, **eminent domain**. The language related to eminent domain in the Fifth Amendment is generally called the *takings clause*.

Eminent domain The authority of the government to take private property for public use, given just compensation to the owner.

Conditions for the Use of Eminent Domain

Eminent domain might sound like bad news to you: "You mean government can come in and just seize my property any time it wants?" Thankfully, the remainder of the takings clause limits government's ability to exercise that power. First, the takings clause indicates *why* private property can be seized: Such seizures are to be undertaken only if the property in question is being taken for public use. Second, the takings clause outlines *how* public property must be seized. Namely, if government seizes your land, it must pay you fairly for it. We'll revisit those parameters and discuss them in greater detail soon. For now, suffice it to say that if government wants a property, within certain bounds, it can take it.

How exactly would eminent domain help society solve the road problem we discussed at the beginning of the chapter? Recall that Bill was unable to build a road on his own because Ben was holding out for a disproportionately large, project-killing share of the gains the road would create. And even if Bill could get Ben to be more reasonable, high negotiations costs with all the landowners might have killed the project as well. But using eminent domain to acquire land keeps negotiation costs low.

Application 11.1

Steel Company Can't Get Homeowner to Sell

Steel Pipe & Supply, Inc., in Manhattan, Kansas, was growing by leaps and bounds, and it desperately needed a new warehouse. The managers wanted to put the new warehouse next to the railroad tracks to make it easy to ship products. This is the warehouse they envisioned:

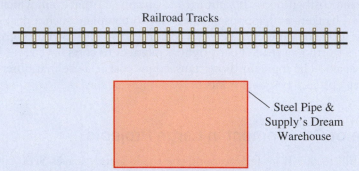

Railroad Tracks

Steel Pipe & Supply's Dream Warehouse

To amass the land for the warehouse, Steel Pipe & Supply started buying up tiny prefab homes that were well past their prime. But one holdout resisted all attempts to acquire his property. Rather than knuckle under, Steel Pipe & Supply had its architects alter the warehouse's building plan and built that warehouse right around the home of the holdout:

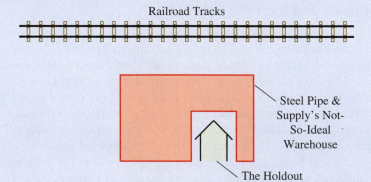

Railroad Tracks

Steel Pipe & Supply's Not-So-Ideal Warehouse

The Holdout

If you keep your eyes open, you'll eventually notice commercial and residential properties in such unlikely places that they just *have* to have been the result of a conflict like the one between Steel Pipe & Supply and the homeowner. The photo at right is just one example.

Steel Pipe & Supply had the luxury of designing its warehouse to fit the available space. But what if the rules had prevented it from building in such a way? The Colorado Rockies Major League Baseball organization faced just such a problem when it tried to build a new stadium in the early 1990s. In a neighborhood of empty warehouses and vacant lots, the Rockies began to acquire land to build what would one day be Coors Field.

And then the inevitable holdout appeared. Denver's wealthy Cowperthwaite

family owned property that had to be acquired. Their 2-acre plot of land included Coors Field's future home plate. The Cowperthwaites wanted $3.4 million and a luxury box in the stadium in exchange for their land. The Rockies weren't willing to pay more than $1.5 million. After a prolonged battle, an arbitrator settled the claim for $2.3 million.

Governments have extraordinary "muscle" to solve problems; they can do things that private individuals often cannot. Both Steel Pipe & Supply and the Colorado Rockies could have asked the government to exercise its takings power. Yet they didn't. Instead, they chose to work out their problems for themselves.

Throughout this course, you've seen instances where a government could step into the marketplace and make the world work better. But Steel Pipe & Supply and the Colorado Rockies remind us that sometimes it can be just as effective to think creatively about how to solve problems for ourselves. Their examples suggest that invoking the takings power of government might well be regarded as a genuine last resort, something to be relied on only when all else has failed.

See related problem 2.18 on page 228 at the end of this chapter.

Based on "Strong Politician Had Style," *The Denver Post*, June 28, 2009; "New Trouble for Rockies: Reaching 1st," *Palm Beach Post*, May 22, 1993; and "Legal Cost of Land Dispute: $360,000," *The Denver Post*, September 3, 1994.

The government simply pays $150,000 to each landowner for his or her land and says, "Take it, or else." If a landowner tries to hold out for more money, the government simply puts the money into that person's checking account and fires up the bulldozers.

Virtually all governments use eminent domain. The U.S. federal government has used eminent domain to take land to build such projects as the interstate highway system and the Tennessee Valley Authority's series of flood control and hydroelectric dams.[1] State governments use eminent domain to acquire land for roads and parks. Cities use eminent domain to acquire land for new schools and swimming pools. And it's not just used in the United States: To a greater or lesser extent, most federal governments maintain some right to take property for public use. Earlier, we talked about how creating and protecting property rights benefits society (see Chapter 6). Now we know that *limiting* those property rights in certain instances may also be beneficial. But we do want to be careful about the injudicious use of eminent domain: A government that uses its takings power too frequently, arbitrarily, or capriciously establishes a reputation for disrespecting private property. Knowing that their property may be seized on a whim may discourage households and firms from conserving, improving, or investing in that property, and the economic pie may shrink as a result.

The Public Use Requirement Let's take a closer look at the conditions under which the government may use its takings power. The first condition is that the property being taken must be intended for public use. Under this criterion, taking private property for the government to build a road that the public could use would certainly be a reasonable interpretation, as would taking property to build a new courthouse or a military base or a park that the public could enjoy.

But the term *public use* is fairly vague, and one might be tempted under certain conditions to apply it more broadly. In fact, there is a fairly well-established history of doing so in the United States. For example, in 1832, the Supreme Court ruled that it was allowable for a mill owner to dam a stream and flood his upstream neighbors' properties as long as he compensated them. In this case, "public use" did not require

---

[1] Much of the land taken for the TVA is now underwater!

direct use by the public as long as the project conferred some benefit to the public—namely, a more efficient mill in an agrarian society where mills were both necessary and scarce.

Such justification has been given in other instances as well. Following World War II, it was deemed in the public's interest to condemn large tracts of blighted slums in Washington, D.C., bulldoze the buildings, and then turn the land over to private developers to erect new housing and commercial properties. In that case, the justification for the taking was that the condition of the neighborhood was "injurious to the public health, safety, morals, and welfare." In other words, the neighborhood was a hotbed of crime, disease, and moral decay, and the city of Washington, D.C. was better off without it. For a multitude of reasons, a private developer might never undertake such an enormous redevelopment. The most practical way to achieve such a change, should the community decide that's what it wants, is to use the power of eminent domain.

So we have some conception that eminent domain might reasonably be applied to improve the lives of those living in a community. We now know something else, too: When the government takes land, it's not necessary for the government itself to improve the land for public use—it can transfer it to a company or an individual to make the improvements. Let's take this one step further by supposing that instead of building a road, enterprising economist Bill Duncan decides he'd like to open an IKEA franchise and needs the land presently occupied by 20 homes in order to do it. Because Bill is a numbers geek, he's calculated that the value of the IKEA is much higher than the value of the homes; the only hurdle in his way is acquiring the parcels of land that the new furniture superstore will occupy.

The problem Bill faces in this case is identical to the problem he faced when he wanted to build the road from Tuscola to Charleston: The holdout problem and high transactions costs might well defeat the project. Once again, the government's power of eminent domain can save the day. The government can condemn the houses, take the land, resell it to Bill, and watch his IKEA bring in customers from hundreds of miles in any direction. The fact that we're dealing with private parties (as we were in the case of the mill owner) and the fact that the battle being waged is between a corporation and a handful of homeowners is relatively immaterial to the economic analysis.

It was exactly this kind of problem that arose in the early 2000s in Connecticut, when the city of New London condemned houses in a working-class neighborhood and then leased the ground to a developer for comprehensive development. The city of New London justified the takings based on the economic benefits the project would provide: some 3,000 new jobs and $1.2 million in additional tax revenues to the city each year. The condemnation was challenged, and by 2005 those challenges reached the Supreme Court of the United States in *Kelo v. City of New London*. In *Kelo*, the Supreme Court ruled much in the way that a practical economist might: Because of transactions costs and the holdout problem, a project that would yield net benefits to society would be unlikely to go forth without the intervening hand of government. So while it may offend your sensibilities to know that government can take your home and turn it into a furniture store, the economic analysis won't let us deny the practical benefits of doing so.

As we have explained, it is important for a government to use the takings power carefully and for property owners and citizens to keep a watchful eye on their governments. Here's why: Suppose that Steve, the owner and CEO of some nameless, faceless retail giant (hereafter referred to as NFRG), decides that he wants to open an NFRG franchise that will confer $300,000 of benefits to society (at least some of which Steve hopes to capture and stick in his own wallet, in the form of profits). Suppose further that the houses that occupy the space Steve would like to build on are worth a total of $400,000. That last fact may be immaterial to Steve, who is interested only in the value of the NFRG project and couldn't care less about the value of the land needed for the project. Steve goes to the town's city council and tells the council

Application 11.2

The Robber Barons of Merriam, Kansas

Baron Automotive sells luxury cars in Merriam, Kansas. The hill that Baron Automotive dominates once housed two lots: a smaller lot that the company owned and a used car lot owned by William Gross. When the demand for luxury cars boomed in the 1990s, the owners of Baron Automotive were anxious to expand and started eyeing Gross's lot with envy.

After private negotiations between the owners of the two car lots crumbled, Baron Automotive proposed a deal to Merriam's mayor, Irene French: Condemn Gross's lot and resell it to Baron Automotive, which would expand its BMW franchise and add Volkswagen-brand vehicles to its lineup. In a decision that would later be highly criticized, French agreed, noting that luxury cars would generate more sales tax revenues for Merriam than Gross's used cars.

Eminent domain is best used when the transactions costs of a deal are high and the potential for holdouts is high as well. But because Baron Automotive was trying to purchase the property of only one landowner, the holdout problem was not nearly as serious as it is in many eminent domain–type situations; oftentimes, dozens or even tens of thousands of landowners are involved. The transactions costs associated with Baron Automotive and William Gross's deal were also likely to be low. The failure to reach a deal privately, then, can likely be attributed simply to Gross valuing his property more than Baron Automotive valued it—or at least more than Baron was willing to pay for it.

But French didn't care who valued the property more. She cared about the tax revenues the project would create—both from the sales of luxury vehicles and from the higher property taxes the redeveloped property would generate. She justified her decision by saying that Gross refused to improve his property to increase the tax. That sets a dangerous precedent of government pursuing not what is best for society but what is best for government.

Consider an analogy: Suppose you buy your dream home, a cozy bungalow. Later, an Internet billionaire decides he'd like to build a McMansion on your lot. When you refuse his offer, your mayor says, "You're living in this dinky house that generates only $1,000 in property taxes. This other guy will build a million-dollar home that brings in $10,000 in property taxes. I'll tell you what: Add a second story and install an in-ground pool, and maybe I won't use my takings power." It's as if the mayor believes you only want to own a home so you will have a reason to send her money!

Condemning your home and turning it over to the billionaire is bad for society. First, it moves a resource from someone who values it more to someone who values it less. But, more importantly, property rights encourage people to build things worth having. If your town regularly takes homes to bolster its tax revenues, people may choose to live in other towns that might not necessarily be their first choice to live in but where they don't face the risk of having their property taken. Or they might build houses that are bigger than they want just to make them less likely targets for a taking. In both of those cases, people are given incentives to make second-best choices, so the economic pie shrinks.

In Merriam, the government stepped in to create a bargain that, for good reason, the parties couldn't agree to themselves. For BMW drivers and Baron Automotive, that was a great deal. But for everyone else, the bargain represented everything people hate about the injudicious use of eminent domain.

See related problem 2.22 on page 228 at the end of this chapter.

Based on "Take and Give: Condemnation Is Used to Hand One Business Property of Another," *Wall Street Journal*, December 2, 1998; "Hearne: Merriam's French Connection; Deceased Mayor Leaves Controversial Legacy," *KC Confidential*, December 6, 2013; and "Longtime Merriam Mayor Irene French Dies," *Kansas City Star*, December 3, 2013.

members that bringing a new big-box store to town will create jobs and enhance the town's income and sales tax revenues.

If the city doesn't carefully compare the value of the land if put to alternative uses, the council might condemn the ground, lease it to Steve at an attractive rate (as cities often do when attempting to lure commercial enterprises to an area), and let the income and sales tax dollars start flowing in. Steve wins, the city wins, consumers in town get another fun place to shop, and if the city uses the funds to build schools or put MRI machines in the local hospital, there may be other benefits besides. But those benefits are received on the backs of the people whose homes used to occupy the NFRG parking lot, and the costs those homeowners bore, you'll remember, were greater than the benefits of the project. If the city is more focused on maximizing its tax revenues than it is on creating value for the community, the city might make decisions like this one that make society as a whole poorer rather than richer.

Just Compensation Let's return for a moment to the road Bill wanted to build. Let's now assume that the government has crunched the numbers, has carefully evaluated the worth of the project, and indeed wishes to build the road itself for the public's use. Consequently, the government condemns the land owned by Erin, Jim Bob, Mary Ellen, and Ben. Now it's time to follow the letter of the Constitution and offer them just compensation.

But how does the government decide what is just? The Supreme Court requires the payment to be sufficient to make the persons whose property will be taken "whole" and asserts that, generally, paying the property owner *fair market value* for the property will accomplish that. Under the fair market value standard, "the owner is entitled to receive 'what a willing buyer would pay in cash to a willing seller' at the time of the taking."[2] The standard method for determining fair market value, called the *comparable sales method*, is for a government to survey comparable properties that have sold in the recent past and use those prices as a baseline. In other words, a government that pays displaced landowners fair market value goes through essentially the same process Bill Duncan went through when planning to build his road. If the government does a nice job of crunching those numbers, the value it sets for the properties in question should be roughly equivalent to the price they would fetch if the owners put them on the market themselves.

The problem is that the people whose homes the government used to establish the price of the homes being taken were the ones who *wanted* to—and did—leave their homes. And after seeing what houses in the neighborhood were selling for, the homeowners the government wants to displace decided they'd rather *stay*. One can imagine, for example, a homeowner who lives in a small home built by her great-great-great-great grandfather—a home that has been occupied for seven generations by her family. This homeowner may value her home more than her former next-door neighbor, who moved in last year and out again last week. Clearly, the homeowners who didn't move value their homes more than the market price dictates, and if that's the case, shouldn't government pay them more?

It would seem fair—and also be just plain nice—if governments would pay homeowners what they truly thought their homes were worth. In fact, the Supreme Court has stated that the ideal outcome would put "the owner of the condemned property in as good a position pecuniarily as if his property had not been taken." In other words, the payment would be sufficient to make the victim subjectively indifferent between staying and going.

But for practical reasons, governments cannot work by that rule. That is because neither a government nor anyone else can tell the difference between someone who values her home at $200,000 but *claims* she values it at $300,000 and someone

---

[2] See *United States v 564.54 Acres of Land*, 441 U.S. 506 (1979), and *United States v Chandler-Dunbar Water Power Co.*, 229 U.S. 53 (1913).

who actually *does* value her home at $300,000 and would be unwilling to sell at any lower price.

Because of that difficulty, offering to pay homeowners what they think their homes are worth gives those homeowners an incentive to shade their self-valuations upward. If a government were to adopt such a policy, it might well find the cost of a project mounting far beyond expectations, the practical result of which might be the abandonment of a project that truly is in the public's best interest. For that reason, the government is forced to ignore considerations like sentimental value, the fact that the same family has lived in the home since before the Constitution was ratified, and the fact that the homeowner's beloved deceased cat is buried in the backyard. Doing otherwise would leave the government open to an inflation of home values that resembles in many ways the holdout problem that Bill faced.

In other words, paying fair market value is a compromise between what is ideal and what is workable. Like all other compromises, it's imperfect. Victims of takings often complain, as indicated above, that their emotional attachment to their property goes uncompensated. They also complain that the fair market value standard doesn't compensate them for any legal fees they might have incurred or for relocation costs.

One final objection is that the takings process doesn't allow landowners to share in the gains that result from the taking of their property. When road-builder Bill bargains with landowners directly, the landowners can potentially capture some of the value of the road for themselves in the bargaining process. That opportunity disappears if the government takes the property and resells it to Bill. In that instance, Bill captures all of the gains.[3]

Some governments, especially in the wake of the controversial *Kelo* decision, have chosen to address those concerns. Some have adopted statutes that require, in certain instances, governments to pay attorney's fees and relocation costs. Others have attempted to incorporate direct payments for sentimental attachments. Still others have mandated payments above fair market value. For example, Michigan amended its constitution in 2006 to require payment of at least 125% of fair market value for taking a home; Kansas requires payment of 200% of fair market value if the legislature authorizes a taking for private economic development, with a 25% bonus if the land will be devoted to an auto race track or special bond project. But those above-market proposals, too, are a compromise: They may push the amount of money required for a taking beyond the true value of the property, and because of that, pie-increasing projects may be rejected.

Conclusion

Using eminent domain is a way for a government to reduce the transactions costs associated with acquiring the large parcels of contiguous land that some projects require. Eminent domain is also a simple solution to the holdout problem. It's useful if a government plans on completing a project, and it's equally useful if the government plans to transfer the land to a private entity to complete the project.

Earlier in the book, we devoted extensive time to discussing how property rights make the economic pie bigger. Here, by contrast, we see that *abridging* those rights through the takings process has the power to increase the size of the pie. But that power must be used with caution: The pie will increase only if the benefits of the project outweigh the costs.

---

[3]A terrific guide to these issues can be found in Katrina Miriam Wyman's "The Measure of Just Compensation," *UC Davis Law Review*, 2007.

Key Terms

Holdout, p. 217   Eminent domain, p. 219

11.1 ## The Role of Individuals in Large Projects, pages 216–219

List the difficulties private individuals may face when acquiring property from multiple owners.

Summary

When providing a good involves assembling several parcels of contiguous land, private individuals may encounter difficulty negotiating the purchase of those parcels. Landowners may ask unreasonable prices for their land, far beyond what their land is worth in any alternative use. If one or more landowners do this, it may drive the price of the land out of reach, and the good will not be provided. Even if there are no holdouts, the transactions costs involved in dealing with multiple landowners may be sufficiently high that the good will not be provided.

Review Questions

All problems are assignable in MyEconLab.

1.1 A landowner who hopes to get an unusually large amount of money for land necessary for a large project by refusing to come to terms is called a(n) _____.

1.2 Large projects that involve purchasing land from many landowners may not succeed due to the expenses (attorney fees, bank fees, appraisals, and so on) of negotiating so many different deals. These fees are examples of _____.
 a. Just compensation
 b. Transactions costs
 c. The holdout problem
 d. Public use

1.3 In 1901, Macy's built its flagship store at Herald Square in New York City. Macy's acquired most of the land it needed by negotiating with several landowners, but the owner of one small five-story building on the corner of 34th and Broadway refused to negotiate a reasonable price. (Eventually, Macy's simply built its nine-story department store around the building.) This is one example of _____.
 a. The public goods problem
 b. A holdout
 c. Unjust compensation
 d. High transactions costs

Problems and Applications

1.4 You are an entrepreneur, with a vision of creating a NASCAR racetrack in the middle of Nebraska. Discuss, in the context of this chapter, some of the difficulties you might have in acquiring the property necessary to make your vision a reality.

1.5 Why is acquiring 5,000 acres of land for a racetrack more difficult than acquiring 5,000 acres of land to grow corn?

11.2 ## The Role of Government in Large Projects, pages 219–225

Describe how the government implements eminent domain and the conditions for its use.

Summary

Governments can use their power of eminent domain to overcome the difficulties private individuals face. They can take the land that a good requires from the landowners directly, eliminating both the potential for holdouts and vastly reducing transactions costs. In the United States, such takings are to happen only if the land in question is to be devoted to public use. Public use, however, is subject to multiple interpretations that include general economic development. When the government takes land, it is required to pay the landowner just compensation, which is usually interpreted to mean the fair market value of the land. Many people believe fair market value undercompensates landowners, particularly because fair market value does not account for any sentimental attachments landowners may have to their property.

Review Questions

All problems are assignable in MyEconLab.

2.1 The government has an overriding authority to take property, which is referred to as _____.

2.2 When governments take land, they often determine the landowner's compensation by determining what similar properties have sold for in the recent past. This method of determining just compensation is called the _____.

2.3 The _____ of the U.S. Constitution gives the government the authority to take property from individuals.

2.4 The language in the U.S. Constitution that gives the government the power of eminent domain is generally called the _____ clause.

2.5 According to the Constitution, the government can seize property by eminent domain only if that property will be devoted to _____.

2.6 The power of eminent domain is also often referred to as government's _____.

2.7 The _____ is a standard process used to determine fair market value of a property.
   a. Just compensation
   b. Takings power
   c. Fifth Amendment
   d. Comparable sales method

2.8 Which of the following is true regarding the power of eminent domain?
   a. Eminent domain is used only by the U.S. federal government.
   b. Eminent domain is used at federal, state, and local levels in the United States.
   c. Eminent domain is used only in the United States.
   d. a, b, and c are all true statements.

2.9 The _____ standard states "the owner is entitled to receive 'what a willing buyer would pay in cash to a willing seller' at the time of the taking."
   a. Takings clause
   b. Fair market value
   c. Holdout
   d. Eminent domain

2.10 The takings clause states that the government can seize private property only if _____ is provided.
   a. Collateral
   b. Public access
   c. Fair market value
   d. Just compensation

2.11 Government's use of its takings power is a solution to the _____.
   a. Free rider problem
   b. Holdout problem

c. Indivisibility problem
d. The takings power is not a solution to any problem.

2.12 Home Depot is trying to assemble a parcel of land to build a new superstore. There are 50 houses on the land the company needs. (The superstore is more valuable to society than the houses, so the benevolent social planner approves.) Which of the following statements is true regarding Home Depot's ability to buy the land and build the store?
   a. High transactions costs of bargaining with so many homeowners might prevent the superstore from being built.
   b. Some homeowners might ask for far more money than their houses are worth and kill the project.
   c. The government exercising its takings power might be the only possible way to assemble the parcel of land.
   d. All of the above are true statements.

2.13 Government gets its takings power from _____.
   a. The Bill of Rights to the Constitution
   b. A law passed in 1964
   c. An executive order issued by the first president, George Washington
   d. The United Nations

2.14 When governments use eminent domain, _____.
   a. The economic pie always gets larger
   b. The economic pie always gets smaller
   c. The economic pie may get larger or smaller; we don't know for sure

2.15 A professional football franchise is trying to assemble a parcel of land to build a stadium. There are 150 houses on the land the franchise needs. In this case, _____.
   a. Eminent domain can reduce transactions costs and make a pie-increasing stadium possible
   b. Eminent domain can reduce the likelihood of holdouts and make a pie-increasing stadium possible
   c. Both of the above
   d. Eminent domain is not called for; the land can be acquired more efficiently through bargaining

2.16 A tanning salon wants to expand its business by acquiring a neighboring tavern. In this case, _____.
   a. Eminent domain reduces transactions costs and makes a pie-increasing tanning salon possible
   b. Eminent domain reduces the likelihood of holdouts and makes a pie-increasing tanning salon possible
   c. Both of the above
   d. Eminent domain is not called for

2.17 The Constitution stipulates that when government uses eminent domain to acquire land for a project, _____.

    a. The government must use its own resources to complete the project

    b. The government can hire a private company to complete the project

    c. The government can resell the land to a private developer to complete the project

    d. The Constitution makes no stipulation at all; in practice, (a), (b), and (c) are all acceptable ways to complete the project

Problems and Applications

2.18 **[Related to Application 11.1 on page 220]** Andre is attempting to privately acquire a group of properties he needs for a big project. Stubborn Sally, who owns a lot at the edge of those properties, refuses to sell at a price that Andre believes represents fair market value. Andre is thinking about asking the city to use its power of eminent domain to compel Sally to sell. Why might the use of eminent domain be more justifiable if Andre's big project is a racetrack than if his big project is an amusement park?

2.19 Comment on this statement: "Eminent domain allows the government to seize land any time it wants."

2.20 Why must a government be careful about using its takings power too frequently, arbitrarily, or capriciously?

2.21 Does "public use" mean using seized property only for pure public goods or services? Explain your answer.

2.22 **[Related to Application 11.2 on page 223]** John and Carmen are neighbors. Carmen would like to acquire John's property, knock both houses down, and then build a larger home for herself. Unfortunately, John has refused all of her offers. If Carmen's dream house would have a higher market value than her current house and John's house added together, is it appropriate for her to ask her city council to take John's house and resell it to Carmen at fair market value?

2.23 Eminent domain requires that the government provide just compensation to persons from whom the property will be taken. What has the Supreme Court stated would be the ideal standard for determining just compensation? What practical difficulties stand in the way of achieving that ideal?

2.24 One standard method of determining just compensation is the comparable sales method. Why might some individuals perceive this method to be unfair?

2.25 The people in a particular state have demanded that their government change the existing law for eminent domain, which provides fair market value for seized property, to be more "fair" to landowners. Give an example of a change the government could suggest in order to ensure that its constituents are satisfied. What is a potential problem with providing more than fair market value for seized property?

2.26 Klaus owns the oldest house in Montgomery County. His house, a site of historical significance, is the only remaining example of Greek Revival architecture within a 200-mile radius. Visitors often drive through town just to see his house. Lately, Klaus has been complaining about the high cost of heating and cooling such an architectural relic. Yesterday he announced plans to demolish the house and replace it with a small, energy-efficient home.

There are 10,000 people in town, each of whom is willing to pay $30 to save the original structure. Klaus would be willing to sell his house and move to a different neighborhood for $250,000. Explain why Klaus's home is likely to be demolished. Should the county use its takings power to seize Klaus's home? Would such a taking satisfy the constitutional requirements for eminent domain?

2.27 Comment on this statement: "Because of eminent domain's public use requirement, it is illegal for a government to seize property from one private party and transfer it to another private party."

2.28 Use the concepts in this chapter and in Chapter 5 to evaluate this statement: "It is clear that creating and enforcing private property rights always produces the biggest economic pie."

The "Ask and You Might Receive" Game

This chapter highlights eminent domain as a solution to the holdout problem—the problem that sometimes arises when people compete for slices of a limited pie and through their actions prevent that pie from being created in the first place. Without eminent domain, both the people involved and society in general may miss out on an opportunity to benefit from a new product or service.

In the "Ask and You Might Receive" game, you and your classmates will each get to ask for a metaphorical slice of pie—in this case, money. You can ask for either a little bit of money or a lot of money. As long as your class doesn't collectively ask for too much—as long as enough of you are content to request a little bit of money—each of you will get what you asked for. But if too many of you request a lot of money, no one will get anything. So, will you ask for a little bit of money or a lot of money?

MyEconLab

Please visit http://www.myeconlab.com **for support material to conduct this experiment if assigned by your instructor.**

12 The Volunteer's Dilemma: A Collective Inaction Problem

Chapter Outline and Learning Objectives

12.1 **What Is the Volunteer's Dilemma?** page 231

Define *volunteer's dilemma*.

12.2 **If Apathy Doesn't Explain the Volunteer's Dilemma, What Does?** page 233

Discuss how pluralistic ignorance and diffusion of responsibility help explain the volunteer's dilemma.

12.3 **Game Theory and the Volunteer's Dilemma,** page 237

Explain what a mixed strategy is in a game and describe its usefulness.

12.4 **Mixed-Strategy Play and the Volunteer's Dilemma,** page 242

Explain why mixed-strategy play in volunteer's dilemma games can result in collective inaction.

12.5 **Overcoming the Volunteer's Dilemma,** page 244

List three possible solutions to the volunteer's dilemma.

Experiment: The "Save Ferris!" Game, page 251

MyEconLab

MyEconLab helps you master each objective and study more efficiently.

In 1964, in a densely populated New York City neighborhood, a young woman named Kitty Genovese was brutally attacked while on her way home from work late at night. Her attacker, Winston Moseley, stabbed her twice in the back. Her cries for help alerted a resident in a nearby apartment building, who shouted, "Let that girl alone!" Moseley fled the scene, only to return 10 minutes later to resume the attack. Over the next half hour, Moseley stabbed Genovese several more times, raped her, and stole $49 from her purse. Genovese's cries were ignored by at least a dozen neighbors. She died on the way to the hospital later that night.

What Is the Volunteer's Dilemma?

12.1 Learning Objective

Define *volunteer's dilemma*.

Given that Moseley had already run away once when yelled at from an open window, it's not too much of a leap to suggest that Genovese might have been saved if someone had stepped forward during the subsequent attack. The Genovese story, though sensationalized in the press, launched serious academic inquiry into a very important question: When there is a job that clearly needs to be done, a job that benefits large numbers of people, and it's a job that can possibly even be done by a single person, why is it so hard to get someone to step forward and do it? This problem—a situation where a single individual can provide a public good—is known as the **volunteer's dilemma**.[1]

Volunteer's dilemma A situation in which a single individual can provide a public good.

Volunteer's dilemmas appear in a wide variety of situations. Here are a few diverse examples:

- A boat is sinking, and the boat's lifeboat is overloaded. Who will jump out of the lifeboat to save the others?
- Migrating wildebeest must cross a crocodile-infested river. The first wildebeest to cross will likely be killed. As the hungry crocs fight over the dying animal, the other wildebeest will pass unharmed.
- In a war-ravaged country, a farmer finds an unexploded land mine near his village. Who will disarm the mine and search for others?
- Your professor asks a question that almost everybody in the class knows the answer to, but nobody raises his or her hand. It will move things along if someone takes a stab at answering, but that requires effort. Why not let somebody else do it?
- One night the power at your house goes out. You notice that none of your neighbors has power, either. Should you call the power company to report the outage? Or should you wait and let one of your neighbors do it instead?

So common are volunteer's dilemmas that the Yaghan Indians of South America have a single word that captures the essence of all these situations. That word, *mamihlapinatapai*, earned a place in the *Guinness Book of World Records* as the most succinct word in any language. Literally translated, it means, "looking at each other hoping the other will offer to do something that both parties desire to have done but are unwilling to do themselves."

In this chapter, we'll discuss the volunteer's dilemma and how it relates to the provision of public goods and services. Because a public good or service creates benefits everyone shares, no single individual wants to bear the cost of providing it. Of course, if nobody steps forward to provide the good or service, its benefits to society will be lost.

---

[1]Saving Kitty Genovese was, in fact, arguably a public good (or service) in the economic sense: If you save Kitty, a large number of people—her friends, her family, her co-workers, her customers—benefit. Those benefits are largely nonrival in that many people can enjoy her company at the same time. The benefits are also nonexcludable: If you save Kitty for one person, you save Kitty for everybody.

Application 12.1

Curt Flood Knocks the Volunteer's Dilemma Out of the Park

Professional baseball is a game of superstar personalities and multimillion-dollar paychecks. Major League Baseball's highest-paid player, Ryan Howard, of the Philadelphia Phillies, earns $25 million per year, and the average salary is over $3 million. Even the worst players earn a league minimum of $490,000.

Compare these salaries to what they were for professional baseball players in 1968. In 1968, Willie Mays, baseball's top earner, was paid $125,000 (about $800,000 in today's dollars). That's not chump change, but it's modest by today's standards.

Mays's modest salary can be attributed to the reserve clause, a labor rule that governed baseball for the better part of a century. Under the reserve clause, if a player played for a team in one year, he was bound to play for that team the next year unless he was traded. If a player was traded, he was required to play for the team he was traded to. Because players weren't free to seek and accept offers from other teams, players' salaries were low.

Enter Curt Flood, who played 12 seasons with the Cardinals while batting .293 and fielding almost flawlessly. At the end of the 1969 season, Flood was traded to the Phillies. But Flood refused to accept the trade. When asked whom he wanted to play for, Flood replied, "The team that makes me the best offer."

Rather than play ball, Flood devoted the 1970 season to suing Major League Baseball. Flood's suit asked the federal court to overturn the reserve clause and grant players free agency—the right to negotiate a contract and play for any team.

Marvin Miller, the director of the player's association, warned Flood of the consequences. "I told him," Miller told *The Atlantic* magazine, "that given the courts' history of bias towards the owners and their monopoly, he didn't have a chance in hell of winning. More important than that, I told him even if he won, he'd never get anything out of it—he'd never get a job in baseball again." But Flood was determined and asked Miller whether it would help other players. Miller said "Yes, and those to come."

"That's good enough for me," Flood replied.[2]

Flood lost both his suit and his subsequent appeal to the Supreme Court. But Flood's suit gave the free agency movement momentum. By 1976, the players' union had negotiated concessions that effectively killed the reserve clause. Players' salaries subsequently skyrocketed, and professional baseball changed forever.

Flood returned to play for the Washington Senators in 1971. But his lawsuit cost him his career: Hounded by threats from fans who accused him of ruining baseball, Flood left for good after only a few weeks with the Senators.

When Flood died in 1997, MLB players' representatives Tom Glavine and David Cone issued a statement about his legacy: "Every major league baseball player owes Curt Flood a debt of gratitude that can never be repaid. With the odds overwhelmingly against him, he was willing to take a stand for what he knew was right."[3]

See related problem 1.5 on page 247 at the end of this chapter.

Based on "How Curt Flood Changed Baseball and Killed His Career in the Process," *The Atlantic*, July 2011; "Curt Flood Is Dead at 59; Outfielder Defied Baseball," *The New York Times*, January 21, 1997; and Brad Snyder's *A Well-Paid Slave: Curt Flood's Fight for Free Agency in Professional Sports*, Plume, 2007.

---

[2]"How Curt Flood Changed Baseball and Killed His Career in the Process," *The Atlantic*, July 2011.

[3]"Curt Flood Is Dead at 59; Outfielder Defied Baseball," *The New York Times*, January 21, 1997.

If Apathy Doesn't Explain the Volunteer's Dilemma, What Does?

12.2 Learning Objective

Discuss how pluralistic ignorance and diffusion of responsibility help explain the volunteer's dilemma.

Let's return to the case of Kitty Genovese and try to figure out why nobody tried to help her. Newspaper accounts of the murder chalked up the lack of help to a cold indifference that city living breeds. In other words, people living in cities simply don't care about one another.

That explanation left social scientists unsatisfied because strong evidence shows that we, as a people, really do care about one another. We donate to charities, we help little old ladies cross the street, we volunteer our time to further important causes—causes that are certainly no more important than saving the lives of potential murder victims. Simply put, Genovese's death could not be chalked up merely to apathy. So if apathy didn't kill her, what did?

Pluralistic Ignorance

One explanation social scientists offered for Genovese's death was that she was the unfortunate victim of pluralistic ignorance. *Pluralistic ignorance* exists when the members of a group believe one thing but mistakenly assume that most of the other members believe something else. That may cause individuals to doubt their own judgment and go along with what they think the group believes. For example, you might think to yourself, "I don't think Miley Cyrus is a very good musician, but I think my friends like her. Maybe they know something I don't." And your friends might be thinking exactly the same thing. If everyone in the group is unsure whether the others like Miley Cyrus, they may all (incorrectly) think the others are fans; then everyone may end up at a concert *no one* wants to attend!

How might pluralistic ignorance explain what happened to Genovese? Some social scientists theorized that nobody could be sure exactly what was happening or exactly how much danger Genovese was in. Was she being beaten, or was she being stabbed? Was this a minor domestic dispute, or was Genovese in mortal peril? Bystanders, unsure of the answers to these questions, looked to others around them for cues about what behavior might be appropriate. And even though each individual might have suspected that Genovese needed help, because nobody else was intervening on her behalf, people were led to believe—against their better judgment—that everything was all right.

Diffusion of Responsibility

Social psychologists John Darley and Bibb Latane offered a second explanation for Genovese's death: They suggested that *diffusion of responsibility* was responsible for the bystanders' inaction. **Diffusion of responsibility** exists when a group of bystanders all agree that something needs to be done but each feels less personal responsibility for taking action because each perceives there are others who *could* take action. In Genovese's case, each bystander might have agreed that help was needed, but because coming to Genovese's aid could be costly (a person trying to help could be injured or killed), bystanders had an incentive to wait to see if someone else would act first.

Diffusion of responsibility A situation that occurs when a group of bystanders all agree that something needs to be done but each feels less personal responsibility for taking action because each perceives that there are others who *could* take action.

Diffusion of Responsibility and the Failure of Individuals to Act One of the unfortunate implications of diffusion of responsibility is that the larger the group, the more diffuse the responsibility is. As the group grows, each individual becomes a smaller part of the whole. As a result, any single individual becomes less likely to act. So the diffusion of responsibility explanation goes some distance toward explaining why the individuals witnessing Genovese's murder failed to intervene.

Diffusion of Responsibility and the Failure of Groups of Individuals to Act There is a difference between any particular *individual's* failure to act and an entire *group's* failure to act. To shed some light on the subtle difference, consider this example: Two people, Fleming and Yukia, come across a drowning puppy. It takes only one volunteer to save

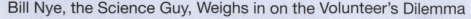

Application 12.2

Bill Nye, the Science Guy, Weighs in on the Volunteer's Dilemma

On November 16, 2010, a crowd gathered at the University of Southern California (USC) to hear William Nye, a.k.a. "Bill Nye, the Science Guy," lecture on the dangers of global warming. Things soon went awry: While walking toward the podium, Nye collapsed in midsentence and fell to the stage.

Yahoo's news account of the incident reports something even more troubling than Nye's collapse: The audience did not rush to help him. USC senior Alastair Fairbanks told the *Los Angeles Times* that he was "perplexed beyond reason" that instead of leaping to Nye's aid, students began texting and updating their Twitter statuses and Facebook feeds.

Why didn't someone rush to help Nye? This chapter's discussion of the volunteer's dilemma mentions three possible explanations. The most innocent is pluralistic ignorance: Maybe audience members saw nobody moving to help Nye, so they incorrectly assumed help wasn't necessary.

A second, less innocent, explanation is diffusion of responsibility: Everyone wanted Nye to be helped but didn't want to do the helping themselves. But diffusion of responsibility is more likely when helping the victim is costly. Helping Nye would have cost just a few steps and a 911 call. Why hope someone else would bear the cost of helping Nye when that cost was close to zero?

One callous explanation is that nobody rushed to help Nye because even idealistic college students couldn't care less for their fellow humans. If that's the case, Bill Nye shouldn't have been speaking about saving the planet for humanity because humanity doesn't deserve to be saved.

Or does it? After reports of students' tweeting went viral, a USC student wrote to Yahoo to contest the assertions. That student wrote that Nye was down for only 5 to 6 seconds, and even though they were shocked they weren't sure whether his collapse was a genuine medical problem or a part of the lecture. After rising, Nye continued his talk, "though it was clear he was really woozy," another student commented in USC's newspaper, the *Daily Trojan*.[4]

In other words, by the time the audience recognized that Nye's collapse wasn't just part of his lecture he had already gotten up. The tweeting and texting largely happened after people knew Nye was okay. It seems as if this was a genuine and innocent case of pluralistic ignorance after all! The best, however, was yet to come, for that same student later wrote that once Nye regained consciousness, everyone realized what was actually happening and the stage hands quickly rushed to assist him.

Faith in humanity restored.

See related problem 2.11 on page 248 at the end of this chapter.

Based on "Bill Nye the Science Guy Faints from Exhaustion at USC," *Los Angeles Times*, November 17, 2010; "Bill Nye Speaks at Bovard About Global Climate Change," *Daily Trojan*, November 16, 2010; "Bill Nye of 'The Science Guy' Fame Collapses During Speech at USC," *Los Angeles Times*, November 16, 2010; and "If the Science Guy Passes Out and Nobody Tweets It, Did It Happen?" *Yahoo News*, November 17, 2010.

the puppy. But because responsibility is diffuse, each person is only 60% likely to try to rescue the puppy.

This scenario has four, and only four, possible outcomes:

- Fleming rescues the puppy, and Yukia doesn't help.
- Yukia rescues the puppy, and Fleming doesn't help.
- Fleming and Yukia both try to rescue the puppy.
- Fleming and Yukia don't move; neither rescues the puppy.

---

[4]"Bill Nye speaks at Bovard about global climate change," *Daily Trojan*, November 16, 2010.

To fully understand the volunteer's dilemma, we need to know how likely each of these outcomes is. While we already have information on how likely any *individual* is to act, each of these outcomes incorporates *two* decisions—Fleming's decision *and* Yukia's decision. This makes figuring out the likelihood of each of these four potential outcomes slightly more difficult.

As a general rule, the probability of two things happening together—this thing *and* that thing—can be found by multiplying together the probabilities of each event happening on its own.[5] Statisticians refer to this as the *multiplication principle*. The key is to multiply when you see the word *and*. So the probability of Fleming rescuing the puppy *and* Yukia not helping can be found by multiplying the probability of Fleming stepping forward (0.6) by the probability of Yukia failing to act (0.4). That equals:

$$0.6 \times 0.4 = 0.24, \text{ or } 24\%$$

Let's examine each of the possible outcomes, see how likely each is to occur, and then determine how likely it is that the puppy will be saved:

- **Possible Outcome 1: Fleming rescues the puppy, and Yukia doesn't help.** As shown above, the probability of this outcome is the probability of Fleming stepping forward (0.6) multiplied by the probability that Yukia does not (0.4). That equals 0.24, so there is a 24% chance Fleming will singlehandedly save the puppy.

- **Possible Outcome 2: Yukia rescues the puppy, and Fleming doesn't help.** Find the probability of this outcome by multiplying the probability of Yukia stepping forward (0.6) by the probability that Fleming does not (0.4). Again, this equals 0.24, so there is a 24% chance Yukia will singlehandedly save the puppy.

- **Possible Outcome 3: Both Fleming and Yukia attempt to rescue the puppy.** Following the examples above, this outcome occurs with probability $(0.6) \times (0.6) = 0.36$; 36% of the time, both Fleming and Yukia will help save the puppy.

Remember that it takes only one rescuer to save the puppy, so the puppy will be saved in each of the three cases listed above. The *overall* probability of the puppy being saved then can be found by adding up the probabilities of the three separate outcomes.[6] Because Fleming saves the puppy alone 24% of the time, and Yukia saves the puppy alone 24% of the time, while 36% of the time they save the puppy together, the probability of the puppy being saved is:

$$24\% + 24\% + 36\%, \text{ or } 84\%$$

There is, however, a fourth possible outcome:

- **Possible Outcome 4: Neither Fleming nor Yukia rescues the puppy.** Fleming fails to rescue the puppy with probability 0.4. Yukia, too, fails to rescue the puppy with probability 0.4. So, the probability of neither Fleming nor Yukia rescuing the puppy is:

$$0.4 \times 0.4, \text{ or } 0.16$$

In other words, there is a 16% chance that the puppy will die.[7]

---

[5]Technically, that is true only if the decisions are statistically independent, which means that one person's decision does not depend on the decision of the other. In an urgent situation where decisions are made simultaneously, or in a situation where the decision makers choose their actions without knowledge of others' choices, statistical independence is a reasonable assumption.

[6]Here we aren't trying to compute the probability of an "and" event; we are determining the probability of an "or" event. That's because the puppy can't be saved in more than one way at a time: Either Fleming saves the puppy alone, *or* Yukia saves the puppy alone, *or* they both save the puppy together. When you have "or" outcomes, to find the overall probability that one of those possible outcomes occurs, simply add up their probabilities: 0.24 + 0.24 + 0.36 = 0.84, or 84%.

[7]You may have noticed that there is another way to arrive at this answer. We showed earlier that one way or another, Fleming and Yukia save the puppy 84% of the time. Because the probability of all possible outcomes must add up to 100%, there must be a 100% − 84% = 16% chance of nobody rescuing the puppy at all.

That's a lot of number crunching, but it highlights the difference between individual inaction and group inaction. Here, any *individual* fails to act with 40% probability, but the *group* collectively fails to act with 16% probability. From the standpoint of the puppy, and from the standpoint of society, it is only the 16% figure that matters: It's not *who* does the rescuing; it's only that *someone* does the rescuing!

How does this analysis relate to diffusion of responsibility? Remember that in the case of the volunteer's dilemma, it takes only one person to do something that benefits everybody. The relevant question, then, is not how diffusion of responsibility affects the willingness of any particular individual to step forward; that is well understood. The relevant question is how diffusion of responsibility affects the chance of nobody at all—not one single person—taking action.

Let's return to the drowning puppy to see how diffusion of responsibility might affect the puppy's chance of surviving. Suppose that a third party, Brandy, joins the group. Now there are three potential volunteers to come to the puppy's rescue, and if all else were equal, that would increase the puppy's chance of rescue. We can call that positive effect of having more potential volunteers on the puppy's chance of rescue the *size effect*.

Unfortunately, all else is not equal. When Brandy joins the group, responsibility becomes more diffuse. That makes any particular individual less likely to step forward. Let's call that reduced likelihood the *diffusion effect*. Holding everything else constant, the diffusion effect makes the puppy less likely to be rescued.

Of course, the size effect and the diffusion effect don't occur in isolation. Rather, the diffusion effect happens *because* the group's size is growing. Because the two effects happen at the same time but work in opposite directions, the net effect of increasing the number of bystanders on the puppy's chance of rescue is uncertain. Let's contrast two possible scenarios to demonstrate how the interaction of the size and diffusion effects might affect the chance of the puppy being rescued:

- **Possible Scenario 1: Adding Brandy to the group reduces the probability of any particular individual stepping forward from 0.6 to 0.55.** In this case, Brandy, Fleming, and Yukia each fail to act 45% of the time. The probability of nobody at all rescuing the puppy can be calculated as:

$$0.45 \times 0.45 \times 0.45, \text{ or } 0.091$$

  In other words, adding Brandy to the group *decreases* the odds of the puppy dying from 16% to 9.1%.

- **Possible Scenario 2: Adding Brandy to the group reduces the probability of an individual stepping forward from 0.6 to 0.4.** In this case, Brandy, Fleming, and Yukia each fail to act 60% of the time. The probability of nobody at all rescuing the puppy can be calculated as:

$$0.6 \times 0.6 \times 0.6, \text{ or } 0.216$$

  In other words, adding Brandy to the group *increases* the odds of the puppy dying from 16% to 21.6%.

As these two scenarios show, adding more people to the group can either decrease the chance of the puppy dying (as in the first example) or increase it (as in the second example). Which way it goes depends, essentially, on whether the diffusion effect is bigger than the size effect. Unfortunately, laboratory experiments designed to test which outcome is more likely repeatedly demonstrate that the larger the group is, the greater the chance that nobody at all will offer help. Why that happens so consistently is a puzzle worth exploring. Unfortunately, the diffusion of responsibility theory simply isn't powerful enough to explain why the diffusion effect seems to dominate the size effect.

Game theory, on the other hand, is. By learning just a little more game theory, you will not only be able to explain why responsibility becomes more diffuse, but you will also be able to *measure* how quickly it happens. That will give you the power to explain why it is, for example, that the bigger a group of potential rescuers is, the smaller the chance of that group actually performing a rescue. The tools of game theory, then, offer one complete explanation of the volunteer's dilemma.

Game Theory and the Volunteer's Dilemma

12.3 Learning Objective

Explain what a mixed strategy is in a game and describe its usefulness.

To explain why the diffusion effect seems to outweigh the size effect, we need to add another item to our game theory toolkit. In particular, we need to add a type of game where the better you are at fooling your opponent, the higher the payoff you are likely to receive. In other words, in games like the ones we'll look at in this chapter, players can improve their payoffs by acting unpredictably. How does this relate to the volunteer's dilemma? If you are ultimately willing to help a victim like Kitty Genovese, but you'd rather someone else did, you might want him or her to believe you won't help so he or she will take on the task.

Mixed-Strategy Games: An Overview

Game theory can help us understand the motives and actions of people facing volunteer's dilemmas. But to help develop the theory we need, let's first consider a simpler type of game that's a bit easier to understand and work with. Suppose that two good friends, George and Jerry, both want the same apartment, but can't decide who should get it. George proposes a game of Odds or Evens. The rules are simple:

- One player is designated as the "odd" player; the other is the "even" player.
- The players each drop one arm to their side.
- Together, they call out "One, two, three, shoot!"
- On "shoot," each raises his arm into a handshake position while simultaneously extending either one or two fingers.
- If the total combined number of fingers is odd, the "odd" player wins.
- If the total combined number of fingers is even, the "even" player wins.

Say that we let George be the "odd" player and Jerry be the "even" player. Next, we assign an arbitrary value of +100 to winning and −100 to losing. Figure 12.1 shows what this game looks like when represented with a payoff matrix.

		Jerry (Even)	
		Shoot 1	Shoot 2
George (Odd)	Shoot 1	−100, 100	100, −100
	Shoot 2	100, −100	−100, 100

◀ Figure 12.1
The Odds or Evens Game
In the Odds or Evens game, each player extends one or two fingers. If the total number of fingers extended is odd, George (in black) wins 100 from Jerry. If the total number of fingers extended is even, Jerry (in blue) wins 100 from George.

As shown in Figure 12.1, if both players shoot 1, the total is even (1 + 1 = 2), and Jerry wins. If one player shoots 1 and the other shoots 2, the total is odd (1 + 2 = 3), and George wins. Finally, if both players shoot 2, the total is even (2 + 2 = 4), and Jerry wins.

This game has two very interesting features that make it different from any other game we've studied so far. First, you'll notice that the game has no obvious Nash equilibria. No matter what the outcome is, one player (the losing player) will want to change his mind. Second, notice that the total payoff in each cell is always equal to zero. A game like this is called a **zero-sum game**, and it reflects the fact that the exact amount that one player wins is the exact amount the other must lose.

Pure Strategies Versus Mixed Strategies Here's what is particularly interesting about a zero-sum game: Because the players are in direct competition with one another, they should avoid playing what game theorists call a pure strategy. A **pure strategy** means playing the same thing time after time. In this game, that means shooting 1 all the time or shooting 2 all the time. The big disadvantage of a pure strategy is that it's

Zero-sum game A game in which the total payoff in each cell of a payoff matrix is equal to zero. In a zero-sum game, one player's winnings equal the other player's losses.

Pure strategy The approach of using the same strategy time after time; a strategy to avoid when players are in direct competition with one another because the strategy is predictable.

Mixed strategy The approach of using a different strategy time after time or randomly selecting a strategy; a strategy to use when players are in direct competition with one another.

predictable, and in a game where the parties are diametrically opposed to one another, being predictable means losing the game. So to be unpredictable and help protect himself from being exploited by Jerry, George should shoot 1 part of the time and shoot 2 the rest. Playing in such a manner is called playing a **mixed strategy**. But what should George's mixture look like? Should he shoot 1 99% of the time and shoot 2 the remaining 1%? Or should he shoot 1 15% of the time and shoot 2 the remaining 85% of the time?

Finding a Player's Ideal Mixed Strategy Finding a player's ideal mixture of strategies for a zero-sum game was one of the big questions John von Neumann, the inventor of modern game theory, found an answer to. Von Neumann observed that if an ideal mixture exists in a zero-sum game, that mixture must simultaneously minimize your opponent's payoff while maximizing yours. If that mixture exists, and if both players are playing their ideal mixtures, neither can do better by altering his or her mixture. In that case, an *equilibrium in mixed strategies* is said to exist.

How do we find a player's ideal mixture? Let's begin by thinking about what George's ideal mixed strategy might look like. Suppose that George and Jerry are to play Odds or Evens 10 times. If George shoots 1 every time (that is, if he adopts a pure strategy of shoot 1), we can represent his round-by-round choices as shown in Figure 12.2.

► **Figure 12.2**
George's Round-by-Round Play in the Odds or Evens Game
In 10 rounds of Odds or Evens, George plays a pure strategy, shooting 1 in every round.

Round	1	2	3	4	5	6	7	8	9	10
George Shoots	1	1	1	1	1	1	1	1	1	1

George has chosen to act predictably, and as a result, his choice of a pure strategy leaves him vulnerable to Jerry. Jerry can simply shoot 1 and win each and every round, as shown in Figure 12.3.

► **Figure 12.3**
Jerry's Counter to George's Pure Strategy in the Odds or Evens Game
Shooting 1 in each round leaves George open to exploitation by Jerry.

Round	1	2	3	4	5	6	7	8	9	10
George Shoots	1	1	1	1	1	1	1	1	1	1
Jerry Shoots	1	1	1	1	1	1	1	1	1	1
Winner (J or G)	J	J	J	J	J	J	J	J	J	J

It's clear that George needs to add a bit of randomness to his play. Suppose he mixes it up just the tiniest bit, shooting 1 90% of the time, and shooting 2 the remaining 10% of the time. This is likely to improve his overall success, but the amount of that improvement depends, too, on how Jerry plays. If Jerry stays the course and continues countering George's play by shooting straight 1s, the overall outcome might look something like what is shown in Figure 12.4.

► **Figure 12.4**
Mixed-Strategy Play in the Odds or Evens Game
Adding a little bit of Shoot 2 to his mixture lets George catch Jerry by surprise. George's winnings rise, and Jerry's fall.

Round	1	2	3	4	5	6	7	8	9	10
George Shoots	1	1	1	1	1	1	1	2	1	1
Jerry Shoots	1	1	1	1	1	1	1	1	1	1
Winner (J or G)	J	J	J	J	J	J	J	G	J	J

The series of plays shown in Figure 12.4 looks much the same as before. But notice what happened in round 8: George broke his pattern and threw a 2, taking Jerry by surprise and sealing up a win.

Should Jerry try to match George's randomness? Suppose that Jerry, noting that George is shooting 2 10% of the time, decides to shoot 2 10% of the time himself. He might get lucky and throw a 2 at exactly the same time George does. But frankly, the odds are stacked against that. A more likely outcome (90% more likely, in fact) is something like the series of plays shown in Figure 12.5.

Round	1	2	3	4	5	6	7	8	9	10
George Shoots	1	1	1	1	1	1	1	2	1	1
Jerry Shoots	1	1	2	1	1	1	1	1	1	1
Winner (J or G)	J	J	G	J	J	J	J	G	J	J

◀ **Figure 12.5**
Countering Mixed-Strategy Play in the Odds or Evens Game
When Jerry adds shooting 2 to his mixture, his winnings fall. To maximize his expected winnings, Jerry should maintain a pure Shoot 1 strategy.

As Figure 12.5 shows, adding a bit of randomness to his own play has cost Jerry even greater losses: He now loses in round 3 *and* round 8. This reveals two subtle and counterintuitive insights:

- **Subtle Insight 1:** Even if George is shooting a few 2s, as long as he isn't doing it too often, Jerry should continue to shoot pure 1s. Doing otherwise reduces Jerry's chances of winning.

- **Subtle Insight 2:** Because Jerry is better off sticking with a pure strategy when George shoots a few 2s, George can improve his performance by adding even more 2s to his mixture. By shooting 2 40% of the time, for example, he can reduce Jerry's winning percentage to 60%.

Of course, George *can* carry shooting 2 too far. If George shoots 2 80% of the time, Jerry can switch to a pure Shoot 2 strategy and guarantee himself victory 8 times out of 10. In that case, by reducing the number of times he shoots 2 to, say, 6 times out of 10, George can once again reduce Jerry's winning percentage to 60%.

A very apparent pattern is forming: When George isn't shooting 2 very often, he can increase his proportion of 2s and reduce Jerry's winnings. When George is shooting 2 a lot, he can decrease his proportion of 2s and reduce Jerry's winnings. Somewhere in the middle, something important happens: Jerry's winnings bottom out, and George's winnings peak. In this simple game, your intuition has probably already guided you to George's ideal mixture: To minimize Jerry's earnings and maximize his own, George needs to shoot 1 50% of the time and shoot 2 the remaining 50%.

Unfortunately, you can't always rely on intuition to guide you to the ideal mixture; not every ideal mixture is a 50/50 blend. A more methodical approach to finding George's ideal mixture begins by modifying the payoff matrix to reflect the fact that George now has three strategies available to him—a pure Shoot 1, a pure Shoot 2, or a mixture of 1s and 2s. Let's call that third strategy George's *p-mix*, with p representing the proportion of the time George shoots 1 and $(1 - p)$ representing the proportion of the time that George shoots 2. After adding that strategy to George's repertoire, the payoff matrix for the game looks like the one shown in Figure 12.6.

In Figure 12.6, the payoffs George and Jerry receive when George plays his p-mix require a brief explanation. Consider the outcome that results when George plays his p-mix against Jerry's shoot 1. Then p percent of the time, George shoots 1 and loses 100, and $(1 - p)$ percent of the time, George shoots 2 and wins 100.

▶ **Figure 12.6**

Adding George's Mixed Strategy to the Odds or Evens Game

George now has a third strategy available, a mixture of shooting 1 and shooting 2. In this game, p represents the fraction of the time George shoots 1 and $(1 - p)$ represents the fraction of the time George shoots 2.

		Jerry (Even)	
		Shoot 1	Shoot 2
George (Odd)	Shoot 1	**−100, 100**	**100, −100**
	Shoot 2	**100, −100**	**−100, 100**
	p-mix	**−100p + 100(1 − p),** **100p − 100(1 − p)**	**100p − 100(1 − p),** **−100p + 100(1 − p)**

The first expression in the corresponding lower-left cell, $-100p + 100(1 - p)$, represents George's average winnings, or the expected value of playing his p-mix against Jerry's pure Shoot 1. The second entry in that cell, $100p - 100(1 - p)$, represents Jerry's expected payoff from playing a pure Shoot 1 against George's p-mix. It indicates that p percent of the time, Jerry wins 100, and $(1 - p)$ percent of the time, Jerry loses 100.

The payoffs for George and Jerry when George plays his p-mix against Jerry's pure Shoot 2 can be found in the next cell to the right and are interpreted in a similar way. In particular, be sure to locate Jerry's expected payoff, $-100p + 100(1 - p)$. That's because Von Neumann's insight into mixed strategies tells us that George's ideal strategy is to find the value of p that minimizes Jerry's expected payoff.

Jerry, of course, is not a passive observer in all this. Jerry has the option of switching strategies if he needs to. Let's quickly summarize Jerry's payoffs from playing his available strategies against George's p-mix:

- When Jerry shoots 1 against George's p-mix, Jerry receives $100p - 100(1 - p)$.
- When Jerry shoots 2 against George's p-mix, Jerry receives $-100p + 100(1 - p)$.

Suppose Jerry can get a higher payoff from shooting 1 against George's mixture than he would get from shooting 2. (This happens when George is shooting a lot of 1s.) Then, as Subtle Insight 1 suggests, Jerry should shoot a pure 1. When Jerry shoots a pure 1, Subtle Insight 2 suggests that George can reduce Jerry's payoff by adding more 2s to his mixture—in other words, by reducing p.

On the other hand, if Jerry can get a higher payoff from shooting 2 against George's mixture than he would get from shooting 1 (as would happen if George were shooting lots of 2s), Jerry should shoot a pure 2. George can reduce Jerry's payoff by adding more 1s to his mixture—in other words, by increasing p.

This suggests that the only time George *can't* reduce Jerry's payoff by adjusting p is when Jerry's payoffs from shooting 1 and shooting 2 are identical. There, Jerry's payoffs are as low as George can make them. That occurs when the following conditions are met:

Jerry's expected payoff from shooting 1 = Jerry's expected payoff from shooting 2

$$100p - 100(1 - p) = -100p + 100(1 - p)$$

We can solve this equation for p by expanding through the parentheses and then simplifying:

$$100p - 100 + 100p = -100p + 100 - 100p$$
$$400p = 200$$
$$p = 1/2$$

In other words, George's ideal mixture is to shoot 1 exactly 50% of the time and to shoot 2 the remaining 50%. There, Jerry gets the same expected payoff no matter whether he shoots 1, shoots 2, or plays a mixture of the two.

Finding the Mixed-Strategy Equilibrium in a Zero-Sum Game

To find the mixed-strategy equilibrium for the game as a whole, we repeat the process of finding the ideal mixture for Jerry. To do that, we create a third possible strategy for Jerry. To differentiate Jerry's mix from George's, you might call Jerry's mixture his q-mix, where Jerry shoots 1 q percent of the time and shoots 2 the remaining $(1 - q)$ percent of the time. The payoff matrix that incorporates Jerry's mixed strategy is shown in Figure 12.7.

		Jerry (Even)		
		Shoot 1	Shoot 2	q-mix
George (Odd)	Shoot 1	–100, 100	100, –100	$-100q + 100(1 - q)$, $100q - 100(1 - q)$
	Shoot 2	100, –100	–100, 100	$100q - 100(1 - q)$, $-100q + 100(1 - q)$

◄ **Figure 12.7**
Adding Jerry's Mixed Strategy to the Odds or Evens Game
Jerry, too, has a mixed strategy available. In this game, q represents the fraction of the time Jerry shoots 1, and $(1 - q)$ represents the fraction of the time Jerry shoots 2.

Jerry can find his ideal mixture by adjusting q until *George's* expected payoffs from playing his pure strategies are identical. That occurs when:

George's expected payoff from shooting 1 = George's expected payoff from shooting 2

$$-100q + 100(1 - q) = 100q - 100(1 - q)$$

Solving for q:

$$-100q + 100 - 100q = 100q - 100 + 100q$$
$$-400q = -200$$
$$q = 1/2$$

Given the symmetric nature of the game, it shouldn't be too much of a surprise that Jerry's ideal mixture mirrors George's: 50% of the time shoot 1, and 50% of the time shoot 2.

Recall that George found his ideal mixture by adjusting his p-mix until he couldn't reduce Jerry's payoffs any further. Now Jerry has adjusted his own mixture until he can't reduce George's payoffs any further. When both play their ideal mixtures against one another, neither has any incentive to adjust his mixture any further, and we say that George and Jerry have found an equilibrium in mixed strategies.

If you're a player in this game, what exactly does playing this mixture earn you? You can determine George's and Jerry's expected earnings by simply plugging the values you found for p and q into the payoffs in the matrixes above. When Jerry shoots 1 against George's p-mix, Jerry earns:

$$100 \times 0.5 - 100(1 - 0.5) = 0$$

When Jerry shoots 2 against George's p-mix, Jerry earns:

$$-100 \times 0.5 + 100(1 - 0.5) = 0$$

So both of Jerry's pure strategies give Jerry an expected payoff of 0, and because Jerry's q-mix is just a weighted average of his pure strategies, when Jerry plays his own mixture against George's p-mix, Jerry will *still* receive an expected payoff of 0.

You might be wondering, "If Jerry's average earnings from shooting 1 are zero, and his average earnings from shooting 2 are also zero, then why should Jerry bother to mix at all?" The answer, of course, is that once he stops mixing, or even if he mixes in the wrong proportions, George can alter his mixture to take advantage of him, and Jerry's earnings will fall *below* zero.[8] As bad is it seems, zero, or breaking even, is the

---

[8]It's easy to see that playing the same thing time after time will cause you to lose. It's harder to see why playing a less-than-ideal mixture does. Suppose that you're the odd player, and you adopt a less-than-ideal mixture: You shoot 1 30% of the time and shoot 2 the remaining 70% of the time. Your opponent can take advantage of that by always shooting 2. You'll win 30% of the time and lose 70% of the time, giving you an expected payoff of $0.3 \times (+100) + 0.7 \times (-100)$, or -40. In other words, adopting a less-than-ideal mixture will cost you 40.

best Jerry can expect to do in this game, and the only way to average zero is to use his ideal mixture.

As shown on the previous page, Jerry's ideal mixture is to shoot 1 half the time and shoot 2 the other half. It is important, however, that Jerry do more than simply alternate 1s and 2s. That's a pattern George can take advantage of. So how can Jerry maintain the ideal 50/50 mixture but do so without establishing an exploitable pattern? One simple way is for him to turn his back on George and discreetly flip a coin: If it comes up heads, Jerry should shoot 1; if it comes up tails, he should shoot 2.

The Odds or Evens game illustrates mixed-strategy play in a game that is repeated over and over. The advantage of randomization is readily apparent in that context: Repeated predictability can lead to exploitation. But being unpredictable can be useful even if the game is to be played only once. If George and Jerry are to play only one round of the Odds or Evens game—winner take all—Jerry may still want to rely on a coin toss to determine his play because the sheer randomness of the coin toss can help him remain unpredictable. In the words of game theorist Avinash Dixit of Princeton University, "The best way to surprise your opponent is to surprise yourself."

Mixed-Strategy Play and the Volunteer's Dilemma

Understanding the basics of mixed-strategy equilibria in zero-sum games can help us understand more complicated situations like the volunteer's dilemma. Let's consider an easy-to-model game theory illustration of the volunteer's dilemma. A good friend of yours, Rena Elle, needs a kidney. You and all the other people in your town each happen to have a spare. If Rena gets a kidney, any kidney, she lives, and each person in town gets 5,000 units of satisfaction. If Rena doesn't get a kidney, she dies, and nobody gets anything. (For simplicity's sake, let's ignore the fact that the donor would have to be a match, tissue-wise, to Rena.)

But donating a kidney is costly. There's great pain and suffering involved for both donor and recipient, not to mention the cost of the procedure itself. Let's suppose that those costs add up to −4,000 units of satisfaction.

If it were just you and Rena living on a desert island, she'd get your kidney. You'd compare your costs of donating (4,000) to your benefits of doing so (5,000), and because the benefits outweigh the costs, you'd be on the operating table in the blink of an eye. In other words, with only one potential volunteer, Rena's chance of getting her transplant is 100%.[9]

The game changes if you add another potential volunteer to the mix. In this case, if one volunteer donates a kidney to Rena, the other potential volunteer gets to enjoy the benefits without sharing the costs. We model this as a game between two potential volunteers, Cameron and Simone, in Figure 12.8.

In Figure 12.8, if one donates and the other does not, the one who free rides gets 5,000 of benefit; the one who donates gets 5,000 of benefit but suffers 4,000 of costs, for a net gain of 1,000. If Cameron and Simone *both* donate, surgeons take both their

▶ **Figure 12.8**

The Organ Donation Game
Rena needs a kidney. Both Cameron and Simone benefit if she receives a donation, but each would like the other to do the donating.

		Simone	
		Donate	Don't Donate
Cameron	Donate	+1,000, +1,000	+1,000, +5,000
	Don't Donate	+5,000, +1,000	0, 0

---

[9]This is purposefully constructed as a best-case scenario—one in which the benefits to the volunteer outweigh the costs. If it can be demonstrated that the volunteer's dilemma exists even under these rosy conditions, then it's even easier to understand why it arises in situations where the costs to the volunteer outweigh the benefits. Wading into a violent situation like Kitty Genovese's, where a volunteer runs the risk of injury or even death, is one example.

kidneys and choose the healthiest one for Rena. Then, both Simone and Cameron get a net benefit of 1,000 each. Finally, if neither donates, Rena dies, and nobody gets any payoff at all.

Practice and experience have taught you to identify the type of game Cameron and Simone are playing on sight. But in case you're not seeing it, let's look for some of its characteristics. A best-response analysis shows that this game has two Nash equilibria in pure strategies—one where Cameron donates and Simone does not, and the other where Simone donates but Cameron does not. Given these numbers, each prefers a different Nash equilibrium.

For any individual, it's far better to have Rena live while you retain both of your kidneys than it is to have Rena live while you keep only one of your kidneys. Consequently, both players in this game have a tough strategy that leads them to the equilibrium they prefer. Cameron prefers the outcome where Simone donates and he does not, so not donating is his tough strategy. Alternatively, giving in and offering Rena a kidney might direct the game to the other Nash equilibrium (the one Cameron doesn't like so well), so donating is Cameron's weak strategy.

In this game, when both players play their weak strategy, Rena lives. Everyone benefits from that, although the social benefits are smaller than if just one had donated. But what happens if both players play their tough strategy? Rena dies, and neither Cameron nor Simone gets anything at all. This is a disastrous outcome for both Cameron and Simone . . . not to mention Rena! There is only one type of game that has all of the characteristics we've discussed: Cameron and Simone are playing chicken.

So now we see that the essence of the volunteer's dilemma, so brilliantly stated by the Yaghan Indians, is captured in the game of chicken. Everybody wants a volunteer to provide something everyone values—some form of public good. But everyone would prefer the volunteer to be someone other than himself—in other words, each volunteer prefers a different Nash equilibrium. If more than one volunteer steps forward, that's not ideal, but at least the outcome is okay; if nobody steps forward, disaster results.

Here's where the previous discussion of mixed strategies becomes important. Remember that when you play the Odds or Evens game, the element of surprise is important. You don't want to be predictable because your opponent could use that to take advantage of you. The same is true with the organ donation game. You don't always want to volunteer to do the hard jobs, or pretty soon everyone will just stand around waiting to free ride on your efforts. But you don't want to say no all the time either because sometimes that leads to a disastrous outcome. The way to get the most benefit at the lowest overall cost is to volunteer some of the time and decline the rest. In other words, the best way to play this game of chicken is to use a mixed strategy.

Of course, chicken is not a zero-sum game where one person's loss is another's gain. When Rena is saved, everyone wins; when she dies, everyone loses. Despite that additional complication, you can still find a mixed-strategy equilibrium in this game, and you find it in the same way as you did in Odds or Evens. Let's look for Cameron's ideal p-mix, recognizing that because this game is symmetric, Simone's q-mix will be fundamentally identical. The matrix reflecting the payoffs available when Cameron plays his mixture is shown in Figure 12.9.

		Simone	
		Donate	Don't Donate
Cameron	Donate	+1,000, +1,000	+1,000, +5,000
	Don't Donate	+5,000, +1,000	0, 0
	p-mix	$1000p + 5000(1-p),$ $1000p + 1000(1-p)$	$1000p, 5000p$

◀ **Figure 12.9**
Mixed Strategies in the Organ Donation Game
Playing a mixed strategy balances Cameron's desire to see Rena saved with his desire to see Simone do the saving.

Just as in the Odds or Evens game, Cameron's ideal mixture is found by equating the payoffs *Simone* receives from playing each of her pure strategies against Cameron's *p*-mix:

$$\text{Simone's payoff from donating} = \text{Simone's payoff from not donating}$$
$$1000p + 1000(1 - p) = 5000p$$
$$1000p + 1000 - 1000p = 5000p$$
$$-5000p = -1000$$
$$p = 0.2, \text{ or } 20\%$$

In other words, Cameron's ideal mixed strategy has him donating his own kidney with 20% probability and waiting for someone else to donate the remaining 80% of the time. This mixture balances Cameron's desire to see Rena saved with his desire to see Simone do the saving. Ultimately, Cameron can expect a higher payoff from playing this ideal mixture than he can by playing a pure strategy.

Here's what's interesting about this result: If Cameron is stepping forward 20% of the time, and Simone is stepping forward 20% of the time, then once in a while (4% of the time) both will step forward, and about 32% of the time one or the other, but not both, will end up stepping forward. This means that with two volunteers playing the game, the chance of Rena being saved is only about 36% . . . and 64% of the time, she will die.[10]

Recall that one of the defining features of the volunteer's dilemma is that as the group gets larger, not only is any individual less likely to volunteer, but also the likelihood of no one at all volunteering tends to increase. The theory of mixed-strategy play has enabled us to quantify both of those phenomena. First, we can measure the magnitude of the diffusion effect: When the pool of potential volunteers grows from one to two, the chance of any particular individual stepping forward falls from 100% down to 20%. Second, we can measure how the size of the volunteer pool affects the overall chance of Rena getting a kidney. As the pool of potential volunteers grows from one to two, Rena's chance of being saved falls from 100% down to 36%.

But what happens if the group gets even bigger? What if we add a 3rd, or 4th, or 400th person to the pool of potential volunteers? As it turns out, no matter what the size of the group, it is possible to calculate each player's ideal mixture.[11] With 3 players, for example, any individual should step forward only 11% of the time, and 89% of the time she should sit back and wait for someone else to volunteer. If everyone follows these guidelines, 0.1% of the time there will be 3 donors, 3% of the time there will be 2 donors, and 26% of the time there will be 1 donor. This means, of course, that about 71% of the time, Rena will die. Adding more donors (the 4th, the 5th, the 5,000th) makes responsibility more diffuse and at the same time continues to increase the likelihood that nobody will step forward at all.

In other words, Kitty Genovese didn't die because there were too few people to help; she died because there were too many.

Overcoming the Volunteer's Dilemma

How can society overcome the volunteer's dilemma? Honestly, there is no easy answer to this question, and the ubiquity of volunteer's dilemmas is a testament to humanity's lack of success in solving them. But one thing is certain: Under certain circumstances,

---

[10]Here's how that calculation is made: The probability of both Cameron and Simone stepping forward at the same time is $0.2 \times 0.2 = 0.04$, or 4%. The probability of Cameron stepping forward while Simone free rides is $0.2 \times 0.8 = 0.16$, or 16%. Similarly, the probability of Simone stepping forward while Cameron free rides is also 16%. In each of these cases, Rena lives. However, the probability of no one stepping forward at all is $0.8 \times 0.8 = 0.64$, or 64%. In this, the most likely outcome of all, Rena dies.

[11]Calculating ideal mixtures in *n*-player games is substantially more complex. For students who want to learn how that's done, see Avinash Dixit, Susan Skeath, and David Reiley's *Games of Strategy* (W.W. Norton and Co., 2009), which is an excellent reference.

governments can help by harnessing powers that individuals don't possess and by doing things ordinary people are not allowed to do.

Compulsory Volunteerism

Suppose your country is being attacked by an evil foreign empire, and your very way of life is threatened. Repelling the enemy brings benefits to everyone in your country, but it might be hard to find enough citizens willing to fight, and perhaps die, for their country. So the government overcomes this dilemma by *compelling* people to fight. If they refuse, they face severe penalties. Compelling people to serve in the military is called *the draft*, and it's been used to enlist soldiers for most of our biggest wars.

Or consider an army that is trying to capture the top of a hill. The general wants his soldiers to attack, fight ferociously, and achieve a victory that can be shared by many. The last thing the general wants to see is his troops retreating. But soldiers aren't fools, and wading into certain death seems silly when there are so many others who could do it. So how, if you're the general, do you keep your army from falling apart? The army of the Roman Empire had a unique solution to this problem: changing the payouts to people who retreated to certain death. If you were a member of the army, you had a standing order to kill any soldier who retreated. In addition, if you saw someone fail to kill a retreating soldier, you were ordered to kill both the retreating soldier and the soldier who failed to kill him. And if you failed to do so, you could be killed yourself!

Coalition Building and Bargaining

A second tactic that can be used to overcome the volunteer's dilemma is coalition building. In our kidney example, Simone and Cameron can form a "Save Rena" alliance that refuses to let her die. Essentially, Simone and Cameron might say to one another, "Hey, *I* don't want to do this, and *you* don't want to do this, so let's both agree to do it together." If they have enough time to talk it through, both donate, and Rena lives. Of course, it would be best if one donated and the other didn't, but it's better for both to donate than for nobody to donate at all.

Coalition building can be taken one step further: Instead of both Simone and Cameron donating a kidney apiece, they can bargain over who will go under the knife. Cameron can tell Simone, "Hey, I really, really want to see Rena saved, but I'm scared of needles. I'll pay you enough money to bring you 3,000 units of satisfaction if you'll make the donation." In that way, Cameron and Simone share the cost of saving Rena but spare society the waste of donating a second kidney Rena won't need.

Both coalition building and bargaining have transactions costs, however. It's worth noting that those costs are lower the smaller the number of parties involved—yet another reason that it may be better to have a small group of potential volunteers than to have a larger group. Further, both coalition building and bargaining work best when the pool of volunteers has time to think things through, evaluate, and negotiate with one another. So in the case of a kidney transplant, maybe coalition building and bargaining aren't terrible solutions. They work worse, however, in situations that arise suddenly and require immediate action. Building coalitions might help find a kidney but won't be of much use in saving Kitty Genovese.

Conclusion

Unfortunately, there really isn't a single solution to the volunteer's dilemma. We simply can't rely on government to compel someone every time a volunteer is needed, and coalition building and bargaining are often slow and difficult processes. Ultimately, our best weapon may be a thorough understanding of the root of the problem, the kind of understanding and insight that game theory can give us. We now know that

Application 12.3

Should There Be a Duty to Rescue?

On December 3, 2012, an argument on a crowded New York City subway platform took a tragic turn: Naeem Davis shoved Ki Suk Han off the platform and into the path of an oncoming train. Although onlookers waved their hands to get the train to stop, none of them attempted to help Han back onto the platform. The train slowed down too late, and Han was fatally crushed.

Han's death may make you wonder: Doesn't the law require bystanders to help in cases like Han's? Don't bystanders have what lawyers call a "duty to rescue"?

Surprisingly, no. With few exceptions, you can't be prosecuted or sued for failing to help someone in distress, no matter how ridiculous your inaction may seem. If you walk by an infant drowning in a puddle, you may be a horrible person, but you won't be liable in court. In legal terms, you don't owe the baby any "duty of care."

Why not? Because it's hard to hold someone to a legal standard when the standard isn't clear. "It's a classic slippery slope problem," law professor Jonathan Turley told the *Wall Street Journal*. "Once we begin to hold people to an affirmative duty act, it's difficult to draw a line where that duty would end." [12] If you're required to save Han from the subway, are you equally obliged to donate a kidney to save someone else? The obligation to rescue is fuzzy in other ways, too: If you're in a group, does everyone have a duty to rescue? Is everyone's duty the same, regardless of how capable he or she may be?

There appears to be a limit to how much morality society is willing to codify into law, especially when behaving morally puts a person in danger. The good news is that most of the time, people *do* try to rescue others, even without a legal duty.

In fact, Americans might even be *too* eager to help when others are in danger. Consider, for example, what happens when someone starts drowning. Often, someone attempts to save the victim. Unfortunately, it's not uncommon for the rescuer to drown, too. Law professor David Hyman analyzed every reported incident where a victim needed rescue between 1994 and 2004 and concluded that "Americans appear to be too willing to undertake rescue if one judges by the number of injuries and deaths among rescuers. Indeed, proven rescuer deaths outnumber proven deaths from non-rescue by approximately 70:1." [13] Further, when Hyman compared the 3 states that do have duty-to-rescue statutes (Minnesota, Rhode Island, and Vermont) to the other 47, he found no discernible difference in the number of rescues and non-rescues.

In other words, we don't really need a legal duty to overcome the volunteer's dilemma: When it really matters, we generally help one another. And, reassuringly, we do it for the best of reasons.

See related problems 5.5 and 5.6 on page 250 at the end of this chapter.

Based on David A. Hyman's "Rescue Without Law: An Empirical Perspective on the Duty to Rescue," 84 Tex. L. Rev. 653 (2006); "The Duty to Rescue," *The Wall Street Journal*, December 4, 2012; and "Suspect Confesses in Pushing Death of Queens Dad in Times Square Subway Station," *New York Post*, December 4, 2012.

when it comes to pools of potential volunteers, bigger is not always better. That insight might, at some critical moment, help us overcome our inner economist and mobilize our inner volunteer.

---

[12] "The Duty to Rescue," *The Wall Street Journal*, December 4, 2012.

[13] David A. Hyman's "Rescue Without Law: An Empirical Perspective on the Duty to Rescue," 84 Tex. L. Rev. 653 (2006.)

Chapter Summary and Problems

Key Terms

Diffusion of responsibility, p. 233

Mixed strategy, p. 238

Pure strategy, p. 237

Volunteer's dilemma, p. 231

Zero-sum game, p. 237

12.1 What Is the Volunteer's Dilemma? pages 231–232

Define *volunteer's dilemma*.

Summary

The volunteer's dilemma is a special case of the public goods problem where a good or service that brings benefits to everybody can be provided by just one person. But because everybody benefits when the good is provided—in other words, because property rights are not well defined—individuals face tension between their desire to see the good provided and their desire to have someone else do the providing. That tension and the strategic behavior it causes create the unfortunate possibility that nobody will provide the good at all.

Review Questions

All problems are assignable in MyEconLab.

1.1 The _____ is a situation in which a single individual can provide a public good.
  a. Public good problem
  b. Holdout problem
  c. Prisoner's dilemma
  d. Volunteer's dilemma

1.2 *Mamihlapinatapai* is a one-word summary of the volunteer's dilemma from
  a. The Inuit Eskimos of arctic North America
  b. Mongolia
  c. The Yaghan Indians of South America
  d. Ancient Cambodia

Problems and Applications

1.3 Consider the examples of the volunteer's dilemma listed in Section 12.1. Explain why the volunteer in each instance provides an economic public good.

1.4 One or more meerkats act as sentries while others forage for food. If a predator approaches, the sentry meerkat lets out a warning call so that others can burrow to safety. However, noise the meerkat sentry makes puts it at risk of being discovered by the predator. Explain why this constitutes a volunteer's dilemma.

1.5 [Related to Application 12.1 on page 232] Read Application 12.1 closely. Explain why Curt Flood's actions constituted a public good.

12.2 If Apathy Doesn't Explain the Volunteer's Dilemma, What Does? pages 233–236

Discuss how pluralistic ignorance and diffusion of responsibility help explain the volunteer's dilemma.

Summary

Early study of the volunteer's dilemma suggested two explanations for bystanders' failure to attempt rescues. First, bystanders may fall victim to pluralistic ignorance, a condition in which a bystander might believe that help is needed, but because nobody else appears to be alarmed, the bystander second-guesses himself or herself and fails to act. Second, bystanders may experience diffusion of responsibility: Because there are others nearby, each person in a group feels less personal responsibility to help. The chance of a rescue may depend on the number of potential rescuers. A larger group means more potential rescuers (the size effect) but also reduces each potential rescuer's feeling of responsibility (the diffusion effect). The diffusion effect seems to be larger than the size effect, meaning that as the group of rescuers grows, the odds of a rescue get smaller.

Review Questions

All problems are assignable in MyEconLab.

2.1 _____ exists when a group of bystanders all agree that something needs to be done, but because each perceives there are others who could help, each feels less personal responsibility for helping.

2.2 Suppose that individual members of a group believe one thing but mistakenly assume that most of the other members believe something else. Each member goes along with what he or she thinks the other members of the group believe. This phenomenon is referred to as _____.

2.3 The positive effect of having more potential volunteers in a volunteer's dilemma situation is called the _____.

2.4 The likelihood of one or more people volunteering in a game of volunteer's dilemma will _____ when the diffusion effect is greater than the size effect.

2.5 A college student who does not intend to drink heavily finds himself drinking more than he intended because he believes that is what his friends want to do. In reality, his friends also wish they drank less heavily and less frequently. This illustrates a situation of _____.

   a. Mixed-strategy play

   b. Diffusion of responsibility

   c. Pluralistic ignorance

   d. The size effect

2.6 A volunteer is needed to perform some onerous task. As the size of a group increases, any particular individual becomes less likely to step forward. This phenomenon is known as _____.

   a. The diffusion effect

   b. The size effect

   c. Pluralistic ignorance

   d. The volunteer's dilemma

2.7 Suppose that in the case of a particular volunteer's dilemma, the size effect is greater than the diffusion effect. As the group of potential volunteers grows, _____.

   a. It is more likely that a volunteer will be found

   b. It is less likely that a volunteer will be found

   c. The chance of a volunteer being found will not change

   d. We cannot determine the likelihood of finding a volunteer with the information given.

2.8 A man has fallen from a subway platform. It takes only one person to save him from an oncoming train. If there are two bystanders who can help, and each bystander is willing to volunteer with a probability of

0.7, what is the probability that nobody at all helps the fallen man?

   a. 0.7

   b. 0.49

   c. 0.09

   d. 0.3

Problems and Applications

2.9 There is a woman yelling, "Someone please help me!" outside your large apartment complex. It is nighttime, but many residents of the apartment complex have their windows open. What are two reasons that the woman may not get the aid she seeks, based on information from this chapter?

2.10 After World War II, some German officers were prosecuted for war crimes. Many of those officers used a defense that basically amounted to "I cannot be held accountable because I was following a superior's orders." What is this an example of?

2.11 [Related to Application 12.2 on page 234] In 2011, Simone Back posted a suicide message on Facebook. The January 5, 2011, issue of *The Guardian* reports that of her 1,048 Facebook friends, "no one who lived nearby contacted police or sought her out in time to save her." Instead, Facebook friends commented that Back was "a liar" and that "she does it [takes all her pills] all the time."[14] It was only the next day that a Facebook user texted Back's mother about the suicide status; by then it was too late. Use the material in this chapter to explain why Back's cry for help was ignored. Then compare and contrast this situation to the discussion of Bill Nye in Application 12.2.

2.12 Read Application 12.1 and problem 1.5 carefully. Then, discuss whether pluralistic ignorance or diffusion of responsibility best explains the failure of major league baseball players to challenge the reserve clause.

2.13 Three potential rescuers witness a drowning puppy. Each is willing to rescue the puppy with probability 0.75. What is the probability that the puppy is rescued?

12.3 **Game Theory and the Volunteer's Dilemma, pages 237–242**

Explain what a mixed strategy is in a game and describe its usefulness.

Summary

Game theory can help explain why the diffusion effect may outweigh the size effect. Mixed-strategy games are the key to understanding this phenomenon. In a mixed-strategy game, players use each of the strategies available to them in various proportions. They do this to remain unpredictable because if they behave predictably, their opponent can take advantage of them. There is an ideal mixture for each player to play. A player's ideal mixture equalizes the payoffs her opponent receives from each of his pure strategies.

Review Questions

All problems are assignable in MyEconLab.

3.1 A _____ is when a player chooses the same strategy time after time.

---

[14]"Facebook 'friends' did not act on suicide note," *The Guardian*, January 25, 2011.

3.2 In a _____ game, there are no obvious Nash equilibria, and one player's losses are equal to the other player's gains.

3.3 Rock–Paper–Scissors is a zero-sum game in which success depends on being unpredictable: Instead of playing a pure strategy, players should play a blend of rock, paper, and scissors. Such a blend is referred to as a _____ .

3.4 When a player in a game changes his or her strategy from round to round, that player is said to be playing a _____ .
   a. Pure strategy
   b. Zero-sum game
   c. Mixed strategy
   d. Hybrid game

3.5 In a _____ game, the total payoff in each cell is always equal to zero.
   a. Chicken
   b. Prisoner's dilemma
   c. Zero-sum
   d. Positive sum

3.6 _____ was the inventor of modern game theory.
   a. John von Neumann
   b. John Nash
   c. Adam Smith
   d. Milton Friedman

Problems and Applications

3.7 Explain what it means to have equilibrium in mixed strategies.

3.8 George and Jerry are playing Odds or Evens but with a unique set of rules. George suggests, "Jerry, if we both shoot one finger, I'll give you 3 points. If we both shoot two fingers, I'll give you 1 point. But if one of us shoots one finger and the other shoots two, you give me 2 points. After a dozen rounds, the one with the most points wins." Construct a payoff matrix that illustrates this game. Then compute George's and Jerry's ideal strategies.

12.4 ## Mixed-Strategy Play and the Volunteer's Dilemma, pages 242–244

Explain why mixed-strategy play in volunteer's dilemma games can result in collective inaction.

Summary

The volunteer's dilemma is a game of chicken played between potential volunteers. To prevent free riders from taking advantage of them, potential volunteers may choose to play a mixed strategy in this game of chicken. Unfortunately, if both players adopt mixed strategies, some percentage of the time, neither of them will volunteer. If players are playing their ideal mixture, that percentage will increase as the number of potential volunteers grows. Game theory, then, offers an explanation for why the diffusion effect outweighs the size effect.

Review Questions

All problems are assignable in MyEconLab.

4.1 In the volunteer's dilemma, each player has a tough strategy and a weak strategy. Disaster occurs when both players play their tough strategy. What type of game is the volunteer's dilemma?
   a. Prisoner's dilemma
   b. Chicken
   c. Battle of the sexes
   d. Zero-sum

4.2 In the case of Rena's kidney discussed in the text, it is clear that the _____ .
   a. Size effect outweighs the diffusion effect
   b. Diffusion effect outweighs the size effect
   c. Size effect and diffusion effect are equal in magnitude
   d. Neither (a) nor (b) nor (c) is necessarily true.

Problems and Applications

4.3 In the case of Rena's kidney discussed in Section 14.4, determine what would happen to Cameron's and Simone's ideal strategies if the benefit to having Rena saved were 4,500 instead of 5,000.

4.4 In problem 4.3, is the answer you got consistent with your intuition? Explain why or why not.

4.5 Explain why the kidney donation problem faced by Rena, Cameron, and Simone is neither a prisoner's dilemma nor a battle of the sexes.

12.5 Overcoming the Volunteer's Dilemma, pages 244–245

List three possible solutions to the volunteer's dilemma.

Summary

There are a few ways to overcome the volunteer's dilemma. First, the government can compel people to volunteer, even against their wishes. This essentially amounts to government changing the available payoffs in the game. Second, groups of potential volunteers might form a coalition in which everyone agrees to help together. Third, potential volunteers can bargain with one another over who will step forward and volunteer. Both coalition building and bargaining, however, might involve transactions costs that prevent potential volunteers from reaching an agreement. And because coalition building and bargaining take time, they are less useful when the crisis is urgent.

Review Questions

All problems are assignable in MyEconLab.

5.1 When individuals form an alliance to ensure that all members will volunteer in a case of volunteer's dilemma, this is called _____.

　　a. Bargaining

　　b. Coalition building

　　c. Compulsory volunteerism

　　d. A mixed strategy

5.2 In some places, the law requires bystanders to come to the aid of people in mortal danger. That legal obligation is called _____.

　　a. Eminent domain

　　b. Mandatory volunteerism

　　c. The categorical imperative

　　d. The duty to rescue

5.3 Under attack by Axis forces in World War II, the United States compelled young men to serve in the nation's defense. That compulsory military service is referred to as _____.

　　a. The draft

　　b. Eminent domain

　　c. Mandatory volunteerism

　　d. The duty to rescue

Problems and Applications

5.4 What are some ways that a government or group can ensure that the economic pie is maximized when a volunteer's dilemma arises? Are there barriers to the effectiveness of these tools?

5.5 [Related to Application 12.3 on page 246] The Brazilian penal code states that it is a crime not to rescue (or call emergency services, when appropriate) injured or disabled people, including those found in grave and imminent danger, as long as it is safe to do so. Unlike in Brazil, as Application 12.3 points out, there is no such duty to rescue in the United States. Why is this the case? Do you believe that there should be such a law? Why or why not?

5.6 [Related to Application 12.3 on page 246] In 2007, 50-year-old construction worker Wesley Autrey became a hero by rescuing a man who had fallen onto the subway tracks.[15] According to *The New York Times*, the man, who was having a seizure, fell from the nearly deserted platform to the tracks below. With a train fast approaching, Autrey leapt to the tracks and moved the man's body between the rails. Then, Autrey laid on top of the man as the speeding train passed overhead. Use the theory developed in this chapter to explain why somebody leapt to rescue the potential victim in this case, but not in the case described in Application 12.3.

---

[15]"It's Hard to Be a Hero" *The New York Times*, December 7, 2012.

The "Save Ferris!" Game

This chapter highlighted how difficult it is for society to find an individual volunteer to provide a good or service that could benefit many people. In this game, you and your classmates have the opportunity to save a student everyone loves, a student who makes everyone's world a little bit richer: Ferris Bueller.

No one has seen Ferris on campus recently, and rumor has it that he needs a kidney transplant. Your class has been asked to locate a donor. If a single donor is found, Ferris will live and everyone will benefit. But donating a kidney is costly and exposes the donor to the risk of medical complications. Will you offer one of your kidneys to Ferris? Will one of your classmates?

MyEconLab

Please visit http://www.myeconlab.com **for support material to conduct this experiment if assigned by your instructor.**

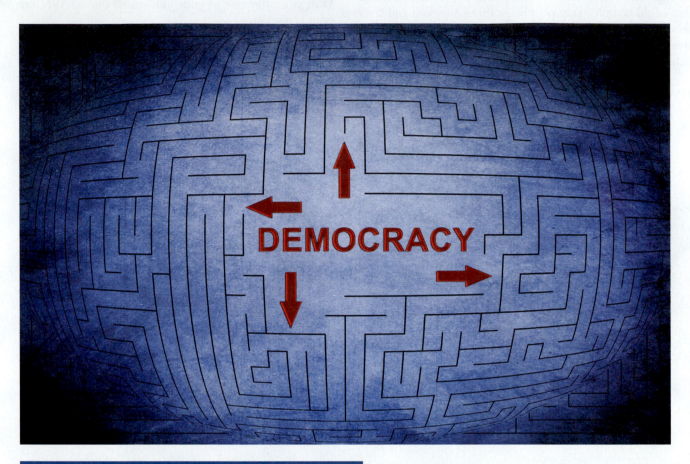

Chapter Outline and Learning Objectives

13.1 An Introduction to Voting Methods, page 253

Use different voting methods to determine the winner of an election.

13.2 Conventional Political Elections and the Median Voter Theorem, page 261

Define *median voter theorem* and explain how it works.

13.3 Strategic Voting and the Order of Events in Runoff Elections, page 268

Demonstrate how the order of events in a runoff election can affect the outcome.

Experiment: Looking for a "Goldilocks" Location, page 274

MyEconLab

MyEconLab helps you master each objective and study more efficiently.

If there's a single underlying theme to the topics in this book so far, it's this: You will face many situations in your life that require you to make a choice about taking some kind of action. In some cases, one choice will be best for you personally, but another choice will be best for society: You might be tempted to control garden pests with an insecticide that also kills beneficial honeybees, for example, or you might be asked to donate a kidney to an anonymous stranger. Regardless of what you choose to do in these cases, there are often enough other people in the world looking out for their own self-interests that as a society, we get a less-than-desirable outcome.

When what's best for the individual isn't what's best for society, we often turn to the government to compel or induce people to behave in certain ways. The good news is that, at least in theory, the government can sometimes achieve outcomes individuals can't achieve on their own. But before the government can come racing to the rescue, society must first choose *who* is going to do the governing.

It would be nice if the people society elected to govern passed laws that reflected society's collective preferences. But as this chapter unfolds, you'll discover that sometimes the very fact that government officials are elected dooms society to outcomes that the typical voter doesn't really like. So, even if everyone generally agrees about what they'd like the government to do, they might have a difficult time getting the government to actually do it. Because of that, it's often the case that even government can't give us what we want.

An Introduction to Voting Methods

Virtually all of us have had some experience with voting. Even if you haven't yet voted in a political election, you've surely been a member of a club or a class that's used a vote to decide something—maybe to elect officers or choose the location of a field trip. And even if you haven't done that, maybe your family voted to decide what movie to rent or where to go for dinner or whose job it was to clean the bathroom. Because you're so comfortable with the *idea* of voting, you might be wondering what's so hard about understanding the *process* of voting. When you vote, don't you just pick the option you like best, tally up the votes, and go with the option that most people prefer?

Well, sometimes. That type of voting does a pretty good job of allowing people to express their preferences when there are only two options or candidates being voted on. But when the world gets even slightly more complex—such as when voters have to choose from three options instead of two—such a simple voting system has the potential to create a great deal of dissatisfaction. In those circumstances, alternative voting procedures may do a better job of expressing the will of the people.

To illustrate, consider an example.[1] A hospital is to be built. It will serve the residents of four towns: Northfield, Easterbrook, Southtown, and West Egg. The residents in these four towns are all retirees, and they all agree that they need a hospital now. The only conflict is over where to build the hospital: Every resident wants to live as close to the hospital as possible.

And so, the powers that be decide to put the location of the hospital up for a vote. To ensure reliable power, water, and sewer, the hospital's board of directors has determined that the facility must be built in a town and not out in the middle of nowhere. The board has assured the residents of the four towns that the hospital will offer exactly the same services no matter where it is built, so the only criterion residents need to consider when voting is the distance that they live from the proposed site. Figure 13.1 is a map that shows the four towns, the major roads between the towns, and the number of residents (voters) in each town. The mileage between towns is shown in italics.

[1] James Madison University professor Scott Stevens developed this example, and it's used here with his permission. Professor Stevens's delightful video introduction to game theory is highly recommended and is available from The Teaching Company (www.thegreatcourses.com).

13.1 Learning Objective
Use different voting methods to determine the winner of an election.

▶ **Figure 13.1**

A Hospital Location Problem
This map shows the four towns where a hospital may be located, with the driving distances between the towns indicated in italics. For example, West Egg is 22 miles away from Southtown, Easterbrook is 13 miles away from West Egg, and Northfield is 30 miles from Southtown.

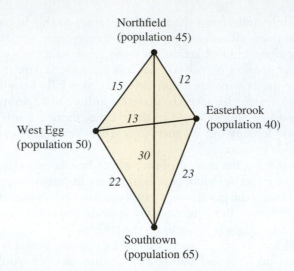

Plurality-rule method A voting procedure in which the alternative that receives the most votes wins, even if that alternative doesn't receive a majority of the votes.

The Plurality-Rule Method

To facilitate the vote on the hospital, its board of directors holds a public meeting that all the residents of all the towns attend. Clara Nightingale, the president of the board, opens the meeting with the suggestion to immediately vote on where to locate the hospital. She explains the rules: "Everybody in attendance gets to cast one vote for the town where they'd like to see the hospital located. We'll be passing out ballots, so just mark an *X* by the town of your choosing. When all of the ballots have been returned, we'll tally the votes, and the town that receives the most *X*s will be the winner." Such a voting procedure is called the **plurality-rule method**, and it's notable that the winner doesn't have to receive a majority of the votes to win but just needs to get more votes than any other alternative.

The votes come rolling in. As you'd expect, everybody votes for the hospital to be located in his or her town. When the votes are tallied, Easterbrook receives only 40 votes, Northfield comes in with 45, West Egg receives 50 votes, and the winner is Southtown, with 65 votes.

Although Southtown is the clear winner under the plurality-rule method Clara has used, that outcome is more than a little problematic. Here's why: Regardless of whether you live in Northfield, West Egg, or Easterbrook, a hospital in *any* of those towns would be closer to you than a hospital in Southtown. Given the population of each town, it turns out that over two-thirds of the people who participated in the election would rather have the hospital *anywhere else* but Southtown! In other words, the plurality-rule method has created what many might view as an undesirable social outcome.

The problem for the residents of Northfield, Easterbrook, and West Egg is that they split their votes among their respective towns. Those residents could have orchestrated a solution superior to Southtown by all agreeing to vote for one of the three northern towns. But beyond the difficulty of deciding which town everyone should vote for (which presents its own set of voting problems), organizing such an effort is costly and difficult. As a result, individuals are left with no better choice than to vote for their own towns, and 135 out of the 200 retirees walk away dissatisfied.

Does this problem sound familiar? It should, because it's just another version of the general scenario we've been talking about throughout this book. The context is different (this problem applies also to global warming, the depletion of fisheries, and rounding up enough organ donors), but the problem is the same: Because of high transactions costs, individuals who could cooperate fail to do so. As a consequence, they receive an undesirable social outcome.

The Condorcet Method

After the vote, Clara Nightingale realizes from the grumbling in the room that most people are dissatisfied with the outcome. Hastily she gathers the other board members around her to figure out a solution. When they break their huddle, Clara announces, "Most of the people in the room are displeased with the choice of Southtown. It's clear that I made a mistake in setting the rules of this election. I'd like a do-over, please, with a different set of voting procedures."

Over the strenuous objections of the 65 residents of Southtown, the vote is nullified, and a new set of rules is announced. "We believe that the winner needs to be clearly better than each of the other alternatives," Clara says. "I propose we pit the towns against one another in head-to-head pairings. The town that can beat all the other towns in such matchups will be declared the winner, and we'll locate our hospital there." Such a set of rules constitutes what political scientists and game theorists call the **Condorcet method**. The winner of such an election is called a *Condorcet winner*.

Let's see how the hospital election will unfold with Condorcet rules in place. To begin, pick a pair of towns—perhaps West Egg and Southtown. Now let the residents of all four towns vote for either West Egg or Southtown; then determine the winner of that pairing. It's pretty clear that the Southtown residents will vote for Southtown (giving them 65 votes), and the West Egg residents will vote for West Egg (giving them 50 votes). Northfield residents would rather drive 15 miles to West Egg than 30 miles to Southtown to get to the hospital, so West Egg picks up Northfield's 45 votes, too. And Easterbrook residents would rather drive 13 miles to West Egg than 23 miles to Southtown to the hospital, so West Egg picks up Easterbrook's 40 votes as well.

In the end, West Egg defeats Southtown 135–65. Southtown, the winner of the plurality-rule vote, cannot defeat all the other towns in head-to-head matchups, and therefore Southtown will most definitely *not* be the Condorcet winner. It's possible (though not yet guaranteed) that West Egg might be.

In order to be the Condorcet winner, West Egg must also defeat Northfield and Easterbrook in head-to-head matchups. When West Egg faces Northfield, West Egg gets 50 votes from its own residents and 65 votes from the residents of Southtown. Northfield gets 45 votes from its residents, and 40 votes from Easterbrook. Therefore, West Egg wins the head-to-head pairing with Northfield, 115–85. Therefore, West Egg might still be a Condorcet winner; but Northfield is definitely not.

West Egg has now defeated both Southtown and Northfield in head-to-head contests. Let's see how West Egg fares against Easterbrook. Again, each town garners its own votes, giving West Egg 50 and Easterbrook 40. Northfield casts its 45 votes for Easterbrook, and Southtown residents cast their 65 votes in favor of the 1-mile-closer West Egg. When the votes are tallied, West Egg defeats Easterbrook, 115–85. West Egg has defeated each of the other towns in head-to-head contests and is declared the Condorcet winner in this election.

The Condorcet method has a great deal of intuitive appeal because in the end, a majority of voters prefers the Condorcet winner to any other single alternative. That's a very strong endorsement, which is nice. So if it's such a good method, why don't we see it used more often?

To shed some light on that question, let's step away from the hospital example for a moment. Instead, consider a group of nine college students—math majors who are burned out after a week of learning about partial differential equations and Hilbert spaces. They've all agreed that they'd like to celebrate the end of the week by going out together. The options available to them are to go to a movie (the student union will be showing *Good Will Hunting*), hang out at the pub in the basement of the math building, or head to baby back ribs night at the local BBQ joint.

It goes without saying that all the people in the group have their likes and their dislikes, and that they don't necessarily agree on what the best option might be. As it turns out:

- Four of the nine prefer the movie to the bar and the bar to the ribs (movie > bar > ribs).

Condorcet method A voting method in which the winner must defeat each of the other alternatives in head-to-head contests.

- Three of the nine prefer the bar to the ribs and the ribs to the movie (bar > ribs > movie).
- Two of the nine prefer the ribs to the movie and the movie to the bar (ribs > movie > bar).

The group decides to use the Condorcet method to determine where to go. First, the group evaluates the bar against the ribs. The four people in the first group prefer the bar to the ribs, as do the three in the second group. Only the two people in the third group prefer the ribs to the bar. So, by a vote of 7–2, the bar wins.

The group then evaluates the movie/bar pairing, and the movie defeats the bar by a vote of 6–3. At that point, Danica, a senior, says, "The bar beats the ribs, and the movie beats the bar. So it's clear, by the transitive property, that the movie is a Condorcet winner!" And the movie lovers rejoice. (You might remember the transitive property from your algebra class. It says that if A is greater than B, and B is greater than C, then A must be greater than C.)

They rejoice, that is, until Marquise steps forward and says, "I hate to be a stickler, but we'd better follow the rules and see this through. Let's pit the movie against the ribs, just for the sake of completeness." Everybody groans, partly because Marquise always second-guesses everything, and partly because the movie is already starting, and they might miss the part where Matt Damon writes out a proof of Fermat's last theorem on the cafeteria floor using only a mop and a bucket of Pine-Sol. But much to everyone's surprise, when the votes are cast, the ribs beat the movie 5–4!

This is wild: A majority of the group prefers the bar to the ribs. And a majority of the group prefers the movie to the bar. And a majority of the group prefers the ribs to the movie. That means that the ribs beat the movie, which beats the bar, which beats the ribs. Either these students are attending the M.C. Escher Academy of Mathemagic, or everything they know about the transitive property has been called into question.

One important implication of this odd puzzle, which is called the *Condorcet paradox*, is that even if each individual in a group has transitive preferences, the group's collective preferences might *not* be transitive. So this paradox should serve as a caution to policymakers: When you design a policy that affects an entire group of people, you can't figure out what the group prefers by simply adding up the preferences of the group's members. It's possible that no matter which policy option you choose, a majority of your constituents would prefer that you do something else. Simply put, you can't please everybody, and often it's hard to please even half of them.

The second implication of the Condorcet paradox is this: When you use the Condorcet system of voting, *there may not be a Condorcet winner*. Think carefully about the mathematicians: The movie can't be a Condorcet winner because the ribs beat it. And the ribs can't be a Condorcet winner because the bar beats them. And the bar can't be a Condorcet winner because the movie beats it. So among these three options, there is no Condorcet winner. And the problem gets worse because, as a general rule, the more options a group is considering, the lower the likelihood that there will actually be a Condorcet winner. In short, an election method that doesn't consistently produce a winner isn't a very useful election method.

The Borda-Count Method

Let's leave the world of collegiate math and go back to the huddle in which Clara Nightingale and her board were overturning the results of the plurality-rule election. We know, of course, that if Clara and the board use the Condorcet method, West Egg will emerge a strong winner. But Clara is a game-theory aficionado, and so she whispers to the board, "I don't like the fact that plurality-rule voting produced a winner that most people don't like. We could use the Condorcet method, but there's no guarantee that there would be a winner. I'd like to recommend a different system. . . ."

And so the board members hammer out a voting system that makes a great deal of sense to them. When they break out of their huddle, Clara announces to the room, "Friends, neighbors, and retirees: My apologies for the bizarre results in our first election. The board would like to redo the election with an alternate set of rules. We would like everybody to take a ballot. On that ballot, you'll see four numbered spaces that are otherwise left blank. As you know, there are four possible locations for the hospital. Please rank those choices by placing your first choice in the blank marked #1, your second in the blank marked #2, etc."

"And then what?" asks Thomas, a resident of Easterbrook.

"Each town will be awarded points based on how each citizen ranks it: Three points for a #1 ranking, two points for a #2 ranking, and one point for a #3 ranking. And if a town gets ranked last, it won't get any points at all. At the end of the tallying, the town with the most points will be declared the winner."

"You're going to have to do an awful lot of math to figure out a winner," Thomas says. "I doubt it's worth it."

"Well, it *is* a lot of trouble," Clara replies, "but this way we'll get information about what locations you like best. Plus, we'll also be able to account for what locations you like *least*, which was a big part of the problem with our plurality-rule vote."

This type of election system is called the **Borda-count method**. And Thomas is right: Determining a winner in this type of election requires a bit more work. But the nice thing about the Borda method is that it allows voters to express, to some degree, the intensity of their preferences. Something that is strongly disliked by a substantial number of voters will not receive many points. And something that is liked best by a small majority of voters but strongly disliked by a large minority may be beaten by an alternative that is a bit more palatable to everybody.

With Thomas appeased, voting begins, and the ballots start to roll in. Because voters' preferences are based on how close the hospital is to their hometowns, the voters of Northfield rank Northfield first. They rank Easterbrook second because it is the second closest location to them, and West Egg third and Southtown fourth for the same reason. Because there are 45 voters in Northfield, Northfield receives $45 \times (3 \text{ points})$, or 135 points. Easterbrook receives $45 \times (2 \text{ points})$, or 90 points; West Egg receives $45 \times (1 \text{ point})$, or 45 points. Southtown receives no points from Northfield's residents.

That process is repeated for each of the other three towns:

- The 40 voters in Easterbrook award themselves 120 points, Northfield 80 points, West Egg 40 points, and Southtown nothing.

- West Egg's 50 voters award themselves 150 points, Easterbrook 100 points, Northfield 50 points, and Southtown nothing.

- The 65 residents of Southtown award themselves 195 points, West Egg 130 points, Easterbrook 65 points, and Northfield nothing.

After all the ballots have been cast and counted, the big winner is Easterbrook, which edges out West Egg by a score of 375–365. Thomas was right: Figuring out the winner did take a bit of effort. But surely the payoff shows that the Borda-count method doesn't have the inherent weaknesses of the other voting methods, right?

Wrong! In fact, the Borda method is just as flawed as the others. To demonstrate this, let's again go back in time to the point where Clara Nightingale was announcing the rules. She's just outlined the Borda-count procedures, and the residents in attendance have taken a few minutes to discuss them. That's when Olson Johnson, the current mayor of Northfield, stands up and makes an important announcement: "We, the proud residents of Northfield, recognize that the great distance between our town and Southtown dooms us to lose this election. We would like to leave this room with our heads held high, so we're doing the honorable thing and removing our town from contention."

Borda-count method A voting method in which each voter ranks alternatives and awards more points to higher-ranked alternatives and fewer points to lower-ranked alternatives. The alternative that receives the most total points from all voters wins.

"Olson Johnson is right," declares Clara. "Northfield cannot win. So, voters, rank the three remaining towns, Southtown, West Egg, and Easterbrook. We will give 2 points to a town receiving a first-place ranking, 1 point for a second-place ranking, and nothing for a third-place ranking. Let the voting begin!" And when the results are tallied, Southtown finishes with 130 points, Easterbrook ends up with 220, and the winner is West Egg, with a whopping 250 points.

But wait! Last time we used the Borda count, Easterbrook was the winner. And now, just because we threw out a town that wasn't going to win anyway, the winner switches to West Egg? That doesn't seem like a very good thing, does it?

No, it doesn't. In this case, the outcome of the election depends on the inclusion or exclusion of what economists call an *irrelevant alternative*—a choice voters might face that won't win under the best of circumstances. Throw out that alternative, and voters pick an entirely different town—despite the fact that the excluded alternative was irrelevant.

This is such a disturbing phenomenon that economists have given it a special name. They call it the *reversal paradox*, and it is incredibly odd and troublesome. To demonstrate, consider this analogy: You walk into a restaurant to order a piece of pie, and the waiter says, "We have apple, peach, and pecan."

"Fine," you reply. "I'll take pecan."

"Oh, hold on," the waiter says. "My mistake—we're out of apple."

"Well in that case," you say, "I'll have peach."

The point is that ideally the winner of an election should not depend on alternatives and choices that can't possibly prevail. In the words of Stanford University's Nobel Prize–winning economist Kenneth Arrow, in a good voting system, the outcome should be *independent of irrelevant alternatives*. That's clearly not the case with the Borda count, nor is it the case with many other systems.

The Instant Runoff Method

Once again, let's turn back the clock on our gathering, back to when Clara Nightingale gathered her board to discuss an alternative set of procedures in the wake of the original Southtown victory. Clara informs the board that the Condorcet method might not produce a winner, and that the results of the Borda count could prove sensitive to the inclusion of irrelevant alternatives. So she proposes a fourth method that seems to have a lot of appeal in that it systematically eliminates irrelevant alternatives. The system Clara announces is called an **instant runoff method**, which is sometimes called a *single transferrable vote system*.

"Okay, voters!" Clara says. "I'd like each of you to rank the cities in order. When we've received your ballots, we'll find the city with the fewest first-place votes and eliminate it. Anyone who voted for that city will have their first-place vote transferred to the town they liked next best. We'll continue to eliminate cities until there's only one left, and at that point, the surviving city will be named the winner."

And when the ballots come in, the results look as shown in Table 13.1.

Instant runoff method A voting method in which voters initially rank alternatives, and the alternative with the fewest first-place votes is eliminated. That alternative's votes are transferred to each voter's next-favorite choice, and the process repeats until a winner emerges.

Table 13.1	Hospital Location Preferences of Residents			
Based on where a particular voter lives, the possible locations for the hospital are ranked, in order, from most preferred to least preferred.				
	Northfield (45 votes)	**Easterbrook (40 votes)**	**Southtown (65 votes)**	**West Egg (50 votes)**
1st choice	Northfield	Easterbrook	Southtown	West Egg
2nd choice	Easterbrook	Northfield	West Egg	Easterbrook
3rd choice	West Egg	West Egg	Easterbrook	Northfield
4th choice	Southtown	Southtown	Northfield	Southtown

Table 13.1 indicates that Northfield voters prefer Northfield to Easterbrook, Easterbrook to West Egg, and West Egg to Southtown. So Northfield gets Northfield's 45 first-place votes. The other ballots end up giving Easterbrook 40 first-place votes, Southtown 65 first-place votes, and West Egg 50 first-place votes. "Easterbrook has only 40 votes, and is therefore eliminated," Clara announces. "Let's transfer everyone's Easterbrook votes to their next-best choice."

If you're seeing this for the first time, the process isn't easy to visualize. Taking it step by step helps. First, erase the word *Easterbrook* everywhere it appears in the table. (But don't delete it from the header, because residents of Easterbrook still get to vote; they just can't win.) Table 13.2 shows how the results look with Easterbrook eliminated.

Table 13.2 Hospital Location Preferences with Easterbrook Removed from Contention				
Easterbrook, with the fewest first-place votes, is eliminated from contention. Blank spaces now appear where Easterbrook appeared previously.				
	Northfield (45 votes)	Easterbrook (40 votes)	Southtown (65 votes)	West Egg (50 votes)
1st choice	Northfield		Southtown	West Egg
2nd choice		Northfield	West Egg	
3rd choice	West Egg	West Egg		Northfield
4th choice	Southtown	Southtown	Northfield	Southtown

Now, move the towns that were ranked below Easterbrook up a slot, and remove the row for 4th choice, as shown in Table 13.3:

Table 13.3 Hospital Location Preferences with Easterbrook's Votes Transferred				
After Easterbrook is eliminated, each resident's Easterbrook vote is transferred to the next-best town still in contention.				
	Northfield (45 votes)	Easterbrook (40 votes)	Southtown (65 votes)	West Egg (50 votes)
1st choice	Northfield	Northfield	Southtown	West Egg
2nd choice	West Egg	West Egg	West Egg	Northfield
3rd choice	Southtown	Southtown	Northfield	Southtown

At this point, the process begins again. Notice that Northfield now has 85 first-place votes (45 from Northfield and 40 from Easterbrook), Southtown has 65, and West Egg has 50. So we can eliminate West Egg. The remaining two contenders and their associated vote counts are shown in Table 13.4:

Table 13.4 Final Vote Counts in the Hospital Voting Problem				
Vote tallies for the hospital-location problem, with Easterbrook and West Egg eliminated and their votes transferred to the next-best contender.				
	Northfield (45 votes)	Easterbrook (40 votes)	Southtown (65 votes)	West Egg (50 votes)
1st choice	Northfield	Northfield	Southtown	Northfield
2nd choice	Southtown	Southtown	Northfield	Southtown

As Table 13.4 indicates, in the final runoff election, Northfield clinches the victory with 135 votes to Southtown's 65.

U.S. Presidential Elections and the Will of the People

If the goal of a voting system is to reflect the will of the people, the system the United States uses to elect its presidents is certainly a curiosity. That's because the U.S. electoral system contains provisions that seem to deliberately drive a wedge between the ballots voters cast and the outcome of the election. Consider these features of the U.S. electoral system:

- Americans don't vote directly for president. Instead, they vote for electors from their state who are affiliated with a particular presidential candidate. Those electors constitute the electoral college and will later cast *their* votes—the votes that count—for president.

- In the electoral college, each state is allocated as many electors as it has members of Congress—one for each senator and representative. Because each state, no matter how large or how small, has exactly two senators, the electoral college gives people from small states a disproportionately large voice in choosing the president. Wyoming, with about 570,000 residents, has three electoral votes; Rhode Island has about twice as many residents as Wyoming but has only one more electoral vote.

- In almost every state, the presidential candidate who wins the popular vote gets all of that state's electoral votes: Win a state 50.01% to 49.99%, and you receive 100% of the state's electoral votes. This "winner take all" system mathematically separates the vote that elects the president from the vote of the people, and it dramatically increases the influence of "spoilers," candidates who cannot win a state but who can draw enough votes away from one candidate to swing that state's electoral votes to another candidate.

- Electors generally pledge to vote for a particular candidate. But sometimes, "faithless electors" abdicate their responsibility and either abstain entirely or switch their vote to another candidate. There have been about 150 documented cases of faithlessness in the electoral college.

- To be elected president, a candidate must win a majority of the 538 electoral votes. If there are more than two candidates, it is possible to have no majority winner. In that case, the election is turned over to the House of Representatives. There, each state delegation casts a single vote for one of the top three contenders to determine the winner.

Separating the outcome of the election from the ballot box in the way the electoral college does has caused problems that many people believe are quite serious. Three presidents—Rutherford B. Hayes, Benjamin Harrison, and George W. Bush—won in the electoral college despite losing the popular vote. In 1800, Thomas Jefferson won in the House of Representatives after tying with *vice-presidential* candidate Aaron Burr in the electoral college. Finally, in 1824, Andrew Jackson lost the popular vote, but when no candidate gained a majority of electoral votes, Jackson was elected president by the House of Representatives.

In other words, about 10% of the time, the winner of the popular vote walked home in defeat, beaten not by his opponent but by the machinery of the electoral college.

See related problem 1.13 on page 272 at the end of this chapter.

Based on William Poundstone's *Gaming the Vote* (Hill and Wang, 2008), George C. Edwards's *Why the Electoral College is Bad for America* (Yale University Press, 2011), and William Kimberling's "The Electoral College," available at the Federal Election Commission website, www.fec.gov.

Voting Methods and Arrow's Impossibility Theorem

We've now used four different ways to count the votes in an election. Table 13.5 recaps the outcome each method produces.

Table 13.5 The Outcome of the Hospital Voting Problem Under Various Election Methods	
In the hospital voting problem, each different election method produces a different winning city.	
Election Method	**Winning City**
Plurality rule	Southtown
Condorcet method	West Egg
Borda count	Easterbrook
Instant runoff	Northfield

As Table 13.5 shows, each method produces a different winner. That seems problematic, doesn't it? And doesn't it beg the question, "Which way is the right way?" Or maybe, "Which way is the *best* way?"

Unfortunately, the answer (thanks to some heavy mathematical wrangling by Kenneth Arrow) is that there *is* no voting system that can consistently make a fair choice among three or more candidates: All voting systems contain some inherent drawback that may prevent them from accurately capturing the preferences of the electorate in all circumstances. In other words, there is no best system. That startling conclusion is formalized as **Arrow's impossibility theorem**.[2]

That's pretty discouraging. It's even more discouraging when we consider the implications from a strategic perspective: Given that four different voting methods can produce four different outcomes, if Clara Nightingale happens to be a resident of Easterbrook, she can get the hospital located in her hometown by choosing the Borda-count method to tabulate the election results. In other words, she who sets the election rules can also (at least sometimes) determine the outcome. *That's* strategic behavior.

If you guessed that we haven't discussed every possible voting system, you're right: There are virtually an infinite number of possible voting systems. But looking at these four basic systems has allowed us to uncover the flaws that Arrow proved are common to *all* voting systems.

Arrow's impossibility theorem The conclusion that all voting systems used to choose from three or more alternatives contain some inherent drawback that can prevent them from accurately capturing the preferences of the electorate in all circumstances.

Conventional Political Elections and the Median Voter Theorem

13.2 Learning Objective

Define *median voter theorem* and explain how it works.

You may be wondering if the hospital example we discussed is realistic. After all, it seems a bit simplistic to vote for one town just because it's a little closer to you, doesn't it? And truthfully, you'll probably never have occasion to vote on the location of a regional hospital. What on Earth does this geography lesson have to do with how we vote, for example, in presidential elections or on school board referenda? Actually, more than you might think.

To answer this question, let's look at a more conventional type of election. For simplicity, assume that there are exactly seven voters (Lilith, Diane, Woody, Sam, Norm, Rebecca, and Cliff), and they're voting to elect someone to represent them in Congress. The voters have different views about social and economic issues: Some are liberal (L) and some are conservative (C), in varying degrees. If we wanted to, we could order these voters based on their political views, with the most liberal voter on

---

[2]More specifically, Arrow's 1950 *Journal of Political Economy* paper "A Difficulty in the Concept of Social Welfare" showed that no voting system can exist which satisfies four minimal conditions: transitivity, unanimity (if everyone prefers A to B, A wins), non-dictatorship (there is more than one voter), and independence of irrelevant alternatives.

the far left and the most conservative voter on the far right. A picture of that ordering might look something like this:

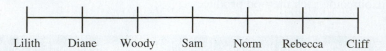

Note that Sam is the voter in the middle of the pack. He's a political moderate. The technical name for Sam is the *median voter*—literally, the voter in the middle. On the far left is Lilith, an extreme liberal. Cliff, an extreme conservative, is on the far right.

Now let's add a label to each position that indicates the voter's political inclinations. Sam gets a big M, since he's the median voter. To his left, Woody, Diane, and Lilith receive labels of L1, L2, and L3, respectively, with L3 representing Lilith, who is the most liberal voter. To Sam's right, let's label Norm C1, Rebecca C2, and Cliff C3. Now the spectrum of voters looks like this:

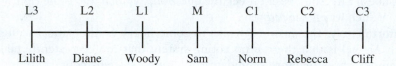

The voters are in position, and their preferences have been indicated. What happens when some candidates are added to the ballot? Running for Congress in the Big First Congressional District today will be Les and Charles, who are, at heart, liberal and conservative, respectively.

Who will each voter vote for? It makes sense to conclude that the voters will vote for the candidate whose platform is most closely aligned with their own preferences. In other words, if the candidates were positioned on the political preference line we've drawn, a voter would choose the candidate closest to him or her. That's why the discussion of voting began with an example based on geography: When it comes to voting, distance is distance, whether it's measured in miles or in some unit of social policy. This is so true that economic and political science studies of voting don't rely on a foundation of politics but instead are built on the tools of geometry—literally, "Earth measuring"—the study of sizes, shapes, positions, and, of course, distances.

Candidate Positioning and the Median Voter Theorem

When it comes to an election, a town can't easily change its location, but it's possible for a politician to change his or her political position. If the candidates can position themselves where they'd like on the political preference line, exactly where will they choose to locate? Remember that Les is liberal and Charles is conservative. Let's position them on the line. First, let's put each candidate at the most extreme position consistent with his internally held views. The political preference line now looks like this, with Les at L3 and Charles at C3:

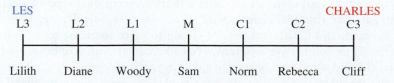

How will this election play out? As it turns out, the answer is uncertain. Norm, Rebecca, and Cliff will vote for Charles because he's closer to their positions than Les is. Lilith, Diane, and Woody will vote for Les because he's closer to their positions than Charles is. But Sam is equidistant from both Les and Charles, and as a result he'll have a hard time deciding whom to vote for. For all intents and purposes, this election will be decided by a coin toss.

Of course, if you're a political candidate, you hate to leave something as fat as a congressional pension up to a coin flip. Is there any way you might increase your odds of winning this election?

Yes, there is. Consider Les: He's taken an extreme position and has captured the votes of all the liberals. To win this election, though, he's going to have to capture at least the moderate vote, which is represented by Sam, the median voter. Les can garner the necessary votes by shifting his position one position to the right. In a real-world context, he might do this by making an unexpected statement that he supports a stronger national defense or that he vows to cut income taxes (both of which are policies that would be unexpected coming from a hardcore liberal candidate). Now the political preference line looks like this:

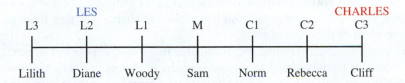

When the voting begins, Charles will still capture the votes of Norm, Rebecca, and Cliff, and Les is still *way* closer to Lilith, Diane, and Woody than Charles is. But look at what Les's move has done to Sam, who now says to himself: "Wow, Les came out in support of a 600-ship navy; he's not as liberal as I thought he was. I agree that we need a stronger national defense, and I thought only Charles would support that. And Charles's policy on the estate tax is *way* too conservative for my tastes, so I'm voting 'Yes for Les' in this election!" And if you measure carefully, you'll find that Sam is only two positions away from Les, but he's three from Charles. Les's strategic statement has sealed up the win!

Or has it? It's sealed up the win as long as Charles stays where he is. But if moving toward the middle can help Les win the election, then moving toward the middle is likely to help Charles, too. So suppose that Charles hears Les's strong pro-defense message and responds with a statement about public health care that is so liberal, it repositions him *two* notches to the left. Here's what the preference line looks like now:

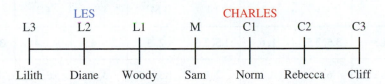

Making this political move has brought Charles large gains. Now Sam, Norm, Rebecca, and Cliff hold values closer to his stated position, while Lilith, Diane, and Woody are closer to Les's. Voila! Charles's repositioning allows him to steal the election away from Les by a vote of 4–3.

But, of course, Les isn't locked into his L2 position. With one single press conference, he can come out in favor of school vouchers and shift his position two slots to the right, and the preference line shifts:

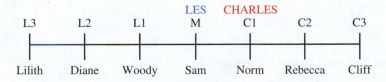

That political maneuvering will allow Les to recapture the election, winning 4–3, unless Charles responds. And the only response that will do Charles any good at all is to also move toward the center, positioning himself in *exactly the same place* as Les! Here's what it looks like:

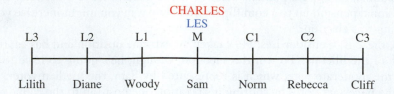

Once again, the election has become a virtual toss-up between the two candidates. But notice what has happened: Natural forces have induced the two candidates, who were quite extreme at the outset, to advocate policies that are palatable to the more typical, median voter. Economists and political scientists call this move toward the center the **median voter theorem**; it states that in an ordinary election between two candidates, the candidates will position themselves in such a way that their platforms reflect the views of the median voter.

It is worth noting that once the candidates move to the political center, neither has an incentive to move back toward one of the extremes. This result resembles a Nash equilibrium—an outcome where both parties are playing their best responses to one another and where neither party has an incentive to change his or her mind (see Chapter 3).

In fact, the moves Les and Charles made can easily be represented as a game, as shown in Figure 13.2. The two players are Les and Charles, and each can choose from one of the seven available positions on the political spectrum, from L3 to C3. The payoffs in the cells represent the number of votes each player will receive, given his position versus his opponent's. (When the two candidates are equidistant from a particular voter, each receives half a vote.)

That's a very large payoff matrix. But a best-response analysis shows that despite its size, this game has a single Nash equilibrium: It's right where both candidates choose position M. In other words, the median voter theorem is just another way of saying that candidates will gravitate to the only Nash equilibrium in the game.

Median voter theorem The conclusion that in an ordinary election between two candidates, the candidates will position themselves in such a way that their platforms reflect the views of the median voter.

▶ Figure 13.2
The Median Voter Theorem as a Two-Player Game
In this game, Les (in black) and Charles (in blue) can choose any position on the political spectrum. The single Nash equilibrium is found where both Les and Charles locate themselves at the median voter's position.

		Charles						
		L3	**L2**	**L1**	**M**	**C1**	**C2**	**C3**
Les	**L3**	3.5, 3.5	1, 6	1.5, 5.5	2, 5	2.5, 4.5	3, 4	3.5, 3.5
	L2	6, 1	3.5, 3.5	2, 5	2.5, 4.5	3, 4	3.5, 3.5	4, 3
	L1	5.5, 1.5	5, 2	3.5, 3.5	3, 4	3.5, 3.5	4, 3	4.5, 2.5
	M	5, 2	4.5, 2.5	4, 3	3.5, 3.5	4, 3	4.5, 2.5	5, 2
	C1	4.5, 2.5	4, 3	3.5, 3.5	3, 4	3.5, 3.5	5, 2	5.5, 1.5
	C2	4, 3	3.5, 3.5	3, 4	2.5, 4.5	2, 5	3.5, 3.5	6, 1
	C3	3.5, 3.5	3, 4	2.5, 4.5	2, 5	1.5, 5.5	1, 6	3.5, 3.5

Why the Median Voter Theorem Might Fail

It's not just researchers and economists who believe in the power of the median voter theorem. Anecdotal evidence suggests that the theorem works pretty well in the real world. For example, people often complain that political candidates look too

Application 13.2

Dangerous Voters: Rational, Irrational, or Both?

Democracy gives power to the people, but, paradoxically, democracies often adopt policies that are harmful to most people. This chapter shows why various voting methods might result in poor policies. However, it's possible that there's another culprit to blame: Voters themselves may cause the paradox of democracy.

Some people believe poor government is the result of low voter turnout and wonder why more people don't vote. Oddly, economists wonder why so many people *do* vote. After all, voting requires both time and effort, and the tangible benefits of voting are small: Your vote matters only if you cast the *deciding vote* that tips the election from the candidate you don't like to the candidate you do like. Because that's generally unlikely, cost–benefit analysis suggests that it's perfectly rational not to vote.

Other people believe poor government is the result of ill-informed voters. These people wonder, "How can society expect good policy when voters don't know what good policy is?" To economists, however, voter ignorance makes perfect sense: Researching the issues is costly, and one vote is unlikely to be decisive, so why study the issues if you can't change the outcome? In other words, it's completely rational for voters to remain ignorant. Economists refer to that as *rational ignorance.*

Here's some good news: If the voters' ignorance is random, the mistakes they make may cancel each other out. For example, if one voter overestimates the benefits of a school voucher program, whereas another underestimates those benefits, their votes will negate one another at the ballot box. Voters who measure the program's benefits correctly will then ultimately decide the issue. In other words, rational ignorance may still result in good policy.

Economist Bryan Caplan of George Mason University, however, isn't so optimistic that this is what happens. Caplan has collected a considerable amount of survey evidence that suggests that voters' ignorance isn't random. Rather, voters bring systematic biases to the ballot box. Caplan points to four types of bias:

- **Anti-market bias:** Underestimating the economic benefits of the market system
- **Anti-foreign bias:** Underestimating the economic benefits of interaction with foreigners
- **Make-work bias:** Assuming that job creation implies economic progress
- **Pessimistic bias:** Underestimating the performance of the economy

Consider free trade. Voters may understand that free trade makes society richer. But in their hearts, they hold an anti-foreign bias that predisposes them to favor restricting trade. Because they know their votes are unlikely to be decisive, these voters sometimes ignore the fact that free trade makes them better off and do something that feels good to them: Indulge their anti-foreign bias by voting to restrict trade. Caplan says, "Why control your knee-jerk emotional and ideological reactions if you can't change the outcome?"[3]

Caplan calls such behavior *rational irrationality* and warns that because those biases are systematically one-sided, voter errors don't cancel one another out. When the ballots are counted, votes that were perfectly harmless when made individually add up and result in laws and policies being passed that everyone agrees are bad for society. That explanation of the paradox of democracy echoes the words of 20th-century journalist and social critic H. L. Mencken: "Democracy is the theory that the common people know what they want, and deserve to get it good and hard."

See related problems 2.4 and 2.5 on page 273 at the end of this chapter.

Based on Bryan Caplan's *The Myth of the Rational Voter: Why Democracies Choose Bad Policies*, Princeton University Press, 2008; "Fractured Franchise: Are the Wrong People Voting?" *The New Yorker*, July 9, 2007; and "Clueless," *The New York Times*, May 27, 2007.

[3]Bryan Caplan, *The Myth of the Rational Voter: Why Democracies Choose Bad Policies*, Princeton University Press, 2008.

much alike, which is consistent with the predictions of the median voter theorem. Furthermore, political candidates often say one thing today and another thing tomorrow, as if they're repositioning themselves along the political preference line. But at the same time, if candidates are supposed to be moving toward political positions that represent the views of the typical, most moderate, voter, then it's curious that so many people are unsatisfied with the politicians the theorem predicts they'll get. Is the median voter theorem flawed, too?

Immobile Candidates   To determine whether there is a flaw in the median voter theorem, let's go back to Les and Charles. Recall that they originally positioned themselves at points consistent with their true beliefs—Les on the far left and Charles on the far right. Now suppose that suddenly, just before the filing deadline, a third candidate, Glen, enters the race. Glen, like Charles, is an arch-conservative. But there's a major difference between Glen and Charles. Charles is willing to modify his political stance to cater to the voters, which makes him sound pretty shifty but really helps the bulk of voters get what they want. But Glen is a mighty oak of conservatism who will not bend. He has publicly vowed to drop out of the race before he will consider changing his platform. With Glen's agenda cast in stone (well, at least in hardwood), let's revisit the political preference line to see how the campaigning will unfold:

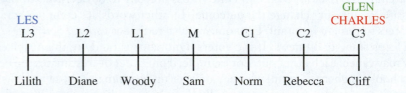

At the beginning of the election season, Les is on the far left, and Glen and Charles are on the far right. If the election were to be held today, Les would end up with three votes from Lilith, Diane, and Woody; Glen and Charles would split Norm's, Rebecca's, and Cliff's votes, for one and a half each; and Sam would be unable to decide among the three (so let's split Sam's vote three ways and give each of our candidates an equal share). The point is that when Glen enters the race, his candidacy tips the election in Les's direction.

The only way for Charles to regain the ground Glen cost him is to alter his position. He could choose just about any of the remaining positions and improve his chances of winning (except for L3, of course—then he'd just end up splitting votes with Les instead of Glen). To do this, suppose Charles makes a moderate political pronouncement that moves him exactly to the middle. The political preference line now looks like this:

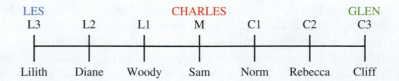

This really is an advantageous position for Charles; if the election were to be held right now, Les and Glen would walk away with two votes each, from the extreme liberals and conservatives from the ends of the spectrum. But Charles, by moving to the center, has Woody, Sam, and Norm walking through neighborhoods and carrying "Charles in Charge" signs. With their three votes, he's headed for victory.

But there's still time left to campaign, and although Glen's campaigning was essentially over the minute he made his "mighty oak" speech, Les still has a chance to regain lost ground. But where should Les position himself? If he moves to the right of Charles, the entire liberal side of the spectrum and Sam will end up voting for conservative Charles, and Les will split the conservative vote with Glen. So Les can go no further than the median. If he positions himself at the median, he and Charles will split everything on the left two ways, and they'll split everything on the right in a three-way division with Glen. That will put Les and Charles in a statistical dead heat, with Glen bringing up the rear.

However, suppose that Les positions himself just to the left of Charles:

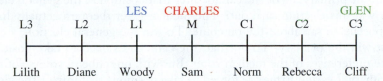

Now Les will pick up three votes from Lilith, Diane, and Woody; Rebecca and Cliff will vote for Glen; and Sam and Norm will vote for Charles. "Les is More," the liberals shout, as they prepare to carry their champion off to the inaugural ball.

"But wait!" Charles says. "I'm not done changing my views! And I'd like to come out in favor of a new government jobs bill, my support for which will move me the teensiest bit to the political left!" Here's what the political preference line looks like now:

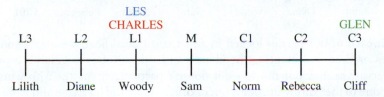

And with this final maneuver, the die is cast. Les and Charles split the votes of Lilith, Diane, Woody, and Sam, getting two votes each. Glen walks away with Rebecca and Cliff's votes, and Norm can't decide among the three candidates. They are all equidistant from him on the political line, so no one is preferable to the others. If you check very carefully, you'll find that neither Glen nor Les can improve the outcome by changing positions; Glen, the only candidate who can make a move and make himself better off, won't. That turns the race into a three-way tie, where each candidate has an equal chance of winning. In the end, a majority of the time, one of the mainstream candidates will win, but every once in a while (one-third of the time, to be precise) Glen, the dark horse, will bring home the victory.

That's all well and good, but remember that the purpose of this exercise is to show why so many voters are displeased with the product of the political system. In other words, we wanted to explain why the median voter theorem might not work in the real world. Now there appears to be at least one valid explanation. Look at the political line again: Any one of the three candidates might win this election, yet *none* of them are positioned at the center. Charles, in particular, had to take great pains to distance himself from the arch-conservative Glen (not because arch-conservatism is necessarily unpalatable but simply to avoid splitting votes with him). In fact, to achieve that distance, Charles actually had to become a moderate liberal! That, in turn, gave Les room to remain a bit more liberal than he would have been in a two-candidate election. So, our voters will end up with a moderate liberal or an extreme conservative in office. The one thing they *won't* get is a candidate who reflects the views of the median voter.

Runoff Elections Even if a race doesn't have an arch-conservative or an arch-liberal who pushes the more moderate candidates toward the extremes of the political line, we may *still* end up with candidates who are less representative of the typical voter than we'd like.

To understand how this can occur, let's modify our election rules just a smidge. Let's make our election a *runoff election*, where liberal and conservative candidates are chosen in primary elections, and the winners of the primaries face off in a general election.

Let's again let Les be a liberal and Charles be a conservative. But now let's add two more candidates to the fray—Ernie on the left and Robin on the right. Les and Ernie will be vying for the liberal nomination, and Charles and Robin will be vying for the conservative nomination. Let's also assume that only liberal voters (Lilith, Diane, and Woody) can vote in the liberal primary between Les and Ernie, and only conservative voters (Norm, Rebecca, and Cliff) can vote in the conservative primary between Charles and Robin. Sam, the moderate, has registered as an independent and cannot vote in either primary. Finally, assume that if a candidate establishes a political position in the primary, he or she cannot alter that position in the general election.

How will this election turn out? The median voter theorem actually has something important to say about the outcome. To win the general election, a candidate must first win the primary. To do that, the candidates need to take positions that reflect the preferences of the median voter. But with only liberal voters voting in the liberal primary, Les and Ernie are forced to take positions that mirror the view of the median *liberal* voter, Diane. Over on the right, Charles and Robin are maneuvering into a position that reflects the preferences of Rebecca, the median conservative voter:

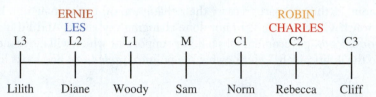

With each of our parties locked in a statistical dead heat, we could end up with either Les or Ernie representing the liberals and either Robin or Charles representing the conservatives. For our purposes, it doesn't particularly matter who wins, so let's throw a bone to the "throw the bums out of office" folks and let Ernie and Robin prevail:

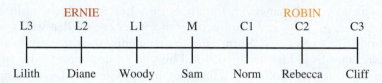

Most important for our purposes is that the candidates established their positions in the primaries, and so there isn't any wiggle room to change those positions in the general election. Consequently, voters in the general election see a slate of candidates whose platforms are quite different than the views of the typical voter.

13.3 Learning Objective

Demonstrate how the order of events in a runoff election can affect the outcome.

Strategic Voting and the Order of Events in Runoff Elections

We've explored a number of reasons elections may yield outcomes that are unsatisfactory to the general electorate. One reason mentioned in Section 13.1 is that the person running the election might choose an election method that's favorable to the outcome she desires. But that's not the only power the person running the election has. Even if the person running the election is forced to use a particular method, sometimes just controlling the order of events in that election can steer the election toward her desired outcome.

To illustrate, consider three roommates, Janet, Jack, and Chrissy, who want to determine an official beverage for the household. The three candidates are beer, wine, and pink lemonade. The roommates do a quick survey of their preferences and discover the following:

• Janet prefers beer to wine and wine to pink lemonade.
• Jack prefers wine to pink lemonade and pink lemonade to beer.
• Chrissy prefers pink lemonade to beer and beer to wine.

Chrissy, who owns the house, says, "Clearly there is no Condorcet winner among these choices. And if we used a Borda count, we'd get a tie. So it looks like our only option is to have a runoff election. We'll pit two of the choices against one another in a preliminary round, and the winner will face off against the remaining choice in the finals." The others, dazzled by Chrissy's ability to assess the outcomes of Condorcet and Borda-count elections without a calculator, spreadsheet, or even pencil and paper, wordlessly nod their heads in awe.

The Agenda Paradox

Chrissy is pretty sharp, and she really likes pink lemonade. Therefore, she contemplates the following: "As the homeowner, I'm in charge of setting up the runoff election. I wonder if I can use that power to engineer the outcome in favor of pink lemonade." And after a few moments of deliberation, she realizes she can. She tells Janet and Jack, "Okay, in the first round, we'll pit beer against wine. The winner of that contest will face pink lemonade for the win."

The first-round ballots roll in, and as expected, Janet and Chrissy vote for beer, and Jack votes for wine. "Beer it is," Chrissy announces. She then passes out slips of paper for the second-round vote between beer and pink lemonade. When the ballots come in, Chrissy and Jack have voted for pink lemonade, and Janet's favorite, beer, has lost the election.

The election did not have to turn out this way. If the group had pitted wine against pink lemonade in the first round, then wine would have won, only to lose to beer in the second round. Alternatively, if the group had pitted pink lemonade against beer in the first round, pink lemonade would have prevailed but would have been beaten by wine in the finals. So Chrissy, by setting the *agenda*—the order of events—played a key role in determining the outcome. The fact that the outcome of an election is sensitive to the order of events is called the **agenda paradox**, and it's one more reason voters in an election might get an outcome that they dislike.

You now know something about Chrissy: She's sharp, cunning, and manipulative. But you don't yet know much about Janet and Jack. Frankly, the way things have been presented so far, they don't look like the brightest crayons in the box. But maybe that's because we just assumed that Jack and Janet would simply sit idly by and let Chrissy steal the election away from them. What if Jack and Janet know that Chrissy is going to try to manipulate the election? Is there any way they can stop her?

Strategic and Naive Voting

If the power to set the agenda is Chrissy's, the only option Janet and Jack have is to somehow change the way they vote. Until this point, we've assumed that Janet and Jack would vote in accordance with their true preferences. Such voting is called **naive voting**. However, it's possible for them to cast votes inconsistent with their preferences (vote for something they don't really like in a round) to get an outcome they prefer to pink lemonade. Such voting is called **strategic voting**.

Assume for now that the agenda is set: Beer will meet wine in the first round, and the winner will face pink lemonade in the second. How can Jack or Janet use strategic voting to counter Chrissy's power play?

You'll remember that in the first round, beer was pitted against wine, with beer pulling down votes from Janet and Chrissy. Although Jack prefers wine to beer, he has no incentive to vote strategically; changing his vote from wine to beer simply turns a 2–1 beer victory into a 3–0 beer victory, with no effect on the outcome of either the first round or the second round. In other words, if anyone can benefit from casting a strategic vote, it must be Janet.

Let's see what that might accomplish. In reality, Janet prefers beer to wine, and when she was voting naively, beer is what she chose. But by doing that, she cemented a first-round beer victory, only to see beer lose to pink lemonade in the finals. In the end, Janet got the drink that she liked the least of the three.

But suppose that Janet votes strategically in the first round. In other words, even though she likes beer more than wine, she votes for wine. Janet's strategic vote changes a 2–1 win for beer into a 1–2 loss for the frothy amber beverage. Now wine advances to the finals, where it faces pink lemonade. With everyone voting their true preferences in the finals, Janet and Jack vote for wine, and wine walks away with

Agenda paradox A situation in which the outcome of an election is sensitive to the order of events.

Naive voting Voting in accordance with one's true preferences.

Strategic voting Voting against one's preferences in the initial rounds of a runoff election in order to prevent the selection of an undesirable alternative in the final round.

Application 13.3

Choosing Planes: Agenda Influence in the Real World

Amateur pilot Michael Levine had been given a tough job: The Los Angeles area flying club he belonged to was replacing the airplanes it rented to its members. Club members asked Levine, a professor at the California Institute of Technology (CalTech), to design the voting system the club would use to choose the new fleet.

Levine wasn't sure how to design a fair voting system, so he called economist Charlie Plott, a fellow club member and colleague at CalTech, for advice. Plott told him that there is no "best" system and that different systems can easily generate different outcomes. He suggested that Levine should develop a system that would yield the type of fleet Levine, himself, desired. "Let's see if we can arrange things that way," Plott said.

The club had already narrowed the choices to four types of aircraft: the Beechcraft A36 six-seater (denoted A), the Beechcraft F33 four-seater (F), the Beechcraft E33 four-seater (E), and the Cessna 210 six-seater (C). Levine wanted a fleet of five four-seaters (three Es and two Fs) and two six-seat Cessnas (two Cs); he hoped to avoid the expensive Beechcraft A36. Based on anecdotal knowledge of members' preferences, Levine and Plott set about writing an agenda designed to steer the club's choice toward Levine's ideal fleet. "This was no simple task," they write. "There were many alternatives, there were over fifty members, and tastes . . . differed radically."[4] Ultimately, they created the following 4-question agenda, to be voted on in order:

Which aircraft (A, F, E, or C) should be in the primary fleet? (decided by a Borda count)

How many planes (six or seven) do we want?

Do we want a mix of four- and six-seat planes?

What type of aircraft (C or A) should be in our secondary fleet?

During voting, the club's president repeatedly attempted to reorganize the agenda in ways that favored his own preferred fleet. But the club stuck to Levine's plan, and in the end, Levine got exactly what he wanted, defeating what he and Plott believed to be the most popular option—a mixed fleet containing two of the expensive A36s.

Later, Plott and Levine sent members a follow-up questionnaire that asked more precise questions about their preferences. What that questionnaire revealed is stunning. First, had the club president been successful in hijacking the agenda, he would have secured his ideal fleet—a fleet that contained two of the costly A36s. Second, a fleet consisting of three Es, three Fs, and one A would have been a Condorcet winner, beating all other options in head-to-head pairings. By carefully arranging the order of events in the election, Levine had defeated an indisputable favorite and in the process had documented for the first time the potential power an agenda setter has in manipulating the outcome of an election.

See related problem 3.6 on page 273 at the end of this chapter.

Based on Michael E. Levine and Charles R. Plott's "Agenda Influence and Its Implications," *Virginia Law Review*, May 1977; Plott and Levine's "A Model of Agenda Influence on Committee Decisions," *American Economic Review*, March 1978; William H. Riker's *The Art of Political Manipulation (Yale University Press, 1986)*, and personal correspondence with professors Plott and Levine.

the win.[5] Jack, who gets his first choice, rejoices. Janet is quite pleased to receive her second choice rather than her third. Only Chrissy, her beloved pink lemonade replaced by the drink she likes least, walks away sad. Strategic voting substantially alters the results of the election and reduces Chrissy's power to manipulate the outcome.

---

[4]Michael E. Levine and Charles R. Plott's "Agenda Influence and Its Implications," *Virginia Law Review*, May 1977.

[5]There is never an incentive to vote against your true preference in the final round of voting in a runoff election; by doing so, you can only make yourself worse off.

Conclusion

We are taught from an early age to put the concept of voting on a pedestal. We hear endless talk about the virtues of democracy, about how it's not just our right but also our duty to go out and vote. We hear about how our votes represent the voice of the people.

Now we know the ugly truth: Voting is far from perfect. One reason is because the person in charge of setting the rules of the election has the power to influence the outcome. Moreover, even if that person does not abuse that power, the winner we elect might be more a reflection of the voting procedures than the preferences of the electorate. Even if the rules of the election are set in stone, simply changing the order of events within that election can influence the results. It is also disheartening that our two-party system often produces candidates whose views don't reflect the views of the average voter and that an election's outcome can be determined by an irrelevant alternative.

In short, voting may be a wonderful thing, and you may feel that it's better than any other possible system for collective decision making. But as Kenneth Arrow proved, *it ain't perfect!*

Chapter Summary and Problems

Key Terms

Agenda paradox, p. 269

Arrow's impossibility theorem, p. 261

Borda-count method, p. 257

Condorcet method, p. 255

Instant runoff method, p. 258

Median voter theorem, p. 264

Naive voting, p. 269

Plurality-rule method, p. 254

Strategic voting, p. 269

13.1 An Introduction to Voting Methods, pages 253–261

Use different voting methods to determine the winner of an election.

Summary

Plurality-rule voting does a good job of capturing the preferences of voters, but only when there are just two candidates. When there are three or more options, plurality-rule voting may result in a winner that a majority of the electorate doesn't like. Alternative voting systems have been developed for elections with three or more candidates. The Condorcet method chooses as its winner the candidate who can beat all others in head-to-head pairings. The Borda count asks voters to rank the entire slate of candidates and then awards points to candidates based on how highly each voter ranked them. The instant runoff method also asks voters to rank the candidates. One by one, the weakest candidates are eliminated, and those candidates' votes are transferred to the next-best candidate on each voter's ballot. Arrow's impossibility theorem demonstrates that none of these methods is universally better than the others.

Review Questions

All problems are assignable in MyEconLab.

1.1 In the _____ voting system, each voter gets one vote, which may be cast for whichever candidate he or she chooses. The candidate who gets the most votes wins.

1.2 When the _____ of voting is used, the winner is the candidate who can beat all others in head-to-head elections.

1.3 According to Kenneth Arrow, in an ideal voting system, the outcome should be independent of _____.

1.4 The _____ occurs when voters switch their vote because an irrelevant alternative is thrown out.

1.5 One drawback to the Condorcet method of voting is that _____.

   a. The results are sensitive to irrelevant alternatives

   b. It is possible that the winner is disliked by a majority of voters

   c. The results are sensitive to the order of voting

   d. There may not be a winner

1.6 Each member of a group has transitive preferences. But when a vote is taken, the collective preferences of the group are not transitive. This anomaly is referred to as the _____.

   a. Agenda paradox

   b. Independence of irrelevant alternatives

   c. Condorcet paradox

   d. Reversal paradox

1.7 In a particular voting system, voters initially rank candidates. One by one, the weakest candidates are eliminated, and those candidates' votes are transferred to the next-best candidate on each voter's ballot until one candidate emerges as a majority winner. This method of voting is referred to as the _____.

a. Instant runoff method

b. Plurality rule method

c. Condorcet method

d. Borda-count method

1.8 Arrow's impossibility theorem lets us conclude that _____.

a. Candidates often have the power to position themselves in order to appeal to the greatest number of voters

b. The agenda can potentially alter the outcome in elections with stages

c. Voters should vote strategically, instead of naively

d. There is no voting system that can consistently make a fair choice among three or more candidates

1.9 In the _____, voters rank all candidates, and points are awarded based on how highly each voter ranked candidates. The winner is the candidate with the most points.

a. Plurality rule method

b. Instant runoff method

c. Borda-count method

d. Condorcet method

1.10 Voters might be able to vote for a candidate who will not win under the best of circumstances. This candidate is often referred to as a(n) _____.

a. Nonstarter

b. Median voter

c. Game changer

d. Irrelevant alternative

Problems and Applications

1.11 Four candidates are running for a resident assistant position in their residence hall. The following table indicates the number of voters and their preferences. (For example, nine voters prefer Brent to Chad to Ralph to Dave.) Determine the winner under each of the four voting schemes discussed in Section 13.1: plurality rule, Condorcet, Borda count, and instant runoff.

	Number of Voters and Their Preferences			
	20	12	9	5
1st choice	Dave	Chad	Brent	Ralph
2nd choice	Ralph	Brent	Chad	Brent
3rd choice	Chad	Ralph	Ralph	Chad
4th choice	Brent	Dave	Dave	Dave

1.12 Twenty-one fraternity brothers are trying to choose a place to vacation. Their choices are Panama City, Cancun, Breckenridge, and San Diego. Their subjective rankings of those cities are given in the table below:

	Number of Voters and Their Preferences		
	8	7	6
Really like	Panama City	Cancun	San Diego
A very close second	Breckenridge	Breckenridge	Breckenridge
Only so-so	San Diego	Panama City	Cancun
Hate	Cancun	San Diego	Panama City

The fraternity brothers have decided to use the instant runoff method. Which destination will win the election? Does the table above suggest a potential drawback to the instant runoff method?

1.13 [Related to Application 13.1 on page 260] Your friend says to you, "America is one of the fairest countries in the world because we have a democracy, and we are able to vote for most of our politicians." What information do you think he or she may want to consider, relative to this chapter?

1.14 Arrow's impossibility theorem allows us to conclude that if there are three or more candidates, there is no system of voting that can consistently produce a fair choice. While this is discouraging, it is probably not too surprising that we would have some trouble determining "fairness" in relation to voting. All the voting systems we considered gave each individual the same amount of voting power (not considering individuals who may be setting the agenda). Is this truly fair? Certain individuals may have a greater stake in an issue: Should they have more voting power? Can you think of any other criteria that may warrant giving certain individuals greater voting power on certain issues?

13.2 Conventional Political Elections and the Median Voter Theorem, pages 261–268

Define *median voter theorem* and explain how it works.

Summary

In conventional political elections with two candidates, those candidates often have the power to position themselves in order to appeal to the greatest number of voters. The median voter theorem suggests that both candidates will eventually gravitate to the views held by the median voter. However, the presence of a third, less mobile, candidate may cause the original candidates to position themselves away from the political center. Further, when candidates are chosen in a primary election, they may have to position themselves to win the primary election, leaving them left or right of center in the general election.

Review Questions

All problems are assignable in MyEconLab.

2.1 In races for the U.S. Senate, states usually hold a primary election. The winners of the primary election then face off in a final round of voting called the general election. This method of voting is called a(n) _____ election.

2.2 The _____ states that in an ordinary election between two candidates, the candidates will position themselves in such a way that their platforms reflect the views of the voter in the middle.

Problems and Applications

2.3 Figure 13.2 presents a game-theoretic illustration of the median voter theorem. First, perform best-response analysis on the game presented and verify that the Nash equilibrium is found where both candidates position themselves at the median. Then construct a similar matrix for a five-voter, two-candidate election and repeat the analysis.

2.4 **[Related to Application 13.2 on page 265]** Explain what *rational ignorance* and *rational irrationality* mean in the context of Application 13.2. Which do you think is more dangerous to democracy? Why?

2.5 **[Related to Application 13.2 on page 265]** Carefully review the definition of a collective action problem in Section 1.4 on page 11. Then explain why rational irrationality represents a clear characterization of a collective action problem. Create an example to illustrate the problem.

2.6 In some countries, such as Brazil and Australia, it is mandatory for citizens to vote. Discuss some potential costs and benefits of compulsory voting. Would you argue in favor of compulsory voting in the United States?

2.7 The median voter theorem suggests that both candidates will eventually gravitate to the views held by the median voter. Explain how the U.S. system of electing presidents tends to create candidates who might be labeled as "flip-floppers."

13.3 Strategic Voting and the Order of Events in Runoff Elections, pages 268–270

Demonstrate how the order of events in a runoff election can affect the outcome.

Summary

In an election with stages (such as a runoff election), the order of voting (the agenda) can potentially alter the outcome. That gives extra power to the person who sets the agenda; he or she may reorder the vote in order to produce the outcome he or she prefers. Voters can potentially reduce the agenda setter's power by voting strategically instead of voting naively.

Review Questions

All problems are assignable in MyEconLab.

3.1 _____ refers to a situation in which a person votes in accordance with his or her true preferences.
  a. Rational irrationality
  b. Strategic voting
  c. The reversal paradox
  d. Naive voting

3.2 A particular election's outcome happens to be sensitive to the order of events. If A happens before B, X will win. But if B happens before A, Y will win. This sensitivity is referred to as the _____.
  a. Agenda paradox
  b. Condorcet paradox
  c. Median voter theorem
  d. Reversal paradox

3.3 In a particular election, Jamie decides not to vote for her favorite candidate. Instead, she votes for a candidate she doesn't like in order to prevent someone even worse from winning. Jamie's voting against her true preferences is referred to as _____.

  a. Naive voting
  b. Strategic voting
  c. Intransitivity
  d. A reversal

Problems and Applications

3.4 In Section 13.3, three roommates were trying to decide on an official drink. Janet preferred beer to wine and wine to pink lemonade; Jack preferred wine to pink lemonade and pink lemonade to beer; and Chrissy preferred pink lemonade to beer and beer to wine. Chrissy, the agenda-setter, offered up this observation: "Clearly there is no Condorcet winner among these choices. And if we used a Borda count, we'd get a tie." Was Chrissy correct? Verify both claims.

3.5 In Section 13.3, Janet and Jack foil Chrissy's plans for pink lemonade domination by voting strategically. Suppose Chrissy knows that both Janet and Jack plan to vote strategically if the opportunity presents itself. Can Chrissy rearrange the agenda to once again yield a pink lemonade victory? If so, describe that agenda.

3.6 **[Related to Application 13.3 on page 270]** Consider the information in this chapter on naive versus strategic voting and work through problem 3.5 carefully. Now consider the problem faced by Plott and Levine in Application 13.3. Without giving specific detail, explain how not knowing whether flying club members would vote naively or strategically likely made constructing the agenda more difficult.

Experiment

Looking for a "Goldilocks" Location

This chapter highlighted the notion that it's hard to satisfy all of the people, all of the time. Today, you'll get to test that notion for yourself. Your class has been charged with choosing the site for a new sports arena, which will be located somewhere along a long stretch of highway. You and your classmates live in various locations along that same highway. The closer the arena is placed to your house, the better off you'll be. One by one, students will propose locations for the arena and one by one, everyone in the class will vote on those proposals. Will the arena be placed in your neighborhood? You will need to use your persuasive powers to ensure the highest possible payoff!

Please visit http://www.myeconlab.com for support material to conduct this experiment if assigned by your instructor.

14 The Economics of Health Insurance and Health Care

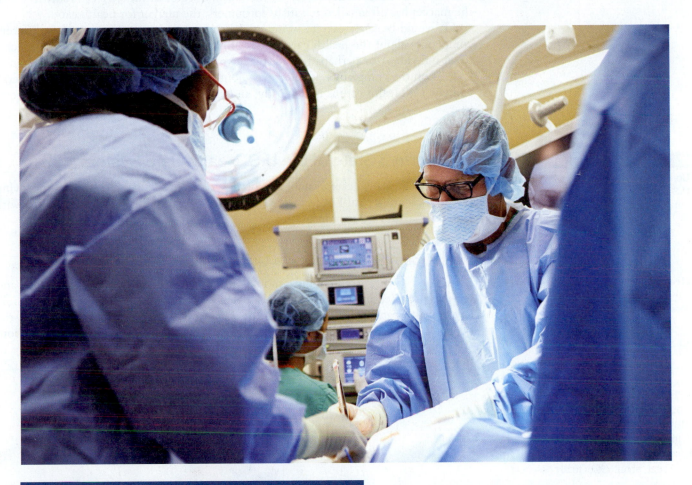

Chapter Outline and Learning Objectives

14.1 The Current State of the U.S. Health Care System, page 276

Compare the cost-effectiveness of the U.S. health care system to those in other developed countries.

14.2 Health Care Delivery and Finance Systems: An International Comparison, page 281

List the key features of the health care systems in Japan, Canada, the United Kingdom, and the United States.

14.3 How Health Care Finance May Affect the Affordability of Health Care, page 284

Explain three reasons why the way the United States pays for health care may result in less-affordable health care than other systems.

Experiment: The Restaurant Game, page 299

MyEconLab

MyEconLab helps you master each objective and study more efficiently.

Well-functioning markets can produce amazing goods and services that make our lives extraordinarily rich. During the past three decades, markets have brought forth life-altering products such as personal computers, portable music, cellular phones, antilock brakes, movies on demand, and high-speed Internet service. Generally speaking, peoples' lives are richer, fuller, easier, and more connected than they have ever been before. Yet there is one sector of the U.S. economy in which the market has often failed to satisfy consumers: the market for health care.

It would be fairly easy to write volumes enumerating various people's different complaints about the health care system. But many of those complaints are specific to an individual, or perhaps to a particular provider or insurer. Instead, this chapter focuses on the complaints people have about the U.S. health care system in general, namely: (1) Health care is quite costly, and (2) not everyone has or can afford access to it.

14.1 Learning Objective

Compare the cost-effectiveness of the U.S. health care system to those in other developed countries.

Health care The goods and services provided by doctors, hospitals, pharmacies, and therapists.

The Current State of the U.S. Health Care System

Today's U.S. health care system can be described in five simple words: Improving care at increasing cost. Let's explore each of those two trends in turn, beginning with a look at health care spending.

Health Care Spending in the United States

Americans spend a tremendous amount of money on **health care**—the goods and services provided by doctors, hospitals, pharmacies, and therapists. At the household level, health care spending accounts for over $3,600 per year, or about 7% of the typical household's total spending.[1] Spending on health insurance accounts for about 60% of that $3,500. Figure 14.1 compares household spending on health care to spending on the other goods and services that households buy.

▶ **Figure 14.1**

Household Spending in the United States, 2013

In the United States, the typical household spends $3,631 on health care each year, about 7% of total household spending.

Source: Bureau of Labor Statistics. Data are most recent available at time of publication.

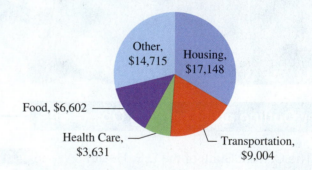

Figure 14.1 makes it appear as if health care spending accounts for a fairly small share of overall spending. That might be true at the household level, but households' spending doesn't account for *all* health care spending—or even a majority of it. Table 14.1 breaks down health care spending by source.

The first two rows of Table 14.1 represent private spending on health care services, both by households and by businesses that pay for private insurance on behalf of their employees. Together, these private sources of spending account for 47.3% of all health care spending. Federal, state, and local governments account for the remaining 52.7%, with the lion's share of that spending originating with the federal government.

Altogether, total health care spending amounts to $2.633 trillion annually, or over $8,000 for every person in the United States.[2] That represents more than 17% of total

---

[1] The typical household consists of about 2.5 people, which means that annual per-person health care spending is about $1,400.

[2] That $2.633 trillion figure includes only the consumption of health care services by individuals, and does not account for investment spending by businesses. That investment spending includes new buildings and facilities and purchases of medical equipment.

Table 14.1 Health Care Consumption Spending by Source

Total annual spending on health care services is over $2.6 trillion in the United States. The majority of that spending originates with federal, state, and local governments.

	Source of Spending	2012 Total (in billion dollars)	Percentage of Total Expenditures
Private Spending	Out-of-pocket spending	$328.2	12.5%
	Private insurance	$917.0	34.8%
	Total private spending	**$1,245.2**	**47.3%**
Government Spending	Medicare	$572.5	21.8%
	Medicaid: federal spending	$237.9	9.0%
	Medicaid: state spending	$183.3	6.9%
	Other federal insurance programs	$103.8	4.0%
	Other federal and state programs	$290.8	11.0%
	Total federal and state government spending	**$1,388.3**	**52.7%**
	Total health care spending	**$2,633.5**	**100%**

Source: Centers for Medicare and Medicaid Services. Data are most recent available at time of publication.

spending in the United States. In other words, Americans spend $1 out of every $6 on health care. That's more than they spend on transportation, more than they spend on food, and about as much as they spend on housing.

Americans haven't always spent so much: In 1960, health care spending amounted to only about 5% of total spending. Health care's share of total spending has increased steadily since that time. Part of the increase in total spending can be accounted for by increases in the amount of health care Americans buy. But increases in total spending can also be attributed to increases in the price of health care. Since 1960, the prices of the other goods and services that the typical American buys have risen 8-fold. But the price of medical care has increased an astonishing 19-fold. In other words, relative to the price of other goods and services, health care is more than twice as expensive today as it was in 1960, which explains in part why it is occupying an ever-larger share of our budget.

Unfortunately, as the price of health care services has increased, so has the price of health insurance, making access to health care difficult for many people to afford. (You will learn more about how health insurance prices are determined later in this chapter.) Before the federal government passed national health care reforms in 2010, the Bureau of the Census estimated that there were 48 million Americans (about 15% of all Americans) without health insurance. Not all of those Americans completely lacked access to the health care system. Some could probably afford health insurance but chose not to buy it: The Census Bureau reports that 18 million of the uninsured (over one-third of all uninsured) had annual household income over $50,000, high enough to place them in the top half of the income distribution. Others had no private health insurance but were eligible to apply for the government's Medicaid program. But even after accounting for those groups, there were still millions of Americans who found obtaining either health insurance or direct access to health care unaffordable.

Health Care Outcomes in the United States

So why is health care so expensive and therefore sometimes unaffordable in the United States?

One quick and convenient answer is that health care services have greatly improved in quality. Just in the past few decades, scientists have made amazing advances in their understanding of the human body and how to treat its maladies. A partial list of those advances includes arthroscopic surgeries, SSRI antidepressants, coronary stents, the coding of the human genome, test-tube babies, artificial hearts, and treatments for many types of cancer.

Developing these advances has been expensive, requiring the training and talents of highly specialized doctors and scientists. It has also been very expensive to develop hundreds of thousands of other medicines, regimens, and surgeries that have turned out not to work well. The costs of those failures have to be built into the price of the successes, and the result is that health care is expensive, but it is also very good. And it is much better than it was just a short time ago.

The improvements we've made in health care have paid noticeable dividends in terms of measurable health care outcomes. Since 1960, for example, Americans' life expectancy at birth has risen almost 10 years, from 69.9 years to 78.7 years. A big portion of that gain can be attributed to improvements in infant mortality, which has dropped from 26 deaths per 1,000 live births to just over 6. We're doing a better job of taking care of our babies, but we're also doing a better job of taking care of our seniors: In 1960, the average 65-year-old man could expect to live another 12.8 years; today, he can expect to live 17.8 years. Four decades of medical progress, in other words, has bought seniors an extra half-decade of life.

We can measure the benefits of improved health care in dimensions other than just life expectancy. The past few decades have brought almost universal progress against the biggest killers: Since the early 1980s, cancer deaths have fallen by 20%, and deaths from cardiovascular disease have fallen in half. Not all of these gains can be attributed to better health care; some of the gains stem from lifestyle changes like the dramatic decrease in smoking in the United States. But certainly, some of the decline in mortality stems from advances in diagnosis and treatment.

The numbers indicate that the U.S. health care system has made great strides in improving measurable outcomes. But those improvements have come at substantial and increasing cost. This raises an important question: Do the benefits justify all those costs? This is a difficult question, but a good first step to answering it is to see if other countries that experience similar health outcomes also have such high levels of spending. In other words, could the United States do just as well without spending so much?

An International Comparison of Health Care Costs and Outcomes

To explore the question of whether the benefits of improved health care justify all the costs, let's see what other countries—countries similar to the United States in terms of their level of development—spend on health care. Table 14.2 presents information about health care costs for a sample of developed countries, drawn from the member nations of the Organisation for Economic Co-operation and Development (OECD).

Table 14.2 shows that the United States devotes more resources to health care than do other developed nations, both in terms of spending per person and in

Table 14.2   OECD Health Care Expenditures

The United States spends more on health care in both absolute and relative terms than do other developed nations.

Country	Spending per Capita in U.S. Dollars, 2012	Total Health Care Spending, % of GDP, 2012
Australia	$3,997	9.1%
Canada	$4,602	10.9%
Germany	$4,811	11.3%
Japan	$3,649	10.3%
The Netherlands	$5,099	11.8%
United Kingdom	$3,289	9.3%
United States	$8,745	16.9%

Source: Based on data from OECD Health Statistics, 2014, http://www.oecd.org/els/health-systems/oecdhealthdata 2013-frequentlyrequesteddata.htm. Data are most recent available at time of publication.

terms of health care's share of overall spending. In fact, no matter whether you measure spending in absolute terms (dollars per capita) or relative terms (health care spending's share of total spending, which is commonly referred to as GDP), the United States spends about half again as much as the second-biggest spender in the OECD, the Netherlands.

Does that extra spending result in better health outcomes? Table 14.3 summarizes some of the key measures of overall physical health for the same countries listed in Table 14.2.

Table 14.3 OECD Health Outcomes

Despite spending more on health care than other nations, the United States doesn't perform appreciably better than those nations on several standard measures of overall health and wellness.

Country	Life Expectancy at Birth, Total Population	Male Life Expectancy at 65 (Additional Years of Life)	Infant Mortality (deaths per 1,000 live births)
Australia	82.1	19.1	3.3
Canada	81.5	18.8	4.8
Germany	81.0	18.2	3.3
Japan	83.2	18.9	2.2
The Netherlands	81.2	18.0	3.7
United Kingdom	81.0	18.5	4.1
United States	78.7	17.8	6.1

Source: Based on data from OECD Health Statistics, 2014, http://www.oecd.org/els/health-systems/oecdhealthdata 2013-frequentlyrequesteddata.htm. Data are most recent available at time of publication.

The numbers in Table 14.3 demonstrate that, relative to the United States, other nations are able to generate superior health care outcomes with fewer resources. Among the nations in the table, the United States ranks dead last in general life expectancy, in life expectancy at 65, and in infant mortality, despite spending about 50% more on health care as a whole. Yet these numbers present something of a paradox, because in many dimensions, U.S. health care is outstanding:

- The United States has the best breast cancer and prostate cancer survival rates in the world and generally scores well for other types of cancer as well.

- The United States scores very well in terms of screening for cancer and gives outstanding access to advanced imaging technologies such as CT and MRI scans.

- In the United States, survival rates following strokes and heart attacks are very good.

- The United States is at the forefront of medical innovation. The top five U.S. hospitals conduct more clinical trials than all the hospitals in any other country you might name, and Americans win more Nobel Prizes for medicine than the rest of the world *combined*.

So if U.S. health care is so good, why don't Americans live longer? Some economists argue that poor life expectancy numbers in the United States may be due not to a lack of exceptional care but to behavioral choices. Consider this: Among developed countries, the United States has the highest obesity rate. Americans are also far more likely to be killed in traffic accidents or by gunfire than are residents of other countries. Further, the United States has a higher rate of teen pregnancy than its OECD counterparts, which may be responsible for a higher incidence of low-birthweight babies. That, in turn, may adversely impact infant mortality, a key health indicator often used to judge the effectiveness of the health care system.

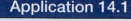

Application 14.1

Explaining the Gap in Measured Health Care Outcomes Between the United States and Canada

The U.S. health care system stacks up poorly against other countries in terms of life expectancy and infant mortality. But many economists believe that at least some of the differences in those outcomes can be attributed to factors other than the health care system. The important question, then, is how much?

Baruch College economists June O'Neill and Dave O'Neill dug into data on U.S. and Canadian health care outcomes to figure out the answer. They examined three sources of mortality that lie at least partially outside the health care system: obesity, accidental deaths, and low-birthweight babies.

Consider obesity: In the United States, the obesity rate exceeds 30%. In Canada, it is below 20%. Notably, Japan's obesity rate is only about 3%, and the Japanese have the longest life expectancy in the OECD. Of course, very few people die directly of obesity, so O'Neill and O'Neill examined deaths due to heart disease (which is highly correlated with obesity) to see how much of the gap in U.S.–Canadian life expectancy might be obesity related. They determined that at older ages (50+), about one-third of the gap in mortality rates can be traced to heart disease. They suggest that, because of obesity, the United States has more heart disease than Canada, and that drags down U.S. life expectancy numbers.

Americans, and especially young Americans, are also far more likely to be victims of homicide or to die in accidents, including traffic accidents. Overall mortality rates for men in their 20s are about 50% higher in the United States than in Canada. But O'Neill and O'Neill show that accidental deaths and murder account for about 75% of that gap. In other words, Americans may not live as long as Canadians, but it's not primarily because of the health care system—it's mostly because lots of young people die of unnatural causes.

The United States compares unfavorably to Canada on another commonly cited health outcome, too: infant mortality. O'Neill and O'Neill's data suggests that the gap in infant mortality is driven by deaths of low-birthweight babies, who have a mortality rate 10 times higher than typical-birthweight babies.

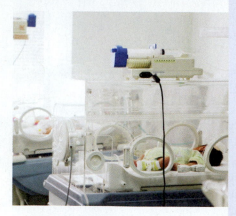

The United States actually does a better job than Canada of helping any particular low-birthweight baby survive. But the U.S. system is simply overwhelmed by the number of those babies: As a proportion of total births, the United States has about 50% more low-birthweight babies than Canada, attributable in part to a 300% higher teen pregnancy rate. That drags down the infant mortality statistics: O'Neill and O'Neill estimate that if the United States and Canada had the same distribution of low-birthweight babies, their infant mortality rates would be roughly identical.

The U.S. health care system has plenty of flaws, but those flaws are not wholly responsible for the country's relatively poor showing in life expectancy. The health care system cannot be held fully responsible for people eating too much, driving too much, shooting too much, and having babies too young. When those factors are accounted for, much, but not all, of the gap that has been attributed to a poor health care system disappears.

See related problems 1.3 and 1.4 on page 295 at the end of this chapter.

Based on June O'Neill and Dave O'Neill's "Health Status, Health Care, and Inequality: Canada vs. the U.S.," *NBER Working Paper*, September 2007; Samuel Preston and Jessica Ho's "Low Life Expectancy in the United States: Is the Health Care System at Fault?" *PSC Working Paper Series*, 2009; and David Cutler, Edward L. Glaeser and Jesse M. Shapiro, "Why Have Americans Become More Obese?" *Journal of Economic Perspectives*, 2003.

Depending on which metric you choose to judge the effectiveness of the health care system, the United States may or may not be doing better than its developed peer nations. One thing is certain, however: The United States devotes substantially more resources to its system than other countries do. Is it possible, as the numbers suggest, that the United States might be able to do more with less?

Health Care Delivery and Finance Systems: An International Comparison

14.2 Learning Objective
List the key features of the health care systems in Japan, Canada, the United Kingdom, and the United States.

Many people believe that the U.S. health care system could benefit from a fundamental reorganization: that the method the United States uses to deliver and pay for health care is the source of the system's apparent lack of cost-effectiveness. With this in mind, let's explore some of the major models of health care delivery and finance currently in use in the developed world.

The United Kingdom's Nationalized Health Care System

In the United Kingdom, almost all health care services are provided directly by the government's National Health Service (NHS), which owns most of the country's hospitals and employs most of its doctors. The NHS provides health care services free of charge to patients and pays for the resources needed to provide those services through income taxes.[3] This type of health care delivery system is often called **nationalized health care** or **socialized medicine**.

Although the government runs the NHS, even governments have scarce resources: The NHS doesn't have enough doctors and hospital beds to give all its patients everything they want when they want it. So the NHS focuses its scarce resources on delivering preventive care and on treating acute conditions. Noncritical conditions that require treatment or surgery are given lower priority, and as a result, patients in the United Kingdom often have to wait for elective surgeries—joint replacements, hernia operations, and knee surgeries, for example—for months or even years, if those procedures are covered at all. As a result, many people in the United Kingdom also purchase additional private insurance that they can use to pay for elective procedures.

Nationalized health care A system of health care in which a government provides health care services free of charge to patients and pays for the resources needed to provide those services through income taxes; also called socialized medicine.

Canada's Single-Payer System

Canada's model for providing health care services to its citizens is different from the United Kingdom's. In Canada, most doctors are privately employed, and most hospitals are private businesses. But in Canada, each provincial government provides its residents health insurance that meets federally determined standards. Doctors and hospitals are required to provide patients with medically necessary care; they are reimbursed for that care by the government at rates set by the government. The insurance system is funded by taxes paid to Canada's federal and provincial governments.

Systems like Canada's are called **single-payer systems** because the government alone is responsible for paying health care providers for delivering medically necessary procedures. That gives the government a lot of power to hold down overall health care costs: Doctors are required to deliver necessary care, regardless of how much the government reimburses them. As is the case with the United Kingdom's nationalized system, one practical consequence of the single-payer system is that elective procedures receive lower priority, often resulting in longer waiting times than one might find in the United States.

Single-payer system A health care system in which the government alone is responsible for paying health care providers for delivering medically necessary procedures.

---

[3] Patients are assessed a small charge for prescription medicine.

Japan's Universal Care System

Japan's government is somewhat less involved in providing and paying for health care than the Canadian and British governments. Japan has a system under which every resident is required to obtain health insurance either from a nonprofit health insurance provider (often one that serves a particular industry or profession, with insurance provided to employees by employers) or from the government. Japan's system (like Canada's and the United Kingdom's systems) is one version of universal health insurance. **Universal health insurance** (also referred to as universal health care) means that a country's health care system provides access to basic medical services for all residents.

In Japan, many hospitals are privately owned but must operate as not-for-profit businesses. Most doctors do not work for the government. To help control overall costs, the government generally regulates fees for medical procedures; the reimbursement rate is periodically renegotiated between the government and physicians. Unlike in Canada and the United Kingdom, the Japanese system doesn't provide all care to all people at essentially zero cost: In Japan, residents are responsible for paying for most routine and preventive care, and they also pay a substantial share (up to 30%) of the cost of covered medical expenses.

The U.S. Private Health Care System

The health care systems described above stand in stark contrast to the U.S. system. In the United States, private doctors and hospitals deliver almost all health care services. Many of those hospitals are nonprofit organizations, but a substantial number are run for profit. Many, but not all, people have some form of health insurance.

A majority of those who are insured receive health insurance coverage from a private insurance company, which may be run as a nonprofit firm or a for-profit firm. Most people with private insurance obtain it through their employer as part of their overall compensation. But about 10% of people purchase insurance privately, on their own initiative, and about one-third of Americans are insured through the government's Medicare and Medicaid programs. In sum, the U.S. system primarily depends on privately delivered health care services, paid for by a blend of private and public insurance.

Due to concerns about rapidly rising costs, and out of concern for millions of uninsured people who had limited access to health care, the U.S. government passed major health care reforms in 2010. Those reforms were gathered under the umbrella of the **Patient Protection and Affordable Care Act (ACA)**, commonly referred to as *Obamacare*. Reforms were largely implemented by 2014, though some pieces of the ACA were designed to be fully phased in only by 2020.

The ACA was an enormous bill, totaling more than 10,000 pages of rules and regulations. These are some of the major highlights of the ACA:

- **The individual mandate.** Under the ACA, every resident of the United States must have health insurance that meets certain basic requirements. By 2016, failure to obtain qualifying insurance will result in a tax penalty of $695 or 2.5% of income, whichever is greater.

- **The employer mandate.** When fully phased in, any business that has more than 50 full-time employees will be required to offer health insurance to its employees. Failure to provide health insurance to employees can result in a tax penalty of up to $3,000 for each employee who obtains health insurance on a government health insurance exchange.

- **Regulation of private insurers.** Insurance companies may not deny coverage to anyone because of a preexisting medical condition. Insurance companies may vary premiums only on the basis of age, tobacco use, family size, and geography; in addition, they may not raise premiums on the basis of claims history, gender, or overall health status. Insurance companies are forbidden to cap lifetime payments made on behalf of particular policyholders.

Universal health insurance A health care system that guarantees access to basic health care services for all of its residents.

Patient Protection and Affordable Care Act (ACA) A set of health care reforms enacted in the United States in 2014.

Application 14.2

Why Do Americans Get Health Insurance from Their Employers?

In the United States, most people with private health insurance obtain that insurance through their employer. Americans may think that's quite commonplace, but in fact, no other industrialized country has an arrangement quite like it.

There are several disadvantages to the employer-based health insurance model that has been the norm in the United States for the past half-century. First among them is this: When your employer pays for health insurance, if you lose your job, you lose your insurance. That leaves people who have lost their job doubly vulnerable to accident or illness: Not only do they lack an income to help pay their medical bills, they also lack insurance.

Employer-provided health insurance also tends to reduce job mobility. You may be reluctant to leave your current job for a better one if doing so means losing your health insurance coverage. Before the ACA, that was particularly true for people who were already sick: Even if your new employer offered health insurance, the insurer could reject or delay coverage for people with preexisting conditions.

A third big disadvantage of employer-provided health insurance is related to how insurance companies set premiums. Often, premiums are based on the overall healthiness of a particular company's employees. For small companies, that means if even a single employee contracts an illness that is costly to treat, premiums for every employee could skyrocket the next year.

So if employer-based insurance has such big drawbacks, how did we end up with this model of health insurance provision in the first place? The roots of the system can be traced back to World War II. In an effort to control rising prices and to promote a sense of shared sacrifice, the U.S. government passed wage controls that prohibited employers from increasing workers' pay. Those wage controls made it difficult for firms to attract and retain the best workers, so those firms began exploiting a loophole in the law: Rather than offer higher wages, they offered to pay for health insurance and other fringe benefits. The loophole in the wage control law dovetailed neatly with a loophole in the tax code: The money firms spent on health insurance was tax deductible to the firm, but health insurance benefits were not considered taxable income to the employee. That made employer-provided insurance financially attractive to both employer and employee, and it caused insurance coverage to skyrocket from just 9% of the population in 1940 to 63% by the early 1950s.

In other words, the primary reason the U.S. system of paying for health insurance looks so different from just about every other country's system—and the reason we have a system that has created such significant problems for so many people—can be traced to a historical accident in which employers and employees were simply trying to evade the law.

See related problem 2.5 on page 296 at the end of this chapter.

Based on Uwe Reinhardt's "Is Employer-Based Health Insurance Worth Saving?" *New York Times*, May 22, 2009; Laura Scofea's "The Development and Growth of Employer-Provided Health Insurance," *Monthly Labor Review*, March 1994; and "Accidents of History Created U.S. Health System," *NPR Planet Money*, October 22, 2009.

- **State health exchanges.** The ACA required each state to create a *health insurance exchange*, an online marketplace where competing private insurers offer regulated and standardized health care plans for purchase by the public.[4] The exchanges help consumers comparison shop for insurance and should help pool risk and reduce administrative overhead. Low-income individuals are eligible for tax credits to help offset the cost of purchasing health insurance on the exchanges.

[4]A number of states declined to create their own exchanges, deciding instead to let the federal government run the exchanges in their states.

Each of these major pieces of the ACA has been hotly contested—in fact, the personal mandate has already survived a challenge in the U.S. Supreme Court.[5] Yet each was designed to deal with a particular problem inherent in a health care system that relies on private insurance to fund privately provided health care services. The remainder of this chapter is devoted to discussing those problems. As the chapter unfolds, we will refer to these particular pieces of U.S. health care reform and explain the rationale for their inclusion in the ACA.[6]

14.3 Learning Objective

Explain three reasons why the way the United States pays for health care may result in less-affordable health care than other systems.

How Health Care Finance May Affect the Affordability of Health Care

We now know that there are big differences between the U.S. health care system and the systems used in other countries. The biggest differences don't necessarily lie in how health care services are delivered; many of the countries discussed above rely on private doctors and hospitals, just like the United States does. Rather, the most notable differences lie in how U.S. residents *pay* for their health care. In particular, relying on a system of private insurance causes a number of potential problems that can drive up prices to patients and costs to the country as a whole.

So in order to understand the difficulties society faces in ensuring everybody access to reasonable and affordable health care, the place to begin is not with hospitals and clinics but with insurance companies. In this section, you will learn how an insurance company operates and how relying on insurers to pay your medical bills can contribute to the high cost of medical care.

Insurance: The Fundamentals

Cedric, Joey, Miaya, Kate, and Susan live in a major eastern U.S. city. They play together on a basketball team and earn their living playing for money against teams from other neighborhoods.

Street ball is a rough game. There are no referees and no athletic trainers. Cedric, Joey, Miaya, Kate, and Susan have seen people get hurt, and each harbors a secret fear: "*What on Earth would happen if I take a fall and tear a ligament?*" One morning, Miaya lays it on the table. "We're all just one bad jump from an expensive knee reconstruction. If I get hurt, I can't come up with tens of thousands of dollars on the spot. I think I'm going to have to quit playing basketball and get another job instead."

A week later, the team's unofficial statistician, Susan, announces that she's discovered a solution to the problem. "Every season, each of us faces exactly a 1-in-5 (0.2) chance of tearing a ligament. Corrective surgery costs $10,000, which means that in any given year, our expected injury cost is $2,000 (0.2 × $10,000) per person. So, every year let's each contribute $2,000 to an account in a local bank. We'll use that account to pay the medical bills for any of us that tear a ligament. In some years, nobody will get hurt, and the account will build. And in other years, two or three of us might get hurt, and we'll have to draw down the account a little bit. But on average, just one of us will get hurt in a given season, and on average, we'll have collectively contributed exactly enough to pay for surgery." The other four players think this is a good idea and agree to the plan.

This arrangement resembles the basic framework of an insurance company. Each player contributes money to a pool (in the real world, that contribution is called a

---

[5]One provision of the ACA that is both less controversial and more popular lets young adults remain on their parents' family insurance plan until age 26. Prior to the ACA, insurers typically refused young adults such coverage after age 19 or, for college students, after graduation.

[6]The new U.S. system created under the ACA bears a strong resemblance to Switzerland's health care system. Like the United States, Switzerland delivers health care services via a combination of public, subsidized private, and private health care providers. Further, the Swiss have a personal mandate to obtain insurance, and insurers cannot deny coverage to anyone who applies.

premium) that will pay medical expenses for those who sustain injuries. Insurance arrangements like this help people avoid the life-changing financial catastrophes that often accompany medical catastrophes. They do this by spreading the financial cost of a medical catastrophe among a large number of people.

Notice in our basketball example that if the probability of being injured in any given year is one in five, then *on average*, each player will get hurt once every five years. If no insurance existed, each player would therefore end up spending $10,000 out of pocket once every five years. With insurance, each player ends up spending $2,000 each year for five years, or $10,000 total. But by doing so, they avoid finding themselves in a position where they have to come up with $10,000 all at once. By sharing risk with their teammates, the players can avoid suffering a potentially catastrophic financial setback.

In the real world, of course, insurance companies have to hire employees, buy buildings, install computers, and do the countless things large commercial enterprises do. All those things cost money. So an insurance company set up to insure the five basketball players might actually end up charging each player $2,200 a year rather than $2,000. The fact that the players would rather pay the premiums (which amount to $11,000 over five years) than suffer a sudden $10,000 loss indicates that they so dislike risk that they're willing to pay people extra to share it with them.

Asymmetric Information and the Adverse Selection Problem

When the basketball players in our example created their insurance arrangement, Susan, the number-cruncher, had access to a great deal of information, including the very important knowledge that each player had an equal 1-in-5 chance of tearing a ligament each year. But what if that weren't true? What if some players were more injury prone than others? Suppose that Joey and Cedric are very susceptible, with a 2-in-5 chance of a torn ligament each year, whereas Miaya, Kate, and Susan have only a 1-in-10 chance of an injury. Each year then, Cedric and Joey have expected medical claims of $4,000 (0.4 × $10,000) apiece, and Miaya, Kate, and Susan each have expected medical claims of $1,000 (0.1 × $10,000). Therefore, the expected medical claims for the group would add up to $11,000 each year. Dividing the total cost equally among the five members of the group, each player would pay an annual premium of $2,200.

Adverse Selection and the Unraveling of Insurance Markets Here's the problem with forming an insurance arrangement when people have different risks of illness: At $2,200 per year, insurance is going to look like a bargain to high-risk customers like Joey and Cedric. On average, they receive $4,000 of medical care for only $2,200. On the other hand, insurance is going to look like a horrible deal to low-risk customers like Miaya, Kate, and Susan. They each pay $2,200 in insurance premiums but on average receive only $1,000 of medical care.

This imbalance can become problematic: After a while, Miaya begins feeling like she's pouring money down the drain. "Wow, every year I pay thousands of dollars in premiums, but I almost never make a claim. Maybe I'd be better off just parking my money in a savings account," she thinks to herself.

And so Miaya cancels her insurance and drops out of the pool. That's fine for Miaya, but it has an unintended consequence for the others. Because Miaya was super-healthy, when she leaves the pool, the healthiness of the "typical" member falls just a bit. Now there are four members, two of whom are low risk and two of whom are high risk. Because there's one fewer athlete to cover, the expected annual medical expenses for the pool fall from $11,000 to $10,000. But now those expenses are being divided among four people, not five, and to cover those expenses, the annual premium must rise from $2,200 to $2,500.

When the premium rises, insurance begins to look less attractive to another low-risk player, Kate. She, like Miaya, leaves the pool, and the pool gets, on average, just a bit more injury prone as a result. Again, total expected medical costs for the pool fall, but because they're only being divided among three people, the premium must rise to $3,000.

Adverse selection The tendency for the people who pose the greatest risks to insurers to buy insurance.

Asymmetric information A situation that occurs when one party to a transaction has more or better information than the other.

Premium death spiral An effect of adverse selection on insurance premiums. As healthy people leave the pool of the insured, premiums must rise, causing more people to leave the pool and driving premiums even higher.

And that causes Susan to drop out, so premiums rise even further. As the price of health insurance continues to increase, it may become unaffordable to higher-risk individuals, too. In the end, society ends up with expensive health insurance and a substantial fraction of the people in the group uninsured.

In insurance markets, economists refer to **adverse selection** as the tendency for the people who pose the greatest risks to insurers to buy insurance (because it looks like a good deal), while those who pose the least risks do not. Adverse selection is one unfortunate result of asymmetric information. **Asymmetric information** means that one party to a transaction has more or better information than the other. The health care market is plagued with information asymmetries, and here is a big one that lies at the root of the adverse selection problem: Patients tend to know more about their overall healthiness than insurance companies do. Your insurance company doesn't know if you're prone to ACL tears, or whether you're arthritic, or if you have a case of terminal cancer. All the insurance company can do is charge its customers an average premium based on the out-of-pocket medical costs that it thinks they might incur. That premium will look like a great deal to people with weak ligaments or chronic joint pain, and it will look like a poor deal to super-healthy people who never get ill or engage in risky behavior. The high-risk people therefore buy the insurance, and the low-risk people don't, which drives premiums even higher, which causes still more healthy people to drop out, which drives premiums higher . . . in what health economists refer to as a **premium death spiral**.

Generally speaking, it's probably a good thing for more people to have insurance rather than fewer; even super-healthy people get sick, suffer injuries, and have accidents. Insurance shouldn't look like such a bad deal that people drop their insurance coverage, only to find out later that dropping out was a life-ruining decision. And insurers want healthy people in the pool they insure—not only because they are inexpensive to serve but also so their premiums can help cover the more exorbitant medical expenses of less-healthy people.

Private Insurers and Adverse Selection Prior to ACA Despite the dire prediction of a premium death spiral, the market for private health insurance hasn't entirely collapsed. How did insurance companies keep that from happening?

First, the majority of people with private insurance obtained that insurance through their employer.[7] Often, employers would pay part of the insurance premiums for the employee as part of the employee's compensation. That decreased the *apparent* price of insurance to the employee, which helped keep healthy people in the pool of the insured. In that way, employer-provided insurance helped reduce the problems of adverse selection.

But not all employers offered their employees health insurance. So if those employees wanted health insurance (and if they weren't eligible for Medicaid), they had to obtain an individual insurance policy. Insurance companies kept the individual insurance market from completely unraveling by obtaining more information about their customers. If you applied for an individual health insurance policy, you would be subjected to a battery of tests: You would have blood drawn and cheeks swabbed. You would have to provide a medical history—your own *and* your parents'. And you would have to answer questions about your lifestyle that might be relevant to the decision to insure you, such as, "Are you a professional bull rider?"

Armed with that information, the insurance company would set premiums based on how healthy the information indicated you were likely to be. For example, in the case of the basketball players, an insurer might notice that males are more prone to ACL tears than females. A profit-conscious insurer might then set the annual premium for a man slightly above $4,000 and charge a woman (who has expected annual medical bills of $1,000), say, $1,100, enough to cover her expected costs with a bit left over to cover the insurer's administrative expenses.

---

[7]Typically, the employer would deal with a single insurance company that agreed to insure every employee of the company and to charge an identical premium, regardless of the employee's health characteristics. Such an arrangement is called *group insurance*.

Unfortunately, this information hunt and risk-based pricing is not an ideal solution to the adverse selection problem—at least not if society wants everyone to have insurance. If insurers gather such information and set premiums based on risk, they can keep low-risk patients in the pool by charging them reasonable premiums. But then insurers have to charge high-risk policyholders high premiums that may price them out of the market.

On the other hand, if insurers *don't* gather extensive information about their clients, the market begins to unravel, and premiums begin to increase anyway. Gradually both low-risk and high-risk people get priced out of the market. So in either case, we find that the people most likely to need some kind of insurance are put in a position where they are unlikely to be able to afford it; society ends up with some fraction of its population uninsured.[8]

How Different Health Care Systems Deal with Adverse Selection The adverse selection problem exists because healthier people choose not to pay for insurance. Fixing the adverse selection problem, then, generally requires taking some action that removes that choice and requires healthier people to obtain and pay for insurance. Single-payer systems like Canada's and nationalized health care systems like the United Kingdom's accomplish this by providing blanket insurance coverage for residents directly and extracting payment through the tax system. Japan's universal health care system takes a different approach: It contains a personal mandate that requires all individuals to obtain health insurance.

In the United States, the ACA takes an approach similar to Japan's. The employer and individual mandates are central to keeping the pool of the insured as large as possible to reduce the adverse selection problem. The employer mandate requires every large employer to provide health insurance for its full-time employees. The individual mandate requires every individual to obtain health insurance, either through his or her employer or by purchasing an individual policy, or through eligibility in a government-sponsored (and tax-funded) program such as Medicare or Medicaid.[9] These mandates, together, ensure that the pool of the insured will contain both high- and low-risk people, an essential ingredient to keeping health insurance affordable for the people most likely to need it.

The ACA also mandates state-level health insurance exchanges where individuals who do not have government or employer coverage can comparison shop for standardized insurance plans issued by private insurers. Coupled with the stipulation that private insurers cannot refuse to issue an insurance policy to anyone because of preexisting conditions or charge them different premiums based on characteristics other than age, tobacco use, family size, or geography, the state insurance exchanges, too, keep high- and low-risk individuals in the same health insurance pool to reduce the adverse selection problem.

The personal mandate forces Americans to purchase health insurance. That provision of the ACA hasn't been overwhelmingly popular: Americans aren't used to being forced to buy things. After all, government doesn't tell people how many cheeseburgers to buy. The aversion to the compulsory purchase of a service from a private-sector business has resulted in a constitutional challenge to the personal mandate. But health care, you'll remember, really *is* different from a cheeseburger. Fail to buy a cheeseburger, and the only person who does without is you. Fail to buy

---

[8]Oddly, while perfect information enhances the functioning of most markets, it can destroy insurance markets. If insurers knew everything about their customers, they would deny coverage to those they knew would get expensive illnesses and offer policies only to people who never get sick. (This is why insurers have been generally forbidden to require genetic testing before issuing policies.) Likewise, if people had perfect knowledge of their own wellness, the healthiest people would never purchase insurance because insurance is not cost-effective for them. Ultimately, insurance companies would want to issue coverage only to the very people who don't want it. This is why it is often said that the proper functioning of any system of insurance depends on mutual ignorance.

[9]There are actually a limited number of exceptions to the individual mandate. For more detail, see "The Requirement to Buy Coverage Under the Affordable Care Act" at the Kaiser Family Foundation, kff.org.

Application 14.3

How Big a Problem Is Adverse Selection?

The Affordable Care Act mandated many changes to the U.S. health care system. One key provision of the ACA is motivated largely by fairness: It requires insurers to issue insurance to all customers, regardless of whether they have a preexisting medical condition. By itself, such a requirement would create an adverse selection problem that could easily cause the insurance market to unravel: No one would buy insurance until he or she got sick. To keep healthy people in the pool, the ACA added the personal mandate: All U.S. citizens are required to buy health insurance.

But the unprecedented and fairly intrusive nature of the personal mandate has caused many people to wonder exactly how big the adverse selection problem actually is. In other words, does the end justify the means?

Yale economists Martin Hackmann and Amanda Kowalski and University of Pennsylvania economist Jonathan Kolstad wanted to find out. They dug into data from Massachusetts, which enacted its own state-level personal mandate in 2006. Comparing the price of insurance in Massachusetts to the price in other states both before and after the individual mandate in Massachusetts went into effect, Hackmann, Kolstad, and Kowalski found that premiums decreased significantly in response to the mandate. They also discovered that the mandate helped hold down premium increases in subsequent years.

On the whole, Hackmann, Kolstad, and Kowalski estimate that the personal mandate made the typical Massachusetts resident better off to the tune of $442 per year. This indicates that the adverse selection problem may be both real and substantial. As objectionable as the personal mandate may be to some people, the work of Hackmann, Kolstad, and Kowalski shows that it may be effective in making insurance more affordable.

See related problem 3.19 on page 298 at the end of this chapter.

Based on Martin Hackmann, Jonathan Kolstad, and Amanda Kowalski's "Adverse Selection and an Individual Mandate: When Theory Meets Practice," *NBER Working Paper*, 2013; and Jonathan Graves and Jonathan Gruber, "How Did Health Care Reform in Massachusetts Impact Insurance Premiums?" *American Economic Review Papers and Proceedings*, 2012.

---

insurance, and your actions spill over to others through adverse selection. Because of that spillover effect, the personal mandate survived a 2012 constitutional challenge in the Supreme Court.[10]

The Moral Hazard Problem

In addition to causing an adverse selection problem, asymmetric information contributes to expensive medical care in a second way. Return to the original scenario in which each basketball player had an equal chance of suffering a torn ligament. The group agrees that all medical expenses will be covered by their cost-sharing arrangement, with each member contributing $2,000 per year to help cover those costs.

Moral Hazard and Risky Behavior The very existence of an insurance agreement may cause the players to alter their behavior. Before the insurance pool was formed, the players were cautious, knowing that one misstep could result in a costly surgery. But when the group shares costs, they play more aggressively. And some of the group's

---

[10]The personal mandate was upheld in part because the penalty for noncompliance is assessed through the tax system. In other words, the Supreme Court ruled not that the government can force you to buy health insurance but that it is within government's power to tax you if you do not.

members begin doing additional things that put their health at risk: Cedric takes up ski jumping, and Susan begins taking gymnastics lessons.

Economists call this a problem of moral hazard. **Moral hazard** is a change in behavior that occurs after a person becomes insured against loss. Moral hazard isn't just limited to risky physical activities: We may eat more poorly, exercise less, and generally take worse care of ourselves if someone else picks up the tab for our neglect. Moral hazard is a concern because when people are less careful, the probability of illness or injury increases, along with the associated medical bills. To cover those higher costs, insurance companies have to increase premiums, making insurance coverage less affordable.

Moral Hazard and the Quantity of Care There is a second way that insurance may cause moral hazard problems and contribute to high individual insurance premiums and high overall health care costs for the country as a whole. Insurance creates an incentive for people to consume more health care than may be socially ideal: They may make too many visits to the doctor's office, order too many tests, and have too many surgeries.

To demonstrate why that happens, consider the decisions made by Rachel and Linda, two tennis buffs who regularly play one another. They've both come down with tennis elbow and are considering how many appointments to schedule with their respective sports therapists. From experience, they know that the most relief comes from the first visit. An additional visit makes them feel better, but the second visit has a smaller impact than the first. To make cost–benefit analysis easier, let's convert the relief they receive from therapy into dollars: The first visit brings a patient $100 of relief; the second gives $30 of additional relief.

Suppose that Rachel and Linda do not have health insurance and that each will bear the full cost of physical therapy. At the therapist's office, the receptionist informs them that each visit will cost exactly $50. She asks how many appointments they'd like to schedule. Rachel runs through the alternatives in her head:

- If she schedules one appointment, she'll get a $100 benefit for $50. So, she'll end up with a $50 net benefit.
- If she schedules two appointments, she'll get $130 of relief ($100 from the first, and another $30 from the second) for a cost of $100. In this case, she'll end up with a $30 net benefit.

Given that the cost–benefit analysis for Linda is identical, the net benefits for the two women can be summarized by inserting the values above into a payoff matrix, as shown in Figure 14.2:

Linda

		1 Appointment	2 Appointments
Rachel	1 Appointment	+50, +50	+50, +30
	2 Appointments	+30, +50	+30, +30

◄ **Figure 14.2**
A Health Care Game with No Cost Sharing
When Rachel (in black) and Linda (in blue) pay for their own health care, the equilibrium outcome is for each to schedule only one appointment.

Notice that no matter what Linda does, Rachel receives the greatest net benefit ($50) from scheduling only one appointment. Linda, too, has a dominant strategy of scheduling just one appointment. So both Linda and Rachel schedule one appointment, which keeps them on the court for another year or so.

Time passes, and tennis elbow returns. This time, it hits Rachel first, and it happens to catch her in financially lean times. She mentions it to Linda, who says, "I'd hate to lose you as a tennis partner. Why don't we split your therapy bill this time, and when my elbow acts up again, you can return the favor."

Moral hazard A change in behavior that occurs after a person becomes insured against loss.

How will that cost-sharing arrangement, which resembles the structure of a typical insurance arrangement, affect Rachel's behavior? Let's figure out what a course of therapy will cost over a period of time in which both Rachel and Linda experience a bout of tennis elbow. We begin by making a list of possible combinations of intensity of usage, combined with the respective payoffs to Rachel and Linda:

- If Rachel and Linda each visit the therapist once, each will receive $100 of benefits. The total cost to the group will be $100, or $50 each. Each will emerge $50 better off than when she began.

- If Rachel and Linda each visit the therapist twice, each will receive $130 of benefits. The total cost to the group will be $200, or $100 each. Each will emerge $30 better off than when she began.

These payoffs mirror the payoffs from before. But important differences appear when we consider other combinations of therapy. Those differences are critical to understanding the fourth fundamental reason that health insurance is so costly:

- Suppose Rachel visits the therapist once, but Linda visits twice. Rachel will receive $100 of benefits, and Linda will receive $130. The total bill will be $150, so each will pay $75. That leaves Linda $55 ($130 − $75) better off and Rachel $25 ($100 − $75) better off. (You can reverse the payouts for a scenario in which Rachel visits the therapist twice and Linda only once.)

We have now accounted for all possible combinations of usage intensity. Inserting the payoffs calculated above into a payoff matrix creates the game shown in Figure 14.3:

▶ **Figure 14.3**

The Health Care Game with Cost Sharing

When Rachel and Linda agree to share costs equally, the dominant strategy for each player changes from scheduling one appointment to scheduling two. The equilibrium outcome is worse for both Rachel and Linda than if they had each scheduled one appointment.

		Linda	
		1 Appointment	2 Appointments
Rachel	1 Appointment	+50, +50	+25, +55
	2 Appointments	+55, +25	+30, +30

Look closely at this game and notice the transformation. Rachel and Linda, through the kind and simple gesture of agreeing to share medical bills, have transformed a game in which one trip to the therapist was a dominant strategy for each into a game in which both players have a dominant strategy of two appointments. That arrangement has changed the equilibrium outcome from one in which everybody gains $50 to one in which everyone gains only $30.

With a shared payment system in place (and remember that health insurance is basically a shared payment system), Linda knows that she's responsible for only half of the cost of her therapy. This makes relatively low-valued therapy look cost-effective. When she paid for everything herself, the second visit cost her more ($50) than it did good ($30), so she made only one visit. But when Rachel picks up half the tab, that next visit *appears* to cost only $25, which is less than the $30 of benefits Linda receives. So Linda makes an appointment for the second visit.

What is true for Linda is also true for Rachel. Both make two appointments, and both stare in shock at the tab they're collectively running up, but both realize that there's little they can do about it: Even if Rachel cancels her own treatments, she's still on the hook for half the cost of Linda's. Taken together, the small "society" consisting of Rachel and Linda ends up consuming a lot of medical care, and that's not altogether bad: They're healthy, and they feel great. But treatments are expensive, and as a result, everyone bemoans the high cost of care, and everybody would actually be happier if they would all consume a bit less. Rachel and Linda are trapped in a classic prisoner's dilemma, with an equilibrium outcome that everyone agrees is horrible but that nobody can figure out how to escape.

The preceding example suggests that because of the cost sharing inherent in insurance arrangements, we consume more health care services than is ideal. In the real world, patients may make more office visits, demand more prescriptions and more diagnostic procedures, and choose more surgeries than they otherwise would. Likewise, doctors have an incentive to overtreat and overprescribe. It may be better for a doctor to recommend a course of treatment that may not work very well than to recommend nothing and expose himself or herself to malpractice liability—a practice known as *defensive medicine*. And because insurance makes such courses of treatment look cheap to the patient, the patient has little financial incentive to refuse. Ultimately, that cost has to show up somewhere, and it generally shows up in higher premiums.

How Private Insurers Deal with the Moral Hazard Problem Moral hazard is a problem in any insurance program, and there really is no completely effective way to make individuals behave in the same way after they've obtained insurance as they did before. But even if moral hazard can't be eliminated, there are provisions in insurance plans that can reduce the problem.

One such provision is called a deductible. A **deductible** is a specified amount of money that an insured person must pay before the insurance company begins to help cover expenses. For example, an insurance company might require you to pay for the first $1,500 of your medical expenses in any given year, and then it will cover any medical costs you have that go above and beyond your deductible.

Another way that insurers help contain the moral hazard problem is through the use of copayments and coinsurance. A **copayment** is a fixed amount the insured pays when obtaining medical care. For example, if the insured visits the doctor, the insured may owe a copayment of $30, regardless of the amount or type of services received. **Coinsurance** is an arrangement under which the insured pays for some fraction of his or her own medical expenses, with the insurance company picking up the other portion. For example, if you break your leg skiing, you might be required to pay 20% of your medical expenses out of your own pocket, and your insurance company will cover the remaining 80%.

Deductibles, copayments, and coinsurance give insured patients a substantial financial stake in their own behavior. That financial stake helps reduce the moral hazard problem: If you are going skiing and know that you will have to pay absolutely nothing if you break your leg, you will use less caution than if your insurance company requires you to pay $1,500 before it chips in a dime on your behalf. Similarly, if you are responsible for chipping in $1 every time your insurance company pays $4, you are likely to be more careful about activities and behaviors that may necessitate medical care.

Similarly, deductibles and coinsurance help reduce problems of overuse. Remember in the tennis example that Rachel asked for a second $50 appointment because her insurance arrangement made that appointment appear to cost only $25. But what if Rachel's arrangement with Linda were restructured slightly so that each were solely responsible for the first $100 of her own therapy, and only after that would Linda and Rachel begin to split costs equally? That would make Rachel responsible for the full $50 cost of the second appointment, and because that second appointment would bring Rachel only $30 of benefit, she wouldn't schedule it.

How Different Health Care Systems Deal with Moral Hazard Many countries have created health care systems that do little, financially, to reduce moral hazard problems. Both Canada's single-payer system and the United Kingdom's nationalized health care system provide care that is free or almost free at the time of delivery. Further, those systems are funded by taxes rather than by premiums, which means that on the whole, peoples' behavior will have essentially zero effect on how much they pay for health care overall. As a consequence, patients have less of an incentive to think carefully about their behavior.

However, one of the most common complaints about both Canada's and the United Kingdom's systems is that patients often have to wait for elective care. That waiting time may help reduce the moral hazard problem: You may not want to play

Deductible A specified amount of money that an insured person must pay before his or her insurance company begins to help cover expenses.

Copayment A fixed amount an insured person pays when obtaining medical care.

Coinsurance An arrangement under which an insured person pays for some fraction of his or her own medical expenses, with the insurance company picking up the other portion.

Application 14.4

Using Information to Overcome Moral Hazard

Adverse selection arises because of asymmetric information: People who apply for insurance know more about how badly they need insurance than the insurance company does. Moral hazard, too, is a problem of asymmetric information: People know more about how obtaining insurance will alter their risky behaviors than the insurance company does.

If adverse selection and moral hazard problems are caused by the insurer's lack of information, then the solution lies in gathering more information—and the right information. Consider, for example, how Progressive Auto Insurance reduces these problems by harnessing the power of information. In 2009, Progressive rolled out a new program to its drivers: If drivers agreed to install a telematics device (similar to an airplane's black box) in their car, Progressive would offer them a substantial discount on their insurance premiums. The size of the discount depended on the data the box collected: the number of miles driven, the time of day the miles were being driven, and information about speed, acceleration, and braking.

Progressive's drivers didn't have to install a black box. In fact, making the box optional gave Progressive power to overcome adverse selection. Drivers who knew they were safe chose to install the box; drivers who knew they were worse risks chose not to. Ultimately, about one-third of drivers chose to participate, and armed with that information, Progressive tailored insurance premiums to drivers based on their self-assessed riskiness.

But the true power of the little black box is in overcoming moral hazard. Knowing that your insurance company is constantly monitoring your level of care gives you a strong incentive to avoid recklessness. And in 2014, drivers who opted for the black box began to pay for that recklessness: Too many miles, driven too recklessly, at the riskiest times of day (generally, between midnight and 4 a.m.) would earn drivers a surcharge rather than a discount. Jacques Amselem, CEO of a company that makes telematics devices, summed up the power of the black box to *Forbes* magazine: "Bad drivers will at some point need to improve their driving or accept [having] to pay for the real risk they represent."[11]

See related problem 3.22 on page 298 at the end of this chapter.

Based on "Progressive Uses 'Black Box' to Monitor Drivers," *PC Magazine*, July 31, 2008; "Data Monitoring Saves Some People Money on Car Insurance, but Some Will Pay More," *Forbes*, September 2, 2013; and "Motorists Tap the Brakes on Installing Data Devices for Insurance Companies," *Chicago Tribune*, September 15, 2013.

basketball on the weekends if you know that a knee injury won't be treated for a period of weeks or months.

Both Japan and the United States rely on financial incentives to reduce the moral hazard problem. In Japan, residents pay for most routine and preventive care out of their own pockets, and they face substantial copayments for other forms of care. In the United States, the ACA largely retained the private insurance system, which uses copayments and deductibles to deal with moral hazard problems.

How Pricing Variability May Contribute to High Health Care Costs

One reason the market for health care services is so vastly different than the market for ordinary goods and services is because almost every piece of the health care puzzle is shrouded in uncertainty. Patients don't know if or when they will get sick or have

---

[11]"Data Monitoring Saves Some People Money On Car Insurance, But Some Will Pay More," *Forbes*, September 2, 2013.

an accident. Doctors and patients alike don't know for certain which treatments will work and which will not. Without certain knowledge of those things, it is hard for doctors and patients to make good cost–benefit calculations.

Oddly, even if doctors and patients know exactly what course of treatment to follow, it may be hard for them to pin down how much that treatment will cost. That kind of information is necessary for markets to work well. Without inexpensive access to good information about the prices of available alternatives, consumers can't comparison shop and make cost-effective decisions about how and where to spend their money. This reduces the competitive discipline of the marketplace and helps keep prices high (see Chapter 6).

Information about health care prices may be more difficult to obtain than the price of just about any other product you can name. Especially in the case of hospitalizations and surgeries, it is often the case that neither doctor nor patient knows the exact cost of a procedure. What's more important, they don't have to: The exchange of funds takes place between the hospital's billing department and the patient's insurance company.

There are, of course, lots of doctors, hospitals, and clinics—enough that a reasonable person might conclude that there's a lot of competition in health care. But without information, competition disappears (see Chapter 6). Evidence of this became public in May 2013, when the Centers for Medicare & Medicaid Services released from a massive government database information about what 3,000 different hospitals charge for 100 of the most common medical procedures. That database revealed pricing discrepancies that would never persist in a world where people had an incentive and ability to comparison shop. Consider these examples:

- A pacemaker implant at Phoenixville Hospital in Pennsylvania costs $211,534. At nearby Uniontown Hospital, it costs only $19,747.

- In California, the typical cost to treat respiratory infections is $101,844; in Maryland, the cost is $18,444.

- A joint replacement in Ada, Oklahoma, can be done for $5,300. That's 97% less than the $223,000 charged in Monterey Park, California.

These incredible price gaps demonstrate that the market for health care isn't nearly as competitive as it looks: If it were, no hospital would be able to charge almost a quarter of a million dollars for a surgery that could be performed elsewhere for less than $6,000. Such pricing disparities persist only because the system the United States uses to pay for health care removes both doctor and patient from the process.

Such hidden pricing has undesirable effects on the overall affordability of health care. First, because prices aren't common knowledge, health care providers can charge prices for procedures that greatly exceed the actual cost of care. That directly drives up the overall cost of health care at a societal level. In other words, the lack of information about prices prevents competition from keeping the price of health care as low as possible. Further, the lack of pricing information hits the uninsured particularly hard: Break your femur in the wrong city, and you can suffer a financial setback that may take decades to recover from.

Second, the lack of information about prices for various treatments contributes to patients' and physicians' inability to perform any kind of cost–benefit analysis before making decisions. Compounding the lack of information about costs is the fact that in many cases, the benefits of various courses of treatment are uncertain or difficult to quantify. That lack of information, coupled with a system where a third party—the insurer—is responsible for the actual payment, creates an environment where doctors and patients may be encouraged to try treatments that they otherwise would not try.

How Different Health Care Systems Deal with Pricing Variability The pricing disparities seen in the United States appear to be unique among developed countries. In nationalized health care systems like the United Kingdom's, there *are* no prices, essentially, because government owns the health care resources and directly provides care, largely free of charge. In single-payer systems like Canada's, health care can be delivered by private doctors and hospitals, but those doctors and hospitals are paid for that care according to a fixed schedule of fees that is set by the government. Reimbursement according to a fixed schedule is referred to as a *fee-for-service* system. When applied at a national level, a fee-for-service system keeps prices uniform; doctors and hospitals know exactly how much each procedure is worth in dollar terms. Japan's universal health care system mimics Canada's single-payer system in this dimension. There, prices for health care services are set periodically through negotiations between the government and physicians. Once those prices are set, they are uniformly applied.

The United States has a blend of both public and private insurance. Medicare, the largest public insurance program, reimburses health care providers on a fee-for-service basis. On the other hand, different private insurers reimburse health care providers in different ways. Some private insurers use a fee-for-service system. Others offer variable reimbursement to health care providers: An insurance company might, for example, reimburse a doctor for 80% of the "usual and customary fees" associated with a procedure, with usual and customary fees being determined by what the typical doctor in a particular area might charge for the same procedure. Other insurers are organized as health maintenance organizations (HMOs); those insurers pay doctors a flat fee per patient per year, regardless of how much or how little care the doctor delivers. This implies that the effects of the pricing variability documented by the Centers for Medicare & Medicaid Services are not felt equally. People who pay for health care out of pocket and insurance companies that use variable reimbursement systems are likely to bear the brunt of the pricing variability documented by the Centers for Medicare & Medicaid Services.

Insurance Reimbursement Methods and Perverse Incentives The different systems of reimbursement have unique implications for overall health care costs and overall patient healthiness. For example, compare two doctors, one of whom (Dr. Grey) is reimbursed on a fee-for-service basis and the other of whom (Dr. Brown) has patients that are members of an HMO. Because Dr. Grey is paid for each service she performs, for any particular patient, Dr. Grey is likely to schedule more visits, administer more tests, and prescribe more treatments than Dr. Brown. Dr. Brown, on the other hand, gets the same total payment, regardless of the course of treatment he prescribes: He has an incentive to minimize the amount of care his patients receive. At a social level, fee-for-service reimbursement may result in healthier patients but at higher cost.

In short, then, the U.S. system contains a number of unique features that combine to make the way health care is priced problematic: The lack of information about the prices of various health care services coupled with the manner in which health care providers are reimbursed may give providers the ability and incentive to charge prices for various services that drive up insurance premiums and the overall cost of health care. And the reimbursement methods themselves may encourage providers not to focus on the quality of care or the health outcomes it generates but rather on the amount of care they deliver.

Conclusion

The United States has been less successful than many other developed countries in making health care available to everybody at a reasonable cost. Pinpointing a single reason why is difficult. Part of that difficulty lies in the fact that the U.S. system has so many different institutional features to account for and keep track of: The blend of public and private insurance, the different ways that insurance companies reimburse health care providers, the fact that some people get health insurance through their employer while others buy insurance privately, and the extreme variability in pricing and why that occurs. Couple that institutional complexity with the difficulty of obtaining good data, and that leaves even the best health care economists at odds over the true cause of high health care costs. Which is the biggest problem: adverse selection; moral hazard; non-uniform, non-transparent prices; or some other factor? There is no definitive evidence that singles out a main culprit, nor is there a consensus among health care economists.

If it's hard to pinpoint a cause of problems in U.S. health care, then it's even harder to design a solution. Because of the many different ways health care is delivered and paid for in the United States, any plan to fix the health care system is bound to create some new problems while reducing others. Fixing the system while retaining incentives to deliver timely and high-quality care is a real challenge. Fixing it and retaining incentives for U.S. companies and research institutions to develop new drugs, new treatment protocols, and new procedures may be even harder.

Chapter Summary and Problems

Key Terms

Adverse selection, p. 286

Asymmetric information, p. 286

Coinsurance, p. 291

Copayment, p. 291

Deductible, p. 291

Health care, p. 276

Moral hazard, p. 289

Nationalized health care, p. 281

Patient Protection and Affordable Care Act, p. 282

Premium death spiral, p. 286

Single-payer system, p. 281

Socialized medicine, p. 281

Universal health insurance, p. 282

14.1 The Current State of the U.S. Health Care System, pages 276–281

Compare the cost-effectiveness of the U.S. health care system to those in other developed countries.

Summary

U.S. residents spend a significant portion of their incomes on health care services, and that portion has been increasing. Compared to other developed countries, the United States spends about 50% more in both absolute and relative terms. In the United States, people are living longer, and infant mortality is declining. However, despite spending more on health care than other developed countries, the United States has lower life expectancy and higher infant mortality than other developed countries. Some portion of the gap in life expectancy and infant mortality can likely be attributed to behavioral choices and other factors rather than the quality of the U.S. health care system.

Review Questions

All problems are assignable in MyEconLab.

1.1 Compared to the rest of the world's developed countries, the United States spends _____ on health care and has _____ outcomes.
   a. More; better
   b. More; worse
   c. Less; better
   d. Less; worse

1.2 Over the past half-century in the United States, health care spending has _____, and health care outcomes have _____.

   a. Increased; improved
   b. Decreased; improved
   c. Increased; worsened
   d. Stayed about the same; improved

Problems and Applications

1.3 **[Related to Application 14.1 on page 280]** The United States compares very unfavorably to Japan in life expectancy. In the United States, average life expectancy at birth is less than 79 years; in Japan, life expectancy is almost 83 years. However, the United States spends 250% more on health care per person than Japan does. Read Application 14.1 and explain clearly why these numbers may not be evidence of the superior cost-effectiveness of the Japanese health care system.

1.4 **[Related to Application 14.1 on page 280]** The heart attack recovery rate in the United States is better than the heart attack recovery rate in Canada. Yet relatively more people die of heart attacks in the United States than in Canada. Reconcile these results, drawing on statistics in Application 14.1, and explain the effect these factors have on life expectancy.

14.2 Health Care Delivery and Finance Systems: An International Comparison, pages 281–284

List the key features of the health care systems in Japan, Canada, the United Kingdom, and the United States.

Summary

Different countries organize their health care systems differently. In nationalized health care systems, the government directly employs health care providers, and residents can access those providers at low out-of-pocket expense. In single-payer systems, doctors and hospitals may be private, but the government insures residents and reimburses doctors and hospitals for the care they deliver. In Japan's universal health care system, residents are required to obtain health insurance from the government or a nonprofit insurer. Doctors and hospitals are reimbursed at rates set by the government. In the United States, health care providers are largely private, and their services are paid for by a blend of private and public insurance. The Affordable Care Act (ACA) made major reforms to health care, including personal and employer mandates.

Review Questions

All problems are assignable in MyEconLab.

2.1 In a _____ health care system, government owns the hospitals and directly employs the health care providers.

2.2 A health care system with private doctors and hospitals but government-provided insurance is known as a _____ health care system.

2.3 In a single-payer system, the price of health care services is determined by _____.
   a. Market forces
   b. Doctors
   c. The government
   d. Private insurance companies

2.4 Which of the following is not a provision of the ACA?
   a. A personal mandate
   b. An employer mandate
   c. Creation of government-run health clinics
   d. Creation of state health insurance exchanges

Problems and Applications

2.5 [Related to Application 14.2 on page 283] Most people who have private insurance obtain it through their employers, and those who obtain it in this way are generally happy about not having to buy it on their own. What would likely happen to wages if a law that banned employer-provided insurance went into effect? Should employees be so happy about having their employer choose and fund their health insurance? Explain your reasoning.

2.6 Comparing countries with private health care systems to countries with nationalized health care or single-payer systems, where do you suppose it is easier to control overall health care costs? Explain your reasoning.

2.7 Enumerate and briefly explain at least two potential drawbacks of nationalized health care relative to privately delivered and financed health care. Then, do the same for single-payer systems.

14.3 How Health Care Finance May Affect the Affordability of Health Care, pages 284–294

Explain three reasons why the way the United States pays for health care may result in less-affordable health care than other systems.

Summary

The way the United States pays for health care may contribute to high overall health care costs and high insurance premiums that may make health care unaffordable to some people. One problem that creates high premiums is adverse selection, which occurs when healthier people choose not to obtain insurance. In the United States, the Affordable Care Act's personal mandate reduces adverse selection. A second problem is moral hazard, which occurs when people engage in riskier behaviors or overutilize the health care system after obtaining health insurance. Insurers use copays and deductibles to reduce moral hazard problems. One final problem that may contribute to high health care costs arises because often neither doctor nor patient is aware of the price of various treatments. This leads to extreme variability in prices and prevents competition from keeping prices as low as possible.

Review Questions

All problems are assignable in MyEconLab.

3.1 Your insurance policy requires you to cover the first $5,000 of your medical care out of your own pocket before your insurer begins paying benefits. That $5,000 is known as a(n) _____.

3.2 _____ occurs when only the sickest people sign up for insurance.

3.3 _____ exists when one party to a transaction knows more than the other.

3.4 Your health insurance requires you to chip in $1 toward your medical care costs for every $3 your insurer pays. The $1 you pay is known as a _____.

3.5 When obtaining insurance causes a person's behavior to change, _____ is said to exist.

3.6 A car insurance company has five customers who have taken out policies against auto damage. The drivers are all alike. On average, each year, two customers will file claims with the company, and the average payout made by the company will be $5,000 per claim. In order to break even, the insurance company needs to charge each of its customers an annual premium of _____.

   a. $5,000

   b. $2,000

   c. $10,000

   d. $1,000

3.7 Suppose that, in problem 3.6, two drivers are very careful and three are reckless. The "average" premium set by the insurance company will look relatively unattractive to the _____ drivers and will look like a good deal to the _____ drivers.

   a. Careful; reckless

   b. Reckless; careful

   c. The average premium will look like a good deal to both careful and reckless drivers.

   d. The average premium will look relatively unattractive to both careful and reckless drivers.

3.8 Given your answer to problem 3.7, the careful drivers _____.

   a. Will be more prone to seek out insurance than the reckless drivers

   b. Will be more prone to drop out of the insurance market

   c. Will be no less and no more likely to seek out insurance than the reckless drivers

3.9 Insurance companies are designed to spread the cost of accidents around. When the cost of an activity is shared by others but the benefits are received by only one person, that person has an incentive to _____.

   a. Overindulge in the activity

   b. Underindulge in the activity

   c. Engage in the socially optimal amount of that activity

3.10 The ACA makes insurance mandatory for everybody. This is a forceful solution to the _____.

   a. Moral hazard problem

   b. Prisoner's dilemma problem

   c. Third-party payment problem

   d. Adverse selection problem

3.11 Sally takes out a homeowner's insurance policy that protects her against burglary. Shortly after obtaining the policy, she begins neglecting to close and lock her windows. This is an example of the _____.

   a. Moral hazard problem

   b. Prisoner's dilemma problem

   c. Third-party payment problem

   d. Adverse selection problem

3.12 Billy, who has a family history of cancer, is more likely to seek out insurance than Joe, whose parents and grandparents all lived to the ripe old age of 112. This is an example of the _____.

   a. Moral hazard problem

   b. Prisoner's dilemma problem

   c. Third-party payment problem

   d. Adverse selection problem

3.13 Deductibles and copayments are tools insurance companies use to overcome the _____.

   a. Moral hazard problem

   b. Prisoner's dilemma problem

   c. Third-party payment problem

   d. Adverse selection problem

3.14 Adverse selection problems may cause insurance premiums to increase and healthier people to drop their insurance. This is commonly referred to as the _____.

   a. Premium death spiral

   b. Premium inflation problem

   c. Health insurance dropout problem

   d. Third-party payment problem

3.15 _____ problems appear before insurance is issued; _____ problems appear after.

   a. Adverse selection; price variability

   b. Moral hazard; premium inflation

   c. Adverse selection; moral hazard

   d. None of the above are accurate.

Problems and Applications

3.16 Explain how a country with a single-payer health care system has more power to control overall health care costs than a country with private health care provision and private insurance. Is there a disadvantage to the single-payer system?

3.17 The ACA contains a provision that requires insurers to issue policies to applicants regardless of preexisting conditions. Explain why that provision of the ACA necessitated the personal mandate.

3.18 Curling is a sport where teams slide stones on ice and attempt to hit targets. Teams consist of four players. Suppose that Bob, Carol, Ted, and Alice are on a team.

Bob and Carol have a 50% chance of slipping on the ice; Ted and Alice have a 25% chance. Each slip results in a bruise that costs $100 to treat. If each member were offered bruise insurance, how much would the premium be?

3.19 [Related to Application 14.3 on page 288] Refer to problem 3.18. Which players are most likely to drop their insurance coverage? If one member of the pool drops out, what will the premium become? After calculating the answer, explain how the ACA's personal mandate can help keep health insurance affordable.

3.20 Gus and Eleanor run marathons together. After a marathon, each requires physical therapy to recover. The first visit brings each $100 of benefit; the second brings $40. Each visit costs $70. How many visits will Gus and Eleanor schedule if they pay for their own therapy? How many visits will they schedule if they split the cost of therapy equally?

3.21 Consider problem 3.20. If Gus and Eleanor split the cost of therapy equally, is their predicted behavior socially optimal? Explain why or why not. How much of a deductible would their agreement require in order to generate a socially ideal outcome?

3.22 [Related to Application 14.4 on page 292] Read Application 14.4 carefully. If more information is better than less information, why do you suppose the U.S. government prohibits insurers from performing genetic tests on their potential clients?

The Restaurant Game

This chapter has highlighted the idea that some of the problems with the U.S. health care system stem from the way people in the country pay for health care. This game explores the incentives that different payment systems create by asking you and your classmates to order something that is every bit as essential as health care—food.

In this game, you will spend two evenings dining at the same fancy restaurant. You will order a selection of food from a menu. Each item on the menu brings you a different amount of pleasure, and each item has a different price. It's your job to order the dinner that brings you the greatest pleasure at the lowest cost.

On the first evening, you will be dining alone. On the second evening, you will be dining with three companions; you have all agreed to split the check equally. How will you decide how much food to order each evening? Will you place the same order on the first evening and the second evening, or will your order change?

MyEconLab

Please visit http://www.myeconlab.com for support material to conduct this experiment if assigned by your instructor.

Chapter Outline and Learning Objectives

15.1 **The Segregation of Neighborhoods and Schelling's Checkerboard,** page 301

Describe the process of neighborhood self-segregation and explain why it happens.

15.2 **Does Your Neighborhood Determine Your Future Well-Being?** page 304

Summarize the Moving to Opportunity program and list its general findings.

15.3 **Labor Market Discrimination,** page 308

Explain the difference between taste-based discrimination and statistical discrimination.

15.4 **How Economists Detect and Measure Discrimination,** page 312

Discuss how economists use the audit method and regression analysis to detect discrimination.

15.5 **Anti-Discrimination Legislation,** page 316

List three justifications for affirmative action programs and list four ways affirmative action is implemented.

Experiment: Schelling's Checkerboard, page 324

MyEconLab
MyEconLab helps you master each objective and study more efficiently.

All people may be created equal. But they don't live equally, nor are they treated equally. Sometimes in society, the way people live and how others treat them depends on their race, ethnicity, gender, or religion. This chapter discusses two important topics: the causes and consequences of neighborhood segregation, and discrimination in the labor market and how to detect and measure it.

The Segregation of Neighborhoods and Schelling's Checkerboard

The Civil Rights Act of 1964 outlawed discrimination based on race, ethnicity, gender, religion, or national origin and also ended racial segregation in schools, workplaces, and facilities that serve the general public. But take a long drive through any major city today, and you might notice that despite passage of the Civil Rights Act, the United States still appears to be a divided country—at least in terms of where Americans live. You will see many predominantly white neighborhoods, black neighborhoods, Chinese neighborhoods, Hispanic neighborhoods, Italian neighborhoods, and other neighborhoods that appear to be segregated by people's races and ethnicities. In fact, it is surprisingly difficult to find a neighborhood that consists of less than two-thirds of people of one race or ethnicity. Americans don't live in a melting pot; they live in a cafeteria tray with different compartments for meat, veggies, bread, and dessert.

Segregation is the sorting and separation of people by various characteristics including, but not limited to race, ethnicity, gender, and religion. Segregation can result from explicit government policies, but it can also be the result of social pressures and individual choices.

Extreme racial segregation during the 1970s motivated future Nobel Prize winner Thomas Schelling to study the phenomenon. Schelling was curious about whether segregation was the result of intense dislike for people of different colors. On a long flight, he began doodling with pencil and paper to uncover the answer. Filling a grid with Xs and Os, he began moving symbols around the paper to see what resulted when a symbol moved from one square to another to avoid being alone in an area dominated by other symbols.

But erasing and redrawing was slow, so when Schelling's plane landed, he got out a checkerboard and raided his son's piggy bank for pennies and dimes. With his son helping, Schelling set some ground rules for how the pennies and dimes would behave. First, they would start with equal numbers of pennies and dimes. Second, neighborhoods would be defined as adjacent squares on the checkerboard. Third, each coin would be assigned a mild preference to live in a neighborhood with coins of the same type as itself—specifically, at least one-third of them should be of the same type.[1] If that preference wasn't satisfied, the coin would move to the nearest square where its preference would be satisfied.

Schelling began by alternating the pennies and dimes on the checkerboard so that they were perfectly integrated and every coin's preferences were satisfied. The corners were left open in case a coin wanted to move, but no coin did. That initial arrangement is shown in Figure 15.1.

Then Schelling did something interesting: Just as the real world sometimes does, he threw in a bit of randomness. He removed 20 coins from the board at random and then placed 5 of the coins he had just removed back on the board, but in randomly assigned locations. In his 1978 book *Micromotives and Macrobehavior*, Schelling

15.1 Learning Objective
Describe the process of neighborhood self-segregation and explain why it happens.

Segregation The sorting and separation of people by various characteristics including, but not limited to, race, ethnicity, gender, and religion.

---

[1] In particular, Schelling set out these parameters: To be happy, if a coin has one neighbor, it must be of the same type. If it has two neighbors, at least one must be of the same type. If a coin has three, four, or five neighbors, two must be of the same type. And if a coin has six, seven, or eight neighbors, at least three must be of the same type. While these parameters are quite rigidly structured, Schelling encourages people who replicate this exercise to make them stronger or weaker as desired.

► Figure 15.1

Schelling's Initial Neighborhood Arrangement

In Schelling's checkerboard model, pennies and dimes are initially perfectly integrated, and each penny or dime is happy with the composition of its neighborhood because at least one-third of each coin's neighbors are of similar type.

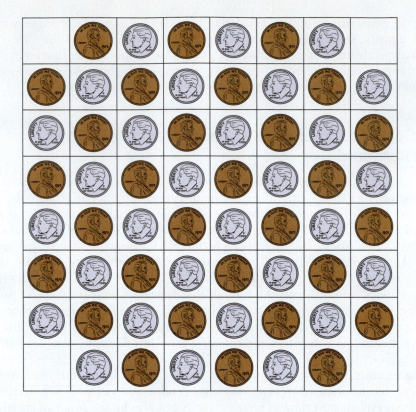

presented one possible outcome of this random removal and replacement process. That outcome is shown in Figure 15.2.

The highlighted squares in Figure 15.2 show the coins that are unhappy with their locations because their preferences are no longer satisfied.

► Figure 15.2

Schelling's Checkerboard After Some Random Rearrangement

A small number of random changes to Schelling's checkerboard causes some of the pennies and dimes to become unhappy with their neighborhoods. Unhappy pennies and dimes are shown in yellow.

Unraveling and Equilibrium

To satisfy the discontented coins, one by one, Schelling moved them to neighborhoods where their preferences were satisfied. But each coin that moved affected other coins, both in the neighborhood that it left and in the neighborhood that it moved to. Some coins in the neighborhoods that were initially content found themselves sufficiently outnumbered so that they, too, desired to leave. Bit by bit, Shelling's checkerboard unraveled as coins sorted out of neighborhoods where they weren't satisfied and into neighborhoods where they were.

Eventually the board returned to equilibrium. In other words, the preferences of each and all of the coins were sufficiently satisfied that none desired to move. That equilibrium, as Schelling points out, isn't unique: Depending on which coins you move, in which order, and to which location, the arrangement shown in Figure 15.2 can ultimately produce thousands of different outcomes.[2] The outcome in Figure 15.3 is one of them.

◀ **Figure 15.3**
An Equilibrium Outcome in Schelling's Checkerboard
In Schelling's checkerboard, dissatisfied pennies and dimes continue to move until the board returns to equilibrium. This equilibrium, which is one of many possible equilibria, displays visible segregation.

The pennies and dimes in Figure 15.3 are all happy: Their "neighborhoods" satisfy Schelling's parameters. Yet this checkerboard is much more segregated. There are clusters of pennies and clusters of dimes, whereas before those pennies and dimes were well mixed. You can measure the segregation quantitatively, too. Before coins started moving, only 3 coins had no neighbors of the opposite type. Now 14 of them do.

The extreme segregation Schelling found didn't result from outright hatred, or even dislike. Rather, it was the result of each coin's mild preference not to be too outnumbered. If you draw a parallel between Schelling's checkerboard and the real world, you might feel discouraged. Segregation, even when it's not enforced like it used to be in parts of the United States, appears to be the unavoidable outcome of a genuine collective action problem: Individuals, in pursuing their own interests, create an outcome that most people agree is less than ideal.

---

[2]Schelling notes that even though there are many possible outcomes, most of those outcomes will display the pattern of extreme segregation shown in Figure 15.3.

Is Neighborhood Segregation Inevitable?

Neighborhoods, of course, aren't segregated on a completely voluntary basis. There are landlords who won't rent to people of some races or ethnicities; there are realtors who won't show houses in predominantly white neighborhoods to blacks or houses in predominantly black neighborhoods to whites. What Schelling's checkerboard shows is that even if those kinds of segregation disappeared from society, people would likely still segregate themselves.

There may, however, be some reason for optimism when it comes to peoples' self-segregation. First, Schelling's checkerboard tells us something positive about ourselves: Just because neighborhoods display extreme segregation doesn't mean that people of different colors and ethnicities necessarily hate one another. That is an encouraging implication.

But there are other reasons for optimism, too. If you return to the initial randomly arranged neighborhood shown in Figure 15.2, you'll find that only 9 of the 45 coins on the board are dissatisfied with their locations. If they could be persuaded to stay, then self-segregation wouldn't occur. Or, with a little bit of ingenuity, it might be possible to strategically relocate some of the coins on the board or bring in some new pieces from outside the board to create a stable "society."

The real-world analogue to such tinkering is for governments to relocate individuals, either forcibly or by creating incentives for relocation. That's something governments have generally been reluctant to do, but it is not unprecedented. Consider, as an example, busing programs that transport schoolchildren from one neighborhood to schools in other neighborhoods in order to integrate schools. Major cities with ethnically segregated school systems initiated busing programs during the years following the landmark 1954 *Brown v. Topeka Board of Education* decision. In *Brown*, the Supreme Court established that "separate educational facilities are inherently unequal." Busing was seen as a means to provide minorities with access to better educational opportunities—with the practical effect of taking segregated societies like the one shown in Figure 15.3 and forcibly turning them, at least for schoolchildren, into integrated societies like the one in Figure 15.1.

In *Micromotives and Macrobehavior*, Schelling offers hope that segregation might, at some point, diminish without such heavy-handedness on the part of government. He observed that at the Dodgers's spring training camps in the late 1960s, tables in the major league dining hall were often segregated, but tables in the minor league dining hall were not. According to the general manager, in the minor league dining hall, the rule was that "A boy takes the first seat available. This has been done deliberately. If a white boy doesn't want to eat with a colored boy, he can go out and buy his own food. We haven't had any trouble."[3]

You might interpret the differences between the major and minor league dining halls as nothing more than evidence that people will eat with people of other races if they are forced to. But perhaps that's too pessimistic. As Schelling notes, even in the 1960s, racial preferences—at least among professional athletes in the minor leagues—must not have been too intense; the players could have avoided eating with people of other races for the price of a meal outside the league dining halls. Or the players could get together with people of the same color and enter the dining halls together. The fact that the athletes, by and large, didn't expend much effort to do so shows that the segregation in major league dining halls probably stemmed from racial preferences that were very mild.

15.2 Learning Objective

Summarize the Moving to Opportunity program and list its general findings.

Does Your Neighborhood Determine Your Future Well-Being?

How much does your neighborhood matter in terms of your well-being, education, and the opportunities you face? If your neighborhood is poor, are you destined to be poor, too? If your neighborhood schools aren't up to snuff, will that prevent you from achieving academic success and doom you to a life of unhappiness?

[3] Thomas C. Schelling, *Micromotives* and *Macrobehavior*, New York: Norton, ©1978.

The People Behind the Theory

Thomas Schelling

Thomas Schelling's model of neighborhood segregation has been highly influential in understanding racial dynamics. But his most notable work didn't deal with neighborhoods; it dealt with nuclear annihilation. This is a story about how two iconic pieces of atomic-era pop culture came into being at Schelling's hands.

After completing his Ph.D. coursework in 1948, Schelling left for Europe, where he helped administer the Marshall Plan for post–World War II reconstruction. He returned to a foreign policy position with the White House and then joined the faculty of Yale University, where he began an intensive study of cooperation and conflict—the essential elements of game theory.

At that time, economists and military strategists were enthusiastically applying game theory to analyze the possibility and strategy of nuclear war. But game theory generally assumes rational, mechanical actors—in Schelling's eyes, a key weakness. According to Schelling, human interactions are characterized by behaviors—posturing, communicating, warning, threatening—that limit the effectiveness of game theoretic models to explain and predict.

Schelling began to study these behaviors in earnest. His 1960 book *The Strategy of Conflict* pioneered the study of *strategic moves*—commitments, threats, and promises that are made "outside" a formal game to gain a strategic advantage over one's rival. His study of conflict and strategy and his research's emphasis on communication led him to the realization that a nuclear war could possibly begin as a result of an accident—a mistake by a radio operator, a miscommunication, or a loose-cannon general.

Schelling suggested something novel to keep such accidents from escalating into all-out nuclear war: a permanent hotline—widely referred to as the "red phone"—between Washington and Moscow that leaders could use to communicate in the event of such a mistake. The red phone was installed in 1963 and is still in use today—although it was never really a phone. It began as a teletype machine, which was later replaced with a fax machine; today, it is a secure email link.

Schelling's second contribution to popular culture came about due to an article he wrote about the possibility of accidental nuclear war. His article, which praised the realism of a novel titled *Red Alert*, caught the eye of film director Stanley Kubrick. Kubrick tracked down *Red Alert* author Peter George, and they began to adapt the novel for film. When they needed advice on some critical strategic issues, Kubrick and George sought out the most obvious expert: Schelling. The film, about how a failure of communication could cause an all-out nuclear war, was eventually released as the darkly comedic, award-winning masterpiece *Dr. Strangelove or: How I Learned to Stop Worrying and Love the Bomb*.

Schelling, the progenitor of the red phone and *Dr. Strangelove*, was awarded the 2005 Nobel Prize "for having enhanced our understanding of conflict and cooperation through game-theory analysis." His Nobel Prize lecture began, "The most spectacular event of the past half century is one that did not occur. We have enjoyed sixty years without nuclear weapons exploded in anger."

Based on Sharon Ghamari-Tabrizi's "The Worlds of Herman Kahn: The Intuitive Science of Thermonuclear War," Harvard University Press, 2005; Matt Cadwallader's "Tom Schelling, Stanley Kubrick and Dr. Strangelove," found at hks.harvard.edu; and biographical information found at www.nobelprize.org.

The Link Between Neighborhoods and Outcomes: Correlation or Causation?

There is little doubt that the characteristics of the neighborhood you grow up in are *correlated* with your life outcomes. In other words, there seems to be a connection between the two. This is particularly true when it comes to neighborhood poverty:

Your health, your mental well-being, your educational outcomes, and certainly your economic prospects appear to be shaped by the typical income in your neighborhood. However, correlation is not the same as causation. The question is, does your neighborhood directly *determine* what your outcome in life will be, or are the two conditions merely related?

Researchers have used statistics to compare the life outcomes of poor families living in poor neighborhoods to the life outcomes of similarly poor families living in wealthier neighborhoods. By statistically sorting through families whose characteristics are otherwise similar (for example, race, gender, marital status, and age), researchers are essentially able to make direct comparisons between families that for all intents and purposes look alike except for where they choose to live.

However, where a family chooses to live indicates something about that family that may muddle the findings. Consider two families that are identical in every way. Each has small children. Suppose that Family A stays in an impoverished neighborhood, and Family B chooses to leave that neighborhood and move to a richer neighborhood with better schools, less crime, and better job prospects. The very fact that Family B made the conscious decision to leave the old neighborhood and seek out a "better" neighborhood says something about Family B—something that might not be easily measured by social scientists. We might use the word *optimism* to capture that intangible characteristic.[4]

Researchers studying Families A and B might observe that Family B performs better on a number of measures, and they might attribute those performance differences to the fact that the families live in different neighborhoods. But those researchers might be wrong: At least part of the difference might be because Family B is more optimistic than Family A. If the people in Family B are optimistic enough to move to a better neighborhood, then their optimism might also be sufficient for them to devote more resources to other things that matter, too—things that social scientists might have trouble measuring. For example, the family might spend more time each evening doing homework; they might pursue scholarship opportunities more aggressively; they might devote more of their resources to eating healthily, and so on. The problem for social scientists, then, is sorting out the effects of living in a different neighborhood from the effects of the indefinable-and-impossible-to-measure quality, optimism.

Moving to Opportunity: A Housing Experiment to Determine Causation

The difference a neighborhood makes in a person's life outcome could be isolated if social scientists had a way to make sure the families they were comparing were identical in every characteristic, including optimism. Researchers could, for example, take families from the same neighborhood and forcibly relocate some of those families—families that had displayed no intention of moving away—to a different neighborhood.

Of course, no family is ever going to change neighborhoods because a mad-scientist economist threatens them. Economists just aren't that threatening. But economists *did* have the opportunity to observe the outcomes from a carefully controlled experiment similar to this: In 1994, the U.S. Department of Housing and Urban Development launched a novel program in five major cities called *Moving to Opportunity* (MTO). Families with children living in public housing or receiving public housing assistance were eligible to participate, provided that they lived in a census tract where more than 40% of residents were below the poverty line.

The Design of the Experiment The families that applied for MTO were randomly assigned into three equal groups. People in the first group received nothing but were able to continue to live in public housing with their rents fixed at 30% of their

---

[4] Use whatever word you would like here, but note that it is important, for rhetorical purposes, to keep the word you choose as neutral as possible. Remember that Family A and Family B are identical in every other measurable respect, including how much they work and how hard they work.

household incomes. People in the second group received a voucher they could use to help pay for private housing; the voucher would pay any rent beyond 30% of their household incomes.[5] Those in the third group received a similar voucher for private housing, but that voucher was good only if the family moved to a neighborhood with a poverty rate of less than 10%. In addition, members of the third group were given assistance in finding suitable housing and counseling to help deal with the stresses of moving to new neighborhoods.

The MTO program gave many families a chance to leave their old neighborhoods behind. Thousands leapt at the chance. Those that applied emphasized that their primary motivation was escaping drugs and gangs: In the six months prior to being assigned to their groups, 25% of the applicants had had purses, wallets, or jewelry snatched; 25% had had a family member threatened with a knife or gun; nearly 25% had been beaten or assaulted; and a full 10% had been stabbed or shot. Applicants' secondary motivations were to find bigger or better apartments and to send their children to better schools.

To economists, MTO provided a natural experiment that they could use to learn about the effects of neighborhoods on life outcomes. Randomly assigning participants to their respective groups ensured that there would be no systematic differences among the three experimental "treatments." Even intangible factors like optimism should have been divided equally among the three groups. As a result, any differences in outcomes could be attributed solely to differences in locations.

The Results of the Experiment The results of this grand housing experiment were mixed. Despite lots of hypothesizing that moving to better neighborhoods would open up employment opportunities and give children access to better educational opportunities, MTO had little effect on either measure. Fifteen years after the program began, children who had moved to low-poverty neighborhoods scored no better on math and reading proficiency tests than the children who hadn't. Their parents had no better luck finding jobs while living in wealthier neighborhoods than they did when they lived in impoverished neighborhoods. Nor did MTO reduce the number of families receiving welfare payments and other forms of public assistance.

Lest that evidence tempt you to conclude that someone's neighborhood doesn't matter, MTO *did* lead to noticeable improvements in other performance measures. In adults, the families that moved to low-poverty neighborhoods had a lower prevalence of severe obesity and diabetes than families in high-poverty neighborhoods. They also suffered less from depression and psychological distress.

Their children benefited, too, but in different ways. Their overall physical health did not generally change as a result of the move, but the program had a profound effect on the mental health of girls: Girls who had moved to a low-poverty neighborhood experienced a lower incidence of psychological distress, panic attacks, and oppositional defiant disorder. They also had fewer behavioral difficulties. Boys who had moved displayed less cruel or mean behavior and experienced less sadness and depression; they also got into slightly less trouble at school and at home. Both boys and girls were less likely to be injured or to be victims of crime. Unfortunately, MTO appears to have had no effect on the likelihood of a child being arrested: Children were just as likely to get in trouble with the law after moving as they were before.

Thomas Schelling demonstrated that societies are likely to fragment into distinct neighborhoods. The MTO experiment shows that the separation Schelling predicted matters: The neighborhood you live in *does* matter. People who live in wealthier neighborhoods are safer, healthier, and happier. Yet your neighborhood does not determine your destiny. Living in a good neighborhood won't improve your test scores. It won't keep you out of jail. It won't guarantee you economic self-sufficiency. Explaining intergroup differences in those key outcomes requires an explanation that goes beyond geography.

---

[5] HUD restricted these payments to housing that was both reasonably priced and of reasonable quality.

15.3 Learning Objective

Explain the difference between taste-based discrimination and statistical discrimination.

Labor Market Discrimination

It is no secret that in the United States, different demographic groups experience different treatment. Those differences are widespread and sometimes show up in unusual places. In the real estate market, realtors tend to show white homebuyers more houses than they show black homebuyers. Realtors also tend to show white people houses in predominantly white neighborhoods and black people houses in black neighborhoods. Symphony orchestras have been shown to discriminate against female musicians during auditions. Even the federal government's National Institutes of Health has been shown to discriminate against African-American scientists applying for grants.[6]

It would be possible to devote an entire book to the various differences in outcomes across race, gender, ethnicity, age, and even sexual identity. But in the minds of economists, one area stands out as most prominent: the labor market. That is because almost everyone will work or will want to work at some point during their lifetimes. The job and earnings opportunities they have will bear directly on their material well-being and the quality of life they enjoy.

An Initial Observation: Outcomes Differ Across Demographic Groups

The raw data paint a disparate picture when it comes to the outcomes different demographic groups experience in the labor market. First, consider the opportunity to participate in the labor market. One measure of that opportunity is the unemployment rate, which is the percentage of people who are actively seeking work but do not currently have jobs (the unemployment rate is explored in depth in Chapter 17). In October 2014, the U.S. unemployment rate for whites was 4.8%; for blacks it was over twice as high, at 10.9%. In other words, 1 out of every 20 whites who wanted to work couldn't find work, compared to 1 out of every 9 blacks. The contrast is even greater when you focus on the young: For whites between the ages of 16 and 19, the unemployment rate was a depressing 16.3%. But as bad as that number appears, it's twice as bad to be black: The teen unemployment rate for blacks was an astonishing 32.6%. In other words, if you're black and young and want a job, your chances of finding work are only slightly better than one in three.

The races also weather recessions differently. Consider the Great Recession of 2007–2009. During that disastrous economic episode and the recovery that followed, the white unemployment rate rose from 4.4% to 9%, an increase of 4.6 percentage points. In contrast, the black unemployment rate rose from 9% at the beginning of the Great Recession to 16.8% as the recovery began, an increase of 7.8 percentage points. In other words, as hard as the recession was for everybody, it was particularly hard for blacks.

Labor market disparities show up in different ways when we compare people by gender, too. Although the unemployment rate for women is consistently a few tenths of a percentage point lower than it is for men, there are dramatic differences in the labor outcomes of the two groups, as measured by earnings. For example, if you look at data from the U.S. Bureau of Labor Statistics, in the third quarter of 2014, the median weekly earnings were $880 for men but only $722 for women. In other words, the typical woman makes about 80% of what the typical man makes. That disparity is more noticeable among the old: When the data are restricted to compare men and women between the ages of 16 and 24, the pay differential decreases from almost 20% to less than 10%. In other words, the typical young woman makes slightly more than 90% of what the typical young man makes.

That's a lot of numbers—numbers that aren't worth memorizing because they change from month to month and year to year. However, the *general pattern* is this: Blacks have a harder time in the labor market than whites, teens fare worse than adults, and women earn less than men.

---

[6]See "NIH Uncovers Racial Disparity in Grant Awards," *Science*, August 2011; Claudia Goldin and Cecelia Rouse, "Orchestrating Impartiality: The Impact of 'Blind' Auditions on Female Musicians," *American Economic Review*, September 2000; and the Department of Housing and Urban Development's *Housing Discrimination Against Racial and Ethnic Minorities 2012*.

Application 15.1

Can You Avoid Being Short-Changed in the Labor Market?

Lest you be led to believe that wage differentials exist only across race and gender lines, the economics literature is loaded with other examples. Left-handers, for example, earn 5% more than right-handers. People with a full set of teeth earn more than people who are missing teeth. Drinkers earn more than teetotalers. And people regarded as beautiful earn about 5% more than people who are simply ordinary.

One interesting case of earnings disparity is found in the labor market's treatment of height. In short, it's good to be tall. Labor market studies find that each extra inch of height is worth about $1,000 in extra earnings each year, which means that if you are a fairly typical 5'11" male, your 6'4" cubicle-mate is more likely than not to earn about $5,000 more than you.

This raises an interesting question: Can you increase your earnings by wearing lifts in your shoes to make you look taller? Economists Nicola Persico and Andrew Postelwaite of the University of Pennsylvania and Dan Silverman of the University of Michigan say no. They explored three theories about why height creates extra earnings:

- **Pure discrimination.** Tall people garner more respect from employers, leading to higher starting salaries and bigger raises.

- **Occupational segregation.** Being tall qualifies someone to do highly paid work that short people just can't do as well.

- **Self-esteem.** Height increases a person's self-esteem, making tall people more assertive and therefore better leaders. Because they bring more value to their employers, they receive bigger rewards.

Determining whether any of these theories explains the height premium is tough. But Persico, Postelwaite, and Silverman discovered something in their data that enabled them to do just that. They found that earnings of short men who were tall as teenagers are similar to the earnings of men who are tall as adults. And the earnings of tall men who were short as teenagers are similar to the earnings of men who are short as adults.

That observation alone rules out the first theory: While employers might discriminate based on today's height, there's no reason to expect them to discriminate based on *past* height. Furthermore, if short men who were once tall earn as much today as tall men, then the occupational sorting hypothesis also fails.

That leaves self-esteem. Persico, Postelwaite, and Silverman note that tall teenagers develop an esteem that they carry with them even when they stop growing. That esteem makes them more likely to play on sports teams and join other groups in which important leadership and social skills are developed. Participation in high school sports alone can account for about a 10% wage premium in adulthood, whereas other activities account for a 5% bump in adult pay.

The importance of self-esteem leads to an interesting conclusion: If your earnings depend on your past height, and not on your current height, putting lifts in your shoes won't garner you any raises. Your money may be better spent on a therapist.

See related problem 3.8 on page 322 at the end of this chapter.

Based on Nicola Persico, Andrew Postelwaite, and Dan Silverman, "The Effect of Adolescent Experience on Labor Market Outcomes: The Case of Height," *Journal of Political Economy*, 2004; Sherry Glied and Matthew Neidell, "The Economic Value of Teeth," *Journal of Human Resources*, 2010; Daniel Hamermesh, *Beauty Pays: Why Attractive People Are More Successful*, Princeton University Press, 2013; and Christopher S. Ruebeck, Joseph E. Harrington, Jr., and Robert Moffitt, "Handedness and Earnings," *NBER Working Paper Series*, 2006.

The big question is why people of different races, genders, and ages earn different wages. Are the pay gaps clear evidence of discrimination? Or can they be explained by fundamental differences in characteristics that affect on-the-job productivity?

Types of Discrimination in the Labor Market

Labor market discrimination
Rewarding or penalizing personal characteristics of a worker that are unrelated to his or her productivity.

Labor market discrimination can be defined as rewarding or penalizing personal characteristics of a worker that are unrelated to his or her productivity. In other words, discrimination exists when employers pay members of one group less than they pay members of another group who have different characteristics, even though members of both groups are equally productive. Discrimination also exists when an employer hires a member of one group when another applicant, who happens to belong to a different group with different characteristics, has better qualifications and is likely to be more productive. Employers can be sued for discrimination, so the question is, why do they do it? Economists have theorized that there are two possible rationales: taste-based discrimination and statistical discrimination.

Taste-based discrimination
Discrimination that occurs because the discriminator dislikes another person's gender, race, or some other personal characteristic.

Taste-Based Discrimination Consider a business owner who discriminates against women for the simple reason that he doesn't like women. Nobel Prize–winning economist Gary Becker called this **taste-based discrimination**. The business owner essentially says, "I've got a job to fill, and Alice is the best qualified. But I like men better than women, so I'm going to hire Ted instead."

As odd as it sounds, when it comes to taste-based discrimination, there's bad news and good news. The bad news (which in no way should be minimized) is that Alice doesn't get hired. The good news is that the business owner pays for his decision. By hiring less-productive Ted instead of more-productive Alice, he hurts his own profitability. If he routinely chooses less-productive men over more-productive women, his profits will decline even more.

That the discriminator pays for his discrimination is some consolation, though it's small consolation (and it's no consolation whatsoever to Alice). But Becker suggested that there are larger implications: Firms engaged in cutthroat competition with rivals operate on slim margins. There just isn't much room to indulge in taste-based discrimination in such an environment. If you are a personnel manager who consistently hires less-productive employees than your rivals do, you are hurting your firm. If the competition in your industry is so intense that some firms will be driven out of business, there's a better-than-average chance it will be yours. Even if your firm survives, you may not: In a cutthroat environment, managers who hire poorly qualified people may not stay managers for very long. The same is true for discriminating managers who are willing to hire women but insist on paying them less: Firms that don't discriminate will be able to hire those well-qualified women away from firms that insist on paying subpar wages. In the end, nondiscriminating firms end up with a more talented labor pool and higher profits.

Anecdotal evidence suggesting that Becker's hypothesis is right can be found in professional sports. There are very few industries where competition is as intense and where there are such clear winners and losers. At the end of every season, you can see which teams were consistently better than others. So the managers of pro sports teams pursue the top talent, regardless of non-performance-related characteristics. As a result, no industry is as visibly color-blind.[7]

Of course, not every industry is as competitive as professional sports. And some industries aren't very competitive at all. The less competitive a particular industry is,

[7]In the National Basketball Association (NBA), for example, hiring decisions appear to be generally color-blind, and there is little systematic evidence of discrimination in pay; some studies find a white salary premium, while others do not. See the *Handbook of Sports Economics Research* and David Berri's *The Wages of Wins* for a review of the literature on salary discrimination. But even pro sports is not entirely free of discrimination: There is, for example, evidence that referees discriminate against players of the opposite race when calling fouls. For evidence, see Joseph Price and Justin Wolfers's "Racial Discrimination Among NBA Referees," *The Quarterly Journal of Economics*, 2010.

the longer taste-based discriminatory behavior can last. And it is likely to: Even pro sports didn't integrate overnight. In fact, even stiff competition is no guarantee that taste-based discrimination will disappear, as long as the discriminators are willing to foot the bill. Further, there exists the possibility that business owners discriminate not because *they* personally dislike a particular group of people but because *their customers* do. If hiring a minority would drive away customers, then discriminating against that minority—even if it results in hiring a less-qualified person—might increase profits rather than decrease them. That, in turn, implies that this particular form of taste-based discrimination is more likely to persist.

Statistical Discrimination The second general type of discrimination isn't based on personal distaste. It's based on numbers. Suppose that on average blacks are less productive workers than whites. That may be true for a number of reasons, including, but not limited to, the fact that blacks don't generally acquire as much education and training as whites.

Now suppose that a black man (Michael) and a white man (Larry) reply to a help-wanted advertisement. Michael may well be better qualified than Larry. But a personnel manager may have a hard time determining that based on a resume and a brief initial interview. So the personnel manager may take a mental shortcut when making her decision: "I don't have enough information to determine whether Michael or Larry is better qualified for this position. However, I know that blacks are typically less productive than whites, and since Michael is black and Larry is white, odds are I'll be best off hiring Larry."

The personnel manager has just practiced statistical discrimination. **Statistical discrimination** is assigning to a particular individual the properties of a group—the labor market equivalent of racial profiling. It is the result of an information problem: If the personnel manager knew Michael was better qualified than Larry, he would have hired him. But because it can be quite difficult to gather information about the potential productivity of an employee from a piece of paper and a short interview, the personnel manager plays the averages. A less-qualified individual gets the job, and the better-qualified applicant is shown the door.

Statistical discrimination isn't only a problem when just two candidates are being compared. It happens when hundreds of candidates are being compared as personnel managers sort through applications quickly to cull them. Eliminating everyone who belongs to a group with lower-than-average performance ratings is a useful way to do this.

A third scenario doesn't involve hiring someone new but promoting from within. Suppose a pharmaceutical firm is considering promoting a woman to an area sales manager position, a job that might require extensive travel. If that woman is in her late 20s or early 30s, she may be passed over on the belief (which may be correct, on average) that she won't stay long in that position because it will interfere with her desire to have and raise a family. This might occur in spite of the fact that she may have no desire to have or raise a family, or that she may remain committed to her job even if she has a family, or that she may be incapable of having a family altogether.

Although it may seem less insidious than taste-based discrimination, statistical discrimination is the more troubling of the two types of discrimination. Here's why: The personnel manager who hires white Larry over black Michael made a mistake—on that particular hire. But if that personnel manager makes a practice of hiring white workers, the law of averages works in his favor. So, compared to a firm that doesn't statistically discriminate but has equally poor information about candidates' true qualifications, the firm that discriminates is likely to be *more* profitable rather than less. In other words, no amount of competition is going to make statistical discrimination go away. Rather, the edge that statistical discrimination gives a firm becomes relatively *more* important the more competitive that firm's industry happens to be.

Statistical discrimination A type of discrimination that occurs when someone assigns the properties of a group to a particular individual who is a member of that group.

How Discrimination Harms Individuals and Society

Discrimination has several important economic effects. From a social standpoint, the immediate effect of discrimination is that society fails to fully utilize the talents and abilities at its disposal. That makes everybody poorer, on average. As bad as that is for society, it's even worse to be on the receiving end of discrimination because it does direct and immediate harm to you. That's true whether the discrimination is taste-based or statistical.

Another insidious effect of discrimination is its indirect and long-term effect on incentives. To illustrate, return to Michael and Larry for a moment. Michael had just lost a job to Larry, despite being a better-qualified applicant. He goes to the next firm, and the next, and the next, and because statistical discrimination is a profitable strategy, at each firm, the outcome is the same. Michael is being held back by the average characteristics of his race, and in the process, he is given this message: "It doesn't matter that you've taken time to invest in your skills, training, and education. Because we can't directly observe the value that those skills, training, and education created, we're going to assume that you are average. And on that basis, we're going to have to say, 'No, thanks.'"

When Michael's children, neighbors, friends, and relatives see that investing in training, skills, and education still can't land Michael a good job, they get the message that training, skills, and education really aren't worth acquiring. Rather than repeat Michael's "mistake," they forgo the opportunity to improve their productivity, and as a result the average ability of the black labor pool declines. A vicious downward spiral can begin as a result: As the average ability falls, the rewards for education and training fall; as the rewards for education and training fall, fewer blacks acquire education and training; as fewer blacks acquire education and training, the average ability falls even further.

15.4 Learning Objective

Discuss how economists use the audit method and regression analysis to detect discrimination.

How Economists Detect and Measure Discrimination

Discrimination is difficult to detect on a case-by-case basis because often the circumstances surrounding the decision to discriminate are highly subjective. For example, the employer who hired Larry over Michael only has to offer a plausible reason for hiring Larry, even if Michael appears to be a better fit in many ways.

Rather than focus on a case-by-case analysis, with all the subjectivity that entails, economists interested in measuring the extent of discrimination tend to look for *systematic* differences in outcomes across groups containing large numbers of people. In other words, economists are not interested so much in isolated cases of discrimination as in discrimination that is pervasive enough that it shows up time and time again. Generally, they use two approaches to look for those large-scale differences: the audit method and regression analysis.

The Audit Method

One way to detect discrimination is to create fake identities for people who are essentially alike but differ in race or gender or some other characteristic of interest to the researcher. Then those people are deliberately placed in a position where they can be discriminated against. If there is significant disagreement about how people with different characteristics are treated, that disagreement is taken as evidence of discrimination. This method of detecting discrimination is called the **audit method**. It is widely applied in many different contexts. For example, Ian Ayres of Yale University and Peter Siegelman of the American Bar Foundation used the audit method to look for discrimination among car dealerships.[8] They sent 38 subjects (including white males, white females, black males, and black females) to more than 150 Chicago car dealers to purchase new cars. Each test subject was young, attractive, well-educated, and

Audit method A method of detecting discrimination that involves researchers faking identities for people who are essentially alike but differ in race, gender, or some other characteristic; deliberately placing those people in a position where they can be discriminated against; and observing whether there is significant disagreement in how they are treated.

---

[8]Ian Ayres and Peter Siegelman, "Race and Gender Discrimination in Bargaining for a New Car," *American Economic Review*, June 1995.

well-dressed, and they all drove similar rental cars. Each indicated that he or she did not need dealer financing for his or her new car. Yet the audit uncovered significant discrepancies in the price offers the new car dealers made: White men were quoted prices that were, on average, $1,100 lower than the prices quoted to black men, $410 lower than the prices quoted to black women, and $92 lower than the prices quoted to white females.

Economists Marianne Bertrand of the University of Chicago and Sendhil Mullainathan of Harvard University conducted one of the most notable recent labor market audit studies. Drawing on examples pulled from job-hunting websites, Bertrand and Mullainathan generated 5,000 realistic-looking resumes, which fell into two groups: high-quality resumes and low-quality resumes. Then they randomly assigned names to each resume. Some of the names sounded distinctly black (Latonya and Kareem, for example) and others sounded very white (Carrie and Neil).

Bertrand and Mullainathan then used the fictitious resumes to apply for jobs advertised in Boston and Chicago newspapers. They sent four resumes in response to each ad: one high-quality black resume, one high-quality white resume, one low-quality black resume, and one low-quality white resume. Then they waited to see who among their fictitious applicants would be selected for interviews.

The results were discouraging:

- As a whole, white names received 50% more interview requests than black names.
- High-quality resumes with white names received 30% more interview requests than low-quality resumes with white names.
- High-quality resumes with black names received no more interview requests than low-quality resumes with black names.

This was true in corporate America, but it was also true in government, where protection from discrimination is arguably taken more seriously.

Perhaps the most interesting result from Bertrand and Mullainathan's study is this: Improving your resume by acquiring new skills and job experience matters for whites, but it doesn't appear to matter at all for blacks. That gives whites an incentive to invest more in improving their quality but sends a discouraging message to blacks: Why invest in training, education, and acquiring experience if there's no payoff? And if blacks don't make that investment, it reinforces employers' prior beliefs about the lower overall quality of the black workforce, perpetuating an unfortunate stereotype.

Regression Analysis

Relying as it does on the creation of fictitious identities, the audit method is a useful tool for detecting discrimination in situations where the discriminator and the person discriminated against are unacquainted. So it is perhaps most useful at measuring discrimination regarding opportunities—the chance to get a job interview, or to see an available apartment, for example. The audit method, however, is less useful in detecting discrimination in situations where the discriminator is familiar with the person being discriminated against—say, in cases of giving employees raises or promotions.[9] Rather than use the direct comparison methods of audit studies, economists instead turn to statistical methods to detect and measure these kinds of discrimination.

Suppose you are interested in examining the effects of gender on income. There are, of course, a lot of characteristics beyond gender that affect income, such as education and work experience. There are measurable differences between men and women across many of those characteristics. For example, on average, women don't remain in their jobs as long as men: Women's lower job tenure may reflect movement from job to job. It may also reflect movements into and out of the labor force that may cause women's skills to deteriorate and delay the training and promotions they earn relative

---

[9]Even in the best of circumstances, the audit method may suffer from a few drawbacks too technical to discuss here. For more information, see James Heckman's "Detecting Discrimination," *Journal of Economic Perspectives*, Vol. 12, No. 2. (Spring, 1998), pp. 101–116. American Economic Association.

to their male counterparts. While at work, men tend to work longer days than women do, which may account for part of their higher pay. Men and women also make distinctly different college and career choices. Women are overrepresented in relatively low-paying occupations like social work and education, and they are underrepresented in higher-paying fields like computer science and engineering. Table 15.1 highlights the magnitude of these differences.

Table 15.1	Work-Related Characteristics of Men and Women	
Women and men differ systematically across a host of earnings-related characteristics, including job tenure, hours worked, and chosen occupational field.		
Job-Related Characteristic	**Women**	**Men**
Median job tenure among workers ages 45–54	7.3 years	8.5 years
Time spent working on days worked	7.8 hours	8.2 hours
College major	77% of all education majors	88% of all computer science majors
Career choice	81% of all social workers	86% of architects and engineers

Sources: Bureau of Labor Statistics; Basit Zafar's "College Major Choice and the Gender Gap," *Federal Reserve Bank of New York Staff Report No. 364*, 2009; and "Computing Degree and Enrollment Trends," *2010–2011 Computing Research Association's Taulbee Survey*.

A cursory look at the female–male earnings statistics (like the 20% gap discussed earlier in this chapter) might convince you that women are being discriminated against. But it is possible that part of that earnings gap can be explained by differences in the productivity-related characteristics of men and women. Many of those characteristics, in turn, result from the personal and job-related choices that men and women have made, which may mean that a portion of the earnings gap can be explained by what economists call *rational choice*.

Regression analysis A statistical technique used to isolate the individual effects of a number of factors on a single outcome.

How Regression Analysis Works It can be difficult to separate the effects of productivity-related characteristics from the effect of gender alone. Generally, economists employ regression analysis to do that. **Regression analysis** is a statistical technique used to isolate the individual effects of a number of factors on a single outcome. Here's how regression analysis does that: Imagine a big building with a line of men and women outside.[10] They enter, and immediately the people with college degrees are sent to a big room on the right, and the people without degrees are sent to a big room on the left.

Then a carpenter builds a wall that divides each of those big rooms into two smaller rooms. In each half of the building, everyone *with* experience goes into one of the small rooms, while everyone *without* experience stays in the other.

There are now four rooms:

- One contains people with both college degrees and experience.
- One contains people with college degrees but no experience.
- One contains people without college degrees but with experience.
- One contains people with neither college degrees nor experience.

The process of wall building and worker sorting continues. Each time, both men and women are divided according to some characteristic other than gender (college major, choice of occupation, or another characteristic) that affects productivity and potential earnings. Eventually, all those characteristics are exhausted, and the pool of

---

[10]Credit for this explanation goes to economist Charles Wheelan of Dartmouth College. His primer on statistical reasoning, *Naked Statistics*, is a lively and interesting read.

Application 15.2

What's in a Name? Comparing Regression Analysis and Audit Studies in Detecting Discrimination

The audit study done by Marianne Bertrand of the University of Chicago and Sendhil Mullainathan of Harvard University demonstrates stark differences in how potential employers treat people with black-sounding names. The evidence suggests that parents who give a child a black-sounding name may limit that child's opportunities. That, in turn, may impose substantial costs on that child over his or her lifetime.

Economist Roland Fryer of Harvard University was interested in how big those costs might be. Instead of looking at how black-sounding names affect *opportunities*, he teamed with economist Steven Levitt of the University of Chicago to explore how black-sounding names affect *outcomes*. Fryer drew on a data set containing birth certificate information for millions of children born in California since 1961. Each birth certificate included the child's name, race, zip code (an indicator of economic status), and gender. Each certificate also included the exact name, maiden name, marital status, and educational attainment of the child's mother.

That information allowed Fryer to link the birth certificate of every child to the birth certificate of his or her mother. He used that data in a compelling way: He looked at the "blackness" of the *mother's* name and then, referring to her own birth certificate, which described the economic circumstances *she* was born into, studied how those circumstances changed between the time she was born and the time she gave birth to her own children.

Fryer used the sorting abilities of regression analysis to compare mothers who had identical characteristics *except* for the blackness of their names. What he found was surprising, especially when compared to Bertrand and Mullainathan's study: The innate characteristics—such as race, education, and socioeconomic status—of a particular mother mattered a great deal in terms of her overall life outcomes, but once regression analysis was used to account for those characteristics, the blackness of her name *didn't matter at all.*

Women with black-sounding names *did* have poorer-than-average life outcomes. But that's because a woman with a distinctively black name was also more likely to be disadvantaged: born into a poor home, to undereducated and unmarried parents. Those factors were likely to have affected her development and education, which in turn affected her overall life outcomes. But her name did not.

So rest easy and name your children whatever you'd like: Regression analysis shows that a Roneisha by any other name is likely to do just as well in the labor market.

See related problem 4.5 on page 322 at the end of this chapter.

Based on Roland Fryer and Steven Levitt, "The Causes and Consequences of Distinctively Black Names," *Quarterly Journal of Economics*, August, 2004; Kristie M. Engemann and Michael T. Owyang's "What's in a Name? Reconciling Conflicting Evidence on Ethnic Names," *Federal Reserve Bank of St. Louis Regional Economist*, January 2006; and Maria Konnikova's "Why Your Name Matters," *The New Yorker*, December 20, 2013.

---

workers has been sliced and divided so completely that there are hundreds of rooms, each containing workers fundamentally identical in every respect *except* for the one the researcher is interested in—in this case, gender. So, for example, one room in the very big building might contain only inexperienced workers (both male and female) with master's degrees in political science working as paralegals in big city law firms. Another might contain experienced welders (again, both male and female) who are employed by aircraft companies in the Midwest.

The process of determining the size of the female–male pay gap is almost complete. Because each room contains identical people doing identical work with identical qualifications, any systematic pay difference between men and women can only be chalked up to the irrelevant gender difference. Regression analysis essentially goes room by room and measures the pay gap between men and women and then summarizes that information by producing the average pay gap across all rooms.

Using Regression Analysis to Determine How Much of the Earnings Gap Is Due to Discrimination Armed with the knowledge of how regression analysis controls for differences in the typical qualifications between males and females, you're now prepared to answer this question: How much of the male–female wage gap is due to discrimination? If women earn only 80 cents for every $1 a man earns, is that 20-cent difference attributable solely to discrimination?

The answer is a solid no. Dozens of labor market studies find that productivity-related characteristics account for about 15 cents of the 20-cent wage gap. The news is even better for young women with college degrees: Once regression analysis is used to sort people by relevant characteristics, young and educated women earn 98 cents for every $1 earned by a man. (Of course, even this "near equality" isn't perfect: It's still equivalent to an extra 2% tax on female labor.)

It is certainly possible that the remaining pay difference is attributable to gender discrimination. But some researchers suspect that the remaining gap might be attributed to women intentionally taking jobs that pay less but that offer child-friendly fringe benefits. Others suggest that at least some of the remaining difference can be accounted for by other productivity-related attributes that labor economists simply haven't thought to include in their regression analyses. As evidence, those researchers offer this observation: There is no measurable difference between the earnings of men and the earnings of women who never married and never had children. The fact that so much of the male–female pay gap can be explained by characteristics reveals something important: For whatever reason, women do not make the same choices as men. Those choices are affecting their earnings. To the extent that those choices are made freely, the measured wage gap mostly disappears.[11]

Using regression analysis to account for productivity-related characteristics shrinks the measured pay gap across races, too. Consider college graduates: In the United States, Asians earn 15% to 25% more than whites, who in turn make about 25% more than blacks. These numbers might lead you to believe that employers are discriminating against whites and blacks in favor of Asians. But once you use a regression analysis to control for (or sort by) educational attainment, the Asian–white gap disappears. Asians earn more because, on average, they have more education. The same explanation can be applied to the white–black gap. After controlling for geography (a disproportionate number of blacks live in the South, where wages are lower for blacks and whites both) and educational test scores (which are an indicator of educational quality), the black–white wage gap for college graduates greatly narrows. In the words of Nobel Prize winner James Heckman, "Most of the disparity in earnings between blacks and whites in the labor market of the 1990s is due to differences in the skills they bring to the market, not to discrimination in the market."[12]

15.5 Learning Objective

List three justifications for affirmative action programs and list four ways affirmative action is implemented.

Anti-Discrimination Legislation

The theory and evidence from economists are mixed on discrimination. The theory establishes that statistical discrimination is not only possible but also profitable and that employers that discriminate based on taste may be able to do so for long periods

---

[11]There is, of course, a very reasonable argument that those choices are not made freely (or, at the very least, that they were not made freely in the past). Women, not men, are equipped for childbearing. Even if they would prefer to have a male partner carry their child so they could remain on a career trajectory, that option is simply unavailable. Further, to the extent that women's expectations and abilities are shaped early in life by parents, teachers, and others ("Doctors are men, and nurses are women," for example, or Barbie's infamous "Math is hard."), they may fall victim to gender stereotyping that stays with them for a lifetime. See msnbc.com's "White House Economist Lays Out Women's Economic Agenda," April 1, 2014, for more.

[12]See James Heckman's "Detecting Discrimination," *The Journal of Economic Perspectives*, Vol. 12, No. 2. (Spring, 1998), pp. 101–116. American Economic Association.

of time, until competition makes it too costly. The evidence, however, is mixed: Audit studies suggest that there may be stark differences in the opportunities available to minorities and women. At the same time, regression analyses confirm that there is a small wage gap but suggest that, by and large, people of every color and gender earn what they can expect to earn, given their characteristics.

Attempting to reconcile the findings of audit studies with those of regression analyses might lead you to the following conclusion: People earn what they earn largely based on their characteristics. However, their characteristics are partially shaped by their opportunities, and audit studies tend to show that those opportunities are not equally available.

If that's the case, what can be done to eliminate the effects of discrimination? Part of the answer, historically, has been for the government to protect minority classes. Table 15.2 presents some key laws designed to prevent discrimination.

Most employment discrimination disputes are resolved through civil action (lawsuits). If a person believes he or she has been a victim of discriminatory treatment, the individual can file a complaint with the Equal Employment Opportunity Commission (EEOC). If the EEOC cannot resolve the complaint directly, it will file a suit on behalf of the complaining party or will issue a *Notice of Right to Sue* letter that will enable the complaining party to file suit on his or her own.

This procedure is straightforward on paper, but unfortunately, filing a complaint in the real world is substantially messier. Suing someone can be costly in terms of time, money, and frustration. An anti-discrimination lawsuit can often take years to resolve. And just because you have filed a lawsuit doesn't mean you will win: Proving discriminatory behavior can be extremely difficult. As a result, for many victims, it is simply easier to walk away from the situation and look for a new job.

Affirmative Action Programs

Rather than wait for discrimination battles to be resolved in the courts, the federal and state governments have also created affirmative action programs. **Affirmative action** is the practice of governments or firms actively improving the educational and

Affirmative action The practice of governments or firms actively improving the educational and job opportunities of members of groups that have not been treated fairly in the past.

Table 15.2   Key Anti-Discrimination Laws

These federal laws are designed to protect women, minorities, and the disabled from discrimination. Each is enforced by the Equal Employment Opportunity Commission (EEOC).

Law	When It Was Passed	Intent of the Law
Equal Pay Act (EPA)	1963	Requires employers to pay men and women equivalent wages for equivalent work.
Civil Rights Act	1964	Prohibits discrimination by employers on the basis of race, color, religion, gender, or national origin.
Age Discrimination in Employment Act (ADEA)	1967	Protects employees and job applicants 40 years of age and older from employment discrimination based on age.
Equal Employment Opportunity Act	1972	Gave the Equal Employment Opportunity Commission the authority to conduct its own enforcement litigation.
Rehabilitation Act of 1973	1973	Prohibits discrimination against qualified individuals with disabilities who work in the federal government.
Americans with Disabilities Act (ADA)	1990	Prohibits, under certain circumstances, discrimination based on disability.
Civil Rights Act of 1991	1991	Provides monetary damages in cases of intentional employment discrimination.
Genetic Information Non-discrimination Act (GINA)	2008	Prohibits employment discrimination based on genetic information.

job opportunities of members of groups that have not been treated fairly in the past. Affirmative action programs are meant to speed up the process of achieving equality.

As often as affirmative action is discussed in the media, you might be led to believe that such programs are widespread. However, federal affirmative action programs are mandatory only within a tightly circumscribed set of applications: Private firms with more than 50 workers that have more than $50,000 worth of contracts with the federal government are required to develop and maintain affirmative action plans. Elsewhere, affirmative action is generally not mandatory, and where affirmative action programs exist, they are largely voluntary.

Affirmative action programs, which are generally oriented toward the hiring and promotion process, take many different forms. Most have a goal of attracting qualified job applicants in reasonable numbers from members of minority groups. At its most basic, a program may consist of policies to ensure that all potentially qualified workers know about a particular job opening. So an employer may post a job ad in the local newspaper, but affirmative action guidelines suggest that the employer also post the same advertisement in a Spanish-language newspaper, or place an advertisement on an Internet bulletin board that attracts a black demographic. This basic form of affirmative action simply ensures that everyone has equal information and equal access to the application process.

A different interpretation of affirmative action suggests that if two applicants have the same qualifications for a particular job, but one happens to be from a disadvantaged class (generally, due to race or gender), the job should be offered to the disadvantaged applicant.

A third form of affirmative action suggests that the labor pool should be representative of the community of qualified applicants. So, if the proportion of people with Ph.D.s in math is 33% female and 67% male, a college math department might attempt to mimic those proportions in its hiring. This helps ensure that the proportion of minorities doesn't drop too low.

Quota Numerical targets companies must meet for the hiring of minorities.

The most restrictive form of affirmative action is a **quota**, which sets numerical targets companies must meet for the hiring of minorities. Although quotas are what most people think of when they think of affirmative action, quotas are generally against the law when it comes to hiring and are *only* used when mandated by a court to remedy long-standing discrimination by a particular entity.

Affirmative action programs serve three purposes. First, they may redress past wrongs. For example, people denied entrance to college 60 years ago simply because of their race may have had to take jobs that paid less and, as a result, may not have been able to send their children to college, either. In that light, affirmative action may be viewed as a means to return a family to a trajectory that it was once denied.

Second, affirmative action programs may address current issues of discrimination. As the theories discussed earlier suggested, discrimination may well exist, and it may well persist. Consequently, the labor market fails to deliver as much productivity as it is capable of. By giving applicants access to the jobs for which they are qualified, affirmative action programs help ensure that the economic pie is as large as it can be. At the same time, those policies may also give members of protected classes an incentive to invest in their skills, education, and training—all costly endeavors that don't pay as large a dividend in a discriminatory environment.

Finally, affirmative action programs can enhance diversity in places where it is of particular value. Diversity may be especially valuable, for example, on a college campus: There, students are asked to view issues from many perspectives, and being exposed to alternative viewpoints can be educationally valuable.

Some Benefits and Costs of Affirmative Action Programs

Affirmative action programs have both benefits and costs. If, without affirmative action programs, qualified minorities are being passed over in favor of less-qualified applicants, then affirmative action programs will be of benefit to the firm as a whole and society as well. To the extent that affirmative action policies help ensure a fundamental sense of fairness in hiring and promotion, they are beneficial. More tangibly, when differences in opportunity and earnings reflect worker characteristics, affirmative action policies may provide an incentive and a means for members of historically underperforming groups to intentionally change their characteristics—to invest in education, acquire experience, and seek out unique training opportunities.

There are also costs associated with affirmative action programs. Some of those costs are administrative; it takes effort to seek out minority applicants, for example, or to ensure compliance with affirmative action guidelines.[13] But there are potential costs beyond the administrative burden. One argument against affirmative action programs is related to economic efficiency: If qualified applicants are passed over in favor of less-qualified minorities, the economic pie will shrink. The more restrictive affirmative action programs are, the greater the likelihood of this happening.

Recent efforts to generate greater diversity in higher education also highlight another potential cost. Affirmative action programs in college admissions promote two admirable goals: First, they promote greater campus diversity, which benefits everybody, and second, they improve educational opportunities for disadvantaged classes. But such programs generally involve relaxing admissions standards, which lowers the average preparedness of entering students. Most significantly, lowering admissions standards may result in a mismatch between the academic capabilities of entering minorities and the demands placed on them. In other words, those entering minority students are being set up for failure. This is particularly true at more selective schools: Evidence indicates that marginally qualified students have dramatically better outcomes if they go to schools where their level of academic preparation is much closer to that of the typical student.

As mentioned above, by opening the door of opportunity, affirmative action programs may produce desirable incentives for historically disadvantaged minorities to invest in education and training. Unfortunately, affirmative action programs may also create perverse incentives that *discourage* such investment. For example, a college-bound high-school student might rely on his affirmative action eligibility to get him into the college of his choice rather than work hard to improve his SAT scores. So, do colleges' diversity programs encourage high school minorities to work harder (because more doors are open) or to work less (because those doors are easier to walk through)? Theory provides no guide; the answer to that question will have to be determined by looking at data.[14]

Ultimately, whether affirmative action programs are effective and worth having may depend on your goal. Consider, for example, programs that increase the number of African-American students admitted to law schools. Increased minority admissions may create a mismatch that eventually causes a disproportionate number of black law students to drop out of their program. That may be a bad thing, but there is an upside: Some of those affirmative action students will probably make it through. If the goal is "more African-American lawyers," then the program—despite its cost to those that failed—will have been successful.

Conclusion

People of different races, ethnicities, and genders often have dramatically different life experiences. They live in different neighborhoods. They are offered different opportunities. They have different jobs, and they receive different pay. None of those facts should come as a surprise to a reasonably aware person.

---

[13] University of Wisconsin–Madison emeritus professor W. Lee Hansen estimated the cost of maintaining the university's diversity program at $40 million per year.

[14] University of Chicago economist Brent Hickman has made a preliminary exploration into the data. He has concluded that affirmative action programs in college admissions encourage high school students in the middle of the distribution to study harder but discourage students at the top and bottom of the distribution. In other words, there is not yet a clear-cut answer to the question of what incentives affirmative action creates. See Hickman's working paper "Pre-college Human Capital Investment and Affirmative Action: A Structural Policy Analysis of U.S. College Admissions," available at his website, http://home.uchicago.edu/hickmanbr.

But do those differences arise because people of different races, ethnicities, and genders vary systematically in their education, training, and other characteristics? Do those differences arise because of conscious choices people have made for themselves? Or do those differences arise because of discrimination? The answers to these questions are not obvious to the casual observer. But economic models like Schelling's checkerboard and statistical techniques like audit studies and regression analysis can help us understand the complex origins of those differences and measure the true impact of discrimination.

Chapter Summary and Problems

Key Terms

Affirmative action, p. 317

Audit method, p. 312

Labor market discrimination, p. 310

Quota, p. 318

Regression analysis, p. 314

Segregation, p. 301

Statistical discrimination, p. 311

Taste-based discrimination, p. 310

15.1 The Segregation of Neighborhoods and Schelling's Checkerboard, pages 301–304

Describe the process of neighborhood self-segregation and explain why it happens.

Summary

Many neighborhoods in the United States are highly segregated by race and ethnicity. Thomas Schelling's model of neighborhood segregation shows that individuals' mild preferences for neighbors not too different from themselves can result in the extreme segregation we observe in the real world.

Review Questions

All problems are assignable in MyEconLab.

1.1 The sorting and separation of people by various characteristics is called _____.
   a. Discrimination
   b. Self-selection
   c. Segregation
   d. Distillation

1.2 The economist who developed the checkerboard model of neighborhood segregation was _____.
   a. John Nash
   b. John von Neumann
   c. Adam Smith
   d. Thomas Schelling

Problems and Applications

1.3 Explain why the neighborhood self-segregation in Schelling's model meets the definition of a collective action problem.

1.4 What was the major takeaway from Thomas Schelling's study of segregation? What does his model suggest the cause of segregation to be?

1.5 Does Schelling's model of segregation lead you to be optimistic or pessimistic regarding the possibility of an integrated society? Explain your reasoning.

15.2 Does Your Neighborhood Determine Your Future Well-Being? pages 304–307

Summarize the Moving to Opportunity program and list its general findings.

Summary

The neighborhood you grow up in is highly correlated with life outcomes such as job opportunities, your educational attainment, and your lifetime income. Does your neighborhood cause those outcomes? A unique housing experiment assigned families with similar characteristics to different neighborhoods. Fifteen years later, families in different neighborhoods had significantly different life experiences regarding crime victimization and physical and mental health. But there were no systematic differences in financial status or educational achievement.

Review Questions

All problems are assignable in MyEconLab.

2.1 The _____ randomly assigned families who applied into three groups and gave families the chance to leave their old neighborhoods.
  a. Affirmative action program
  b. Moving on Up program
  c. Schelling's checkerboard program
  d. None of the above

2.2 The research done regarding the Moving to Opportunity program found which of the following?
  a. Children who moved to low-poverty neighborhoods scored better on math and reading proficiency.
  b. Adults who moved to low-poverty neighborhoods had better luck finding jobs.
  c. Female children who moved to low-poverty neighborhoods experienced a lower incidence

of psychological distress, panic attacks, and oppositional defiant disorder.
  d. The overall physical health of children who moved to low-poverty neighborhoods improved.

Problems and Applications

2.3 In the Moving to Opportunity experiment, one-third of the participants were assigned to remain in public housing; one-third received vouchers to move to private housing; and one-third received vouchers to move to private housing provided that the housing was in a low-poverty neighborhood. Explain the importance of assigning people to each of these groups randomly.

2.4 How was the Moving to Opportunity experiment a success? How was it a failure? Explain.

2.5 Suppose that you have been recently elected president of the United States. You are extremely concerned with ability of the poorest members of society to escape poverty. Discuss how the results of the Moving to Opportunity experiment might inform your policy decisions. What programs might you give additional emphasis in the coming four years? What programs might you de-emphasize?

15.3 ## Labor Market Discrimination, pages 308–312

Explain the difference between taste-based discrimination and statistical discrimination.

Summary

There are many types of discriminatory behaviors. In the labor market, discriminatory behavior might arise from bigotry; that type of discrimination is called taste-based discrimination. Taste-based discrimination generally imposes costs on the employer that discriminates; as a result, the more competitive an industry is, the less likely such discrimination is to persist. In contrast, statistical discrimination is assigning the average characteristics of a group to a particular individual. On average, statistical discrimination makes an employer who discriminates more profitable. Discrimination of either type creates poor incentives for minority individuals to invest in developing desirable labor market characteristics.

Review Questions

All problems are assignable in MyEconLab.

3.1 _____ exists when employers pay members of one group less than members of another group with different characteristics, even though members of both groups are equally productive.

3.2 A business owner who prefers not to work with women and discriminates in hiring based on this preference is engaging in _____ discrimination.

3.3 _____ exists when an employer rewards or penalizes an employee for personal characteristics that are unrelated to his or her productivity.
  a. Affirmative action
  b. Segregation
  c. Discrimination
  d. Prejudice

3.4 If an employer hires a man who is less qualified than a female applicant because she believes the female applicant is likely to take maternity leave, the employer is engaging in _____.
  a. Taste-based discrimination
  b. Statistical discrimination
  c. Fact-based discrimination
  d. Racial profiling

3.5 A firm that engages in taste-based discrimination will generally be _____ profitable than its nondiscriminating rivals.
  a. Less
  b. More
  c. Both discriminating and non-discriminating firms will be equally profitable.

3.6 A firm that engages in statistical discrimination will generally be _____ profitable than its nondiscriminating rivals.

    a. Less

    b. More

    c. Both discriminating and nondiscriminating firms will be equally profitable.

Problems and Applications

3.7 Describe the two types of discrimination discussed in this chapter.

3.8 **[Related to Application 15.1 on page 309]** Read Application 15.1 carefully. A friend of yours is considering plastic surgery to remove an unsightly mole because he recently read a study which said that attractive individuals make more money than unattractive individuals. What advice might you give him?

3.9 Explain the effects of discrimination on the size of the economic pie. Be sure to discuss the role of incentives.

3.10 Taste-based discrimination is grounded in bigotry. Statistical discrimination is not. Explain why society should be more concerned about statistical discrimination.

How Economists Detect and Measure Discrimination, pages 312–316

Discuss how economists use the audit method and regression analysis to detect discrimination.

Summary

Economists use two methods to determine whether opportunity differences or pay differences are due to discrimination or due to systematic differences between members of various groups. The audit method creates fake identities for people of different races or gender. By assigning the subjects similar (fake) characteristics and observing how members of different groups are treated, the audit method can pinpoint discriminatory behavior. In contrast, regression analysis is a statistical method that is used to sort out whether the pay and opportunity differences individuals experience are due to differences in characteristics or due to discriminatory treatment.

Review Questions

All problems are assignable in MyEconLab.

4.1 _____ is a statistical technique used to isolate the individual effects of a number of factors on a single outcome.

4.2 When fake identities for people who are essentially alike but differ by race are created in order to detect discrimination, the _____ is being used.

4.3 Bertrand and Mullainathan's audit method study revealed which of the following?

    a. On the whole, white names received 10 times as many interview requests as black names.

    b. High-quality resumes with white names received no more interview requests than low-quality resumes with white names.

    c. High-quality resumes with black names received no more interview requests than low-quality resumes with black names.

    d. High-quality resumes with white names received 7 times as many interview requests as high-quality resumes with black names.

Problems and Applications

4.4 "Women make about 80 cents for every dollar a man earns." Explain whether this (true) statement constitutes, on its own, evidence of the discriminatory treatment of women. Then, explain the importance of regression analysis in determining whether discrimination actually exists.

4.5 **[Related to Application 15.2 on page 315]** Read Application 15.2 and the discussion of Bertrand and Mullainathan's audit study in section 15.4 carefully. Suppose two black men, D'Andre and Neil, send resumes to a company in response to a help-wanted ad. If the employer dislikes black men and takes every opportunity to discriminate against them, what is likely to happen at the resume screening phase? What is likely to happen in the interview phase? How do your answers help reconcile the results of Bertrand and Mullainathan and those of Fryer and Levitt?

4.6 This chapter explains that much of the difference in earnings between men and women can be attributed to college major, occupational choice, hours worked, educational attainment, and other productivity-related factors that affect earnings. If that is the case, should it matter to society that men make more than women? Explain your reasoning.

4.7 Several economic studies are described in this chapter. Select one and provide a follow-up research question that you find interesting.

Anti-Discrimination Legislation, pages 316–319

List three justifications for affirmative action programs and list four ways affirmative action is implemented.

Summary

In the United States, various laws make discriminatory behavior illegal. Those laws generally make discrimination actionable in civil court. In addition, the federal government, many state governments, and many private organizations have created affirmative action programs designed to enhance the opportunities of historically oppressed classes and speed the process to equality. Depending on circumstances, those programs may enhance economic efficiency or reduce economic efficiency. By creating opportunities, those programs may create positive incentives for minorities to work hard and invest in education and training; but by making it easier for minorities to achieve success, they may reduce incentives for hard work and investment in skills.

Review Questions

All problems are assignable in MyEconLab.

5.1 The practice of actively improving the educational and job opportunities of members of groups that have been treated unfairly in the past is called _____.

5.2 _____ discrimination occurs when a hiring agent selects one candidate over another due to assigning the properties of a group to the particular individual who was not chosen.

5.3 Affirmative action programs may be used to _____.

  a. Redress past wrongs

  b. Address current issues of discrimination

  c. Enhance diversity in places where it is of particular value

  d. All of the above

5.4 A(n) _____ is the most restrictive form of affirmative action, in which an employer sets a numerical target for the hiring of an underrepresented group.

  a. Audit

  b. Quota

  c. Schedule

  d. Allocation

Problems and Applications

5.5 Describe four types of affirmative action.

5.6 Aside from affirmative action programs, what kind of efforts/programs might have a positive impact on increasing equality of opportunity and equality of outcomes for the different groups?

5.7 Why might affirmative action programs be valuable on a college campus?

5.8 An individual can sue his or her employer for discrimination on the basis of a protected class. What type of barriers might prevent this from happening?

Schelling's Checkerboard

This chapter highlighted Thomas Schelling's research on neighborhood self-segregation. In this experiment, you will replicate Shelling's pioneering work. Armed with a checkerboard and two bags of different-colored candies, you will create an integrated neighborhood. Then, following Shelling's guidelines, you will start moving candies until every candy is content with its neighbors.

What will your checkerboard look like when you're done? If you have time, work through the process two or three times. Do the checkerboards you end up with look alike each time?

MyEconLab

Please visit http://www.myeconlab.com **for support material to conduct this experiment if assigned by your instructor.**

Gross Domestic Product and the Wealth of Nations: An Introduction to the Macroeconomy

Chapter Outline and Learning Objectives

16.1 Macroeconomics and How It Differs from Microeconomics, page 326

Distinguish macroeconomics from microeconomics.

16.2 Material Well-Being and Gross Domestic Product, page 326

List the components of GDP and explain how it is calculated.

16.3 Nominal GDP and Real GDP, page 333

Explain the importance of adjusting GDP for the effects of rising prices.

16.4 Shortcomings of GDP, page 335

Discuss why GDP is an imperfect indicator of material well-being.

16.5 Economic Growth, page 340

List key characteristics that help an economy grow.

16.6 Business Cycles and Recessions, page 343

Explain how supply and demand shocks may lead to recessions.

MyEconLab Real-Time Data Activity: Gross Domestic Product and Business Cycles, page 354

MyEconLab

MyEconLab helps you master each objective and study more efficiently.

For most students, the next step after finishing college is to find a job. Your ability to land a good offer will depend primarily on your performance in school as well as on your skills, abilities, and determination. But it will also depend on other factors—factors that are largely beyond your control. Getting a job offer is far more likely in an economy where employers are lined up to hire available graduates than it is in an economy where graduates are lined up to apply for the few available jobs. When consumers and businesses are buying lots of goods and services, employers sometimes have a hard time keeping up with demand for their products. Employers facing this situation often aggressively hire new employees—and pay higher wages to attract them. On the other hand, when the sales of businesses stagnate, hiring generally slows.

The quality of life you will enjoy after college also depends on the overall state of the economy. If prices of the goods and services you buy are rising quickly, you may find that your paycheck purchases fewer of the things you want. High interest rates may increase the size of your car payment and force you into a used car instead of a new one. For those reasons, graduating into a robust, vibrant, and growing economy is probably important to you.

Macroeconomics and How It Differs from Microeconomics

16.1 Learning Objective

Distinguish macroeconomics from microeconomics.

Macroeconomics The study of the economy as a whole. Macroeconomics attempts to evaluate or summarize the performance of all markets simultaneously.

Microeconomics The study of decisions made by individuals, businesses, and other entities such as governments. Microeconomics often focuses on a single market.

The issues that will affect your prospects and lifestyle after graduation—employment, strong sales, rising prices, and high interest rates, among others—are related to the overall functioning of the economy. Economists call the study of the economy as a whole **macroeconomics**. Macroeconomists are interested in issues like the national unemployment rate, the indebtedness of nations, and foreign exchange rates.

Those issues are different than the ones we've studied so far, which have largely been microeconomic issues. **Microeconomics** is the study of decisions made by individuals, businesses, and other entities such as governments. Microeconomics often focuses on one market at a time, such as the market for bread. (See Chapter 6 for more on markets.)

Macroeconomists care less about what happens in the bread market than they do about evaluating the performance of *all* markets—the bread market, the fighter jet market, the market for tickets to *Wicked*, and hundreds of thousands of other markets—all at the same time. In addition to understanding the interconnections among all those markets and summarizing their collective performance in a way ordinary people can understand, macroeconomists gather and study a lot of numbers and data for policymakers so that those policymakers can manipulate the macroeconomy to keep it growing and keep people employed.

If the description of macroeconomics and the idea of gathering and studying data sound daunting to you, fear not. It doesn't take an advanced degree in economics to understand the basics of the macroeconomy. By the time you are done reading the next few chapters, you'll have an educated lay understanding of how the macroeconomy functions, who the big players are, and what exactly the Federal Reserve does, among other things. You will also be able to speak the language of macroeconomists.

Material Well-Being and Gross Domestic Product

16.2 Learning Objective

List the components of GDP and explain how it is calculated.

Macroeconomists are interested in lots of different things, but most of them would probably agree that at its core, the field is devoted to studying how well society meets the material needs of its citizens.[1] With that in mind, let's start digging into the story of a society's material well-being. Begin by imagining a sailor marooned on a desert island.

---

[1]Some macroeconomists have devoted their study to more subjective measures of well-being. Those economists work to quantify overall happiness in a society, or measures of an economy's performance that might include adjustments for civil liberties, educational attainment, access to clean drinking water, and a host of other important qualitative measures. Application 16.1 discusses some of the debate surrounding these measures.

Left with only a few supplies, he carefully considers his options. He's tempted to lie on the beach and listen to the waves roll in. But he knows that if he wants to enjoy material comforts like food, shelter, and a warm bed, he's going to have to put in some hours gathering food, constructing a shelter, and trying to make a fire. In other words, his material comfort depends on him becoming a *producer*.

That's true for the sailor's tiny economy, and it's also true for larger and more complex economies. Material comforts—cars, medicines, and action movies—don't appear out of thin air. Someone, somewhere, must devote time and effort to producing those material comforts. All else equal, the more you work, the smarter you work, and the harder you work, the greater the material comforts you are likely to enjoy.

Gross Domestic Product: A Measuring Stick for Production

If production is the key to material comfort, figuring out how much "stuff" society produces seems to be a worthwhile piece of data to gather. The particular piece of data macroeconomists use to capture the overall production in an economy is called **gross domestic product (GDP)**; GDP is the market value of all final goods and services produced in a country in a given year.

Gross domestic product (GDP) The market value of all final goods and services produced in a country in a given year.

The definition of GDP may seem straightforward to you, but there are actually a lot of nuances hidden in it. Let's begin by looking at the term *market value*. Remember that the goal is to measure how much stuff gets produced. Consequently, it's natural to think in terms of quantities of stuff produced. If that's the case, you might think to yourself, "I made three dozen brownies today, and two dozen yesterday, so I increased the nation's GDP by five dozen brownies." But were we to attempt to express GDP statistics this way, GDP would end up being quoted something like this: "In the last quarter of 2013, GDP was . . . four calling birds, three French hens, two turtle doves, and a partridge in a pear tree." That's not very useful: If you tried to list every item produced in the entire economy, you'd never finish. The point is that GDP is a number we use to *summarize* the performance of an economy, so that we can *avoid* having to enumerate every single item produced in the economy. Consequently, it's much less cumbersome to combine all the things the economy produces into one compact piece of data—the total market (dollar) value of all those items.

Why does using market values make sense? Because not all things an economy produces are created equal. Suppose an artist spends her days making garden gnomes that sell for $1 apiece at the local farmers' market. Meanwhile, her next-door neighbor, a mechanic, builds automobiles that sell for $30,000 each. There's a big difference between an economy that produces 1 car and 5 garden gnomes (let's call this Economy A) and an economy that produces 1 garden gnome and 5 cars (let's call this Economy B). Yet both Economy A and Economy B produce 6 items each. Combining cars and gnomes in a way that accounts for the fact that the typical person gets a lot more value from a car than from a gnome requires a common denominator—some convenient unit that can be used to compare both products. The easiest unit to use is their total market (dollar) value.

Using GDP to Measure Market Value To calculate GDP, you simply add up the *market value* of each type of product produced and sold in a particular year. This is as easy as summing the number of units of each type of item that gets sold and multiplying by their market prices. The formula for the 2015 GDP of the previously mentioned gnome- and car-producing economy is this:

$$GDP_{2015} = Q_{gnomes} \times P_{gnomes} + Q_{cars} \times P_{cars}$$

where Q_{gnomes} and Q_{cars} are the quantities of gnomes and cars, respectively, produced in the economy in 2015, and P_{gnomes} and P_{cars} are their respective market prices.

Because Economy A produced 5 gnomes and 1 car, its GDP was:

$$5 \times \$1 + 1 \times \$30,000 = \$30,005$$

In other words, it produced about $30,000 worth of items for its residents to enjoy. By contrast, because Economy B produced 1 gnome and 5 cars, its GDP was:

$$1 \times \$1 + 5 \times \$30,000 = \$150,001$$

In terms of monetary value, Economy B is nearly five times the size of Economy A. Put another way, Economy B produced about five times the material comfort for its citizens as Economy A.

GDP Includes Both Goods and Services Note that the definition of GDP includes both goods *and* services. When someone buys a new RV, GDP rises, but it also rises when someone rents a night in a luxury hotel (which is a service). When you buy a mop, GDP rises, but it also rises when you hire someone to mop for you. Both goods and services are included in GDP because both goods and services bring people comfort and satisfaction, and both goods and services can be obtained in the marketplace.

GDP Includes Only Final Goods and Services So you know that GDP includes both goods *and* services. However, the goods and services included in GDP must be *final* goods and services. This means that if a purchase is to be counted in GDP, the buyer must be the ultimate consumer of the product. Remember that the purpose of GDP is to measure the material comforts people enjoy. So if the buyer of a garden gnome values it at $1, by including only the $1 value of the final good in GDP, we get a pretty accurate reflection of the material comfort the gnome provided.

But suppose the garden gnome producer buys 70 cents worth of plaster and 25 cents worth of paint in order to produce a garden gnome that sells for $1. The plaster and paint are called *intermediate goods*—raw materials or components that will eventually be transformed into a finished product. GDP doesn't include the 70-cent transaction that occurred when the artist bought the plaster, nor the 25-cent transaction that took place when she bought the paint. If we included the plaster and paint transactions in GDP, the gnome would be valued at $1 + $0.70 + $0.25 = $1.95. This overstates the actual value the gnome buyer receives by 95 cents. Another way to view why intermediate goods are not included is to note that the market price of the finished gnome already accounts for, or embodies, the value of the raw materials; if we were to include intermediate goods in GDP alongside final goods, we would end up counting the plaster and paint twice.

GDP Measures Production at the Time It Occurs When we formulate GDP, we need to be sure that we're counting things only at the time they're being produced and not counting things that don't correspond to any production. So when your next-door neighbor builds a new house, GDP rises, but when your sister buys an already existing home, GDP does not rise because that house was already included in some previous year's GDP. The same is true of used cars, thrift-shop clothing, and any other good that has already been counted at some other point in time. GDP also excludes the purchase of stock (which represents ownership in a company) because the purchase of stock is simply the transfer of an existing asset from person to person (just like passing down an old pair of shoes to your little brother), and because stock represents the ownership of a company that produces things but does not represent production itself. Still, the services provided by the realtor that matched your sister and the seller whose house she bought, and the services of the broker that matched you with a seller of Apple stock are both valuable and currently produced; those fees *do* show up in this year's GDP.

GDP Is Specific to a Particular Time and Place There are two additional qualifiers to address regarding GDP. First, GDP includes only the value of items produced *in a particular country*. The United States has its own GDP; so do Japan, Somalia, and Vanuatu. Each of these countries' respective GDPs measures productive activity that occurs within its own borders. That is true no matter who is responsible for that activity, whether they are citizens or noncitizens. When a German cellist plays a concert at Kennedy Center in Washington, D.C., the box office receipts are included in U.S. GDP. When foreign-owned Toyota builds Tacoma pickups at its Texas mega-plant,

U.S. GDP rises. Conversely, when a U.S. resident crosses into Canada to pick beans, or when a U.S. businessperson produces shoes in a Taiwanese factory, those activities are *not* included in U.S. GDP, even though the proceeds end up in the pockets of U.S. residents.

Finally, GDP measures the economic activity that takes place in a given period of time—one year, to be exact. In the United States, our roughly $17 trillion GDP indicates that we're producing about $17 trillion worth of final good and services *each year*. In practice, GDP is actually estimated four times a year by the U.S. Bureau of Economic Analysis (BEA), which is a part of the U.S. Department of Commerce. The BEA multiplies that quarterly GDP figure by four to estimate how much is being produced annually.

GDP is, of course, an estimate because keeping track of $17 trillion worth of transactions is too big a job if we want to count every transaction. So the BEA estimates GDP based on a large sample, and, as you might expect, estimates are rarely spot-on. In fact, the BEA generally publishes revised estimates as more information trickles in. As you might suspect, this makes it difficult for policymakers to make informed decisions about whether the economy might need a dose of stimulus, and, in turn, on how big that stimulus might need to be. We will visit that issue shortly.

The Components of GDP and the Expenditures Approach

GDP is the market value of a country's production, and as you saw, we can measure GDP by adding up the amount spent on final goods and services by various buyers. Those expenditures are:

- Consumption expenditures made by households (C)
- Investment expenditures made by businesses (I)
- Government spending (G)
- Net purchases by foreigners of domestically produced goods and services (NX)

Adding them up, GDP can be expressed as:

$$GDP = C + I + G + NX$$

This method of computing GDP is known as the *expenditures approach*. Table 16.1 shows the size of each of these components of GDP, as well as their total.

As shown in Table 16.1, gross domestic product in the United States is over $17 trillion. Table 16.2 compares GDP in the United States to GDP in a handful of other countries around the world.

As Table 16.2 shows, U.S. GDP is the largest in the world. In dollar terms, the U.S. economy is about twice the size of the world's second-largest economy, China. Let's take a closer look at each component of U.S. GDP to see where all that spending comes from.

MyEconLab Real-time data

Table 16.1 The Components of GDP Expenditures

GDP is the sum of consumption spending, investment spending, government spending, and net exports. Consumption is by far the largest component of GDP.

Type of Spending	Estimate of Annual Spending, Third Quarter, 2014
Consumption	$11,973.0 billion
Investment	$2,890.7 billion
Government spending	$3,207.7 billion
Net exports	–$516.2 billion
Gross domestic product (GDP)	**$17,555.2 billion**

Source: Data reflects estimates from third quarter 2014. Data is seasonally adjusted and was obtained from the Bureau of Economic Analysis.

Table 16.2 GDP in Selected Countries, 2013

The United States has the world's biggest economy, as measured by GDP.

Country	GDP (millions)	Rank in World
United States	$17,089,600	1
China	$9,330,000	2
Japan	$5,007,000	3
Canada	$1,825,000	10
Mexico	$1,327,000	14
Switzerland	$646,200	20
Peru	$210,300	51
Tunisia	$48,380	81
Trinidad and Tobago	$27,130	101
Guinea	$6,544	148
Tuvalu	$38	193

Source: Bureau of Economic Analysis and CIA World Factbook.

Consumption Spending by households on goods and services; also called consumption spending.

Consumption News reports about the economy often use the term *consumer spending* to refer to the goods that people purchase. Economists use the term **consumption**, which is defined as spending by households on goods such as:

- Food and clothing, which are called *consumer nondurables* because they do not last long

- Washing machines and cars, which are called *consumer durables* because they generally last for several years

- College tuition, which is a service

As Table 16.1 shows, consumption spending is the biggest component of GDP, accounting for almost $12 trillion, or about 68% of all spending. Consumption expenditures are generally quite stable through time, but because consumer spending represents such a big share of GDP, when it does increase or decrease sharply, it has a large impact on the economy. This is why you often see consumer spending numbers reported in the news.

Investment Spending by businesses on final goods and services that will be used later to produce more goods and services.

Investment GDP also includes expenditures made by businesses on final goods and services that will be used later to produce more goods and services. That spending is called **investment**, and it can be lumped into a few important subcategories. The first is called *fixed investment*, which includes expenditures on physical plants—factories and other facilities. Fixed investment also includes equipment like drill presses, computers, and sewing machines—things used to produce other things. Be sure to note the distinction between *investment goods* (which are expenditures by businesses and households on final goods and services) and *intermediate goods* (which are materials purchased by businesses that are later transformed into a different final good). These two terms are easily confused.

The second subcategory is *inventory investment*. When Hershey produces a chocolate bar, we want GDP to rise to reflect the production, even if the chocolate bar doesn't sell right away. So we say that Hershey has made an investment in inventory, and we mark up GDP by the market value of the candy bar. Later, when someone actually buys the candy, the BEA marks up the consumption category and marks down the inventory investment category by an equal and opposite amount. This ensures that GDP rises at the time of production and not at the time of sale. This sounds like hair-splitting, but as it turns out, inventory investment is actually something that policymakers pay a lot of attention to because, as you will soon see, sudden buildups of inventory may indicate a looming economic slowdown.

The third subcategory of investment spending that is noteworthy, particularly in light of the events of the past few years, is investment spending on housing, which economists call *residential fixed investment*. To the rest of us, that means people are building new houses. Remember that residential fixed investment does not include spending on the purchase of *existing* houses, as those houses were already counted in GDP at the time they were built.

Finally, the investment category of GDP includes spending on *intellectual property*—creations of the mind that can become someone's property through patents, trademarks, or copyrights. Investments in intellectual property include research and development expenditures by individuals and firms, as well as expenditures made in producing or acquiring the rights to music, films, and artistic and written works. Intellectual property was once considered an intermediate good and was, therefore, not directly included in GDP. But in 2013, the BEA reclassified it as investment spending because, like factories and equipment, intellectual property can last a long time and can potentially generate profits for its owners.

Taken all together, investment amounts to $2.9 trillion, or 16% of GDP. Despite being much smaller than consumption spending, investment spending is very important both because it represents the purchase of things that will contribute to future GDP and because it is the most volatile of the components. In part, that's because investment spending can be more easily adjusted than other types of spending. For example, someone who is worried about losing his or her job may have a tough time cutting back on monthly food or fuel purchases but can more easily hold off signing a contract for construction on a new house. A business owner worried about the overall economic outlook still has salaries to pay and raw materials to buy but can perhaps delay spending on a new factory, if necessary. By contrast, when the economy is booming, residential investment and business fixed investment often rise rapidly, reflecting optimism about the future.

Government Expenditures The third major category of expenditures consists of all the goods and services that government buys. *Government spending*, which includes spending at federal, state, and local levels, is substantial, amounting to over $3 trillion. That makes government responsible for 18% of total spending—about $1 out of every $5. Governments spend money on roads; they spend money on parks; they spend money on tanks; they spend money hiring the services of politicians and police officers and soldiers. This measure of government spending includes only spending on final goods and services. It excludes payments to Social Security and welfare recipients. Those payments, called *transfer payments*, simply shift dollars from person to person; they do not indicate the production of goods and services that GDP is designed to capture.

Government expenditures are special for two reasons. First, the government doesn't always have the funds it needs to pay for its expenditures, so it often borrows the difference. Over the past half-century, that has become the rule rather than the exception for the U.S. government. This, of course, has led to great concern about the government's indebtedness and repayment burden. Second, as you will learn, government expenditures are one of the tools used to combat economic recessions. For now, it's enough to understand that when your local flower shop sells a centerpiece for a fancy dinner, it doesn't particularly matter to the owner whether the buyer is:

- An ordinary person putting together a dinner party, in which case the transaction will be recorded in the consumption category

or

- The U.S. president's personal assistant putting together a state dinner, in which case the transaction would be counted in the government expenditures category

Either way, the spending is part of GDP.

Net Exports If there's little difference between selling flowers to an ordinary person or to the president's personal assistant, then there is probably little difference between selling them to a person from Cleveland, Ohio, in the United States and to a person

Net exports The sum of the goods produced domestically and sold abroad (U.S. *exports*), minus the goods and services that were produced abroad but purchased domestically (U.S. *imports*).

from Calgary, Canada. This brings us to the fourth category of GDP expenditures: net exports. **Net exports** are the sum of the goods produced domestically and sold abroad (U.S. *exports*, denoted X), minus the goods and services that were produced abroad but purchased domestically (U.S. *imports*, denoted M). Therefore, we can rewrite the expression for GDP as:

$$GDP = C + I + G + (X - M)$$

It is easy to understand why exports are included in GDP: When we produce a good in the United States and sell it to a consumer in Azerbaijan, the transaction reflects U.S. production and is therefore included in U.S. GDP. Imports enter the GDP calculation with a minus sign in front of them, which might lead a casual observer to conclude that they cause U.S. GDP to fall. Conclusions of that sort are often used to argue against allowing or encouraging imports from abroad.

However, such a conclusion is incorrect. Here's why: When you buy a smartphone made in Japan, the BEA increases the consumption expenditures portion of GDP because you spent money on a phone, which is a consumption good. This increase in consumption might lead you to believe that GDP has increased. But clearly GDP has *not* increased because the phone was not produced on U.S. soil. So the BEA needs to adjust the numbers so that the increase in consumption doesn't cause GDP to rise. The BEA does this by making an equal entry in the imports category of GDP, and because imports have a minus sign, that entry cancels out the increase in consumption. In the end, GDP *does not fall* by the amount of the imports; rather, the combined effect of increasing consumption and increasing imports leaves GDP unchanged.

As Table 16.1 shows, net exports are smaller than the other types of spending. Interestingly, in 2013, net exports were also negative. The total shown, coupled with the negative sign, means that U.S. imports outweighed U.S. exports by $456.9 billion. When imports are larger than exports, economists say the United States is running a *trade deficit*. On the other hand, if the United States imported less than it sold abroad, it would be running a *trade surplus*.

The Income Approach

Every transaction has two sides—a buyer's side and a seller's side. If the purchase of a bagel represents $1 of expenditure to the buyer, it's just as accurate to say that it represents $1 of income to the seller. Reinterpret every transaction in the economy in this way, and you'll conclude that in addition to measuring a society's total expenditures, GDP also measures the total income a society generates. You can calculate GDP by adding up everyone's expenditures, but it's just as accurate to calculate GDP by adding up everyone's income. That method of computing GDP is called the *income approach*.

We can break income into categories just as we do when we compute GDP using the expenditures approach. Think about $1 earned by Einstein's Bagels. Some of it (say, 60 cents) will go to pay the worker who got up at 3 a.m. to make the bagel. That's called *wage* income. Another 20 cents will go to pay the lease on the kitchen and storefront. Payments to landlords are called *rents*. Whatever is left over will go into the owner's pocket as *profit*, which is her reward for risking her savings buying ovens and mixers and tables and chairs.

Of course, even Einstein's can't produce matter out of nothing; bagels are made from flour and other ingredients. Suppose the owner of Einstein's has to spend 5 cents on ingredients for every bagel it makes. The remaining 95 cents is then divided up: 60 cents to the workers as wages and 20 cents to the landlord for rent, leaving 15 cents for the owner as profit. This makes it appear that only 95 cents' worth of income is generated by the $1 transaction.

But the 5 cents that Einstein's spent on ingredients shows up as income to somebody, too. Maybe 1 cent goes to pay the workers who grew the wheat and milled it into flour (wages); 3 cents goes to the owner of the land where the farm and the mill are located (rents); and the remaining 1 cent is profit to the person who bought the tractors and put up the mill. In this alternative scenario, the original $1 worth of expenditure is still split into $1 worth of income: 61 cents in wages, 23 cents of rent, and 16 cents of profit.

In other words, GDP does measure income, even though the recipients of that income may be scattered throughout the economy.

Nominal GDP and Real GDP

16.3 Learning Objective

Explain the importance of adjusting GDP for the effects of rising prices.

Because people are so used to thinking about their personal well-being in terms of their income, GDP is a logical piece of data to use to assess how well the economy is doing. GDP falls, and people tremble. GDP rises, and they rejoice. But here's a big complication to deal with: Increases in GDP don't always mean that an economy is producing more or doing better.

How Rising Prices Affect Nominal GDP

When GDP is calculated in the way we've done up until now, it's often referred to as nominal GDP. **Nominal GDP** measures a country's production of goods and services, valued at current market prices. But as time passes, both the prices and quantities used to calculate nominal GDP are likely to change, and unfortunately, that may create confusion about how much material well-being an economy is actually producing.

Nominal GDP A measure of a country's production of goods and services valued at current market prices.

To illustrate why, consider two small isolated island economies, Tobi and Sonsorol.[2] Each island produces only two goods, pineapple and coconuts. In 2015, they both produced 10 pineapples and 10 coconuts, and in both places, pineapple and coconuts sold for $1 each. Based on that, Tobi and Sonsorol each had a nominal GDP of $20 in 2015.

Suppose that in 2016, Tobi produces 20 pineapples and 20 coconuts, each of which still sells for $1. As a result, Tobi's nominal GDP doubles to $40. Life is good! Across a few hundred miles of dangerous sea, the Sonsorolese continue to produce 10 pineapples and 10 coconuts, but for reasons we'll deal with later, the price of both pineapple and coconuts doubles to $2. Consequently, Sonsorol's nominal GDP for 2016 doubles to $40, too!

The fact that nominal GDP doubled in both places masks important differences between Tobi and Sonsorol. In Tobi, every resident has twice as much pineapple and twice as many coconuts to enjoy this year than he or she had last year. The residents are probably a lot happier!

Compare that to what happened in Sonsorol. Residents there are *materially* no better off in 2016 than they were in 2015: They have exactly the same amount of pineapple and coconuts to enjoy. Their island's nominal GDP has risen not because they are producing more but simply because the prices of everything happened to double. You might be led to believe that's a good thing, that the sellers of pineapple and coconuts will be making twice as much. But remember that when it comes time to spend the money they earned, they'll be dismayed to find that the things they want to buy cost twice as much. Their paychecks, though bigger in dollars by a factor of two, buy them no more goods and services in 2016 than they did in 2015.

The point is that GDP is really designed to measure production because material well-being depends on what and how much is being produced. But increases in prices in an economy will cause nominal GDP to rise, too. So we are left with the hard job of figuring out whether an economy looks rich because it actually is rich or whether it looks rich just because the few things it produces fetch ridiculously high prices.

---

[2] Many advanced economic models are based on "island economies." This scenario keeps things simple because there are limited production opportunities, and no international trade has to be accounted for.

Adjusting GDP for Increasing Prices: Real GDP

Real GDP A measure of the output of final goods and services in a country, holding prices constant from year to year.

Economists have created a statistic that they call *real GDP* that filters out the effects of rising prices. **Real GDP** measures the output of final goods and services in a country, holding prices constant from year to year. To do that, the people who compute real GDP must choose which year's prices they want to use initially. That year is known as the *base year*. For any given year, real GDP can be calculated as:

$$\text{Real GDP} = Q_{\text{pineapple}} \times P_{\text{pineapple}}{}^{\text{base year}} + Q_{\text{coconut}} \times P_{\text{coconut}}{}^{\text{base year}}$$

Let's visit a third island, Merir, to see how real and nominal GDP compare. Table 16.3 outlines Merir's production of pineapple and coconuts in 2015 and 2016, the prices of each product in each year, and both nominal and real GDP for each year.

Table 16.3 Real and Nominal GDP on the Island of Merir: An Example

Between 2015 and 2016, nominal GDP more than doubles. But real GDP rises by just 50%, matching Merir's increase in production.

	Production of Pineapple	Production of Coconuts	Price of Pineapple	Price of Coconuts	Nominal GDP	Real GDP, Base Year = 2015
2015	20	40	$4	$2	$160	$160
2016	30	60	$6	$3	$360	$240

In Merir, nominal GDP rises 125% (from $160 to $360) between 2015 and 2016. But is this large increase due to increased production or the effects of rising prices? Let's see how real GDP can filter out the effect of rising prices and give us insight into the improvement in Merir's material well-being. Remember that real GDP uses current-year quantities and base year prices. So:

Real GDP for 2015 is (20 pineapples × $4) + (40 coconuts × $2) = $160.
Real GDP for 2016 is (30 pineapples × $4) + (60 coconuts × $2) = $240.

Notice that while nominal GDP rose 125% between 2015 and 2016, real GDP rose by only 50% (from $160 to $240). If you check further, you'll notice that the production of pineapples and coconuts each increased by 50%, too. In other words, increases in real GDP are proportional to increases in actual production, and because it's actual production that produces material well-being, economists generally focus their attention on real GDP, not nominal GDP.

Adjusting for a Country's Size and Real GDP per Capita

You now know what GDP is, and you know how to adjust GDP to account for the effects of rising prices. There's one other adjustment to make to GDP if it is going to be used to evaluate how well societies meet the material needs of their people. To shed light on this, consider the economies of Japan and India, which are of roughly equal size in terms of their production[3]. Does this mean that Japan and India are doing an equally good job of caring for their people?

Absolutely not. Although India and Japan produce about the same amount of stuff, that stuff gets split among about 125 million people in Japan, but gets divided among 1.23 *billion* Indians. Not surprisingly, the typical person in Japan is about 10 times better off than the typical person in India!

GDP indicates the size of the economic pie. But if you're interested in GDP as an indicator of how well society meets the material needs of its people, you need to account for the number of ways the pie must be split. So, to give us the best indicator of the material standard of living of the typical person in society, we focus on *real GDP per capita*, which is real GDP divided by the population.

---

[3] Estimates of GDP in India and Japan adjusted for purchasing power parity (a measure of real GDP that allows for international comparisons) are from the CIA *World Factbook*.

Shortcomings of GDP

Let's recap what you've learned so far. You have learned that how successful economies are at providing material comforts to their residents depends on how much the economies produce. You've learned how GDP captures the value of the items an economy makes in its quest to provide those material comforts. You've learned how real GDP filters out the effects of rising prices in general and allows us to compare the amount of production in any given year to the amount of production in an arbitrarily chosen base year. Finally, you've learned how to divide GDP to reflect the level of well-being a typical resident enjoys. Surely, after all that calculation, after all those adjustments, GDP must do a great job of measuring what we want it to measure.

Sadly, it doesn't. GDP, to paraphrase Sir Winston Churchill's famous quote about democracy, is the worst possible statistic we might use to assess the performance of an economy . . . except for any other that you might name. In other words, GDP is still pretty imperfect.

GDP Doesn't Include the Underground Economy

What are the flaws that render GDP such an imperfect measure of economic performance? For starters, consider that for very practical data-collection reasons, GDP measures only legitimate market transactions. The fact is, however, that many transactions are neither recorded nor reported. Sometimes it's because the seller wishes to avoid paying sales and income taxes on the transaction. Sometimes it's because the data would provide evidence that could be used against the buyers and sellers in court. Consider, for example, a drug deal. The seller gains from the transaction: He values the money more than the drugs. The buyer, who values the drugs more than the money, gains, too. From that standpoint, an illicit exchange of heroin is little different than a legal exchange of milk. But because milk is legal and heroin is not, the sale of a gallon of milk will show up in reported GDP, and the sale of heroin will not.

Additionally, in most places around the globe, and particularly in developing countries, many legal transactions go unrecorded. This often occurs because government lacks the resources to track transactions and enforce tax codes, and it's often the case that the businesses involved are miniscule, unlicensed, cottage-scale businesses run by individuals. In many places, there are more workers in this "informal" sector than there are in what we would generally refer to as the organized economy.

Economists refer to these unreported, but wealth-creating, transactions collectively as the *underground economy*. The underground economy is not small: In the United States, it is estimated that the underground economy might amount to as much as $2 trillion. That's about 15% of the legitimately recorded transactions contributing to GDP. In places where governments are even more strict about what their residents may or may not do, or where tax rates are higher than in the United States, underground transactions may account for a huge proportion of all final expenditures: That's the case in Bolivia and Peru, for example, where the underground economy is estimated to be about two-thirds the size of the official economy[4]. So, although GDP might measure a great deal of the production of a country, it doesn't measure it all, which throws off the numerical measure of our well-being.

That makes inter-country comparisons of well-being difficult. Suppose, hypothetically, that the U.S. economy has GDP per capita of $50,000 and no underground economy at all, while the economy of Iceland has an official GDP per capita of $40,000 and a large underground economy that generates an additional $20,000 per person. When you compare the *official* statistics, the United States looks about 25% richer than Iceland. But when you compare the *actual* size of the economies—$50,000 per person in the United States and $60,000 in Iceland—it turns out that the United States is actually quite a bit poorer than Iceland in per capita terms. Speaking more

---

[4] Estimates of the size of the underground economy discussed in Section 16.4 are from Friedrich Schneider's "Shadow Economies of 145 Countries All over the World: What Do We Really Know?" *Brookings Institution Working Paper*, 2006.

generally, because the underground economy in the United States is smaller than it is in most other places on the globe, that suggests that other countries are not quite as poor, relative to the United States, as a simple comparison of GDP numbers might lead you to believe.

GDP Doesn't Include Household Production

There's another set of productive activities that goes unreported as well: the activities that take place within a household. Consider the process of laundering clothes. You can take your clothes to a dry cleaner for laundering, and someone will wash them. Or you can take your clothes home and have your parents launder them for you for free (assuming that they are willing to do that). Exactly the same service is produced either way, but when your dry cleaner does your laundry, GDP rises by $25 or $50 or whatever you get charged. When your parents do your laundry, GDP doesn't rise at all. This leaves us with an odd statistical artifact: If you happen to marry your dry cleaner, GDP is likely to fall—unless he charges you for laundering your clothes!

The household production problem is important for a couple of reasons. First, GDP is supposed to be a numerical indicator of how well people live. In the United States, GDP has risen fairly steadily over the past half-century, and we might be led to conclude that we are much better off than we used to be. But some of those gains are phantom gains—an artifact of an exodus of women into the workforce during the 1960s and 1970s. Simply put, when women went to work in the marketplace, their production was counted as part of GDP. Their work at home was not. In other words, we started to actually measure the production of these new entrants into the labor force.

However, because GDP figures are often used to compare standards of living across nations, measuring household production is important. There are countries that rely on lots of household production—of food, of cleaning, of childrearing, among other things. These countries will have artificially low GDP figures, which makes them look, in relative terms, poorer than they actually are.

GDP Doesn't Account for the Value of Leisure

In addition to the criticisms already mentioned, GDP has several other flaws that cast doubt on its ability to measure how well we live. Consider this paradox: Bill likes pie, and every time he buys a piece of pie, his happiness rises, and GDP rises, too. Bill also likes naps. Every time he takes a nap, his happiness rises, but nothing happens to GDP. In fact, if Bill knocks off work to take a nap, GDP might even fall! In other words, GDP accounts for the fact that well-being depends on the consumption of *things* but fails to account for the fact that well-being also depends on the consumption of *leisure*.

This is a surprisingly big problem because lots of leisure gets consumed. Some people choose to work only part time (and consume leisure the rest of the time), or people from households with two potential workers might decide that it's better to bring home a bit less and have the "second earner" stay home. In addition, leisure gets consumed more in some countries than in others. For example, in America, including all people between the ages of 16 and 65, the average number of hours worked per week is just over 25. In Italy, the average number of hours worked per week is slightly less than 17. In other words, the typical American works about 50% more than the typical Italian. Such a discrepancy in workweek hours distorts the picture of well-being that GDP projects. Using measured market production, Americans produce and earn much more than Italians, so they should be better off. But one of the reasons that Americans earn so much more is because they spend so much more time working—and remember, leisure can be as much fun as bringing home a big paycheck! So, if we're truly interested in measuring the well-being of Italians compared to Americans, using GDP as the basis of comparison may make Italians look poorer (and perhaps, by inference, unhappier) than they really are.

GDP Doesn't Account for Economic "Bads"

In each of the previous scenarios, GDP did a bad job because it failed to measure something people value that just happens not to be valued or measured in the market-place: clean clothes, heroin, informal production, and power naps. But the opposite is true, too: GDP does a bad job because it fails to account for things that we *don't* value or like. We call those things *economic bads*.

To shed light on this issue, consider China. Many major cities are booming with construction, lots of activity, and lots of production. The growth in China is occurring in a much different way than in Singapore, which is also booming (and which has *been* booming for the past 30 years or so). Whereas Singapore is almost spotlessly clean, visitors to China almost invariably mention the extraor-dinary pollution, including smog so heavy you can almost cut it with a knife. The smog comes at a very real cost to China's people. If we're truly interested in measuring the well-being of the typical Chinese citizen, we should account not only for the fact that China produces lots of things but that people there are breathing nasty air.

In the case of environmental degradation, production causes the economic bad. But in other cases, economic bads may cause production. Consider what happens when property crime begins to rise in your neighborhood. Your neighbors might begin installing car alarms, home security systems, and stronger door locks. Those expenditures cause GDP to increase, but the apparent increase in material well-being suggested by the GDP numbers is illusory: Buying an alarm system doesn't make you materially much better off than you were before; it simply helps protect the things you've already acquired. In other words, GDP includes some preventive spending on goods and services we would rather not purchase.

GDP Reveals Nothing About the Distribution of Income

There is one more reason that GDP fails to capture a country's well-being, and it's a big one—so big that an entire chapter of this book is devoted to it: GDP reveals nothing about the *distribution* of income (see Chapter 21). Consider two five-person islands out in the middle of the Pacific Ocean. There's a big difference between one island, where all five people make $200,000 apiece, and the other island, where one person makes $960,000 and the other four make $10,000. Neither GDP nor GDP per capita accurately depicts those differences. In other words, GDP doesn't paint an accurate picture of the material comforts the *typical* person enjoys: The GDP statistic overstates the lifestyle of the typical person on the second island.

GDP Redeemed

All the criticisms just discussed might lead you to conclude that GDP doesn't do a good job of reporting anything meaningful. Admittedly, it's imperfect, but it's none-theless widely used for a couple of reasons. The first reason is that economists haven't come up with any other summary measure of an economy's performance that is less flawed. The second reason is more compelling: GDP may not measure all the things we really care about, but it is so strongly statistically correlated with many of the things we do that it's a reasonable indicator of how we're doing.

To demonstrate, consider an indicator of well-being that virtually everyone agrees matters to the average person but is not included in GDP: child mortality. If you decide to have children, you will desperately want your child to have the greatest possible chance of reaching adulthood.

Figure 16.1 shows child mortality statistics compiled by Gapminder.org. The countries are arranged left to right in order of real GDP per capita. On the far left is the Democratic Republic of the Congo, where real GDP per person is just over $400 per year. As you look to the right, the countries get richer. At the far right is Qatar, where on average, real GDP per capita is more than $90,000 per year.

▶ **Figure 16.1**

Income and Child Mortality in 186 Countries, 2012

Income per person is highly correlated with meaningful life outcomes such as child mortality. Generally speaking, the richer a nation is, the lower its child mortality rate. In Iceland, real GDP per capita is $34,371 and child mortality is 2.3 out of every 1,000 children. By comparison, in Sierra Leone real GDP per capita is around $1,000 a year and child mortality is 182 out of every 1,000 children.

Data Source: Free material from www.gapminder.org.

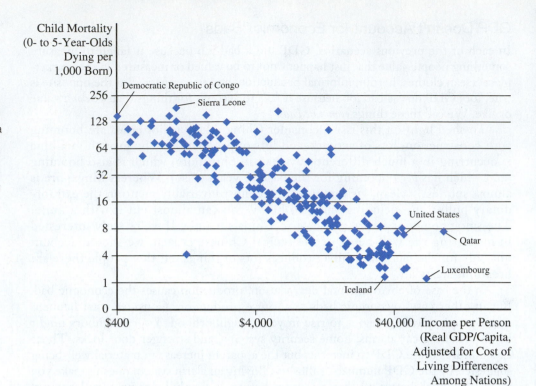

From top to bottom, each country's position represents the number of children out of every 1,000 who will die before turning age five. Based on this information, the worst place in the world to have a baby is Sierra Leone, where an astonishing 182 out of every 1,000 children will perish before five years of age. Not far behind Sierra Leone is the Angola, where 163 out of every 1,000 children born will die before reaching age five.

If Sierra Leone and Angola are the worst places in the world to rear children, what are the best? Luxembourg and Iceland, where only 2.3 children out of 1,000 die before age five. In other words, if your employer forces you to transfer from its Reykjavik office to its office in Freeport, Sierra Leone, from a purely statistical perspective your child's chance of dying goes up 60-fold.

Here's why GDP is so important to this story: There's a distinct pattern to these dots. When you draw a line through them, the line runs sharply downhill. The downward slope tells you something: The safest places to rear children are also the richest.

Figure 16.1 is a snapshot of the income/child mortality relationship taken at a particular point in time. But the relationship between wealth and health can also be established by looking at how the data have evolved *across* time. In the early 1800s, most people in the world were quite poor—even in the most developed countries. Infant mortality, even in the richest places, was often in the neighborhood of 600 deaths per 1,000 children. That's stunning: At a point in time within the relatively modern, industrial era, most kids in the world didn't stand a 50–50 chance of reaching school age. Even in 1900, there was no country in the world where a child's risk of death was lower than 1 in 10. But as the 20th century unfolded, many, if not most, countries got a lot wealthier, and as incomes increased infant mortality rates began to fall: Today, the child mortality rate in worst-ranked Sierra Leone is only one-third the mortality rate in the *typical* country in 1800. But, as you may have guessed, the gains in child mortality weren't spread evenly: The largest improvements were found in the countries that were getting the richest the fastest.

There are many reasons higher incomes correlate with lower infant mortality rates. Some of the reasons are causal: Earning more money gives you the ability to buy more and better food, clean water, and good health care. Some of the correlations are

Application 16.1

Don't Care Too Much for Money

In 2006, the British economist Richard Layard wrote that unhappiness was a bigger problem in England than unemployment. Layard has long believed that GDP is an overrated measure of well-being and that policymakers should focus more on creating happiness and less on generating economic growth. British Prime Minister David Cameron paid heed to Layard's argument. In November 2010, Cameron asked the Office of National Statistics to create a measure of Britain's general well-being that would, in addition to GDP, become a focus of policy.

Layard's argument rests on decades-old work which showed that a nation's per capita income and self-reported happiness tend to rise together until income reaches about $15,000 (in today's dollars). There, happiness appears to level off even as income continues to rise.

Economist Justin Wolfers of the University of Michigan disagrees, telling *The Economist* magazine that he has heard arguments like Layard's "hundreds of times, and it irritates me so much." Unable to find a formal statistical test of the proposition, Wolfers teamed with economist Betsey Stevenson of the U.S. Department of Labor to conduct one. Examining decades of survey data on happiness and life satisfaction, they found that a given percentage increase in GDP buys at least as much happiness in a rich country as it does in a poor one.

That finding directly contradicts Layard: "We present evidence that well-being rises with absolute income, period. This conclusion suggests that economists' traditional interest in economic growth has not been misplaced."

Wolfers and Stevenson then took a closer look at one survey in particular, the Gallup World Poll (GWP), an extraordinarily comprehensive global survey about ordinary peoples' subjective life experiences. The GWP asks questions such as, "Did you smile or laugh a lot yesterday?" and "Were you treated with respect all day yesterday?"

Wolfers and Stevenson grouped GWP data by country and compared that data to each country's GDP. They found that as GDP increased, respondents reported:

- Significantly less physical pain, depression, anger, and boredom
- Significantly more smiles, laughter, and general enjoyment
- Significantly more choice over how they spent their time
- Being treated with greater respect

GDP, however, is not the answer to *all* of the world's problems. Wolfers and Stevenson report that on a typical day, people in rich countries were *no more or less likely* than people in poor countries to feel well-rested, learn or do something interesting, or experience worry or sadness. Nor were people in rich countries any more likely to experience feelings of personal closeness and intimacy, verifying an assertion that has been circulating unproven since at least 1964: Money really can't buy you love.

See related problem 4.10 on page 352 at the end of this chapter.

Based on Betsey Stevenson and Justin Wolfers, "Economic Growth and Subjective Well-Being: Reassessing the Easterlin Paradox," Brookings Papers on Economic Activity, Spring 2008; and "The Joyless or the Jobless: Should Government Pursue Happiness Rather than Economic Growth?" *The Economist*, November 25, 2010.

not causal: For example, the GDPs of countries embroiled in civil wars are generally low, and in those nations, infant mortality rates are high. In such cases, it's likely that the low GDPs aren't the sole *cause* of high infant mortality but that these findings are merely correlated to a certain extent. Civil wars tend to disrupt markets (along with a lot of other things) and interfere with the process of generating income. The wars also lead to people, including children, dying in greater numbers.

Even if other factors such as civil wars skew the well-being equation, GDP is still a useful tool. It is so strongly correlated with so many things that we're genuinely concerned about (child mortality not the least among them) that, despite its flaws, GDP tells us much about how well we are doing.[5]

16.5 Learning Objective

List key characteristics that help an economy grow.

Economic growth The increase in the overall value of goods and services produced in an economy across time; usually measured as the percentage increase in a country's real GDP or real GDP per capita.

Economic Growth

The general standard of living around the world 2,000 years ago was very low: The typical person worked very hard, was very poor, and lived a very short life. That standard of living didn't change much over the next 1,600 years: The typical person in the 17th century lived much like the typical person in the first century. But about 300 years ago, something interesting happened: Global production and global standards of living began to increase. Those increases eventually created a general prosperity that has made many—but not all—nations incredibly wealthy by historical standards. Economists call increases across time in the overall value of goods and services produced in an economy **economic growth**. Economic growth is generally measured as the percentage increase in a country's real GDP or, alternatively, as the percentage increase in a country's real GDP per capita.

Economic growth isn't generally explosive; the increases in prosperity many countries have experienced didn't happen all at once. Rather, those gains reflect modest increases in output sustained over long periods of time. That's certainly been the U.S. experience, as Figure 16.2, which shows U.S. real GDP from 1947 to 2014, demonstrates.

Between 1947 and 2014, U.S. real GDP grew eightfold—from about $2 trillion to about $16 trillion. That's a tremendous increase in production in just a few decades.

MyEconLab Real-time data

▶ **Figure 16.2**
U.S. Real GDP, 1947–2014
Large increases in real GDP don't happen overnight. Rather, increasing prosperity is the product of modest increases in output sustained over long periods of time. *Note:* Shaded areas represent recessions, which are periods of slow economic activity.

Source: FRED Economic Database
(http://research.stlouisfed.org/fred2/series/GDP/).

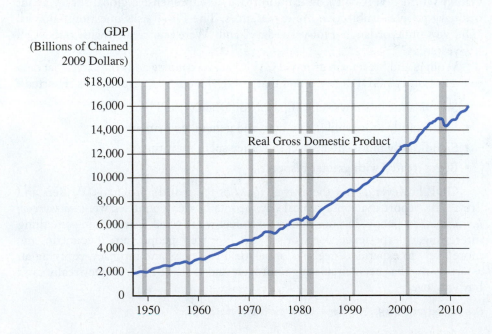

[5] Numerous alternatives to GDP attempt to incorporate quality-of-life indicators. The most prominent is the UN's Human Development Index. But there are several others, including Bhutan's Gross National Happiness, the OECD's Better Life Index, and the New Economics Foundation's Happy Planet Index. These indexes generally subjectively weight production with other measures of well-being, such as education, access to clean water, and life expectancy, among others.

Yet that increase reflects an *annual* growth rate of only about 3% per year. In other words, small increases in output sustained over long time horizons can turn poor countries into rich ones.

How Small Differences in Growth Rates Can Cause Large Differences in Well-Being

Not all countries have shared equally in the global prosperity of the past few centuries. Some countries have grown much richer than others. You might conclude that the slower-growing countries have made mistakes that stunted their growth—and in some cases that's probably true. But over long time spans, even small differences in year-over-year growth rates can lead to huge differences in long-term economic performance. To illustrate, consider a popular shortcut from business finance that you can use to estimate a country's long-term growth; it's called the Rule of 70. The **Rule of 70** states that the number of years it takes for a country to double its real GDP is approximately equal to 70 divided by the country's annual real GDP growth rate:

$$\text{Number of years to double real GDP} \approx \frac{70}{\text{Annual real GDP growth rate}}$$

Rule of 70 A formula used to determine how long it will take a country to double its real GDP. The number of years it will take to double real GDP is approximately equal to 70 divided by the annual growth rate of real GDP.

If a country's real GDP grows at 5% per year, its real GDP will double about every $70 \div 5 = 14$ years. Now, think about how that country's real GDP will change over longer time horizons. Suppose that real GDP is initially $1 trillion:

- In 14 years, real GDP will double to $2 trillion.
- In 14 more years, that $2 trillion will double again, to $4 trillion.
- And in yet another 14 years, real GDP will double again, to $8 trillion.

Taken in total, over a time span of 42 years, GDP will grow eightfold.

Now compare two economies with slower growth. Economy A has an annual growth rate of 2%; its real GDP doubles about every 35 years. Economy B has an annual growth rate of 1%; its real GDP doubles about every 70 years. What will happen in these two countries over a long period of time—say, 210 years? Suppose each country starts with an arbitrary but identical amount of wealth. Let's call it "one dollar sign's worth." Table 16.4 shows, with an appropriate number of dollar signs, exactly what to expect in each country over the next 210 years:

Table 16.4 Economic Growth over Long Time Horizons		
Modest differences in growth, sustained over long periods of time, result in tremendous differences in standard of living. Starting with identical standards of living, if Country A grows at 2% per year and Country B grows at 1% per year, over two centuries, Country A will become eight times richer than Country B.		
Date	**Country A's Real GDP**	**Country B's Real GDP**
Today	$	$
In 35 years . . .	$$	$$
In 70 years . . .	$$$$	$$
In 105 years . . .	$$$$ $$$$	$$$
In 140 years . . .	$$$$ $$$$ $$$$ $$$$	$$$$
In 175 years . . .	$$$$ $$$$ $$$$ $$$$ $$$$ $$$$ $$$$ $$$$	$$$$ $$
In 210 years . . .	$$$$ $$$$ $$$$ $$$$ $$$$ $$$$ $$$$ $$$$ $$$$ $$$$ $$$$ $$$$ $$$$ $$$$ $$$$ $$$$	$$$$ $$$$

As shown in Table 16.4, over 210 years, Economy A will see its output grow by a factor of 64, and Economy B will grow by a factor of only 8. A small difference in two countries' growth rates, sustained over a long time horizon, makes a huge difference in those countries' well-being.

Essential Ingredients for Economic Growth

If small differences in growth rates can lead to large differences in well-being, then a natural policy question is, "What can we do to make the economy grow as fast and sustainably as possible?" In other words, is there a recipe that countries can follow that will eventually make them rich?

Unfortunately, there is no single magic formula. Rather, the countries that have grown most rapidly over the past few hundred years have drawn various items from a set of practices and institutions that have proven to promote growth. In Chapter 6, we discussed some of the characteristics necessary for a market to function well: honesty, competition, and property rights. Because economic growth measures increases in market activity, it's no surprise that these same characteristics are positively related to growth at the macro level.

Honesty and the Rule of Law If buyers and sellers don't trust one another, they'll complete fewer transactions than they otherwise would. That stunts economic activity and growth. At a macro level, the importance of honesty manifests itself in a second way: Public corruption can interfere with a country's economic growth and development. That's because corrupt public officials may make decisions not on what's best for the economy but instead on what's best for their pocketbooks, friends, and family members. In addition, officials who demand bribes in exchange for doing their jobs (such as issuing building permits or issuing tax identification numbers) often interfere with the process of opening and running a business.

Countries with legal institutions designed to encourage and foster honesty tend to grow more sustainably; countries with fewer of those institutions and with significant public corruption may not grow at all. Each year, Transparency International compiles a global index of public corruption. In 2013, the least corrupt nations were Denmark, New Zealand, Finland, Sweden, and Norway—five countries with track records of sustained economic growth. In contrast, the five most corrupt countries— Somalia, North Korea, the Sudan, South Sudan, and Libya—have had little or no economic growth over a period of many decades.

Competition and International Trade Competition disciplines producers, encouraging them to minimize wastefulness in production and to specialize in producing the goods and services that they are relatively best at making. At the macro level, countries that expose themselves to competition with the rest of the world—through openness to international trade—tend to grow more rapidly than countries that wall themselves off: The fastest-growing countries of the past few decades include a disproportionate number of open traders, including the rapidly growing Asian economies of South Korea, Taiwan, Singapore, and Hong Kong. Trade spurs growth in part because of the discipline that foreign import competition provides domestic producers and also because openness to trade creates a global market for the goods and services a country specializes in producing for export.

Property Rights The countries that have exhibited the strongest and most consistent growth have almost invariably been countries with market economies. The fundamental function of market economies is to facilitate the transfer of property from one party to another. Well-defined and well-protected property rights encourage those transactions: When you buy a new car, it's nice to know a neighbor or a government official won't take it from you. Otherwise, you'd likely never buy a car in the first place.

So property rights are the foundation on which market transactions are built. But they are also a critical component of the market system in that the right to own and operate a business provides an incentive—the profit motive—for entrepreneurs to create new goods and services, explore new ideas, and produce more efficiently. People work smarter, harder, and more creatively when they get to keep the rewards of their efforts for themselves. To that end, institutions that create and protect property rights—patents, trademarks, copyrights, and the right to own a business—are key institutions in the formula for economic growth.

Physical Capital In addition to honesty, competition, and property rights, economists have identified a few other essential ingredients in the formula for growth. The first is a large stock of physical capital, which can include:

- Investment goods, such as factories, tools, and other equipment used to produce other goods and services
- Infrastructure, such as roads, bridges, and railroads, necessary to move goods from place to place
- Communications networks, such as the telephone system and the Internet, that help facilitate the buying and selling of goods and services

Physical capital makes workers more productive, so an expanding capital stock helps the economy grow. This is why policymakers emphasize the investment component of GDP. Of course, business owners don't generally pay for factories out of their own pockets; instead, they typically borrow money from banks or sell shares in their business to people—investors—who have some savings set aside that they'd like to earn a return on. So a high savings rate and a stable, well-functioning financial system that helps businesses access households' accumulated savings are important prerequisites for a large and growing stock of physical capital.

Human Capital If investing in machinery can spur growth, so can investing in people. Economists call the knowledge and skills that people accumulate through experience, education, and training **human capital**. The more human capital a country's labor force has, the more productive and efficient it is likely to be. Basic literacy enables workers to read and follow instructions. Mathematical training helps them with basic job tasks: *How many boxes do I have left to stack on the truck?* It also helps them analyze problems: *If I've got a 5 acre plot and can grow one corn plant per square foot, how many seeds do I need to buy?* Additional education pays dividends in other ways; for example, those who are educated may develop critical reasoning skills, learn construction methods, or understand essential business practices. Not surprisingly, countries that have educated and literate labor forces tend to have stronger and more sustained growth than countries that don't.

> **Human capital** The knowledge and skills people accumulate through experience, education, and training.

Political Stability One of the most important ingredients in creating and sustaining economic growth is political stability. It is hard to convince people to invest in consumer goods, houses, and farms when the next government might seize them. It is hard to convince multinational corporations to build factories in a country if the next government might confiscate those factories. It is hard to convince people to save money if the next government might appropriate that savings or replace the currency with a new one. In other words, political instability creates uncertainty about honesty and property rights that discourages economic growth. Not surprisingly, over longer time horizons, the world's slowest-growing economies are often found in countries that have experienced significant civil unrest.

Business Cycles and Recessions

16.6 Learning Objective

Explain how supply and demand shocks may lead to recessions.

Although low, steady growth over decades and centuries does a pretty good job of describing the U.S. economy, it doesn't show the complete picture. U.S. GDP has actually fallen many times—sometimes precipitously and for significant lengths of time. There have also been periods during which GDP grew *too* quickly, at paces that were unsustainable. Other countries have had similar experiences.

Business cycle The ordinary fluctuation of real GDP around its long-run trend.

Recession An economic downturn in a business cycle.

Depression A particularly severe and protracted recession.

Business Cycles and Recessions Defined

Economists use the term **business cycles** to refer to the ordinary fluctuation of real GDP around its long-run trend. In lay terms, business cycles represent the economy's ups and downs. Business cycles are of great concern to policymakers. Even an economy that grows too quickly can lead to problems. (That case will be discussed more thoroughly in Chapter 19.) Consider the opposite case—the case of stagnating or declining economic activity. These economic downturns are called **recessions**. A particularly severe and protracted recession is called a **depression**.[6] Application 16.2 describes the criteria that have to be met for a downturn to be considered a recession.

For many people, even the mildest recession can have dire economic consequences. Before digging further into why recessions can be so nasty, it's worth noting that the term *business cycle* can be misleading. After all, a cycle somehow implies a high degree of regularity and predictability. For example, the phases of the moon constitute a cycle, and with about 30 seconds' access to a smartphone, you can tell what phase the moon will be in on a specified date 1,000 years in the future.

But business cycles are different. They happen unpredictably, and no two cycles are alike, either in terms of how big they are or how long they last. During the 70-odd years since the end of World War II, the United States has had 11 downturns bad enough to be classified as recessions. Refer again to Figure 16.2 on page 340, which shows the behavior of real GDP from 1947 to 2014 and indicates periods of recession with shaded bands.

The long, steady trend in real GDP is clearly upward, though it is periodically interrupted by periods of recession. On average, the United States has experienced a recession about every 6 years. But that is misleading, because as Figure 16.2 shows, some of the recessions occurred one right after another. (Two back-to-back recessions are often referred to as a "double-dip.") Take, for example, the double-dip recessions in the early 1980s. A 6-month recession began in January 1980, followed by 12 months of recovery, followed again by an unusually severe 16-month recession that began in July 1981. Between other recessions, there are substantial periods of economic growth: After a short and mild recession that began in July 1990 and ended in March 1991, the economy experienced 10 solid years of sustained economic growth.

Recessions also differ in their severity: The recessions that began in 1990 and 2001 lasted only 8 months each, and increases in the unemployment rate were fairly mild. (See Chapter 17 for more about unemployment.) In fact, during the recession of 2001, the unemployment rate stayed well below 6%, which is not far from its long-run average when the economy is growing. However, recessions can be both severe and protracted. The big recession of 1981 saw the unemployment rate top out at almost 11%. It climbed almost that high during the recession that began in 2007 (which is now being called the Great Recession), and 3 years after the recession ended, unemployment was still well above 8%.

Not only do we not know exactly when a recession is coming, we also have little indication how bad one is going to be once it's begun. In fact, sometimes we even have trouble figuring out whether we're in a recession, largely because it is so difficult to collect accurate macroeconomic data, especially over short time horizons. Therefore, one important thing to remember about economic policy designed to prevent recessions is this: If policymakers can't see recessions coming, it's pretty hard to stave them off.

---

[6] The National Bureau of Economic Research (NBER) declares the start and end dates of recessions. However, there is no organization that officially declares a depression. Rather, that term arises through public consensus and use. The difference between even a large recession like the Great Recession of 2007–2009 and a depression is stark: In the Great Recession, unemployment peaked at about 10%, and output fell by less than 5%. In the Great Depression of the 1930s, unemployment rose to about 25%, and output fell by 25%.

Application 16.2

Who Says We're in a Recession?

For all the pain and suffering recessions cause, and all the attention recessions receive in the press, one fairly obvious question often remains unasked: How exactly do we know when the economy is in a recession?

The responsibility for making that determination rests with the National Bureau of Economic Research (NBER), a private nonprofit organization based in Cambridge, Massachusetts, dedicated to studying the science of economics. At the NBER, a select group of eight economists known as the Business Cycle Dating Committee determines when recessions begin and end. Those economists are all academics at the top of their game: Two are from Harvard, two are from Berkeley, and there is one economist each from Stanford, MIT, Northwestern, and Princeton.

The popular press often defines a recession as two consecutive quarters of falling real GDP. But that's just a rough guideline: The Business Cycle Dating Committee takes a far more exhaustive approach. The committee defines a recession as "a period between a[n economic] peak and a trough. During a recession, a significant decline in economic activity spreads across the economy and can last from a few months to more than a year."

In other words, the NBER doesn't even *mention* GDP in the definition of a recession! But although it may go unmentioned, it does not go unnoticed. The "significant decline in economic activity" the NBER refers to encompasses real GDP as well as economy-wide employment, real incomes (incomes adjusted for inflation), industrial production, and other useful indicators of economic performance. So the beginning of a recession isn't determined by a hard-and-fast rule but rather by a preponderance of the evidence, carefully weighed.

But that evidence rolls in slowly because data are collected infrequently and are often subject to substantial revision. As a result, a recession isn't generally declared until 6 to 21 months after the recession began. Sometimes this means the NBER is too late in declaring one: The July 1990 recession was declared in April 1991—a month after it ended!

You might think that such a lack of timeliness is a problem. You might also think that the weighty responsibility of declaring recessions should belong to the government and not a bunch of college professors. Truthfully, though, very little rides on whether a recession is accurately declared: Announcing a recession doesn't trip any governmental policy triggers, and it doesn't launch any relief programs or set off alarm bells at the Federal Reserve Bank. It really wouldn't even matter if we stopped announcing recessions altogether. They would still happen, and they would be just as long or short as they would be if they were announced. Consequently, allowing a group of professors to pinpoint the beginning and end of a recession seems perfectly reasonable: All they're responsible for is giving a name and a birthdate to the economic malaise people were already feeling.

See related problems 6.8 and 6.9 on page 353 at the end of this chapter.

Based on information obtained from the National Bureau of Economic Research (NBER) at www.nber.org.

Supply Shocks as a Cause of Recessions

One of the reasons it's hard to know whether a recession is coming is because economists aren't absolutely certain *why* many of them begin in the first place. Sometimes, economists attribute recessions to supply shocks. **Supply shocks** are events that fundamentally reduce society's ability to produce goods and services. Supply shocks can manifest themselves in many ways. For example, in Iowa, a major producer of

Supply shocks Events that fundamentally reduce society's ability to produce goods and services.

corn, economic performance depends on the weather: Too much moisture, too little moisture, or maybe one bad night of hail, and a significant share of Iowa's output can simply disappear. Production falls, and incomes fall with it.

Changes in the availability or cost of energy can also constitute supply shocks. As an oil importer, America is vulnerable to global swings in crude oil prices. Because petroleum-derived energy is a key input into the production and delivery of goods and services, an increase in oil prices raises producers' costs and reduces their ability to make and distribute the goods and services consumers want. When energy prices rise quickly and dramatically, production can fall so much that a recession results. The recession of 1973–1975, for example, has been largely attributed to a 300% increase in the price of oil engineered by the Organization of Petroleum Exporting Countries (OPEC).

Demand Shocks as a Cause of Recessions

Despite the ability of supply shocks to explain changes in our production and income, most economists agree that most recessions probably originate on the buyers' side of the market, not the sellers'. **Demand shocks** are events that reduce the willingness or ability of buyers to purchase goods and services. Sometimes those demand shocks are fairly easy to explain. But more often, those shocks arise spontaneously and unpredictably as a result of changes in the confidence consumers and businesses have about the economy.

Demand shocks Events that reduce the willingness or ability of buyers to purchase goods and services.

Here's how the process might begin. Suppose that you work in the jet aircraft industry, building passenger planes. Now suppose you and your fellow workers become worried about the future of the industry. Maybe there's a real reason for this, such as a series of airplane hijackings that generates uncertainty about the future of air travel. But maybe there's no real reason at all, perhaps just an intangible sense of bad things to come, or water-cooler gossip that a few aircraft manufacturers are thinking about layoffs. You and your coworkers aren't sure if a downturn is going to occur. However, with rumors floating around that it will, you decide it's not the best time to spend $500 on a new watch, take a cruise, or even go out for dinner a third time in a single week. Ultimately, anxiety and uncertainty about the future might lead you to consume a bit less and save a bit more. If the uncertainty is widespread, substantial numbers of people are likely to act the same way.

When you and thousands of people like you cut back on spending, fewer income-producing transactions get completed. The jeweler, the cruise line owners, and the owners of your favorite steakhouse suddenly notice that there are unsold watches, vacant cabins, and too many steaks left in the restaurant's freezer. The cutbacks by individuals then cause GDP as a whole to fall.

And although that's where the problem begins, it's certainly not where it ends. The jeweler, the cruise line owners, and the couple who run the steakhouse unexpectedly find their incomes falling, so they, in turn, postpone concerts and oil changes and convince their children to attend cheaper colleges. Each adjustment brings further declines in GDP and reduces the incomes of performers, mechanics, and universities. A downward spiral has begun—not because society's ability to produce goods and services got fundamentally worse but simply because of caution.

Things can get worse because cutting back on spending is only *one* way that the jeweler and the owners of the steakhouse adjust to falling sales. Put yourself in the shoes of a business owner: Every morning you fill your shelves with items you've produced, and every night those shelves are depleted by the day's sales. But now something different is happening: Each morning your fill your shelves, and by night, you still have lots of items left over that you didn't sell. This tells you that you don't need to produce as much; there's no sense making items that aren't selling. So, you cut back on production and lay off some of your employees.

The people who were laid off, in turn, cut their expenditures, and those cutbacks are felt at coffeehouses and hardware stores and hundreds of other places. Eventually, spending may slow to the point that even the aircraft business—the business you happen to be in and the origin of this vicious chain reaction—begins to suffer. The next thing you know, you're laid off, too.

Application 16.3

The Origins of the Great Recession

The United States has experienced many recessions. However, the last one, which began in December 2007 and lasted for 18 months, was anything but typical: It was dubbed the "Great Recession." Real GDP fell by 4.3%, the largest drop since the Great Depression. The effects also lingered long after the recession was over: Per capita real GDP didn't return to its pre-recession level until midway through 2013, and millions remained jobless after years of unemployment.

The scale of this catastrophe has led many people to wonder exactly how such a crisis began. Those beginnings aren't to be found in 2007, however. They're found back in the 1990s, a period of unprecedented economic calm: Prices were stable and GDP grew, uninterrupted, for an entire decade. Part of the credit for that prosperity (and part of the blame for what followed) belonged to former Federal Reserve Chairman Alan Greenspan, who kept interest rates at low levels throughout the late 1990s and well into the 2000s. Those low interest rates stimulated three types of spending that contributed to the boom: Consumer durables, business fixed investment, and residential investment all grew at unprecedented rates.

Of particular interest is residential investment, which grew rapidly during the 1990s and even faster in the 2000s. In hindsight, it is apparent that a speculative bubble fueled the housing boom. In lay terms, a *bubble* exists when things like houses are being bought at unnaturally high prices by people who believe that prices will rise even higher. Believing that housing prices could not fall and fueled by low interest rates and lax mortgage lending standards, consumers began borrowing money to buy more and more expensive homes—homes that in many cases were beyond their true ability to afford. Many people, too, started flipping houses—buying homes with the intent of quickly reselling them at a higher price.

Rising home values fueled other consumption spending, too. A homebuyer who borrowed to purchase a house for $200,000 and saw its value rise to $350,000 could refinance the home loan and draw out up to $150,000 in cash. That cash could then be used to buy clothes and cars and other consumer goods, especially consumer durables.

The bubble popped in the fall of 2007, after many consumers began defaulting on their home loans. Eventually, home prices fell—by up to 40% in many places. More and more homeowners found themselves "underwater," owing more on their homes than their homes were worth. Many simply walked away from their mortgages, and almost overnight, residential construction disappeared.

That set off a chain reaction. As housing wealth evaporated and uncertainty increased, spending on consumer durables plummeted. Increased pessimism made businesses more cautious about expanding or starting new ventures. Consequently, real GDP fell by over $600 billion. That amounted to a decline in real GDP of 4.3%, which is enormous by modern standards.

This is a short and incomplete story of how the Great Recession began: falling residential investment, falling consumer durables spending, and falling business investment. Still more of this story will be told in chapters to come, as we learn more about the financial system and the role it played in the economy's collapse.

See related problem 6.10 on page 353 at the end of this chapter.

Interestingly, the upheaval spending cuts cause doesn't reflect a change in the economy's ability to produce things. Rather, it was touched off on the buying side of the economy by an uneasy feeling—a feeling that may not have been grounded in fact but only in fear. Those fears then became reality—a self-fulfilling prophecy. It is for this reason that during the Great Depression of the 1930s, U.S. President Franklin Delano Roosevelt tried to reassure Americans by declaring, "We have nothing to fear but fear itself."

The preceding example paints just one picture of how a demand shock can start a recession. But there are others. Regardless of where the demand shock originates, the common denominator is that somewhere in the economy, for some reason, somebody cuts spending; that spending cut snowballs until a recession results.

Consumers make cutbacks in response to economic uncertainty, but they also do so for other reasons, such as the following:

- **If an increase in taxes leaves consumers with less *disposable income* to spend.** Disposable income is defined as income minus taxes. Suppose you make $100 per week, and the government takes $10 in taxes. Your disposable income is $90. If government raises your taxes to $40, your disposable income falls to $60, which may cause you to reduce your consumption.

- **If consumers see some of their wealth evaporate.** In 2008, both the stock market and the housing market collapsed. If you had a lot of wealth in the form of stocks and housing, you probably saw a lot of that wealth disappear. Such a loss might make you more careful about how you spend your paycheck: You may cut your consumption and postpone the purchase of a new car. Such a response is called a *wealth effect*.

- **If rising interest rates make it more costly for consumers to borrow money.** This is likely to have a particularly strong impact on purchases of consumer durables like cars and appliances because many consumers borrow money to pay for such purchases.

Spending cuts don't have to originate with households. They can also originate with businesses. Businesses are less likely to make investment expenditures in order to increase their production or initiate new ventures under the following conditions:

- **If the economy appears to be weakening.**
- **If corporate income taxes increase.** This makes businesses less profitable and reduces the incentive to invest.
- **If interest rates increase.** Rising interest rates raise the cost of borrowing; as a result, borrowing for new equipment and new construction of homes and factories and other ventures may decrease.

A demand-side recession can also be triggered by decreases in government spending or by lower net exports. If government decides to cut its spending on Jeeps, the effect is just the same as when households cut their spending on Jeeps. Likewise, net exports will fall if foreigners decide to stop buying Jeeps. Drops such as these, just like decreases in consumption or investment, can also spiral into recessions.

Conclusion

You learned in earlier chapters that perfectly rational actions by individual people can lead to collective outcomes that are undesirable. This theme is certainly echoed in this chapter. Cutting your spending when you are worried about losing your job is perfectly sensible. But when many people cut their spending, an undesirable recession can result. This phenomenon is easy to understand. What's harder to understand is how to pinpoint what causes recessions in the first place, predict them, and prevent them from happening. The ways in which policymakers attempt to do that are addressed in upcoming chapters.

Chapter Summary and Problems

Key Terms

Business cycle, p. 344
Consumption, p. 330
Demand shocks, p. 346
Depression, p. 344
Economic growth, p. 340
Gross domestic product (GDP), p. 327

Human capital, p. 343
Investment, p. 330
Macroeconomics, p. 326
Microeconomics, p. 326
Net exports, p. 332
Nominal GDP, p. 333

Real GDP, p. 334
Recession, p. 344
Rule of 70, p. 341
Supply shocks, p. 345

16.1 Macroeconomics and How It Differs from Microeconomics, page 326

Distinguish macroeconomics from microeconomics.

Summary

Macroeconomics is the study of the large-scale functioning of the economy. Microeconomics, by contrast, looks at decision making in a small slice of the economy. A microeconomist might be interested in what happens in the market for a single product. A macroeconomist might be interested in the total output of an economy, across all markets.

Review Questions

All problems are assignable in MyEconLab.

1.1 The study of the economy as a whole is called _____ .

1.2 _____ is the study of decisions made by individuals, businesses, and other entities such as governments.

1.3 _____ are interested in issues like the national unemployment rate, the indebtedness of nations, and foreign exchange rates.
   a. Microeconomists
   b. Macroeconomists
   c. Sociologists
   d. Aggregationists

1.4 _____ focus on studying one market at a time, such as the market for television programs.
   a. Microeconomists
   b. Macroeconomists
   c. Isolationists
   d. Political scientists

Problems and Applications

1.5 "Labor economists study the labor market. Because they study only one market, they must be microeconomists." Indicate whether you feel this statement is true or false, and explain your reasoning.

1.6 "The job of the macroeconomist is simple: All he must do is summarize what happens in microeconomic markets." Do you feel this statement is true or false? Why?

1.7 Name three specific topics macroeconomists study that microeconomists generally do not.

16.2 Material Well-Being and Gross Domestic Product, pages 326–333

List the components of GDP and explain how it is calculated.

Summary

An economy's material well-being depends on the amount and value of output the economy produces. Gross domestic product (GDP) is a summary statistic that attempts to measure society's material well-being by totaling the market value of all final goods and services produced in an economy. GDP can be measured by adding up a country's total consumption, investment, and government expenditures, as well as its net exports. This approach to measuring GDP is called the expenditures approach. A second, equivalent, approach to calculating GDP totals all income received by workers, landlords, and business owners. This approach to measuring GDP is called the income approach.

Review Questions

All problems are assignable in MyEconLab.

2.1 Raw materials or components that will eventually be transformed into a finished product are called _____ .

2.2 A person buys a new set of sheets for his bed. That purchase is counted in the _____ component of GDP.

2.3 _____ is the market value of all final goods and services produced in a country in a given year.

2.4 _____ are the sum of the goods produced in America and sold abroad, minus the goods and services that were produced abroad but purchased in America.

2.5 _____ include spending by businesses on factories, tools, and research and development.

2.6 The _____ to calculating GDP adds up wages, rents, and profits to determine GDP.

2.7 _____ are income earned by landlords, _____ are income earned by business owners, and _____ are income earned by workers.

  a. Profits; rents; wages

  b. Rents; wages; profits

  c. Wages; profits, rents

  d. Rents; profits; wages

2.8 Expenditures on physical plants and equipment, which are then used to produce other goods, are referred to as _____ .

  a. Fixed investment

  b. Consumer durables

  c. Inventory investment

  d. Intermediate goods

2.9 The _____ adds up total spending on final goods and services made by the various types of spending units in order to compute GDP.

  a. Income approach

  b. Expenditure approach

  c. Goods and services approach

  d. Factor approach

2.10 If an automobile is produced by Chevrolet in 2008 but is not sold until 2010, the automobile is included in which year's GDP?

  a. 2008

  b. 2010

  c. Both 2008 and 2010

  d. 2009—the average of the two

2.11 Building houses, or residential fixed investment, is a type of _____ expenditure.

  a. Consumption

  b. Investment

  c. Government spending

  d. Inventory investment

2.12 Which of the following transactions is included in the calculation of U.S. GDP?

  a. General Mills buys oats to make Cheerios.

  b. General Motors builds a pickup truck at a manufacturing facility in Brazil.

  c. General Colin Powell purchases a Victorian-era mansion from former Vice President Al Gore.

  d. General Electric purchases a machine that will be used to produce LED light bulbs.

2.13 When Josie, a U.S. resident, buys an imported bottle of wine from France, _____ .

  a. U.S. GDP increases, but French GDP stays the same

  b. U.S. GDP decreases, and French GDP increases

  c. U.S. GDP stays the same, and French GDP increases

  d. Both U.S. and French GDP increase

2.14 In discussing the recovery from the Great Recession, several economists stated they were in favor of greater government involvement in the economy because government constitutes one of the components of GDP. Yet the government does not produce many tangible goods. What approach to calculating GDP were these economists referring to?

  a. Absorption approach

  b. Expenditures approach

  c. Income approach

  d. Accounting approach

Problems and Applications

2.15 Explain the difference between an intermediate good and an investment good. Why don't economists include the sale of intermediate goods and services in the calculation of GDP?

2.16 Give an example of an export that is a consumer non-durable good and of an import that is a consumer durable good.

2.17 The money you spend on college tuition is included in the consumption category of expenditures. Can you make an argument that it should be counted elsewhere in GDP? Explain.

2.18 If the goal of GDP is to measure a country's production of goods and services, why do we quote GDP in terms of dollars rather than in terms of physical goods?

16.3   **Nominal GDP and Real GDP, pages 333–334**

Explain the importance of adjusting GDP for the effects of rising prices.

Summary

Nominal GDP values current production at current prices. This means that if prices rise, GDP will rise, even if production doesn't. Real GDP measures current production at an unchanging set of prices. Increases in real GDP represent true increases in the productivity of an economy. To get an accurate picture of the material well-being enjoyed by the typical person in a country, economists divide real GDP by the country's population. That common measure of standard of living is called per capita real GDP.

Review Questions

3.1 _____ measures the output of final goods in a country in a given year, valued at a particular base year's prices.

3.2 The best measure of a country's standard of living discussed in this chapter is _____ .

3.3 GDP for a given year valued in that year's prices is called _____ .
  a. Per capita GDP
  b. Adjusted GDP
  c. Nominal GDP
  d. Real GDP

3.4 Suppose that between the years 2524 and 2525, U.S. production remains unchanged, but prices increase by 6%. Then _____ .
  a. Nominal GDP increases, and real GDP increases
  b. Nominal GDP is unchanged, and real GDP increases
  c. Nominal GDP increases, and real GDP decreases
  d. Nominal GDP increases, and real GDP is unchanged

Problems and Applications

3.5 A small island economy produces 10 rafts in 2015 and sells them at a price of $20 per raft. In 2016, the island produces 12 rafts and sells them at $25 per raft. What is the nominal GDP in 2015 and in 2016? What is the real GDP in 2015 and 2016, using 2015 as the base year?

3.6 Why is real GDP a better indicator of economic progress than nominal GDP? Give an example to explain your answer.

3.7 "It is impossible for nominal GDP to decrease while real GDP increases." Is this statement true or false? Explain your reasoning.

16.4 ## Shortcomings of GDP, pages 335–340

Discuss why GDP is an imperfect indicator of material well-being.

Summary

The various measures of GDP are the most widely used indicators of material well-being. But they are not perfect. GDP measures do not include transactions made in the underground economy. They are not adjusted to reflect production that takes place inside the household. Nor do they account for the value of leisure. Standard GDP measures do not account for economic bads such as pollution. Nor do they reveal anything about the distribution of income in a country. Yet GDP measures do correlate well with many life indicators that are highly valued by society, such as infant mortality and life expectancy.

Review Questions

4.1 The _____ is what economists call unreported but wealth-creating transactions, collectively, that are not included in GDP.
  a. Black market
  b. Illicit transactions
  c. Underground economy
  d. Formal economy

4.2 In Japan, real GDP per capita is higher than it is in Greece. However, people in Japan work much longer hours than people in Greece. This disparity in work hours suggests that _____ .
  a. Greece looks poorer, relative to Japan, than it really is
  b. Greece looks richer, relative to Japan, than it really is
  c. The real GDP per capita numbers accurately capture the well-being of Greece and Japan.

4.3 In places where production causes a great deal of pollution, _____ .
  a. Society is richer than GDP numbers suggest
  b. Society is poorer than GDP numbers suggest
  c. GDP numbers accurately measure society's well-being

4.4 Health experts note that _____ .
  a. As countries get richer, life expectancy increases
  b. As countries get richer, infant mortality decreases
  c. Both (a) and (b) are true
  d. Neither (a) nor (b) is true

Problems and Applications

4.5 In the United States, the typical worker works about 32 hours per week; in Singapore, the typical worker works about 43 hours per week. In the United States, GDP per capita is about $52,000; in Singapore, it is about $60,000. Discuss the effect of workweek length on the relative well-being of people in the United States and Singapore. Are Americans worse off than GDP numbers suggest, or are they better off?

4.6 List and discuss three problems with using GDP to assess the performance of an economy.

4.7 Given all the problems in using GDP as a measure of performance of an economy, why is it still widely used to measure both the economy's performance and as an indicator of standard of living? Explain your answer.

4.8 Bolivia has an official GDP per capita of $5,300; the country's underground economy is estimated to be two-thirds the size of its official economy. Cambodia has an official GDP per capita of about $2,650, and its underground economy is about half the size of its official economy. Do these numbers suggest that the typical Bolivian is about twice as well off as the typical Cambodian? If not, is the typical Bolivian more than twice as well off or less than twice as well off as the typical Cambodian? Explain.

4.9 Go to Gapminder.org and generate graphs of each of the following variables against real GDP per capita: children per woman; life expectancy; and mean years in school (females 25 and over). Is there a pattern to your results? Find some other variable that is strongly correlated with real GDP per capita and report your results.

4.10 **[Related to Application 16.1 on page 339]** Read Application 16.1. How do the results of Wolfers and Stevenson's study differ from the previous prevailing opinion? What does Wolfers and Stevenson's work suggest economic policymakers should focus their attention on?

16.5 Economic Growth, pages 340–343

List key characteristics that help an economy grow.

Summary

Economists refer to increases in real GDP across time as economic growth. Over long time horizons, even small differences in the rate of economic growth can lead to large differences in material well-being. The countries that have experienced the strongest and most sustained growth have a general set of characteristics in common: honest business practices and government; a competitive business environment and openness to international trade; respect for property rights; investment in physical and human capital; and political stability.

Review Questions

All problems are assignable in MyEconLab.

5.1 The economy of Paulonia grows at 3.5% per year. How many years will it take for real GDP in Paulonia to double?
   a. 70
   b. 35
   c. 20
   d. 2

5.2 Suppose that in the economy of Tilden, real GDP per capita grows at 10%, doubling every 7 years. In 35 years, the typical resident of Tilden will be _____ times as rich as the typical resident today.
   a. 2
   b. 5
   c. 10
   d. 32

5.3 Which of the following statements best captures the story of the world's economic growth?
   a. Most of the world's wealthy economies have had slow and sustained growth for the last 1,000 years.
   b. People in 1900 lived about the same as people in the year 1000.
   c. Most of the world's economic growth has taken place in the past 300 years.
   d. The world's most developed countries were fortunate to experience large spurts of growth that catapulted them to wealth.

5.4 The countries that have experienced the most rapid economic growth are the countries that _____ .
   a. Are most open to international trade
   b. Close their borders and reserve the domestic market for domestic producers
   c. Export primary products like coal, while importing high-tech products like iPods
   d. None of the above statements are true

5.5 Which of the following has been shown to positively affect countries' economic growth?
   a. A large stock of physical capital
   b. A more educated workforce
   c. Government that establishes and protects property rights
   d. All of the above positively affect countries' growth.

Problems and Applications

5.6 Indicate whether the following statement is true or false, and give an example to support your answer: "Over long time horizons, small differences in economic growth between countries lead to correspondingly small differences in standard of living."

5.7 List three institutions that are vital ingredients for experiencing economic growth.

5.8 Explain why countries that open their borders to international trade tend to grow more rapidly than countries that do not.

5.9 Explain the differences and similarities between physical and human capital. Which do you think is more important? Why?

16.6 Business Cycles and Recessions, pages 343–348

Explain how supply and demand shocks may lead to recessions.

Summary

The ups and downs in an economy are called business cycles. An economic downturn is called a recession; a particularly severe downturn is called a depression. Recessions may be caused by supply shocks—fundamental reductions in an economy's ability to produce goods and services. Or recessions may be caused by demand shocks. Demand shocks are decreases in the willingness or ability of buyers—consumers, businesses, governments, or foreigners—to purchase goods and services.

Review Questions

All problems are assignable in MyEconLab.

6.1 Deviations from the long, steady trend of GDP are called _____ .

6.2 Events that fundamentally reduce society's ability to produce goods and services are called _____ .

6.3 A _____ is a downturn of the economy, as determined by the NBER.
  a. Bust
  b. Depreciation
  c. Recession
  d. Boom

6.4 _____ shocks arise spontaneously and unpredictably, often as a result of changes in the confidence consumers and businesses have about the economy.
  a. Supply
  b. Real
  c. Demand
  d. Energy

6.5 Who declares when the U.S. economy officially enters a recession?
  a. The president of the United States
  b. The Department of Commerce
  c. The Bureau of Economic Analysis
  d. The National Bureau of Economic Research

Problems and Applications

6.6 Give three examples of shocks that could originate on the buyers' side of the market. Identify the origin of (reason for) the shock and then identify the type of spending that is affected (consumption, investment, government purchases, or net exports).

6.7 How might the news media affect the economy? Discuss whether the news media is more likely to be responsible for a demand shock or a supply shock.

6.8 **[Related to Application 16.2 on page 345]** Application 16.2 suggests that there's no harm in having the group that declares recessions be independent of government. Can you think of one reason why, in a democracy, it might be a good thing to separate the managers of the economy from the body that evaluates how that economy is doing?

6.9 **[Related to Application 16.2 on page 345]** "The NBER uses GDP to determine whether we are in a recession." Is this statement true or false? Explain your answer.

6.10 **[Related to Application 16.3 on page 347]** Describe at least one shock that contributed to the Great Recession of 2007. Did the shock you describe affect consumption, investment, government expenditures, or net exports?

Gross Domestic Product and Business Cycles

This chapter introduced you to gross domestic product (GDP), which is the most fundamental and important indicator of a country's economic performance. You learned that GDP has four components: Consumption, investment, government spending, and net exports. Here are some news headlines about GDP that you may have noticed:

- U.S. GDP expanded in last quarter.

- Ireland's GDP leads the Eurozone.

- Hong Kong's GDP contracted last quarter.

The chapter also discussed the nature and origins of business cycles, which refer to the ups and downs of the economy. Here are some news headlines about business cycles that you may have noticed:

- Fears of recession linger.

- Is the Eurozone recession over?

- Economic recovery expected, but uncertain.

Collecting and analyzing data about GDP and business cycles are an important part of what economists do and are of great interest to government officials and the general public. The activities at the ends of Chapters 16–20 therefore focus on data.

In this real-time data analysis activity, you'll revisit the fundamental ideas of GDP and business cycles using data from Federal Reserve Economic Data (FRED), a comprehensive, up-to-date data set maintained by the Federal Reserve Bank of St. Louis.

1. Visit the FRED website located at www.stlouisfed.org/fred2.

2. Examine the data for each component of GDP and track how each component has changed over time.

3. Explore how each component of GDP behaves during economic recessions, paying particular attention to the behavior of consumption and investment spending.

MyEconLab
Please visit http://www.myeconlab.com for support material to conduct this experiment if assigned by your instructor.

CHAPTER

17 Unemployment

Chapter Outline and Learning Objectives

17.1 **What Is Unemployment?** page 356

Use employment status information to compute the unemployment rate.

17.2 **Shortcomings of the Measured Unemployment Rate,** page 359

List three reasons the measured unemployment rate is inaccurate.

17.3 **Types of Unemployment,** page 362

Describe the differences among frictional, structural, and cyclical unemployment.

17.4 **Policy Implications of Unemployment,** page 370

Explain how policymakers might use the actual and natural unemployment rates to determine appropriate economic policy actions.

MyEconLab Real-Time Data Activity: **Unemployment Rates,** page 377

MyEconLab

MyEconLab helps you master each objective and study more efficiently.

If a society is to produce the greatest material wealth for its population, it must use resources fully and in the best possible way. The most precious resource a society possesses is its people: They come up with the brilliant ideas, they invent the machinery, they till the soil. When human power isn't fully utilized, society fails to realize its potential, and the world gets poorer. That seems horribly wasteful. The purpose of this chapter is to develop an understanding of why society sometimes fails to take advantage of the human power at its disposal—a phenomenon that macroeconomists call unemployment.

What Is Unemployment?

Unemployment exists when people who are willing and able to work cannot find jobs. It's fairly easy to understand the importance of unemployment at the micro level: It would be a terrible setback if you were to spend years going to college and then couldn't find work in your chosen field. Losing a job can ruin a family's financial future, as unemployment often forces families to drain their savings. And unemployment is likely to place workers on a permanently lower earnings trajectory. But unemployment extracts a tremendous human toll in other dimensions. Unemployment can tear apart families: Economists Kerwin Charles of the University of Michigan and Melvin Stephens of the Carnegie Mellon University found that the probability of a divorce rises 18% following a husband's job loss and 13% after a wife's. Unemployment is linked to an increased risk of mental disorders such as depression, insomnia, and anxiety. It is linked to an increased risk of physical illnesses, too, including both heart attacks and cancer. Those effects, together with an increased risk of suicide, combine to produce significantly lower life expectancy for victims of unemployment. Economists Daniel Sullivan of the Federal Reserve Bank of Chicago and Till von Wachter of Columbia University estimated that job losses increased death rates for older male workers who were previously consistently employed by 50% to 100%. In other words, unemployment can kill.

At the macro level, unemployment vexes policymakers for two reasons. First, if policymakers are interested in producing wealth for society, unemployment represents a tremendous productive resource (humanpower or, as economists call it, *labor*) that is sitting idle instead of creating things people value. Second, policymakers are faced with the difficult question of why unemployment exists at all. After all, there will never be a shortage of work to be done, and if there are people who are willing to do that work, what on Earth is preventing potential workers from being matched up with potential work? Each of those issues will be addressed in this chapter. But because it's fairly easy to see that having productive workers sit idle represents an inefficient use of a valuable resource, we'll spend more time talking about the causes of unemployment.

Determining a Person's Labor Status

Our first step when it comes to studying unemployment is to look at the data economists use to summarize labor market conditions. Every month, the U.S. Bureau of Labor Statistics (BLS), a division of the U.S. Department of Labor, releases new data about unemployment in the United States. The BLS numbers are widely publicized and of grave concern to politicians, whose chances of reelection often depend on the state of unemployment. Of all the statistics that the BLS releases, none receives more attention than the **unemployment rate**, which measures the percentage of people in the labor force who are not working but are actively seeking work.

How does the BLS figure out what the unemployment rate is? Each month, the bureau surveys around 60,000 households about their employment status. Based on the responses, each of the roughly 110,000 adults in those 60,000 households is lumped into one of three categories:[1]

- *Employed.* The person being surveyed has a job or is self-employed.
- *Unemployed.* The person being surveyed does not have a job but is currently available for work and has taken active steps to find a job in the past four weeks.
- *Not in the labor force.* The person being surveyed does not have a job and has not taken active steps to find one in the past four weeks.

Figure 17.1 shows the labor market status of the adult population in the United States as of March 2014. At that time, 145.7 million adults were officially classified as employed, 10.5 million adults were unemployed, and 91.0 million adults were not in the labor force.

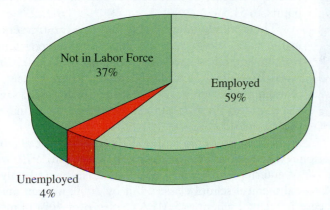

MyEconLab Real-time data

◀ **Figure 17.1**
Employment Status of the U.S. Adult Population, March 2014
Most U.S. adults are either employed or not in the labor force. A relatively small percentage of the adult population is classified as unemployed.
Source: Bureau of Labor Statistics.

Calculating the Unemployment Rate

Using the data from the monthly survey it conducts, the BLS computes several statistics. First among them is the size of the labor force, which is the number of people who are either working or who want to be working and have tried to find jobs:

Labor force = Number of people employed + Number of people unemployed

The second statistic the BLS calculates is the **labor force participation rate**, which measures the percentage of the adult population that is in the labor force:

$$\text{Labor force participation rate} = \frac{\text{Labor force}}{\text{Adult population}}$$

Labor force participation rate A measurement of the percentage of the adult population that is in the labor force.

The third statistic the BLS calculates is the unemployment rate, which is the fraction of the labor force that is unemployed. The formula for the unemployment rate is:

$$\text{Unemployment rate} = \frac{\text{Number of unemployed}}{\text{Labor force}}$$

or

$$\text{Unemployment Rate} = \frac{\text{Number of unemployed}}{(\text{Number of employed} + \text{Number of unemployed})}$$

The previous equation expresses the unemployment rate as a decimal. You can multiply the equation by 100 as follows to convert it to a percentage:

$$\text{Unemployment rate} = 100 \times \left[\frac{\text{Number of unemployed}}{(\text{Number of employed} + \text{Number of unemployed})} \right]$$

The unemployment rate tells us the fraction of people who want to be working (including those with jobs and those who don't have jobs but who are actively seeking

---

[1]Officially, the BLS categorizes people over age 16 who are not in the military or institutionalized in a prison, a nursing home, or a mental care facility.

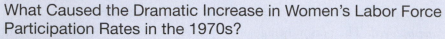

Application 17.1

What Caused the Dramatic Increase in Women's Labor Force Participation Rates in the 1970s?

In the years following World War II, women began entering the formal labor market in unprecedented numbers. The female labor force participation rate, which measures the fraction of the adult female population that is officially in the labor force, rose steadily from 32% in 1945 to 43% in 1970, an 11-percentage-point gain. The growth was even more rapid in the 1970s. By 1980, the labor participation rate of women had risen an additional 8 percentage points, to 51.5%.

These numbers are a testament to the tremendous change in the status of women. But despite the increasing numbers of women working in the labor force, prior to the 1970s, they were rarely found practicing law, dentistry, or medicine—professions that required a significant investment in advanced schooling. Nor were women often found in managerial positions, which often require an MBA.

Then, beginning in the 1970s, the number of women enrolling in professional degree programs began to skyrocket. In 1970, women made up less than 5% of entering MBA and dental school classes and only about 10% of entering law and medical school classes. But by 2000, women made up about one-third of entering dental school and MBA classes, over 40% of medical school classes, and almost half of entering law school classes. The bulk of the increases occurred between 1970 and 1980.

Economists Claudia Goldin and Lawrence Katz, both of Harvard University, wondered what was responsible for the dramatic change. Their answer is intriguing: The increase in women's representation in the professions could, in great part, be attributed to the contraceptive pill.

First approved by the Food and Drug Administration (FDA) in 1960, the pill is an extraordinarily effective family-planning method. Nonetheless, in 1960, 30 states banned advertisements for contraceptives entirely, and 22 had some general prohibitions on contraceptive sales. It wasn't until 1965 that the Supreme Court said that states couldn't ban the sale of contraceptives to married couples, and in 1972 the Supreme Court extended that ruling to single persons.

Goldin and Katz argue that the pill fundamentally changed the way women structured their lives. First, graduate school is both expensive and time-intensive. The pill dramatically reduced the risk that the graduate education of a woman would be interrupted by a pregnancy that would make that education difficult or impossible to complete. That gave young women an increased incentive to invest in a professional degree.

Second, Goldin and Katz observe that the pill enabled couples to be intimate without long-term commitments. That gave women the power to delay marriage, which is something women entering graduate school often wish to do. Goldin and Katz assert that this also increased women's entry into the professions.

Goldin and Katz caution that not all of the changes in women's labor force participation rates can be attributed to the pill. But they present compelling evidence that greater reproductive control played an important role in it and in the entry of women into the professions in particular.

See related problem 1.10 on page 374 at the end of this chapter.

Based on Claudia Goldin and Lawrence Katz, "The Power of the Pill: Oral Contraceptives and Women's Career and Marriage Decisions," *Journal of Political Economy*, vol. 110, no. 4, 2002; the Milken Institute's "On the Pill: Changing the Course of Women's Education," *Milken Institute Review*, 2001; and "The Liberator," *The Economist*, December 23, 1999.

work) but aren't. What the unemployment rate doesn't tell us is the fraction of people who aren't working but don't want to, don't have to, or have quit looking for jobs. In other words, the rate doesn't reflect in any way the number of retirees who aren't working, the number of idle rich, or the number of people who have stopped searching for jobs.

Figure 17.2 shows the historical behavior of the unemployment rate in the United States from 1948 to 2014. On average, the unemployment rate is about 6%. But it is quite volatile, having dipped below 3% in the early 1950s and peaked at 10.8% in 1982. In Figure 17.2, the gray bands show periods of economic recession. Note that the unemployment rate rises sharply during those periods. Unemployment is said to be *countercyclical*: As GDP decreases during recessions, unemployment generally increases.

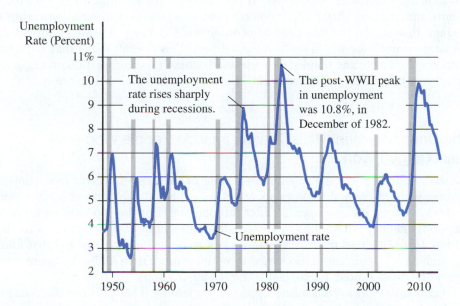

MyEconLab Real-time data

◄ **Figure 17.2**
The Historical Behavior of the U.S. Unemployment Rate, 1948–2014
The unemployment rate in the United States fluctuates, rising in recessions and falling in expansions. On average, it is about 6%.

Note: Shaded areas indicate periods of recession.

Source: Bureau of Labor Statistics.

Shortcomings of the Measured Unemployment Rate

17.2 Learning Objective

List three reasons the measured unemployment rate is inaccurate.

Like GDP, the unemployment rate is far from a perfect measurement. Generally the number is lower than the "real" unemployment rate. Let's explore some of the ways in which the measured unemployment rate fails to capture a true picture of what's going on in the economy—specifically, how it may understate the true amount of unemployment.

The Unemployment Rate Doesn't Include People Who Work Part Time

When the unemployment rate is calculated, people who work part time are counted as employed, just the same as full-time workers are. Why is this a problem? Consider the following scenario: Shelton is a construction worker who loses his job with one construction company but is able to find part-time employment with another construction company. The unemployment rate takes a quick blip upward when Shelton loses his job with the first company, and then the unemployment rate returns to its original level when Shelton gets hired by the second company. This indicates that everything is A-OK.

Except everything is not A-OK because the two jobs aren't equal. In the first job, society benefited from 40 hours of Shelton's talents each week; in the second job, society only gets to enjoy what Shelton can produce in 20 hours. In other words, half of Shelton's productivity has disappeared, and society is undoubtedly worse off as a result, but the unemployment numbers indicate that everything is just as good as it was before. Consequently, the unemployment rate paints an inaccurate picture of the true jobs situation.

The Unemployment Rate Doesn't Include People Who Are Underemployed

Here's a second scenario: Courtney is a nuclear engineer who works at a power plant on the coast of Louisiana. A massive hurricane destroys the plant's reactors, and Courtney is out of a job. Because she has a huge student loan payment due next month, she scrambles to find work and quickly comes up with a full-time job arranging flowers.

Once again, the unemployment numbers don't budge when Courtney shifts from one job to another. Yet the fact that the unemployment numbers don't move is problematic because we want those numbers to be tied in some way to how fully and how well society is employing its labor resources. Although Courtney continues to work full time after switching jobs, society is not receiving the full benefits of Courtney's talents and training. After all, it doesn't take a degree in nuclear engineering to arrange flowers. In the language of economists, Courtney is **underemployed**— performing work for which she is overqualified. This doesn't mean that arranging flowers isn't honest and honorable work, and it doesn't mean that it doesn't take any training or talent. It simply means that Courtney is trained for a far more specialized occupation.

Underemployed Performing work for which a person is overqualified.

The Unemployment Rate Doesn't Include People Who Are Discouraged Workers

To shed light on the third major shortcoming of the unemployment rate, consider Jerome, whose factory shut down about a year and a half ago. Jerome really wanted to work. He pursued job opening after job opening. But the economy in his town was slowly failing, and nothing materialized. After meeting with failure day after day, Jerome finally realized that there were no jobs to be had in his town and that filling out endless job applications amounted to nothing more than killing innocent trees. Angry and disappointed, he stopped filling out applications.

Economists have a special name for people like Jerome. They call them **discouraged workers**—people who have given up actively seeking work after an extended period of unemployment. Discouraged workers are not counted in the unemployment rate. From a policymaker's standpoint, discouraged workers are particularly problematic: Here are people who want to work but who have met with so little success that even if society does manage to create a job that is perfect for them, they'll have trouble being matched to it simply because they have given up seeking work.

Discouraged workers distort the unemployment rate statistics in a perverse way. Consider a village with five workers: Abel, Baker, Charlie, Victor, and Jerome. Suppose that Abel, Baker, and Charlie are working, and Victor and Jerome are not working but are actively seeking work. Two of the five members of the labor force are unemployed, so the unemployment rate is:

Discouraged workers People who have given up actively seeking work after an extended period of unemployment.

$$\text{Unemployment rate} = 100 \times \left[\frac{2}{(3 + 2)} \right] = 40\%$$

An unemployment rate of 40% is incredibly high by any standard. The members of the village council will surely be wringing their hands, trying to figure out how to solve this unemployment problem before the next election.

Then things go from bad to worse: Jerome gets so discouraged that he stops looking for work. Labor market conditions are really bleak now. To see just how bleak, let's incorporate Jerome's new status as a discouraged worker into the measurement of the unemployment rate. Abel, Baker, and Charlie continue to work and are classified as employed. Victor continues to look for work and is classified as unemployed. But Jerome has thrown up his hands, and four weeks after he stops looking for work, he is no longer considered unemployed; rather, the BLS counts him as "not in the labor force." As a result, the unemployment rate changes. On the top part of the formula, only one person is unemployed. On the bottom, the labor force consists of the three who continue to work and the one who continues to look:

$$\text{Unemployment rate} = 100 \times \left[\frac{1}{(3 + 1)}\right] = 25\%$$

Is this cause for celebration? Despite the fact that the unemployment rate has dropped, it should be clear that *at best* the employment picture is no better than before, and it's probably much worse because an able-bodied person who really wants to work has withdrawn from active participation in a job search.

The Unemployment Rate Doesn't Include People Who Work in the Underground Economy

Each of the potential inaccuracies discussed in the previous sections tends to cause the measured unemployment rate to paint an overly rosy employment picture. There is, however, one more source of measurement error, and it causes the unemployment rate to present an artificially bleak picture of joblessness: Not everybody who is working cares to report it to the government when asked. Some people, for example, work for cash to avoid paying taxes. Others are employed in illicit activities like selling drugs or sex. Still others are undocumented workers. Such individuals are more likely to report being unemployed than is someone who has a job in the formal sector. This means that the measured unemployment rate will tend to overstate the actual number of unemployed. Most economists, however, generally agree that the effects of part-time employment, underemployment, and discouraged workers outweigh the effect that workers in the informal sector have on the unemployment rate. In other words, the measured unemployment rate tends to understate the unemployment problem.

Why Not Fix the Shortcomings of the Unemployment Rate?

So why doesn't the BLS incorporate the complexities we've discussed into the unemployment rate? Why doesn't the bureau count discouraged workers as unemployed? Why doesn't it count someone who wants to work full time but can only find part-time work as half-unemployed? Why doesn't it count someone who is underemployed as being partially unemployed?

In fact, the BLS regularly publishes alternative measures of unemployment that incorporate adjustments such as these. But they aren't relied on heavily because the survey questions used to calculate those alternative numbers are more a matter of opinion than fact. "Are you employed? Have you looked for a job in the past month?" These are yes or no questions used to calculate the basic unemployment rate.

By contrast, determining whether someone is a discouraged worker is more subjective. The BLS survey taker who is trying to count discouraged workers has little way to tell the difference between Jerome, who really *wants* to work and has tried to find work to no avail, and his cousin Jeremiah, who really doesn't want to work but says he does because he doesn't want to admit that he's sort of a slacker. For the same reason, distinguishing between part-timers who would like to work full time and people who work only part time because they want to is hard as well. So is determining who is underemployed and who is not: Picture a 5'8" economics professor who firmly believes he should be playing NBA basketball and pulling in millions instead of teaching economics for much less. In his own mind, he is underemployed. His office mates, however, might argue that not only should he not be playing pro basketball, but his student evaluations indicate that he's not really qualified to teach economics, either. In their minds, he is overemployed! So who's right, and who's wrong? Who knows?

Adjusting the unemployment rate to accurately reflect these factors is not only difficult, it's impossible. The subjective nature of the questions required to calculate these alternative measures introduces error into those measures. So economists generally rely on the flawed but completely objective measure of the unemployment rate that this chapter began with. If that number is less than wholly satisfactory, it's possible to draw on the alternative measures the BLS publishes.

Types of Unemployment

You now know how the unemployment rate is calculated and understand some of its shortcomings. Because of its shortcomings, you now know that the unemployment rate cited in the news is likely to understate the severity of the unemployment problem. But there are other questions about unemployment that remain to be asked, not least among them the big question raised earlier: If there is plenty of work to be done, and if unemployed people are genuinely interested in doing work, then why can't we place those people in jobs? Because not all unemployment is the same. Different types of unemployment occur for different reasons. Let's take a closer look at the three different types of unemployment and what causes them.

Frictional Unemployment

Frictional unemployment
Unemployment that exists because it can be difficult and time-consuming to match unemployed persons to existing vacancies.

Frictional unemployment arises because it can be difficult and time-consuming to match workers to jobs for which they are qualified. Frequently, workers have a number of interviews scheduled and are waiting to complete them before deciding which jobs they will choose. The same is true for employers: They may have many interviews to complete and take some time deciding who will get the jobs. In either case, the market mechanism discussed earlier in this book may not work as smoothly as it should. People may not find out about jobs as rapidly as society wishes they would, and employers may not make employment decisions as rapidly as is ideal.

Frictional Unemployment May Be Good Unemployment Frictional unemployment isn't a terrible thing. As a society, we want workers to choose jobs that maximize their energy and enthusiasm and that match their talents. This is how we ensure that we're making the most of the available resources we have. It is far better to have Albert Einstein, Jr., teaching physics than dunking fries at the nearest Burger King. So, if he takes a little longer to get a physics job, that's probably a good thing.

Frictional unemployment is also evidence of a dynamic economy. In a dynamic economy in which new businesses pop up while others whither, there will always be some frictional unemployment. It simply takes time to shift workers from one industry to another. In the Middle Ages, most people went into the same professions as their parents—they became carpenters, masons, and farmers, for example—and there was very little unemployment. But there was also very little economic progress. New industries and technologies weren't being created. Life was static. Another good thing about frictional unemployment is that spells of it don't typically last very long. We'll look at some data on the duration of the typical spell of unemployment in Application 17.3.

Reducing Frictional Unemployment Frictional unemployment isn't that much of a problem, but this doesn't mean that all efforts to reduce it are wasted. Policymakers, businesses, and private individuals may be able to do some simple things to speed up the search process. Some of them involve using communication and technology to make sure people who lose their jobs can easily search for new employment options. Thirty years ago, the only good source of information about vacancies was the help wanted ads in the local paper. Finding a job out-of-state took *real* effort! Those days are gone: Now there are a thousand different ways to find out about new jobs, both across the country and around the globe, spurred mainly by the growth of the Internet.

If, upon your graduation, you want to go to work for Zappos, you can find out about employment opportunities just by visiting the company's website. There are also Internet enterprises like monster.com and craigslist.com that are devoted to directly matching workers and jobs. Similarly, brick-and-mortar employment agencies such as Manpower and corporate headhunters also are likely to speed the transition between jobs and reduce frictional unemployment. More subtly, networking sites like LinkedIn and even social networking sites like Facebook help people connect to people who know people that are related to people who might know something about employment opportunities.

The innovations just discussed are largely private. But government helps job-seekers, too. The U.S. Department of Labor operates CareerOneStop, a one-stop shop that offers training referrals, career counseling, access to state job bank listings, and similar employment-related services. The U.S. government has also centralized its own job postings online: You can find thousands of available jobs at www.usajobs. gov. Many state and local governments also offer services similar to those offered by the federal government. In addition, many governments devote resources to improving information flow to the public; one way they do so is by improving access to libraries, computers, and the Internet.

Structural Unemployment

There is a second type of unemployment that we're likely to find at any given time. **Structural unemployment** is longer-term unemployment that exists when there are more people looking for work in some labor markets than there are jobs available, at the existing wage rate. This is a very different type of unemployment than frictional unemployment: Frictional unemployment exists even when there is a vacancy for every job hunter. Because there aren't enough jobs to go around, spells of structural unemployment are likely to last much longer than spells of frictional unemployment.

In theory, such surpluses of labor shouldn't exist. Here's why: Imagine that there are 20 potential workers who are all applying for one job that pays $20 an hour. Doug, who is first in line, gets hired; the remaining 19 potential workers are left unemployed. But before Doug can unpack his lunchbox, one of the remaining 19 (call her Keisha) pipes up, "I'll do that job just as well for $10!" Faster than you can say "undercut the competition," Doug's out, and Keisha's in.

Something interesting happens when Keisha undercuts Doug and drives the wage down to $10: The line gets shorter. This happens for two reasons. First, business owners say to themselves, "At a wage of $20 an hour, I could only afford to hire 1 worker. But with wages coming down, maybe I'll hire 2!" The line also gets shorter because of how the job seekers react. Some of the remaining 18 say to themselves, "I was only standing in line because I thought I could pull down $20 an hour. But if the job's only going to pay $10, I'd rather go fishing."

That exit shrinks the surplus of labor. At $20 an hour, there were many people seeking work who couldn't find it. At $10, there are fewer of them. And if workers continue to undercut one another, sooner or later the wage falls to the point that there are just enough workers to fill the available vacancies. No surplus labor; no unemployment. When this happens, economists say the labor market *clears*. This means that wages fall low enough so that everyone who is willing to work for that amount has a job, and the people who aren't willing to work for that amount drop out of the labor force and pursue other interests instead, such as fishing, or childrearing, or volunteer work. Recall that people who drop out of the labor force are *not* considered unemployed.

Of course, the wage mechanism also works in reverse. If businesses begin offering wages of only $3 an hour, it will be difficult to find people who will want to work for them. So, instead of having a surplus of workers, the economy will have a shortage of them. Consequently, firms offer wages sufficiently high to lure enough applicants to fill existing vacancies, and a super-sneaky firm might even offer a wage generous enough to lure talented workers from other firms; those firms are forced to respond

Structural unemployment Longer-term unemployment that exists when there are more people looking for work in some labor markets than there are jobs available, at the existing wage rate.

by offering higher wages, too, just to retain their best workers. In other words, in a market economy where workers are free to switch jobs and firms are free to compete for workers, the wage that prevails is the one that results in luring just enough workers to the workforce to staff the available jobs.

Ignoring frictions—the time it takes to find out about vacancies and fill them—the unemployment rate if wages are free to move up and down should, at least in theory, be zero. If there is a surplus of workers, competitive forces should push wages down until that surplus disappears. A surplus persisting suggests that wages are not fully adjusting to their market-clearing levels. In other words, structural unemployment exists because something is holding wages artificially high.

Minimum Wage Laws May Cause Structural Unemployment What is it that holds wages artificially high? Sometimes, the government is responsible. Take, for example, minimum wage laws. Most countries around the world have passed such laws. They do so, supposedly, to help people at the bottom end of the socioeconomic ladder be as self-sufficient as possible. In other words, if you have a job, minimum wage laws help ensure that you will be able to afford basic necessities like food, clothing, and shelter.

But in order to have any effect, the minimum wage must be set above the market-clearing wage. If the government thinks that everyone should be making $7.50 an hour, and the market-clearing wage set by workers and firms is already $9 an hour, then the minimum wage doesn't accomplish anything. Establishing a minimum wage above the market-clearing level creates a potential trade-off for policymakers: The minimum wage helps poorer people who are working afford basic necessities, but it may also cause businesses to hire fewer workers.

That's because firms don't generally hire people out of the goodness of their hearts. They hire people because they add more value to the firm in an hour than the firm has to pay them. The difference goes into the owner's pocket as profit. So think about someone just starting out in the labor force. Will that person be able to add a lot of value to the company he works for? If he brings only $5 of value to a potential employer, but the minimum wage mandates that he be paid $7.50, his job application is likely to be greeted with, "Thanks, but no thanks." So minimum wage legislation makes it easier to live if you have a job. But minimum wage legislation may make it more difficult to *find* a job! In other words, minimum wage legislation may create structural unemployment.

The good news for Americans is this: Most people make more than the minimum wage already, so they are unlikely to fall victim to the unemployment created by it. The bad news is that the minimum wage can make it hard for young and untrained workers to acquire the skills and experience they need to eventually leave minimum wage territory.

Though theory suggests that minimum wage laws create structural unemployment, especially among younger workers, there is considerable debate among economists about how much, if any, unemployment such laws create. That debate began with research by economists David Card of Berkeley and Alan Krueger of Princeton. They studied neighboring counties in Pennsylvania and New Jersey during a time when New Jersey increased its state minimum wage. They found that the increase in New Jersey's minimum wage had no adverse impact on fast-food employment. They hypothesize that there was no impact because a higher minimum wage reduced labor turnover, which saved fast-food restaurants the cost of locating and training replacement workers. In other words, the minimum wage drove up the cost of paying workers, but those costs were offset by lower costs elsewhere in the firm.

After Card and Krueger's unexpected findings were published, other economists began to investigate the question more seriously. Some, like Card and Krueger, found that increasing the minimum wage had little impact on employment. A recent study by Barry Hirsh and Bruce Kaufman of Georgia State University and Tetyana Zelenska of the Jameel Latif Poverty Action Lab highlighted some of the other ways that fast-food employers adjust to mandatory increases in the minimum wage. Some employers, for example, increase performance standards for their workers—paying them more but asking for more in return. Others deal with minimum wage increases by cutting hours, discouraging costly overtime work, or passing cost increases along to their customers. Ultimately, Hirsch, Kaufman, and Zelenska concluded that employers find other ways to deal with minimum wage increases than cutting jobs: They found no systematic effect of a minimum wage increase on employment at 81 fast-food restaurants in Georgia and Alabama.

However, the results of those studies conflict with the results of other studies. Joseph Sabia of San Diego State University, Richard Burkhouser of Cornell, and Benjamin Hansen of the University of Oregon applied Card and Krueger's methods to investigate the effects of an increase in the New York State minimum wage. In contrast to Card and Krueger, Sabia, Burkhouser, and Hansen found that raising the New York minimum wage "significantly reduced employment rates of less-skilled, less-educated New Yorkers." And economists David Neumark of the University of California–Irvine and William Wascher of the Federal Reserve surveyed the literature on the effects of the minimum wage and reported that of the most credible studies, the majority suggest that increasing the minimum wage reduces employment.

Ultimately, the impact of the minimum wage on employment has yet to be determined: Many studies suggest that there is a strong impact; many others suggest that there is none. Economists have yet to reach a consensus on the "right" data to use to test the theory and the right statistical methods to apply to that data. Until such a consensus is reached, we can say only that theory suggests that the minimum wage *may* cause unemployment among low-skilled workers.

Labor Unions May Create Structural Unemployment Minimum wage laws can create structural unemployment at the lower end of the wage ladder. In a similar way, labor unions create structural unemployment at the higher end of the wage ladder. A *labor union* is an organization of employees who as a group agree to negotiate their salary and benefits and working conditions. The process of doing so, which is referred to as *collective bargaining*, is based on the idea that there is strength in numbers. Unions began forming in the mid-1800s, in response to the social and economic impacts of the Industrial Revolution. Unions played a critical role in establishing workers' rights, ensuring safer working conditions, and eliminating child labor.

Today, unions play a less prominent role than they once did; union membership has declined from about one worker in every three to one worker in every six. But unions still have substantial bargaining power: They are effectively able to raise wages above what would be paid to their members if salary negotiations were conducted on a person-by-person basis. Empirical evidence suggests that the salaries of employees who are union members are about 15% higher than the salaries of non-unionized employees. But the higher salaries take a toll on unemployment: Firms may hire fewer workers than they otherwise would because of the artificially high wages, and structural unemployment results.

Labor Protections May Cause Structural Unemployment Sometimes structural unemployment exists not because wages are artificially high but because benefits are. One benefit to which economists attribute a great deal of structural unemployment is employment protection. Employment protection regulations are designed to make it more difficult for businesses to lay off employees. For example, many European Union countries have adopted very strict labor protections that require businesses to notify government if they dismiss a worker and that require government's permission to lay off a group of workers. In addition, regulations may require that, in the event of a layoff, the most junior workers are let go first and that dismissed workers receive a severance package.

It's nice to know your employer can't get rid of you easily. Have you ever heard anyone complain, "I'm getting tired of all this job security?" However, there are many circumstances in which employers need to let workers go—sometimes quickly. When firms' products aren't selling well, being forced to keep idle employees on payroll can drive the companies into bankruptcy. Worse, employment protection makes it difficult to get rid of employees who are not a good fit for the job or who choose to take advantage of their job security and avoid work by napping in a closet.

You may be wondering how laws that make it hard for firms to get rid of even the most worthless employees contribute to unemployment. After all, it appears as if they might even *reduce* unemployment! To help understand why this is the case, consider this question, posed by economists Tyler Cowen and Alex Tabarrok: Would you ever go out on a first date if the law said that at the end of the evening, you were required to get married? That is exactly what employment protection laws do: They make it more risky for firms to hire people, even if they appear to be stellar employees. In that environment, many firms choose to operate with fewer employees than they otherwise would. This can result in too many people looking for too few jobs, which means structural unemployment.

Labor protection tends to increase the overall rate of unemployment: Countries that have greater labor protection generally have higher overall unemployment rates. But more importantly, in countries that have greater labor protection, spells of unemployment tend to last a lot longer. Figure 17.3 shows the impact of labor market protections on long-term unemployment. The horizontal axis groups nations by their degree of labor protection, as measured by the World Bank's Rigidity of Employment Index. The vertical axis measures the percentage of the unemployed who have been unemployed for longer than one year. In low-protection countries that have fewer labor protections, about 16% of those who are jobless have been unemployed for longer than a year. In high-protection countries where labor protection is strong, about 43% have been unemployed for longer than a year. The pattern evident in the chart—greater labor protection resulting in longer-term unemployment—is testament to the impact of labor protection on structural unemployment.

▶ **Figure 17.3**

Labor Protection and Long-Term Unemployment

In countries that have stronger labor protections, the proportion of the jobless who have been unemployed for one year or longer is higher.

Source: World Bank and OECD data, 2008.

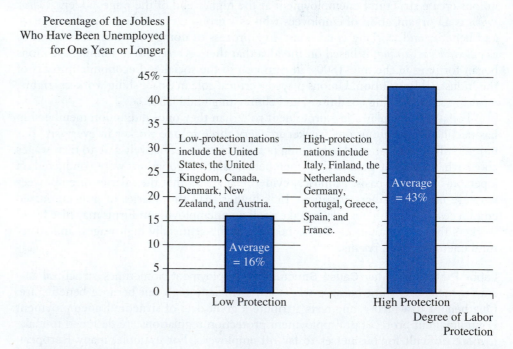

Fundamental Changes in the Economy May Cause Structural Unemployment Economists often lump one more type of unemployment into the category of structural unemployment: unemployment that occurs as a result of changes in the nature and structure of the economy. As an example, go back to the mid-1980s, when people began mothballing their typewriters in favor of word processors and personal computers. The change in how people produced written documents was a structural change, similar in nature to the popularization of the automobile in the early 1900s and air travel in the 1950s.

One of the side effects of the structural change in the 1980s was that jobs disappeared in the typewriter industry and appeared in the computer industry. It might have been tempting to label the laid-off workers from the typewriter industry as frictionally unemployed: "They just haven't been matched with one of the new openings in the computing industry yet!" But it took a different set of skills to make or repair a computer than it did to assemble a typewriter, and until the laid-off employees could obtain those skills, there was a surplus of workers in one industry and a shortage in the other. Because of that surplus, economists considered those workers to be structurally unemployed.

Application 17.2

Mixed Blessing: Unemployment Insurance Makes the Labor Market Work Better. And Worse.

If you lose your job, it's good to know someone's got your back. The American system of unemployment compensation is designed to provide workers with income during periods of temporary unemployment. The system, which dates back to the 1930s, pays benefits based on a worker's prior wages. Though the benefits vary by state, they typically replace 40% to 50% of a worker's salary for six months to a year.

By reducing the cost of remaining unemployed, unemployment insurance reduces the incentive for laid-off workers to quickly find a new job. As a result, frictional unemployment increases. There's plenty of evidence of this: Several studies have found that a disproportionate number of unemployed persons find work just before or just after their unemployment benefits expire. This could be interpreted as lack of effort on the part of job seekers.

Economist Dale Mortensen of Northwestern University, who shared the 2010 Nobel Prize with Peter Diamond of MIT and Christopher Pissarides of the London School of Economics for their work studying labor market frictions, might disagree. Mortensen's work shows that unemployment insurance affords workers the opportunity to look for the best work at the highest pay rather than take early offers out of desperation. Ultimately, this allows the economy to best utilize workers' training and talents, which makes the economy better rather than worse.

However, if the benefits are too generous, they can backfire. As an example, consider the labor market experience of the United States and Germany over a 25-year period ending in 2005. Over that time horizon, U.S. unemployment insurance replaced about 40% of income in the first year of unemployment and less than 15% in subsequent years. In contrast, German unemployment insurance replaced about 75% of lost income in the first year and continued to replace over 70% for at least the next four years.

Partly as a result of such generous unemployment benefits, the unemployment rate was 3.6% higher in Germany than in the United States—for decades. More telling, over half of the unemployed in Germany had been out of work for more than one year; only 13% of American unemployed had been out of work that long.

Mortensen, Diamond, and Pissarides view the German experience as problematic: When workers remain unemployed for so long, their skills deteriorate. The more their skills deteriorate, the more difficult it is to find work. So Mortensen, Diamond, and Pissarides caution against too much of a good thing. Unemployment benefits may be good for society when they simply fill a gap while workers are between jobs. But unemployment benefits that are too generous can turn relatively painless short-term frictional unemployment into chronic and costly structural unemployment that adversely affects the unemployed, taxpayers, and society as a whole.

See related problem 3.17 on page 375 at the end of this chapter.

Based on "Peter Diamond, Dale Mortensen and Christopher Pissarides Share Economics Nobel Prize for Jobs Study," *The Guardian*, October 11, 2010; "Economists Share Nobel for Studying Job Market," *The New York Times*, October 11, 2010; and "The Work Behind the Nobel Prize," *The New York Times*, October 11, 2010.

The good news is that this type of structural unemployment need not persist forever. But because the retraining is likely to take some time, this type of unemployment fits with the general theme of structural unemployment being more persistent than frictional unemployment.

Structural unemployment, like frictional unemployment, can be difficult to solve directly, however. When structural employment is a result of an economy undergoing fundamental structural changes, the government might aid workers' transition from declining industries to growing industries by offering or encouraging (often through subsidies) retraining or education. In fact, the U.S. government has a number of programs designed to do this. However, the government cannot compel people to take advantage of such programs, which means that this type of structural unemployment may be quite persistent.

When structural unemployment is a result of wage rigidity, the only permanent solution is to get rid of the rigidity itself. So the government could get rid of the structural unemployment caused by the minimum wage simply by eliminating the minimum wage or outlawing labor unions. Those options, however, are unpalatable to large numbers of people, which means that some structural unemployment may simply be the trade-off we accept for meeting other social goals.

The Natural Rate of Unemployment

Natural rate of unemployment The sum of the frictional and structural unemployment rates.

Both frictional and structural unemployment are likely to exist in some amount at any given point in time. There will always be workers moving from one job to another; there will always be new industries springing up while others die; and it's difficult to get rid of laws designed to protect employees once those laws are in place. Because these types of unemployment occur naturally in a dynamic economy, economists often refer to them collectively as the economy's "natural" level of unemployment. More specifically, they say that the **natural rate of unemployment** is the sum of the frictional and structural unemployment rates, where the frictional unemployment rate is the number of workers frictionally unemployed divided by the labor force, and the structural unemployment rate is calculated the same way:

$$\text{Natural rate of unemployment} = \text{Frictional unemployment rate} + \text{Structural unemployment rate}$$

Full employment A situation that occurs when unemployment is at its natural rate.

When unemployment is at its natural rate, the economy is often said to be operating at **full employment**. Note that full employment does *not* mean that the unemployment rate is zero. Rather, it means that the unemployment rate is at a level that we could reasonably expect, given that sometimes people are between jobs, sometimes people don't have quite the right training, and sometimes labor market rigidities keep wages from adjusting.

Cyclical Unemployment

Cyclical unemployment Unemployment that is related to downturns in the economy during business cycles.

You are now acquainted with the first two types of unemployment. But there is a third type of unemployment that economists pay particular attention to. **Cyclical unemployment** is unemployment that is related to downturns in the economy during business cycles. Business cycles, and recessions in particular, occur every now and then (see Chapter 16). People cutting their spending are both a cause of and consequence of the recession: When people spend less, sales at firms decline. When sales at firms decline, people earn less income. When people earn less, they spend less. Suddenly the economy is in a downward spiral of falling earnings, and all the while policymakers and politicians are breaking into a cold sweat wondering how to stop the spiral.

An economic spiral like this creates a situation that is ripe for cyclical unemployment. Firms see their sales falling and their inventories of unsold products rising. It doesn't do the firms any good to pay workers to make more widgets when there are 20 million widgets already on the shelves that apparently nobody wants to buy. Sooner or later, it is likely that the firm will lay off some employees. Those employees are then cyclically unemployed.

Okun's Law and the Link Between Output and Unemployment As the name might lead you to suspect, there is a link between cyclical unemployment and the business cycle, which is the ordinary fluctuation of real GDP around its long-run trend. The causation runs both ways: As cyclical unemployment increases, fewer workers are producing goods and services, and real GDP falls below its trend. As real GDP falls, firms feeling pinched lay off workers, and so the cyclical unemployment rate rises. The late economist Arthur Okun, a professor at Yale and chair of the President's Council of Economic Advisors in the 1960s, quantified the link between cyclical unemployment and real GDP growth with a rough rule of thumb that macroeconomists know as *Okun's law:* For every 1-percentage-point increase in the cyclical unemployment rate, real GDP growth decreases by about 2 percentage points.

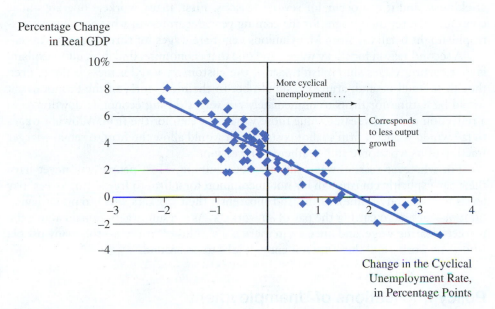

◀ **Figure 17.4**
Okun's Law, 1950–2014
Each dot plots one year's measured change in the cyclical unemployment rate and the percentage change in real GDP. The general pattern indicates that each 1-percentage-point increase in the unemployment rate causes the growth rate of real GDP to decrease by about 2 percentage points.
Source: FRED Economic Database (http://research.stlouisfed.org/fred2/series /UNRATE/).

Figure 17.4 shows the Okun's law relationship for the United States from 1950 to 2014. In the figure, each dot plots one year's measured change in the cyclical unemployment rate and the percentage change in real GDP. On average, real GDP growth was about 3%. But the downward-sloping line that captures the general pattern apparent in the dots shows a negative relationship between the unemployment rate and real GDP: When the unemployment rate increases (as you move to the right in the graph above), each percentage-point increase reduces real GDP growth by about 2 percentage points. On the other hand, when the unemployment rate decreases, each percentage-point reduction in the unemployment rate corresponds to an increase in GDP growth of about 2 percentage points.

You might be wondering why the swings in GDP are bigger than the swings in unemployment. If we have 1% fewer workers, shouldn't we see 1% less output? In theory, perhaps. But in the real world, things are messier. For example, some laid-off employees will become discouraged workers. The economy loses the output of those workers but does not count them among the unemployed. This is one reason we might expect the output decline to be larger than the unemployment increase. A second reason is that many firms cut their output during recessions but hang onto many of their workers because those workers were hard to find and costly to train. This practice is known as *labor hoarding*. Output falls a lot, but unemployment doesn't decrease nearly as much. Either way, the end result is the same: Empirically, there is about a 2-for-1 relationship between output and unemployment.

Wage Stickiness and Cyclical Unemployment It seems odd to say it, but like structural unemployment, cyclical employment is often the result of wages that are too high compared to market-clearing levels. To understand this, think about how wages are determined when the economy is doing well. With strong sales, firms need to attract workers, and one of the best ways to do so is to offer good wages. Firms are willing to pay good wages as long as workers are adding more value to the firm than it costs to employ them. How do workers add value? By producing lots of products that sell for high prices.

Now think about what happens during a recession. People are not buying as much of the firm's products, so the things that workers produce are bringing in less revenue for the firm. Or perhaps the firm cuts prices to stimulate sales, in which case workers may be producing as much as ever but generating fewer dollars because of the price cut. Either way, the value that workers add to the firm decreases, but their wages probably do not.

Wage stickiness The inability of wages to adjust to market conditions.

Economists call this inability of wages to adjust to market conditions **wage stickiness**, and it can occur for several reasons. First, many workers operate under contracts that set their wages for the coming year, regardless of what economic catastrophe might befall the firm. Many unions negotiate wages for three years at a time.

A second reason for sticky wages, and one that economists find difficult to explain, is that cutting wages simply isn't part of the customary way business is done, even though it could be and, arguably, should be. In the ideal world of the economist, it would be natural for firms to immediately cut wages during economic downturns as a reflection of the decreased value those workers create for the firm. Allowing wages to fall would reduce a firm's labor costs, which would allow the firm to retain a larger fraction of its workforce and weather the recession.

For whatever reason, wage cuts are not common. Most people will never have their pay explicitly cut (though it's not uncommon for a firm to freeze employees' pay levels for a period of time). Firms, and apparently their workers, seem to prefer laying off *some* workers to cutting the pay of *all* workers. As a result, wages remain above the market-clearing wage, and once again there is a surplus of workers—too many people who want work—and there are not enough jobs to go around.

Policy Implications of Unemployment

17.4 Learning Objective

Explain how policymakers might use the actual and natural unemployment rates to determine appropriate economic policy actions.

We can put the three types of unemployment together and see how they relate to the published unemployment rate that we calculated at the beginning of this chapter. The measured unemployment rate is the sum of the frictional, structural, and cyclical unemployment rates:

$$\text{Unemployment rate} = \text{Frictional rate} + \text{Structural rate} + \text{Cyclical rate}$$

The frictional rate and the structural rate, added together, are the economy's natural rate of unemployment:

$$\text{Unemployment rate} = \text{Natural rate} + \text{Cyclical rate}$$

In other words, cyclical unemployment is any unemployment that can't be chalked up to labor market frictions or structural problems. As such, you might calculate the cyclical unemployment rate as:

$$\text{Cyclical rate} = \text{Actual unemployment rate} - \text{Natural unemployment rate}$$

Why the Appropriate Policy Prescription Depends on the Type of Unemployment

You may be wondering why economists bother to distinguish between the different types of unemployment. To people who have just been laid off, the distinctions probably seem immaterial. However, they matter a great deal to policymakers because the recipe for fixing an unemployment problem varies depending on what type of unemployment the economy is experiencing.

If government is interested in reducing unemployment and most of that unemployment is frictional, then the only permanent fix is for government to devise a way to do a better and faster job of matching workers with jobs. On the other hand, if the problem is structural, a job-matching program isn't going to do much good because there aren't enough jobs to match workers to! The way to address structural unemployment is to address the underlying structural problem. Sometimes this can be done in a politically palatable way. Few people object to job retraining programs, for example. But sometimes the underlying structural problem is harder to address: No politician who runs on a platform of "We must reduce the minimum wage!" is likely to get elected.

Solving cyclical unemployment is a different problem altogether. Cyclical unemployment is often the result of insufficient spending on the part of millions of people. To reduce cyclical unemployment, policymakers must either get people to accelerate their own spending or find some way to replace the spending that evaporated. Those solutions aren't easy to implement: The government has a limited number of tools at its disposal, and at different times those tools have varying degrees of effectiveness. The next few chapters devote a lot of attention to understanding those tools and their shortcomings.

Another limitation of government policy is that the government cannot use the tools it draws on to address cyclical unemployment to push unemployment permanently below its natural rate. Experience has taught economists that trying to hold unemployment unnaturally low makes undesirable things happen elsewhere in the economy. The biggest concern is that trying to do so will cause the prices of goods and services throughout the economy to rise rapidly (see Chapter 19).

Data Issues and the Appropriate Policy Prescription

One theme that runs through the overall discussion of the macroeconomy is the availability and the quality of data. This chapter discusses at length the shortcomings of the unemployment rate in depicting conditions in the job market. There is, however, one more layer of complexity to add to the picture: *Policymakers only receive information about the overall unemployment rate.* They have to estimate how much of it is frictional, structural, and cyclical, which is hard to figure out even on a person-by-person basis: Is a recently-laid-off Asian fusion chef frictionally unemployed because there's another fusion job open halfway across the country that he doesn't know about? Is he structurally unemployed because fusion is no longer popular, and he needs retraining in Moroccan grilling? Or is he cyclically unemployed because the only reason more people aren't eating fusion is because of a slack economy? It is genuinely hard to tell. And if it's difficult to determine what kind of employment one person is experiencing, then think how difficult it must be to figure out, with no additional information, how many of the millions of unemployed people are experiencing each type of unemployment.

The uncertainty makes crafting policy difficult. Suppose the chair of the Federal Reserve System is charged with maintaining full employment. This means that she is to eliminate cyclical unemployment, given that there is little she can do to eliminate frictional and structural unemployment. She observes that the unemployment rate is 5.5%. What the chair does with this information depends on what she believes the unobserved natural rate to be. If she believes the natural rate of unemployment is 4.4%, then the cyclical unemployment rate must be 1.1%. That calls for some economic stimulus. The Fed chair, as you will see in later chapters, will try to pump up the economy and stimulate spending by reducing interest rates.

On the other hand, if the Fed chair believes that the natural rate of unemployment is 5.9%, then cyclical unemployment must be –0.4%. The Fed chair's natural response is, "People are working too hard; businesses are producing too much. We must clamp down on this economy before bad things begin happening." The recipe for doing this involves increasing interest rates to slow down spending.

The third and final possibility is that the Fed chair believes the natural rate to be exactly 5.5%, in which case she picks up her newspaper, mixes a dry martini, and tells her employees to knock off early. The point is that the difficulties in measuring the unemployment rate and its component parts make crafting policy difficult. The estimation involved means that even when the Fed chair does the right thing, she is left wondering how much of the right thing to do. It also tells us that unless the Fed chair's estimates of the natural rate are good, she might end up doing the wrong thing and making conditions in the economy worse.

Application 17.3

Unemployment During the Great Recession

One indisputable macroeconomic fact is that the unemployment rate rises when the economy slides into recession. Sometimes the increase is small; for example, during the 2001 recession, unemployment rose from 4.3% to a modest 5.5%. Sometimes, however, the increase is large.

During the Great Recession of 2007–2009, the unemployment rate rose from 5.0% to 9.5%. It continued to rise after the recession ended, peaking at 10% in late 2009. A 10% unemployment rate is both harsh and unusual, but it is not unprecedented. In the double-dip recessions of the early 1980s, the unemployment rate peaked at an alarming 10.8%.

This presents a puzzle: Why is the 2007–2009 recession called the Great Recession when the 1980–1981 recessions appear to have been worse? A good part of the answer lies in how long the typical unemployed person remained jobless in the years following the recession.

Consider this: From 1948 to November 2007, the average duration of unemployment averaged 13.5 weeks. It had never gone higher than 22 weeks. So, during the painful recessions of the early 1980s, someone who was laid off could reasonably expect to find work in less than half a year.

Compare that to what happened from the beginning of the Great Recession in December 2007 until September 2013. Over that entire time horizon, the average duration of unemployment averaged an astonishing 31.3 weeks, 18 weeks longer than the pre-recession average and 9 weeks longer than the pre-recession *record*.

But even this doesn't tell the entire story: In 2011, the average duration of unemployment peaked at almost 41 weeks. In other words, it took almost twice as long for the typical unemployed person to find employment two years *after* the Great Recession ended as it did at the *peak* of the 1980s recessions. It shouldn't be a surprise that many job losers eventually gave up the search and left the labor force.

The exit of these people from the labor force makes the calculated unemployment rate look artificially low. In August 2013, the published unemployment rate was 7.3%. But the BLS also publishes an alternative measure of the unemployment rate that accounts both for workers who accepted part-time work out of necessity and for discouraged workers. In August 2013, that measure of the unemployment rate stood at 13.7%, almost double the official rate. In other words, long after the recession was over, one out of eight people who wanted to work were either unemployed or not fully employed.

The 2007 recession was undeniably severe. But the reason it gets called the Great Recession isn't because of its severity but because of its staying power. It deserves its name because, unlike all other recessions in the postwar era, its effects dragged on, and on, and on.

See related problems 3.17 and 4.5 on pages 375 and 376 at the end of this chapter.

Based on data from the Bureau of Labor Statistics at bls.gov.

Conclusion

Unemployment can be devastating to workers. It can also be bad for society: An economy that underutilizes its labor resources fails to produce the greatest possible material wealth for society. For these reasons, most governments around the world try to actively manage their economies in order to keep unemployment, especially cyclical unemployment, as low as they can. The chapters ahead focus on this policy piece of the macroeconomy: You will be formally introduced to the policymakers, learn what tools lie at their disposal, and learn more about the difficulties of using those tools to their fullest potential.

Chapter Summary and Problems

Key Terms

Cyclical unemployment, p. 368

Discouraged workers, p. 360

Frictional unemployment, p. 362

Full employment, p. 368

Labor force participation rate, p. 357

Natural rate of unemployment, p. 368

Structural unemployment, p. 363

Underemployed, p. 360

Unemployment, p. 356

Unemployment rate, p. 356

Wage stickiness, p. 370

17.1 What Is Unemployment? pages 356–359

Use employment status information to compute the unemployment rate.

Summary

Unemployment exists when people who want to work can't find work. Each person in the economy 16 or older can be classified as employed, unemployed, or not in the labor force. The unemployment rate measures the percentage of the labor force that is unemployed.

Review Questions

All problems are assignable in MyEconLab.

1.1 When individuals are willing and able to work but cannot find jobs, _____ exists.

1.2 The _____ measures the percentage of people in the labor force who are not working but are actively seeking work.

1.3 The _____ measures the percentage of the adult population that is in the labor force.

1.4 An individual who is self-employed is considered to be _____.

a. Employed

b. Unemployed

c. Not in the labor force

d. Underemployed

1.5 In order to be considered unemployed, an individual must not have had a job, must have been available for work, and must have taken active steps to find a job in the past _____.

a. Two weeks

b. Three weeks

c. Four weeks

d. Six weeks

1.6 Individuals who do not have a job, are available for work, but who have not taken active steps to find a job in the four weeks preceding the survey are considered _____.

a. Employed

b. Unemployed

c. Not in the labor force

d. Underemployed

1.7 There are 5 million people in an economy. If 3 million are employed and 1 million are unemployed, the size of the labor force is _____ people.

a. 5 million

b. 4 million

c. 3 million

d. 2 million

1.8 There are 5 million people in an economy. If 3 million are employed and 1 million are unemployed, the unemployment rate is _____.

a. 20%

b. 25%

c. 33%

d. 40%

1.9 The _____ measures the percentage of the labor force that is unemployed.
   a. Employment rate
   b. Labor force participation rate
   c. Natural rate of unemployment
   d. Unemployment rate

Problems and Applications

1.10 **[Related to Application 17.1 on page 358]** As discussed in Application 17.1, the contraceptive pill contributed to a dramatic change in the women's labor force participation rate. Do you think a highly effective contraceptive drug for men would have any impact on men's participation in the labor market?

1.11 This chapter presents data on the overall state of unemployment. But the Bureau of Labor Statistics also breaks down unemployment data by race and gender. Visit the BLS website at www.bls.gov and compare unemployment rates and labor force participation rates for men and women. Then make the same comparison for whites, blacks, Hispanics, and Asians. What are the big differences in the data? Can you think of anything that might account for those differences?

17.2 Shortcomings of the Measured Unemployment Rate, pages 359–362

List three reasons the measured unemployment rate is inaccurate.

Summary

The measured unemployment rate is not a perfect indicator of how well society is using its workers. It treats part-time and full-time employment equally. It does not account for underemployment. It also fails to measure discouraged workers who have dropped out of the labor force entirely. Unfortunately, adjusting the unemployment rate for these shortcomings introduces an element of subjectivity into the adjusted rate, making it unreliable.

Review Questions

All problems are assignable in MyEconLab.

2.1 An individual who is performing work for which he or she is overqualified is _____.

2.2 _____ are individuals who have given up actively seeking work after a spell of long-term unemployment.
   a. Underemployed workers
   b. Employees
   c. Redundant workers
   d. Discouraged workers

2.3 Because the unemployment rate counts people who are underemployed as being employed, the measured unemployment rate probably _____ the true state of unemployment.
   a. Overstates
   b. Understates
   c. Neither overstates nor understates

2.4 When discouraged workers leave the labor force, the unemployment rate _____.
   a. Increases
   b. Decreases
   c. Is unaffected

Problems and Applications

2.5 Explain why, from society's point of view, it is problematic that the measured unemployment rate fails to distinguish between part-time and full-time employment.

2.6 Discuss the ability of the measured unemployment rate to capture the true jobs picture in a place with a large underground economy (see Chapter 16). Does the measured unemployment rate tend to overstate or understate the true unemployment rate? Explain.

2.7 As economies emerge from recessions, it is often the case that both the number of persons employed and the unemployment rate increase. Reconcile this apparent paradox in the data.

17.3 Types of Unemployment, pages 362–370

Describe the differences among frictional, structural, and cyclical unemployment.

Summary

There are three types of unemployment. Frictional unemployment stems from the difficulty of matching existing workers with existing jobs. Structural unemployment exists when there are more people looking for work than there are jobs available. Together, the frictional and structural unemployment rates constitute the natural rate of unemployment. The third type of unemployment is cyclical unemployment. Cyclical unemployment is related to fluctuations in the business cycle: Recessions cause cyclical unemployment to increase, and expansions cause cyclical unemployment to decrease.

Review Questions

3.1 Unemployment that exists because it takes time to match workers to jobs for which they are qualified is called _____.

3.2 A(n) _____ is an organization of employees who as a group agree to negotiate their salary, benefits, and working conditions.

3.3 Unemployment that is related to downturns in the economy during business cycles is called _____.

3.4 The natural rate of unemployment is the sum of the _____ and the _____.

3.5 _____ unemployment exists when there are more people looking for work than there are jobs available at the existing wage rate.

3.6 The ordinary fluctuation of real GDP around its long-run trend is called a(n) _____.

3.7 The economy is often said to be operating at full employment when unemployment is equal to _____.
   a. Zero
   b. The frictional unemployment rate
   c. The natural rate of unemployment
   d. The structural unemployment rate

3.8 Okun's law says that for every 1-percentage-point increase in the cyclical unemployment rate, _____.
   a. Real GDP growth will increase by 1 percentage point
   b. Real GDP growth will decrease by 2 percentage points
   c. The natural rate of unemployment will increase by 2 percentage points
   d. The natural rate of unemployment will increase by 0.5 percentage points

3.9 Dan recently reentered the labor force after 15 years at home raising his children. Unfortunately, he cannot find a job in his field, computer science, because his skills have deteriorated during his hiatus from the labor force. Dan is probably considered _____ unemployed.
   a. Cyclically
   b. Frictionally
   c. Structurally
   d. Naturally

Problems and Applications

3.10 If the unemployment rate is 8%, the cyclical unemployment rate is 4%, and the frictional rate is 3%, what is the structural employment rate?

3.11 If the cyclical unemployment rate is 3% and the unemployment rate is 8%, what is the natural rate of unemployment?

3.12 Explain the potential trade-off inherent in minimum wage legislation.

3.13 Why do you think firms may be slow to lay off workers during a recession?

3.14 What are two reasons that wages tend to be sticky in the downward direction?

3.15 What is the cost of employment protection regulations? What are some benefits?

3.16 The percentage of workers affiliated with unions has fallen in half over recent decades. Discuss the potential impact of this change on the natural rate of unemployment.

3.17 [Related to Applications 17.2 and 17.3 on pages 367 and 372] Explain the effects of unemployment insurance on frictional and structural unemployment. Then consider this: During the Great Recession, governments extended unemployment benefits dramatically—up to 99 weeks. Do you suppose that extending unemployment benefits during the Great Recession was a good idea or a bad idea? Argue some pros and cons of the benefits extension.

17.4 | **Policy Implications of Unemployment, pages 370–372**

Explain how policymakers might use the actual and natural unemployment rates to determine appropriate economic policy actions.

Summary

Policies to reduce unemployment must be targeted to the type of unemployment being experienced. Reducing frictional unemployment requires improving information flow and speeding up job matching. Reducing structural unemployment may require job retraining or removing laws or institutions that keep wages above market-clearing levels. Reducing cyclical unemployment requires more macro measures, such as stimulating the economy during recessions or slowing the economy when it is expanding too quickly. But unemployment data is not perfect, and its imperfections may make it difficult for policymakers to diagnose the true state of cyclical unemployment and craft an appropriate policy response.

Review Questions

4.1 Suppose that the measured unemployment rate is 4.8%, and the natural rate of unemployment is 5.2%. Then policymakers should _____.
   a. Stimulate the economy
   b. Work to slow the economy
   c. Not intervene in the economy

4.2 The type of unemployment the Federal Reserve is best suited to alleviating is _____.

  a. Frictional unemployment

  b. Structural unemployment

  c. Cyclical unemployment

  d. Natural unemployment

4.3 Suppose that today's measured unemployment rate is 6%, and the true natural rate of unemployment is 4.8%. If the chair of the Fed believes the natural rate of unemployment to be 6.2%, then the chair will _____.

  a. Stimulate the economy when it should be slowed

  b. Slow the economy when it should be stimulated

  c. Stimulate the economy, exactly as called for

  d. Slow the economy, exactly as called for

Problems and Applications

4.4 As discussed in the chapter, it can be very difficult to pinpoint the structural, frictional, and cyclical unemployment rates. If politicians pass laws that attempt to encourage spending at the individual level, will this affect the unemployment rate if most of the unemployment is structural?

4.5 [Related to Application 17.3 on page 372] During the Great Recession of 2007–2009, the unemployment rate peaked at 10%, and the average duration of unemployment reached postwar highs. Use credible Internet resources such as the Bureau of Labor Statistics (www.bls.gov) and the Bureau of Economic Analysis (www.bea.gov) to obtain data that explains why the Great Recession, as severe as it was, didn't constitute a depression.

4.6 On March 7, 2014, *The Guardian* reported "U.S. economy adds 175,000 jobs but unemployment rate rises to 6.7%." Explain this apparent paradox in the U.S. labor market as the economy continued its recovery from the Great Recession.

4.7 During the 1990s and early 2000s, the United States experienced a residential construction boom. In the Great Recession, the housing market collapsed, and millions of construction workers lost their jobs. In hindsight, it became apparent that the nation had overbuilt housing during the boom and that the construction industry would not be so big in coming decades. Discuss the nature of the unemployment that the laid-off construction workers faced. Was their unemployment frictional, structural, or cyclical? Does your answer depend on the time frame you consider?

Unemployment Rates

This chapter introduced you to the unemployment rate: what it is, how it is measured, and how it behaves over the course of the business cycle. The chapter also discussed some of the shortcomings of the measured unemployment rate. This real-time data analysis activity touches on each of those areas.

In this real-time data analysis activity, you'll revisit the fundamental ideas of unemployment using data from Federal Reserve Economic Data (FRED), a comprehensive, up-to-date data set maintained by the Federal Reserve Bank of St. Louis.

1. Visit the FRED website located at www.stlouisfed.org /fred2.

2. Using FRED data, calculate today's unemployment rate.

3. Explore how unemployment behaves during recessions—not only for the economy as a whole, but also for distinct groups of people within the economy, such as men, women, blacks, and Hispanics.

4. Examine the measured unemployment rate's failure to account for part-time and discouraged workers.

MyEconLab

Please visit http://www.myeconlab.com for support material to conduct this experiment if assigned by your instructor.

Notes

1.1 In Section 17.1, the reference to the link between unemployment and a person's permanent income trajectory comes from See Mai Dao and Prakash Loungani, "The Human Cost of Recessions: Assessing It, Reducing It," *International Monetary Fund Staff Position Note*, 2010. The effect of unemployment on divorce is discussed in "Job Displacement, Disability, and Divorce," *Journal of Labor Economics*, 2004, and the impact of joblessness on mortality is found in "Job Displacement and Mortality: An Analysis Using Administrative Data," *Quarterly Journal of Economics*, 2009.

1.2 Card and Krueger's study of the minimum wage discussed in Section 17.3 can be found in "Minimum Wages and Employment: A Case Study of the Fast Food Industry in New Jersey and Pennsylvania," *American Economic Review*, 1994. Follow-up research includes Hirsch, Kaufman, and Zelenska's "Minimum Wage Channels of Adjustment," *IZA Discussion Paper No. 6132*, 2011, and Sabia, Burkhouser, and Hansen's "Are the Effects of Minimum Wage Increases Always Small? New Evidence from a Case Study of New York State," *Industrial and Labor Relations Review*, 2012. A survey of the literature surrounding the minimum wage can be found in John Schmitt's "Why Does the Minimum Wage Have No Discernable Effect on Employment?" CEPR Working Paper, 2013.

An Introduction to Money, Banks, and the Financial System

Chapter Outline and Learning Objectives

18.1 Money and Its Functions, page 380
Describe the three key functions of money.

18.2 The Evolution of Money and the Origins of the Modern Banking System, page 381
Describe the evolution of money, from commodity money to fiat money.

18.3 Commercial Banks, Central Banks, and Money Creation, page 384
Explain the essential functions of commercial banks and of central banks.

18.4 The Banking System and the Money Supply, page 385
Contrast the roles of the central bank and of commercial banks in creating money.

18.5 Financial Instruments and Their Functions, page 388
List the four key functions of financial instruments.

MyEconLab Real-Time Data Activity: Money and the Financial System, page 399

MyEconLab
MyEconLab helps you master each objective and study more efficiently.

The previous two chapters introduced you to the large-scale functioning of the economy. Chapter 16 discussed the market for goods and services. Chapter 17 exposed you to some key elements of the labor market. Both chapters emphasized how important it is for a country to utilize its resources as effectively as possible in order to create wealth for its residents.

A third market, called the *financial system*, helps the market for goods and services and the labor market work up to their potential. A smoothly functioning financial system makes it easier to complete transactions. When the financial system isn't working well, people have to devote more effort to arranging transactions—effort that could instead be used to produce material wealth. A well-functioning financial system also makes it easier to open and expand businesses. The financial system not working well may prevent entrepreneurs from bringing new ideas to the marketplace, resulting in lost opportunities for society. The financial system collapsing (as financial systems sometimes do) can touch off a chain reaction that results in rapid decreases in real GDP and dramatic increases in unemployment. Recessions accompanied by banking crises and other financial system failures are typically deeper and longer-lasting than ordinary recessions.

This chapter is devoted to understanding the basics of the financial system. In this chapter, you'll learn about the evolution and functions of money, the structure of the banking system, and the role of a country's central bank in controlling the supply of money. You'll also learn about the functions of financial markets, where stocks, bonds, and other financial assets are issued and traded.

Money and Its Functions

Perhaps the best way to begin studying the financial system's role in the macroeconomy is by discussing the nature and functions of money. **Money** is anything that is commonly acceptable as payment for goods and services. In the words of economists, money serves as a *medium of exchange*. But money does more than just serve as a medium of exchange: It also serves as a yardstick that people use to measure the value of the things they buy, and it helps people store wealth across time. These functions are discussed in detail next.

The Medium of Exchange Function

The medium of exchange function of money just means that money is something people use to help ease the process of trading goods and services. Imagine how miserable your economics professor would be if there were no such thing as money, and every time she wanted a hamburger, she had to find some rancher so desperate to listen to an econ lecture that he'd be willing to trade ground chuck for it. Economists call that a *double coincidence of wants* problem, which means that in a world without money, you have to find someone who has what you want and who wants what you have. Money fixes that problem: Your econ professor sells her lectures to college students and uses the money they pay her to buy beef from ranchers. There doesn't have to be a single cattleman interested in economics for her to eat a hamburger. And because money's medium of exchange function reduces the amount of time people have to spend looking for suitable trading partners, it allows them to devote more time to producing things society values. In other words, money is a convenience that makes the economic pie bigger.

The Store of Value Function

In addition to being a medium of exchange, money also serves a second function: It helps people store value across time, which allows them to separate the sale of the goods and services they produce from the purchase of the goods and services they want. In other words, because money is a store of value, people don't have to spend their income immediately upon earning it. Money's ability to store value depends on how fast prices in the economy are increasing. In countries where prices don't change much from year to year (such as Japan, where prices have been quite stable over the past half-century or so), you can stick a candy bar's worth of money under your mattress, and it will still buy you a candy bar in a year. In other countries, money is a lousy store of value: During the Zimbabwean monetary crisis of 2008, prices increased at a rate that, during one month, approached an annualized 6 sextillion percent. (Counting that high requires some numerical dexterity: *million, billion, trillion, quadrillion, quintillion, sextillion*. To phrase it differently, prices rose six billion trillion percent.) In an environment like that, if you cashed your monthly paycheck on Tuesday afternoon and hid it in your mattress overnight, it would buy you almost nothing by Wednesday morning. Prices and money are inextricably entwined: Rapid increases in the amount of money circulating in the economy often cause rapid increases in prices, an interconnection explored in Chapter 19.

The Standard of Value Function

In addition to being a medium of exchange and storing value, money serves a third important function: Money serves as a standard of value. In other words, money is a yardstick you can use to measure how much something is worth. This saves people a tremendous amount of time figuring out how much of this they should trade for how much of that. Can you imagine walking into a store and picking up a bag of chips with an enormous price tag that said, "This bag of chips can be exchanged for 10 french fries, or 4 pickled eggs, or one-tenth of a quartz watch . . ." and so on? With all prices measured in units of money, you don't have to do that. This cuts down tremendously on the amount of information you need to process when deciding how to fill your shopping cart.

Money's standard of value function helps us compute one very important piece of information: the real value of our labor. *"How many hours' worth of work will that new flat-screen TV cost me?"* That's a useful question if you happen to like TV, and it's a question that's much easier to answer if you convert both your labor at the factory and the value of the TV into dollars first.

The problem with using money as a yardstick is that the value of money changes over time. This is not a trivial issue, which is why a good chunk of the next chapter is devoted to it. Having a monetary yardstick that gets shorter each year adds confusion to the process of figuring out what things are worth. Can you imagine if the government did this with *actual* yardsticks—this year, the yard is 36 inches, but next year only 32? Measuring your vertical leap would not only require you to specify how high you jumped but also which year's yardstick you used to do the measuring.

The Evolution of Money and the Origins of the Modern Banking System

18.2 Learning Objective

Describe the evolution of money, from commodity money to fiat money.

Money helps you measure value, money helps you store that value, and money helps you convert your stored value into goods and services when you want. Now you know what money *does*, but you still don't really know what money *is*. And despite the common view that money consists of green sheets of paper printed with pictures of dead presidents, those sheets of paper are not money everywhere, and they're not the only kind of money even here in the United States.

Commodity Money

Paper money is a relatively new idea. For most of recorded history, money consisted of physical items other than pieces of paper. For example, the ancient Romans used bronze coins as money, Mexicans once used cocoa beans, and pre-revolutionary Americans used tobacco. Figure 18.1 shows one of the enormous stone disks that residents of the Pacific islands of Yap used as money.

In addition to being used as money, these items could also be used for other things. Economists say these early monies had *intrinsic value*, or *value in use*, as well as value in exchange. Money with intrinsic value is called **commodity money**. The

Commodity money Money that has intrinsic value.

▲ **Figure 18.1**

The Giant Stone Money of Yap
For hundreds of years, residents of the Pacific islands of Yap used gigantic stone disks like this one as money. The disks were quarried in distant Palau and returned 300 miles to Yap in fragile sailing canoes. The value of any particular stone depended on its size, the difficulty of the voyage, and the number of people who died quarrying it and returning it home. These disks are still in limited use today.

Representative commodity money Paper currency that could be redeemed for a specific quantity of an underlying commodity.

currency we have today has little intrinsic value—it consists of slips of paper that are not good for much of anything other than making exchanges.

Of course, the gold standard of commodity monies is gold itself. Gold served, in some form, as the domestic currency of the United States until the 1930s, and it was the international currency nations used to settle their accounts as late as 1971. Gold deserves particular attention because events in the gold trade led to our modern system of banking, and an understanding of the modern system of banking is crucial to understanding how a country's central bank controls the supply of money and attempts to stabilize the economy.

Representative Commodity Money

To understand how the gold trade evolved into our modern banking system, let's travel back in time to England in the 1600s. Gold was the currency of choice. Unlike paper money, gold could be used for multiple purposes. Artisans called goldsmiths were capable of turning gold ingots into shiny pretty things like vases, necklaces, and gilded picture frames. Goldsmiths were special because they worked with the medium of exchange and because they had secure storage facilities.

Ordinary people used gold, too, to help facilitate buying and selling. To keep their gold safe, they took their money to the secure storage facilities of a goldsmith, who would issue them a receipt for any gold they deposited with him. Then, when it was time to buy something, people would take their receipts to the goldsmith, redeem them for the gold they had on deposit, and use that gold to make their purchases.

It didn't take long for people to figure out that when they wanted to buy something, they could cut out a lot of legwork by making the *seller* fetch the gold. They began to make payments by simply circulating the goldsmith-issued receipts. *"Here's my receipt from Revere's shop for an ounce and a half of gold. Cash it in yourself. Now hand over those potatoes."* This marked another stage in the evolution of money: We moved from commodity money to **representative commodity money**, paper currency that could be redeemed for a specific quantity of an underlying commodity. The paper currency retained its value because it could be exchanged for an actual substance, gold.

Sellers of potatoes discovered that they didn't have to go to the trouble of cashing in the receipts they were paid, either. They passed them on to the next person, who passed them on to the person after that, and so on. And when a receipt started to wear out, whoever was holding it could take it into Revere's shop and redeem it—not for gold but for a fresh receipt. This greatly simplified the transactions people were conducting, and it greased the wheels of commerce.

Partially Backed Representative Commodity Money

The evolution from commodity money to representative commodity money was a marvelous innovation because of what happened next. Some enterprising goldsmith discovered that although his receipts were circulating like wildfire, nobody was actually bothering to cash them in for gold. That meant that the goldsmith was guarding a gigantic pile of gold that was just sitting there doing nothing. And so the goldsmith decided to put that gold to work for himself, lending it out at interest to someone who wanted to borrow it. Surely, he must have felt a bit guilty—after all, the gold didn't even belong to him. But he knew that few people were likely to redeem their receipts for gold, and if someone did do so, as long as the goldsmith didn't lend out the entire pile of it—that is, as long as he held some *in reserve*—there would probably be enough left in the stack to cover the receipt.

You've probably already made the mental leap between goldsmiths and banking. There are a lot of parallels. There are also some very important subtleties worth exploring. To help explain those subtleties, let's simplify the world a bit. Let's go to a desert island with three inhabitants, Shelby, Rose, and Taylor. Suppose Shelby has 100 gold coins, the only money on the island. She takes them to Taylor, a goldsmith, for storage in her basement; Taylor then issues Shelby a receipt showing that she has 100 gold coins on deposit. Shelby can use that receipt to pay her bills on a neighboring island, or she can stuff it in her mattress if she pleases. The important thing is that Shelby still has 100 coins' worth of money at her disposal, 100 coins she can spend either by redeeming her receipt or by simply giving that receipt away.

Now let's have Taylor do what she is likely to do after looking at Shelby's gold day after day: She lends the gold to Rose. Interestingly, Taylor doesn't actually have to give Shelby's gold coins to Rose. Instead, as soon as Rose has signed her legally binding promise to repay the coins (with interest), Taylor simply issues Rose a receipt saying that Rose now has 100 gold pieces deposited, or locked away, in the basement.[1]

Remember that money is defined as anything that is commonly acceptable as a form of payment for goods and services. So, if everybody is willing to hand over something they've worked hard to produce in exchange for a goldsmith's receipt, then that receipt is, by definition, money. With that in mind, observe what has happened to the amount of money on the island. Originally, Shelby had 100 pieces of money. She put that money in storage with Taylor, who locked it away and removed it from circulation. However, Shelby was able to use the receipt she received from Taylor as money. That means that the supply of money on the island was 100 pieces of coin, embodied in slips of paper that were fully redeemable for gold.

But then Taylor gets crafty and makes a loan to Rose, issuing yet another receipt for the same pile of coins. With the stroke of a pen, there are now 200 coins' worth of receipts circulating in the economy.[2] The **money supply**, the quantity of items circulating in the economy that can be used as money, has increased!

Another aspect of the story that may not be immediately obvious is that the receipts circulating throughout the economy are no longer fully backed in gold. Before Taylor made the loan, there were 100 coins' worth of receipts, redeemable for the 100 pieces of gold in her basement. After Taylor made the loan, there were 200 coins' worth of receipts, each of which claimed to be redeemable in gold. Yet there were still only 100 pieces of gold. In other words, each receipt is backed only 50% by gold. Such *partially backed representative commodity money* was the next step in the evolution of our modern banking system.

Money supply The quantity of items circulating in the economy that can be used as money.

Fiat Money

Partial backing of money may have been the next step in money's evolution, but it wasn't the last step. If money doesn't have to be fully redeemable for some sort of commodity, you might ask why it needs to be redeemable for any commodity at all. Such monies are called **fiat monies**—monies that are backed by nothing but the faith and confidence that if you accept them in exchange for something, you will be able to exchange them for something else.

For about the past 100 years, most of the world's currencies have had no backing in an underlying commodity. There's nothing backing the money in your wallet—no gold in Fort Knox, no silver at the Federal Reserve, no anything, anywhere—except the confidence you and 300 million other Americans have that you'll be able to spend it tomorrow if you accept it today.

Fiat money Money that is backed by nothing but the faith and confidence that if you accept it in exchange for something, you will be able to exchange it for something else.

[1] If you wish, you can jump through all the hoops and end up with the same result. Taylor lends Rose the actual coins. Rose exits the building, reenters, and says, "I'd like to put these coins on deposit," at which time Taylor carts the 100 coins back to the basement and issues Rose a receipt.

[2] If you wish, you can envision Taylor lending Rose the actual coins, in which case there are 100 coins' worth of receipts circulating as money, and there are 100 coins as well. Either way, we find that the economy now has a money supply of 200 coins.

Application 18.1

Funny Money Meets Serious Need

You're already aware that a society's money doesn't need to be backed by any physical commodity. You may also find it surprising that a society's fiat money doesn't have to be issued by a sanctioned monetary authority.

In the tumultuous years surrounding World War II, Sumatra (part of Indonesia today) bounced from colonial power to colonial power. Sumatra was seized from the Dutch by the Japanese and then occupied by the Allied powers after Japan's surrender. When British soldier Edward Behr landed on Sumatra as part of the Allied occupation, there was no uniform currency. Dutch guilders circulated side-by-side with Japanese yen and Indian rupees, as did currency from England, the United States, and China. Less common, but still acceptable, were notes from Australia and Thailand, and Behr noted that locals even used "some Allied postwar 'mad money,' printed, by the looks of it, on a home press in the back streets of Calcutta."

Behr's job was to obtain fresh food for his men in a place where fresh food was scarce. At one point, he discovered ample quantities of chicken and vegetables on a nearby island. He tried to purchase some with Japanese-occupation guilders, but the island chiefs refused to deal. Unable to think of anything to trade for the food his troops so desperately needed, Behr was about to give up.

> *Suddenly, I had a brain wave. Promising to replace a Monopoly set, I bought it off the Royal Navy. I then explained to the island headman that I could let him have some of the new currency that was being introduced elsewhere in Indonesia, but that—since the release date of the currency was to come only in a few days' time—he was not to mention this to anyone.*[3]

The Monopoly money looked a good deal more genuine than anything the island chiefs had seen during the Japanese occupation, and they parted with a sizable amount of chickens and vegetables in exchange for some Monopoly bills.

Fiat money's only backing is confidence in its general acceptability. Behr took measures to establish that confidence:

> *A few days later, I got another officer to go back to the island, with my remaining stock of Monopoly money. The fact that different people would brandish Monopoly money and handle it as though it were the real thing put the islanders' suspicions to rest.*[4]

Behr's battalion soon left, but the Monopoly money remained. Trust in its general acceptability was so great that when an acquaintance of Behr's returned to the island six months later, the Monopoly money was still circulating, and the locals refused to accept anything else.

See related problems 2.5, 2.6, and 2.7 on page 396 at the end of this chapter.

Based on Edward Behr's 1978 memoirs, *Anybody Here Been Raped and Speaks English?* Edward Behr publisher.

18.3 Learning Objective

Explain the essential functions of commercial banks and of central banks.

Commercial Banks, Central Banks, and Money Creation

The previous section exposed you to the origins of the modern banking system. A country's banking system plays a key role in that country's economic well-being. In particular, the banking system consists of two financial entities that *can't* be ignored in a discussion of the financial system in particular and the macroeconomy in general because those two institutions together have special power that can potentially help stabilize the economy when it's heading into recession.

---

[3]Edward Behr's 1978 memoirs, *Anybody Here Been Raped and Speaks English?*
[4]Ibid.

Commercial Banks

The first of the institutions with the power to potentially help stabilize the economy is what economists call a **commercial bank**. To ordinary people, that's the bank on the corner: The First National Bank, Commerce Bank, or Community Savings Bank. When it's time to talk about stabilizing the economy, we'll discuss the collection of all banks, known as the *banking system*, and we'll include among them the financial institutions that technically *aren't* banks but that function like banks, such as credit unions and savings and loan associations.

One important function of a bank is to accept deposits. It accepts them from people like you who have a bit more money than you're willing to spend (or perhaps a bit more than you want to carry around). In the United States, banks' checking account and savings account deposits amount to somewhere on the order of about $9 trillion. The other important thing that a bank does is make loans. It takes the money that you deposited and gives it to someone else for a period of time. It makes commercial loans to businesses, and it makes **mortgage loans** to people who want to buy land, houses, or other buildings. It makes consumer loans to people who want to buy cars and washing machines. It makes student loans to people who want to invest in their education.

Those two functions—accepting deposits and making loans—are the vital functions of the banking system. Of course, banks do other things, too. But those other things aren't the *essence* of a bank the way accepting deposits and making loans are. Also, those other functions aren't critical to the key role that banks play in stabilizing the economy.

Central Banks

As mentioned earlier, there are two different financial institutions that play a critical role in stabilizing the economy. The first of those is the commercial banking system. The second type is a bank, too, but it serves a different set of clients. Such a bank doesn't accept deposits from ordinary people like you and me. It doesn't accept deposits from businesses like the restaurant down the block. This bank is special: The vast bulk of its deposits come from the federal government and, oddly, from commercial banks. This institution, which macroeconomists call a **central bank**, serves as a bank to the government and as a bank to other banks.

In the United States, the central bank is called the **Federal Reserve System**, or "The Fed" for short. Other nations have central banks as well. Among others, England has the Bank of England, the Philippines has the Central Bank of the Philippines, and Hong Kong has the Hong Kong Monetary Authority. In some countries, a large privately owned bank might serve as the central bank. In other countries, the government itself controls the central bank. Some countries have no central bank at all, and they rely instead on the currency and central banking facilities of some other country.

The reason people pay so much attention to central banks is not because they serve as banks to governments but because they are responsible for issuing currency and controlling the amount of money that circulates throughout the economy and because they have considerable influence over the level of interest rates. For those reasons, a country's central bank is often referred to as that country's *monetary authority*.

The Banking System and the Money Supply

We have learned something important about the financial system in general and the banking system in particular: Banks have a special power, the power to create money. In fact, every time a bank makes a loan (as happened in our island economy), the money supply rises by the amount of the loan. The opposite is true, too: Every student loan payment you make for the next 15 years is going to cause the money supply to fall.

Commercial bank A financial institution that accepts deposits and makes loans.

Mortgage loan A loan extended for the purpose of purchasing real property, such as land, houses, or other buildings.

Central bank A financial institution that is responsible for issuing currency and controlling the amount of money in circulation. The central bank generally serves as a bank to the government and as a bank to other banks.

Federal Reserve System The central bank of the United States.

18.4 Learning Objective

Contrast the roles of the central bank and of commercial banks in creating money.

You might have been wondering exactly why we spent so much time talking about the evolution of money. Now you know: Tracing the evolution of money has allowed us to understand the origins and functions of the modern banking system. That's important because banks are vital to the functioning of the economy: Banks are by far the largest source of credit for people who want to go to college, get a car, buy a house, or travel with a credit card. In other words, banks help create real economic activity, and in the process of doing that, they create money, too. The importance of money creation will be discussed in detail in the chapters to come. Careful management of the money supply can potentially help stabilize the economy and minimize the effects of recessions.

The Central Bank's Role in Money Creation

In the real world, somebody has to make that critical first deposit into the banking system before new money can be created. Recall that in our island economy, Shelby had deposited some gold coins with Taylor that would soon be lent to Rose, setting off a spurt of money creation. But where did Shelby's coins come from in the first place?

In the days of the gold standard, that initial deposit could have come from any crusty old miner looking to protect his stash of nuggets from robbers and thieves. Because gold backed the currency, a 1-ounce gold nugget was worth just as much as a 1-ounce gold coin, which meant that people could literally dig money out of the ground! Placed on deposit in a bank, that 1-ounce gold nugget could be lent, and re-lent, and lent again until 5 or 10 ounces' worth of money were created.

In the age of fiat money, figuring out exactly where that initial deposit comes from isn't quite so straightforward. You certainly can't dig it out of the ground: If you take a 1-ounce gold nugget into the bank, they might put it in a safety deposit box for you, but the bank won't use it to make loans or create money. Nor can you print that first dollar of fiat money yourself without ending up in federal prison. But that money has to come from somewhere, and if it doesn't come from private individuals, then where *does* it come from?

The money comes from the central bank, which alone among all our various and assorted financial institutions has been given the power to issue currency. To see how that is done, use your imagination for a moment and envision the United States without any money whatsoever. Now imagine Janet Yellen, who is the chair of the Board of Governors of the Federal Reserve System, climbing aboard a bright-green Chinook helicopter. Just as the helicopter passes Toledo, Ohio, Yellen takes a single $100 bill from the inside breast pocket of her jacket and drops it out the cargo door. The bill lands in the backyard of Carrie, a resident of Toledo, who promptly deposits it in her neighborhood bank.

The Commercial Banking System's Role in Money Creation

Carrie's bank can now take the $100 she deposited and lend it to Simon, who wants to buy a fishing boat from Andrew:

- Note that the economy has $200 worth of money: Carrie has $100 in her checking account (the modern version of goldsmith receipts), and Simon has a $100 bill.
- After Simon pays Andrew for the boat, Andrew deposits that $100 bill in *his* bank. That bank then lends that $100 to Lowell, who wants to buy a new Audi.
- The money supply has grown again: Now Carrie, Andrew, and Lowell each have $100.

The Federal Reserve's injection of $100 in new currency has created $300 worth of money, and if the cycle of deposits and loans continues further, even more money can be created. The mechanics of the money supply process will be explored further in the next chapter. For now, it's sufficient to note that in our modern financial system, money is *created* by both the central bank and the banking system. Yet all money *originates* with the central bank. The banking system can't simply create money without a jumpstart from the Fed. In reality, Janet Yellen is not going to shovel pallets of new money out the cargo door of her Chinook helicopter if the Fed decides to increase the money supply in the economy. There are other ways for her to increase the money supply, which you will learn about shortly. There are also ways the Fed can remove money from the economy, and you will learn how the Fed does that, too.

Measuring the Money Supply

You now know how the central bank and the banking system together determine the supply of money. How big is the supply of money? Unfortunately, there is no simple answer to this question because how big the money supply is depends on what things you choose to consider as money.

The Federal Reserve actually computes a few different measures of the money supply, each of which includes some different financial assets. The first measure the Fed computes is called the M1 money supply. **M1** consists of currency in circulation, checking account balances, and traveler's checks. The currency component of M1 includes only currency held by members of the public outside the banking system: If currency is locked up in a bank vault, it is neither circulating nor creating economic activity, so it is not included in M1. Therefore,

M1 A measure of the money supply that includes currency in circulation, checking account balances, and traveler's checks.

M1 = Currency + Checking Account Balances + Traveler's Checks

Figure 18.2 shows the magnitude of M1, broken down into its three components. As of April 2014, just over $1.2 trillion was circulating in the form of currency and almost $1.6 trillion was in checking accounts. Altogether, the M1 money stock totaled about $2.8 trillion.

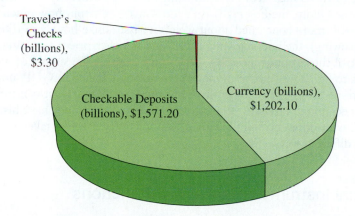

Traveler's Checks (billions), $3.30

Checkable Deposits (billions), $1,571.20

Currency (billions), $1,202.10

MyEconLab Real-time data

◄ Figure 18.2
The Components of M1, 2014
The M1 money supply totaled about $2.8 trillion in April 2014. Currency accounted for about 43% of M1, and checkable deposits accounted for 57%. Traveler's checks are a negligible fraction of the M1 money stock.

Source: Federal Reserve System, April 2014.

Remember that money is defined as anything that is commonly acceptable as payment for goods and services—in other words, anything that can serve as a medium of exchange. Certainly the M1 measure of the money supply fits that definition: You use cash and traveler's checks to buy goods and services, and you can also use checks or debit cards to access your checking account balance in order to complete transactions.

You can also use a credit card to buy goods and services. So are credit cards included in M1? No, and here's why: When you purchase an item using your American Express card, American Express pays for the item on your behalf, using money from its own checking account. Those checking account balances have already been counted in M1, so including your credit card balance in the money supply would result in counting the same money twice. Credit cards are a means of using someone *else's* money to complete your transactions, but they are not money in and of themselves.

M2 A measure of the money supply that includes everything in M1, plus savings account balances, money market mutual fund balances, and small certificates of deposit.

MyEconLab Real-time data

▶ **Figure 18.3**
The Components of M2, 2014
M2 includes everything in M1, plus the dollar value of some highly liquid financial assets. M2 is many times the size of M1, totaling $11.2 trillion in April 2014.
Source: Federal Reserve System, April 2014.

In addition to the M1 money supply, the Fed also publishes a second measure of the money supply, called M2. **M2** includes everything in M1, plus some other financial assets that can be easily converted to cash or checking account balances. Those assets include savings account balances, money market mutual fund balances, and small certificates of deposit.[5] Because those assets can be easily converted to cash or checking account balances, they are often referred to as *near monies*. Figure 18.3 summarizes the components of M2 and shows their relative magnitudes as of April 2014.

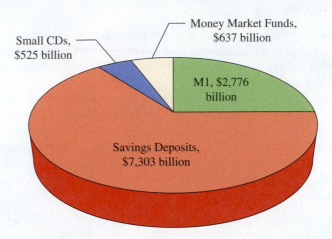

Small CDs, $525 billion

Money Market Funds, $637 billion

M1, $2,776 billion

Savings Deposits, $7,303 billion

As noted, M2 includes everything in M1, plus more. And those extra assets are very large, which means that the M2 money stock is much bigger than M1. In April 2014, the M1 money stock was about $2.8 trillion; the M2 money stock was $11.2 trillion, almost four times as large.

Why does the Fed publish different measures of the money supply, especially when one of those measures includes things that can't directly be used to complete transactions? Oddly, the Fed really isn't too concerned about how much money there is. The Fed is more concerned about weightier issues like how big GDP is (and how fast it is growing), the unemployment rate, and how fast prices are rising. But the Fed can't control those things directly—it can only control the supply of money. So the Fed wants to find a measure of money that is strongly linked to GDP, unemployment, and inflation: It hopes that by controlling the money supply, it can influence those important economic variables. The different measures of money have historically been correlated with different Fed objectives, which is why the Fed takes care to measure money in different ways.

18.5 Learning Objective

List the four key functions of financial instruments.

Financial instruments Documents that represent agreements between two or more parties about rights to payments of money.

Financial Instruments and Their Functions

The banking system plays a critical role in the macroeconomy. But there are other financial institutions, and they play important roles, too. Those institutions produce a wide array of financial products and services. But all **financial instruments**—documents that represent agreements between two or more parties about rights to payments of money—perform the same few jobs. People can use financial instruments to raise the money they need to open or expand a business, for example. Other people might use financial instruments to save money for their retirement. Some individuals and businesses use financial instruments to reduce risk. Others, called *speculators*, use financial instruments to take on more risk in hopes of earning large profits.

---

[5]Money market mutual funds function a lot like interest-bearing checking accounts. In fact, money market funds generally allow limited check-writing privileges. Small CDs are savings accounts whereby the saver promises not to withdraw their savings for a certain amount of time. However, some small CDs can be sold early in financial markets and immediately converted to cash.

Raising Capital

The first thing financial instruments are used for is to raise financial capital (money). Financial capital is different than the capital referred to earlier in this text (see Chapter 1). That type of capital, *physical capital*, consists of tools and equipment that can be used to produce other products or services. But factories and tools and equipment can be very expensive, so business owners often need help paying for them. The money that business owners raise to purchase physical capital or to fund new business ventures is called **financial capital**.

Suppose that transportation networking guru Garrett Camp wants to expand headquarters at his company Uber.com, and he needs a few million dollars to do it. Camp might turn to financial markets to raise the money. **Financial markets** are simply places, physical or electronic, where financial instruments are traded. There, Uber can request money from people all over the world in order to amass the enormous financial capital that it takes to crush taxi companies and car rental services like Enterprise and Avis.

Stocks One way that Uber can raise money is by selling stock. A **stock** is a financial asset that represents partial ownership of a corporation. That ownership is easily transferrable from person to person because stock can be easily bought and sold at exchanges—centralized trading places—such as the New York Stock Exchange and the London Stock Exchange. That's what most of the activity on the stock market is about—people buying and selling small pieces of existing companies like General Motors and Apple. If you purchase stock in Uber, and Uber earns huge profits, you (as partial owner) will get a part of those profits. But if Uber does poorly, you will also share in its losses.

A special type of financial institution known as an *investment bank* can assist Uber in raising the money it needs. An investment bank helps firms sell newly created shares of stock to the public. Often, the investment bank will purchase a large number of shares for itself, which it then gradually resells to investors. By doing so, investment banks make the process of raising the money an entrepreneur needs to start or expand a business much easier and much faster.

Bonds Instead of selling off ownership of his company by issuing stock, Garrett Camp might borrow the money he needs. He could take out a loan at a bank, or he could print up a bunch of legally binding IOUs and sell them to people who are willing to lend Uber money. Those IOUs come in many forms, the most common of which is called a bond. A **bond** is an IOU that, in exchange for using a person's money today, obligates the borrower to pay back a specified amount of money at a particular point in the future. The advantage from Uber's standpoint is that it has to pay back only what the contract specifies. If Uber has phenomenal earnings, its owners don't share them with bondholders. On the other hand, if Uber has an abysmal year, Uber's bondholders are entitled to their contractual payment, whereas Uber's owners may not receive anything.

Bonds come in all shapes and sizes. Some *mature*, or come due (require full repayment), in a year or less; others mature in 20 or 30 years. Some require the borrower to make periodic payments to the lender; others simply require a single lump-sum payment at maturity. Like stocks, existing bonds can be bought and sold on organized exchanges: If you buy one of Uber's bonds and later decide you'd rather not wait 30 years for the bond to mature, you can sell your bond to someone else for cash today.

Regardless of whether Uber borrows money from a bank or issues bonds, Uber will have to pay back more money than it borrowed. The difference is called interest. **Interest** is the price a borrower must pay for the use of other peoples' money. It is also the reward to the people who postponed spending money on things that they wanted in order to let Uber spend their money on the things *it* wanted. Often, interest is expressed as a percentage of the amount borrowed, which is called the **interest rate**.

Financial capital The money that business owners raise to purchase physical capital or to fund new business ventures.

Financial markets Places, physical or electronic, where financial instruments are traded.

Stock A financial asset that represents partial ownership of a corporation.

Bond A financial instrument that represents a debt contract and obligates a borrower to pay back a specified amount of money at a particular point in the future.

Interest The price a borrower must pay for the use of other peoples' money.

Interest rate Interest expressed as a percentage of the amount borrowed.

Businesses often borrow money by issuing and selling bonds. (Again, investment banks help businesses bring those bonds to market.) Governments do, too: The U.S. federal government generally issues bonds when it spends more on its programs than it takes in from taxes; state and local governments borrow money to build roads and schools and parks.

This kind of large-scale credit is essential for the development and functioning of both businesses and government. But credit doesn't have to be measured in millions to be useful. Many people lend money $25 or $50 at a time to budding entrepreneurs in developing countries through organizations such as kiva.com. These small loans, which are referred to as *microcredit*, enable small businesswomen, in particular, to put together the few hundred or few thousand dollars necessary to launch their own enterprises. Microcredit, a lending practice that began gaining momentum in the 1970s, has been instrumental to both launching economic development and empowering women in countries in which they are often considered second-class citizens. Microcredit has had such an impact in both of those arenas that in 2006, Muhammad Yunus, the Bangladeshi banker and economist who pioneered its innovation, received a Nobel Peace Prize for his efforts.

Storing Wealth Across Time

Using financial markets is an easy way for Uber to borrow other peoples' money for its own use. But why do people want to lend Uber their money in the first place? Part of the answer is that people wish to trade the chance to buy things today for the chance to buy a larger quantity of things tomorrow. But even if you're not motivated by the lure of "more," you may still want to consume less than you earn now and send the rest of your earnings to financial markets. This is because buying financial instruments can help you store your wealth across time.

Consider Maleah, who wants to buy a nice used car and is setting aside some of her earnings until she has enough to buy one. She could store those earnings in her mattress, but that's not a great system, and here's why: Because the prices of the things people buy generally increase each year (a phenomenon known as *inflation*), she'll find that the dollar she stuffs in her mattress today will buy fewer things when she pulls it out next year.

Maleah can use financial markets to help ensure that the value of her savings increases over time instead of falling. She could use the money to buy shares of stock in Facebook, or she could lend it to Twitter in the bond market if she senses her friends are doing more tweeting and less liking. She could deposit it in a savings account or buy a certificate of deposit (CD). The interest or profits those financial instruments generate will help offset the effects of inflation.

When it's time for Maleah to purchase the car she's been saving for, she'll have to convert her savings into cash. Sometimes that's easy: If Maleah stored her wealth in a savings account, all she needs to do is visit her bank and make a withdrawal. On the other hand, if Maleah stored her wealth by purchasing antique furniture, she may have trouble finding a willing buyer right away. Savings accounts, antique furniture, and other assets have different degrees of **liquidity**—the ease with which they can be converted to cash. From a saver's standpoint, liquidity is a very desirable quality: It makes it easy to get into and out of different investments if a better opportunity comes along, and it makes it easy to convert your savings into cash if you need to pay rent or buy a used car.

Liquidity The ease with which an asset can be converted to cash.

Another reason people want to store wealth is to help smooth their consumption of goods and services over time. Nobody wants to consume exorbitantly during their high-earning years and then go on a starvation diet once they retire. Financial markets help people prevent that: When you're earning a lot of money, you can buy stocks and bonds and CDs from your bank, and you can cash them in or sell them later, when you're retired.

Financial markets also help smooth consumption when you're young. Many college students, for example, live in decent places, drive nice cars, and study abroad in distant lands. If they had to live on their actual incomes, their lives might be pretty bleak. But often, they take out student loans that let them borrow against their future earnings to finance a better lifestyle today. A student loan is a financial instrument, just as shares of stock and government bonds are.

Reducing Risk

For people who watch, wide-eyed, as the stock market makes huge surges followed by deep dives, it may not be intuitively obvious that one of the major functions of financial markets is to help people reduce risk. But that's exactly what some of the most volatile financial instruments were actually designed to do.

Consider Cecil, a Kansas farmer. Every September, Cecil plants wheat that won't be harvested until the next June. Without financial markets, his decision about how much wheat to plant depends on his guess about what wheat will be selling for in nine months. Unfortunately, if the price of wheat is lower than he'd thought it would be, Cecil might have trouble paying back the money he borrowed for seed and fuel and fertilizer.

To avoid that possibility, Cecil turns to financial markets: He sells some of his wheat *at the time he plants it*, with the promise to deliver it and receive payment in July. That promise is a financial instrument called a **futures contract**, and it's especially well suited for commodities like wheat.

Suppose Cecil sells some wheat to Gold Medal Flour in September for delivery in July at $8 per bushel. If the price of wheat ends up being $12, Cecil is worse off than he would have been if he had waited to sell it. But if the price of wheat ends up being $4, he can pat himself on the back for avoiding financial catastrophe. Either way, the contract stabilizes his income: He's willing to forgo the possibility that the price might rise to eliminate the risk of it falling. This helps him smooth his consumption and soothes his anxiety. Gold Medal Flour, too, reduces its uncertainty by locking in the price of the wheat early.

Via diversification, financial markets help investors reduce their exposure to risk in a second way. **Diversification** is the practice of spreading your wealth across multiple investments. Economist James Tobin won the Nobel Prize largely for his work on diversification, expressing mathematically what rural housewives have known for centuries: Don't put all your eggs in one basket.

Here's why diversifying is such a good idea. Suppose that you have $1 million stuffed inside your mattress. Anxious to put that money to work, you use it to buy stock issued by Uber. In doing that, you're putting your life savings in the hands of the company's CEO, Garrett Camp. One bad decision on his part, and your savings could disappear. But if you divide your savings between Uber and the Werner ladder company, you'll substantially reduce your risk of losing it all. If Uber tanks, you've still got your Werner holdings. If Werner tanks, you've still got your Uber holdings. You are much safer because the chance of *both* companies going under at the same time is much smaller than the chance of just either company going under.

Financial markets make it easy to diversify—to spread your investments over 2, 20, or 200 different companies. In fact, you don't have to be an investment expert to own a piece of even *thousands* of companies. All you have to do is buy shares in a financial instrument called a mutual fund. A **mutual fund** is a financial asset that is essentially an investment club in which the pooled savings of investors is used to buy stock or bonds or other financial assets issued by thousands of firms and governments around the globe. If you buy a share of a mutual fund, you are entitled to a proportionate share of the earnings of all the companies the fund has invested in. One of the neat things about buying mutual funds is that there's one to satisfy every taste: If you want to invest in gold mining, or green companies, or companies that do not allow their subcontractors to employ child labor, there's a fund for each.

Futures contract A financial instrument that establishes the terms of a sale that will take place at a later time.

Diversification The practice of spreading wealth across multiple investments.

Mutual fund A financial asset in which the pooled savings of many investors is used to buy stock, bonds, or other financial assets.

Enabling Speculation

There is one remaining need that financial markets fill, and it's a need that's not always looked upon positively. Financial markets make it easy for people to indulge in their desires to speculate. Just as a gambler might feel that the next spin of the roulette wheel will turn up red, speculators might feel that the price of wheat (or the value of gold, or the stock market, or even the rainfall total in Sonoma) will go up or down. Financial markets make it easy to put your money where your hunch is.

Suppose you believe the price of wheat is going to rise from $3 per bushel today to $10 per bushel by July. Here's one way to act on that hunch:

- Buy 5,000 bushels of wheat today for $3 per bushel and have it delivered to your home.

- In July, buy a shovel and rent a truck. Use the shovel to fill the truck with the wheat.

- Drive the wheat to a grain elevator, sell it for $10 per bushel, and earn a $35,000 profit.

Here's an easier way:

- For a small fee, buy a futures contract for 5,000 bushels of wheat, priced at $3, to be delivered and paid for in July.

- On June 30, if wheat is selling for the $10 you guessed it would, your futures contract will be worth a net of $35,000. Call your commodities broker and offer to sell your contract for $34,000 to a flour mill that needs the wheat.

- The next day the flour mill takes delivery from the seller and pays him the $15,000 specified in the contract.

With this arrangement, the mill gets its wheat for $49,000 ($1,000 less than it would otherwise have to pay), the farmer gets $15,000 (which is what he originally wanted for his wheat), and you earn $34,000 without ever having to lift a shovel.

Of course, you could be wrong. If wheat turns out to be $1 a bushel in July, you'll lose $10,000, regardless of whether you stored the wheat in your basement or used a futures contract. But whether you win or lose, it's worth remembering that the person on the other end of your contract may not be speculating at all: The same financial instrument you are using to indulge your risk might be used by a farmer or baker or miller to *reduce* his!

Speculators are often criticized for their ability to destabilize markets. For example, in 1600s Holland, speculators began buying up tulip bulbs on the belief that their prices would rise in the future. Speculators' hoarding drove bulb prices higher, which sustained their belief in ever-increasing tulip prices and created more hoarding at ever-higher prices. At the height of the tulip craze, a single bulb sold for 10 times the annual salary of a skilled worker.

When prices are driven not by the intrinsic value of an item but rather by such a speculative spiral, a *speculative bubble* is said to exist. The problem with bubbles is that they pop, and when they do, prices plummet, and wealth evaporates. If large numbers of people are involved, those wealth effects can plunge an entire economy into recession (see Chapter 16).

While speculators *have* been responsible for some notable economic catastrophes, on a day-to-day basis, they actually stabilize prices rather than destabilize them. Suppose, for example, that pecans are plentiful and cheap today but that you and a handful of others believe that a drought will ruin next year's pecan harvest, creating a scarcity that will drive prices skyward. You can profit from that belief by buying lots of pecans today, storing them, and then selling them next year.

That's a speculative endeavor, but it does society a lot of good. First, it makes more pecans available at a time when they are particularly scarce. In other words, it moves pecans from a time when they have relatively low value (today) to a time when they will have relatively high value (next year). This helps society get more happiness out of each pecan. Second, your speculative gamble helps stabilize prices. Buying up pecans today, when pecans are cheap, drives up their price a bit; making them available next year when pecans are scarce helps push down their price at that time. (See Chapter 6.) So, as a result of speculation, price swings in the pecan market are smaller than they would otherwise be.

Application 18.2

Financial Instruments and the Origins of the Great Recession

MyEconLab Real-time data

The story of the Great Recession didn't begin with the housing collapse of 2007. Its roots can be traced back a decade earlier, to *financial innovations*—the development of new financial instruments.

Not long ago, if you borrowed money to buy a house, you would have made monthly payments to the bank that loaned you the money until the loan was paid off. Thirty years ago, however, banks began making loans and then selling the stream of future loan payments to third parties in exchange for immediate lump sums of cash.

Banks often sold their loans to large investment banks and to two quasi-governmental corporations created to encourage home ownership by providing funds for home loans to the banking system: the Federal National Mortgage Association (Fannie Mae, created in 1938) and the Federal Home Loan Mortgage Corporation (Freddie Mac, created in 1970). Fannie Mae and Freddie Mac purchase mortgages from lenders and repackage large blocks of those mortgages into special bonds called "mortgage-backed securities," which are then sold to pension funds and other large investors. Homeowners' mortgage payments are then used to make the scheduled interest payments to bondholders. Each bond, backed by a small slice of many home loans, is diversified and presumably low risk.

If diversifying once is good, diversifying twice is better. In the 1990s, investment bankers combined the payments from multiple mortgage-backed securities into yet another financial instrument called a collateralized debt obligation (CDO). Believed to be extremely safe, CDOs were wildly popular. Trillions of dollars' worth were sold to investors and investment banks. Those investors and investment banks often insured their CDOs against default by purchasing a second financial instrument called a *credit default swap* that would compensate them if a CDO they had purchased went into default.

Those financial instruments provided massive funds to the housing market, fueling the housing boom of the 1990s and 2000s. At the same time, under direction from the federal government, Fannie Mae and Freddie Mac increased their purchases of mortgage loans that had been extended to less credit-worthy borrowers. (Those loans are referred to as *subprime loans*.) Banks and other mortgage lenders were happy to play along. They pursued high-risk borrowers by issuing them adjustable-interest-rate mortgages with low introductory, or *teaser*, rates, knowing the mortgages would be quickly sold to someone else for conversion to CDOs. They also encouraged existing homeowners to refinance their existing mortgages, often offering homeowners a chance to borrow more than their house was actually worth and take the difference in cash. Cheap credit also fueled a speculative "flipping" craze in which people would buy homes in hopes of quickly reselling them for a higher price.

And then the Federal Reserve began raising interest rates—from 2% in 2004 to 5% in May 2006. As interest rates increased, mortgage payments for homeowners with adjustable-rate mortgages increased, too. Millions of homeowners, subprime and otherwise, found themselves unable to make their payments. As shown in the following figure, at the peak of the crisis, more than 10% of mortgage holders had failed to make all their scheduled payments. Those defaults dragged the mortgage-backed securities and CDOs that relied on their monthly payments into default with them.

(continued)

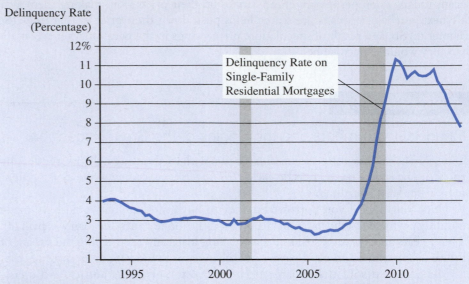

Delinquency Rate (Percentage)

Shaded areas represent U.S. recessions.

Source: Board of Governors of the Federal Reserve System (http://research.stlouisfed.org/fred2/series /DRSFRMACBN).

The effects were immediate and devastating. Three Wall Street investment banks with major CDO holdings collapsed, threatening to take the entire financial system with them. The world's largest insurance company, American International Group (AIG), which had issued $400 billion of credit default swaps to insure CDOs against loss, needed a government bailout to pay its claims. With so many homes in foreclosure, housing values plummeted. Banks, concerned about spreading foreclosures and worried about the fragile state of the economy, dramatically reduced lending even to highly qualified homeowners, consumers, and businesses. Home construction dried up overnight, and consumption and business investment spending both fell precipitously. The Great Recession had begun.

See related problems 5.16 and 5.17 on page 398 at the end of this chapter.

Based on Lloyd B. Thomas's *The Financial Crisis and Federal Reserve Policy*, Palgrave Macmillan, 2013, and the CNBC documentary *House of Cards*.

Speculation helps stabilize prices in the pecan market. Financial instruments like futures contracts make it easier for speculators to perform this valuable function. In addition, speculation may help stabilize prices in financial markets themselves: You can buy shares of Apple stock speculatively just as easily as you can speculate in the market for real apples.

Conclusion

At this point, you know a lot about the financial system. You know what functions financial markets perform, and you have some idea how they do it. You know about the history and evolution of the most interesting financial instrument of all: cold, hard cash. You know how the banking system works and how it has the special power to create money. You have a barebones acquaintance with central banking and the Federal Reserve System, and you know that in a modern monetary system, the money supply begins and ends with the central bank.

This chapter ends with an observation and a question. The observation comes from the example in which Janet Yellen dropped a $100 bill from a helicopter. That helicopter drop initiated something more than just the creation of $200 worth of additional money. It also enabled the purchase of a boat and a car. In other words, it initiated what economists call *real* economic activity—the kind of activity that creates jobs and raises living standards.

Now, the question: If dropping $100 created that kind of real activity, why not drop thousands, or millions, or billions? In the next chapter, we'll take a close look at how the central bank attempts to manage the economy by increasing and decreasing the money supply. Those actions, called *monetary policy*, are perhaps the most important part of the Federal Reserve's mission. By the end of the next chapter, you will understand how and why the Fed implements those actions, and you will understand the strengths, weaknesses, and limitations of monetary policy.

Chapter Summary and Problems

Key Terms

Bond, p. 389

Central bank, p. 385

Commercial bank, p. 385

Commodity money, p. 381

Diversification, p. 391

Federal Reserve System, p. 385

Fiat money, p. 383

Financial capital, p. 389

Financial instruments, p. 388

Financial markets, p. 389

Futures contract, p. 391

Interest, p. 389

Interest rate, p. 389

Liquidity, p. 390

M1, p. 387

M2, p. 388

Money, p. 380

Money supply, p. 383

Mortgage loan, p. 385

Mutual fund, p. 391

Representative commodity money, p. 382

Stock, p. 389

18.1 Money and Its Functions, pages 380–381

Describe the three key functions of money.

Summary

Money is anything that is commonly acceptable as payment for goods and services. Money serves as a medium of exchange, a store of value, and a standard of value. By making transactions easier to complete, money creates more opportunity for a society to devote more time to production. In that way, money increases material wealth.

Review Questions

All problems are assignable in MyEconLab.

1.1 Money has three primary functions; it serves as _____, _____, and _____.

1.2 Money's function as a _____ ensures that individuals will be able to purchase goods and services without having to fulfill a double coincidence of wants.
   a. Store of value
   b. Medium of exchange
   c. Standard of value
   d. None of the above

1.3 Money's _____ function means that money can be reliably saved now and used later.
   a. Store of value
   b. Medium of exchange

   c. Standard of value
   d. None of the above

1.4 Money serves its store of value function worst when prices are _____.
   a. Increasing
   b. Stable
   c. Falling
   d. Prices do not affect money's ability to store value.

Problems and Applications

1.5 John grows apples and desires peaches. Josie grows peaches and desires pears. Myron grows pears and desires apples. Discuss the difficulties these three people would face satisfying their desires in a world without money.

1.6 Explain the importance of money's standard of value function. Is this standard of value always 100% reliable? What can the central bank do to enhance this standard of value function?

The Evolution of Money and the Origins of the Modern Banking System, pages 381–384

Describe the evolution of money, from commodity money to fiat money.

Summary

Originally, people used substances with intrinsic value as money. Those commodity monies evolved into representative commodity monies—pieces of paper redeemable in a real commodity. Eventually, most countries adopted fiat monies—monies with no intrinsic backing.

Review Questions

All problems are assignable in MyEconLab.

2.1 Money that is backed by nothing but the faith and confidence that it will serve as a medium of exchange is called _____.
  a. Representative commodity money
  b. Commodity money
  c. Fiat money
  d. None of the above

2.2 Paper currency that could be redeemed for a specific quantity of an underlying commodity is called _____.
  a. Representative commodity money
  b. Commodity money
  c. Fiat money
  d. None of the above

2.3 The money currently in use in the United States is backed by _____.
  a. Gold
  b. Silver
  c. Some substance other than gold or silver
  d. Nothing

Problems and Applications

2.4 Modern money is backed only by the faith and confidence that if you accept it from someone today, someone else will accept it from you tomorrow. Explain the role that a country's central bank might play in maintaining that common acceptability.

2.5 [Related to Application 18.1 on page 384] Read Application 18.1 carefully. Then go to the Internet and search for *Bloomberg Businessweek*'s "The Bitcoin-Mining Arms Race Heats Up," at www.businessweek.com. Draw some parallels between bitcoin and the Monopoly money used in Indonesia. Do you think bitcoin is money? What functions of money does it serve? What functions does it not serve?

2.6 [Related to Application 18.1 on page 384] "Money must be officially issued by government or sanctioned by government if it is to serve as money." Do you agree or disagree with this statement? Explain your reasoning.

2.7 [Related to Application 18.1 on page 384] Why was Edward Behr able to use monopoly money to purchase goods in Sumatra?

2.8 Go to the Internet and search for *Bloomberg Businessweek*'s "The Bitcoin-Mining Arms Race Heats Up," at www.businessweek.com. Do you consider bitcoin to be a commodity money or a fiat money? Explain your reasoning.

2.9 How did the evolution of partially backed representative commodity money fundamentally change the nature of economic activity? What are some potential consequences of that evolution?

Commercial Banks, Central Banks, and Money Creation, pages 384–385

Explain the essential functions of commercial banks and of central banks.

Summary

Commercial banks are institutions that accept deposits and make loans. A central bank provides banking functions to government and also serves as a bank to banks. Perhaps more importantly, a country's central bank is responsible for controlling that country's money supply. In the United States, the central bank is called the Federal Reserve System.

Review Questions

All problems are assignable in MyEconLab.

3.1 _____ are loans that banks make to people who want to buy land, houses, or other buildings.

3.2 A _____ serves as a bank to the government and as a "banker's bank."

3.3 The central bank of the United States is called _____.
  a. The Bank of the United States
  b. The Department of the Treasury
  c. The Bureau of Printing and Engraving
  d. The Federal Reserve System

3.4 A financial institution that accepts deposits and makes loans is generally referred to as a(n) _____.
  a. Central bank
  b. Investment bank
  c. Commercial bank
  d. None of the above

Problems and Applications

3.5 In the United States, both commercial banks and the central bank (the Federal Reserve) accept deposits and make loans. Explain the key differences between commercial banks and the Federal Reserve.

3.6 Comment on the following statement: The Federal Reserve, like all central banks, is a part of the federal government.

18.4 ## The Banking System and the Money Supply, pages 385–388

Contrast the roles of the central bank and of commercial banks in creating money.

Summary

A country's central bank has the unique power to inject new money into the economy. When that money is deposited in a bank, the bank can subsequently lend it to customers. Each time that happens, the money supply grows. The Federal Reserve measures the total amount of money in the economy. The M1 money stock consists of currency, checking account balances, and traveler's checks. The M2 money supply consists of everything included in M1, plus some highly liquid assets that can be easily converted to cash.

Review Questions

All problems are assignable in MyEconLab.

4.1 The quantity of items, such as coins, paper money, and checking account balances, circulating in the economy that can be used as money is called the _____.

   a. Stock
   b. Money supply
   c. Exchange rate
   d. Commodity market

4.2 When a bank makes a loan to Maleah for the purchase of a new car, the money supply _____.

   a. Increases
   b. Decreases
   c. Remains the same

4.3 The M1 money supply consists of _____.

   a. Currency
   b. Checking account balances
   c. Traveler's checks
   d. All of the above

4.4 The M1 measure of the money supply emphasizes money's _____ function; the M2 measure increasingly emphasizes money's _____ function.

   a. Standard of value; store of value
   b. Store of value; medium of exchange
   c. Medium of exchange; standard of value
   d. Medium of exchange; store of value

4.5 Which of the following is not included in M2?

   a. Currency
   b. Money market mutual fund accounts
   c. Savings account balances
   d. a, b, and c are all components of M2

4.6 M2 is _____.

   a. Always larger than M1
   b. Sometimes larger and sometimes smaller than M1
   c. Always smaller than M1

Problems and Applications

4.7 Money is created by the central bank and by commercial banks. How does money creation at the central bank differ from money creation in the commercial banking system? Are there any similarities?

4.8 If consumers were to shift funds from their savings accounts to their checking accounts, what would happen to M1? To M2?

18.5 ## Financial Instruments and Their Functions, pages 388–394

List the four key functions of financial instruments.

Summary

There are many different financial instruments. But they all serve one or more of the same few functions. First, they may be used to raise financial capital. Second, they may be used to store value. Third, they may be used to reduce risk. Finally, they may be used to speculate. A few special financial instruments are stock (which represents ownership of a corporation), bonds (which represent a loan to a business or government), and futures contracts (which represent a promise to buy or sell an item in the future at a specified price).

Review Questions

All problems are assignable in MyEconLab.

5.1 Documents representing legal agreements that involve some sort of monetary value are called _____.

5.2 Bonds are essentially IOUs. When they reach the date on which they require full payment, they are said to have reached _____.

5.3 _____ loans are very small loans that are most frequently made to impoverished female entrepreneurs who may not have access to loans from traditional sources.

5.4 The practice of spreading wealth across multiple investments is called _____.

5.5 The physical or electronic places where financial instruments are traded are called _____.

5.6 When the central bank increases or decreases the money supply in an attempt to manage the economy, those actions are referred to as _____.

5.7 A _____ represents partial ownership of a corporation, and a _____ obligates the borrower to pay back a specified amount of money at a particular point in the future.
  a. Bond; stock
  b. CDO; bond
  c. Stock; CDO
  d. Stock; bond

5.8 Which of the following is a type of financial instrument?
  a. Bonds
  b. Mortgage-backed securities
  c. Savings accounts
  d. All of the above are financial instruments.

5.9 The price a borrower must pay for the use of other peoples' money is called _____.
  a. Interest
  b. Savings
  c. Dividend
  d. Rebate

5.10 A(n) _____ is an arrangement in which a farmer sells some of his product when it is planted, with the promise to deliver it and receive payment after it is harvested.
  a. Insurance policy
  b. Savings contract
  c. Futures contract
  d. Contingent sale

5.11 The reward for individuals who choose to postpone spending now in order for their money to be lent out is called _____.
  a. Interest
  b. Speculation

  c. Hedging
  d. Diversification

5.12 Purchasing something today in the hope of reselling it tomorrow at a higher price is known as _____.
  a. Diversification
  b. Speculation
  c. Indemnification
  d. Financial innovation

Problems and Applications

5.13 Financial instruments exist for the following reasons: to raise capital, store value, reduce risk, or facilitate speculation. Give an example of a financial instrument that is well suited for each of these functions and explain why it is well suited.

5.14 Microlenders have been the subject of some criticism because, although one of the goals of microcredit is to provide impoverished borrowers access to affordable loans, in many cases, the interest rates that are charged for the loans can be quite high. Why might the interest rates be high? What are some consequences of very high interest rates?

5.15 Why do individuals prefer to smooth out their consumption? What tools exist for helping individuals do so?

5.16 [Related to Application 18.2 on page 393] The Fed began raising interest rates between 2004 and May 2006. This resulted in mortgage defaults, and in July 2007, the first major bank failed. The Fed began lowering interest rates shortly thereafter, and by November 2008, the rate was back down to 1%. Why do you suppose reversing the course of interest rates didn't solve the growing economic problems?

5.17 [Related to Application 18.2 on page 393] The U.S. government chose to encourage homeownership by creating Fannie Mae (1938) and Freddie Mac (1970), which purchase home loans made by banks for lump sums of cash. For banks, this created an incentive to make higher-risk loans than they would have had they been fully responsible for the loans. Can you think of a different way for government to have encouraged homeownership that would not have created such a disastrous set of incentives?

Money and the Financial System

This chapter introduced you to the financial system. It explained the functions of money and illustrated how a well-functioning financial system makes it easier for individuals and businesses to buy and sell goods and services and invest money. In this real-time data analysis activity, you'll measure the current money supply and explore the role the financial system played in the Great Recession of 2007–2009, using data from Federal Reserve Economic Data (FRED), a comprehensive, up-to-date data set maintained by the Federal Reserve Bank of St. Louis.

1. Visit the FRED website located at www.stlouisfed.org/fred2.

2. Locate current data about the size of the money supply and its components.

3. Examine how events in the financial sector touched off the Great Recession, and see how those financial-sector events spilled over into the market for goods and services.

MyEconLab

Please visit http://www.myeconlab.com for support material to conduct this experiment if assigned by your instructor.

19

The Federal Reserve: Monetary Policy, Economic Activity, and Inflation

Chapter Outline and Learning Objectives

19.1 **The Origins of the Federal Reserve and Its Tools of Policy,** page 401

Describe how the Fed's four tools of policy affect bank reserves and the money supply.

19.2 **The Money Supply, Interest Rates, and Monetary Policy,** page 406

Explain how the Fed uses its power over interest rates to influence real economic activity.

19.3 **The Art and Implementation of Monetary Policy,** page 409

List and define the three lags of monetary policy.

19.4 **Money and Inflation,** page 415

Discuss the harms that inflation and deflation can do to an economy.

MyEconLab Real-Time Data Activity: Monetary Policy and Inflation, page 425

MyEconLab
MyEconLab helps you master each objective and study more efficiently.

The previous chapter introduced one of the cornerstones of modern financial systems: central banks. The central bank of the United States is called the **Federal Reserve System**, or the Fed. Established by Congress in 1913, the Fed has the sole authority to manage the money supply. Aided by the commercial banking system, the Fed injects money into the economy in carefully metered amounts. By doing so, the Fed tries to gently steer the economy toward goals such as full employment, stable prices, and economic growth. Economists call the Fed's actions to achieve those goals **monetary policy**.

Using monetary policy to achieve economic goals can be quite difficult. This chapter will acquaint you with the mechanics of how monetary policy is conducted, what it is meant to achieve, and the real-world difficulties of designing and implementing monetary policies that are effective. Along the way you'll take a closer look at the origin, structure, and mission of the Fed and also at the role commercial banks play in the money supply process.

Federal Reserve System The central bank of the United States.

Monetary policy The central bank's manipulation of the money supply in order to achieve economic goals such as full employment, stable prices, and economic growth.

The Origins of the Federal Reserve and Its Tools of Policy

As you have learned, a country doesn't actually have to have its own central bank but can instead use another nation's currency to conduct its business. You might be surprised, for example, to discover that the U.S. dollar is the official currency of Ecuador, Palau, Panama, the British Virgin Islands, and a number of other countries, and it is commonly acceptable in many others, including Cambodia, Nicaragua, and Vietnam. So if a country doesn't have to have a central bank, what made the United States decide it needed one? Following a series of banking crises in the late 1800s and early 1900s, the United States created a central bank to help shore up confidence in its banking system.

To understand how a central bank can stabilize the banking system, let's revisit the scenario in which Shelby deposited a hundred coins in the Bank of Taylor (see Chapter 18). Taylor issued Shelby a receipt for those coins and then promptly lent those very same coins to Rose. What happens if Shelby pops into the Bank of Taylor the very next day and asks to redeem her receipt—that is, *withdraw* her money from the bank? Suddenly, Taylor finds herself in a tight spot. She could ask Rose for the money, but it's possible that Rose has already spent it. Besides, Rose's loan contract probably indicates that she doesn't have to pay the money back until some specific date in the future.

Even though our example is simple, it captures the essence of what banks do: They borrow money from depositors and then they lend that money to other people. But if depositors like Shelby can demand their money at any time, how can a bank feel comfortable lending out money for long periods of time to other people—perhaps, say, for car or home loans? How can a bank ensure that it has enough money on hand to meet its customers' withdrawals?

First, on any given day, there are lots of people withdrawing money from their bank, but there are also lots of people depositing money. That helps ensure that the bank has enough money on hand. But there's a second explanation: Banks don't lend out everything they take in as deposits. Instead, they keep some of those deposits safely tucked away in their vaults or in their deposit accounts at the Federal Reserve. The money a bank does not lend out is referred to as its **reserves**. Banks hold reserves for two reasons. First, the Federal Reserve requires them to hold a portion of their deposits in reserve. Those reserves are called *required reserves* and, generally speaking, they must amount to 10% of a bank's total checking account balances.

Banks often hold extra reserves above and beyond what the Federal Reserve requires. Those reserves are called *excess reserves*. Banks hold them because they want to have some funds around in case of unusually large withdrawals. If a bank doesn't hold enough excess reserves, and unexpected withdrawals force it to dip into its required reserves, the bank will have to take action to replenish its reserves or face a fine levied by the Fed.

19.1 Learning Objective
Describe how the Fed's four tools of policy affect bank reserves and the money supply.

Reserves Money that banks do not lend to customers but instead hold in their vault or in their account at the Federal Reserve.

Runs, Clearinghouses, Panics, and the Fed

Let's go back to the pre-Fed days of the early 1900s and combine what you've just learned about banking with a bit of historical perspective. By today's standards, people in those days were relatively poor and didn't have access to the financial markets modern Americans take for granted—like the stock and bond markets, 401(k) plans, and mutual funds. Investing was largely a rich person's game. Nevertheless, there were a lot of ordinary people who had *some* money to save, and often the only way to do that securely aside from burying cash in a coffee can was to deposit that money in a bank.

Bank Runs Money was generally safer in a bank than it was in a coffee can, but there was a cost to putting money in a bank. In the days before the Fed's creation, there was no such thing as deposit insurance: Today's largest insurer, the Federal Deposit Insurance Corporation (FDIC), was created 20 years *after* the Fed. Deposit insurance is a program that guarantees that depositors will be able to recover their money if their bank goes under. FDIC deposit insurance covers up to $250,000 in losses per account.

Without deposit insurance, if your bank went under, you lost your savings. Because of that, bank runs were fairly common. A **bank run** occurs when a bank's depositors all line up at the same time and ask to withdraw their money. Bank runs may be justified when the banks experiencing them are insolvent.[1] *Insolvency* means a bank owes more money to its depositors than it has in cash, loans, and other assets (like its building and its holdings of bonds and other financial instruments).

It makes perfect sense that an insolvent bank's depositors want to get their money back before the bank goes under. But in the early 1900s, a lot of financially sound banks experienced runs, too. In those days, a run could be triggered just by unfounded rumors of insolvency. If you *think* your bank is going to fail, it makes good sense to try to get your money out, even if your bank is actually healthy.

A run is a real and potentially devastating problem for a bank. It wouldn't be a problem, of course, if banks simply took your deposits and sat on them. *"You have $100 to deposit? I'll just wrap it up with this yellow ribbon and write your name on it. It'll be waiting in our vault when you need it."* But banks don't do that; they lend your deposits to people who won't repay those loans for years and years. Remember that one reason banks feel comfortable using their deposits to make loans is because on any given day, new deposits generally offset any withdrawals. That doesn't happen when a bank experiences a run: Its withdrawals greatly exceed its deposits.

Clearinghouses The problem a banker faces during a run is finding cash to pay off the bank's depositors. The cash isn't sitting in the vault with a yellow ribbon around it. It's been loaned out and is moving through the economy to pay for houses, cars, and college tuitions. If you're the banker, you really *do* want to pay off any depositor who asks for his money because if you don't, this will happen: *"Bill! I went down to Security First Trust today to get some cash, and they didn't have enough money to pay me. I think they're in trouble. You'd better get down there and try to get your money before the place goes under!"*

That's all it takes to create a bank run. To stave off such an event, a banker has a few choices. First, she might call in some loans, which means that she pressures some of the bank's borrowers into paying off their loans early. That's tough on everybody and logistically difficult to pull off. Another option is for the banker to sell some of the bank's loans to someone else for cash. That's easier to do because there's already an established market where banks sell loans to one another for reasons unrelated to financial distress.

Many banks also invest their deposit dollars in bonds. The banker could try to sell off some of those bonds to raise the cash the bank needs. But if the bonds have fallen in value since the time the bank acquired them, the banker might have to unload an *extra-large* bunch of bonds to raise enough cash. For example, if the bank sells bonds

Bank run A situation that occurs when many or all of a bank's depositors attempt to withdraw their money at the same time.

---

[1]Bank runs were much more common in the days before deposit insurance, but they still occur today. On September 25 and 26, 2008, depositors ran on Washington Mutual Savings Bank (the sixth-largest bank in the United States) and Wachovia National Bank (the fourth-largest bank in the United States), collectively withdrawing over $20 billion in deposits.

for $400 that it paid $1,000 for, it suffers a $600 loss. This kind of "buy high, sell low" activity can quickly drive even a healthy bank into insolvency.

To avoid that possibility, in the late 1800s and early 1900s, banks often got together and formed clearinghouses. A **clearinghouse** is a group of banks that agree to lend one another money in case of unexpectedly large withdrawals. If a bank in the clearinghouse were experiencing a run, instead of selling off loans or bonds, it could temporarily borrow funds from other banks. Those funds would be paid back later, when the bank's customers, realizing that the bank really *could* meet its obligations, re-deposited their money.

Clearinghouse A group of banks that agree to lend one another money in case of unexpectedly large withdrawals.

Application 19.1

The Fed's Role as a Lender of Last Resort During the Great Recession

The Federal Reserve acts as a lender of last resort to banks. This was critical during the Great Recession of 2007–2009. In the last few months of 2008, banks stopped lending to other banks because they weren't sure about each other's true financial condition. Banks were also reluctant to borrow from the Fed because that might send a bad signal about their stability to their depositors and shareholders.

To overcome the reluctance of banks to borrow money and make loans, the Fed created the *Term Auction Facility (TAF)*. Ordinarily, the Fed's loans to banks are short term. But via the TAF, banks were allowed to borrow money for an extended period of time at attractive interest rates. The favorable terms of the TAF overcame the reluctance banks felt about borrowing from the Fed: Within 18 months, the TAF extended nearly $500 billion of desperately needed credit to the banking system.

Ordinarily, the Fed lends money only to banks. But in the Great Recession, it extended its lender-of-last-resort role to other financial institutions that badly needed cash. The Fed lent money to:

- **High-quality corporations.** The Fed created the Commercial Paper Funding Facility, which lent money to high-quality corporations that were having trouble obtaining short-term credit or honoring their short-term bond obligations.

- **Securities dealers.** The Primary Dealer Credit Facility and the Term Securities Lending Facility lent money to certain securities dealers to stimulate purchases of government bonds and other securities.

- **Investment banks.** The Fed's Money Market Investor Funding Facility lent money to large investment banks so they could, in turn, buy assets from troubled money market mutual funds that badly needed cash.

- **Other investors.** To stimulate consumer and business lending, the Term Asset-Backed Securities Loan Facility extended loans to a variety of investors for the purchase of bonds backed by consumer loans, student loans, and small business loans.

The Fed's mission has evolved over time. But during the Great Recession, the Fed returned to its roots as a lender of last resort, providing about $1.5 trillion in emergency cash to a variety of critical financial institutions. The Fed's creative interpretation of that role may well have prevented a collapse of the financial system.

See related problem 1.14 on page 422 at the end of this chapter.

Based on Lloyd B. Thomas's *The Financial Crisis and Federal Reserve Policy*, Palgrave Macmillan, 2013, and Alan Blinder's *After the Music Stopped: The Financial Crisis, the Response, and the Work Ahead*, Penguin Press, 2013.

Panics Clearinghouse arrangements were an effective means to deal with runs on individual banks. But clearinghouses were ill suited to deal with situations in which many banks in the clearinghouse experienced runs at the same time. How can Fourth National plan on borrowing from Second Guaranty to stave off a run when Second Guaranty is hoping to borrow from Fourth National to stave off a run of its own?

A run on a large number of banks, even those that are financially sound, is called a **panic**. It's called a panic for good reason: You see your neighbor's bank failing, and you start to worry that your bank will fail, too. History is loaded with bank panics. In the United States alone, bank panics occurred in 1819, 1837, 1857, 1873, 1893, 1896, and 1907. Each panic was marked by a large number of bank failures and major losses of wealth, and each resulted in a deep recession or depression.

The Federal Reserve as a Lender of Last Resort During a panic, the banking system needs a source of *new* money that banks can tap into. Following the Panic of 1907, a consortium of banks and the government got together and created that source. They called it the Federal Reserve System, and at its inception in 1913, its mission was to be a **lender of last resort** to the banking system. In other words, if the banking system couldn't come up with enough money during a panic, the Federal Reserve had the power to *create* new money and lend it to troubled banks.

The Federal Reserve, Its Tools of Policy, and the Money Supply

For the first 20 years of the Federal Reserve's existence, serving as a lender of last resort and creating money was basically all the Fed did. But its role in the economy evolved over time, driven by the growing realization that by managing the money supply, the Fed had the power to influence peoples' spending. Peoples' spending, in turn, was linked to things that policymakers and society really cared about, like how fast prices were rising and how many jobs the economy could provide for people who wanted to work. Three decades after the Federal Reserve was created, Congress passed the Employment Act of 1946, which extended the Fed's mission: The Fed was to use its powers of money creation not only to provide new cash to the banking system during panics but also to manage the overall money supply to achieve full employment, stable prices, and a host of other economic objectives.

Chapter 18 described a scenario in which Federal Reserve Chair Janet Yellen dropped $100 bills out of a helicopter in an effort to stimulate the economy. Of course, Janet Yellen doesn't actually drop money from a helicopter. Instead, the Fed uses four distinct tools of policy to influence the money supply: discount window policy, reserve requirement policy, open market operations, and adjustments to the interest it pays banks on their reserve holdings.

Discount Policy Consistent with its original mission as a lender of last resort, the Federal Reserve can lend money. Loans that the Fed makes to commercial banks are called discount loans, and the interest rate the Fed charges for use of those funds is called the **discount rate**.

When a bank borrows $100 from the Fed, either the Fed gives the bank $100 in cash or (more likely) simply credits the bank's reserve account at the Fed with $100. Either way, the bank receives new reserves that weren't previously circulating. The bank can now lend those reserves to its customers, and when it does, the money supply rises.

So if the Fed wants to use discount policy to increase the money supply, it needs to convince banks to borrow more money from the Fed. It does that by reducing the discount rate, making it cheaper for banks to borrow. On the other hand, if the Fed wants to suck some money out of the economy, it can raise the discount rate, which discourages new borrowing and encourages banks with outstanding discount loans to pay them back more quickly.

Reserve Requirement Policy A second way the Fed can influence the money supply is by changing reserve requirements. Suppose that the Bank of Whiskey River has

Panic A run on a large number of banks, even those that are financially sound.

Lender of last resort A function of the central bank to loan money to banks during banking panics.

Discount rate The interest rate the Federal Reserve charges commercial banks for loans.

$1,000 in checkable deposits. Recall that every bank is required to hold 10% of its deposits in the form of reserves, so the Bank of Whiskey River keeps $100 locked away in its vault.

Now suppose that the Fed reduces the reserve requirement from 10% to 4%. The Bank of Whiskey River, which was holding $100 in reserves, is now required to hold only $40. It can lend out the remaining $60, and when it does, the money supply will increase. Note that reserve requirement policy works differently than discount policy: When banks borrow from the Fed, new reserves are created. When the Fed adjusts reserve requirements, no new reserves are created, but some required reserves turn into excess reserves. In either case, however, banks suddenly find themselves with money to lend.

Of course, the reserve requirement doesn't just apply to the Bank of Whiskey River. Exactly the same thing is happening with every other bank in the country, so the change in reserve requirements can potentially unleash a large and rapid increase in bank lending and the money supply. In practice, the reserve requirement is such a powerful tool that the Fed chooses not to use it very often: Reserve requirements were last changed in 1990.

Open Market Operations While it is possible for the Fed to influence the money supply by adjusting the discount rate and the reserve requirement, the Fed has a third policy tool that it has found to be easy to use, direct, and effective. When the Fed wants to increase the money supply, it simply buys something and pays for the purchase with new money. But the Fed needs to buy billions and billions of dollars' worth of things, which cuts down on the time available for comparison shopping. So the Fed buys something there is plenty of—something it can purchase without being particularly choosy: The Fed buys government bonds. Sometimes it buys the bonds directly from a bank, and sometimes it buys them from a securities broker who then deposits the money in his bank. But in either case, the purchase of bonds results in a bank having more money on hand. The purchase or sale of bonds to manipulate the money supply is called **open market operations**.

Open market operations The purchase or sale of bonds by the Federal Reserve to manipulate the money supply.

Suppose the Fed buys $1 million worth of bonds. Some of the money the Fed uses to pay for those bonds will stay in banks' vaults and reserve accounts because the Fed requires banks to hold money in reserve against their deposits. But the bulk of the money the Fed has injected into the banking system can be used to extend loans, and each time a bank makes a new loan, the money supply grows even more. In fact, each new dollar of cash the Fed injects into the economy can create up to $10 of additional money: The Fed's $1 million bond purchase could ultimately cause the money supply to grow by $10 million.[2]

If the Fed decides there's too much money in circulation, it simply reverses the process: It sells some of the hundreds of billions of dollars' worth of bonds that it has purchased in the past. When the public pays for the bonds, the cash spent on the bonds disappears into the Fed, and the money supply falls.

Adjusting Interest on Reserves The fourth tool of policy at the Fed's disposal is a relatively new one. In 2008, the Fed began paying interest on banks' required and excess reserve balances. Remember that banks are free to lend out their excess reserves and that every time a bank makes a loan, the money supply grows. Suppose the Fed is interested in reducing lending activity and money supply growth. With this new tool of policy, the Fed can convince banks to hold on to excess reserves instead of lending them to customers simply by increasing the interest rate paid on reserve deposits. If

---

[2]What economists call the "money multiplier" can, under ideal theoretical conditions, be as high as 10. However, in the real world, it is much lower. That's because banks don't lend out all the money they could; they choose instead to keep excess reserves on hand. It's also because people like to keep some money in the form of cash rather than put it in the bank, where it is available for making loans and, consequently, creating more money. For that reason, the real-world money multiplier generally hovers at about 2.0: Every dollar the Fed injects into the banking system results in one additional dollar being created by the banking system.

instead the Fed wants to stimulate lending and money growth, it can reduce the interest it pays on reserves.

The Money Supply, Interest Rates, and Monetary Policy

The Fed manages the money supply for a reason: It wants to influence the economy. But how exactly does that happen? The Fed sends money coursing into the banking system at the touch of a button. Then banks put that money into peoples' hands by making loans. But how does a bank, sitting on a pile of cash, convince people to borrow that cash?

The Money Supply and Interest Rates

A bank can convince people to borrow more money by reducing the interest rates it charges for borrowing money. That sends a visible signal to the public that money is available. It also makes borrowing money for cars or houses or college tuitions less expensive, which convinces more people to buy cars and houses and send their kids to college.

The Fed starts the ball rolling by injecting the banking system with cash. In the words of economist and public policy expert Charles Wheelan, "Money is like apartments: when there's too much, the rent goes down." Of course, the rent on money is the interest rate, and when the Fed pumps money into banks by buying bonds, it causes that rent to go down.

The rent doesn't go down in just those few banks. It goes down at virtually every bank across the country. Here's how that happens. A big bank finds itself with extra money as a result of the Fed's bond buying. That big bank may well try to get rid of the extra money by dropping its interest rate. But that causes interest rates to go down everywhere else—for two reasons. The first is competition: There are lots of places people can go to obtain loans. If Security First Trust is charging 4% while everyone else is charging 5%, Security First is going to find itself with a long line of people asking for money. Meanwhile, loan departments at other banks are going to look more like mortuaries . . . until they bring their rates down to 4%, too.

The second reason injecting one or two big banks with money causes interest rates to go down everywhere else is because that money doesn't stay in those one or two big banks very long. Do you remember the clearinghouse arrangements banks created, where one bank could borrow money from another in an emergency? Today, there is one gigantic electronic clearinghouse where any bank in the United States can borrow money from any other bank in the United States, for any reason. That clearinghouse is called the *federal funds market*. Despite its name, it doesn't really involve either the Federal Reserve or the federal government in any meaningful fashion: It's a market that consists of loans from one ordinary bank to another. The interest rate that banks charge each other for these loans is called the **federal funds rate**. The federal funds rate is particularly noteworthy because it is a target of Fed policy: The Fed injects or withdraws cash from the economy to push the fed funds rate to the level it desires.

When the Federal Reserve injects a major bank with new cash, rather than wait for its own customers to come in and borrow those funds, the bank often makes those funds immediately available to banks across the country through the federal funds market. To get the attention of banks that might otherwise not know that they have a few billion dollars of new money available, Security First might signal that to the market by dropping the interest rate it charges other banks. To the thousands of banks that might be interested in borrowing in the federal funds market, that interest rate cut signifies something important: Banks now have a cheaper source of funds than they did yesterday. Competition among those banks will force them to pass some of that cost savings along to their customers by reducing the interest rate they charge for loans.

Federal funds rate The interest rate that banks charge each other for loans.

Interest Rates and Real Economic Activity

So, by pumping new cash into the banking system, the Fed can push down the federal funds rate, and other market interest rates tend to follow.[3] As they do, important things begin to happen. First, consumers accelerate their purchases of consumer durables like cars and dishwashers because the cut in interest rates lowers their monthly payments. Second, those same consumers start thinking about buying and building houses: A cut in interest rates not only makes the monthly payment on a new mortgage loan lower than it otherwise might be, but it also encourages homeowners to build bigger and more expensive houses. It's not just consumers that take notice when interest rates start falling. Businesses do, too. Lower interest rates make it cheaper for them to open new businesses, buy new equipment, and expand their facilities.

The Natural Limits of Monetary Policy

More money means lower interest rates, and lower interest rates stimulate more spending. In turn, more spending means more jobs. So should the Fed open the money tap all the way and let everyone have money interest free? Isn't more spending—more homebuilding, more automaking, more venture capital for things like iPods and Facebook, more kids going to college—a good thing?

That kind of spending is problematic for two reasons. One reason is that it assumes that the economy can produce everything consumers want in unlimited amounts. But it can't. Producing bedroom sets and earthmoving equipment requires resources like machinery, land, energy, technology, and labor power, none of which is available in unlimited quantity. As long as society's resources are limited, there's an upper limit to how many goods and services the economy can produce. This means that there's a practical limit to the amount of *real* spending that can occur in an economy. You can pump money into the economy until everyone's houses are filled with trillion-dollar bills, but nobody can use those bills to buy things if those things haven't been produced. In other words, you can't increase the productive potential of the economy by printing more pieces of green paper.

A second problem is this: What happens if everyone has buckets and wheelbarrows full of cash, but there are a limited amount of things to spend that cash on? Suppose 10 very hungry people show up at the only bakery for miles, each carrying $1,000. At the bakery, they find only one loaf of bread available, priced at $2.99. One person snaps up that loaf of bread and takes it to the counter. "I'd like to buy this bread, please," he says. But before the sale can be rung, another customer says, "I'll give you $4 for it!" And the lady behind him says, "$4? I'll pay $5!" Before you know it, those 10 people, who had loads of money but only one loaf to spend it on, have bid up the price of bread to $1,000.

When this happens in an economy, economists say that "too much money is chasing too few goods." In other words, once we bump up against the economy's speed limit—that is, when the economy is producing the maximum amount that it can—adding money to the economy causes prices, not output, to increase.

In the real world, the mechanisms by which prices go up are a bit more subtle. When the Fed pushes interest rates down, that might encourage Southwest Airlines to buy some new airplanes, so it might place an order with Boeing. So far, so good. Boeing might hire some extra workers and start pumping out extra 737s, which is exactly what the Fed wanted to happen. As more orders come in, however, Boeing has a harder time finding new workers. Boeing tries to lure workers away from Airbus, but to do that, Boeing has to offer higher wages. To cover those extra costs, Boeing raises the price it charges for planes.

The same phenomenon also happens in other areas of the economy. In an effort to get their hands on workers and raw materials like steel, automakers try to outbid heavy equipment manufacturers like John Deere and Caterpillar. Facebook tries

---

[3]The Fed's influence over the federal funds rate is powerful but indirect. In contrast, the Fed has complete and direct control over the discount rate. But it chooses not to use that direct control; instead, the Fed simply sets the discount rate a small percentage above the federal funds rate.

to steal programmers from Microsoft, while Microsoft tries to outbid Google for graduating computer science majors. Across the country, the prices of labor and raw materials shoot up as everyone competes for scarce productive resources; businesses then raise the prices of their products to cover those increased resource costs. This is referred to as inflation. We will talk more about inflation later in Section 19.4.

Application 19.2

The Fed's Job Is Easing, but It Isn't Easy

As the Great Recession of 2007–2009 unfolded, borrowers were unsure of their ability to repay loans, and banks were wary of extending credit. As lending by banks faltered, so did spending, and GDP began to plummet. Default-driven bank failures also began to mount: In 2008, 25 banks failed. In 2009, 140 failed. And in 2010, 157 failed.

A well-functioning financial system is vital to the economy. Recessions that are accompanied by banking crises tend to be unusually long and deep. Anxious to stimulate spending and stabilize the faltering banking system, the Federal Reserve began injecting new money into the economy by purchasing short-term government bonds. As the money supply grew, the federal funds rate fell. In August 2007, the rate was 5%. By December 2008, it was just 0.16%.

But decreasing short-term interest rates didn't cause spending to rise, in part because people don't borrow short term to finance homes and durable goods. And because short-term rates were almost zero, the Fed didn't have room to push them much lower. So the Fed reoriented its target and embarked on a program of long-term government and mortgage-backed bond purchases designed to bring down long-term interest rates. That program was called *quantitative easing*.

Quantitative easing, an aggressive three-stage program, began in November 2008 and ended in October 2014. In the first phase, called QE1, the Fed purchased $1.75 trillion of Fannie Mae and Freddie Mac bonds and mortgage-backed securities. In the second phase, QE2, the Fed purchased $600 billion of long-term government bonds. In the third phase, QE3, the Fed pledged to continue large-scale purchases of long-term securities each month until overall conditions in the labor market improved.

As quantitative easing progressed, the 30-year mortgage rate dropped from over 6% to an all-time low of 3.35% in December 2012. During the same time period, the interest rate on 10-year government bonds fell by half, to 1.65%.

When the Fed buys a bond, the *monetary base*, which measures the amount of money the Fed has injected into the banking system, rises. When the recession began, the base was $859 billion. As quantitative easing progressed, the base skyrocketed, surpassing $3 trillion in April 2013.

Those huge cash infusions caused many people to fear inflation. But during the Great Recession, the economy had excess capacity: Many workers and machines sat idle. That gave the Fed room to stimulate the economy with little fear of rising prices. In addition, much of the new cash didn't result in further money creation by the banking system. Rather, banks hung onto a lot of it as excess reserves. That cash was good insurance and a confidence booster for banks, but because it didn't circulate, it couldn't cause inflation. In fact, over the entire QE program, inflation averaged a modest 1.6%.

The Fed held nothing back in fighting the Great Recession. Quantitative easing was unprecedented in scope and magnitude. It provided desperately needed cash to the troubled financial sector and helped drive long-term interest rates to historic lows. Through the forceful and imaginative use of the available tools of policy, the Fed may have prevented the Great Recession from becoming much worse.

See related problem 2.7 on page 423 at the end of this chapter.

When Monetary Policy Is Most Effective

You shouldn't discount the possibility that pumping money into the economy can help create jobs. When the economy *isn't* making full use of its labor and capital (in other words, when there is unemployment and resources are going unused), firms don't have to compete so hard for resources. Pumping a little bit more cash into the economy can temporarily boost its output without creating much inflationary pressure. Economists call actions like this *expansionary monetary policy*. Alternatively, when the economy is at capacity and inflation is mounting, removing some money from the economy can reduce some of the inflationary pressure, with little detrimental impact on output. Economists call actions like this *contractionary monetary policy*.

Let's take a minute to review and synthesize exactly what we know so far about monetary policy:

- If the economy isn't fully using its inputs, like labor and capital, pumping money into it and pushing interest rates downward can stimulate consumption and investment spending. That, in turn, causes businesses to expand production and create jobs.

- If the economy's resources are fully employed, pumping more money into the economy cannot increase output any further. Those extra dollars just increase prices instead.

- If the economy is bumping up against its speed limit in terms of what it can produce and prices are starting to rise, the Fed can remove some money from the economy. A well-calculated action such as this can reduce inflationary pressure but leave output near its potential level.

The Art and Implementation of Monetary Policy

Now you have a picture of what the Fed can do and how it goes about it. It seems pretty simple. The economy is underperforming? Pull some levers, push some buttons, and nudge the economy back up to 100%. The economy is overheating? Push some levers, spin some dials, and remove just enough money to eliminate the inflationary pressure without killing jobs.

Unfortunately, in the real world, monetary policy is less precise and powerful than you've been led to believe. The practical reality is that figuring out which levers to pull—and how far to pull them—is extraordinarily difficult. In other words, being an effective Fed chair is no easy job.

19.3 Learning Objective
List and define the three lags of monetary policy.

The Lags of Policy

The late Milton Friedman of the University of Chicago, who in addition to being a Nobel laureate was perhaps the preeminent macroeconomist of the past half-century, explained why conducting effective monetary policy is so difficult.

Friedman recognized that monetary policy holds great potential power and can do tremendous good if properly applied. But he also pointed out that monetary policy can do great harm to the economy, even when kindhearted and benevolent policymakers try to use monetary policy for the powers of good. If monetary policy isn't conducted in a "Goldilocks" fashion—not too hot, not too cold, but just right—then not only will it fail to "fix" recessions, but it also has the power to make those recessions even more severe and long-lasting.

Friedman based this assertion on his observation that the conduct of monetary policy is hampered by long and variable lags of policy. This means that there is a long time between the time when the need for the judicious application of monetary policy arises and the time when monetary policy actually begins to affect the economy. Think of it in terms of baseball: If you're a batter, and you wait to see where the pitch is going before you start your swing, you're guaranteed to strike out. Good monetary policy requires anticipating the pitch.

The Recognition Lag Friedman's critique of monetary policy breaks down the lags of policy into three types. The first is the recognition lag. The **recognition lag** is the length of time before policymakers realize they need to intervene in the economy. The recognition lag exists because of the timing and quality of the economic data needed to make these decisions. To illustrate, consider GDP data, which is just one of the indicators the Fed uses to determine how the economy is doing. (Similar issues exist with many other indicators, too.) The U.S. Bureau of Economic Analysis produces a GDP number only four times each year, and that number is an estimate based on a sample of the transactions that take place in the economy. But estimates aren't perfectly accurate: More often than not, the Bureau of Economic Analysis later revises the GDP data it has published. It's entirely possible that the original data indicates that the economy is peachy, while the revised data shows the peaches have gone rotten.

> **Recognition lag** The length of time before policymakers realize they need to intervene in the economy.

Another problem with economic data is that even when the values are observable and accurate, it's hard to tell what they could *potentially* be. As you know, the economy has a speed limit. The Fed wants to keep the economy near that speed limit. But it's handcuffed because it doesn't know exactly what that speed limit is. Can GDP potentially grow at 3% this year, or can it grow at only 2.2%? If the economy is capable of growing at 3%, then 2.6% growth is pretty lackluster, and perhaps the Fed should step in. If the economy is capable of permanent growth of only 2.2%, the economy is overheating in an unsustainable way, and there's a danger of inflation, so the Fed should pull back. So, to recap, the recognition lag includes not only the length of time required to figure out how well the economy is doing but also the length of time it takes to figure out how well the economy *could* be doing.

The Implementation Lag Suppose that Fed Chair Janet Yellen has done it: She's gained a true and accurate picture of the state of the economy and determined that it needs a booster shot of monetary stimulus. By pushing down interest rates, she can create an incentive for people to buy more cars, build more factories, and move into larger homes, leaving a trail of job creation in their wake. However, the Fed must deal with some practical and procedural hurdles before it can begin fixing the economy. Friedman called the time it takes to overcome those hurdles the **implementation lag**.

> **Implementation lag** The practical and procedural hurdles that take time and delay the Fed in implementing monetary policy.

First, consider the practical hurdles. By how much will interest rates have to be pushed down to bump GDP up to its potential? Will a quarter of a percentage point do it? Or is a two percentage point reduction the right amount? It can take time to determine the appropriate stimulus because every business cycle is a bit different, and because what works in one downturn may not work in another, and because such a determination relies on the careful statistical analysis of data—data that, you'll remember, may be infrequently gathered or of less-than-hair-splitting accuracy.

There are also procedural issues to deal with. Yellen doesn't make the big decisions at the Fed by herself; a committee makes them. The committee that determines the course of monetary policy is called the *Federal Open Market Committee (FOMC)*, and it consists of the Fed chair, the other six members of the Federal Reserve's Board of Governors (who would, in the real world, be called a board of directors), and, on a rotating basis, the presidents of 5 of the Fed's 12 district banks.

Every six weeks or so, the FOMC meets to discuss the economy and the Fed's stance on monetary policy. After a few days of deliberation and a vote on an appropriate course of action, the FOMC issues a *directive* that tells the New York Federal Reserve District Bank what to do. Specifically, it might tell the New York Fed (which conducts the vast majority of the Fed's financial transactions) to pump money into the economy until interest rates fall by half a percentage point or to suck money out of the economy until interest rates ratchet up a quarter of a percentage point. The time it takes to meet, formulate, and enact policy is the implementation lag.

The Impact Lag Even after the Fed has recognized a need for action and has crafted and implemented a policy response, it takes time for the policy to have an impact. Economists call the period between the time monetary policy is implemented and the time it actually begins to affect the economy the **impact lag**.

Suppose the Fed pumps money into the banking system in an attempt to stimulate the economy. Banks will try to signal their customers that they've got money to lend by reducing the interest rates they charge for money. But the Fed's action won't stimulate the economy until consumers and businesses actually borrow that money and use it to make purchases. Sometimes consumers are receptive to lower interest rates and take advantage of them. But even if consumers and businesses are willing to borrow, economic activity may not begin right away; potential homeowners have to line up funds and satisfy some time-intensive legal requirements before buying; businesses don't immediately start building new factories

But sometimes, even as interest rates fall to lower and lower levels, consumers are still so concerned about their ability to repay loans—perhaps because they are worried that they could lose their jobs during a recession—that they refuse to borrow money. In that case, the Fed's move to pump new money into the banking system will not be immediately effective. In the worst case, individuals and banks simply hoard the new money the Fed injects into the economy and don't spend it at all. That case is generally called a **liquidity trap**, and in such a case, monetary policy is rendered completely ineffective.

Why the Lags of Policy Make Monetary Policy Difficult

Lags of policy are a source of frustration for economic policymakers. To see why the lags make implementing monetary policy so difficult, consider Figure 19.1. The nice straight line represents the long-run potential growth of the economy, or *potential real GDP*, and its upward slope tells us that society is generally capable of producing more goods and services each year than it was the year before. One reason that the economy's potential grows is because the labor force gets bigger each year due to population growth and immigration. A second reason is because the stock of physical capital (tools and equipment used to produce goods and services) generally grows over time. A third reason is that production technology improves over time, allowing society to produce more output (clothes, cars, furniture) with the same amount of inputs (cotton, steel, or lumber).

The economy doesn't always perform exactly at its potential. The wavy line in Figure 19.1 shows the actual behavior of real GDP. Actual GDP is often below potential GDP, and every now and then, the economy superheats and actual GDP rises above potential GDP.

In the real world, however, **business cycles**—the fluctuations of actual GDP above and below potential GDP—are not nearly as regular as shown in Figure 19.1. If you examine the data on expansions (the times when real GDP is increasing) and recessions

Impact lag The period between the time monetary policy is implemented and the time it actually begins to affect the economy.

Liquidity trap A situation in which money created by the Fed to stimulate the economy is hoarded rather than being put to use. The liquidity trap renders monetary policy ineffective.

Business cycle The ordinary fluctuation of real GDP around its long-run trend.

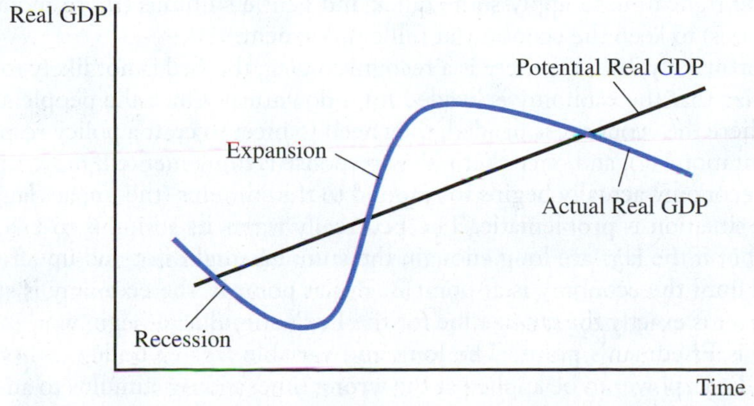

MyEconLab Real-time data

◀ **Figure 19.1**
Actual Real GDP, Potential Real GDP, and the Business Cycle
Over time, an economy's productive potential generally increases due to population growth, capital accumulation, and improvements in technology. Fluctuations of real GDP around its potential are called the business cycle. Recessions drive real GDP below its potential; expansions can temporarily push GDP above its potential.

(the times when, generally speaking, real GDP is falling), you will find that expansions are typically much longer than recessions. Further, sometimes only a few months pass between recessions, while at other times almost an entire decade separates them.

Figure 19.1 can be used to illustrate what the Fed hopes to achieve and the difficulties it faces. When actual GDP is below potential GDP, society is not only creating fewer material things to bring people joy but is also underutilizing its resources. Society is likely to have cyclical unemployment and idle machinery. That can be devastatingly costly to those who want to work but can't find a job, as well as to business owners who have risked substantial chunks of their savings to buy machinery that isn't working to pay them back. It is less obvious, but no less true, that producing above capacity can be bad for society. When actual GDP is above potential GDP, the economy is exceeding its speed limit, and inflation is likely to result. There are real costs associated with rapidly increasing prices, and we will explore them later in this chapter.

If operating below potential GDP is costly and operating above potential GDP is costly, then it seems reasonable that the Fed should try to keep actual GDP as close to potential GDP as it can. That's not easy. So the Fed has settled for a more pragmatic approach. It tries to reduce the size of the business cycle by "leaning against the wind." If the economy is heating up, the Fed tries to slow it down a bit. If the economy is spiraling downward, the Fed tries to give it a little burst of adrenaline. If we were to illustrate what the Fed realistically hopes to achieve, it might look something like Figure 19.2.

▶ **Figure 19.2**

The Practical Goal of Monetary Policy

Through the careful implementation of monetary policy, the Fed hopes to reduce the waviness (or *amplitude*) and duration of the business cycle. This is often referred to as leaning against the wind. Here, stimulus is called for at A, where actual GDP begins to fall below potential GDP. At B, the Fed hopes to restrain the economy as actual GDP rises above potential GDP.

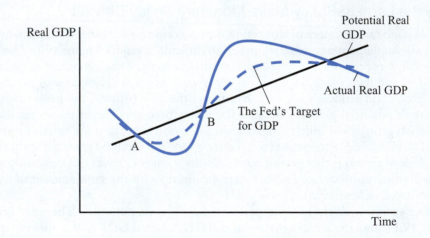

In other words, the Fed hopes to reduce the waviness (or *amplitude*) of the business cycle and keep the economy's actual growth rate close to its potential growth rate. That sounds good in theory, but it's hard to implement in practice, mostly because of the policy lags we discussed. Suppose that the economy is at point A in Figure 19.2: Output is just beginning to fall below its long-run potential. In an ideal world, this is exactly the right time to apply some quick and gentle stimulus (more money, lower interest rates) to keep the economy at full employment.

Unfortunately, because there is a recognition lag, the Fed is not likely to immediately realize that the economy is headed for a downturn. Once the people at the Fed realize where the economy is headed, they need to meet to craft a policy response (the implementation lag), and once that policy response is implemented, more time passes until the economy actually begins to respond to the stimulus (the impact lag).

This situation is problematic. The Fed really wants its stimulus to take effect at point A, but if the lags are long enough, the stimulus might not end up affecting the economy until the economy is at point B. But at point B, the economy is starting to overheat—it is exactly the *wrong* time for the Fed's stimulus to begin working!

This is Friedman's point: The long and variable lags of policy can potentially cause the Fed's power to be applied at the wrong time, adding stimulus to an economy that's already gulped down the equivalent of a double espresso. Perhaps even worse, in an inflationary phase, the Fed's efforts to restrain the economy might not be felt until the economy is already headed downhill on its own. Friedman suggested that the Fed's attempts to steer the economy don't make business cycles smaller but might instead actually make them bigger.

For that reason, Friedman, who believed in the strength and potential power of monetary policy, advocated a Federal Reserve that avoids trying to fine-tune the economy. Instead, he suggested that the Fed follow a *monetary rule* whereby it increases the money supply just enough to pay for the additional goods and services the economy produces without causing any price pressure. If the economy is growing at 3% on average, then the Fed should set a rule whereby it circulates 3% more money each year and promises not to try to react to the ordinary ups and downs of the business cycle. Such restraint, in Friedman's view, may prevent the Fed from making some business cycles smaller, but it also prevents the Fed from making business cycles bigger.

Now you know why the Fed chair's job is so difficult. People tend to think of the Fed chair as an all-seeing, all-knowing, all-powerful Wizard of Oz type who, by turning knobs and pushing buttons, can micromanage the $17 trillion U.S. economy like a tugboat bumping a supertanker up to the dock. But now you know that the Fed really has only one dial to turn: It can pump money into the economy or drain money out, and through those indirect means, it can push interest rates downward or upward. Sometimes that works well, and the Fed provides a stabilizing influence. But sometimes monetary policy might not work so well. Further, during economic downturns, critics often blame the Fed for not reacting properly, quickly, or strongly enough. And when the Fed does respond aggressively to a downturn, it is often criticized by someone else for creating a risk of inflation. The Fed simply can't please all people at all times.

So let's summarize what we know about the Fed's powers to make the business cycle disappear:

- The Fed has a limited but powerful toolkit. Often, the economy responds well to those tools. But if the economy refuses to respond to the Fed's few tools of policy, there's not much else the Fed can do.

- Even if the economy does respond to the Fed's policy measures, because of the lags of policy, the response can potentially come too late to do any good.

- If the economy's response is delayed enough, Fed policy may actually push "with the wind," making business cycles worse.

- The Fed chair, who attempts to manipulate the machinery of a $17 trillion economy, makes less than most university presidents. It's a thankless job for which she is, by market standards, grossly underpaid.

And so, if implementing monetary policy is so difficult, are we out of luck? Or is there something else we can do to fight the business cycle? We'll answer that question in Chapter 20, which is all about taxes, government spending, and the role the federal government plays in keeping the economy healthy.

The People Behind the Theory

Milton Friedman

Milton Friedman was a man of many accomplishments. But his achievements and influence extended far beyond his academic work at the University of Chicago. Friedman is also known for his applied work in economic policy and for his ability to communicate economic ideas to ordinary people. Here is a brief snapshot of these three facets of the late Milton Friedman.

(continued)

Friedman the Academic

Few economists dispute Friedman's position as the most prominent macroeconomist of the latter half of the 20th century. His influence extends to almost every corner of macroeconomic theory. You've seen some of those theories scattered throughout this text, from the theory of the natural rate of unemployment, to the lags of policy, to this famous adage: *"There is no such thing as a free lunch."*

Despite the prominence of his theories, Friedman is perhaps most famous for his research in economic history. Written with Anna Schwartz, his *Monetary History of the United States* presents a scathing critique of Federal Reserve policy during the Great Depression. In Friedman's eyes, bungled policy by the Fed turned what would have been an ordinary recession into a worldwide economic catastrophe:

> *The Great Depression, like most other periods of severe unemployment, was produced by government mismanagement rather than by any inherent instability of the private economy.*[4]

Friedman the Policy Expert

As a founder of the free market–oriented Chicago school of economic thought, Friedman was committed to libertarian ideals and was skeptical of the effectiveness of government planning and programs, no matter how well-meaning. While visiting a developing country in Asia, Friedman accompanied a government official to the site of a new public works project. There, workers with shovels were digging a new canal. When Friedman expressed his surprise at the lack of modern earthmoving equipment, the bureaucrat told him that the project was a jobs program. Friedman calmly replied that if the government was really interested in creating jobs instead of building a canal, it shouldn't have provided the workers shovels; it should have given them spoons: *"One of the great mistakes is to judge policies and programs by their intentions rather than their results."*[5]

Friedman spoke and consulted widely on matters of policy, serving as an advisor to Presidents Richard Nixon and Ronald Reagan and playing a prominent ideological role in economic reforms in Iceland, Chile, Estonia, and the United Kingdom.

Friedman the Apostle

Friedman's commitment to economic education and libertarian ideals made him a media darling. An outstanding speaker and long-time columnist for *Newsweek*, Friedman was asked to create a television program presenting his social and economic philosophies. The resulting series, *Free to Choose*, aired on PBS in 1980; the companion volume Friedman authored with his wife Rose was the bestselling nonfiction book that year. Friedman the apostle was known for the logic of his argumentation, the gentleness of his manner, and his belief in the power of the market to create both opportunity and wealth for ordinary people.

For his devotion to individual liberty, President Reagan awarded Friedman the Presidential Medal of Freedom in 1988. In 2002, President George W. Bush paid tribute to Friedman with these remarks:

> *He has used a brilliant mind to advance a moral vision: the vision of a society where men and women are free, free to choose, but where government is not as free to override their decisions. That vision has changed America, and it is changing the world. All of us owe a tremendous debt to this man's towering intellect and his devotion to liberty.*[6]

Based on Milton Friedman's *Capitalism and Freedom*, University of Chicago Press, 2002; Niall Ferguson's "Friedman's Century," *The Spectator*, July 14, 2012; and Stephen Moore's "Missing Milton: Who Will Speak for Free Markets?" *Wall Street Journal*, May 29, 2009.

---

[4]Milton Friedman's *Capitalism and Freedom*, University of Chicago Press, 2002.

[5]Milton Friedman, Interview with Richard Heffner on The Open Mind (7 December 1975).

[6]www.gpo.gov/fdsys/pkg/WCPD-2002-05-13/html/WCPD-2002-05-13-Pg782-2.htm.

Money and Inflation

As you have learned, when the economy is at full employment, injecting money into it simply drives up prices. Economists call a general increase in the prices of the goods and services people buy **inflation**. Runaway inflation is a serious economic ill. Countries that live with high inflation for a few decades often develop a very strong aversion to it and are willing to take strong measures to get rid of it.

Inflation is so destructive that many of those countries (and other countries as well) have switched to *inflation-targeting* regimes, under which the central bank is committed to maintaining modest inflation. Under such regimes, central banks often face severe penalties, including the termination of key officials, if they fail to meet their low-inflation targets. What's interesting about such arrangements is that those countries have explicitly told their central banks that it is generally more important to keep prices stable than it is to try to fix recessions.

How Is Inflation Calculated?

If policymakers are going to be celebrated for stable prices or castigated for increasing prices, it's probably a good idea to know how the overall level of prices is calculated. In the United States, the most commonly cited measure of the price level is the **consumer price index (CPI)**, which measures the overall cost of living for the typical consumer.

The Bureau of Labor Statistics (BLS) is responsible for computing the CPI. To do that, it first determines what the typical consumer buys; that *basket* of goods and services remains unchanged through time. Then the BLS sends its agents to shopping malls and e-tailers to determine how much it costs to purchase items in that basket.

The cost of maintaining a particular, fixed standard of living can be tracked by comparing the cost of the basket at various points in time. To make snap comparisons simpler, the BLS converts the cost of living into the CPI, which is, as you'll see, slightly easier to interpret than odd dollar amounts. To do that, the BLS designates an arbitrary year as a base year; it then uses the following formula to compute the CPI, which compares the cost of living in any particular year to the cost of living in the base year:

$$\text{CPI} = \frac{\text{Cost of living in current year}}{\text{Cost of living in base year}} \times 100$$

Suppose that the basket costs $464.80 this year, and it cost $332 in the base year. The CPI this year would be:

$$\text{CPI} = \frac{\$464.80}{\$332} \times 100 = 140$$

If you also calculate the CPI for the base year, you'll find that it is 100. Taken together, the calculated value of 140 for the CPI tells you that, on average, what cost $100 in the base year now costs $140. Alternatively, it tells you that prices have risen 40% since the base year.

The CPI can then be used to calculate how fast prices are rising. Specifically, the **inflation rate** measures the percentage change in prices from one year to the next. That can be calculated with this general formula:

$$\text{Inflation rate} = \left[\left(\frac{\text{CPI this year}}{\text{CPI in previous year}} \right) - 1 \right] \times 100$$

So if the CPI in 2015 is 140, and the CPI in 2014 was 132, the inflation rate can be calculated as:

$$\text{Inflation rate} = \left[\left(\frac{140}{132} \right) - 1 \right] \times 100 = 6.06\%$$

19.4 Learning Objective

Discuss the harms that inflation and deflation can do to an economy.

Inflation A general increase in the prices of the goods and services people buy.

Consumer price index (CPI) A measure of the overall cost of living for the typical consumer.

Inflation rate A measure of the percentage change in prices from one year to the next.

The Link Between Money Growth and Inflation

Now you know how the inflation rate is measured. But how is it *determined*? Over longer time horizons, governments have the power to set the long-run rate of inflation wherever they desire. To accomplish that, they don't have to set prices by decree, as is done in lots of developing economies today and has been done for thousands of years

---

Application 19.3

Should the United States Return to the Gold Standard?

In July 2013, Kentucky Senator Rand Paul addressed FreedomFest, an annual convention devoted to discussing libertarian ideals. Paul noted that in the last 100 years, the U.S. dollar had lost 95% of its value to inflation and that the Federal Reserve had failed to maintain the dollar's purchasing power. Paul concluded by expressing interest in exploring the possibility of the United States returning to the gold standard.

The impetus for Paul's remarks was quantitative easing, wherein the Fed was responsible for vast and potentially inflationary increases in the money supply. Under the gold standard, the government would be required, on demand, to redeem dollars for an equivalent amount of gold. That would link the money supply to the government's stock of gold and prevent excessive money growth. Gold proponents assert that such a link would create price stability and prevent the government from using the printing press to pay for excessive spending.

Those potential benefits seem straightforward, but returning to the gold standard would also bring costs. First, the government has less than $400 billion of gold reserves, not nearly enough to back the $2.8 trillion in circulation. Returning to the gold standard would require government to acquire vast amounts of bullion, at tremendous expense.

Further, returning to the gold standard would prevent the Fed from responding to economic crises. Former Fed Chair Ben Bernanke questions the wisdom of outsourcing monetary policy decisions to the quantity of shiny rocks that can be dug from the ground: "[Committing to the gold standard] would mean we are swearing that no matter how bad unemployment gets, we aren't going to do anything about it." That prospect is alarming to many: A recent poll of 40 prominent economists found them unanimously opposed to returning to gold.

Many economists note that gold proponents appear to have false notions of what life under the gold standard was like. Nobel Prize winner Paul Krugman of Princeton University notes that in the gold standard era there were severe financial panics in 1873, 1884, 1890, 1893, 1907, 1930, 1931, 1932, and 1933. James Hamilton, of the University of California, San Diego, further notes that under the gold standard, recessions were more frequent, longer, and deeper than they have been in the fiat money era.

And what about price stability? While there was virtually no long-term inflation in the gold standard era as a whole, there were many shorter cycles of rapid inflation followed by rapid and devastating deflation. Those wildly variable prices lead Krugman and other prominent economists to suggest that people who advocate a return to the gold standard in the name of price stability simply haven't examined the evidence.

See related problem 4.9 on page 424 at the end of this chapter.

Based on Rand Paul's "Why I Plan to Grill Yellen," *Time*, October 11, 2013; "Bernanke: Returning to Gold Standard Would Not Be Feasible for Practical and Policy Reasons," at thinkprogress.org; Paul Krugman's "Gold Instability," *The New York Times*, August 26, 2012; and "Gold Standard," a survey from the University of Chicago's IGM Forum, January 12, 2012.

around the globe. Governments don't have to make it illegal to raise prices. All they have to do is make sure their central banks exercise an appropriate degree of restraint when it comes to printing new money.

To see why, look at Figure 19.3, which plots the average inflation rates for 156 countries over about a decade against the corresponding average rate of growth in each respective country's money supply. The strong correlation between the two demonstrates that countries where the money supply grows the fastest experience higher inflation rates, and a country's central bank has the power to wipe out inflation just by hitting the "off" switch on the printing presses for its currency.

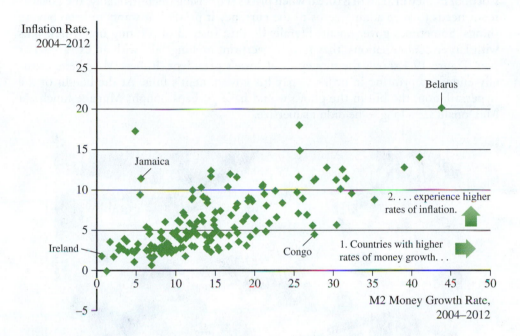

◄ **Figure 19.3**
Money Growth and Inflation in 156 Countries, 2004–2012
The more rapidly a country's money supply grows, the faster prices rise. This suggests that a country can eliminate most inflation simply by limiting the amount of new money it circulates.
Source: World Bank.

The Costs of Inflation

So why might a country want to hit the monetary "off" switch? Why is inflation so bad that nations hate it so much? After all, although inflation makes things more expensive, there *is* more money floating around to help pay for those things. So maybe it's a wash.

That observation contains more truth than you might realize: After all, inflation is an increase in the price of goods and services that get sold, and one of the biggest things anyone sells is his or her labor. The data shows that wages and prices track one another quite well; in periods of inflation, workers are generally successful in obtaining cost-of-living adjustments to their wages that compensate for higher prices.

So if more expensive goods and services aren't the problem, what is? To illustrate, consider Zimbabwe, the site of the planet's most recent **hyperinflation**—a period of very high and accelerating inflation. Over the course of a year, from 2007 to 2008, prices rose so quickly that the Zimbabwe dollar (Zim dollar) lost 99.9% of its value. In 2007, the international business newspaper *The Economic Times* noted that in Zimbabwe, "a loaf of bread now costs what twelve new cars did a decade ago."

Zimbabwe's inflationary spiral was caused by the same thing that causes all major inflationary spirals: The central bank went wild with the printing presses in order to pay the government's bills. In an undeveloped economy like Zimbabwe's, it's often logistically difficult for the government to collect enough sales and income taxes to fund its operations. It's far easier to indirectly collect taxes from money holders. Here's how that works: If the government wants $10 worth of new ribbon for the presidential podium, it simply prints a $10 bill. After government buys its

Hyperinflation A period of very high and accelerating inflation.

ribbon, the $10 continues to circulate, passing from person to person throughout the economy. Of course, a government that's broke is going to have to print a lot more than $10 to stay afloat. It's going to have to print a lot of money. Eventually, the new money printed by the government drives up the price of every other good in the economy, making anyone who had wealth stored in the form of money just a little bit poorer in terms of what that money will buy. No wonder printing money to pay a government's bills is often referred to as an *inflation tax*: Government gets richer, and money holders get poorer.

One of the prices that increases is the price of ribbon. The next time government wants to festoon the presidential podium, it finds that it needs to print $15 worth of money instead of $10. So when prices start rising uncontrollably, the government needs to keep adding zeros to the currency it prints if it wants to keep buying things. Sometimes governments literally do this: Instead of printing brand-new bills with larger denominations, they simply overprint existing bills with an extra zero or two. Figure 19.4 shows the money Zimbabwe's president, Robert Mugabe, eventually ended up printing in order to pay his government's bills. At the height of the hyperinflation, the bill in the photo would have perhaps bought Mugabe lunch. At McDonald's. As long as he didn't supersize.

▶ **Figure 19.4**
Big Money and Rising Prices
At the height of the Zimbabwe hyperinflation, the government was printing $100 trillion dollar bills. Those bills had about the same purchasing power as four U.S. dollars.
Source: Wikimedia commons.

Shoeleather Costs When prices are stable, you can store value across time just by sliding money into your mattress. But when prices are rising, the money you shove in your mattress will buy you less every day that it sits there. So in high-inflation environments, people tend to spend more time than usual trying to protect themselves from rising prices. One way they do this is by looking for financial instruments that can protect them against inflation better than their mattresses can. So people store their money in assets like interest-bearing accounts, gold, or the stock market and then make frequent trips to their banks and brokers to convert those assets to cash when it's needed. Economists call the costs of making those extra trips *shoeleather costs* because that term paints a picture of people wearing out the leather soles of their shoes by running from place to place trying to manage their money.

In Zimbabwe, which lacks the sophisticated financial markets of the developed world, people sought to trade their Zim dollars for other currencies that were better stores of value: the South African rand, Botswana's pula, or the U.S. dollar. Workers were often paid multiple times per day and released from work several times per day so they could convert their earnings into more stable currencies. That's time that could have been spent producing things people value; instead it was wasted as workers scrambled to hang onto the value of the work they'd already performed.

Inflation Distorts Consumption Choices There is, of course, another way that people can prevent their wealth from deteriorating when inflation begins rising. Instead of converting their money into more sophisticated financial assets or foreign currencies, they can simply convert it into goods and services. After all, if everything is getting more expensive, you might as well buy what you can now before prices go up. So inflation causes people who wish to store wealth over time to abandon that goal and spend their money earlier. This doesn't sound so bad, but remember that those people were storing wealth for a reason: Storing wealth helps people smooth out their consumption over their lifetimes. Janet Koech of the Federal Reserve Bank of Dallas reports that in Zimbabwe, store shelves quickly emptied as people rushed to convert the savings they were counting on to fund their retirements into enough groceries to feed their family for the next day or two. How they will be able to buy food when they are old is a real problem. It's likely that many will pay for the actions of their government by working not until retirement but until death. Robert Mugabe is a thief of time, having stolen decades of work from the people he governs.

Inflation Arbitrarily Redistributes Income How would you feel if your professor reached into your wallet without your permission, took out a $20 bill, and gave it to the person sitting next to you? You'd probably be pretty upset.

Although it's subtle, inflation can result in the same kind of indiscriminate redistribution of wealth. The redistribution occurs in a number of ways. As an example, consider how an unexpected burst of inflation may redistribute wealth to people who owe other people money. Suppose you are a hard-working person living in Zimbabwe in 2005. You've amassed 100,000 Zim dollars by working and saving for several decades. By local standards, you are quite wealthy. One day, your cousin, an egg farmer, asks to borrow your 100,000 Zim dollars so that he can build a new house. You agree, he builds the house, and you start receiving a steady stream of repayments.

A short time passes, and Robert Mugabe starts the monetary Xerox machine. Prices rise, and before long, a dozen eggs cost a million Zim dollars. The next thing you know, your cousin the egg farmer shows up at your door with his loan contract in one hand and a 100,000 Zim bill in the other. "I'm ready to pay off my loan," he says. The 100,000 Zim dollars that you worked your entire life for won't buy you a decent meal. That work has been taken from you and embodied in a house that your cousin paid for with about a minute's worth of his earnings. *That's* how an unexpected burst of inflation redistributes money: Borrowers of money win, and lenders lose.

The End of Inflation

A hyperinflation eventually shuts down the economy. As prices rise, the value of accumulated wealth erodes; eventually people are forced to stop buying things. Stores selling goods and people selling their labor eventually refuse to accept payment in currency that is likely to become worthless within a few minutes. Some people resort to inefficient barter; those lucky enough to hold some foreign currency may use that to conduct transactions instead. Others withdraw from market activity entirely. With few people buying and selling, economic activity may collapse, as it did in Zimbabwe. The unemployment rate eventually hit an astonishing 80%. Eventually, Mugabe gave up printing new Zim dollars because he couldn't find anyone willing to accept them, no matter how many zeros he put on them.

Milder inflations, of course, have milder consequences. But the costs we've described can still be felt even when prices aren't rising at a million billion percent each year. Economies with sustained high inflation also generally have very low GDP growth rates. The hidden costs of the inflation manifest themselves in distorted incentives to save and invest, which stifle growth. When inflation isn't rising rapidly, businesses find it easier to plan for the future: They like to know what they'll be selling their products for in the future, and how much they'll be paying for their inputs. That's much easier to do in a low-inflation environment. As inflation escalates, it also becomes more volatile, bringing with it uncertainty about future prices that causes businesses to be overly cautious when it comes to building new factories and launching new product lines. It comes as no surprise to economists, then, that the greatest economic miracles of the 20th century—the economies of Germany and Japan, which rose from the rubble at the end of World War II to become economic superstars—happened in two of the countries most determined to stabilize their prices.

One key to ending inflation (or to keeping it low in the first place) is separating the central bank from the government. That keeps the government from treating the central bank like its own personal Visa card every time it wants to buy something, and it also keeps the government from leaning on the central bank to aggressively stimulate the economy every time there's an election. An independent central bank is free to pursue monetary policy goals without pressure or interference from a self-interested government.

The creators of the U.S. Federal Reserve System took great pains to ensure its independence:

- The Federal Reserve Act of 1913 divided the country into 12 regions, each with a Federal Reserve branch that was originally charged with implementing policy in that region.
- Federal Reserve governors (the major policymakers at the Fed) are appointed by the president to long, 14-year terms, and they cannot be fired. This frees them to conduct policy without fear of reprisal.
- Federal Reserve governors cannot be reappointed. This eliminates the incentive for governors to curry favor with the government at reappointment time.
- The Federal Reserve is not a part of or under legal control of any branch of the government.
- The Fed does not depend on government funding. Rather, it funds its operations from the interest it earns on its bond holdings.

It's clear that even in 1913, when the Fed was established, people understood the importance of separating monetary policy from government. A century's worth of evidence supports that understanding: Over long time horizons, the more independent a country's central bank is, the lower the inflation that country experiences.

Inflation does not generally fix itself: It can continue for decades, all the while extracting a meaningful toll on a country's economic performance. Fixing inflation requires discipline and restraint, which is why so many high-inflation countries have freed their central banks from the obligation of fixing business cycles and directed them to concentrate solely on stabilizing prices. In Zimbabwe, the government eventually sought outside help in exercising that restraint: It stopped printing Zim dollars and adopted a new and much more stable currency in the hope that arresting inflation would help revitalize the economy. The dollars circulating in Zimbabwe today are U.S. dollars.

If Inflation Is Bad, Is Deflation Good?

Rising prices can take a heavy toll on an economy. But falling prices can, too. When prices of goods and services in an economy are falling, economists say we are experiencing **deflation**. Here's why deflation can be a devastating phenomenon. First, economic activity tends to slow as consumers attempt to postpone purchases: Why buy today what you can buy cheaper tomorrow? As a result of its impact on spending, deflation can lead to recession.

Second, deflation tends to be accompanied by lots of loan defaults. To explain why, suppose that you are a doughnut maker, and your doughnuts sell for $1 each. You decide to take out a $40,000 loan for a new car. Paying off that loan is going to require you to sell 40,000 of your doughnuts (assuming that you got 0% financing on the car!). Now suppose that deflation forces the price of your doughnuts down to $0.80. Instead of having to sell 40,000 doughnuts to pay off your car, you'll have to sell 50,000; you'll have to work harder and sell more, and you'll have to do this at a time when your customers are actually trying to postpone their purchases and buy less.

Deflation A period of falling prices of goods and services in an economy.

If you fail to sell those extra doughnuts, you'll go into default. In other words, deflation affects peoples' behavior in the market for goods and services, and it also affects financial markets.

The Federal Reserve was deeply concerned about the possibility of deflation during and immediately after the Great Recession. That concern was one justification for the massive scale of quantitative easing. The Fed drew its lessons from Japan, where policymakers did not aggressively fight deflation following a financial system collapse in the early 1990s. Two decades later, Japan was still wrestling with chronic deflation, and the Japanese economy, one of the most dynamic and rapidly growing economies in the world between 1950 and 1990, was stagnant. Between 1991 and the beginning of Japan's own version of the Great Recession in 2007, Japan's real GDP grew at a paltry 1.1% annually. Japanese citizens are now calling those years the "lost two decades."

Conclusion

It is extremely difficult for the Federal Reserve to implement successful monetary policy. With a limited set of tools, the Fed attempts to smooth the ups and downs of the business cycle. The effectiveness of Fed policy in doing that depends on the power of the Fed's tools and the length of the lags of policy. In stabilizing business cycles, the Fed must also be mindful of the effects of its policy on prices. Too much stimulus can cause inflation; too little can contribute to deflation. Unfortunately, there is no set prescription for the Fed to follow: Every business cycle is different. This means that conducting monetary policy is part science, but is also part art.

Chapter Summary and Problems

Key Terms

Bank run, p. 402

Business cycles, p. 411

Clearinghouse, p. 403

Consumer Price Index (CPI), p. 415

Deflation, p. 420

Discount rate, p. 404

Federal funds rate, p. 406

Hyperinflation, p. 417

Impact lag, p. 411

Implementation lag, p. 410

Inflation, p. 415

Inflation rate, p. 415

Lender of last resort, p. 404

Liquidity trap, p. 411

Monetary policy, p. 401

Open market operations, p. 405

Panic, p. 404

Recognition lag, p. 410

Reserves, p. 401

19.1 The Origins of the Federal Reserve and Its Tools of Policy, pages 401–406

Describe how the Fed's four tools of policy affect bank reserves and the money supply.

Summary

When a commercial bank experiences a bank run, it needs to come up with cash quickly. In the past, banks supported one another by lending emergency cash to banks in trouble. But in a panic, when many banks need emergency cash at the same time, banks cannot look to one another. Congress created the Federal Reserve in 1913 to supply the banking system with new emergency cash during panics. The Fed's mission has evolved, and the Fed is now charged with stabilizing the macroeconomy. It has four tools at its disposal: discount policy, reserve requirement policy, open market operations, and adjusting the interest rate it pays on bank reserves.

Review Questions

1.1 The actions the Fed takes in order to gently steer the economy toward goals such as full employment and stable prices are referred to as _____.

1.2 _____ are reserves held by banks due to Federal Reserve requirements. Additional reserves beyond those are called _____.

1.3 If a bank owes more money to its depositors than it has in loans and other assets, it is considered to be _____.

1.4 A(n) _____ is a run on a large number of banks, even those that are financially sound.

1.5 The purchase or sale of bonds to manipulate the money supply is called _____.

1.6 A _____ exists when a bank's depositors try to withdraw their money at the same time.
   a. Bank run
   b. Panic
   c. Clearinghouse
   d. Portfolio imbalance

1.7 In addition to serving as a lender of last resort, the Fed's powers were expanded with the _____, which directed the Fed to use its powers to achieve full employment, stable prices, and other economic objectives.
   a. Employment Act of 1946
   b. Federal Reserve Act of 1944
   c. Banking Act of 1935
   d. Federal Reserve Reform Act of 1956

1.8 A _____ serves as an extra source of money if the banking system does not have enough in its reserves during a panic.
   a. Mutual fund
   b. Depository
   c. Lender of last resort
   d. Clearinghouse

1.9 Which of the following policy actions can the Fed implement to stimulate the economy?
   a. Increasing the money supply
   b. Increasing the discount rate
   c. Increasing the reserve requirement
   d. All of the above will stimulate the economy.

1.10 The interest rate the Federal Reserve charges when it lends money to banks is the _____.
   a. Federal funds rate
   b. Prime rate
   c. Treasury rate
   d. Discount rate

1.11 If the Fed wants to decrease the money supply, it should _____.
   a. Buy bonds
   b. Sell bonds
   c. Neither buying nor selling bonds will affect the money supply.

Problems and Applications

1.12 Explain the difference between a bank panic and a bank run. Is one more serious than the other? Why?

1.13 List three options a bank can use to raise cash when it experiences significant withdrawals.

1.14 **[Related to Application 19.1 on page 403]** Explain how, during the Great Recession of 2007–2009, the Fed went beyond its mandate to serve as a lender of last resort to the banking system. List one potential negative consequence that might have occurred had the Fed not gone beyond its mandate.

19.2 ## The Money Supply, Interest Rates, and Monetary Policy, pages 406–409

Explain how the Fed uses its power over interest rates to influence real economic activity.

Summary

The focus of the Fed's policy is the federal funds rate. When the Fed injects new money into the economy, the federal funds rate decreases. Other interest rates tend to follow. By lowering the cost of borrowing, interest rate decreases encourage consumers and businesses to make new purchases. However, if the economy is already at its productive limit, new money simply drives up prices. To slow a booming economy, the Fed can withdraw money from the economy, increase interest rates, and discourage consumer and business purchases.

Review Questions

2.1 The modern clearinghouse where any bank in the United States can borrow money from any other bank in the United States is called the _____.

2.2 Increasing the money supply to boost an ailing economy is known as _____.
   a. Contractionary monetary policy
   b. Recessionary monetary policy
   c. Aggressive monetary policy
   d. Expansionary monetary policy

2.3 When the Fed aggressively increases the money supply, interest rates tend to _____.
   a. Increase
   b. Decrease
   c. The money supply has no effect on interest rates.

2.4 To slow down an overheating economy, the Fed needs to _____.
   a. Increase interest rates
   b. Reduce interest rates
   c. Hold interest rates steady but reduce reserve requirements
   d. Buy bonds

Problems and Applications

2.5 When the economy is headed into recession, should the Fed increase interest rates or reduce them? Explain how the change you recommend will influence consumers and businesses.

2.6 Suppose that the economy is overheating. What actions do you recommend the Fed take? Specifically, address the desired level of interest rates, money growth, and bond purchases or sales.

2.7 **[Related to Application 19.2 on page 408]** How did the Fed's program of quantitative easing in response to the Great Recession differ from an ordinary expansion of the money supply? Be sure to address both its goals and its implementation.

19.3 **The Art and Implementation of Monetary Policy, pages 409–414**

List and define the three lags of monetary policy.

Summary

Fine-tuning the economy with monetary policy is difficult because of long and variable lags of policy. The recognition lag is the time it takes to discover that monetary policy is needed. The implementation lag is the time it takes to formulate and implement an appropriate policy. The impact lag is the time it takes for the policy to work. Lags reduce the effectiveness of monetary policy, and because of lags, monetary policy can possibly be destabilizing.

Review Questions

3.1 The length of time that passes between when the economy moves away from full employment and when policymakers realize that this move has occurred is called the _____.

3.2 The period of time between when monetary policy is implemented and when it begins to affect the economy is called the _____.

3.3 A central bank that was under the direction of Milton Friedman would follow a(n) _____, whereby it would increase the money supply just enough to pay for the additional goods and services the economy produces without causing any price pressure.

3.4 The fluctuations of actual GDP around potential GDP are called _____.
   a. Waves of pessimism
   b. Economic phases
   c. Financial progressions
   d. Business cycles

Problems and Applications

3.5 Suppose newspapers are printing stories stating that the country is heading for a recession. A friend who has read these newspapers believes that the Fed should immediately expand the money supply to prevent a downturn. What arguments might you make to help him understand why the Fed might take some time to respond? What arguments might he make in favor of immediate action?

3.6 Suppose that Friedman's hypothesis about the long and variable lags of policy is correct—that rather than being a stabilizing influence, the Fed is *destabilizing*. Replicate Figure 19.1 on page 411, and then add a new curve to show what the business cycle looks like when a destabilizing Fed implements monetary policy.

3.7 Summarize the pros and cons of using a monetary rule instead of discretionary monetary policy.

19.4 Money and Inflation, pages 415–421

Discuss the harms that inflation and deflation can do to an economy.

Summary

The CPI measures the overall level of prices. Inflation is an increase in that overall level of prices. Hyperinflation is very high and accelerating inflation. Deflation is a decrease in the overall level of prices. Over longer periods of time, the inflation rate is strongly related to how quickly a country increases its money supply. Inflation imposes costs on society: People devote more resources to protecting wealth and accelerate their consumption of goods and services. Inflation also redistributes income from lenders to borrowers. Inflation can be stopped by slowing the growth of the money supply. The more independent a country's central bank is, the more easily it can prevent inflation.

Review Questions

All problems are assignable in MyEconLab.

4.1 A general increase in the price of goods and services is called _____.

4.2 A central bank that is committed to maintaining modest inflation is said to have a(n) _____ regime.

4.3 _____ is a period of pronounced and accelerating inflation.
- **a.** Deflation
- **b.** Expansion
- **c.** Hyperinflation
- **d.** Superinflation

4.4 When high inflation causes people to spend more time managing their money, the costs of that extra management are called _____.
- **a.** Commissions
- **b.** Adjustment costs
- **c.** Shoeleather costs
- **d.** X-inefficiencies

4.5 The more closely tied a country's central bank is to its government, _____.
- **a.** The lower its inflation rate tends to be
- **b.** The higher its inflation rate tends to be
- **c.** The relationship between the central bank and the government has no impact on the inflation rate.

Problems and Applications

4.6 Explain why printing money to pay a government's bills is often referred to as an inflation tax.

4.7 The Fed increases the money supply with the goal of increasing economic activity. Does this policy prescription work for increasingly larger increases in the money supply? Why or why not?

4.8 Inflation is generally regarded as a serious economic ill. Who suffers when inflation accelerates? Does anybody benefit?

4.9 **[Related to Application 19.3 on page 416]** During the past few years, it has become more popular for people to invest in gold and other precious metals. What actions taken by the Fed in the past decade or so have contributed to the popularity of gold? Why?

4.10 Suppose that in 2025, the basket of goods and services purchased by the typical consumer cost $882. In 2026, the same basket cost $965. Compute the CPI for both 2025 and 2026, using 2025 as the base year. Then calculate the inflation rate between 2025 and 2026.

4.11 Suppose there is a massive deflation. Discuss how that deflation redistributes income between borrowers and lenders.

Monetary Policy and Inflation

This chapter introduced you to the art and practice of monetary policy. The chapter highlighted discretionary monetary policy, which refers to the central bank's manipulation of the money supply and interest rates to moderate the business cycle. The chapter emphasized both the promise of discretionary policy and its potential pitfalls. In this real-time data analysis activity, you'll explore the conduct and effectiveness of monetary policy using data from Federal Reserve Economic Data (FRED), a comprehensive, up-to-date data set maintained by the Federal Reserve Bank of St. Louis.

1. Visit the FRED website located at www.stlouisfed.org /fred2.

2. Examine how the Federal Reserve used its tools of policy to manage the money supply and interest rates during the Great Recession of 2007–2009.

3. Explore some of the factors that limited the Federal Reserve's ability to stimulate the economy when the Great Recession was at its worst.

4. Gather current data to calculate today's inflation rate.

MyEconLab

Please visit http://www.myeconlab.com for support material to conduct this experiment if assigned by your instructor.

The potential losses that banks face when selling bonds discussed in Section 19.1 depend on the way banks account for changes in the value of their assets. Today, banks are required to value bonds at current market value and account for potential losses on a day-to-day basis. But in the early 1900s, banks valued bonds at their historical costs and were not required to account for losses until the bonds were sold. Because this section focuses on the historical reasons for creating the Federal Reserve, the second accounting approach is discussed in the text.

For more information about the relationship between central bank independence and economic performance, see Alberto Alesina and Lawrence Summers's "Central Bank Independence and Macroeconomic Performance: Some Comparative Evidence," *Journal of Money, Credit and Banking*, 1993; and Jeroan Klomp and Jakob de Haan's "Inflation and Central Bank Independence: A Meta Regression Analysis," *Journal of Economic Surveys*, 2010.

The Federal Government: Taxes, Spending, and Fiscal Policy

Chapter Outline and Learning Objectives

20.1 Government Revenue, page 428

List and define the major sources of federal government revenue.

20.2 Government Expenditures, Deficits, and Debt, page 435

Explain the difference between mandatory and discretionary expenditures and between the federal government's budget deficit and the federal debt.

20.3 The Future of the Federal Budget, page 440

Discuss how changes in the age of the U.S. population will affect the federal budget over the next four decades.

20.4 The Federal Government and Fiscal Stabilization Policy, page 442

Describe two fiscal policy tools that government can use to help fight recessions and explain when those tools are likely to be most effective.

MyEconLab Real-Time Data Activity: Budget Deficits and the Federal Debt, page 453

MyEconLab

MyEconLab helps you master each objective and study more efficiently.

In July 2011, the government of the United States was almost forced to shut down because it was running out of money. By the end of the month, it wouldn't be able to pay its employees, power its air conditioners, or shuttle the president between the White House and Capitol Hill. The president and Congress, fighting over future taxation and spending policies, played a dramatic game of chicken during that critical July. The stakes were high: If they could come to an agreement, Congress would enact legislation enabling the government to borrow what it needed. Otherwise, the government would cease operating. Each refused to yield. As the end of the month drew near, the government's financial reserves drew ever closer to exhaustion.

Funding-related shutdowns (and near shutdowns) aren't that uncommon—there were several in the 1980s and 1990s, and another in 2013. You might think it odd that the government can run out of money. After all, the federal government takes in almost $3 *trillion* dollars in taxes each year. If you counted ten $100 bills each second for your entire lifetime, you still couldn't get close to what government takes in during a single year. But as good as government is at collecting money, it's even better at spending it: During the period from 2005 to 2014, the federal government spent about $800 billion more each year than it took in from taxes.

This chapter discusses the federal government's taxing and spending policies. You'll learn where the government gets its revenue and how it has structured the tax code. You'll also learn how the government spends its money. In addition, this chapter addresses several important questions:

- When the government spends more than it takes in, how does it make up the difference?
- Is the U.S. government's pattern of spending more than it takes in sustainable? If not, why not?
- Can a government's tax policy stimulate or slow economic growth?
- Can a government's taxing and spending practices be used to revive a struggling economy?

Fiscal activities Activities related to how the federal government raises revenue and manages its spending.

Discussing a government's **fiscal activities**—how it raises revenue and how it spends that revenue—almost invariably involves facts and figures that will undoubtedly change after you complete the course. However, what you will learn in this chapter about the U.S. government's current fiscal activities will help you understand the challenges the United States will face in the future. This is important because those challenges are very much *your* challenges: The government you elect today will make choices that will materially affect the way you live when you are middle-aged and older.

20.1 Learning Objective

List and define the major sources of federal government revenue.

Government Revenue

The federal government of the United States raises about $2.9 trillion to fund its operations each year. It only seems natural to ask where that $2.9 trillion comes from. It turns out that the government has its fingers in lots of pies. Figure 20.1 shows the sources of federal government revenue for 2014.

The federal government collects money through fees, fines, and registrations. It collects still more money via taxes of various kinds, including excise taxes on products like gasoline, taxes on many imported goods, and taxes on the estates of the deceased. But as Figure 20.1 shows, those are *very* small pies, accounting for only about 6% of the total revenue the government collects annually. The big revenue sources are the ones that are both obvious and familiar to you: income taxes and payroll taxes. Both of those taxes are generally based on what you earn. However, they are applied differently, both in terms of how much the government collects per dollar of earnings and, oddly, in terms of where those earnings actually came from.

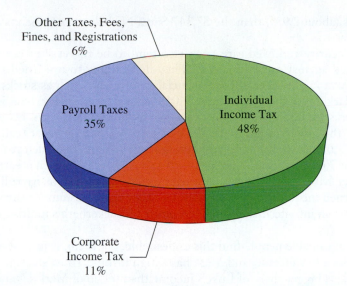

Other Taxes, Fees, Fines, and Registrations 6%

Payroll Taxes 35%

Individual Income Tax 48%

Corporate Income Tax 11%

◀ **Figure 20.1**
Sources of Federal Government Revenue, 2014
The largest part of the federal government's revenue comes from individual and corporate income taxes and payroll taxes.
Source: Office of Management and Budget.

Payroll Taxes

If you've ever worked for a paycheck and then taken a close look at your pay stub, you've probably noticed that before you were paid, a little less than 10% of your paycheck disappeared into something called "FICA." FICA stands for *Federal Insurance Contributions Act*, which dates back to 1935. The money collected as a result of the act funds the nation's Social Security and Medicare programs. FICA contributions are mandatory **payroll taxes** that both you and your employer must pay if you work for money in the United States. They are called payroll taxes because your employer will submit them on your behalf each payday. Payroll taxes are collected only on *earned income* and are calculated as a percentage of that income. Earned income is income from paid work, the kind you receive a paycheck for. Payroll taxes are *not* collected on investment income, inheritances, or, if you're so lucky, lottery winnings.

Here's how payroll taxes work: Every time you earn $1 at work, the government takes 6.2 cents from you and directs it to the Social Security Administration. The government also takes an additional 6.2 cents from your employer, for a total of 12.4 cents. The government keeps doing this until your earnings reach about $118,500, at which point the government says, "This guy has paid in enough. We won't collect any more from him or his employer this year." This means that the typical college president, who earns $250,000 each year, and Satya Nadella, who is the CEO of Microsoft and who makes well over $1 million, pay exactly the same amount annually (about $7,347) to the Social Security Administration.

The government goes through the same process to fund the Medicare program, which provides medical care for senior citizens. The Medicare tax is smaller than the Social Security tax: The government takes only 1.45 cents per dollar earned from the employee, plus a 1.45-cent match from the employer. However, there is no threshold on earnings beyond which the Medicare tax collections stop. As a result, Satya Nadella pays much more to Medicare than does the typical university president.

For many people, the payroll taxes related to FICA are the biggest taxes they pay. And unlike income taxes (which will be discussed soon), there is absolutely no way to reduce the amount of payroll taxes you pay except to earn less.

A notable feature of these payroll taxes is that they are regressive. A **regressive tax** takes a larger share of the income of low-income taxpayers than it does from high-income taxpayers. Social Security taxes are regressive for two reasons. First, because government stops collecting tax on earned incomes above $118,500, people who make less than that will pay 6.2% on *everything* they earn, whereas people who make more than that will pay 6.2% on just part of their earnings. In other words, the $7,347 the typical university president pays represents a much bigger fraction of

Payroll tax A mandatory tax that both workers and employers in the United States pay to fund Social Security and Medicare; calculated as a percentage of each worker's pay.

Regressive tax A tax that takes a larger share from the income of low-income taxpayers than it does from high-income taxpayers.

her earnings (about 2.9%) than the $7,347 Satya Nadella pays (which is about 0.7% of his earnings).

Social Security and Medicare taxes also tend to be regressive because they are only collected against earned income. They don't apply to unearned income, like the income you might receive from financial investments such as stocks and bonds. Consider Mark Zuckerberg, the owner of Facebook. Zuckerberg, who is fabulously wealthy, works for a salary of $1 per year but makes millions from his investments. In contrast, the guy who mops the floor at the local burger joint (call him Luke) works for $15,000 per year and earns nothing from investments. Each year, Luke pays $1,147.50 (or 7.65%) in payroll tax against that income, all of which is earned income. On the other hand, Mark Zuckerberg pays exactly 7.65 *cents* in payroll tax against his $1 of earned income. That's not only a smaller absolute amount than Luke pays, but it's almost an infinitesimally small *percentage* of Zuckerberg's multi-million-dollar income.

Lots of reasonable people find this undesirable. To them, it just *sounds* wrong to say, "Luke has a low income, and Mark has a high income, so let's design a tax policy where we take a bigger share of Luke's income than we do of Mark's."

Of course, neither the Social Security program nor the Medicare program is all cost and no benefit. People pay into those programs during their working years, but they draw money out of the same programs once they retire. To determine whether a program as a whole is regressive, we also need to know how much Luke and Mark receive in benefits. For now, however, let's focus only on the "paying in" side of things and deal with the "drawing out" side when we talk about the federal government's spending. It's sufficient for now to say that payroll taxes are a major source of government revenue, accounting for about 35% of all the money the government takes in.

Income Taxes

Income tax Tax on the income of individuals, families, and corporations.

In addition to the payroll tax, the other major source of government revenue is the **income tax**, which is collected against the earnings of individuals, families, and corporations. The income tax works exactly like it sounds: Earn a dollar of income, and the government claims a piece of that dollar for itself. Fail to deliver what the government claims, and you'll find yourself enjoying an all-expenses-paid vacation in a federal correctional resort. Unlike payroll taxes, income taxes apply to both earned income *and* unearned income. That unearned income includes income from investments as well as other sources, such as large gifts and, of course, your lottery winnings. Some types of investment income, however, are treated specially and are taxed at a lower rate than other forms of income.

The Individual Income Tax In the United States, income taxes are collected from two different sources. *Individual income taxes* are collected from households. *Corporate income taxes* are levied against the earnings of corporations. By far the bigger of the two is individual income taxes, which alone make up about 48% of the government's revenues. Corporate income taxes make up a much more modest 11%.

Marginal tax rate The tax rate you pay on an *additional* dollar of income.

Not every dollar of your income is taxed at the same rate. You might never realize that if you use TurboTax to compute your tax bill each year, or if you simply consult the tax tables that the Internal Revenue Service (IRS, the government's official tax collector) prints for you. There, you simply look up your taxable income, and in the next column you find printed exactly how many dollars you owe. But all those numbers are defined by a carefully constructed formula that is based on marginal tax rates. The **marginal tax rate** is the tax rate you pay on an *additional* dollar of income.

A look at the tax code may help explain what this means. Table 20.1 illustrates the 2014 marginal tax brackets for a single taxpayer.[1]

---

[1]If you are married and file your taxes as a couple, or if you file your taxes as a head of household, the dollar thresholds change, but the structure of marginal rates is the same.

Table 20.1   U.S. Marginal Tax Brackets, 2014

In the United States, the more you earn, the higher the applicable marginal tax rate. The top marginal tax rate is 39.6%.

Taxable Income Range	Marginal Tax Rate
$0 to $9,075	10%
$9,076 to $36,900	15%
$36,901 to $89,350	25%
$89,351 to $186,350	28%
$186,351 to $405,100	33%
$405,101 to $406,750	35%
$406,750 and above	39.6%

Source: Internal Revenue Service, www.irs.gov/pub/irs-drop/rp-13-35.pdf.

Suppose that after you graduate from college, you get a good job that pays $80,000 a year. How much money will you owe in income taxes? To figure this out, you need to break your income into chunks that will be taxed at different rates. The first $9,075 is taxed at 10%. The next $27,825 of your income ($36,900 − $9,075) will be taxed at 15%. And the remaining $43,100 ($80,000 − $36,900) will be taxed at 25%. Table 20.2 illustrates how your total tax is computed.

Table 20.2   Hypothetical Tax Calculation for an $80,000 Income

The total tax owed is found by breaking down income into chunks taxable at different rates, computing the tax owed on each chunk, and adding the chunks to find the total.

$80,000 Income, Sorted into IRS Income Ranges	Income Taxable	Applicable Marginal Tax Rate	Tax Owed
$0 to $9,075	$9,075	10%	$907.50
$9,076 to $36,900	$27,825	15%	$4,173.75
$36,901 to $80,000	Remaining $43,100	25%	$10,775.00
	Total Income: $80,000		Total Tax Due: $15,856.25

Your total tax due is $15,856.25. That includes the $907.50 you owe on the first chunk of your income, the $4,173.75 you owe on the second chunk, and the $10,775 you owe on the third chunk.

You may have noticed that the more money you make, the higher the marginal rate that applies to your income. That suggests that the income tax system, unlike the payroll tax system, may not be regressive. To determine if that's true, let's do an additional calculation. Instead of looking at the marginal tax rate you face, let's look at your **average tax rate**, which indicates how much of the *typical* dollar you take in must ultimately be sent to the government.

Calculating the average tax rate is easy. Simply take your total tax bill and divide by your income. Then multiply your answer by 100 to convert it to a percentage:

$$\text{Average tax rate} = \frac{\text{Total tax}}{\text{Taxable income}} \times 100$$

Using this formula, your average tax rate is: ($15,856.25 ÷ $80,000) × 100 = 19.82%. In other words, on average, you need to send $1 out of every $5 to the federal government.

Notice that there's a difference between your marginal and average tax rates: The marginal rate is higher. That is important for two reasons. First, the fact that the marginal

Average tax rate How much of the *typical* dollar of your income that must ultimately be sent to the government; calculated as your total tax bill divided by your income.

Progressive tax A tax that takes a larger share from the income of high-income taxpayers than it does from low-income taxpayers.

rate is higher means that the more you earn, the higher your average tax rate will be. In other words, the tax code is **progressive** in that the government takes a larger share of the income of high-income taxpayers than it does from the income of low-income taxpayers.[2]

The second reason it's important to distinguish between marginal and average rates is because it is the marginal rate that shapes people's behavior. When you're considering working for another hour, you may want to know that the government's going to take $1 out of every $4 you earn (your marginal rate), not $1 dollar out of every $5 (your average rate). Big jumps in the marginal rate can potentially cause big changes in behavior. Consider France, where the marginal rate changes from 14% to 30% at an income of €26,632. You might be willing to put in some overtime if your next dollar of income were taxed at 14%; you would likely be less willing to do so if that next dollar were taxed over twice as much, at 30%. Many people complain that high marginal rates separate effort from reward and therefore stifle hard work, innovation, and entrepreneurship—or cause it to move elsewhere. During the 1960s, when England had extremely high (95%!) marginal tax rates on the super-rich, both the Beatles and the Rolling Stones moved to countries with lower taxes.

There are some ways you can reduce the taxes you owe. One way is to claim *exemptions*, which are automatic reductions in taxable income, based on the characteristics of your household. You are automatically entitled to a $3,950 *personal exemption*. If you have kids or other dependents, you can reduce your income by an extra $3,950 for each one.

A second way you can reduce your taxable income is by claiming deductions. *Deductions* are reductions in your taxable income you get for spending money in certain ways. Unlike exemptions, deductions are not automatic; you have to spend money to claim them, and you have to spend that money in prescribed ways.

The tax code is full of possible deductions. One huge deduction for homeowners is the mortgage interest deduction. If you borrow money from a bank to buy a house, any money you spend to pay interest on your home loan can be deducted from your taxable income. Second, the IRS lets you deduct any money you donate to charity from your taxable income. You may have heard something like this on the radio: "The Association to Enhance Scholastic Achievement Among the Elderly is a 501(c)(3) organization." That designation means that the association is a nonprofit entity, and so donations to it are eligible for the charitable deduction. Third, the IRS lets you deduct contributions to certain pension and retirement plans from your current taxable income: When you graduate and get a job, any contributions to your company's 401(k) retirement plan will not be taxed until you withdraw those funds during your retirement.

Recall that you can automatically claim a $3,950 personal exemption. Suppose you can also deduct from your taxable income $22,000 in interest you paid on your home loan, $12,000 in contributions to your retirement plan, and $8,000 in charitable contributions to the American Cancer Society. Those exemptions and deductions reduce your taxable income from $80,000 to a much more modest $34,050, dropping you from the 25% marginal tax bracket into the 15% marginal bracket, and decreasing your tax bill from $15,856.25 to only $4,653.75. Your average tax rate falls from almost 20% to a much more modest 13.7%. Avoiding taxes is pretty easy, if you're willing to use your income in certain ways.

The Corporate Income Tax Just as the government levies a tax on individuals' incomes, it also levies a tax on corporations' incomes. A *corporation* is similar to a business partnership where the partners agree to share any profits the company earns. There are a few differences, however, between corporations and partnerships. One of those differences is the scale of ownership: A corporation may have thousands of partners, called *shareholders*. A second difference is that in a partnership, often the partners make the key business decisions; in a corporation, shareholders generally elect a board of directors to make those decisions. Third, corporations have a life of their own: If one

---

[2]To get a complete picture of the progressivity or regressivity of taxes, it's important to consider the entire set of taxes people pay as a whole: income taxes, payroll taxes, property taxes, fuel taxes, sales taxes, and so on. Issues of fairness and redistribution are discussed further in Chapter 21.

Application 20.1

Why Do Americans Work So Much?

Americans might be proud to learn that, on average, they work more than people in many of the world's other developed countries—namely, Canada and countries in Western Europe. In some cases, the differences are startling: The typical American works almost 60% more than the typical Italian, 50% more than the average French citizen, and 33% more than the average German.

Nobel Prize–winning economist Edward Prescott of the Federal Reserve Bank of Minneapolis thought he knew why: marginal tax rates. Prescott measured the average workweek in each country, accounting for all adults between 15 and 64. Then Prescott constructed an estimate of the true marginal tax rate faced by the typical worker in each country. The true marginal rate measures the amount of the last dollar earned that goes to the government—any part of the government. That rate includes income taxes, of course. But it also includes payroll taxes and consumption taxes such as Europe's Value Added Tax and American sales taxes.

Prescott was struck by the strength of the relationship between hours worked and marginal tax rates. In Italy, the typical worker gets to enjoy only 36 cents of consumption for every $1 earned. There, workers choose to work less and enjoy lots of leisure. At the other end of the spectrum, the Japanese keep 63 cents out of each $1 they make. As a result, they work much more. Almost invariably, the higher the marginal tax rate a country has, the less its people work.

Country	True Marginal Tax Rate Faced by Typical Worker, 1993–1996	Average Number of Hours Worked per Week, 1993–1996
Italy	64%	16.5
France	59%	17.5
Germany	59%	19.3
Canada	52%	22.9
United Kingdom	44%	22.8
United States	40%	25.9
Japan	37%	27.0

Prescott expected to find that other factors, such as the generosity of European unemployment compensation and institutional labor market rigidities, also contributed to American–European workweek differences. He was surprised to discover that those factors didn't matter much at all: Almost all of the difference in workweek lengths could be explained solely by differences in the applicable marginal tax rates.

Should Americans be proud of their work ethic? Prescott's research suggests that Americans don't work so much because they're more virtuous than Europeans. Rather, their long hours are almost solely the product of living in a place where the tax system does less to discourage work than do tax systems elsewhere.

See related problems 1.13 and 1.14 on page 450 at the end of this chapter.

Based on Edward Prescott, "Why Do Americans Work So Much More Than Europeans?" *Federal Reserve Bank of Minneapolis Quarterly Review*, July, 2004; "Why Do Americans Work More Than Europeans?" *Wall Street Journal*, October 21, 2004; and "Why Europeans Work Less Than Americans," *Forbes*, May 23, 2006.

of the owners passes on, the corporation survives. That isn't necessarily true of more traditional business partnerships.

A fourth difference between a corporation and a more traditional partnership is the way they are taxed. Partnerships don't generally pay income taxes on their earnings. Instead, the government waits to collect taxes until the partners receive those profits

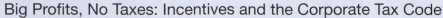

Application 20.2

Big Profits, No Taxes: Incentives and the Corporate Tax Code

The top 2014 average corporate tax rate is officially 35%. But many corporations pay much less. In a study of 280 major corporations, the Citizens for Tax Justice noted that 111 of those corporations paid less than 17% in taxes, while only 71 paid more than 30%. And in a recent survey of 500 major corporations, *USA Today* found that 57—about 1 in 9—paid no taxes at all.

How do corporations reduce their tax burdens so dramatically? First, they take advantage of deductions and credits. The corporate tax code, like the individual tax code, is filled with tax breaks corporations can receive for spending money in particular ways. Second, corporations are essentially allowed to bring forward past losses and deduct them from their taxable income in profitable years.

Finally, many multinational corporations take advantage of legal provisions that allow them to shift foreign profits to subsidiaries located overseas. Apple, for example, funnels two-thirds of its global profits through a foreign subsidiary in Ireland, where corporate income taxes are significantly lower than in the United States. Those profits won't be subject to U.S. taxes until Apple brings them home—if Apple ever does. In the meantime, offshoring profits saves Apple about $10 billion in taxes each year. Apple is not alone: *Forbes* magazine reports, "Apple cut its taxes with the same tools multinationals have been using for years to minimize their worldwide tax liability. And if there is a scandal, I suppose it is the very ordinariness of these transactions."[3]

The complex nature of the corporate tax code encourages socially costly behaviors. Corporations devote tremendous resources to lobbying for deductions, credits, and other tax breaks. They also devote legal resources to offshoring their profits—resources that could be used instead to create and produce goods and services. As *Forbes* suggests, "Just imagine if Apple could replace all those tax lawyers with creative new software geeks or industrial designers."

Many economists believe that it would be easy to get corporations to pay more while discouraging such socially wasteful behaviors: Reduce the high tax rates that encourage corporations to offshore profits and eliminate the deductions, credits, and exemptions that reward special interest lobbying efforts.

Demonizing corporations for responding to the incentives created by the law won't fix the problems of corporate taxation; the only way to truly solve problems created by the tax code is to change the tax code. As Judge Learned Hand said in 1934, "Anyone may arrange his affairs so that his taxes shall be as low as possible; he is not bound to choose that pattern which best pays the treasury . . . [T]here is nothing sinister in so arranging affairs as to keep taxes as low as possible. Everyone does it, rich and poor alike and all do right, for nobody owes any public duty to pay more than the law demands."[4]

See related problem 1.19 on page 450 at the end of this chapter.

Based on "The Real Story on Apple's Tax Avoidance: How Ordinary It Is," *Forbes*, May 21, 2013; "Large Companies Find Ways to a Zero Tax Rate," *USA Today*, February 19, 2014; and CNNMoney's "Many Companies Pay No Income Taxes, Study Finds," November 3, 2011.

---

[3]The Real Story On Apple's Tax Avoidance: How Ordinary It Is," Forbes, May 21, 2013, http://www.forbes.com/sites/beltway/2013/05/21/the-real-story-about-apples-tax-avoidance-how-ordinary-it-is/.

[4]Judge Learned Hand, in the case of *Helvering v. Gregory*, 69 F.2d 809, 810-11 (2d Cir. 1934).

as personal income. That is not true for corporations: Because they have distinct legal lives, they are taxed accordingly. This has a surprising implication: Any profit earned by a corporation gets taxed *twice* by government—once when it is declared as income by the corporation, and a second time when those profits are distributed and declared as personal income by the corporation's shareholders.

The corporate tax code is structured a lot like the personal tax code. It is progressive, with increasing marginal and average rates. The top marginal rate is 38%, and it applies to earnings between $15 million and $18 million. That's the highest top marginal rate in the developed world, but because of liberal allowances for deductions, the average tax rate faced by the typical corporation is much lower. So, despite the incredible earning power of U.S. corporations, their direct tax contributions account for only about 11% of what the federal government takes in.

Government Expenditures, Deficits, and Debt

You now have a fairly complete picture of where the federal government's money comes from. Let's look now at how the federal government spends the money it takes in. Then we'll take a look at the overall budgetary health of the federal government's operations by examining budget surpluses, budget deficits, and the federal debt.

20.2 Learning Objective

Explain the difference between mandatory and discretionary expenditures and between the federal government's budget deficit and the federal debt.

Discretionary Expenditures

In general, government expenditures can be broken down into two broad categories. Some government spending is discretionary. **Discretionary expenditures** are spending that must be authorized by Congress each year. They're the kind of expenditures you are likely to think of when you think of government spending—building roads, buying tanks, funding grants for scientific research, and so on. Those discretionary expenditures include purchases of goods and services, and they also include the wages and salaries of government employees.

Discretionary expenditures
Spending that must be authorized by Congress each year.

All totaled, discretionary expenditures are quite large. They account for about 30% of what government spends. But that's somewhat misleading. If you look at all of the various expenditures, you'll see that they are quite varied: There is funding for public broadcasting, foreign aid for the Federated States of Micronesia, and money to send spaceships to the far reaches of the solar system. However, the biggest part of discretionary spending ($640 billion, or about 55% of 2015 discretionary spending) is devoted to national defense.

Of the 45% of non-defense discretionary spending, the overwhelming majority is devoted to domestic expenditures. Those expenditures include building and maintaining roads and bridges, funding the U.S. national park system, providing federal student loans and grants, paying federal employees, and so on. Those expenditures total about 42% of discretionary spending. The remaining 3% of discretionary spending goes overseas in various forms, including as foreign aid.

Many people worry about wasteful discretionary spending and its impact on the government's fiscal health. And it's certainly easy to find money in the federal budget that gets spent on wasteful discretionary items. The late Wisconsin Senator William Proxmire made great sport of this during the 1970s and 1980s, creating a dubious honor he called the Golden Fleece Award. One winner of the award was the National Science Foundation, which spent $103,000 to study whether sunfish that drank tequila were more aggressive than those that drank gin. Another winner was the National Institute of Mental Health, which spent a similar amount to study what went on in a Peruvian brothel. *The New York Times* reported that "[the institute] made repeated visits in the interest of accuracy."

It is easy to poke fun at spending like that, but it's really not very constructive. Even by 1970s standards, the dollar amounts were pretty small. By today's standards, they're almost meaningless: Nobody can solve our country's fiscal problems $103,000 at a time. Politicians who are really interested in cutting spending will have to look at the items the government is spending really *big* money on. On the discretionary side, one big item is defense spending.

Today's defense spending is, even in inflation-adjusted terms, about as high as it has been in the post–World War II era. Cutting defense spending is often regarded as a political minefield; many people believe that the most important job of government is defending its citizens and that cuts to other programs should be made before cuts to defense. Also, because the defense budget is so large, many states and corporations have a great deal to lose when defense is downsized. As a result, lobbying efforts to maintain the defense budget are often intense. But despite the political difficulties inherent in cutting defense spending, it has been done before. In fact, the pattern of defense spending in the post–World War II era has been quite regular: large increases during wartime followed by large decreases when conflicts end.

Mandatory Spending and Entitlements

The second large category of government spending is called mandatory spending. **Mandatory spending** is spending that is not subject to Congress's annual appropriations process. Figure 20.2 shows total government spending, broken down into discretionary and mandatory components. As Figure 20.2 shows, mandatory spending accounts for more spending each year than all discretionary spending, including defense spending.

Mandatory spending Spending that is not subject to Congress's annual appropriations process.

▶ **Figure 20.2**
Mandatory and Discretionary Government Spending, 2015
Most government spending is mandatory spending. Almost all mandatory spending is devoted to funding entitlement programs.
Source: Office of Management and Budget.

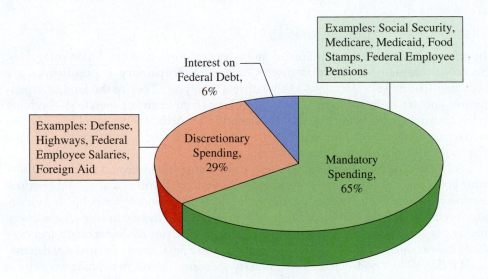

Entitlement programs account for almost all mandatory spending, and their share of the total federal budget has doubled over the last 50 years. One major entitlement program is Social Security. Individuals make themselves eligible to receive Social Security benefits by fulfilling two criteria: They must accumulate a certain number of years' tenure in the workforce, and they must reach an official retirement age. Once those criteria are met, the benefits are automatic and are prescribed by a set formula.[5] The government is largely obliged to fund Social Security to whatever extent is necessary to provide the benefits recipients are eligible for.

Earlier, we discussed the fact that the Social Security tax is regressive. But Social Security *benefits* are progressive. Empirically, the regressive nature of the tax is more than offset by the progressive nature of the benefits. Over a lifetime, a low earner planning to retire in 2030 will pull about $3,000 more out of the Social Security system than he put into it. In contrast, a high earner can expect to pull out over $190,000 less than he contributed. On net, then, the Social Security program is progressive in the sense that it redistributes income from higher earners to lower earners.

---

[5]The amount of benefits depends on the chosen retirement age. The retirement age for full benefits has increased over the years. For people born after 1960, the retirement age is now 67. The Social Security Administration pays reduced benefits to people who choose to retire earlier.

Social Security spending makes up about 31% of mandatory spending. But there are other types of social insurance that collectively account for just as much mandatory spending as Social Security. The biggest fraction of that mandatory spending is devoted to health care. Most of that spending isn't for government-provided health care services. Rather, more often the government pays for (or assists in paying for) privately provided health care services for qualifying individuals.

The two largest government health care programs are Medicare and Medicaid. Recall that payroll taxes fund Medicare. Individuals pay money into Medicare while they work, and they draw money out of it when they retire. In other words, the Medicare program is for older people. Medicaid, by contrast, helps pay for the medical care of lower-income people, regardless of how old they are. Of the two programs, Medicare is the larger. It makes up 25% of mandatory spending. Medicaid is not small, though: It makes up 13% of mandatory spending, which means that health care spending represents a larger fraction of mandatory spending than Social Security does.

There are other mandatory expenditures, as well. About 10% of mandatory spending is used to make interest payments on the federal government's existing debt. Thirteen percent of mandatory spending is for income security programs, such as food stamps, housing assistance, and other forms of government assistance. The remainder is spent on other retirement and disability programs, among them pension benefits for federal government employees.

That's a long laundry list of government expenditures, one that may be hard to remember. And the numbers change a bit from year to year. But there are some big-picture ideas you can glean from a look at the data:

- Over half of government spending is mandatory spending.
- Social Security, Medicare, and Medicaid programs represent the bulk of that mandatory spending.
- The biggest discretionary spending item is defense spending.

Surpluses, Deficits, and Debt

Now that you understand where the government's money comes from and where the government's money goes, let's combine that information and take a bird's-eye look at the government's financial health.

Deficits and Surpluses In 2015, the federal government's expenditures were estimated to come in at $3.9 trillion, while federal government revenues were estimated to come in at $3.3 trillion. In other words, the government was expected to spend more than it takes in—about $600 billion more. Economists call the amount by which annual expenditures exceed annual receipts the federal government **budget deficit**. If the opposite happens and annual revenues exceed annual expenditures, that excess is called the federal government's **budget surplus**. Figure 20.3 shows the government's budget surpluses and deficits going back to the late 1960s. In Figure 20.3, negative numbers indicate deficits; positive numbers indicate surpluses.

For most of the nation's history, the federal government was careful not to spend more, on average, than it took in. As Figure 20.3 shows, that fiscal discipline disappeared in the late 1970s and 1980s and was restored briefly in the 1990s, when the United States had a few years of budget surpluses. Since then, the government has run large and recurring deficits. The largest of those deficits was in 2009, when the government spent $1.4 *trillion* more than the $2.1 trillion it took in.

The government has a few options available when it runs out of money but still has bills to pay. One option is to print enough new money to pay the bills. That seems like a quick and painless way for a government to pay its bills, but it has its costs. When governments print more money, prices tend to increase (see Chapter 19). If prices really begin to spiral upward, the effect can devastate a nation and its economy.

Budget deficit The amount by which annual expenditures exceed annual receipts.

Budget surplus The amount by which annual revenues exceed annual expenditures.

▶ **Figure 20.3**

Federal Government Budget
Surpluses and Deficits

The federal government began running
large deficits in the 1980s. Since that
time, deficits have been the rule rather
than the exception.

Note: Shaded areas indicate U.S. recessions.

Source: FRED Economic Database
(http://research.stlouisfed.org/fred2/series/
M318501A027NBEA).

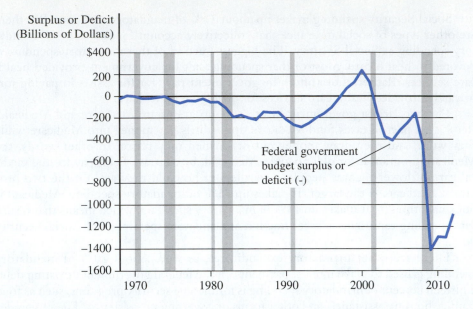

Federal debt The total amount of
money the government owes to its
creditors.

In the United States, the Federal Reserve does adjust the money supply to respond
to changing conditions in the economy, but it has not been common practice to issue
new money to pay the government's bills.

If a government is reluctant to turn on the printing presses, as many governments
are, then there is really only one way to make up for a revenue shortfall: Borrow
money. Government generally borrows the money it needs in the bond market. A
bond is a contract that promises the holder a certain sum of money on some certain
future date. When you lend the government, say, $1,000, the government will issue
you a bond promising to repay you more than $1,000 at some future date. The differ-
ence between what you give the government at the beginning and what government
gives you back at the end is called *interest*. Interest is your reward for postponing your
own consumption and letting the government use your money instead.

The Federal Debt The total amount of money the government owes to its creditors is
the **federal debt**. The federal debt is directly related to the current and past budget
deficits and surpluses. The government accumulates debt by borrowing when it runs
deficits. When the government runs a surplus, that surplus is used to pay off some of
its existing debt. So the total debt (the total amount of bonds outstanding) is the sum
of all past deficits minus the sum of all past surpluses.

As of early 2014, the total federal debt was $16.7 trillion. But part of that $16.7 trillion is money that the government owes to itself. Sometimes a division or department
or agency of government has a bit of surplus cash floating around that it doesn't know
what to do with. That may occur because of the timing of when it receives its money
compared to when it spends its money, or it may occur simply because some government programs take in a lot of money. Rather than sit on a big pile of cash, those
agencies may choose to lend it out and earn interest. One easy and safe way to lend out
that money is to buy government-issued bonds. Because that's money the government
owes to itself, it doesn't really represent a debt to society as a whole. It's as if you borrowed some money from your sister: Your individual debt goes up, but the total net
debt of your family is unchanged.

One large source of credit for the government has been the Social Security Trust
Fund. For decades, people paid into Social Security more than Social Security paid out
to retirees. The excess accumulated in the Social Security Trust Fund, and the trust-
ees of that fund put that cash to work by lending it to the government. One agency of
government borrowed from another, so the government's net debt was unchanged.

In early 2014, there was about $4.4 trillion worth of inter-agency borrowing and
lending within the federal government. So the *net* federal debt—the amount that the

government owes to the public and not to itself—was $12.3 trillion, substantially smaller than the $16.7 trillion figure mentioned earlier.

But $12.3 trillion is a lot of money. However, the United States (and by default, its government) is fabulously wealthy. Suppose that you and Bill Gates both have half-million-dollar balances on your Visa cards. Do you suppose Bill Gates would be as worried about paying his Visa bill as you might be? It seems unlikely; he's got a much bigger income and a lot more wealth to draw on than you do.

Just as Bill Gates is in better shape to pay a huge credit card bill than you are, the U.S. government is in far better shape to handle a $12.3 trillion debt than the government of, say, Turkmenistan. In either case, you can get a far more accurate picture of how much of a burden a debt actually represents by comparing the amount of the debt to the income of the debtor. At the national level, you can measure that income as gross domestic product (GDP). (See Chapter 16.) You might remember that U.S. GDP is enormous—about $17.1 trillion each year. So economists usually account for the burden of the debt by calculating the ratio of a government's net debt to GDP. The net debt/GDP ratio of the United States is $12.3 trillion/$17.1 trillion, or 72%, which means that our net debt is about three-quarters of one year's worth of income.

How does today's federal debt stack up historically? Figure 20.4 shows the total debt/GDP ratio of the federal government over a long span of time.[6] Despite the size of the $16.7 trillion total debt, the debt/GDP ratio is not as high as it was near the end of World War II. The fact that the United States was able to pay down the huge relative debt it had in the 1940s suggests at least the possibility of being able to pay down today's debt to manageable size.

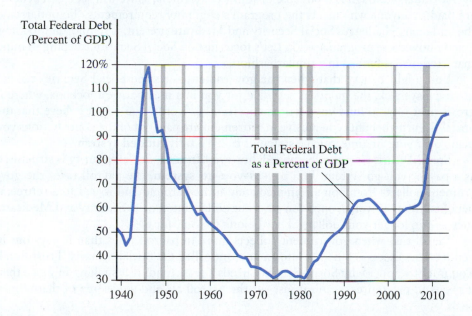

MyEconLab **Real-time data**

◄ **Figure 20.4**
Total Federal Debt/GDP Ratio, 1939–2014
Although the debt/GDP ratio has been increasing since 1980, it has not reached its historical high. After WWII, the debt/GDP ratio fell steadily, then increased during the 1980s and during the wars in Iraq and Afghanistan and during the Great Recession of 2007-2009.

Note: Shaded areas indicate U.S. recessions.

Source: FRED Economic Database (http://research.stlouisfed.org/fred2/series/GFDGDPA188S).

That said, just because it is *possible* to pay down the debt doesn't mean that doing so will be easy or painless. Anyone of modest means who has ever racked up a few thousand dollars in credit card debt knows how painfully slowly that debt disappears, even when the monthly payments on it seem quite significant. One reason those debts disappear so slowly is because a good chunk of each payment is devoted just to paying accumulated interest. That's true for the government, too. In fact, as Figure 20.2 shows, the interest on the debt accounts for 6% of total federal government expenditures. In other words, the government spends a lot of money to pay for the use of other peoples' money, and the bigger that debt becomes, the more the government

---

[6]Figure 20.4 shows the ratio of total debt to GDP rather than net debt to GDP, even though net debt is really the most relevant measure of the burden of the debt. Unfortunately, net debt figures before 1965 are not readily available. Both total debt to GDP and net debt to GDP behave in a similar way.

has to spend to meet its interest payments. In recent years, the U.S. government has benefited from interest rates being quite low by historical standards. That has made it cheap for the government to borrow money and has helped keep down the government's annual interest expenditures.

20.3 Learning Objective

Discuss how changes in the age of the U.S. population will affect the federal budget over the next four decades.

The Future of the Federal Budget

The previous section pointed out some reassuring aspects about the government debt. First, relative to GDP, today's debt is not overly high by historical standards. Second, the government is currently paying an exceptionally low interest rate on that debt. So if the government debt doesn't appear to be such a big deal, why does it receive so much attention?

Demographic Challenges

The government's debt may not be as bad as it appears right now, but America has some enormous new challenges looming in the next half-century. And they're costly challenges; in fact, the borrowing that might be necessary to meet those challenges could make today's debt seem small.

The budget problems the United States faces in the future stem largely from two programs designed specifically for people of retirement age: Social Security and Medicare. Spending on both of those programs, you will recall, is mandatory: It's set by a formula (although it is possible to adjust the formula, as we will see), and benefits are paid to anyone who meets the program's eligibility requirements. To understand the budgetary challenges Social Security and Medicare present, it's important to know exactly how those programs work. Let's focus just on Social Security, keeping in mind that Medicare is funded in a similar fashion.

You might believe that when the government takes the Social Security tax out of your paycheck, the money is set aside for you in a metaphorical lockbox, where it grows over time to fund your retirement. In other words, you might believe that the Social Security benefits you receive in retirement are paid out of the contributions you made over your lifetime. Such a system is called a **fully funded system**.

Fully funded system A retirement system in which the benefits government pays to retirees are paid out of the contributions those retirees made during their working years.

Pay-as-you-go system A retirement system in which the benefits government pays to retirees are paid out of the contributions of current workers.

Social Security is not fully funded, however. Instead, Social Security is structured as a pay-as-you-go system. In a **pay-as-you-go system**, the payroll taxes the government collects from you are immediately turned around and issued to a retiree as benefits. In other words, once you pay your dollars into Social Security and Medicare, they are no longer your dollars: They belong to someone else.

Recall that when government collects more in payroll taxes than it pays out in benefits, the excess is pumped into an account called the Social Security Trust Fund. You might wonder why Social Security needs a trust fund: If it's taking in more than it needs to pay retirees, can't it just cut the payroll tax and give some of that money back?

Think about what would happen if, in some year, the government found itself obligated to pay more out in benefits than it received in payroll taxes. That would result in a shortfall, and retirees wouldn't get the money they were promised. The Social Security Trust Fund was designed so that the Social Security system has reserves to draw on to prevent that from happening. For decades, that system has worked. Americans have been paying into the Social Security Trust Fund ever since it was established in the 1930s, and as of 2014, it was valued at $2.8 trillion. But as big as the Social Security Trust Fund is, it's not big enough to meet the challenges of funding retirement programs over the next few decades.

That's because the age structure of the U.S. population is changing dramatically. In the 1950s and 1960s, there weren't very many retirees, and there were very few people over the age of 85. At the same time, there were relatively large numbers of workers contributing to Social Security and Medicare to fund benefits for those retirees.

In 2010, something important happened: The first of the baby boomers, born in 1945, reached official retirement age. The rest of the baby boom generation will enter retirement over the next 15 to 20 years. And those retirees are expected to live about a decade longer than the retirees of the 1950s and 1960s, largely due to improvements in medical care. But that medical care is becoming increasingly expensive (the cost of care has risen more quickly than the prices of other goods and services), so in the decades to come, the government will be funding both retirement benefits and more expensive health care, for more retirees, for a longer period of time.

Here's another piece of the budget-challenge puzzle: The baby boomers didn't have a lot of children. Remember that Social Security and Medicare are pay-as-you-go programs where contributions by today's workers are immediately paid out as benefits to today's retirees. When there are a large number of workers, providing Social Security and Medicare benefits to a comparatively small number of retirees is relatively easy. But when there are lots of retirees and not many workers paying in, that places a large burden on the workers and can put the system under stress. In 1960, there were five workers per retiree. Today, there are just under three.

To maintain retiree benefits, the Social Security Administration began dipping into the Social Security Trust Fund in 2010. It estimates that the fund will be exhausted by 2036. The Medicare Trust Fund is in even worse shape: The Social Security Administration expects it to be depleted by 2024. Once those funds are depleted, benefits will be funded solely by the contributions of workers. By 2030, when you are entering your prime earning years, there will be only two workers per retiree. At current tax and benefit levels, the contributions of those two workers will be insufficient to support the benefits of retirees. This raises some important questions: Are these entitlement programs beyond hope? Will Social Security and Medicare be gone by the time you reach retirement age?

Meeting Future Demographic Challenges

It is unlikely that either Social Security or Medicare will cease to exist. However, it is clear that something will have to be done to make up for each program's revenue shortfall. Generally speaking, there are only two possible solutions. The government can either increase the amount coming in from workers, or it can reduce the amount flowing out to retirees. In other words, the government can raise payroll taxes or cut benefits.

Unfortunately, neither of those solutions is very politically popular, and since those changes must be initiated by politicians, solving the shortfall in funds for entitlement programs may turn out to be more difficult than it really should be. Recognizing that ultimately one, the other, or both changes will have to be made, politicians have roughly three ways to implement those changes:

- Today, they can make relatively small increases in current payroll tax rates combined with small downward adjustments to benefits. There are a number of ways to implement these changes. The government could increase payroll tax revenues by increasing the payroll tax rate, or in the case of Social Security, by raising the payroll tax cap beyond its current $118,500. Similarly, the government can cut people's entitlement benefits or scale back planned increases in future benefits. The government can also increase the retirement age for full eligibility beyond its current 67 years.

- Politicians can postpone action until the trust funds disappear and then enact more draconian cuts and bigger tax increases to keep both systems solvent.

- Politicians can postpone action until the trust funds disappear and then borrow money to keep both programs afloat. That would push the burden of paying for Social Security and Medicare even further into the future—onto generations of taxpayers who may not have even been born yet.

The last option mentioned—borrowing to cover the shortfall—is the option skeptics say is most likely to appeal to politicians. That's because the people most adversely affected by this option—future generations of taxpayers—may be too young to vote for the politicians who decide to borrow money today.

If government does borrow to cover the shortfall, how big will the impact be? The Congressional Budget Office (CBO), which regularly projects what the federal debt will be in the future, estimates that the ratio of publicly held debt to GDP will rise from today's 73% to about 130% by 2050 if no entitlement reforms are enacted. That may be hard to put into context, so consider this: Today's $12.3 trillion debt, divided among 317 million Americans, represents a current debt burden of about $38,800 per man, woman, and child. If today's debt burden were scaled to 2050 proportions, it would amount to about $69,000 per person. For a family of four, that represents a debt burden of over a quarter-million dollars.

The CBO also publishes an "alternative fiscal scenario" that makes some realistic assumptions about future legislation and the future state of the economy. You might consider the alternative fiscal scenario a realistic worst-case scenario: Suppose the 2050 debt/GDP ratio isn't 130% but is 250% instead. In today's dollars, that's about $132,000 per person, or about $528,000 for a family of four. Just the interest on a debt that size is huge: If the government successfully borrows at a 3% interest rate, the annual interest expense for a family of four—which is paid with taxes that the family sends to the government—amounts to over $15,000.

The Federal Government and Fiscal Stabilization Policy

20.4 Learning Objective
Describe two fiscal policy tools that government can use to help fight recessions and explain when those tools are likely to be most effective.

There is one last dimension of government's fiscal operations left to explore in this chapter: the government's role in stabilizing the economy. With extraordinary taxing and spending power at its disposal, can the government stimulate spending to revitalize a sluggish economy?

Fiscal Policy: The Basics

Fiscal policy Government's use of its taxing and spending powers to influence overall economic activity.

Government's use of its taxing and spending powers to influence overall economic activity is called **fiscal policy**. Consider an economy sliding into recession because consumers have stopped spending money and are saving it instead. Perhaps they are worried about losing their jobs, so they cut their purchases of consumer durables and stop building new homes. Or maybe businesses cut their investment expenditures. Economists call these spending cutbacks *decreases in aggregate demand*. Once the government recognizes that there is a downturn occurring, it can pursue two possible remedies.

First, the government can cut taxes. That leaves consumers with more income after taxes, or *disposable income*. Tax cuts work a little bit of magic: Even though workers don't get an increase in their wages or salaries, their paychecks get bigger. That may help boost their confidence, but even if it doesn't, the mere fact that they have more cash in their pockets means they will probably increase their spending somewhat.

Second, the government can attempt to replace the lost consumption and investment spending with expenditures of its own. Remember that GDP is the sum of consumption spending, investment spending, net spending by foreigners on domestic goods, and government spending. If consumption spending falls by $10 but government spending rises by $10, GDP remains unchanged. So the essence of this approach to fiscal policy is that if the economy is in a recession because people won't spend their money, the government will spend it for them!

Discretionary fiscal policy The act of deliberately cutting taxes or ramping up expenditures to fight an economic downturn. Alternatively, policymakers can increase taxes or slow expenditures to slow an overheating economy.

Deliberately cutting taxes or ramping up expenditures to fight an economic downturn is called **discretionary fiscal policy**. But there are also fiscal measures that are built into the current government structure that automatically work to ramp up overall spending in recessions. First, in recessions, income tax collections automatically decrease. Second, during recessions, government spending on unemployment benefits and government assistance programs tends to increase without any deliberate action by the government. Both the reduction in taxes and the increase in government spending on assistance programs work to increase consumption. These naturally occurring recession fighters are called **automatic stabilizers**.

Automatic stabilizers Built-in changes in taxes and spending that, without any deliberate action by policymakers, stimulate the economy when it is weak or slow the economy when it is overheating.

The Multiplier Effect

Suppose that as part of a fiscal stimulus program, the government purchases $100 of paper clips from Bob, an office supply vendor. All else equal, that purchase increases GDP by $100. But the government's fiscal action may have a larger impact because Bob now finds himself with an extra $100, and he might be tempted to spend some of it. That would increase GDP even more.

Let's suppose that people will generally spend 70 cents out of each dollar's worth of new income. Economists call the proportion spent of each new dollar's worth of income the *marginal propensity to consume (MPC)*. So Bob spends $70 buying a dozen golf balls from Jane; Jane then spends $49 ($70 × 0.7) on a new clock; the clock seller spends $34.30 ($49 × 0.7) on barbeque sauce; the sauce seller spends $24.01 on movie tickets, and so on. At each step, GDP rises.

Will GDP increase indefinitely? No, because each successive round of additional spending is getting smaller. You can find the total potential impact of the government's purchase by applying the following formula:

$$\text{Total impact on GDP} = \text{Initial new spending created} \times \frac{1}{(1 - MPC)}$$

where $1/(1 - MPC)$ is called the *spending multiplier*. So, in our example, $100 of new government spending can ultimately create up to $333.33 of income:

$$\text{Total impact on GDP} = \$100 \times \frac{1}{(1 - 0.7)} = \$333.33$$

In other words, the spending multiplier is 3.33 because $100 of new spending creates about $333 of new income.

The People Behind the Theory

John Maynard Keynes

John Maynard Keynes (pronounced "canes"), widely regarded as the most influential economist of the 20th century, was more than just an economist. He was a modern-day renaissance man: an academic, a self-made man, a prominent social critic, and a prescient diplomat.

Keynes the Economist

In his academic role at Cambridge University in England, Keynes redefined existing economic thinking, departing dramatically from the prevailing *laissez-faire* thought. You are familiar with some of his groundbreaking contributions:

- The notable insight that recessions can result from deficient aggregate demand
- The development of the spending multiplier
- The theory of sticky wages and prices, which prevent recessions from fixing themselves in a timely fashion

Keynes used those ideas to reinvent the role of government in the economy. He stressed that waiting for an economy in recession to recover on its own, as many economists of the day prescribed, could be unnecessarily costly. "In the long run," Keynes remarked, "we are all dead." Rather than wait for the economy to fix itself, Keynes asserted that during demand-induced recessions, government should use fiscal policy to return the economy to full employment, replacing lost consumption and investment spending with government spending. Deficits are often regarded as bad, but Keynes thought the government *should* move into deficit during recessions, cutting taxes and increasing spending.

Keynes the Investor

Keynes the classroom economist was also Keynes the real-world investor. Investing made Keynes fabulously wealthy: In today's money he was worth an estimated £11 million. Despite his apparent Midas touch, Keynes proved himself mortal when he failed to foresee the stock market crash of 1929; only a £10,000 loan from his father saved him from bankruptcy.

Keynes the Iconoclast

Keynes didn't just reject economic orthodoxy; in many ways, he rejected social orthodoxy as well. Keynes was a member of the Bloomsbury Group, an influential group of writers, intellectuals, philosophers, and artists who deeply influenced art, literature, and social criticism. The Bloomsbury Group championed sexual freedom, feminism and women's suffrage, pacifism, and the rejection of bourgeois values. Keynes was also a devoted patron of the arts and a proponent of eugenics.

Keynes the Diplomat

Called to civil service during World War I, Keynes helped represent England at the Treaty of Versailles. Keynes advocated modest reparations for Germany, fearing that strict demands would harm innocent German people and limit Germany's ability to pay. But his advice was ignored, and in his 1919 book *The Economic Consequences of the Peace*, he predicted that the harsh reparations demanded by England, France, and the United States would cause disaster:

> *If we aim deliberately at the impoverishment of Central Europe, vengeance, I dare predict, will not limp. Nothing can then delay for very long that final war between the forces of Reaction and the despairing convulsions of Revolution, before which the horrors of the late German war will fade into nothing.*[7]

Keynes's predictions came to pass: Germany printed money to pay its reparations, and the resulting hyperinflation brought the downfall of the Weimar Republic and the rise of Nazism.

Keynes died in 1946, but his legacy lives on: His theories are still prominent in economics textbooks, are hotly debated by academic and policy economists, and are in widespread use by governments throughout the world.

Potential Pitfalls of Fiscal Policy

Using fiscal policy to remedy recessions seems like it would be both easy to implement and effective, doesn't it? After all, General Motors doesn't care whether it sells a car to your next-door neighbor or to the Pentagon. Either way, it sells a car. Unfortunately, the policies aren't always easy to implement, and some less-than-intuitive complications can reduce the effectiveness of those policies.

The Lags of Policy Just like monetary policy, fiscal policy is hampered by policy lags. Lags are the first hurdles the government must leap if fiscal action is to be effective. Let's briefly discuss those lags and compare the potential effectiveness of fiscal policy versus monetary policy. First, as with monetary policy, there is a recognition lag: Economic data must first be gathered, and then it must indicate to policymakers that a recession is in progress. Generally speaking, economic data is released to policymakers

---

[7]John Maynard Keynes, *The Economic Consequences of The Peace*, 1919.

and the general public at the same time, which means that lawmakers, who design fiscal policy, and the Federal Reserve, which designs monetary policy, face roughly the same recognition lag.

Next, there is an implementation lag: The Federal Open Market Committee, which sets monetary policy, meets only about every six weeks. But once it does and reaches a decision about the appropriate course of action, that course can be rapidly implemented. The implementation lag can be much longer for fiscal policy because fiscal changes often require an act of Congress (though sometimes the president can make fiscal changes by executive order). That can be a slow process. Even when a bill has been passed by Congress and signed into law by the president, it may not go into force until much later: Many laws don't become effective until several months after they are passed.

There is one area where fiscal policy can potentially outdo monetary policy: the impact lag. Fiscal policy's impact lag can be incredibly short. When government purchases $8 million of paper clips to boost the economy, GDP rises by $8 million the second the transaction is complete. So when the government decides to stimulate the economy by ramping up government spending, the impact lag depends in part on how many "shovel-ready" projects are available. If a potential government project has to be developed, approved, and put out for bid, then the impact lag for government purchases can be long.

Crowding Out Even if there were no policy lags, fiscal policy might still not work well. To see why, suppose the government decides that consumption spending is too low. Government decides to make up for low consumption spending by purchasing $1,000 worth of bottled water. But where will government get the $1,000 it needs to pay for the water?

The government can't print the money it needs—that's the Fed's job. One option is for the government to raise taxes by $1,000. Then it can use that $1,000 to buy the bottled water. But here's an important question: If government hadn't increased taxes by $1,000, what would consumers have done with that money?

If consumers would have spent the entire $1,000 anyway, then the government spending hasn't *created* any new income; it has merely *replaced* consumer spending with government spending. There is no spending created; there is no net stimulus. When this happens, economists say government spending has completely **crowded out** consumption spending.

> **Crowding out** Decreased consumer or business spending as a result of increased government spending.

Typically, consumers save at least part of their income and spend the rest. Several studies estimate that in the short run, consumers spend about 75 cents of each $1. This means that if the government collects $1,000 in taxes from consumers, they were probably planning on spending $750 of it anyway. Consequently, the net impact of the government's spending is not a GDP increase of $1,000 but an increase of only $250.[8] In other words, the fiscal policy worked, but it didn't work particularly well.

Suppose instead that government decides to raise the $1,000 by borrowing money instead of raising taxes. That way the government's expenditure won't crowd out consumption spending. Or will it?

Unfortunately, the government spending may *still* crowd out spending elsewhere in the economy. Here's how that happens: The government goes to the financial markets and borrows the $1,000. But it's not likely that the lender of the $1,000 was going to let the money sit idle in a pile anyway: Ultimately, the government prevents that $1,000 from being borrowed by someone else—perhaps a business looking to install a new computer or a homeowner planning to add on a deck. In this case, government spending has crowded out investment spending.

There's a second, more sophisticated way to envision government's crowding out of investment spending. Picture a pool of available cash, waiting to be lent to creditworthy borrowers. Ordinarily, that money would be borrowed by consumers and

---

[8]Apply the multiplier to determine the total impact of that $250 of new spending. In this case, the total impact would be $1,000. Because $1,000 of government spending created $1,000 in total spending, we can say that the multiplier, after being adjusted for crowding out, is 1.0.

businesses. But suddenly government decides it wants a big share of that pool. With more competition for the available funds, the price of those funds—the interest rate—begins to increase. As the interest rate increases, some business projects begin to look less profitable. Firms abandon those projects, and some investment spending doesn't occur—investment spending that would have occurred had government not driven up interest rates.

The effectiveness of fiscal policy hinges on the strength of the crowding out effect. If spending was likely to have occurred anyway, the government expenditures merely

Application 20.3

Fiscal Policy During the Great Recession

When the Great Recession began to unfold in December 2007, few people predicted its extent or duration. Economic conditions worsened throughout 2008, and even after the recession ended in 2009, the economy struggled. By 2013, the economy still had not fully recovered. Ultimately, the Great Recession would be the biggest economic disaster since the Great Depression. Its catastrophic nature begs the question: Did the government do everything it could to combat it?

The standard fiscal policy prescription for combatting recessions is to cut taxes and increase government spending. The government did both. Four months after the recession began, the Bush administration slashed each taxpayer's tax bill by roughly $600 and then mailed each taxpayer a check for the appropriate amount. Though not huge in scale, the Bush tax rebate put more money in consumers' pockets and provided an early boost to spending. The Bush administration also created the Troubled Asset Relief Program (TARP), which authorized the Treasury to engage in large-scale purchases of mortgage loans and various mortgage-backed financial instruments. TARP contributed to the stability of the financial sector by enabling financial institutions to offload risky and illiquid assets that could potentially drive them into insolvency.

By early 2009, the Obama administration brought out the heavy artillery, passing the American Reinvestment and Recovery Act (ARRA), an $800 billion fiscal stimulus package unprecedented in size and scope. The ARRA contained a number of provisions consistent with putting more money in peoples' pockets and elevating spending, including the following:

- A temporary extension in unemployment benefits
- $288 billion in tax cuts, including a 2.5% reduction in employees' payroll tax contributions
- Tax credits for people purchasing new homes
- Expanded tax credits for parents with children and for their children's college tuition
- $357 billion in government-funded spending on infrastructure and science, education, health care, and energy
- $88 billion in aid to state governments, primarily through the Medicaid program

Fiscal policy works best when consumers are holding tightly onto their money and businesses are reluctant to invest. Both of those conditions were true in the Great Recession. Consumption spending had, for the first time in the post–World War II era, taken a large visible dip (see chart) as nervous consumers held onto their cash. Investment spending had plummeted 25% by the time the ARRA took effect, despite interest rates near 0%. In other words, government didn't have to compete for the money it needed to fund the ARRA, and it didn't have to worry about crowding out private consumption and investment spending.

Were the government's fiscal programs a success? Former Federal Reserve Vice Chair Alan Blinder says yes. He and Mark Zandi, the chief economist at Moody's

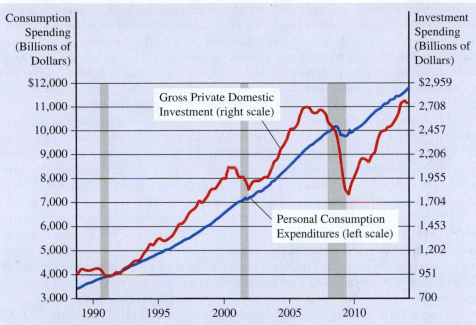

Note: Shaded areas indicate U.S. recessions.

Source: FRED (http://research.stlouisfed.org/fred2/series/PCEC96/ and http://research.stlouisfed.org/fred2/series/GPDI).

Analytics, estimate that by 2010, the fiscal stimulus alone had caused real GDP to increase by 3.4%, reduced the unemployment rate by 1.5 percentage points, and added 2.7 million jobs to U.S. payrolls.

Other economists disagree. Princeton University's Paul Krugman says the stimulus was too small—that despite the increases in federal spending, overall government spending actually declined because of state budget cuts. Stanford's John Taylor notes that actual purchases of goods and services didn't rise much—that much of the federal stimulus was devoted to transfers and tax rebates that were largely saved rather than spent. Still other economists argue that pieces of the government program were actually counterproductive—that extending unemployment benefits, for example, discouraged laid-off workers from aggressively pursuing reemployment. In a full-page ad in the *New York Times* in 2009, 200 high-profile economists argued that government efforts to fix the recession would have been better devoted to "reforms that remove impediments to work, saving, investment and production," including lower tax rates and a reduction in the burden of government.

Why is there so much disagreement about fiscal policy's effectiveness? The lack of consensus stems from two big issues that plague macroeconomists: a lack of good data and a lack of consensus on the statistical techniques used to analyze that data. As a result, of the nine most widely discussed statistical studies of fiscal policy during the Great Recession, three claim either zero or modest impact, while six claim a mostly positive or strong impact.

Economist Russell Roberts of George Mason University notes that economists do agree on many things but that consensus is harder to achieve regarding infrequent, unfamiliar, and complicated events like financial crises. In a podcast about the role of empirical evidence in economics, he remarked on the difficulty of arriving at a "Yes, it worked" or "No, it didn't" answer: "We're trying to tease out the effect of one social policy in the face of hundreds of thousands of other changes."

See related problems 3.10 and 3.11 on page 452 at the end of this chapter.

Based on Alan Blinder and Mark Zandi, "How the Great Recession Was Brought to an End," working paper, 2010; John Taylor's "An Empirical Analysis of the Revival of Fiscal Activism in the 2000s," *Journal of Economic Literature*, 2011; Russell Roberts' *EconTalk* podcast, January 29, 2009; and "Did the Stimulus Work? A Review of the Nine Best Studies on the Subject," *Washington Post*, August 24, 2011.

replace other forms of spending and provide no net stimulus to the economy. On the other hand, if the funds government acquired through taxes or borrowing wouldn't have been spent, then the government spending boosts GDP. This suggests that fiscal policy is most likely to be effective when consumers and businesses are, on a large scale, cautiously holding onto cash instead of spending it. Alternatively, fiscal policy may be effective if consumers and businesses are reluctant to borrow in credit markets or if financial institutions like banks are reluctant to make loans to them.

As mentioned earlier, the government can also attempt to stimulate the economy by cutting taxes. This seems like a more foolproof way for government to stimulate the economy than increasing its own spending. However, tax cuts can be problematic, just as government-spending increases are. Suppose the government cuts taxes by $1,000, and just for the sake of simplicity, assume that consumers spend that entire $1,000. Their consumption therefore increases GDP by $1,000.

However, the tax cut comes at a cost. Because government now finds itself with $1,000 less than it was counting on, it faces two alternatives. First, it can cut its own spending by $1,000. If it does, the tax cut has merely changed the *composition* of spending because the government's spending has been replaced with consumption spending. The total amount of spending hasn't changed. As a result, the tax cut won't stimulate the economy.

A second option for government is to keep its spending steady and borrow $1,000 to cover the shortfall created by the tax cut. But that removes $1,000 from the pool of savings that businesses use to finance their investment spending. So in the end, households end up spending $1,000 more on consumption, government spending remains constant, and business investment spending falls by $1,000. The tax cut, once again, has changed the composition of spending without changing the total amount of spending. So the fiscal action will be ineffective at stimulating the economy.

Can a tax cut stimulate the economy? Yes. But the tax cut has to move money from people who aren't planning on spending it to people who are. In the example above, if government borrows money that businesses weren't planning on using anyway (perhaps because the state of the economy made them too afraid to invest in new plants and equipment) and it places that money in the hands of households that will spend it on consumption goods, the tax cut will successfully stimulate the economy.

On the other hand, suppose the government borrows money to give consumers a tax cut, but consumers are so fearful of the future that they stuff that money in their mattress, just in case. Then the tax cut has done nothing to stimulate the economy; it has simply moved cash from one place where it was sitting idle to another. The same is true if consumers use the tax cut to pay off existing debt rather than spend it on GDP-increasing purchases. This, perhaps, is one reason that the government sometimes opts for spending programs rather than tax cuts: When government borrows money to fund a new spending program, it knows that the money will actually be spent.

Ultimately, no matter what form the fiscal policy action takes, its effectiveness hinges on these two questions: Where did the money to pay for the fiscal action come from? And what would that money have been used for had the fiscal action never occurred?

Conclusion

The federal government is a major player in the macroeconomy, accounting for about $1 out of every $4 that is spent. It goes without saying that government does not exist in a vacuum: How the government funds its operations and what it spends its money on create incentives that shape the behavior of consumers and businesses.

Sometimes the political process creates genuine economic problems, such as the looming entitlement funding problem. But sometimes the government has the power to create solutions, too: By carefully managing its tax and expenditures policies, it's sometimes possible for government to affect the overall level of spending in the economy and fight economic downturns.

This chapter touched on the regressive or progressive nature of particular taxes. The next chapter takes that discussion one step further: Government has, through its power to tax and spend, the ability to change the shape of the income distribution. That power is part of the next chapter's larger discussion of income inequality and the redistribution of income.

Chapter Summary and Problems

Key Terms

Automatic stabilizer, p. 443

Average tax rate, p. 431

Budget deficit, p. 437

Budget surplus, p. 437

Crowding out, p. 445

Discretionary expenditures, p. 435

Discretionary fiscal policy, p. 442

Federal debt, p. 438

Fiscal activities, p. 428

Fiscal policy, p. 442

Fully funded system, p. 440

Income tax, p. 430

Mandatory spending, p. 436

Marginal tax rate, p. 430

Pay-as-you-go system, p. 440

Payroll taxes, p. 429

Progressive tax, p. 432

Regressive tax, p. 429

20.1 Government Revenue, pages 428–435

List and define the major sources of federal government revenue.

Summary

The federal government raises about $3 trillion in revenue each year, largely through payroll and income taxes. Payroll taxes are about one-third of revenue and are used to fund entitlement programs. Income taxes, assessed on individuals and corporations, are the federal government's largest source of revenue. Economists pay particular attention to marginal income tax rates because the marginal rate affects peoples' behavior. In general, taxes are progressive if they take an increasing share of income the richer one is, and they are regressive if they take an increasing share of income the poorer one is.

Review Questions

All problems are assignable in MyEconLab.

1.1 A government's _____ activities include how it raises revenue and spends that revenue.

1.2 _____ are taxes that a worker's employer is required to pay on behalf of the worker every payday.

1.3 A(n) _____ tax takes a larger proportion of a person's income the poorer that person is.

1.4 _____ income is income that you receive from your job, as opposed to income received from financial investments.

1.5 The tax rate you pay on an additional dollar of income is called the _____.

1.6 A(n) _____ tax takes a larger proportion of a person's income the more that person makes.

1.7 Automatic reductions in taxable income based on the characteristics of someone's household are called _____.

1.8 Reductions in a person's taxable income due to particular ways he spends his money are called _____.
  a. Deductions
  b. Exemptions
  c. Progressive taxation
  d. Discretionary taxation

1.9 The biggest source of government revenue is _____.
  a. Individual income taxes
  b. Corporate income taxes
  c. Estate taxes
  d. Payroll taxes

1.10 The tax you pay on the typical dollar you make is called the _____.
  a. Sales tax rate
  b. Marginal tax rate
  c. Average tax rate
  d. Progressive tax rate

Problems and Applications

1.11 Your economics professor earns most of her income from stock investments in corporations. Last year, the average tax rate on her individual income tax was 25%. Explain why her average tax rate understates the true tax she paid on her income.

1.12 Explain two reasons FICA payroll taxes are regressive.

1.13 [Related to Application 20.1 on page 433] Edward Prescott's research indicates that in developed countries, the amount of work performed is directly related to the marginal tax rate. Do you suppose Prescott would find the same results in developing countries? Why or why not?

1.14 [Related to Application 20.1 on page 433] Edward Prescott's research indicates that in developed countries, the amount of work performed is directly related to the marginal tax rate. Can you think of some other economic factors that might account for the differences in hours worked between countries? If so, list and explain them.

1.15 In France, workers face the following individual income tax rates:

Income Range	Marginal Tax Rate
€0 to €6,011	0%
€6,012 to €11,991	5.5%
€11,992 to €26,631	14%
€26,632 to €71,397	30%
€71,398 to €151,200	41%
€151,201 and above	45%

  a. Suppose that you work in Paris, where you earn €26,000. Calculate your tax owed and determine your marginal and average tax rates.

  b. Suppose you receive a €1,000 raise. What happens to your average tax rate? What happens to your marginal tax rate?

1.16 Do a Google search to find the top marginal individual income tax rate in half a dozen countries of your choosing. How does the top U.S. marginal rate compare?

1.17 The U.S. tax code constitutes about 60,000 pages of exemptions, deductions, and loopholes. Conservative estimates place the cost of complying with the tax code (hiring accountants, for example) at well over $150 billion. As a result, several politicians have proposed replacing the current tax code with a simple 17% flat tax applicable to everybody, with no deductions allowed. Discuss some of the pros and cons of this proposal.

1.18 There is a built-in irony in government's use of the income tax to generate revenues: Taxing peoples' earnings discourages work. As a result, several economists have proposed eliminating the income tax and replacing it with a consumption tax—essentially, a national sales tax—sufficiently large to generate the same revenue for the government. Discuss some pros and cons of this proposal.

1.19 [Related to Application 20.2 on page 434] Discuss some pros and cons of eliminating the corporate income tax entirely.

20.2 ## Government Expenditures, Deficits, and Debt, pages 435–440

Explain the difference between mandatory and discretionary expenditures and between the federal government's budget deficit and the federal debt.

Summary

Government expenditures can be divided into two categories, mandatory and discretionary. Mandatory spending is automatically funded; discretionary spending must go through the normal appropriations process. Mandatory spending, composed mostly of spending on social insurance programs, is the biggest type of spending. The government's overall budget is in deficit when government spending exceeds revenues in a given year. Because government generally borrows to cover the shortfall, the federal debt is the sum of all past deficits, less any surpluses.

Review Questions

All problems are assignable in MyEconLab.

2.1 Spending that is not subject to Congress's annual appropriations process is referred to as _____.

2.2 _____ are expenditures that must be authorized by Congress each year.

2.3 Entitlement programs constitute _____ spending, while repairing roads can be considered _____ spending.

  a. Discretionary; mandatory
  b. Mandatory; discretionary
  c. Fully funded; pay-as-you-go
  d. Surplus; deficit

2.4 Which of the following accounts for the largest portion of mandatory spending?

  a. Social Security
  b. Defense spending
  c. Medicare
  d. Foreign aid spending

2.5 As a whole, the Social Security program is _____ because it redistributes income from higher earners to lower earners.
   a. Regressive
   b. Flat
   c. Proportional
   d. Progressive

2.6 The largest portion of discretionary spending is _____.
   a. Social Security
   b. Defense spending
   c. Foreign aid spending
   d. Education spending

2.7 _____ spending is a larger portion of government spending than _____ spending.
   a. Discretionary; mandatory
   b. Medicaid; Social Security
   c. Mandatory; discretionary
   d. Medicare; Social Security

2.8 If annual government expenditures exceed annual government receipts, the government is running a _____; if receipts exceed expenditures, the difference is called a _____.
   a. Debt; deficit
   b. Budget deficit; budget surplus
   c. Budget surplus; debt
   d. Budget surplus; budget deficit

2.9 The sum of all past federal government deficits minus the sum of all past federal government surpluses is called the _____.
   a. Budget deficit
   b. FICA
   c. Debt/GDP ratio
   d. Federal debt

Problems and Applications

2.10 A friend is concerned about the size of the total federal debt. Explain to him why looking at the total federal debt may be overly alarming and suggest some alternative measures for your friend to consider.

2.11 "It is clear that wasteful spending and mismanagement are the sources of the federal government's budgetary woes." Do you agree or disagree with this statement? Explain your reasoning.

2.12 "The federal government always runs a deficit. That's what all governments do." Comment on this statement, and bolster your commentary with data.

2.13 Suppose that government runs a deficit this year, with expenditures running greater than tax revenues. How will government likely pay for the excess spending? Does the government have any other options available to it?

20.3 | **The Future of the Federal Budget, pages 440–442**

Discuss how changes in the age of the U.S. population will affect the federal budget over the next four decades.

Summary

The federal budget faces a daunting set of demographic challenges over the next 50 years. The large population bubble known as the baby boom generation is entering retirement now; their children will be responsible for their benefits in Social Security and Medicare's pay-as-you-go systems. Small increases in payroll taxes today coupled with small cuts in projected benefits could eliminate the looming problems. The longer the government waits, the more dramatic the tax increases or benefit cuts that will be required. Government can also borrow to fund future shortfalls, which could shift the burden of paying for baby boomers' retirements still further onto future generations.

Review Questions

All problems are assignable in MyEconLab.

3.1 A retirement system that pays you benefits out of contributions that you made over your lifetime is called a(n) _____ system.

3.2 In a _____ system, the payroll taxes the government collects from individuals are immediately turned around and issued to retirees as benefits.
   a. Fully funded
   b. Discretionary
   c. Progressive
   d. Pay-as-you-go

3.3 The U.S. Social Security system is a(n) _____ system.
   a. Fully funded
   b. Discretionary
   c. Defined contribution
   d. Pay-as-you-go

Problems and Applications

3.4 The government has begun using the Social Security and Medicare trust funds, and both are expected to be depleted within the next 25 years. That places both programs in fiscal danger. Explain the sources of financial distress in the Social Security and Medicare systems.

3.5 Explain the funding structure of the Social Security and Medicare programs. What is the purpose of the Social Security and Medicare Trust Funds?

3.6 You have been selected by the president to fix the ailing Social Security system. What options are available to you? What are some costs and benefits of each option? Which solution will you choose?

20.4 The Federal Government and Fiscal Stabilization Policy, pages 442–448

Describe two fiscal policy tools that government can use to help fight recessions and explain when those tools are likely to be most effective.

Summary

Aggregate demand decreases when consumers and businesses stop buying the goods and services the economy is capable of producing. The government can use fiscal policy to stimulate the economy in such instances. The government can cut taxes to raise consumers' disposable income and stimulate consumption spending. Or the government can simply spend money itself, replacing the lost demand. Sometimes these fiscal actions happen automatically, via automatic stabilizers. Fiscal policy's ability to stimulate the economy depends on how long the lags of policy are. Fiscal policy's recession-fighting ability also depends on how much consumption and investment spending the fiscal action crowds out.

Review Questions

All problems are assignable in MyEconLab.

4.1 The government's use of its taxing and spending powers in order to fight economic downturns is called _____.

4.2 When government cuts personal income taxes, consumers' _____ income increases.

4.3 Because unemployment payments and welfare payments, which reduce a recession's severity, naturally increase during a downturn, they are called automatic _____.

4.4 _____ occurs when government spending doesn't increase overall spending, but simply displaces consumption or investment spending.

4.5 The economy is sliding into a recession. An appropriate fiscal policy response would be to _____.
  a. Increase the money supply
  b. Cut taxes
  c. Reduce government spending
  d. Both options (a) and (b) are appropriate fiscal policy responses.

4.6 The economy begins sliding into recession. The Senate majority leader proposes a stimulus bill, but the bill gets bound up in committee for three months before coming to a vote. That delay is an example of the _____.
  a. Recognition lag
  b. Implementation lag
  c. Impact lag
  d. Efficiency lag

Problems and Applications

4.7 The economy is sliding into a recession, and the president is calling for fiscal measures to prevent it. What two general recommendations might the president make? What condition is required for those tools to be effective?

4.8 List the lags of fiscal policy and compare their lengths to the lags of monetary policy.

4.9 Explain how government fiscal stimulus may crowd out private spending in each of the following cases:
  a. Government borrows money to buy a new Air Force One.
  b. Government uses tax revenue to expand bridge-building programs.
  c. Government cuts individual income taxes and borrows money to finance the deficit that results.

4.10 [Related to Application 20.3 on page 446] List three fiscal policy tools that were used to fight the Great Recession of 2007–2009. Were those tools effective? Why do you suppose it is so difficult to determine whether the tools worked or not?

4.11 [Related to Application 20.3 on page 446] The American Reinvestment and Recovery Act (ARRA) included a provision that imposed a general requirement that any public building or public works project funded by the ARRA must use only iron, steel, and other manufactured goods produced in the United States. What are the pros and cons of this type of provision?

Budget Deficits and the Federal Debt

This chapter highlighted the financial operation of the federal government, including where the government gets its revenue and how it spends that revenue. The chapter paid particular attention to government budget deficits and the federal debt. In this real-time data analysis activity, you'll examine the federal government's revenues and expenditures and explore their impact on the overall budget deficit and the federal debt using data from Federal Reserve Economic Data (FRED), a comprehensive, up-to-date data set maintained by the Federal Reserve Bank of St. Louis.

1. Visit the FRED website located at www.stlouisfed.org/fred2.

2. Measure the federal government's budget deficit using data on the federal government's receipts and expenditures.

3. Explore cuts to defense spending as a way to reduce the federal government budget deficit.

4. Locate current data on the federal government's debt and calculate the per-person burden of that debt.

MyEconLab

Please visit http://www.myeconlab.com for support material to conduct this experiment if assigned by your instructor.

Notes

Section 20.2

The figures used to gauge the overall progressivity/regressivity of the Social Security system discussed in Section 20.2 are based on a Social Security benefits calculator created by C. Eugene Steuerle and Adam Carasso for *USA Today* in 2004. The numbers account not only for the amount contributed but the hypothetical interest those contributions would have earned if they had been invested in a private savings account.

Section 20.3

Projections of the 130% debt/GDP ratio discussed in Section 20.3 come from the Congressional Budget Office and assume that current laws on other federal government spending will remain unchanged and that overall federal revenues grow at the same rate as GDP. For more information, see "The Budget and Economic Outlook: 2014 to 2024" at www.cbo.gov. This report makes clear that the biggest contributor to future budget problems is entitlement programs.

The alternative fiscal scenario discussed in Section 20.3 assumes that "some policies [such as some temporary tax breaks and temporary spending programs] that are now in place but that are scheduled to change [or expire] under current law would continue instead, and some provisions of current law that might be difficult to sustain for a long period would be modified." The CBO estimates that those changes will result in an extra $2 trillion of federal debt over the next decade.

CHAPTER

21

Income Inequality and the Redistribution of Income

Chapter Outline and Learning Objectives

21.1 **How Is Inequality Measured?** page 456

Summarize the major methods of measuring income inequality.

21.2 **How Unequal Is the Distribution of Income in the United States?** page 461

Using data, describe the income distribution in the United States.

21.3 **What Are the Causes and Effects of Income Inequality?** page 466

List three causes of income inequality and explain two effects it may have on economic efficiency.

21.4 **What Is the Role of Government in Promoting Equality?** page 470

Explain the major philosophical arguments for redistributing income.

Experiment: Unveiling Ignorance, page 478

MyEconLab

MyEconLab helps you master each objective and study more efficiently.

The previous five chapters were about macroeconomics, the functioning of the economy as a whole. We paid special attention to gross domestic product (GDP), which measures both the overall output of an economy and the overall income received by the people in that economy. *Real* GDP is GDP adjusted for the effects of rising prices. Here's the positive story that the history of U.S. GDP—and in particular, real GDP—tells us: In the approximately 70 years since the end of World War II, real GDP in the United States has trended steadily upward. There have been 11 blips in that trend—periods of time when real GDP has fallen. Those 11 *recessions* (periods of declining overall economic activity) were generally fairly short; the average recession lasts about a year. But even short recessions can be costly: During recessions, output and income fall, unemployment rises, and opportunities are lost.

But recessions are temporary. If you look past those painful episodes, the behavior of GDP tells a story of rising prosperity. Consider this: In 1960, real U.S. GDP per capita was less than $18,000. By 2011, it was over $48,000. As measured by real GDP, the typical American in 2011 was 2.5 times better off than he or she was in 1960. Modest growth, sustained for decades, leads to large gains in material standards of living. (See Chapter 16 for more on GDP and growth.) The typical American appears to be getting richer and richer.

But just because the typical American is getting richer doesn't necessarily mean that *every* American is getting richer. After all, not everybody is typical. And even if every American *is* getting richer, some Americans may be getting a little bit richer, whereas others may be getting a *lot* richer. In other words, the standard-of-living gains America is making may not be shared equally.

Income distribution The share of income received by different groups.

These observations reflect concerns about **income distribution**—the share of income received by different groups—and *income inequality*. Several important questions relevant to these concerns will be addressed in this chapter. First, how is the income distribution measured? Second, how unequal *is* the distribution of income? Third, what are the causes and effects of income inequality? Finally, on what basis should we decide to reengineer the distribution of income?

21.1 Learning Objective

Summarize the major methods of measuring income inequality.

How Is Inequality Measured?

To discuss income inequality, you need an understanding of the methods commonly used to measure it. There are many ways to do so, but almost all of them are based on just a handful of methods. Let's look at some of them.

Means and Medians: A First Step Toward Measuring Inequality

This chapter opened by describing the typical American's standard of living, as measured by real GDP per capita (per person). Real GDP per capita is often used to measure how a nation's standard of living has changed over time. It is also used to compare the income inequality of different nations. So understanding what real GDP per capita really says (and what it doesn't say) about the distribution of income is important.

Real GDP per capita can be calculated as real GDP for the entire country, divided by the number of people in the country:

$$\text{Real GDP per capita} = \frac{\text{Real GDP}}{\text{Population}}$$

Real GDP per capita is an average, or mean. It indicates the amount of real GDP each person would receive if it were divided equally among everyone in a nation. But the averaging process tends to disguise information about the distribution of income. For example, consider a small island with five people who each earn an inflation-adjusted $200,000 per year. To calculate real GDP per capita, add up everyone's income and divide by five:

$$\text{Real GDP per capita} = \frac{\$1 \text{ million}}{5}$$

$$= \$200,000$$

This is not a particularly surprising result. Compare it, however, to a different island, where four people earn $10,000 each, and a fifth earns $960,000. On this island, the real GDP per capita is:

$$\text{Real GDP per capita} = \frac{\$1 \text{ million}}{5}$$

$$= \$200,000$$

This is a very interesting result: two identical per capita real GDPs for two *very* different islands. Economists and the popular media both use real GDP per capita to describe what life looks like for the typical resident in a country. Although a real GDP of $200,000 per person does a good job of that on the first island, it does a lousy job of that on the second island. There, most people would agree, the typical resident lives on $10,000, not $200,000.

To overcome this problem, economists discussing income distribution often discard average, or *mean*, measures of income and use a summary measure called median income instead. **Median income** is measured as the income of the middle person in an income distribution. You can find the median income by simply ordering the five people on the first island from least income to greatest and then underlining the income of the person in the middle. On the first island, unsurprisingly, the median income is $200,000:

Median income The income of the middle person in an income distribution.

$200k $200k   <u>$200k</u> $200k $200k

Doing the same for the second island, we find that the median income is $10,000:

$10k $10k   <u>$10k</u> $10k $960k

The median income on the second island is much lower than it is on the first island, but it does a much better job of describing what the typical person's income is.

Using averages can also distort the picture of economic growth. If on the second island the income of the top earner rose by $1 million (to $1,960,000), the average income on the island would double to $400,000. But the median income would still be $10,000. For that reason, when you see people using real GDP per capita to talk about how Americans are getting wealthier, keep in mind that those gains may not be received by everybody; they might go just to the people at the top end of the income distribution.

However, the median statistic has its own ways of distorting the picture of economic growth. Consider a slightly larger island with nine residents with various incomes. If you list them in order as you did before, they look like this:

$5 $5 $5 $5 <u>$1k</u> $1k $1k $1k $1k

On this island, the median income is $1,000. Now suppose economic progress occurs, and the incomes of some of the residents rise, as follows:

$1k $1k $1k $1k <u>$1k</u> $50k $50k $50k $50k

Eight out of the nine residents have been made much better off by the economic progress. Yet if you used median income to measure well-being on the island, it would indicate that absolutely no economic progress had occurred. It is also hard to argue that the typical person on the island makes just $1,000 when almost as many of them earn $50,000. In this case, the mean might actually do a better job than the median of describing the progress of the typical person. Ultimately, no single summary measure of the income distribution is perfect. To get the most accurate picture possible, it's better to look at alternate, or even multiple, summary measures.

Quintiles: A More Detailed Look at the Income Distribution

To get a picture of how well the typical person in an economy is doing, economists and the media often present more detailed summaries that break down the income distribution of people into groups, from the poorest people in society to the richest. Often such a breakdown sorts income earners into quintiles. A *quintile* is a group that contains exactly one-fifth of the population. Consider a society with just five people, with the following incomes:

Bottom Quintile (Dean)	Second Quintile (Sammi)	Middle Quintile (Frank)	Fourth Quintile (Joie)	Top Quintile (Peter)
$4,000	$6,000	$10,000	$16,000	$24,000

Notice that they are sorted from the poorest (Dean) to the richest (Peter) and that each person represents a population quintile, since each is one-fifth of the total number of earners in the society.

The raw numbers in the table make it easy to compare the incomes of any two quintiles directly: The top earner earns six times what the bottom earner does. It's also easy to calculate the median income for the society as a whole: It's the income of the person in the middle of the middle quintile. Since the middle quintile contains only one person in this example, the median income is $10,000.

Often, however, earnings data is converted to make relative comparisons even easier. Notice that the earnings of all five people combined sum to $60,000. Dean takes home $4,000 out of that $60,000, which is 6.66% of all the income earned. In contrast, Peter takes home $24,000 of the $60,000, or 40% of all the income earned. In news stories, you might see this income distribution described like this: "The bottom 20% of all earners took home only 6.66% of the income, whereas the top 20% of earners took home 40% of all income."

Lorenz Curves and Gini Coefficients

It's quite common for income-distribution information to be presented in tables like the one shown above. Sometimes, however, people prefer to view income distributions graphically. The standard tool used for this purpose is a Lorenz curve. A **Lorenz curve** plots, for any given percentage of the population, the proportion of total income earned by that particular group of people.

Lorenz curve A curve that plots, for any given percentage of the population, the proportion of total income earned by that particular group of people.

Constructing a Lorenz Curve Consider, for starters, the island where each person earns exactly $200,000. There, the income distribution is perfectly equal. No one is richer than anyone else, but no one is poorer either. If you lined up all those people in any order and called the person on the far left the "poorest" (noting that nobody here is really poor—that's why it's okay to line them up in any order) and the person on the right the "richest," you would have five people, each representing one quintile, and each earning 20% of the income on the island. We can rephrase that slightly by saying that:

- The bottom 20% of the population earns 20% of the income.
- The bottom 40% of the population earns 40% of the income.
- The bottom 60% of the population earns 60% of the income.
- The bottom 80% of the population earns 80% of the income.
- All of the earners together (100%) earn 100% of the income.

Next, to construct a Lorenz curve that depicts this information, draw a square box and label the vertical and horizontal axes in 20% increments, ranging from

0% to 100%. Label the horizontal axis "Percentage of Total Population" and the vertical axis "Percentage of Total Income."[1] Then plot the points indicated in the previous bulleted list:

- Because 20% of the population earns 20% of the income, plot a point where 20 and 20 intersect and label it with an *A*.
- Because 40% of the population earns 40% of the income, plot a point where 40 and 40 intersect and label it with a *B*.
- Because 60% of the population earns 60% of the income, plot a point where 60 and 60 intersect and label it with a *C*.
- Because 80% of the population earns 80% of the income, plot a point where 80 and 80 intersect and label it with a *D*.
- Fill in the endpoints: 0% of the population earns 0% of the income; 100% of the earners earn 100% of the income.
- When you've plotted all the points, connect the dots. The Lorenz curve for this economy is complete and looks like this:

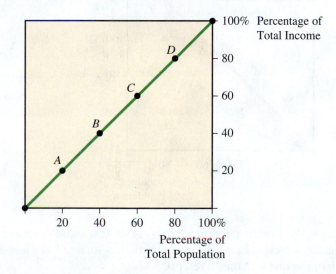

Notice that the Lorenz curve doesn't look like a curve. It looks like a straight line. That's because the economy we are considering is a very special one—one in which everybody's earnings are identical. A straight line of this type in a Lorenz curve is referred to as the *line of perfect equality*. The line of perfect equality describes what the income distribution would look like if everyone had equal earnings.

In the real world, there is no society in which everyone earns the same income. So let's look instead at the group of five earners referred to in the discussion of quintiles and use their incomes to construct a Lorenz curve. The following table presents the incomes earned by each quintile (member) of this small five-person society, as well as the percentage of the total income earned by each quintile:

Bottom Quintile (Dean)	Second Quintile (Sammi)	Middle Quintile (Frank)	Fourth Quintile (Joie)	Top Quintile (Peter)
$4,000	$6,000	$10,000	$16,000	$24,000
6.66%	10%	16.66%	26.66%	40%

---

[1]Lorenz curves are often scaled on the right-hand axis.

You can use this information to calculate the data necessary to build the Lorenz curve in the following figure, which shows the distribution of this society's total income:

- The bottom 20% of earners (Dean) take home 6.66% of the total income, which corresponds to point *A*.
- The bottom 40% of earners (Dean and Sammi) take home 16.66% (6.66% + 10%) of the total income, which corresponds to point *B*.
- The bottom 60% of earners take home 33.33% (6.66% + 10% + 16.66%) of the total income, which corresponds to point *C*.
- The bottom 80% of earners take home 60% (6.66% + 10% + 16.66% +26.66%) of the total income, which corresponds to point *D*.

Use this information to plot points as you did earlier, and then connect the dots. Here's what you should get:

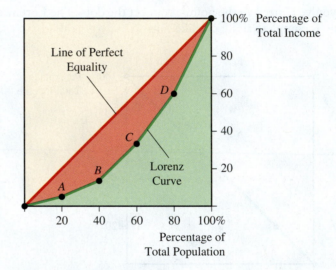

In this figure, the Lorenz curve really is a curve. It is some distance from the line of perfect equality, which indicates that this particular society has a less-equal income distribution than the one we considered previously.

The more top-heavy the income distribution is, the farther the Lorenz curve will be from the line of perfect equality. In the society depicted in the following graph, the distribution of income is even more unequal: 80% of the workers earn just over 20% of the total income, whereas the remaining 20% percent of workers earn 80% of it.

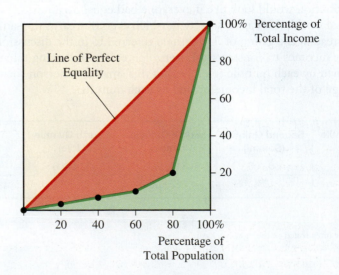

Calculating a Gini Coefficient The Lorenz curve is a nice visual way to depict the amount of income inequality in a society. The greater the gap between the Lorenz curve and the line of perfect equality, the greater the disparity between rich and poor. This information can be summarized numerically as well. Consider the following Lorenz curve, which is identical to the previous one:

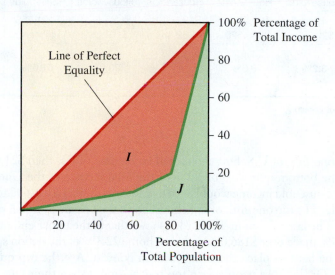

Notice that the letter I has been placed in the gap between the Lorenz curve and the line of perfect equality. The letter J has been placed in the gap between the Lorenz curve and the axes. The more unequal the income distribution, the larger the gap containing I (which we can call "area I") will be relative to *entire* area under the line of perfect equality, which can be measured as area I plus area J. The **Gini coefficient** measures the degree of inequality in society by comparing area I to areas I plus J. Specifically,

$$\text{Gini} = \frac{I}{(I + J)}$$

There are three important things to note about the Gini coefficient. First, because area I is always going to be smaller than (or, at the very most, equal to) areas $I + J$, the Gini coefficient will always be less than 1. Second, the smallest area I can be is 0, so the Gini coefficient will always be greater than or equal to 0. So the Gini coefficient will always be between 0 and 1. Third, the size of the Gini coefficient is directly related to the amount of income inequality. The bigger area I is, the more unequal the income distribution and the greater the Gini coefficient. If a society has perfect equality, both area I and the Gini coefficient will be 0. If a society has complete inequality, in which almost everybody works for nothing and one lone person captures *all* the income, then area J will equal 0, and the Gini coefficient will be 1.

Gini coefficient A number that measures a society's income inequality, based on how income is distributed across quintiles. The Gini coefficient is derived from the Lorenz curve and ranges from 0 (perfect equality) to 1 (perfect inequality).

How Unequal Is the Distribution of Income in the United States?

Your understanding of the ways economists measure and describe the distribution of income is most useful when combined with actual data. So what does the income distribution look like in the United States, and how has the income distribution changed over time?

21.2 Learning Objective

Using data, describe the income distribution in the United States.

U.S. Income Inequality, Past and Present

Let's begin by looking at the income distribution in the United States, arranged by quintile, as well as some additional data for the top 5% of earners. The data is shown in Table 21.1.

Table 21.1   U.S. Household Income by Quintile, 2012

In the United States, the bottom one-fifth of households receive 3.2% of total income. The top one-fifth of households receive 51% of total income.

	Bottom Quintile of Households	Second Quintile of Households	Middle Quintile of Households	Fourth Quintile of Households	Top Quintile of Households	Top 5% of Households
Income Range	$0 to $20,262	$20,263 to $38,520	$38,521 to $62,434	$62,435 to $101,582	$101,583 or more	$186,000 or more
Share of Total Income	**3.2%**	8.3%	14.4%	23.0%	**51.0%**	22.3%

Source: U.S. Census Bureau.

In 2012, one-fifth of U.S. households had an income of less than $21,000 per year. This group, the bottom quintile, got 3.2% of the total income in the United States. In contrast, your household income would have had to have topped $101,000 to make it into the top quintile. The top one-fifth of U.S. households took home over half of the nation's total income. The last column in Table 21.1 shows that at the upper end of the distribution, the top 5% made over $186,000 and took home 22.3% of the nation's income.

It might be hard to place those numbers in context. Are the top quintile's earnings justified? Or do those people earn too much—more than their fair share? These are largely normative questions that don't have objectively clear answers. Gathering additional data to place the 2012 figures in context is perhaps the most honest way to figure out what *your* answers to those questions will be.

If you are forming an opinion about the degree of inequality, one piece of information that might be useful to you is how the incomes in the United States have changed through time. Table 21.2 shows the share of income earned by each quintile over several decades, as well as the U.S. Census Bureau's estimated Gini coefficient.

Table 21.2 helps put the current numbers in historical context. Over the 40 years shown here, the share of income going to the top quintile of households increased from 43% to 51%. Much of that increase can be attributed to the top 5% of households, whose earnings rose from 16.6% of total income in 1970 to 22.3% of total income in 2012. Those gains appear to be occurring at the expense of households at the lower end of the distribution. The increasing inequality is also reflected in the Gini coefficient, which rose steadily from .394 in 1970 to .477 in 2012.

Economists Thomas Piketty of the Paris School of Economics and Emmanuel Saez of the University of California, Berkeley, have data that illuminates the changing income distribution in even greater detail. Using individual income tax returns, Piketty and Saez

Table 21.2   Share of Total U.S. Income, by Quintile

In the United States, the share of income received by the bottom quintile has been shrinking for several decades, while the share received by the top quintile has been growing. Overall inequality, as measured by the Gini coefficient, has been increasing.

Year	Bottom Quintile of Households	Second Quintile of Households	Middle Quintile of Households	Fourth Quintile of Households	Top Quintile of Households	Top 5% of Households	Gini Coefficient
1970	4.1%	10.8%	17.4%	24.5%	43.3%	16.6%	.394
1980	4.2%	10.2%	16.8%	24.7%	41.1%	16.5%	.403
1990	3.8%	9.6%	15.9%	24.0%	46.6%	18.5%	.428
2000	3.6%	8.9%	14.8%	23.0%	49.8%	22.1%	.462
2012	3.2%	8.3%	14.4%	23.0%	51.0%	22.3%	.477

Source: U.S. Census Bureau.

carefully constructed a data series that shows what has been happening at the very top of the income distribution. Between 1973 and 2010, for example, the income share earned by the top 1% of earners rose from 7.7% to 17.4%. Over that same time horizon, the income share earned by the top one-hundredth of 1% (the top 0.0001 of earners) rose sixfold, from 0.5% of all income to 3.3% of all income. In other words, the rich may be getting richer, but the super-rich are getting super-richer. It's no wonder that concerns about income inequality have become increasingly prominent since the Great Recession of 2007–2009. Years after the recession ended, large numbers of Americans were still underemployed, employed part time, or not employed at all. Real GDP per capita still had not returned to pre-recession levels, and yet at the top of the income distribution, the super-rich appeared to be living larger than ever before.

U.S. Income Inequality Compared to Other Countries

It might be informative to see how income inequality in the U.S. compares to income inequality in other countries. The easiest way to do this is to look at each country's Gini coefficient. Recall that a Gini coefficient of 0 means perfect equality, and a Gini coefficient of 1 means perfect inequality. Table 21.3 shows the Gini coefficients of a number of developed and developing countries and regions during the first decade of the 2000s.

Among developed countries, the United States has one of the higher Gini coefficients, which indicates a higher degree of inequality. The highly developed Western European nations almost universally have very low inequality, and the collection of EU nations as a whole has a Gini coefficient of only .306. The EU–U.S. comparison is an interesting one because the economies of the European Union and the United

Table 21.3   Gini Coefficients, Selected Countries and Regions, 2000s

Inequality, as measured by the Gini coefficient, differs widely between countries in all stages of development.

	Country	Gini Coefficient
Developed Countries	Sweden	.230
	Germany	.270
	Australia	.303
	European Union	.306
	Canada	.321
	Japan	.376
	United States	.450
	Singapore	.463
	Hong Kong	.537
Developing Countries	Pakistan	.306
	Egypt	.308
	India	.368
	Tanzania	.376
	Morocco	.409
	Philippines	.448
	China	.473
	Mexico	.483
	Brazil	.519
	Chile	.521
	Central African Republic	.613
	South Africa	.631

Source: CIA World Factbook, 2014.

States are about the same size and they are, generally speaking, at the same stage of development. Yet their measured income inequality differs substantially.

More subtly, the *source* of that measured inequality differs substantially. A significant number of the nations in the European Union have substantially greater equality than the European Union as a whole does. For example, both Germany (Gini = .27) and Slovakia (Gini = .26) have very little inequality within their own borders. But Germany is a very rich EU country (so the typical German has a high income), and Slovakia is a relatively poor EU country (so the typical Slovakian has a low income). This means if you calculated income inequality for the Germany–Slovakia pair, it would likely be higher than measured income inequality in either nation. In other words, in the EU, income inequality is most apparent when you travel from one place to another.

The U.S. experience is quite different. In the United States, each state has a population of rich and poor people living essentially side by side. In other words, the Gini coefficient for each state is in roughly the same range as the Gini coefficient for the country as a whole. Utah, which has the least inequality, has a Gini coefficient of .419. New York, the state with the greatest inequality, has a Gini coefficient of .499. Interestingly, the most unequal place in the United States is the District of Columbia, where the Gini coefficient is a whopping .532. In contrast to the European Union, there are no large-scale pockets of equality anywhere in the United States.

Table 21.3 also tells some important stories about income inequality in the developing world. On the one hand, there are countries such as Pakistan that are quite poor but in which income inequality is low. On the other hand, there are countries such as South Africa in which income inequality is high. Generally speaking, inequality is higher in the developing world than in the developed world: The 10 countries in the world with the highest income inequality and 37 of the top 40 are all developing countries.

Are the Rich Getting Richer and the Poor Getting Poorer in the United States?

The U.S. inequality statistics in the previous section paint a Charles Dickens–like picture of increasing income for the rich at the expense of the poor. But the statistics show only the relative shares of income across the population. To determine whether that assertion is true, you have to look at *how much* income each group earned. Table 21.4 shows the mean real income within each quintile for a number of years since 1970. Table 21.4 also shows by how much it grew over a few key time periods.

Table 21.4   U.S. Mean Household Real Income and Growth Rates, by Quintile

Between 1970 and 2012, the average real income increased for each quintile. Mean incomes for the bottom two quintiles increased more slowly than incomes for the upper three quintiles.

	Year	Bottom Quintile	Second Quintile	Middle Quintile	Fourth Quintile	Top Quintile	Top 5%
Income	1970	$10,512	$28,475	$45,852	$64,633	$114,421	$175,624
	1993	$11,515	$29,192	$48,932	$76,044	$158,434	$271,926
	2006	$12,928	$32,771	$54,917	$86,924	$191,513	$338,686
	2012	$11,490	$29,696	$51,179	$82,098	$181,905	$318,052
Total Growth	1970 to 2006	23%	15%	20%	34%	67%	93%
	1993 to 2012	0%	2%	5%	8%	15%	17%

Source: U.S. Census Bureau.

The data in Table 21.4 illustrates two important points. First, ignoring the effects of the Great Recession and the economy's incomplete recovery afterward, the 1970–2006 data shows that at the household level, both the rich and the poor have improved their absolute standards of living over the past four decades. The richest 5% saw their real earnings rise 93% over those 36 years, or about 1.9% annually. The poorest quintile saw their real earnings rise 23% over the same time span, which corresponds to an annual growth rate of about 0.6%.[2]

In other words, the rich are getting richer. But the numbers don't generally bear out the assertion that the poor are getting poorer. On average, people in the bottom quintile could afford to buy 23% more goods and services in 2006 than they could in 1970. The people in this quintile have been getting wealthier but at an excruciatingly slow pace. Top earners have been on an income-growth rocket ship by comparison.

Second, the data reveals that the technology-related boom that began with the Internet in the early 1990s has largely left the bottom quintile behind. Over the two decades of the tech explosion, the real incomes of the rich rose substantially, even accounting for the effects of the Great Recession and slow recovery. But despite all the wealth those two decades created, the earnings of the poor were unchanged. In fact, the bottom three quintiles appear to have shared very little of the economic benefits of the tech boom.

Is Economic Mobility Decreasing in the United States?

It is clear that economic inequality has been growing in the United States. The raw numbers suggest that, over time, the richest one-fifth of the population made dramatic gains, while the incomes of the poorest one-fifth stagnated. But those numbers may be misleading because the people occupying each quintile change over time. Some of the people who were in the richest quintile this year were in the lowest quintile a few years ago. And some of the people who are in the richest quintile today will fall to a lower quintile in the not-so-distant future. In other words, Americans have **income mobility**—the ability to move to a different part of the income distribution.

Income mobility The ability to move to a different part of the income distribution.

Many people disagree about the degree of inequality a country should have. But in the United States, most people agree that high mobility is better than low mobility. After all, low mobility runs counter to the U.S. image as a land of opportunity. So how low is income mobility?

Economists generally measure income mobility in two ways. First, they look at intergenerational mobility—the ability of a child to escape his or her parents' circumstances—by looking for correlations between parents' and children's incomes. Second, they may follow particular individuals for a long stretch of time to see how those persons' incomes change and then measure the probability of a person jumping from one part of the income distribution to another.

In the most comprehensive study of income mobility to date, Harvard economists Raj Chetty and Nathaniel Hendren, along with Berkeley economists Patrick Kline and Emmanuel Saez and Nicholas Turner of the Department of the Treasury, performed just such calculations for the United States. Their study examined more than 40 million tax records (with identifying information removed) of people born between 1971 and 1993. Contrary to public perception, they find little change in economic mobility over recent decades. In 1971, a child born into the lowest-income quintile had an 8.4% chance of making it to the top quintile. That number changed little between 1971 and 1986, when the chance of making the leap from bottom to top was 9%. Given prior studies that document little change in mobility between 1950 and the 1970s, the authors conclude that income mobility has changed little over the past half-century.

---

[2]Unfortunately, precise annual growth rate numbers can't be calculated using simple division. That's why, for example, the growth rate for the rich isn't just 93% ÷ 36 years, or 2.58%. If you're curious about exactly how the growth rate is computed, your instructor can provide you both the necessary background and formula.

The study does confirm one major conclusion from other studies: Income mobility in the United States is lower than in many other developed countries. And in a second study spun off from the original project, the authors determine that even economic mobility in the United States depends critically on where you happen to live. A child born into the bottom quintile of the income distribution in San Jose has a 12.9% chance of reaching the top quintile; a similar child in Atlanta has only a 4.5% chance.

The authors pinpoint five factors that are correlated with economic mobility:

1. **Segregation by race or income.** The more segregated (by race or income) the city, the lower the associated economic mobility.

2. **Family structure.** A higher prevalence of single-parent households in a community is correlated with lower economic mobility.

3. **School quality.** Areas with higher test scores, lower dropout rates, and smaller class sizes had greater mobility.

4. **Social capital.** Greater religious and civic participation are positively correlated with economic mobility.

5. **Economic inequality.** Smaller income gaps among the middle class were associated with greater income mobility.

It is easy to understand why a widening income distribution is discouraging to those at the bottom of the income ladder. But the work of Chetty, Hendren, Kline, Saez, and Turner suggests that those who start at the bottom of the income ladder don't have to remain there. Their research also informs those who are interested in preserving or improving economic mobility about some potential policy targets.

What Are the Causes and Effects of Income Inequality?

21.3 Learning Objective

List three causes of income inequality and explain two effects it may have on economic efficiency.

If income inequality appears to be high and growing, then it's natural to wonder why it exists in the first place. Economists have explored five major sources of inequality: differences in productivity, increasing globalization, improvements in technology, the increasing prominence of winner-take-all tournament-style markets, and rent-seeking by the incumbent wealthy.

Inequality and Productivity

One big step toward understanding why income inequality exists is recognizing that people's incomes are related to their productivity in the marketplace. Productivity can be reflected along two dimensions. First, suppose that two people do the same job for the same company, but one is very fast and the other is quite slow. The employee who is faster is likely to be paid more simply because he produces more. Even if his company won't pay him more, other companies will want to lure him away because of how fast he works. If he takes advantage of those opportunities, his income will rise. Second, market productivity depends on the value of what is being produced. Consider two restaurant cooks who both work very hard every day. One is a chef at a gourmet restaurant where a typical meal costs $200. The other works as a cook at a diner where a typical meal costs $6. Even if they both produce the same number of meals, the chef at the fancy restaurant is likely to be paid more simply because each meal brings more cash into the restaurant. In other words, the chef adds more value to the ingredients by turning them into delicious gourmet meals, and his pay is likely to reflect that.

Although productivity differences can result in income inequality, that isn't necessarily a bad thing. Consider the following scenario suggested by Harvard economist Greg Mankiw: An island is home to 500 people. Each person earns $100 each year, the island's income equality is perfect, and everyone is happy. Then one person on the island invents something extraordinary—perhaps the iPod, or beer, or a series of novels about a young man who goes to a school for wizards. Everybody loves the new invention, and each person gives $10 to the inventor to obtain one.

The perfect equality on the island is now gone: Although 499 people still have incomes of $100, the inventor sees her income rise by thousands of dollars. Yet this is a good inequality: The inventor is rewarded for coming up with something extraordinary, and the 499 others get something extraordinary that they value more than their $10. In this case, everyone wins.

Inequality, Globalization, and Technology

The previous section may have already planted the idea that the more talented you are and the more you have been trained to use your talents, the more value you are likely to produce, and the more you are likely to earn.

In the past few decades, changes in the structure of the economy have increased the rewards for additional education and training. No change has been more noticeable than the role of technology in our daily lives. The tech sector has created many highly paid jobs for people with the ability and training to work in that sector. People without that level of education and training have largely seen their incomes stagnate because their talents aren't as highly valued as they were a few decades ago, relative to the talents of skilled workers.

A second fundamental change in the economy has been increasing **globalization**, the increasing integration of the world's economies. In many ways, globalization has been a wonderful thing: It has given U.S. producers access to larger markets and brought U.S. consumers a wider variety of goods and services at lower cost. Globalization has also resulted in increased competition that has led to better products. The quality of automobiles today compared to the quality in decades past is a notable example.

Globalization The increasing integration of the world's economies.

Globalization, however, has not been kind to low-skilled workers in the United States. The world is full of low-skilled workers capable of performing the same jobs as these workers, and often at lower cost. In other words, globalization, like everything else, has costs and benefits. It has created opportunities for people with special skills to expand who they sell to, but it has closed doors for people who don't have special skills, and it's widened the gap between rich and poor.

Inequality, Technology, and Tournament-Style Markets

Every year, thousands of talented high-school students head off to college on sports scholarships. Yet out of those thousands of players, only a tiny fraction will become professional athletes. For many, the years of sacrifice and the dream of going pro will end when they receive their diplomas.

Economist Sherwin Rosen likened labor markets such as this to tournaments: The people who enter them know they are likely to lose but are hoping to be lucky enough or skilled enough to win. Winning, of course, takes some luck. But odds are that the winner of a tournament creates success by having exactly the right blend of qualities in sufficient amounts.

It's not just the market for athletes that looks like a tournament market. Think how many people move to California to become actors and actresses, or how many audition for *American Idol* and *The Voice*. Many of those people are talented, but few are so complete and so super-talented that they have the mass appeal necessary to achieve stardom and the income that stardom produces.

The bigger the market, the bigger the rewards to stardom. Globalization, as mentioned before, means bigger markets. But so does technology. The technologically interconnected world gives the especially talented new ways to leverage their stardom. First, technology allows superstars to reach more people. Today, people in Outer Mongolia can watch Miley Cyrus sing on their iPhones; 20 years ago, they wouldn't have known who the top American recording stars *were*. Second, technology has created new ways for superstars to earn income: Miley collects a tiny share of Google's ad revenue each time an Outer Mongolian plays one of her YouTube videos.

So globalization has provided increased opportunities for higher-skilled labor, and growing technology has done the same. But both have produced outsized, exponential rewards for superstar talents. That's true for superstars like Miley Cyrus and Yao Ming, but it's also true for corporate superstars: Since 1982, the pay of corporate chief executive officers (CEOs) has grown from 40 times the typical worker's wages to over 200 times the typical worker's wages. CEOs of the top 350 companies made an average of *$15.2 million* in 2013.

Inequality and Rent Seeking

The explanations of growing inequality in the previous sections present a mixture of good and bad *outcomes*, but in none of those cases does increasing inequality stem from bad *motives*. The fourth explanation for growing inequality, though, might: Growing inequality might be the direct result of rent seeking.

Rent seeking occurs when someone seeks to use the power of government to his or her own private advantage, at the expense of everyone else (see Chapter 1). For example, suppose that a large Florida sugar producer is disappointed with the price his sugar fetches in the market. By lobbying Congress to limit imports of sugar from abroad, that sugar producer creates an artificial scarcity in the market that allows him to sell his sugar for a much higher price. The sugar producer wins; 300 million sugar consumers lose. That's rent seeking.

Nobel Prize–winning economist Joseph Stiglitz makes the case that growing inequality stems from rent seeking in his 2013 book *The Price of Inequality: How Today's Divided Society Endangers Our Future*. Not only might inequality *result* from rent seeking, but inequality gives the richest members of society the financial resources they need to *sustain* their positions at the top of the income distribution: Lobbying legislators for protection from foreign sugar is easier when you have millions of dollars to throw at those legislators.

The Economic Effects of Inequality

Income inequality discussions almost always revolve around normative issues. But many economists are concerned with a more dispassionate analysis of the effects income inequality has on economic *efficiency*—society's ability to extract the greatest value from its scarce resources. In other words, income inequality may affect the size of the economic pie.

There are two major ways that economic inequality may affect economic efficiency. In a world with perfect equality, the benefits of economically virtuous behaviors—investing, inventing, creating, risk taking—are divided among everyone equally, leaving little reward for inventors and entrepreneurs. On the other hand, a wide income distribution opens the possibility of receiving great rewards. This is particularly important to those who are most creative and imaginative—the superstars. But remember that superstars get rich because they create value for their fans, so a wide income distribution can result in everyone being better off. This is the essence of the Mankiw story above.

On the other hand, if inequality results from or encourages more rent seeking, inequality might actually shrink the size of the economic pie. If a government policy such as a restriction on imported sugar results in a sugar baron getting $1 richer but costs society $2, then that inequality is bad for society. This is the essence of the Stiglitz story.

World Bank economist Branko Milanovic summarizes these possibilities with this analogy:[3]

> To understand it, look at inequality, as far as economic efficiency is concerned, as cholesterol: There is "good" and "bad" inequality, just as there is good and bad cholesterol. "Good" inequality is needed to create incentives for people to study, work hard, or start

---

[3]See Branko Milanovic, *The Haves and the Have-Nots: A Brief and Idiosyncratic History of Global Inequality*, Basic Books, 2010.

Application 21.1

Keeping Up with Your Co-workers Is Important

Suppose you are hired to sweep floors. Your employer gives you a broom and instructions to sweep for one hour. When you're done, she gives you a $100 bill.

How happy would you be?

Now, suppose that later in the day you learn that your roommate *also* spent one hour sweeping floors and that he earned *$200*.

How happy would you be now?

In the hyper-rational world of economists, your happiness should depend only on whether the pay you receive is sufficient to offset your displeasure of working. In other words, do the benefits outweigh the costs *for you*? But in the real world, humans' motivations are sometimes more complex. Many people theorize that your job satisfaction depends not only on how much you get paid but also on how your pay compares to your co-workers' earnings.

Princeton economist Alexandre Mas joined Berkeley economists David Card, Enrico Moretti, and Emmanuel Saez to test this theory. They did so using a website created by the *Sacramento Bee* in 2008 that published the salaries of all California state employees, including the employees of state universities. The economists sent an email to about one-third of the employees at three California state universities to let them know about the new website.

About a week later, the economists then sent another email to *every* employee at those three universities, asking them to respond to a survey. In addition to questions about their use of the website, the survey asked employees how satisfied they were with their jobs and their pay and how likely they were to look for a new job in the next year.

The survey responses showed that the economists' initial email greatly increased the employees' awareness of the website: Fifty percent of the group that received that email had accessed the site, compared to 20% of the remaining employees. Eighty percent of viewers indicated they used the site to see what their co-workers made.

Knowing what their co-workers made affected the employees' job satisfaction. Among workers with below-median earnings, those who had accessed the *Bee* site reported significantly less job satisfaction than those who had not accessed the site. Workers who had visited the site were 20% more likely to have said they intended to search for new jobs.

Did those workers follow through on their intentions? Three years later, Card, Mas, Moretti, and Saez searched the universities' personnel directories to see who had actually left their jobs. Workers who had said they intended to search for new employment were 20% more likely to have left their jobs than other workers. Below-median earners who had expressed a desire to leave and who knew of their co-workers' salaries were even more likely to have left their jobs.

In other words, what you make matters. But what your co-workers make matters, too: Being paid less than one's co-workers is so important to many people that they may be willing to leave their jobs because of it.

See related problem 3.7 on page 477 at the end of this chapter.

Based on David Card, Alexandre Mas, Enrico Moretti, and Emmanuel Saez, "Inequality at Work: The Effect of Peer Salaries on Job Satisfaction," *American Economic Review*, October 2012; Alain Cohn, Ernst Fehr, Benedikt Herrmann, and Frederic Schneider, "Social Comparison in the Workplace: Evidence from a Field Experiment," *IZA Discussion Paper No. 5550*, 2011; and Andrew Clark, David Masclet, and Marie Claire Villeval, "Effort and Comparison Income: Experimental and Survey Evidence," *Industrial and Labor Relations Review*, 2010.

risky entrepreneurial projects. None of that can be done without providing some inequality in returns. But "bad" inequality starts at a point—not easy to define—where, rather than providing the motivation to excel, inequality provides the means to preserve acquired positions. This happens when inequality in wealth or income is used to forestall an economically positive political change for the society, or to allow only the rich to get education, or to ensure that the rich keep the best jobs.

21.4 Learning Objective

Explain the major philosophical arguments for redistributing income.

What Is the Role of Government in Promoting Equality?

Many impassioned and intelligent people believe that society would be better off if income distribution were flatter. Often, they argue for active redistribution programs that tax the rich highly and then redistribute the proceeds to the poor. The redistribution can be direct: The government can take $1 from rich Peter and transfer it to poorer Paul. The redistribution can also be indirect: The government can provide programs and services to society as a whole that are funded by a disproportionately heavy tax on Peter. Regardless of whether the transfer is direct or indirect, a system that assesses proportionally higher taxes on the rich than it does on the poor is called a *progressive* tax system. (See Chapter 20 for more on the tax system.)

Philosophical Justifications for Redistribution

People who are in favor of redistribution programs often rely on a few highly persuasive philosophical arguments. Let's look at them.

Utilitarianism The belief that the ethically proper thing to do in any situation is the thing that maximizes society's overall utility (happiness) and minimizes society's overall suffering.

Diminishing marginal utility The belief that having more of something makes you happier but in successively smaller increments.

Utilitarianism   One common argument in favor of redistribution is based on the philosophical framework of utilitarianism. **Utilitarianism** is the belief that the ethically proper thing to do in any situation is the thing that maximizes society's overall utility (happiness) and minimizes society's overall suffering. The utilitarian argument for redistribution depends on the idea of the diminishing marginal utility of income. **Diminishing marginal utility** means that having more of something makes you happier but in successively smaller increments. Think, for example, about doughnuts: The first one you eat is divine, the second one you eat is great, and the third one is merely okay.

Likewise, the last dollar Bill Gates earned probably didn't increase his happiness very much. After all, what can he do with that dollar that he couldn't do without that dollar? So we might evaluate that dollar, in Bill Gates's hands, as merely okay.

But what if you take Bill's dollar and give it to a poorly paid single mother of two, struggling to put macaroni and cheese on the table? That dollar might make a real difference to her and to her family. In other words, we might evaluate that dollar, in our single mother's hands, as divine. By taking a dollar from Bill Gates and redistributing it to someone who values it more highly, society as a whole extracts more happiness from that same dollar. As a result, the world is a better place for the redistribution.

The diminishing-marginal-utility aspect of income makes utilitarianism a compelling argument for redistributing income. But it's not completely convincing because those who make the utilitarian argument often fail to take it to its logical conclusion: People who are very rich should therefore be required to give some of their money to people who are very poor. And where are those poor? Most of them live in developing countries. In fact, even the poorest group of Americans—those in the lowest 5% of the U.S. income distribution—earn more than 60% of the people on the entire planet do. So should all Americans, including the lowest 5% of earners, be heavily taxed and the proceeds sent to extremely impoverished people in another country? In all likelihood, far fewer Americans would be in favor of this alternative than would be in favor of redistribution within their own country. In other words, for many people, utilitarianism stops at a country's borders. Ultimately, if utilitarianism is to provide a moral foundation for redistribution, it must be extended to everybody: In the eyes of a true utilitarian, happiness in Pakistan is no less important than happiness in West Palm Beach, Florida.

The Rawlsian Social Contract Suppose you are abducted by aliens who intend to move you to a strange country on a strange planet. There you will live a life that will be randomly chosen for you. In particular, your unalterable lifetime income will be determined by a roll of the dice: You could end up being one of your new society's wealthiest members. Or you could be at the very bottom of the distribution, the poorest of the poor.

In this scenario, you have been placed in what philosopher John Rawls called the *original position*, a hypothetical place, before you are born, where you don't know anything about what your future life will look like. Will you be rich or poor? Will you be beautiful or homely? Will you be brilliant or will you have low intelligence? In other words, you are situated behind what Rawls called a *veil of ignorance*.

Now imagine that you could buy insurance that would prevent you from being deposited into a position of extreme and enduring poverty. Many people, maybe even most people, in that position would gladly pay for such an insurance policy, even if the policy were pretty costly. They would willingly make themselves somewhat poorer (by spending their money on such a policy) to avoid the chance of being extremely poor.

Real-world redistribution programs can accomplish exactly the same thing as this imaginary insurance contract. The government can collect "insurance premiums" (taxes) from the well-off and then transfer the money collected from the premiums to the poorest members of society. In other words, redistribution by the government enforces a social contract that many or most people would agree to from behind the veil of ignorance.

The Rawlsian argument, like the utilitarian argument, can be compelling. But like the utilitarian argument, it may not be logically complete. Harvard economist Greg Mankiw points out one example: In addition to being concerned about income, in the original position, people might also be concerned about health outcomes. What if you could buy an insurance policy that would guarantee you one working kidney? The same Rawlsian reasoning that justifies taking earnings from the rich could be used to justify taking a kidney from a healthy person and giving it to someone who needs one.

Of course, few people in the United States advocate compulsory organ donation, even if a Rawlsian argument calls for one. But if organs are off the table, Mankiw wonders, why is income still on the table? The point of a moral philosophy is that it should provide consistent and universal guidance: In other words, if you think the Rawlsian social contract should be adopted, fine. However, you don't get to pick and choose where it is applied and where it isn't.

The Benefits Received Principle In 2011, a quote from then Massachusetts senatorial candidate Elizabeth Warren went viral:

> You built a factory out there? Good for you. But I want to be clear: you moved your goods to market on the roads the rest of us paid for; you hired workers the rest of us paid to educate; you were safe in your factory because of police forces and fire forces that the rest of us paid for. You didn't have to worry that marauding bands would come and seize everything at your factory, and hire someone to protect against this, because of the work the rest of us did. Now look, you built a factory and it turned into something terrific, or a great idea? God bless. Keep a big hunk of it. But part of the underlying social contract is you take a hunk of that and pay it forward for the next kid who comes along.

Warren's quote illustrates what public-finance economists call the **benefits received principle**: Higher taxes on the rich aren't being justified on the grounds that the rich can afford to pay more. Instead, they are justified because the rich have received a disproportionately large benefit of the services, infrastructure, and protections the government provides.

Benefits received principle The belief that higher taxes on the rich are justified because they have received a disproportionately large benefit of the services, infrastructure, and protections the government provides.

Such an argument in favor of progressive taxation makes some sense to economists. After all, one big theme in the early chapters of this book is that separating the costs and benefits of an activity generally results in a poor social outcome. The progressive taxation Warren suggests rejoins those costs and benefits.

Application 21.2

What Does the Ideal Wealth Distribution Look Like?

Imagine that you are in Rawls's original position and are asked what the ideal distribution of wealth would look like in your society, where wealth is defined as the total value of what someone owns, minus what that person owes to others. Now suppose you come out from behind the veil of ignorance and compare the actual distribution to your ideal. Do you want a more equitable society? A less equitable society?

Using a carefully designed survey, professors Dan Ariely of Duke University and Michael Norton of Harvard asked 5,500 people to make that comparison. The survey revealed surprising points about the preferences Americans have when it comes to how the nation's wealth should be distributed. As part of the survey, respondents were shown the following table, which depicts the hypothetical wealth distributions in three fictitious countries:

Wealth Shares of Quintiles in Three Hypothetical Countries					
	Fifth (Bottom) Quintile	Fourth Quintile	Third Quintile	Second Quintile	First (Top) Quintile
Country A	20%	20%	20%	20%	20%
Country B	0.1%	0.2%	4%	11%	84%
Country C	11%	15%	18%	21%	36%

Next, respondents were shown various pairings of the three countries and asked to vote for the country they would prefer to live in if they found themselves in Rawls's original position. In those pairings, Country C beat Country A 51% to 49%; Country A beat Country B 77% to 23%; and Country C beat Country B 92% to 8%.

What Ariely and Norton didn't tell respondents was this: Country B's distribution is the same as that of the United States, and Country C's distribution is the same as Sweden's. In other words, Americans vastly prefer Sweden's more equitable distribution. They even prefer the completely egalitarian distribution in Country A to the distribution of wealth in the United States!

Then Ariely and Norton asked respondents to estimate what the current distribution of wealth in the United States is and then create their own ideal distribution. Their responses were as follows:

U.S. Wealth Distributions (Approximate)					
	Fifth (Bottom) Quintile	Fourth Quintile	Third Quintile	Second Quintile	First (Top) Quintile
Ideal Wealth Distribution	11%	14%	20%	23%	32%
Estimated Wealth Distribution	3%	6%	13%	20%	58%
Actual Wealth Distribution	0.1%	0.2%	4%	11%	84%

The results of this exercise are illuminating. First, people created ideal wealth distributions that were much more equitable than they estimated the distribution of wealth in the United States to be. Second, respondents vastly underestimated the amount of wealth inequality that actually exists. Impressively, those results were consistent regardless of the respondent's income or political affiliation.

Ariely and Norton's research shows that Americans have a preference for much greater equality than currently exists. The researchers hypothesize that perhaps Americans don't advocate more strongly for greater equality because, as the second result shows, they don't fully understand how far from ideal the true distribution is.

See related problems 4.9 and 4.10 on page 477 at the end of this chapter.

Based on Michael Norton and Dan Ariely, "Building a Better America—One Wealth Quintile at a Time," *Perspectives on Psychological Science*, 2011; "Americans Want to Live in a Much More Equal Country (They Just Don't Realize It)," *The Atlantic*, August 2, 2012; and "The Inequality Delusion," *Bloomberg Businessweek*, October 21, 2010.

The benefits received principle is a reasonable justification for a highly progressive tax code. But it is not an airtight justification. First, it's hard to quantify exactly how big those government benefits actually are. For example, how big of a benefit does Walmart get by being able to use the nation's roads to transport products to its store? How much benefit does it receive from police and fire protection, or from national defense? An honest use of the benefits received principle requires that those benefits be measured.

A second and more philosophical argument against the benefits received principle is that the benefits the rich receive from government programs are available to everybody. Poor people can drive on government-provided roads just as easily as rich people can. Poor people receive the same benefits from police protection as the rich do. In other words, many government services are what economists call public goods: Once you've provided them to one person, they are available to all. (See Chapter 10.) Just because the rich happened to take greater advantage of roads and police and other public goods doesn't mean that poor people were being denied those benefits. In other words, it may not be fair to penalize the rich for making the most of the government services they received because those services were available to everyone.

Progressive Taxation

If the utilitarian, Rawlsian, or benefits received arguments have convinced you that a progressive tax is justified, exactly how progressive should that tax system be? How high a tax constitutes a fair share for the poor, the middle class, and the rich? And how do we need to alter our current tax code to achieve that ideal?

How Progressive Is the U.S. Tax System? A good place to begin answering the question just posed is by gaining an understanding of exactly how progressive the U.S. tax system is. To do that, economists generally compare the average tax rate applied to rich peoples' incomes to the average tax rate applied to poor peoples' incomes, where the average tax rate is measured as the amount of taxes a person pays divided by his or her income. Table 21.5 shows the average federal tax rate applicable to the incomes of ordinary Americans, ordered by quintile.

Table 21.5 shows that at the federal level, the tax code is progressive: The rich pay a higher share of their income in taxes. And because the rich earn more income and pay a higher rate, the rich pay a disproportionate share of the cost of running the government. The top 20% of earners pay for over two-thirds of the cost. The top 1% alone pay more than one-fifth of the cost.

Now let's compare the tax burden of the rich to the share of income they earn: In 2010, the top quintile earned 51.9% of the country's before-tax income but paid 68.8% of the taxes. The top 5% earned 27.4% of the income but paid 41.4% of the taxes. Whatever one might say about the rich, they pay more taxes, both in absolute and relative terms, than everyone else.

Table 21.5 Average U.S. Tax Rate by Quintile						
The U.S. federal tax system is progressive: The top quintile faces an average tax rate of 24% and contributes 68.8% of all federal tax dollars received. The bottom quintile faces an average federal tax rate of 1.5%, and contributes 0.4% of all federal tax dollars received.						
	Bottom Quintile	Second Quintile	Middle Quintile	Fourth Quintile	Top Quintile	Top 1%
Average Federal Tax Rate	1.5%	7.2%	11.5%	15.6%	24.0%	29.4%
Share of Total Federal Tax Liabilities	0.4%	3.8%	9.1%	17.6%	68.8%	24.2%

Source: Congressional Budget Office, 2010 data. Tax rates and shares include all federal taxes, including income tax, payroll tax, corporate income tax, and excise taxes.

Should the U.S. Tax System Be More Progressive? The rich pay a disproportionate share of the cost of government. But is it disproportionate enough? That is a normative question, but it has a positive component: The question is not whether increasing taxes on the rich is fair, or whether it makes them angry. The question is, how would higher taxes make the rich behave? Would they stop doing the things that generate high amounts of income if the government claimed a larger share of that income? If so, then increasing taxes on the rich may make society worse off.

There is a second way that raising taxes on the rich can harm society. Instead of generating a lot of income in the United States, the rich may just choose to generate it in some other country. That's true for ordinary people, but it's particularly true for superstars, who often have individual talents that are highly portable. Superstars who have moved to avoid taxes in their countries include actors Gerard Depardieu and Sean Connery, rock legends the Beatles and the Rolling Stones, and most recently Facebook co-founder Eduardo Saverin.

So an effective tax policy must balance the desire to have the richest members of society pay for the bulk of the services the government provides with the negative effects the policy has on the desire to be productive. This, then, begs the question: Have we reached that point? Is there room to raise taxes even further? This is a question that must be answered with data.

Nobel Prize winner Peter Diamond, along with Emmanuel Saez, set out to do just that. They argue that the rich should be paying higher rates, on average, than they are and that the *marginal rate*—the percentage tax rate applied to the very last dollar of income earned—should be much higher than the current 39.6%. They suggest that a marginal rate of 73% on incomes greater than $300,000 is the rate that balances revenue generation with disincentive effects.

Conclusion

Ultimately, income-distribution questions are normative questions. No definitive conclusion can be drawn about the relative obligations of the rich and poor. Nonetheless, normative questions can be informed by positive analysis: How big are the disincentive effects of high taxes? How much marginal utility does a dollar bring Bill Gates? How big are the benefits the government confers on the superrich? Gathering data of this sort and analyzing it is a good first step. But until those questions are answered, perhaps the best place for the government to focus its efforts is not on providing more equal outcomes but on ensuring more equal opportunities. Ensuring that everyone has access to cost-effective education can help close the skills gap between workers and reduce inequality. Similarly, clamping down on rent seeking is something that virtually every economist can get behind. Ultimately, your opinion is your own. But being able to back up your opinion with the tools of economics will make whatever position you take more persuasive.

Chapter Summary and Problems

Key Terms

Benefits received principle, p. 471

Diminishing marginal utility, p. 470

Gini coefficient, p. 461

Globalization, p. 467

Income distribution, p. 456

Income mobility, p. 465

Lorenz curve, p. 458

Median income, p. 457

Utilitarianism, p. 470

21.1 How Is Inequality Measured? pages 456–461

Summarize the major methods of measuring income inequality.

Summary

The income distribution describes how total income is divided among the population. Summary measures of the income distribution include the mean income and the median income. More detailed measures illustrate how much income is received by each quintile. The Lorenz curve is a graphical way to illustrate the income distribution; the Gini coefficient summarizes the information in the Lorenz curve in a single number.

Review Questions

All problems are assignable in MyEconLab.

1.1 _____ describes how a nation's income is divided among its people.

1.2 _____ is a measure of the overall output of an economy and the overall income received by that economy's people.

1.3 The _____ measures the income of the person in the middle of the income distribution.

1.4 A(n) _____ is a group containing exactly one-fifth of the population.

1.5 The _____ plots, for any given percentage of the population, the proportion of the income earned by that particular group of people.

1.6 The more unequal the income distribution, the _____ the Gini coefficient.

1.7 The _____ is the share of income received by different groups.

  a. Gini coefficient

  b. Income distribution

  c. Mean income

  d. Median income

1.8 If 90% of the income is earned by the top 1%, the resulting Gini coefficient will be _____.

  a. Near 1

  b. Near 0

  c. Near 100%

  d. Exactly 0.9

1.9 In 2012, the real GDP estimate for Tuvalu, a Polynesian island, was $37 million, and the population estimate was approximately 10,800. What was the approximate real GDP per capita in 2012?

  a. $3,700

  b. $343

  c. $2,919

  d. $3,426

Problems and Applications

1.10 Why is real GDP per capita not an ideal measure of how well off the individuals in a country are?

1.11 Suppose that seven people live on an island. The incomes of the seven are as follows:

Davenport	Reacher	Millhone	Pike	Cole	Scudder	Flowers
$8,000	$44,000	$19,000	$51,000	$32,000	$2,000	$26,000

  a. Compute the median income and mean income. Are they the same?

  b. Construct a Lorenz curve for the islanders.

21.2 How Unequal Is the Distribution of Income in the United States? pages 461–466

Using data, describe the income distribution in the United States.

Summary

In the United States, income is not distributed evenly. The top quintile takes home about half of all income. While incomes in every quintile have been increasing over the past 40 years, quintile data and the Gini coefficient show that inequality has been increasing, too. Compared to most other developed countries, the United States has a high degree of inequality. But inequality is generally higher in the developing world.

2.1 In the United States, the top fifth of all earners take home about _____ of all income.

   a. 1/5

   b. 1/2

   c. 3/4

   d. 9/10

2.2 As indicated by Gini coefficients, the United States income distribution is _____ the income distribution in other developed countries.

   a. More equal than

   b. Less equal than

   c. About the same as

2.3 What the ideal income distribution looks like is a(n) _____ question.

   a. Objective

   b. Positive

   c. Normative

   d. Value-free

2.4 The Gini coefficient in the United States has been _____ over the past 50 years.

   a. Increasing

   b. Decreasing

   c. Roughly constant

   d. Alternately increasing and decreasing

2.5 Generally speaking, Gini coefficients indicate that the income distribution in developed countries is _____ the income distribution in developing countries.

   a. More equal than

   b. Less equal than

   c. About as equal as

   d. There is no general pattern of inequality in developed and developing countries.

2.6 Data indicate that over the last 40 years, income mobility in the United States has _____.

   a. Increased

   b. Decreased

   c. Remained constant

   d. Increased, then decreased

Problems and Applications

2.7 How has income inequality changed in the United States over time? How does inequality in the United States compare to inequality in other countries?

2.8 Are the rich getting richer while the poor get poorer in the United States? Answer this question, and back up your answer with data.

2.9 The United States is often referred to as a land of opportunity. Do mobility data back up that assertion? Explain.

2.10 The United States and Sweden have similar average incomes, but the United States has a wider income distribution, with more people who are very poor, and more who are very rich. Explain, using this information, why income mobility is likely to be lower in the United States than in Sweden.

21.3 What Are the Causes and Effects of Income Inequality? pages 466–470

List three causes of income inequality and explain two effects it may have on economic efficiency.

Summary

Inequality may reflect productivity differences between rich and poor. Growing inequality has been linked to increasing globalization and improvements in technology. Globalization and technology reduce the returns to unskilled labor but increase the returns to those with rare talents. Inequality may also reflect rent seeking, which provides a way for certain parties to capture wealth and a means for the rich to preserve wealth. Inequality can create the incentives necessary to invest and create, which makes society richer. But if inequality results from or causes rent seeking, society can be made poorer.

Review Questions

All problems are assignable in MyEconLab.

3.1 _____ is the increasing integration of the world's economies.

3.2 Someone who seeks to use the power of government to his own private advantage at the expense of everyone else is engaging in _____.

3.3 A labor market where one person rises to superstardom and riches while the others walk away empty-handed is called a _____ market.

Problems and Applications

3.4 Is inequality necessarily a negative for society? If not, when does it become a negative?

3.5 How does increasing globalization affect the incomes of the poor? The rich? Explain the overall effect of globalization on the income distribution.

3.6 List some ways that individuals in the top quintile of an unequal society might engage in rent seeking. Do you think rent seeking is a problem in the United States? Why or why not?

3.7 [Related to Application 21.1 on page 469] From your perspective, why might you be more dissatisfied with your own income if you found out that your coworker is making more than you? Is this economically rational?

3.8 Explain two different ways in which advances in technology have contributed to increasing income inequality.

21.4 What Is the Role of Government in Promoting Equality?
pages 470–474

Explain the major philosophical arguments for redistributing income.

Summary

Government has the power to actively redistribute income. It may justify redistribution on utilitarian grounds—that a poor person will value a particular dollar more than a rich person. Or redistribution may reflect a social insurance policy that people would have agreed to before they knew what their station in life would be. Government may also base redistribution on the benefits received principle—that the rich receive disproportionately large benefits of the services of government. Each of these arguments is compelling, but none is logically airtight.

Review Questions

All problems are assignable in MyEconLab.

4.1 A system that assesses proportionally higher taxes on the rich than it does on the poor is called a _____.

4.2 _____ is a philosophy that says the ethically proper thing to do in any situation is the thing that maximizes overall societal happiness.

4.3 _____ is the belief that the ethically proper thing to do in any situation is the thing that maximizes society's overall utility or minimizes society's overall suffering.
   a. The Rawlsian social contract
   b. The benefits received principle
   c. Utilitarianism
   d. Redistribution

4.4 The first Krispy Kreme donut you ate was amazing, the second was good, and the third was only okay. This is an illustration of _____.
   a. Diminishing marginal utility
   b. Income distribution
   c. Median income
   d. The Gini coefficient

4.5 "Higher taxes on the rich are justified because the rich have received disproportionately greater benefits from services, infrastructure, and protections the government provides." This statement reflects _____.
   a. The benefits received principle
   b. Utilitarianism
   c. The Rawlsian social contract
   d. None of the above

Problems and Applications

4.6 A large and increasing portion of government spending goes to transfer programs (such as Social Security, Medicare, and Medicaid) and national defense, neither of which directly helps the rich get richer. Given those facts, discuss the applicability of the benefits received principle in justifying progressive taxation. Is it possible that the rich do benefit more from national defense? Can you think of any ways that the rich also benefit from transfer payments?

4.7 Changes in technology and globalization have hollowed out some traditionally middle-class jobs and jobs for low-skilled workers. The idea of a basic income has been proposed by some economists and politicians. A basic income guarantees each individual some unconditional, regular sum of money sufficient for basic necessities. Discuss some pros and cons that such a system would have.

4.8 In 2014, economist Thomas Piketty of the Paris School of Economics released a book titled *Capital in the Twenty-First Century*, which focuses on wealth and income inequality. Piketty suggests that in capitalism, those who start out with money have an easier time making more money, and when this system is left unchecked, the top percentage of income holders eventually capture enough wealth that those who are not in the top percentage could never hope to catch up. If this is true, do you think this is fair? Does it matter if it's fair?

4.9 [Related to Application 21.2 on page 472] Research by Ariely and Norton indicates that Americans have a preference for much greater equality than currently exists but also that Americans may not fully understand how far the current distribution is from the ideal income distribution. Why do you think this is the case? Can you think of any cultural factors that perpetuate a belief that the income distribution is more equal than it actually is?

4.10 [Related to Application 21.2 on page 472] Application 21.2 suggests that Americans would prefer a much more equitable wealth distribution than what actually exists. Why do you suppose lawmakers have not enacted policies to give Americans what they prefer?

Unveiling Ignorance

This chapter was devoted to helping you learn about income distribution—how society's income is divided among its people. The chapter highlighted the difficulty in answering an important normative question: What does the ideal income distribution look like?

This experiment gives you a chance to explore that question. Your instructor has a large number of extra credit points that can be applied to the next exam in your class. The points don't have to be divided equally: Instead, your class will be broken into five groups, and each group can make a proposal for how to allocate points to the various groups. The proposal that gets the most votes will determine how your professor will allocate the points on exam day.

But there's a twist: On exam day, your instructor will randomly reassign you and your classmates to new groups. Knowing that there's an equal likelihood of being assigned to any group on exam day, will you propose a very equal distribution of extra credit points today? Or will you propose an unequal distribution of points and hope to win big?

Notes

Section 21.2

The Piketty and Saez results discussed in Section 21.2 come from "Income Inequality in the United States, 1913–1998," *Quarterly Journal of Economics* 118, February 2003. Saez provides updated data on his website, http://elsa.berkeley.edu/~saez/. Piketty and Saez use a different measure of income than the U.S. Census Bureau does, so direct comparison between the two data sets is inexact. Nevertheless, the overall story is largely the same: The income distribution in the United States is heavily skewed toward the top.

Decreasing income mobility, discussed in Section 21.2, is a theme that appears often in the media and in politics—on both sides of the aisle. See, for example, President Obama's 2014 state of the union address, as well as "Republicans Suddenly Can't Stop Talking About 'Mobility,'" *New Republic*, February 19, 2014. The mobility study authored by Chetty, Hendren, Kline, Saez, and Turner is "Is the United States Still a Land of Opportunity? Recent Trends in Intergenerational Mobility," *NBER Working Paper Series 19844*, 2014. That study finds little change in the ability of a person in any quintile to reach the top quintile over a relatively long time horizon. For an international comparison of income mobility, see Miles Corak's "Inequality from Generation to Generation: The United States in Comparison," in *The Economics of Inequality, Poverty, and Discrimination in the 21st Century*, 2012.

Section 21.3

The explanation of good inequality in Section 21.3 is found in Greg Mankiw's "Defending the One Percent," *Journal of Economic Perspectives*, Summer 2013. The theory of tournament-style labor markets is developed in Sherwin Rosen's "The Economics of Superstars," *American Economic Review*, vol. 71, 1981. Claudia Goldin and Lawrence Katz document the increasing returns to education in *The Race Between Education and Technology*, Harvard University Press, 2008.

Due to difficulties in determining average workers' salaries across firms, estimates of the ratio of CEO to average worker salary, as discussed in Section 21.3, vary depending on the source. Generally, however, estimates reflect the same trend across time. See, for example, Bloomberg's "CEO Pay 1,795-to-1 Multiple of Wages Skirts U.S. Law" at Bloomberg.com, April 29, 2013.

Section 21.4

In Section 21.4, there are other, more technical reasons that utilitarianism is less than a completely convincing argument in favor of redistribution. Not least among them is the difficult job of objectively comparing the happiness two different people might receive from the same good, service, dollar, or experience. Microeconomists generally agree that it is impossible to make such comparisons in any consistent way.

Henrik Kleven, Camille Landais, and Emmanuel Saez use data from European soccer players to document the mobility of superstars discussed in Section 21.4 in "Taxation and the International Migration of Superstars," NBER Working Paper 16545, November 2010.

Peter Diamond and Emmanual Saez's analysis of the optimal tax, discussed in Section 21.4, can be found in "The Case for a Progressive Tax: From Basic Research to Policy Recommendations," *Journal of Economic Perspectives*, vol. 25, 2011.

Glossary

Absolute advantage The ability to produce a good using fewer resources than someone else. (*p. 100*)

Adverse selection The tendency for the people who pose the greatest risks to insurers to buy insurance. (*p. 286*)

Affirmative action The practice of governments or firms actively improving the educational and job opportunities of members of groups that have not been treated fairly in the past. (*p. 317*)

Agenda paradox A situation in which the outcome of an election is sensitive to the order of events. (*p. 269*)

Arrow's impossibility theorem The conclusion that all voting systems used to choose from three or more alternatives contain some inherent drawback that can prevent them from accurately capturing the preferences of the electorate in all circumstances. (*p. 261*)

Assurance game A game in which two players want to coordinate on an outcome and in which both agree that coordinating on one particular outcome is preferred to coordinating on the other. (*p. 70*)

Asymmetric information A situation that occurs when one party to a transaction has more or better information than the other. (*p. 286*)

Audit method A method of detecting discrimination that involves researchers faking identities for people who are essentially alike but differ in race, gender, or some other characteristic; deliberately placing those people in a position where they can be discriminated against; and observing whether there is significant disagreement in how they are treated. (*p. 312*)

Automatic stabilizers Built-in changes in taxes and spending that, without any deliberate action by policymakers, stimulate the economy when it is weak or slow the economy when it is overheating. (*p. 443*)

Average tax rate How much of the *typical* dollar of your income that must ultimately be sent to the government: Calculated as your total tax bill divided by your income. (*p. 431*)

Bank run A situation that occurs when many or all of a bank's depositors attempt to withdraw their money at the same time. (*p. 402*)

Battle of the sexes game A game in which both players want to coordinate, but each player prefers coordinating on a different outcome. (*p. 70*)

Benefits received principle The belief that higher taxes on the rich are justified because they have received a disproportionately large benefit of the services, infrastructure, and protections the government provides. (*p. 471*)

Best-response analysis A technique for locating equilibria by marking the best strategy a player can use to counter each of his or her rival's possible moves. (*p. 67*)

Black market A market where goods are sold in violation of governmentally imposed restrictions. (*p. 107*)

Bond A financial instrument that represents a debt contract and obligates a borrower to pay back a specified amount of money at a particular point in the future. (*p. 389*)

Borda-count method A voting method in which each voter ranks alternatives and awards more points to higher-ranked alternatives and fewer points to lower-ranked alternatives. The alternative that receives the most total points from all voters wins. (*p. 257*)

Budget deficit The amount by which annual expenditures exceed annual receipts. (*p. 437*)

Budget surplus The amount by which annual revenues exceed annual expenditures. (*p. 437*)

Business cycle The ordinary fluctuation of real GDP around its long-run trend. (*pp. 344, 411*)

Cap-and-trade system A pollution-reduction scheme in which the government sets an overall limit (cap) on the amount of pollution that can be emitted and then allows polluters to negotiate about who will get to pollute via a system of tradable pollution permits. (*p. 172*)

Capitalism A form of economic organization in which productive resources are privately owned by individuals, who independently decide what to produce. (*p. 130*)

Central bank A financial institution that is responsible for issuing currency and controlling the amount of money in circulation. The central bank generally serves as a bank to the government and as a bank to other banks. (*p. 385*)

Chicken game A version of the battle of the sexes game that results in disaster if each player plays his or her tough strategy. (*p. 72*)

Clearinghouse A group of banks that agree to lend one another money in case of unexpectedly large withdrawals. (*p. 403*)

Club good A good that is nonrival but excludable. (*p. 199*)

Coase theorem A theorem which asserts that under certain conditions, the property right to an activity will be acquired by the party that values it most. (*p. 148*)

Coinsurance An arrangement under which an insured person pays for some fraction of his or her own medical expenses, with the insurance company picking up the other portion. *(p. 291)*

Collective action problem A problem that exists when naturally occurring incentives encourage sufficient numbers of people to act in a way that makes everybody worse off. *(p. 11)*

Command economy An economy in which the government makes production and distribution decisions. *(p. 3)*

Commercial bank A financial institution that accepts deposits and makes loans. *(p. 385)*

Commodity money Money that has intrinsic value. *(p. 381)*

Common pool resource A good that is rival but nonexcludable. *(p. 200)*

Communism A form of economic and social organization in which all property is held in common, and the government decides what to produce and how to distribute it. *(p. 130)*

Comparative advantage The ability to produce a good at a lower opportunity cost than another producer. *(p. 100)*

Compensating differential approach A method of valuing a life that estimates how much money it takes to get the typical person to bear an additional risk of death. *(p. 49)*

Compensating differential The extra pay people earn in exchange for undertaking risky or otherwise undesirable work. *(p. 49)*

Competition A market condition in which buyers and sellers are free to choose with whom to complete their transactions. *(p. 124)*

Complements Goods that buyers like to consume together. *(p. 26)*

Condorcet method A voting method in which the winner must defeat each of the other alternatives in head-to-head contests. *(p. 255)*

Consumer price index (CPI) A measure of the overall cost of living for the typical consumer. *(p. 415)*

Consumer sovereignty The idea that in the market system, consumers ultimately decide which goods and services firms will produce. *(p. 120)*

Consumer surplus The maximum amount a buyer would be willing to pay for a good or service less the price he or she actually pays. *(p. 102)*

Consumption Spending by households on goods and services; also called consumption spending. *(p. 330)*

Cooperative surplus The sum of all the net benefits received by the parties to a transaction. *(p. 102)*

Copayment A fixed amount an insured person pays when obtaining medical care. *(p. 291)*

Copyright An exclusive property right the government grants the creator of an original work to produce and sell that work. A copyright typically lasts for the life of the creator plus 70 years. *(p. 131)*

Cost-justified precaution A safety measure whose benefits outweigh its costs. *(p. 43)*

Cost–benefit analysis A method that decision makers use to evaluate choices among competing alternatives. *(p. 37)*

Crowding out Decreased consumer or business spending as a result of increased government spending. *(p. 445)*

Cyclical unemployment Unemployment that is related to downturns in the economy during business cycles. *(p. 368)*

Deadweight loss Surplus value that is lost because something is keeping the market from functioning as well as it can. *(p. 106)*

Deductible A specified amount of money that an insured person must pay before his or her insurance company begins to help cover expenses. *(p. 291)*

Deflation A period of falling prices of goods and services in an economy. *(p. 420)*

Demand curve A curve that shows how many units of a good or service consumers are willing to buy at various prices. *(p. 20)*

Demand shocks Events that reduce the willingness or ability of buyers to purchase goods and services. *(p. 346)*

Depression A particularly severe and protracted recession. *(p. 344)*

Diffusion of responsibility A situation that occurs when a group of bystanders all agree that something needs to be done but each feels less personal responsibility for taking action because each perceives that there are others who *could* take action. *(p. 233)*

Diminishing marginal utility The belief that having more of something makes you happier but in successively smaller increments. *(p. 470)*

Discount rate The interest rate the Federal Reserve charges commercial banks for loans. *(p. 404)*

Discouraged workers People who have given up actively seeking work after an extended period of unemployment. *(p. 360)*

Discretionary expenditures Spending that must be authorized by Congress each year. *(p. 435)*

Discretionary fiscal policy The act of deliberately cutting taxes or ramping up expenditures to fight an economic downturn. Alternatively, policymakers can increase taxes or slow expenditures to slow an overheating economy. (p. 442)

Diversification The practice of spreading wealth across multiple investments. (p. 391)

Dominant strategy A strategy that is universally best, regardless of the strategy chosen by others. (p. 62)

Economic growth The increase in the overall value of goods and services produced in an economy across time; usually measured as the percentage increase in a country's real GDP or real GDP per capita. (pp. 124, 344)

Economic model A structured and simplified version of reality that we can use to explain real-world behavior. (p. 58)

Economics The study of how society manages its scarce resources to satisfy its wants. (p. 2)

Economy A type of organization that produces goods and services and then allocates those goods and services to its members. (p. 2)

Eminent domain The authority of the government to take private property for public use, given just compensation to the owner. (p. 219)

Excludable good A good that a producer can prevent people from consuming. (p. 199)

Explicit costs Costs that are measured in dollars and that typically involve some exchange of money. (p. 6)

Exports Products produced domestically and sold in foreign countries. (p. 112)

External costs The value of a negative externality borne by those who do not produce the good or service. (p. 165)

Externality A by-product of an activity that hurts or helps someone who is not involved in that activity. (p. 142)

Federal debt The total amount of money the government owes to its creditors. (p. 438)

Federal funds rate The interest rate that banks charge each other for loans. (p. 406)

Federal Reserve System The central bank of the United States. (pp. 385, 401)

Fiat money Money that is backed by nothing but the faith and confidence that if you accept it in exchange for something, you will be able to exchange it for something else. (p. 383)

Financial capital The money that business owners raise to purchase physical capital or to fund new business ventures. (p. 389)

Financial instruments Documents that represent agreements between two or more parties about rights to payments of money. (p. 388)

Financial markets Places, physical or electronic, where financial instruments are traded. (p. 389)

Fiscal activities Activities related to how the federal government raises revenue and manages its spending. (p. 428)

Fiscal policy Government's use of its taxing and spending powers to influence overall economic activity. (p. 442)

Free rider A person who enjoys the benefits of a good without bearing a proportionate share of the cost. (p. 200)

Frictional unemployment Unemployment that exists because it can be difficult and time-consuming to match unemployed persons to existing vacancies. (p. 362)

Full employment A situation that occurs when unemployment is at its natural rate. (p. 368)

Fully funded system A retirement system in which the benefits government pays to retirees are paid out of the contributions those retirees made during their working years. (p. 440)

Futures contract A financial instrument that establishes the terms of a sale that will take place at a later time. (p. 391)

Game theory A method of analyzing the strategic interaction that occurs among small numbers of people, firms, organizations, and even countries. (p. 57)

Gini coefficient A number that measures a society's income inequality, based on how income is distributed across quintiles. The Gini coefficient is derived from the Lorenz curve and ranges from 0 (perfect equality) to 1 (perfect inequality). (p. 461)

Globalization The increasing integration of the world's economies. (p. 467)

Gross domestic product (GDP) The market value of all final goods and services produced in a country in a given year. (p. 327)

Health care The goods and services provided by doctors, hospitals, pharmacies, and therapists. (p. 276)

Holdout A negotiator who hopes to get an unusually large amount of money for land by refusing to come to terms. (p. 217)

Human capital The knowledge and skills people accumulate through experience, education, and training. (p. 343)

Hyperinflation A period of very high and accelerating inflation. (p. 417)

Impact lag The period between the time monetary policy is implemented and the time it actually begins to affect the economy. (p. 411)

Implementation lag The practical and procedural hurdles that take time and delay the Fed in implementing monetary policy. (p. 410)

Implicit costs Costs that do not involve an exchange of money. *(p. 6)*

Imports Products produced in a foreign country and sold domestically. *(p. 112)*

Incentives Inducements to act in certain ways. *(p. 9)*

Income distribution The share of income received by different groups. *(p. 456)*

Income mobility The ability to move to a different part of the income distribution. *(p. 465)*

Income tax Tax on the income of individuals, families, and corporations. *(p. 430)*

Increase in demand A condition in which buyers increase the number of units of a good or service they are willing to purchase at each price. *(p. 23)*

Increase in supply A condition in which sellers increase the number of units of a good or service they offer for sale at each price. *(p. 25)*

Individual Transferable Quota (ITQ) system A system of controlling overfishing whereby the government decides how big the total fish catch will be and then lets fishermen negotiate to determine the share of the total catch each fisherman will be allowed. *(p. 189)*

Inferior good A good that consumers buy less of as their incomes rise. *(p. 27)*

Inflation A general increase in the prices of the goods and services people buy. *(p. 415)*

Inflation rate A measure of the percentage change in prices from one year to the next. *(p. 415)*

Inputs Resources that are used in the production of a good or service. *(p. 27)*

Instant runoff method A voting method in which voters initially rank alternatives, and the alternative with the fewest first-place votes is eliminated. That alternative's votes are transferred to each voter's next-favorite choice, and the process repeats until a winner emerges. *(p. 258)*

Institutions The ground rules, customs, and conventions that govern the behavior of market participants. *(p. 124)*

Interest rate Interest expressed as a percentage of the amount borrowed. *(p. 389)*

Interest The price a borrower must pay for the use of other peoples' money. *(p. 389)*

Investment Spending by businesses on final goods and services that will be used later to produce more goods and services. *(p. 330)*

Labor force participation rate A measurement of the percentage of the adult population that is in the labor force. *(p. 357)*

Labor market discrimination Rewarding or penalizing personal characteristics of a worker that are unrelated to his or her productivity. *(p. 310)*

Law of demand The inverse relationship between the price of a good or service and the quantity of that good or service that consumers want to buy. When the price of a good rises, there is a decrease in quantity demanded, and when the price of a good falls, there is an increase in quantity demanded. *(p. 21)*

Law of supply The positive relationship between the price of a good or service and the quantity of that good or service that sellers are willing to offer for sale. When the price of a good rises, there is an increase in quantity supplied, and when the price of a good falls, there is a decrease in quantity supplied. *(p. 21)*

Lender of last resort A function of the central bank to loan money to banks during banking panics. *(p. 404)*

Liquidity The ease with which an asset can be converted to cash. *(p. 390)*

Liquidity trap A situation in which money created by the Fed to stimulate the economy is hoarded rather than being put to use. The liquidity trap renders monetary policy ineffective. *(p. 411)*

Lorenz curve A curve that plots, for any given percentage of the population, the proportion of total income earned by that particular group of people. *(p. 458)*

Lost-income approach Estimating the value of an injured or deceased person's life by adding up that person's lost future earnings. *(p. 47)*

M1 A measure of the money supply that includes currency in circulation, checking account balances, and traveler's checks. *(p. 387)*

M2 A measure of the money supply that includes everything in M1, plus savings account balances, money market mutual fund balances, and small certificates of deposit. *(p. 388)*

Macroeconomics The study of the economy as a whole. Macroeconomics attempts to evaluate or summarize the performance of all markets simultaneously. *(p. 326)*

Mandatory spending Spending that is not subject to Congress's annual appropriations process. *(p. 436)*

Marginal analysis Arriving at a decision by comparing marginal costs and marginal benefits. *(p. 38)*

Marginal benefit The additional benefit you expect to receive if you undertake an activity. *(p. 38)*

Marginal cost The additional cost you expect to incur if you undertake an activity. *(p. 38)*

Marginal tax rate The tax rate you pay on an *additional* dollar of income. *(p. 430)*

Market A forum where buyers and sellers conduct transactions. (*p. 120*)

Market equilibrium A condition in a market where there is no upward or downward pressure on price, and where quantity demanded equals quantity supplied. (*p. 22*)

Market system A form of economic organization in which individual buyers and sellers are free to exchange goods and services. (*p. 3*)

Median income The income of the middle person in an income distribution. (*p. 457*)

Median voter theorem The conclusion that in an ordinary election between two candidates, the candidates will position themselves in such a way that their platforms reflect the views of the median voter. (*p. 264*)

Microeconomics The study of decisions made by individuals, businesses, and other entities such as governments. Microeconomics often focuses on a single market. (*p. 326*)

Mixed economies Economies where buyers and sellers make some production decisions and governments make others. (*p. 3*)

Mixed strategy The approach of using a different strategy time after time or randomly selecting a strategy; a strategy to use when players are in direct competition with one another. (*p. 238*)

Monetary policy The central bank's manipulation of the money supply in order to achieve economic goals such as full employment, stable prices, and economic growth. (*p. 401*)

Money Anything that is commonly acceptable as payment for goods and services. (*p. 380*)

Money supply The quantity of items circulating in the economy that can be used as money. (*p. 383*)

Monopolistic competition A market with many sellers offering differentiated products. (*p. 121*)

Monopoly A market where there is only one seller, and there is no close substitute for the product being sold. (*p. 121*)

Moral hazard A change in behavior that occurs after a person becomes insured against loss. (*p. 289*)

Mortgage loan A loan extended for the purpose of purchasing real property, such as land, houses, or other buildings. (*p. 385*)

Mutual fund A financial asset in which the pooled savings of many investors is used to buy stock, bonds, or other financial assets. (*p. 391*)

Mutual interdependence The characteristic of games whereby the outcome of the game depends not only on what you do but on what the other players do in response. (*p. 57*)

***n*-player game** A game that helps us evaluate the interaction of four or more players, where *n* is an algebraic variable that can assume any value between four and infinity. (*p. 87*)

Naive voting Voting in accordance with one's true preferences. (*p. 269*)

Nash equilibrium An outcome in which both players are playing their best strategy, given the strategy chosen by the opponent. (*p. 60*)

Nationalized health care A system of health care in which a government provides health care services free of charge to patients and pays for the resources needed to provide those services through income taxes; also called socialized medicine. (*p. 281*)

Natural rate of unemployment The sum of the frictional and structural unemployment rates. (*p. 368*)

Negative externality An externality that imposes a burden or cost on others. (*p. 143*)

Net exports The sum of the goods produced domestically and sold abroad (U.S. *exports*), minus the goods and services that were produced abroad but purchased domestically (U.S. *imports*). (*p. 332*)

Nominal GDP A measure of a country's production of goods and services valued at current market prices. (*p. 333*)

Nonexcludable good A good that a producer finds difficult or costly to prevent people from consuming. (*p. 199*)

Nonrival good A good that many people can use simultaneously. (*p. 199*)

Normal good A good that consumers buy more of as their incomes rise. (*p. 27*)

Normative economics Statements of "what should be" in the economy. (*p. 12*)

Oligopoly A market dominated by a few large sellers, offering identical or differentiated products. (*p. 121*)

Open market operations The purchase or sale of bonds by the Federal Reserve to manipulate the money supply. (*p. 405*)

Opportunity cost What is sacrificed in order to engage in an activity. (*p. 4*)

Panic A run on a large number of banks, even those that are financially sound. (*p. 404*)

Patent An exclusive property right the government gives an inventor to produce and/or market an invention. A patent typically lasts for about 20 years. (*p. 131*)

Patient Protection and Affordable Care Act (ACA) A set of health care reforms enacted in the United States in 2014. (*p. 282*)

Pay-as-you-go system A retirement system in which the benefits government pays to retirees are paid out of the contributions of current workers. *(p. 440)*

Payoff matrix A table that summarizes who the players are, the actions available to each player, and the payoffs available to each player for each action that he or she might choose, given the action chosen by his or her rival. *(p. 58)*

Payroll tax A mandatory tax that both workers and employers in the United States pay to fund Social Security and Medicare; calculated as a percentage of each worker's pay. *(p. 429)*

Perfect competition A market with many sellers who all sell an identical product. *(p. 121)*

Plurality-rule method A voting procedure in which the alternative that receives the most votes wins, even if that alternative doesn't receive a majority of the votes. *(p. 254)*

Positive economics Objective analysis of "what is" in the economy. *(p. 12)*

Positive externality An externality that confers benefits on others. *(p. 144)*

Premium death spiral An effect of adverse selection on insurance premiums. As healthy people leave the pool of the insured, premiums must rise, causing more people to leave the pool and driving premiums even higher. *(p. 286)*

Price elasticity of demand The sensitivity of consumers' buying behaviors to changes in prices, measured as the percentage change in the quantity of a good demanded by consumers for each 1% change in price. *(p. 29)*

Prisoner's dilemma A game in which each player has a dominant strategy of defecting, and each ends up worse off than if they had both cooperated. *(p. 64)*

Private costs Costs that are borne by the producer of a good or service. *(p. 165)*

Producer surplus The amount a seller receives for a good or service beyond the minimum he or she would be willing to sell the good for. *(p. 102)*

Production technology The efficiency with which firms convert inputs into outputs. *(p. 27)*

Progressive tax A tax that takes a larger share from the income of high-income taxpayers than it does from low-income taxpayers. *(p. 432)*

Property right The right to own or control a resource. *(pp. 130, 148)*

Protectionism The process of governments protecting domestic producers from foreign competition by restricting the ability of foreigners to sell their products in domestic markets. *(p. 109)*

Public goods problem The tendency for private individuals to provide pure public goods in less-than-ideal amounts because of free riding. *(p. 204)*

Public policy The collection of laws, regulatory measures, and actions concerning a particular topic that originates with some body of government. *(p. 7)*

Pure coordination game A game in which it only matters that the players coordinate on an outcome, not which outcome they coordinate on. *(p. 67)*

Pure private good A good that is rival and excludable. *(p. 199)*

Pure public good A good that is nonrival and nonexcludable. *(p. 199)*

Pure strategy The approach of using the same strategy time after time; a strategy to avoid when players are in direct competition with one another because the strategy is predictable. *(p. 237)*

Quota A limit on the number of imported goods allowed into the country. *(p. 112)*

Quota Numerical targets companies must meet for the hiring of minorities. *(p. 318)*

Rationality assumption The assumption that given the strategy chosen by the other participant, a player will always choose the strategy that brings him or her the best payoff. *(p. 66)*

Real GDP A measure of the output of final goods and services in a country, holding prices constant from year to year. *(p. 334)*

Recession An economic downturn in a business cycle. *(p. 344)*

Recognition lag The length of time before policymakers realize they need to intervene in the economy. *(p. 410)*

Regression analysis A statistical technique used to isolate the individual effects of a number of factors on a single outcome. *(p. 314)*

Regressive tax A tax that takes a larger share from the income of low-income taxpayers than it does from high-income taxpayers. *(p. 429)*

Rent seeking Attempting to influence the law for one's own private economic advantage. *(p. 107)*

Representative commodity money Paper currency that could be redeemed for a specific quantity of an underlying commodity. *(p. 382)*

Reserves Money that banks do not lend to customers but instead hold in their vault or in their account at the Federal Reserve. *(p. 401)*

Resources Items such as land, labor power, raw materials, fuel, factories, machinery, and people's skills that a society uses to create goods and services. *(p. 2)*

Rival good A good that only one person at a time can enjoy. *(p. 199)*

Rule of 70 A formula used to determine how long it will take a country to double its real GDP. The number of years it will take to double real GDP is approximately equal to 70 divided by the annual growth rate of real GDP. *(p. 341)*

Scarcity A situation in which limited resources make it impossible to fulfill all of our wants. *(p. 4)*

Segregation The sorting and separation of people by various characteristics including, but not limited to, race, ethnicity, gender, and religion. *(p. 301)*

Shortage A condition in which the quantity of a good or service demanded at the existing price is greater than the quantity supplied. *(p. 22)*

Single-payer system A health care system in which the government alone is responsible for paying health care providers for delivering medically necessary procedures. *(p. 281)*

Social cost The full cost of producing a good or service, including the producer's private costs and all the external costs. *(p. 165)*

Socialism A form of economic organization in which individuals may own private property but in which the government owns and operates productive resources. *(p. 130)*

Specialization The process of making the best use of our limited resources by doing the things we are best at and hiring other people to do the things we're not particularly good at. *(p. 99)*

Statistical discrimination A type of discrimination that occurs when someone assigns the properties of a group to a particular individual who is a member of that group. *(p. 311)*

Stock A financial asset that represents partial ownership of a corporation. *(p. 389)*

Strategic interaction Anticipating the decisions others will make in response to your decisions, knowing all the while that they are anticipating your response. *(p. 57)*

Strategic voting Voting against one's preferences in the initial rounds of a runoff election in order to prevent the selection of an undesirable alternative in the final round. *(p. 269)*

Structural unemployment Longer-term unemployment that exists when there are more people looking for work in some labor markets than there are jobs available, at the existing wage rate. *(p. 363)*

Subsidy A payment that a person receives from the government for engaging in a particular activity. *(p. 107)*

Substitutes Goods that can serve in place of one another. *(p. 26)*

Substitutes in production Different goods that can be produced with the same inputs. *(p. 28)*

Supply and demand model A graphical model used to depict the interaction of consumers and producers in the market for a good or service and to explain how the price of that good or service is determined. *(p. 20)*

Supply curve A curve that indicates how many units of a good or service sellers are willing to offer for sale at various prices. *(p. 21)*

Supply shocks Events that fundamentally reduce society's ability to produce goods and services. *(p. 345)*

Surplus A condition in which the quantity of a good or service supplied at the existing price is greater than the quantity demanded. *(p. 22)*

Tariffs Taxes the government imposes on imported products. *(p. 110)*

Taste-based discrimination Discrimination that occurs because the discriminator dislikes another person's gender, race, or some other personal characteristic. *(p. 310)*

Tax A compulsory payment to the government that is generally linked to engaging in some activity. *(p. 105)*

Tragedy of the commons The tendency of a society to overuse and deplete open-access (common pool) resources. *(p. 186)*

Transactions costs The costs of arranging and enforcing a transaction. *(p. 152)*

Underemployed Performing work for which a person is overqualified. *(p. 360)*

Unemployment A situation that occurs when people who are willing and able to work cannot find jobs. *(p. 356)*

Unemployment rate A measurement of the percentage of people in the labor force who are not working but are actively seeking work. *(p. 356)*

Universal health insurance A health care system that guarantees access to basic health care services for all of its residents. *(p. 282)*

Utilitarianism The belief that the ethically proper thing to do in any situation is the thing that maximizes society's overall utility (happiness) and minimizes society's overall suffering. *(p. 470)*

Volunteer's dilemma A situation in which a single individual can provide a public good. *(p. 231)*

Wage stickiness The inability of wages to adjust to market conditions. *(p. 370)*

World Trade Organization (WTO) An international organization dedicated to reducing trade barriers between its member nations. *(p. 114)*

Zero-sum game A game in which the total payoff in each cell of a payoff matrix is equal to zero. In a zero-sum game, one player's winnings equal the other player's losses. *(p. 237)*

Photo Credits

CHAPTER 1: p. 1: Ammentorp/Fotolia; p. 8: Alexander Maximov/Fotolia; p. 19: AntonioDiaz/Fotolia.

CHAPTER 2: p. 36: Silvano Rebai/Fotolia; p. 46: Age fotostock Spain, S.L./Alamy.

CHAPTER 3: p. 56: Image Source/Getty Images.

CHAPTER 4: p. 79: DuongMinhTien/Shutterstock; p. 92: xurzon/Fotolia.

CHAPTER 5: p. 98: Hoda Bogdan/Fotolia; p. 104: Georgios Kollidas/Fotolia; p. 113: Alan Grant.

CHAPTER 6: p. 119: nimon_t/Fotolia; p. 127: aerogondo/Fotolia.

CHAPTER 7: p. 141: Nattesha/Fotolia; p. 147: Library of Congress Prints and Photographs Division [LC-DIG-fsac-1a35422].

CHAPTER 8: p. 159: karichs/Fotolia; p. 166: Pix by Marti/Fotolia.

CHAPTER 9: p. 179: George Spade/Shutterstock; p. 185: Karel Gallas/Shutterstock; p. 190: mrakhr/Fotolia.

CHAPTER 10: p. 197: Ricon16/Fotolia; p. 201: K. Geijer/Fotolia.

CHAPTER 11: p. 215: Serguei Vlassov/123RF; p. 220: rob casey/Alamy.

CHAPTER 12: p. 230: Photographee.eu/Fotolia; p. 234: tiero/Fotolia.

CHAPTER 13: p. 252: alexskopje/Fotolia; p. 265: Marty Haas/Fotolia.

CHAPTER 14: p. 275: Monkey Business/Fotolia; p. 280 (top): Michelaubphoto/Fotolia; p. 280(center): mario beauregard/Fotolia; p. 280(bottom): Nenov Brothers/Fotolia.

CHAPTER 15: p. 300: Kokhanchikov/Fotolia; p. 309: Juice Images/Cultura/Getty Images.

CHAPTER 16: p. 325: Tyler Olson/Fotolia; p. 339: olly/Fotolia.

CHAPTER 17: p. 355: Giuseppe Porzani/Fotolia; p. 358: Pixinoo/Fotolia.

CHAPTER 18: p. 379: WavebreakmediaMicro/Fotolia; p. 382: Alan Grant.

CHAPTER 19: p. 400: adamparent/Fotolia; p. 408: Benjamin Simeneta/Fotolia.

CHAPTER 20: p. 427: Dave Newman/Fotolia; p. 434: Sam Spiro/Fotolia.

CHAPTER 21: p. 455: Rawpixel/Fotolia; p. 469: Jeanette Dietl/Shutterstock.

Index

Note: Key terms and the page on which they are defined appear in **boldface**.

A

Absolute advantage, 100
Absolute property rights, 164
  creating, 189, 191
Access
  granting of, in welfare-maximizing
    way, 189
  proper amount of, 189
  restricting, to endangered
    resources, 188–189
A Civil Action (Hart), 163*n*
Adverse selection, 286
  asymmetric information and,
    285–288
  health care systems in dealing
    with, 287–288
  private insurers and, 286–287
  as problem, 288
  unraveling of insurance markets
    and, 285
Affirmative action, 317–318
  benefits and costs of, 318–319
Against the Tide (Irwin), 110*n*
Age Discrimination in Employment
    Act (1967), 317
Agenda influence, 270
Agenda paradox, 269
Alesina, Alberto, 426*n*
Alternatives
  evaluating, as the margin, 38–39
  using cost–benefit analysis in
    selecting among competing,
    37–38
Amazon.com, gift card from, 58
American Bar Foundation, use of
    audit method to look at
    discrimination, 312–313
American Idol, 467
American Reinvestment and
    Recovery Act (2009), 446
Americans, working habits of, 433
Americans with Disabilities Act
    (1990), 317
Amplitude, 412
Amselem, Jacques, 292
Anti-discrimination legislation,
    316–319
Anti-foreign bias, 265
Anti-market bias, 265

Antwerp, Belgium, diamond market
    in, 120
Apathy, volunteer's dilemma and,
    233, 235–236
Apple, 126, 434
Ariely, Dan, 472–473
Arkansas River, damming of, 187
Arm's length bargaining, 152
Arrow, Kenneth, 261, 271
**Arrow's impossibility theorem,
    261**
Association of Wine Economists
    (AWE), 103
Assumptions
  Ceteris paribus, 26
  rationality, 66
Assurance games, 69–70, 73
  characteristics of, 70, 73
Asymmetric information, 286
  adverse selection and, 285–288
AT&T, 121, 126
Audit method, 312–313
  comparing regression analysis
    and, in detecting discrimina-
    tion, 315
Australia, estate tax law in, 10
Auto emissions, alternative
    approaches to reducing,
    166–167
Automatic stabilizers, 443
Average tax rate, 431
Ayres, Ian, 312

B

Babiker, Mustafa, 166*n*
Bangladesh, specialization in, 101
Bank runs, 402
Banks
  central, 385, 386, 401
  commercial, 385, 386–387, 401
  investment, 389, 403
  money supply and, 385–388
Banks, Ernie, 201
Bargaining, 245
  around the law, 148
  coalition building and, 245
  side, 148
Baron Automotive, 223

**Battle of the sexes games, 52,
    70, 73**
  characteristics of, 72, 73
Beatles, 474
A Beautiful Mind (movie), 61, 85
  game theory in, 85–86
Becker, Gary, 310–311
Behr, Edward, 384
Behrens, William W., III, 180*n*
Benefits, marginal, 38
Benefits received principle, 471
Benevolent social planner, 13
  access and, 189
  holdout problems and, 218
  public versus private goods
    and, 198
  socially optimal amount of pollu-
    tion and, 145
Bernanke, Ben, 416
Berri, David, 310*n*
Bertrand, Marianne, 313, 315
Best-response analysis, 67, 203
  in three-player games, 83–85
  voting and, 264
Bhutan's Gross National
    Happiness, 340*n*
Bias
  anti-foreign, 265
  anti-market, 265
  make-work, 265
  pessimistic, 265
Bieber, Justin, 120
Big sugar, 206
Black market, 107, 185
Blinder, Alan, 403*n*, 446–447
Blooming Nonsense (Carpenter), 108*n*
Bloomsbury Group, 444
BMW, cross–benefit analysis at,
    37–38
Bonds, 389–390
Borda-count method, 256–258,
    257, 261
Bradford, William, 132
Brown and Williamson, 39
Brown v. Topeka Board of Eduction, 304
Bubble, 347
  speculative, 392
Budget deficit, 437
Budget surplus, 437
Buffett, Warren, 4

Bureau of Labor Statistics, 356–357, 361, 362, 415
Burkhouser, Richard, 365, 378n
Burr, Aaron, 260
Bush, George W., 260, 414, 446
Business Cycle Dating Committee, 345
Business cycles, 343–**344, 411**–412
By-product, 142

C

Cadbury, 125
Cameron, David, 339
Camp, Garrett, 391
Canada
  Alberta Tar Sands in, 182
  Competition Bureau in, 125
  health care outcomes in, 280
  obesity rate in, 280
  single-payer systems in, 281, 287, 291–292, 294
  trade between United States and, 112
Cap-and-trade systems, 172
  in bringing fisheries back from the brink, 190
  in regulating pollution, 171–173
Capital, 2
  financial, 389
  human, 48, 343
  physical, 343, 389
Capitalism, 130
Caplan, Bryan, 265
Carasso, Adam, 454n
Card, David, 364, 378n, 469
CareerOneStop, 363
Carpenter, Dick, 108n
Castaldi, R. M., 103n
Caterpillar, 407
Causation
  versus correlation, 305–306
  housing experiment in determining, 306–307
Cell-by-cell inspection, 61, 62
Centers for Medicare & Medicaid Services, 293, 294
Central banks, 385, 401
  role of, in money creation, 386
Ceteris paribus assumption, 26
Charitable deductions, 432
Charles, Kerwin, 356
Chetty, Raj, 465, 466, 479n
Chicago Cubs, Wrigley Field and, 201
Chicken game, 72–73
  characteristics of, 72–73

Chickens, 184
  turning rhinos into, 185
Child safety seat, value of, 42
China
  Cultural Revolution in, 134
  Great Leap Forward in, 134
  gymnastic students in, 130
  property rights in, 134
Cholette, S., 103n
Churchill, Winston, 335
Citizens for Tax Justice, 434
Civil Rights Act (1964), 301, 317
Civil Rights Act (1991), 317
Clark, Andrew, 469n
Class, 163
Clayton Act (1914), 126
Clearinghouses, 402–**403**
Climate change, dealing with, 168
Clubbing game
  equilibrium in a, 91
  payoffs in a, 90
Club goods, 199
Coalition building, 245
  bargaining and, 245
Coase, Ronald, 134n, 148, 153
Coase theorem, 148–151, **149,** 160
  application of, 150–151
  inefficient resource management and, 191
  Nature Conservancy and, 149
  property rights and, 148
  transactions costs and, 151–152
Cohn, Alain, 469n
Coinsurance, 291
Collateralized debt obligation (CDO), 393
Collective action problems, 11–12
Collective bargaining, 365
Colorado River Compact, 187
Colorado Rockies Major League Baseball, 220
Column player, 59
Command economies, 3
Commercial banks, 385, 401
  role of, in money creation, 386–387
Commercial Paper Funding Facility, 403
Commodity money, 381–383
  partially backed representative, 382–383
  representative, 382
Common pool resources, 200
Communication, prices as means of, 122–123
Communism, 130

Comparable sales method, 224
Comparative advantage, 100
  opportunity costs and, 100–101
  specialization and, 99–100
Compelling interest, 108
Compensating differential approach, 48–50, **49**
Compensation, just, 224–225
Competition, 124–126
  government and, 124–126
  international trade and, 342
  monopolistic, 121
  perfect, 121
Complements, 26
  price of, 26
Compulsory volunteerism, 245
Condorcet method, 255–256
Cone, David, 232
Congressional Budget Office (CBO), 442, 454n
Connery, Sean, 474
Conservation, price increases and, 181–182
Constitution, U.S.
  Fifth Amendment in, 219
  protection of free speech in, 9
Consumer durables, 330
Consumer nondurables, 330
Consumer price index (CPI), 415
Consumer sovereignty, 120
Consumer surplus, 102
Consumption, 330
  inflation and choices in, 419
Consumption spending, 446
Contraceptive pill, increase in women's labor force participation rate and, 358
Contractionary monetary policy, 409
Contract laws, 127–128
Convention on International Trade in Endangered Species (CITES), 185
Cooperative strategy, 64
Cooperative surplus, 102
  effects of tariff on, 111
  exchange and, 101–102
  as measure of wealth creation, 102, 105
Copayment, 291
Copyrights, 131, 331
Corak, Miles, 479n
Corporate Average Fuel Economy (CAFE) standards, 166
Corporate income taxes, 432–433, 434

Corporations, 432
    lobbying by, 434
Correlation versus causation,
    305–306
Cost–benefit analysis, 37
    applying to life, 40–41
    as decision making aid, 55
    defined, 37
    in determining appropriate level
        of safety, 41–44
    problems and pitfalls of, when
        life is involved, 44–47
    in selecting among competing
        alternatives, 37–38
    tobacco settlement and, 39
Costello, Christopher, 190
Cost-justified precaution, 43, 45
Costs
    collectivization, 161–162
    explicit, 6, 7
    external, 165
    implicit, 6, 7
    marginal, 38
    monitoring and enforcement,
        162–163
    negotiation, 162
    private, 165
    search, 160–161
    social, 165
    transactions, 151–152, 160–163,
        219
Council on Foreign Relations,
    167
Countercyclical, 359
Cowen, Tyler, 366
Co-workers, keeping up with,
    469
Cowperthwaite family, 220–221
Credit default swap, 393
Crowding out, 445
Crowe, Russell, 61
Cutler, David, 280*n*
Cyclical unemployment,
    368–370
    solving, 371
    wage stickiness and, 369–370
Cyrus, Miley, 233, 467, 468

D

Danish Road Safety Council, 46
Dao, Mai, 378*n*
Darley, John, 233
Davis, Naeem, 246
DDT, 164

Deadweight losses, 106
    of the quota, 114
    as restriction on free exchange,
        106–107
    tariffs and, 111
Death, taxes and, 10
Deciding vote, 265
Decision theory, 57
Declaration of Independence, 104
Decrease
    in demand, 24
    in supply, 25
Deductibles, 291
Deductions, 432
    mortgage interest, 432
Deficits, budget, 437
Deflation, 420–421
Delphi, 121
Demand, 20–21
    decrease in, 24
    increase in, 23
    law of, 21
Demand curve, 20
    factors that shift, 26–27
Demand shocks, 346
    as cause of recessions, 346,
        348
Demand-side recession, 348
Democracy, paradox of, 265
Demographic challenges to
        the federal budget,
        440–442
Demographic groups, differences
        in outcomes across, 308,
        310
Denmark, corruption in, 342
Depardieu, Gerard, 474
Depletion
    dangers of, for resources,
        184–186
    pollution and, 188
    role of prices, in oil, 181–184
    role of society in fixing problems
        of, 188–191
Depression, 344. *See also* Great
        Depression
Diamond, Peter, 367, 474, 479*n*
Differentiated products, 121
Diffusion effect, volunteer's
        dilemma and, 236
Diffusion of responsibility, 233,
        235–236
    failure of groups to act and,
        233, 235
    failure of individuals to act
        and, 233

Diminishing marginal utility,
        470
Director, Aaron, 153
Discount rate, 404
Discouraged workers, 360–361
Discretionary expenditures,
        435–436
Discretionary fiscal policy,
        442–443
Discrimination
    anti-, legislation on, 316–319
    comparing regressional analysis
        and audit studies in
        detecting, 315
    detecting and measuring,
        312–316
    impact on individuals and society,
        312
    labor market, 308–312
    pure, 309
    statistical, 311
    taste-based, 310–311
Disposable income, 348, 442
Diversification, 391
Division of labor, 104
Dixit, Avinash, 244*n*
Dolan, Matthew, 113*n*
Dominance, in three-player games,
        82–83
Dominant strategies, 62–63
Double coincidence of wants
        problem, 380
Double-dip, 344
Doyle, Joseph, 42*n*
*Dr. Strangelove or: How I Learned to Stop
        Worrying and Love the Bomb,*
        305
Draft, 245
Drop Dead Healthy (Jacobs), 46*n*
Durables consumer, 330
Duty to rescue, 246

E

Earnings gap, regression analysis of,
        316
Eastern Illinois University, 216
Economic bads, 337
The Economic Consequences of the Peace
        (Keynes), 444
Economic growth, 124, 340–343
    differences in, as reason for
        differences in well-being,
        341–342
    ingredients for, 342–343
Economic model, 58

Economics, 2–3. *See also* Macroeconomics; Microeconomics
collective action problems in, 11–12
doing, 18
economists' analysis of issues in, 12–13
explicit costs in, 6, 7
governments in, 7
implicit costs in, 6, 7
incentives in, 9–11
normative, 12–13
opportunity costs in, 4–5
positive, 12–13
principles of, 4–6
public policy in, 7
scarcity in, 4
trade-offs in, 4–5, 6, 7–9
uses of, 2
Economics at the Wheel (Porter), 9n
Economies
command, 3
mixed, 3
Economists
analysis of economic issues, 12–13
forensic, 47
Economy, 2
features of, 2–3
fundamental changes in, as cause of structural unemployment, 366–367
key questions for, 3
resources of, 2
underground, 335–336
Edwards, George C., 260n
Effort, connecting reward and, 132–135
Einstein, Albert, 61
Einstein's Bagels, 332
Elasticity, 29
Elections
conventional political, and the median voter theorem, 261
runoff, 267–269
Electoral college, 260
Eminent domain, 219
conditions for use of, 219–224
Employers, as source of health insurance, 283
Employment, 357
full, 368
Employment Act (1946), 404
Endangered resources, restricting the access to, 188–189
Energy, U.S. Department of, estimates on oil, 180

Enforcement costs, 162–163
Engemann, Kristie M., 315n
Entitlements, 436–437
Environmental degradation, 337
Environmental Protection Agency (EPA), 49
Equal Employment Opportunity Act (1972), 317
Equal Employment Opportunity Commission (EEOC), 317
Equal Pay Act (1963), 317
Equilibrium, 21–22
in a clubbing game, 91
finding, in games with more than three players, 88–91
Nash, 60, 61, 63, 67, 70
strategies for finding, 60–63
Equilibrium price, 22
Equilibrium quantity, 22
European Union
restrictions on imports of U.S. agricultural products, 113
restrictions on production and use of genetically modified organisms, 167
Excess reserves, 401
Exchange
comparative advantage and specialization as catalysts for, 99–100
cooperative surplus and, 101–102
link between specialization and, 104
Excludable goods, 199
Exemptions, 432
personal, 432
Exide, 121
Expansionary monetary policy, 409
Expenditures, discretionary, 435–436
Expenditures approach, 329–332
Explicit costs, 6, 7
Exploration, price increases in encouraging, 182–183
Exports, 112
net, 331–332
External costs, 165
Externalities, 142–144
internalizing the cost of, 164–165
negative, 142–145, 168
positive, 143–145
Extra credit game, 88
equilibrium in, 89
Exxon *Valdez*, 163

F

Facebook, 430, 474
breaking stranglehold of, 92
Fair market value, 224, 225
Fargnoli, Andrew, 103
Fatality Analysis Reporting System (FARS), 42
Federal budget, demographic challenges to, 440–442
Federal debt, 438–440
Federal Deposit Insurance Corporation (FDIC), 402
Federal funds market, 406
Federal funds rate, 406
influence of Fed over, 407n
Federal government, 427–453. *See also* Government
discretionary expenditures and, 435–436
fiscal stabilization policy and, 442–448
future of federal budget and, 440–442
government revenue and, 428–435
income taxes and, 430–433, 435
mandatory spending, entitlements and, 436–437
payroll taxes and, 429–430
profits, incentives, and corporate tax code and, 434
surpluses, deficits, and debt and, 437–440
working habits of Americans and, 433
Federal Home Loan Mortgage Corporation (Freddie Mac), 393, 408
Federal Insurance Contributions Act (1935), 429
Federal National Mortgage Association (Fannie Mae), 393
Federal Open Market Committee (FOMC), 410, 445
Federal Reserve Act (1913), 420
Federal Reserve Bank of Dallas, 419
Federal Reserve Economic Data (FRED), 425
Federal Reserve System, 326, 385, 387, **401**–421
adjusting interest on reserves, 405–406
bank runs and, 402
clearinghouses and, 402–403
discount policy of, 404
easing of job, 408

gold standard and, 416
governors in, 420
during Great Depression, 414
inflation and, 415–421
influence over federal funds rate, 407n
as lender of last resort, 403, 404
mission of, 395
monetary policy and, 409–413
money supply, interest rates, and monetary policy, 406–409
open market operations of, 405
origins of, 401–404
panics and, 404
policy tools of, 404–406
reserve requirement policy of, 404–405
Federal Trade Commission Act (1914), 126
Fee-for-service system, 294
Fehr, Ernst, 469n
Ferguson, Niall, 414
Fiat money, 383, 384
Fifth Amendment, 219
Finance systems, health care delivery and, 281–284
Financial capital, 389
Financial instruments, 388
functions of, 388–393
origins of the Great Recession and, 393–394
Financial markets, 389
Financial system, 380
Finland
corruption in, 342
opportunity cost in, 5
Fiscal activities, 428
Fiscal policy, 442–448
automatic stabilizers and, 443
basics, 442–443
discretionary, 442–443
effectiveness of, 447
during the Great Recession, 446–447
multiplier effect and, 443
potential pitfalls of, 444–446
Fixed investments, 330
Flood, Curt, 232
Focal point, 68
Food and Drug Administration (FDA), 50
drug testing procedures of, 50
regulation of tobacco products, 39
Ford Motor Company, 40
cost–benefit calculations of, 47
production and sales of Ford Pinto, 4, 40–44, 47

Ford Transit Connect, 113
Forensic economists, 47
Fort Knox, 383
Fracking, 183
Franklin, Benjamin, 10
Free exchange, restrictions on, 105–109
Free riders, 200, 202–203
government's tax powers and, 205–207
Free to Choose (TV series), 414
French, Irene, 223
Frictional unemployment, 362–363, **370**
as good unemployment, 362
reducing, 362–363
Friedman, Milton, 7, 127, 153, 409–410, 413–414
Fryer, Roland, 315
Fuel-economy mandate, 166
Full employment, 368
Fully funded system, 440
Funding-related shutdowns, 428
Futures contract, 391

G

Gaines, Steven, 190
Gains, measuring, from specialization and exchange, 100
Games
assurance, 69–70, 73
basic structure of, 58–63
battle of the sexes, 52, **70**, 72, 73
chicken, 72–73
clubbing, 90, 91
extra credit, 88, 89
with more than three players
depicting, 87–88
finding equilibria in, 88–91
n-player, 87
prisoner's dilemma, 63–64, 73, 203
pure coordination, 64–69, 73
push–pull, 78
red–green, 97
revised bargaining, 102
setting up, 58–60
three-player (*See* Three-player games)
two-player (*See* Two-player games)
types of, 63–73
zero-sum, 61, 237, 241–242
Game theory, 14, 57–58, 142, 236
in describing human interactions, 71
tobacco advertising ban and, 65
volunteer's dilemma and, 237–242

Gaming the Vote (Poundstone), 260n
Gans, Joshua, 10
Gas tax, 166
Gates, Bill, 4, 439, 470
GDP. *See* Gross domestic product (GDP)
Genovese, Kitty, 231, 233, 242n, 245
George, Peter, 305
Gini coefficient, 461, 463–464
calculating, 461
Glaeser, Edward L., 280n
Glavine, Tom, 232
Glied, Sherry, 309n
Globalization, 467–468
of wine, 103
Global warming, 192
Gokceekus, Omer, 103
Golden Fleece Award, 435
Goldin, Claudin, 308n, 358, 479n
Goldsmiths, 382
Gold Standard, U.S. return to, 416
Goods
club, 199
excludable, 199
inclusion of, in gross domestic product, 328
inferior, 27
network, 92
nonexcludable, 199
nonrival, 199
normal, 27
public, 216–225
versus private, 198–200
pure private, 199
pure public, 199
rival, 199
Google, 408
Google+, 92
Government. *See also* Federal government
guidelines for provision of public goods, 207–208
in large projects, 219–225
in overcoming public goods problem, 205–209
problem solving and, 7
in promoting equality, 470–474
provision of salt in Turkmenistan, 209
in regulating pollution, 160–173
spending by, 331
tax powers and free ridership, 205–207
in well-functioning markets, 124–131

Government revenue, 428–435
  income taxes as, 430–433
  payroll taxes as, 429–430
Graves, Jonathan, 288*n*
Great Depression, 348
  causes of, 414
  Federal Reserve policy during,
    414
Great Recession (2007–2009), 308,
    344, 408. *See also* Recessions
  deflation following, 421
  effects of, 465
  Federal Reserve's role as lender of
    last resort during, 403
  fiscal policy during, 446–447
  income inequality following, 463
  origins of, 347
  unemployment during, 372
Greenhouse effect, 168
Greenspan, Alan, 347
Grimshaw v. *Ford Motor Co.*, 40*n*
Gross, William, 223
Gross domestic product (GDP),
    327, 439, 456
  adjusting, for increasing prices, 334
  business cycles and, 354
  components of, 329–332
  decrease in, during recessions, 359
  goods in, 328
  material well-being and, 326–332
  as measuring stick for production,
    327–329
  nominal, 333
  real, 334, 456–457
  redeemed, 337–338
  services in, 328
  shortcomings of, 335–340
  as specific to particular time and
    place, 328–329
  unemployment and, 369
  using, to measure market value,
    327–328
Growth, economic, 124
Gruber, Jonahan, 288*n*
Guatemala, resources in, 5

H

Haan, Jakob de, 426*n*
Hackmann, Martin, 288
Hamermesh, Daniel, 309*n*
Hamilton, James, 416
Hand, Learned, 434
Hansen, Benjamin, 365, 378*n*
Hansen, W. Lee, 319*n*

Hardin, Garrett, 186*n*
Harford, Tim, 192*n*
Harrington, Joseph E., Jr., 309*n*
Harrison, Benjamin, 260
Hart, Jonathan, 163*n*
Hayes, Rutherford B., 260
Health care, 276
  adverse selection and, 285–288
  affordability of, 284–294
  in Canada, 280
  dealing with pricing variability in,
    293–294
  explaining the gap in measured
    outcomes between the
    United States and Canada,
    280
  finance systems and delivery of,
    281–284
  financing of, 284–294
  international comparison of costs
    and outcomes, 278–279
  moral hazard problem and,
    288–289
  nationalized, 281
    in United Kingdom, 281, 287,
    291–292
  pricing variability and costs of,
    292–294
  private, 282–285
  single-payer system of, 281
  in Switzerland, 284*n*
  in the United States, 276–281
Health insurance
  employers as source of, 283
  exchanges in, 283
  reimbursement methods in, 294
  universal, in Japan, 282, 287, 294
Health maintenance organizations
    (HMOs), 294
Heckman, James, 313*n*, 316
Hendren, Nathaniel, 465, 466, 479*n*
Hermann, Benedikt, 469*n*
Hershey, 125
Hickman, Brent, 319*n*
Hill, Julia "Butterfly," 149
Hirsh, Barry, 364–365, 378*n*
Ho, Jessica, 280*n*
Holdouts, 217
  problem of, 217–220
Honesty, 126–128
  enforcing, in India, 127
  rule of law and, 342
  in well-functioning market,
    126–128
Hong Kong, economic growth
    in, 342

Household production, 336
Housing and Urban Development,
    U.S. Department of, Moving
    to Opportunity, 306
Human capital, 48, **343**
Hume, John, 185
Hussain, M., 103*n*
Hyman, David, 246
Hyperinflation, 417, 418, 419

I

Iacocca, Lee, 40
Ideal world, regulating pollution in
    an, 163–165
IKEA, 222
Impact lag, 411
Implementation lag, 410, 445
Implicit costs, 6, 7
Imports, 112
Incentives, 9
Income
  change in, 26–27
  disposable, 348, 442
  median, 457
Income approach, 332–333
Income distribution, 456
  economic mobility in the U.S.
    and, 465–466
  inequality of, in U.S., 461–466
Income equality, role of government
    in promoting, 470–474
Income inequality, 456
  causes and effects of, 466–467
  economic effects of, 468, 470
  keeping up with co-workers and,
    469
  measurement of, 456–461
Income mobility, 465
  decrease in the U.S., 465–466
Income redistribution
  inflation and, 419
  philosophical justifications
    for, 470–473
Income taxes, 430–433
  corporate, 430, 432–433, 434
  individual, 430–432
Increase in demand, 23
Increase in supply, 25
India
  enforcing honesty in, 127
  GDP in, 334*n*
Individuals
  impact of discrimination on, 312
  role of, in large projects, 216–219

Individual transferable quota (ITQ) system, 19, 189
Industry structure, 120
Infant-industry rationale, 109–110
Inferior goods, 27
Inflation, 415
    calculation of, 415
    consumption choices and, 419
    costs of, 417–419
    end of, 419–420
    income redistribution and, 419
    link between money growth and, 416–417
    money and, 415–416
Inflation rate, 415
Inflation tax, 418
Information
    in overcoming moral hazards, 292
    in well-functioning market, 128–130
Inputs, 27
    price of, 27
An Inquiry Into the Nature and Causes of the Wealth of Nations (Smith), 104
Instant runoff method, 258–259
Institutions, 124
Intellectual property, 331
Interdependence, mutual, 57
Interest, 389
    adjusting, on reserves, 405–406
Interest rates, 389
    money supply and, 406
    real economy activity and, 407
Intermediate goods, 330
Internal Revenue Service (IRS), 430
International trade
    competition and, 342
    not-so-free exchange and, 109–114
Inventory investment, 330
Investment banks, 389, 403
Investment goods, 330
Investments, 330–331
    fixed, 330
    inventory, 330
    residential fixed, 331
iPhone, 126
Irwin, Douglas A., 110n

J

Jackson, Jill, 108
Jacobs, A. J., 46n
James, LeBron, 4

Japan
    deflation in, 421
    GDP in, 334n
    obesity rate in, 280
    real GDP in, 421
    universal health insurance in, 282, 287, 294
Jepbarova, Dilyara, 209n
John Deere, 407
Johnson Controls, 121
Just compensation, 224–225

K

Kahneman, Daniel, 45n
Kansas v. *Colorado*, 187
Karplus, Valerie, 166n
Katz, Lawrence, 358, 479n
Kaufman, Bruce, 364–365, 378n
Kelo v. *City of New London*, 222, 225
Kenya, rhinoceros hunting in, 185
Keynes, John Maynard, 443–444
Kimberling, William, 260n
Kim Jong-il, 8
King, Billie Jean, 70
Ki Suk Han, 246
Kitch, E. W., 153n
Kleven, Henrik, 479n
Kline, Patrick, 465, 466, 479n
Klomp, Jeroan, 426n
Koech, Janet, 419
Kolstad, Jonathan, 288
Kopczuk, Wojciech, 10
Kowalski, Amanda, 288
Krueger, Alan, 364, 378n
Krugman, Paul, 416, 447
Kubrick, Stanley, 305

L

Labor, U.S. Department of
    Bureau of Labor Statistics, 356–357, 361, 362, 415
    CareerOneStop, 363
Labor force participation rate, 357
    increase in women's in 1970s, 358
Labor hoarding, 369
Labor market
    being short-changed in, 309
    impact of unemployment insurance on, 367
Labor market discrimination, 308–312, 310
    types of, 310–311

Labor protections, as cause of structural unemployment, 365–366
Labor services, 130
Labor status, determining, 356–359
Labor unions, 365
    in creating structural unemployment, 365
Lady Bug Flowers, 108
Lags, 411–413, 444–445
    impact, 411
    implementation, 410, 445
    recognition, 410
Laissez-faire, 443
Landais, Camille, 479n
Latane, Bibb, 233
Law of demand, 21
Law of supply, 21
Layard, Richard, 339
Leigh, Andrew, 10
Leisure, value of, 336
Lender of last resort, 404
    role of Federal Reserve as, 403, 404
Levine, Michael, 270
Levitt, Steven, 42, 315
Libya, corruption in, 342
Life
    applying cost–benefit analysis to, 40–41
    approaches to valuing a, 47–50
    mistakes in estimating true value of, 47
    problems and pitfalls of cost–benefit analysis and, 44–47
Life expectancy, 278
Lincoln, Abraham, tariffs and, 110
Linden, Leigh, 143
Line of perfect equality, 459
Liquidity, 390
Liquidity trap, 411
Loans
    defaults of, 420
    mortgage, 385
    subprime, 393
London Stock Exchange, 389
Lorenz curves, 458
    constructing, 458–460
Lorillard, 39, 121
Losses, deadweight, 106–107
Lost-income approach, 47–48
Louisiana, floral-arranging industry in, 108
Loungani, Prakash, 378n
Lynch, Diahanna, 167n
Lynham, John, 190

M

M1, 387
M2, 388
Mamiblapinatapai, 231
Macroeconomics, 326, 456
　differences between microeconomics and, 326
　material well-being and gross domestic product and, 326–332
　Okun's law in, 369
　unemployment in, 356
Make-work bias, 265
Malyshkina, Nataliya, 183*n*
Management, privatization in encouraging efficient, 191
Mandatory spending, 436
Manhattan Project, 61
Mankiw, Greg, 466, 479*n*
Mao Tse Tung, 134
Margin, evaluating alternatives at the, 38–39
Marginal analysis, 38
Marginal benefits, 38
Marginal costs, 38
Marginal propensity to consume (MPC), **443**
Marginal tax rate, 430, 474
Market, 120
Market equilibrium, 21–22
Market failure, 208*n*
Market structure, 120
Market system, 3
　basis of, 99
　communication in, 122–123
　competition in, 124–126
　connecting effort and reward in, 132–135
　functions and structure of, 120–121
　honesty in, 126–128
　information in, 128–130
　measuring desire in, 122
　prices in, 122–123
　production decisions in, 123
　property rights in, 130–132, 134
　role of government in, 124–132
　scarcity in, 122
Market value, 327
　GDP in measuring, 327–328
Mars candy, 125
Marshall Plan, 305
Martin, John, Reservoir, 187
Mas, Alexander, 469
Masclet, David, 469*n*
Material well-being, 326–332

Mays, Willie, 232
McGuire, Mark, 201
McMillan, John, 129
Meadows, Dennis L., 180*n*
Meadows, Donella H., 180*n*
Median income, 457
Median voter theorem, 264
　reasons for failure of, 264, 266–268
　as two-player game, 264
Medicaid, 437
Medicare, 429, 437, 440, 441
Medicare Trust Fund, 441
Medium of exchange, money as a, 380
Megan's law, property values and, 143
Memoirs of an Unregulated Economist (Stigler), 153*n*
Mencken, H. L., 265
Mental disorders, link to unemployment, 356
Merriam, Kansas, robber barons of, 223
Microcredit, 390
Microeconomics, 326, 479*n*
　differences between macroeconomics and, **326**
Micromotives and Macrobehavior (Schelling), 301–302, 304
Micronesia, Federal States of, foreign aid for, 435
Microsoft, 121, 408, 429
Milanovic, Branko, 468, 470
Miller, Marvin, 232
Ming, Yao, 468
Minimum wage laws, as cause of structural unemployment, 364–365
Mixed economies, 3
Mixed strategies, 238
　equilibrium in a zero-sum game, 241–242
　finding player's ideal, 238–240
　games in, 237–240
　pure strategies versus, 237–238
　volunteer's dilemma and, 242–244
Moffitt, Robert, 309*n*
Monetary base, 408
Monetary History of the United States (Schwartz), 414
Monetary policy, 395, **401**
　art and implementation of, 409–413
　business cycle and, 411–412
　contractionary, 409
　expansionary, 409

　goals of, 412
　lags of, 411–413
　natural limits of, 407–408
Monetary rule, 413
Money, 380
　commodity, 381–383
　evolution of, 381–383
　fiat, 384
　inflation and, 415–416
　medium of exchange function of, 380
　spread of value function of, 381
　standard of value function of, 381
　store of value function of, 380–381
Money creation
　central bank in, 386
　commercial banking system in, 386–387
Money growth, link between inflation and, 416–417
Money Market Investor Funding Facility, 403
Money multiplier, 405*n*
Money supply, 383
　banking system and, 385–388
　interest rates and, 406
　measuring, 387–388
Monopolies, 121
Monopolistic competition, 121
Moore, Stephen, 414
Moral hazards, 288–292, **289**
　health care systems and, 291–292
　information in overcoming, 292
　private insurers and, 291
　quantity of care and, 289–291
　risky behavior and, 288–289
Moretti, Enrico, 469
Mortensen, Dale, 367
Mortgage interest deductions, 432
Mortgage loan, 385
Moseley, Winston, 231
Moving to Opportunity (MTO), 306–307
Mugabe, Robert, 418
Mullainathan, Sendhil, 313
Multiplication principle, 235
Mutual fund, 391
Mutual interdependence, 57
Mutually beneficial exchange, 102

N

Nadella, Satya, 429–430
Naive voting, 269
Namibia, rhinoceros hunting in, 185
Nanhe, Mohammed, 127

Nash, John, 61, 85

Nash equilibrium, 60, 61, 63, 67, 70, 133, 169

    finding, in three-player games, 82–86

    tragedy of the commons and, 187

National Basketball Association, hiring decisions for, 310*n*

National Bureau of Economic Research (NBER), 344*n*, 345

National Highway Traffic Safety Administration (NHTSA), 42, 43, 47, 49

National Institute of Mental Health, 435

National Institutes of Health, 308

Nationalized health care, 281

    in United Kingdom, 281, 287, 291–292

National Safety Council, 46

Natural rate of unemployment, 368, 370

Nature Conservancy, 149

Near monies, 388

Negative externalities, 142–143

    climate change and, 168

    disagreements over the competing use of scarce resources and, 144–145

Negotiation costs, 162

Neidell, Matthew, 309*n*

Neighborhoods

    in determining future well-being, 304–307

    link between outcomes and, 305–306

    segregation as inevitable, 301–304

Neilly, Clark, 108

Nestle, 125

Net exports, 331–332

Network goods, 92

Neumark, David, 365

New Economics Foundation's Happy Planet Index, 340*n*

Newton, Isaac, 61

New York City, choice of focal point in, 69

New York Federal Reserve District Bank, 410

New York Stock Exchange, 389

New Zealand, corruption in, 342

Niemeier, Debbie, 183*n*

Nintendo, 121

Nixon, Richard, 414

Niyazov, Saparmurat, 209

Nominal GDP, 333

Nondurables, consumer, 330

Nonexcludability, 200, 202–204

Nonexcludable goods, 199

Nonrival goods, 199

Normal goods, 27

Normative economics, 12–13

North Korea

    command economy in, 8

    corruption in, 342

    decisions made in, 3

    South Korea and, 57

Norton, Michael, 472–473

Norway, corruption in, 342

Not-so-free exchange, international trade and, 109–114

***n*-player games, 87**

Nye, Bill, 234

O

Obama, Barack, 446, 479*n*

Obesity rate, comparison of, in U.S., Canada, and Japan, 280

Occupational segregation, 309

Odom, Bob, 108

OECD's Better Life Index, 340*n*

Ogallala Aquifer, 187

Oil

    price increases in development of substitutes, 183–184

    proven reserves of, 180

    role of prices in the depletion of, 181–184

    running out of, 180–181

Okun, Arthur, 369

Okun's law, 369

Oligopolies, 121

Olsen, Mancur, 206–207

O'Neill, Dave, 280

O'Neill, June, 280

Open market operations, 405

Opportunity costs, 4, 28

    comparative advantage and, 100–101

    money and, 5

    trade-offs and, 4–5

Order of events in runoff elections, 268–269

Organisation for Economic Co-Operation and Development (OECD), 278–279

Organization of Petroleum Exporting Countries (OPEC), 184, 346

Original position, 471

Ostrom, Elinor, 192

Outcomes

    differences across demographic groups, 308, 310

    link between neighborhoods and, 305–306

Output, link between unemployment and, 369

Overfishing, chronic, 190

Owyang, Michael T., 315*n*

P

Palau, 70 Islands Marine Preserve in, 189

Panics, 404

Partially backed representative commodity money, 382–383

Partnerships, 433, 435

part-time, identifying workers, 359

Patents, 131, 331

Patient Protection and Affordable Care Act (2014), **282**

    employer mandate in, 282, 287

    individual mandate in, 282, 287

    private insurers and adverse selection prior to, 286–287

    regulation of private insurers in, 282

    state health exchanges in, 283–284

Paul, Rand, 416

Pay-as-you-go system, 440, 441

Pay gap, size of female-male, 315–316

Payoff matrix, 58–60

Payoffs

    in a clubbing game, 90

    measuring, 66

Payroll taxes, 429–430

Pentagon, terrorist attack on, 45

Perfect competition, 121

Persico, Nicola, 309

Personal exemptions, 432

Perverse incentives, 294

Pessimistic bias, 265

Peters, Shamille, 108

Phillip Morris, 39, 121

Physical capital, 343

Pickrell, John, 185*n*

Piketty, Thomas, 462–463, 479*n*

Pilgrims, private property and, 132

Pissarides, Christopher, 367

Planet Hollywood, 120

Pluralistic ignorance, 233

Plurality-rule method, 254

Polio, Salk vaccine versus Sabin vaccine and, 147

Political stability, 343
Pollution
    depletion and, 188
    disagreements over competing
        uses of scarce resources,
        144–145
    government policies in regulating,
        160–173
    regulating, in an ideal world,
        163–165
    right amount of, 145–147
    socially optimal amount of,
        145–147, 150–151
    types of, 143
Porter, Richard, 9n
Positive economics, 12–13
Positive externalities, 143–145, **144**
Postelwaite, Andrew, 309
Poundstone, William, 260n
Precautions, cost-justified, 43, 45
Preferences, changing, 27
Premium, 285
Premium death spiral, 286
Prescott, Edward, 433
Presidential elections, voting in, 260
Preston, Samuel, 280n
Price(s)
    adjusting gross domestic product
        for increasing, 334
    of complements, 26
    equilibrium, 22
    functions of, in the market system,
        122–123
    increases in encouraging conserva-
        tion, 181–182
    of inputs, 28
    role of, in the depletion of oil,
        181–184
    of substitutes, 26
        in production, 27–28
Price elasticity of demand, 29 –31
Price fixing, 125–126
Price inelastic, 29
*The Price of Inequality: How Today's
    Divided Society Endangers Our
    Future* (Stiglitz), 468
Primary Dealer Credit Facility, 403
Princeton's Institute for Advanced
    Study, 61
Prisoner's delight, 170
Prisoner's dilemma games, 63–64,
    203
    characteristics of, 64, 73
Private costs, 165
Private goods, versus public goods,
    198–200

Private health care system, 282–285
Private insurers, 291
Private property, Pilgrims and, 132
Privatization, in encouraging efficient
    management, 191
Problems, meeting head on, 71
Producers, 327
    changes in the number of, 28
Producer surplus, 102
Production
    gross domestic product as
        measuring stick for, 327–329
    household, 336
    price of substitutes in, 27–28
    prices in coordinating decisions,
        123
    substitutes in, 28
Production technology, 27
Products, differentiated, 121
Profit, 120, 332
Profit maximization, 120
Progressive Auto Insurance, 292
Progressive taxes, 432, 473–474
Projects
    role of government in large,
        219–225
    role of individuals in large,
        216–219
Property rights, 130–132, **148,**
    342–343
    absolute, 164, 189, 191
    Chinese agricultural revolution
        and, 134
    Coase theorem and, 148
    creating absolute, 189, 191
    defined, 130
    public goods problem and,
        204–205
    voluntary exchange of, 148
    in well-functioning market,
        130–131
Property values, Megan's law and, 143
Protectionism, 109
Proxmire, William, 435
Public goods
    guidelines for the government
        provision of, 207–208
    versus private goods, 198–200
    role of government in large
        projects, 219–225
    role of individuals in large
        projects, 216–219
    volunteer's dilemmas and, 231
Public goods problem, 204
    government role in overcoming,
        205–209

    property rights and, 204–205
Public Health Cigarette Smoking
    Act (1970), 65
Public policy, 7
Public use, 221–222
Pure coordination games,
    64–69, **67**
    characteristics of, 68–69, 73
Pure discrimination, 309
Pure private goods, 199
Pure public goods, 199
Pure strategies, 237–238
    versus mixed strategies, 237–238
Push–pull game, 78

Q

QE1, 408
QE2, 408
QE3, 408
Quality of life, 326
Quantitative easing, 408, 416
Quantity demanded, 20, 22
Quantity of care, moral hazards and,
    289–291
Quantity supplied, 21
Quintiles, 458, 465
Quotas, 112, 114, **318**
    deadweight loss of, 114
    individual transferable system,
        189, 190

R

Randers, Jorgen, 180n
Rational choice, 314
Rational ignorance, 265
Rational irrationality, 265
Rationality assumption, 66
Rawls, John, 471
Rawlsian social contract, 471
Read, Leonard, 123n
Reagan, Ronald, 414
Real economy activity, interest rates
    and, 407
Real GDP, 334, 456–457
    adjusting for country's size and,
        334
    fall of, 347
Recessions, 344, 408. *See also* Great
    Recession (2007–2009)
    demand shocks as cause of, 346,
        348
    demand-side, 348
    gross domestic product in, 359

identifying, 345
  supply shocks as cause of, 345–348
  unemployment in, 359
Recognition lag, 410
Red Alert (George), 305
Red-green game, 97
Regression analysis, 313–316, 314
  comparing audit studies and, in
    detecting discrimination,
    315
  in studying earnings gap, 316
Regressive taxes, 429–430
Regulation, need for, and transactions
    costs, 163–164
Rehabilitation Act (1973), 317
Reiley, David, 244n
Reilly, John, 166n
Reinhardt, Uwe, 283n
Rents, 332
Rent seeking, 107
  income inequality and, 468
**Representative commodity money,
  382**
Required reserves, 401
Reserve requirement policy, 404–405
Reserves, 401
  adjusting interest on, 405–406
  excess, 401
  required, 401
Residential fixed investments, 331
Resource depletion, sustainability
    and, 180–192
Resource management, Coase
    theorem and inefficient, 191
Resources, 2
  best use of scarce, 13
  dangers of depletion, 184–186
  disagreements over the competing
    uses of scarce, 144–145
Revised bargaining game, 102
Reward, connecting effort and,
    132–135
Reynolds, R. J., 39, 121
Rhinos, 184
  turning, into chickens, 185
Riggs, Bobby, 70
Risk
  exposing yourself to, 41
  mistakes in estimating, 44–45
  moral hazards and, 288–289
  reducing, 391
Rival goods, 199
Robber barons, 223
Roberts, Russell, 101, 447
Robinson-Patman Act (1936), 126
Rockoff, Jonah, 143

Rolling Stones, 474
Roosevelt, Franklin D., Great
    Depression and, 348
Rosen, Sherwin, 467, 479n
Rouse, Cecelia, 308n
Row player, 59
Royal Gorge, 187
Ruebeck, Christopher S., 309n
Rule of 70, 341
Rule of law, honesty and, 342
Runoff elections, 267–268
  strategic voting and the order of
    events in, 268–269

S

Sabia, Joseph, 365, 378n
Sabin, Albert, 147
Sabin vaccine versus Salk vaccine,
    147
Saez, Emmanuel, 462–463, 465, 466,
    469, 474, 479n
Safety, using cost–benefit analysis in
    determining an appropriate
    level of, 41–44
Salk, Jonas, 147
Salk vaccine versus Sabin vaccine,
    147
Salt, government-provided,
    in Turkmenistan, 209
Saudi Arabia, oil reserves in, 182
Saverin, Eduardo, 474
Scarcity, 4
  best use of, 13
  disagreements over competing
    uses of, 144–145
  prices and, 122
Schelling, Thomas, 68, 301–304, 305,
    307
  checkerboard of, 302–303, 304,
    320, 324
Schmitt, John, 378n
Schneider, Friedrich (same person),
    335n, 469n
Schwartz, Anna, 414
Schwartz, Gary, 40n
Scofea, Laura, 283n
Search costs, 160–161
Securities and Exchange Commission
    (SEC), 129
Securities dealers, 403
Segway, 121
Segregation, 301
  of neighborhoods, 301–304
  occupational, 309
Self-esteem, 309

Self-interest, pursuit of, 104
Services, inclusion of, in gross
    domestic product, 328
Shapiro, Jesse M., 280n
Shareholders, 432
Sherman Act (1890), 125, 126
Shoeleather costs, 418
Shortage, 22
Short-changed, being, in the labor
    market, 309
Side bargains, 148
Siegelman, Peter, 312
Silverman, Dan, 309
Singapore, economic growth in, 342
Single-payer systems, 281
  in Canada, 281, 287, 291–292, 294
Size effect, volunteer's dilemma
    and, 236
Skeath, Susan, 244n
Slemrod, Joel, 10
Smith, Adam, 86, 104, 125
Smith, Vincent, 206
Snyder, Brad, 232n
Social costs, 165
Socialism, 130
Socialized medicine, 281
Socially optimal amount of pollution,
    150–151
Social planner, benevolent, 13, 145,
    189, 198, 218
Social Security, 429, 440, 441
  benefits, 436
  spending on, 437
Social Security benefits calculator,
    454n
Social Security Trust fund, 440, 441
Society, impact of discrimination on,
    312
Somalia, corruption in, 342
Sony, 121
Sorlien, John, 190
South Africa, rhinoceros hunting
    in, 185
South Korea
  economic growth in, 342
  North Korea and, 57
Spears, Britney, 120
Special-interest groups, catering
    to, 107
Specialization, 99, 104
  comparative advantage and,
    99–100
  link between exchange and, 104
  measuring gains from, 100
Speculation, enabling, 392–393
Speculative bubble, 392

Speculators, 388
Spending
  consumption, 446
  government, 331
  mandatory, 436
Sprint, 121
Stakeholders, 37
Standard of value, money as a, 381
Statistical discrimination, 311
Steel Pipe & Supply, 220, 221
Stephens, Melvin, 356
Steuerle, Eugene, 454n
Stevens, Scott, 253n
Stevenson, Betsey, 339
Steward, David, 187n
Stigler, George, 153
Stiglitz, Joseph, 468
Stock market crash of 1929, 444
Stocks, 389
Store of value, money as a, 380–381
Strassel, Kimberly A., 166n
Strategic interaction, 57
Strategic moves, 305
Strategic voting, 268–269
The Strategy of Conflict (Schelling), 305
**Structural unemployment,
    363–367, 370**
  fundamental changes in the econ-
    omy as cause of, 366–367
  labor protections as cause of,
    365–366
  labor unions in creating, 365
  minimum wage laws as cause of,
    364–365
Subprime loans, 393
Subsidies, 107, 171
  in regulating pollution, 169–171
  as restriction on free exchange,
    107–109
  visibility of, 109
Substitutes, 26
  price of, 26
  in production, 27–28
Subway, 6
Sudan, corruption in, 342
Sullivan, Daniel, 356
Summers, Lawrence, 426n
Supply, 21
  decrease in, 25
  increase in, 25
  law of, 21
Supply and demand
  changes in, 23–26
  factors that shift, 26–28
  price elasticity of, 29–31
Supply and demand model, 20

Supply curve, 21
  factors that shift the, 27–28
Supply shocks, 345
  as cause of recessions, 345–348
Surplus, 22, 102
  budget, 437
  consumer, 102
  cooperative, 102
  exchange and cooperative,
    101–102
  producer, 102
Sustainability, resource depletion
    and, 180–192
Swap, credit default, 393
Sweden, corruption in, 342
Switzerland, health care system in, 284n

T

Tabarrok, Alex, 366
Taiwan, economic growth in, 342
Takings clause, 219
Takings power, 219
Tariffs, 110–112
  deadweight losses and, 111
  effects of, on cooperative surplus,
    111
  hidden costs of a, 111–112
**Taste-based discrimination,
    310**–311
Tastes, changing, 27
Taxes, 105
  death and, 10
  gas, 166
  income, **430–433**
  payroll, 429–430
  progressive, 432, 473–474
  regressive, 429–430
  in regulating pollution, 167–169
  as restriction on free exchange,
    105–106
  value added, 433
Tax rates
  average, 431
  marginal, 430–431
Taylor, John, 447
Tennessee Valley Authority (TVA),
    221
Term Asset-Backed Securities Loan
    Facility, 403
Term Auction Facility (TAF), 403
Term Securities Lending facilities,
    403
Tesla Motors, 126
Thomas, Lloyd B., 403n

Three-player games, 80–82, 202–203
  best-response analysis in, 83–85
  dominance in, 82–83
  finding Nash equilibria in, 82–86
T-Mobile, 121
Tobacco advertising ban, game
    theory and, 65
Tobacco Control Act (2009), 39
Tobacco settlement, cost–benefit
    analysis of, 39
Tobin, James, 391
Trade deficits, 332
Trademarks, 331
Trade-offs
  measuring, 9
  opportunity costs and, 4–5
  superheroes and, 6
Trade surplus, 332
**Tragedy of the commons,
    186**–188, 192
Transactions costs, 152, 219
  Coase theorem and, 151–152
  need for regulation and, 163–164
  types of, 160–163
Transfer payments, 331
Transparency International, 342
Travolta, John, 163n
Troubled Asset Relief Program
    (TARP), 446
Truth-in-advertising standards, 129
Tucker, Ross, 185n
Turbo Tap, 99, 105, 114
Turkmenistan, government-provided
    salt in, 209
Turley, Jonathan, 246
Turner, Nicholas, 465, 466, 479n
Tuscola, Illinois, Victorian-era houses
    in, 198
Tversky, Amos, 45n
Two-player games, 56–74
  basic structure of, 58–63
  median voter theorem as, 264
  types of, 63–73

U

Underemployment, 360
Underground economy, 335–336
  size of, 335n
  workers in, 361
Underwriters Laboratories
    (UL), 129
Unemployment, 355–373, 356
  appropriate policy prescription
    and, 370–371

as countercyclical, 359
cyclical, 368–370
data issues and appropriate policy prescription, 371–372
determining a person's labor status, 356–359
frictional, 362–363, 370
during the Great Recession, 372
link between output and, 369
at the macro level, 356
natural rate of, 368, 370
policy implications of, 370–372
structural, 363–367, 370
Unemployment insurance, impact on labor market, 367
Unemployment rate, 308, 356
calculating, 357, 359
reasons for not fixing the shortcomings of the, 361–362
shortcomings of the measured, 359–362
United Nation's Human Development Index, 340n
United States
dollar of, as official currency, 401
health care outcomes in, 280
labor force participation rate of women in, 358
obesity rate in, 280
private health care system in, 282–285
specialization in, 101
trade between Canada and, 112
unemployment rate in, 308
wheat market in, 121
working habits of Americans in, 433
United States v. *Chandler-Dunbar Water Power Co.*, 224
Universal health insurance, 282
in Japan, 282, 287, 294
Utilitarianism, 470

V

Vaccines, Salk versus Sabin, 147–148
Value added taxes (VAT), 433
Veil of ignorance, 471
Verizon, 121
Veseth, Michael, 103n
Villeval, Marie Claire, 469n
Viscusi, Kip, 39
Vogel, David, 167n
The Voice, 467
Voluntary exchange, of property rights, 148

Volunteerism, compulsory, 245
Volunteer's dilemmas, 231–246
apathy and, 233, 235–236
coalition building and bargaining and, 245
compulsory volunteerism and, 245
diffusion of responsibility and, 233, 235–236
duty to rescue and, 246
Flood, Curt, on, 232
game theory and, 237–242
mixed-strategy play and, 242–244
Nye, Bill, on, 234
overcoming, 244–245
pluralistic ignorance and, 233
public goods and, 231
von Neumann, John, 61, 238
Voters, dangerous, 265
Voting, 253–271
Arrow's impossibility theorem and, 261
Borda-count method of, 256–258, 261
candidate positioning and the median voter theorem in, 262–265
Condorcet method of, 255–256
conventional political elections and the median voter theorem, 261–262
instant runoff method of, 258–259
methods of, 253–261
naive, 269
plurality-rule method of, 254
in presidential elections, 260
strategic, 268–270

W

Wachovia National Bank, 402n
Wachter, Till von, 356
Wage income, 332
The Wages of Wins (Berri), 310n
Wage stickiness, 370
cyclical unemployment and, 369–370
Waheed, Abdul, 127
Wang, Ning, 134n
Warren, Elizabeth, 471
Wascher, William, 365
Washington Mutual Savings Bank, 402n
Wealth, storing across time, 390–391
Wealth creation, cooperative surplus as a measure of, 102, 105

Wealth distribution, appearance of ideal, 472–473
Wealth effect, 348
Weiner, Zach, 6n
Well-being
growth rates, as a reason for differences in, 341–342
role of neighborhood in determining future, 304–307
West, Sarah, 166
Wheelan, Charles, 314n, 406
Why the Electoral College is Bad for America (Edwards), 260n
Williams, Roberton, 166
Wine, globalization of, 103
Wine Wars: (Veseth), 103n
Winner-take-all system, 260
Winter, Harold, 12
Wohlgenant, Michael, 206
Wolfers, Justin, 339
Women, increase in labor force participation rate of, 358
Wonder Bread, 122–123
World Bank's Rigidity of Employment Index, 366
World Trade Center, terrorist attack on, 45
World Trade Organization (WTO), 114
Wrigley Field, 201
Wyman, Katrina Miriam, 225n

X

Xiao, Kate, 134n

Y

Yaghan Indians, 231
Yap, giant stone money of, 382
Yellen, Janet, 386, 387, 394, 404, 410
Younkle, Matt, 99

Z

Zandi, Mark, 446–447
Zelenska, Teryana, 364–365, 378n
Zero-sum games, 61, 237
mixed-strategy equilibrium in, 241–242
Zimbabwe
inflationary spiral in, 417–418, 420
rhinoceros hunting in, 185
Zuckerberg, Mark, 4, 430

Flexibility Chart

1. Despite the fact that Chapter 4 is optional, you can conduct the Red/Green Experiment without going through the concepts of that chapter. The experiment is very useful in helping students' understanding of the outcomes of experiments with more than two players.

Core Topics in Micro	Optional Topics in Micro
Chapter 1: Fundamental Concepts in Economics *Experiment:* The Ultimatum Game: Are You Generous or Greedy?	
	Chapter 1 Appendix: Supply and Demand
Chapter 2: Cost–Benefit Analysis and the Value of a Life *Experiment:* The Dictator Game	
Chapter 3: Basic Game Theory: Games Between Two Players *Experiment:* The Push–Pull Game	
	Chapter 4: Game Theory: Games Between Three or More Players *Experiment:* The Red–Green Game
Chapter 5: Free Exchange: Individual and International Trade *Experiment:* The Gains-from-Trade Game	
Chapter 6: The Market System: Functions, Structure, and Institutions *Experiment:* Capitalism and Communism Games	
Chapter 7: The Nature of Pollution Problems *Experiment:* The Herd Immunity Game	
Chapter 8: Government Policies to Regulate Pollution *Experiment:* The Judge-Me-Not Game	
	Chapter 9: Resource Depletion and Sustainability *Experiment:* The "Gone Fishing" Game
Chapter 10: Public Goods and the Role of Government *Experiment:* The Garden Game	
	Chapter 11: Public Goods: Tackling Large Projects and Eminent Domain *Experiment:* The "Ask and You Might Receive" Game
	Chapter 12: The Volunteer's Dilemma: A Collective Inaction Problem *Experiment:* The "Save Ferris!" Game
	Chapter 13: Voting: You Can't Always Get What You Want *Experiment:* Looking for a "Goldilocks" Location
	Chapter 14: The Economics of Health Insurance and Health Care *Experiment:* The Restaurant Game
	Chapter 15: Segregation and Discrimination *Experiment:* Schelling's Checkerboard

2. The macro chapters de-emphasize game theory. You will see game theory in segments of Chapters 5, 6, 10, 13, and 14, but it's not vital to the understanding of most of the material in those chapters. Nevertheless, the collective action material and the material on the divergence between individual and social incentives that Chapter 1 presents can be illustrated with the experiments in Chapters 3, 4, 6, 10, 11, 13, and 14, even if students don't have the formal background in game theory.

Core Topics in Macro	Optional Topics in Macro
Chapter 1: Fundamental Concepts in Economics *Experiment:* The Ultimatum Game: Are You Generous or Greedy?	
	Chapter 1 Appendix: Supply and Demand
Chapter 2: Cost–Benefit Analysis and the Value of a Life *Experiment:* The Dictator Game	
	Chapter 3: Basic Game Theory: Games Between Two Players *Experiment:* The Push–Pull Game
	Chapter 4: Game Theory: Games Between Three or More Players *Experiment:* The Red–Green Game
Chapter 5: Free Exchange: Individual and International Trade *Experiment:* The Gains-from-Trade Game	
Chapter 6: The Market System: Functions, Structure, and Institutions *Experiment:* Capitalism and Communism Games	
Chapter 10: Public Goods and the Role of Government *Experiment:* The Garden Game	
	Chapter 11: Public Goods: Tackling Large Projects and Eminent Domain *Experiment:* The "Ask and You Might Receive" Game
	Chapter 13: Voting: You Can't Always Get What You Want *Experiment:* Looking for a "Goldilocks" Location
	Chapter 14: The Economics of Health Insurance and Health Care *Experiment:* The Restaurant Game
Chapter 16: Gross Domestic Product and the Wealth of Nations: An Introduction to the Macroeconomy MyEconLab Real-Time Data Activity: Gross Domestic Product and Business Cycles	
Chapter 17: Unemployment MyEconLab Real-Time Data Activity: Unemployment Rates	
Chapter 18: An Introduction to Money, Banks, and the Financial System MyEconLab Real-Time Data Activity: Money and the Financial System	
Chapter 19: The Federal Reserve: Monetary Policy, Economic Activity, and Inflation MyEconLab Real-Time Data Activity: Monetary Policy and Inflation	
Chapter 20: The Federal Government: Taxes, Spending, and Fiscal Policy MyEconLab Real-Time Data Activity: Budget Deficits and the Federal Debt	
	Chapter 21: Income Inequality and the Redistribution of Income *Experiment:* Unveiling Ignorance